MASTERPLOTS II

WOMEN'S LITERATURE SERIES

MASTERPLOTS II

WOMEN'S LITERATURE SERIES

3

Gao-Lif

Edited by

FRANK N. MAGILL

SALEM PRESS

Pasadena, California   Englewood Cliffs, New Jersey

Library of Congress Cataloging-in-Publication Data
Masterplots II. Women's literature series / edited by
Frank N. Magill.
    p.   cm.
Includes bibliographical references (p.) and index.
    1. Literature—Women authors—History and criti-
cism. 2. Literature—Stories, plots, etc. 3. Women in
literature. I. Magill, Frank Northen, 1907-   . II. Ti-
tle: Masterplots 2. III. Title: Masterplots two.
PN471.M37   1995
809'.89287—dc20   94-25180
ISBN 0-89356-898-8 (set)   CIP
ISBN 0-89356-901-1 (volume 3)

LIST OF TITLES IN VOLUME 3

LIST OF TITLES IN VOLUME 3

MASTERPLOTS II

WOMEN'S LITERATURE SERIES

THE GAOL GATE

Author: Lady Augusta Gregory (1852-1932)
Type of work: Drama
Type of plot: Tragedy
Time of plot: 1906
Locale: Galway, Ireland
First produced: 1906, at the Abbey Theatre, Dublin, Ireland
First published: 1909

> *Principal characters:*
> MARY CAHEL, the mother of Denis Cahel, who is being held in
> Galway Jail; because she cannot read, she has come bearing a
> letter in order to ask the authorities what it says about her son
> MARY CUSHIN, Denis' wife, who has come on the long journey
> with her mother-in-law
> TERRY FURY and PAT RUANE, Denis' friends, who were also
> arrested; the arresting sergeant boasted that he obtained Denis'
> confession and the implication of his two companions
> THE GATEKEEPER, the guard who tells the women that Denis has
> been hanged and that the letter was giving them permission to
> visit Denis before his sentence was carried out

Form and Content

The story of *The Gaol Gate* is told through the dialogue of two women—the mother and wife of the executed Denis Cahel—which constitutes three-fourths of the entire one-act play; their brief conversation with the gatekeeper takes the remaining one-fourth. Spoken in the "Kiltartan dialect" developed by Lady Augusta Gregory to represent the Gaelic-tinged speech of the people of her district, it is the talk of two ordinary women who have come a long way on foot and who cannot cease worrying and hoping about what they will find when they arrive at the Galway Jail, nor about the truth of the rumors in their home village that Denis has betrayed his comrades, Terry Fury and Pat Ruane.

Through their conversation, one learns the bare facts of the case of Denis Cahel, who was arrested and imprisoned for "firing a shot" in the nighttime—apparently a murder or an attempted murder. From the gatekeeper, they learn that Denis has been executed because his footprint was found "outside the window" and that his two companions have already been released for lack of evidence against them. This news is both a distress and a relief: The two women now know that Denis is irretrievably gone, but they also know that the rumors spread against him as an informer are false.

The dialogue between Mary Cahel and Mary Cushin begins with the end of their journey from Daire-caol, as they remark on the grim exterior of the jail, and—as in any casual conversation—shift by association of word and thought: first to the harsh things that were being said about Denis by the female relatives of Terry Fury and Pat Ruane, then to their certainty that it was in fact Terry who fired the shot and Pat who instigated the deed, and then to the fearful and hopeful speculation about the contents of the letter that Mary Cahel is carrying under her cloak.

The first five speeches of the two women identify Denis Cahel only by the words "he," "him," and "man," introducing his name only after the audience has fully absorbed the grim reality of the jail's exterior and the horror of "He that was used to the mountain to be closed up inside of that!"

The rest of their short dialogue is devoted to plans and speculations based on the assumption that the letter Mary Cahel is carrying is an announcement of Denis' imminent release. Because the rumors at home could be true, and Denis might have implicated his companions while under the influence of alcohol, he clearly cannot return home. Rather than accept the money that the government would presumably pay Denis for being an informer, Mary Cahel is prepared to sell the family's small landholding to pay for passage to America for Denis, Mary Cushin, and their child.

It is at this point in their conversation that the gate of the jail opens and the gatekeeper discovers them waiting outside. After reading their letter for them and reporting Denis' fate, he disappears to fetch the few clothes that they may claim, and his absence is filled with the "keening" of their grief for Denis' life and reputation. His return with the news that Denis' companions were released for lack of evidence is followed by Mary Cahel giving the longest speech of the play, in which she states her intention to tell the world of her son's heroism and sacrifice.

Analysis

The structure of this play is almost invisible, beginning as the continuation of a conversation which has probably been going on all night on the road from Daire-caol to Galway; proceeding seamlessly as a two-sided, then a three-sided conversation; and culminating in a monologue by Mary Cahel. That is not to say that there is no structure, for the organization is very tight and purposeful: first, the exposition of what the two women know, hope, and fear; then, their exploration of possibilities for the future, built on the assumption that the rumors at home are true and Denis has traded his companions for his own life and freedom; and finally, the revelation of the truth and Mary Cahel's triumphant, vengeful determination to have the truth of the matter told far and wide.

Lady Gregory's artistry is proven by the invisibility of the structure, for one is drawn into the very inner lives of Mary Cahel and Mary Cushin by overhearing a conversation between two apparently very ordinary women. The "Kiltartan dialect," which Lady Gregory had already perfected and popularized in *Cuchulain of Muirthemne* (1902) and *Gods and Fighting Men* (1904), is the sound of the peasants and simple folk she knew and loved, and from whom she collected much of her folklore. There are no great dramatic flourishes or technical effects—only the simple and heartbreaking dialogue of two women who are not sure whether they should fear their son's and husband's death or the disgrace of the family name.

While suspense is created by the guesses and hopes of the two women until they learn the truth, tension is provided by the submerged clash of personalities between Mary Cushin and Mary Cahel and the more open clash between the feelings of Mary Cushin and the attitude of the gatekeeper toward criminals.

From the start, Mary Cahel appears to be the stronger of the two main characters. When Mary Cushin reports the sergeant's boast that he had gained a confession from Denis by the use of strong drink, she says there would be no blame for Denis if he had implicated his companions, "his wits being out of him with drink." When Mary Cushin says that it was Terry who fired the shot and Pat who instigated it, her mother-in-law's only comment is that she should be silent and not help the sergeant in his inquiries. It is Mary Cahel who has insisted that they come to Galway to warn Denis of the poisonous atmosphere at home, and it is she who proposes a solution in the sale of the landholding to buy her son, daughter-in-law, and grandson a passage to America. As for herself, she is prepared to go to the workhouse, rather than return to Daire-caol and face the hate of the neighbors. When she learns of her son's death, she falls to her knees and simultaneously grieves for her son and gives thanks that he did not inform against anyone. When she has had her say, she turns to her daughter-in-law and asks reproachfully if she has been left to keen Denis alone. Finally, when the gatekeeper has returned and told them that Denis did not inform, her concluding speech is worthy of any song of praise and mourning in *Gods and Fighting Men*.

Beneath the surface, however, there is more to Mary Cushin than one might suspect, because her finest moments are bracketed by those of her mother-in-law. When Mary Cahel asks if she is to be left alone in the keening, Mary Cushin responds with the second-longest speech in the play, detailing the many ways in which she will miss him and concluding with a complaint that the worst of it is that his name and the name of his child will be blackened by the word that he was an informer. It is to this complaint that Mary Cahel's powerful final speech is addressed.

When she asks if they will receive Denis' body and the gatekeeper replies that he has already been buried, Mary Cushin says that it is a hard thing to have had no kindred at the burial, and this elicits the gatekeeper's harsh reply about the order of things for a man to be hanged. While Mary Cahel stoically accepts the fact of Denis' death and leaves the audience with her ringing determination to retrieve has name, Mary Cushin's last words are a questioning of justice and an all-inclusive curse placed on those who executed Denis and on Terry Fury as well, for firing the shot.

Context

Praised by George Bernard Shaw as the greatest living Irishwoman, friend and literary collaborator of William Butler Yeats, Lady Gregory was cofounder and director of the Abbey Theatre (the beginning of a serious Irish theater), the interpreter and popularizer of the Irish epics whose versions still appear in bookstores and classrooms, and a playwright of note. *The Gaol Gate* was her own favorite among her tragedies and is considered one of her two or three best plays. The play was an early success by a woman who began a serious writing career at the age of fifty, was alternately praised and reviled by both sides in the struggle for an independent Ireland, and maintained her own personal and literary voice throughout.

The play, like much of her work, both epic and dramatic, is unusual in its ability to evoke the spirit of the common people in a land which had spent generations being taught that its own culture and traditions were worthless. While maintaining the traditions and values of the nationally downtrodden, Gregory is also able to show the courage and dignity of Gaelic women, whether in the patriarchal, heroic past or in the oppressed, fervent, revolutionary, and still patriarchal present. It is Gregory's peculiar gift that she can couch such plays as *The Gaol Gate* in the very language that she uses in her heroic epics. Its characters are palpably real and everyday, but their tragedy is invested with no less dignity and pathos than those of Deirdre and Emer at the death of their loved men.

This play is one of Gregory's earliest and was reportedly written at speed. Perhaps because of that fact, rather than in spite of it, this work offers an impelling view of the universal condition of women in a patriarchal society. The patronizing sympathy and rigid self-righteousness of the gatekeeper are suitable foils to the women, whose characters speak of deeper and more human values. Hardly "feminist" in tone, the play nevertheless speaks of how women must face and deal with the results of what their men have wrought.

Sources for Further Study

Adams, Hazard. *Lady Gregory*. Lewisburg, Pa.: Bucknell University Press, 1973. The primary interest of this study, in the chapters entitled "Mythological History," "Cloon," and "Wonder," is the ancient and continuing folk sources of Lady Gregory's characterizations.

Coxhead, Elizabeth. *Lady Gregory: A Literary Portrait*. New York: Harcourt, Brace & World, 1961. A sympathetic and comprehensive treatment of the person and her works, noting, among other things, Lady Gregory's unheralded contributions to Yeats's *Cathleen ni Houlihan* (1902).

Frazier, Adrian. *Behind the Scenes: Yeats, Horniman, and the Struggle for the Abbey Theatre*. Berkeley: University of California Press, 1990. More a history than an analysis, this book describes Gregory's significant part in the founding and maintenance of the theater, as well as in the writing of both *Cathleen ni Houlihan* and *Pot of Broth* (1902).

Gregory, Lady Augusta. *Seven Short Plays*. Dublin: Maunsel, 1909. Lady Gregory's own note describes the three personally witnessed events from which she wove *The Gaol Gate*.

Kohfeldt, Mary Lou. *Lady Gregory: The Woman Behind the Irish Renaissance*. New York: Atheneum, 1985. This may well be the more complete, scholarly work foreseen by Elizabeth Coxhead (above) in her own treatment of Lady Gregory. Carefully researched and replete with documentation from letters and elsewhere, as well as interpretations of the works as they occur in Lady Gregory's life, the book offers a more complete idea of how much of *Cathleen ni Houlihan* is Lady

Gregory's creation and an intimate glimpse into her relationship with Wilfred Blunt (with a suggestion of how his time in prison in Galway served to acquaint her with that jail gate). The definitive study.

Mikhail, E. H., ed. *Lady Gregory: Interviews and Recollections*. London: Macmillan, 1977. Offers Lady Gregory's and others' interpretations of her strengths, trials, and successes.

Robinson, Lennox. *Ireland's Abbey Theatre: A History, 1899-1951*. Port Washington, N.Y.: Kennikat Press, 1968. Presents descriptions of Gregory and her work in the words of contemporaries, notes the initial rejection of her first two plays, and confirms her worth as a writer of comedy and drama, as well as a cultural mediator in her translations and adaptations of Molière's plays.

James L. Hodge

THE GARDEN
New and Selected Poetry and Prose

Author: Bella Akhmadulina (1937-   )
Type of work: Poetry
First published: 1990

Form and Content

Bella Akhmadulina began publishing poetry at the end of the 1950's. After the publication of her first collection, *Struna* (1962; the string), she became a prominent figure in the new generation of Russian poets during the "thaw" period following Joseph Stalin's death. Her poetry also brought expulsion from the Union of Soviet Writers for her "dangerous unconcern" with social questions of the day. Each new collection solidified her position as a leading member among the promising young poets that included Yevgeny Yevtushenko, Andrei Voznesensky, and Robert Rozhdestvensky, among others.

Born in Moscow of mixed Russian-Italian-Tartar origins, Akhmadulina approached poetry in an uncertain fashion, "frail and infantile," as her former husband Yevtushenko put it. At that time, poetry was for her more a matter of personal confession than a matter of a strong social or philosophical statement. As she matured, she was able to leave her cocoon and to assume the role of a voice of conscience that has been traditional in Russian literature. Her inner makeup, however, prevented her from becoming a social bard in the mold of Yevtushenko and Voznesensky, although her concern for the burning issues of the day is no less strong or sincere.

In the following decades, several themes crystallized in her poetry. Throughout her career, she has been searching for her poetic self. A set of thirteen poems under the title "A Fairy Tale About Rain" expresses this quest. The rain, as a life-sustaining substance, is the metaphor for the poetic inspiration accompanying her everywhere, including on a visit to people steeped in a vulgar, materialistic world. Soaked with rain, she feels apologetic for soiling the exquisite furniture ("I've been wallowing about, like a pig in the mud. . . . I'm lost in foggy bubbles. . . . t'was Rain that led me into trouble"). As the party progresses and the philistines and snobs pester her with asinine questions—"Is your husband really rich?" and "Who gives presents to the ones/ God has endowed? And how would it be done?"—the visitor, the lyric persona, loses her temper and answers caustically, all the time watching the rain, which had camped outside. When, finally, the rain comes to her rescue and floods everything inside the house, the poet walks away happily, convinced that the two worlds will never mix and that the enmity between them will always exist. Through this self-realization, the poet finds her rightful place, learning to bear her alienation as the price for being different. A similar theme of alienation is depicted in "Fever," where creativity is presented as illness incomprehensible to, and feared by, mere mortals.

Self-realization leads to a constant search for beauty as the prerequisite for a poet's vocation. Akhmadulina finds it in an artist's studio ("Features of an Artist's Studio"), where "the house, like a lost balloon, / flutters over Boredom Valley"; in the evoking of the artist Raphael ("Raphael's Day"), recollecting her Italian ancestors; in the noble role of Vladimir Vysotsky's theater ("Theater"); in the slender cheetahs embracing in a zoo as a symbol of mindless imprisonment of natural beauty ("Two Cheetahs"); or in the wondrous beauty of the flowers and bees upon them while the poet is writing a poem ("The Secret"). For Akhmadulina, beauty is everywhere.

The discovery of beauty is one role of a poet. It is no wonder that she likens the work of a poet to a garden; yet all the beauty of a garden is useless unless a poet gives expression to beauty through words ("The Garden"). The poet is a magician opening hidden worlds ("Poetry Magic") but is less important than the discovery itself, being only "a Simple Simon" bidding the command from "the conductor somewhere up in heaven." Akhmadulina sums up the relationship between a poet and a poem in this way: "All life and death has been played out in/ the magic theater of a poem."

Love is an inescapable theme in a sensitive young poet such as Akhmadulina. There are many poems in which love is either a central theme or a by-product of other emotions. As in many other poems, she is serious and whimsical at the same time. In "A Summer-House Love Story," a real-life triangle at a dacha is skillfully replaced by that of Akhmadulina, Alexander Pushkin, and his lover. In other love poems ("Don't Spend a Lot of Time on Me," "Hey, Kid!," "Parting"), she is again both serious and playful, as if reminding herself and others that, though blissful, love is transient and that likewise love pain is not the end of the world. Much more important to her is the other kind of love, *agape*. Compassion is a much more sublime feeling for her. Recollecting the inhumanity committed upon children in "Saint Bartholomew's Day," she concludes that "a child born amidst a massacre/ must be willfully immoral." If we cannot feel sorry for "just thirty thousand Huguenots," both the hangman and his victim will end up on the gallows. In "An Owl's Death," the interdependence of all human beings is again emphasized, because the lack of compassion for an ugly child killed by her brother provokes fear that "I will some day be killed." In "The Hospital Christmas Tree," human suffering is again the source of love and compassion; the Virgin's child, symbolized by a Christmas tree, is the last hope, if everything else fails.

There are several poems dedicated to other Russian poets. Pushkin is extolled in the prose piece "An Eternal Presence," Mikhail Lermontov in "Longing for Lermontov," Anna Akhmatova in "I envy the way she was young," Osip Mandelstam in "Back in the days when any villain would do," and Marina Tsvetaeva in "I Swear" and "Return to Tarusa." All these poems show Akhmadulina's reverence for her fellow poets and her kinship with them.

Most of Akhmadulina's poems are in the form of traditional rhymed quatrains in the Russian iambic tetrameter. There are variations in meter, as well as in poem length. She prefers end-rhyme, with some initial and internal rhymes. Sometimes she uses assonance instead of exact rhyme, and there are occasional extreme alliterations. She also employs archaisms, neologisms, and linguistic innovations. By and large, she steers a middle course between experimental and traditional prosody. Her formalistic achievements are considerable.

Analysis

Akhmadulina's poetry displays several distinct features. First, there is a broad range of themes and approaches, ranging from expressing her innermost feelings to showing concern for fellow human beings, especially the sufferers; from her own secluded world to her relationship with other Russian poets; and from a serious, almost classical approach to poetry to the idiosyncratic and whimsical demeanor that is sometimes "recklessly gay, drunk with the joy of life, impetuously kittenish, and even slightly silly," in the words of critic Deming Brown. Yet, she succeeds in striking a balance between her personal preoccupations and her concern for the outside world.

Her lyricism is genuine and intense. Whether stemming from her pronounced femininity, from high emotionality, or from a vulnerability that derives from her intuitive realization of the basically tragic nature of being, her delicately musical lyricism gives the body of her poetry an additional dimension and luster.

Akhmadulina's spiritual vision is another dimension. She is not only a poet but also an individual fully aware of all people's spiritual needs. When spiritual life is lacking or suppressed, she told *The Harvard Advocate* in May, 1988, "people turn to the poet as confessor and priest. . . . People seek something lofty, something spiritual. And that's why people are always striving for what's beautiful, lofty, musical." This spiritual vision is woven into the fabric of her poetry unobtrusively, however, as is almost everything else in her verses.

Similar to the spiritual needs is the need for love, both of the *agape* and the *eros* kind. Humans need the warmth of other human beings, Akhmadulina says in poem after poem. She seems wounded and lonely when love is not reciprocated, which leads to insecurity and withdrawal. At the same time, she stoically rejects pity, as in the poem "An Incantation": "Don't weep over me—I'll keep going on/ poor but happy, a prisoner with goodwill." Caught between the need to love and be loved and the vulnerability of such feelings, she persists: "The snow is high. . . . Immodestly/ I radiate love's inner grace" (in "Hey, Kid!"). "Not pride but a heavy heart makes me/ hold my head high," she says in another poem, "Don't spend a lot of time on me." Thus, whether happy or unhappy—though the latter seems to predominate—love must be consummated and the results must be accepted because, "Still, after centuries, just like that,/ we fall in love at the drop of a hat,/ and hearts keep circling in their flight,/ like vessels passing in the night,/ sweetening verse with samples of/ the true and bitter taste of love" (in "A Summer-House Love Story").

Perhaps the most important feature of Akhmadulina's poetic stature is her high opinion of poetry as art. She elevates the role of a poet to that of a priest or priestess in the temple of beauty and love. At the same time, she rejects the self-centered status of a poet: As she once said, "I don't accept the love and adoration of my admirers as solely my own; I feel that it's for the great Russian poets who preceded me." Akhmadulina is not only a good poet but also a gracious practitioner of the art.

Context

Bella Akhmadulina belongs to a prominent group of women writers in Russian literature of the twentieth century, securing the legitimate place of women in that literature. Considering the fact that there were relatively few women writers in all the preceding centuries, the progress is considerable, especially after the Bolshevik Revolution of 1917. In the beginning, Akhmadulina was only one member of a group of poets—on equal footing, to be sure—but after having established herself, she came to enjoy an independent status.

Her strongly independent spirit has made her respected among her peers from the outset. Her independence is reflected not only in poetic matters but also in her social status. While she has not been prominently involved in the dissident movement in her country, the strength of her character and her achievements have garnered her high esteem, making her a role model for younger Russian women writers. The issues present in her poetry are not revolutionary, but she has shown a remarkable aplomb in voicing them. Perhaps the fact that she has not been very vocal has made her position all the more effective. Her unobtrusive preoccupation with moral issues has enhanced Akhmadulina's status as one of the most respected spokespersons of the new spirit in Russian literature.

Sources for Further Study

Brown, Deming. "The Younger Generation of Poets." In *Soviet Russian Literature Since Stalin*. Cambridge, England: Cambridge University Press, 1978. A brief treatment of Akhmadulina's poetry, together with other poets of her generation such as Yevgeny Yevtushenko and Andrei Voznesensky.

Feinstein, Elaine. "Poetry and Conscience: Russian Women Poets of the Twentieth Century." In *Women Writing and Writing About Women*, edited by Mary Jacobus. New York: Barnes & Noble Books, 1979. Akhmadulina is appraised, along with other Russian woman poets. Examines her contribution and establishes her place in relationship to her contemporaries.

Ketchian, Sonia I. *The Poetic Craft of Bella Akhmadulina*. University Park: Pennsylvania State University Press, 1993. This book-length survey of Akhmadulina's poetry, the first in English, traces in clear and concise terms her development, influences, and contribution to Russian literature, focusing on the main characteristics and formal aspects of her verses.

Rydel, Christine. "A Bibliography of Works by and About Bella Akhmadulina." *Russian Literature Triquarterly* 1 (1971): 434-441. A thorough, unannotated bibliography of books, poems in periodicals and anthologies, translations of and by Akhmadulina, and critical articles in English, Russian, Serbo-Croatian, and Slovak.

_____ . "The Metaphysical World of Bella Akhmadulina." *Russian Literature Triquarterly* 1 (1971): 326-341. A pithy discussion of Akhmadulina's poetry through 1970, establishing its main features and exploring the relationship between the personal and the impersonal nature of her art.

Vasa D. Mihailovich

GATHERING THE TRIBES

Author: Carolyn Forché (1950-   )
Type of work: Poetry
First published: 1976

Form and Content

In his introduction to *Gathering the Tribes*, Stanley Kunitz contends that Carolyn Forché's first volume of poetry is a work preoccupied with the theme of kinship, and while this is certainly true, Forché's vision is of a distinctly woman-centered kinship. In the poetic style that she has described as "first-person free verse lyric-narrative," Forché writes a three-part sequence of poems exploring a woman's connections with her ancestry, the land and its people, and her physical body. Forché opens the volume by invoking memories of her grandmother, Anna, a central figure who functions as a spiritual guide for the poet in her journey toward establishing these essential female connections.

The poems of the first section, "Burning the Tomato Worms," are united by their focus on history, particularly Anna's Slovak roots. "Grandma, come back," the poet writes in the ambiguous first poem, "The Morning Baking." Expressing anger over Anna's death, the majority of the lines berate the grandmother: "I am damn sick of getting fat like you." The ending, however, speaks of reconciliation: "But I'm glad I'll look when I'm old/ like a gypsy dusha hauling milk." These lines foreshadow many of the section's poems, such as "What It Cost" and "Early Night," that connect the poet's identity with that of her grandmother, as well as poems in subsequent sections that reach toward possibilities of regeneration.

In the poem "Burning the Tomato Worms," Forché introduces additional conditions of women's existence that will recur in the volume. In this poem, she intersperses fragments of Anna's history with her own primary poetic themes: cycles of history and nature, cycles of birth and death, and the cycles that govern a woman's body. She also writes about feminine rituals of spirituality, purification, and initiation. The poem ends with an account of the poet's sexual initiation—a subject that Forché writes about ambivalently and to which she will return in the poems of section 3.

The poems of section 2, "Song Coming Toward Us," draw complex relationships between the land and the inhabitants who strive to understand and respect it. Forché writes of predominantly American Indian and Spanish people who live in concord with the earth; kinship with the natural world, as with the past, she suggests, is necessary before people can form bonds with one another. In this section, Forché interweaves metaphors of birth and death with American Indian legends, and she links the poems together with highly visual natural imagery.

The poem "Song Coming Toward Us" tells of a spiritual entity—a song of the earth—which gains an immortality much as Anna has; her mortal death has not erased the poet's memories of her. In "Ha Chi Je Na   I Am Coming," Forché unites a story of an imminent birth with the natural elements of earth, air, fire, and water. Another poem, "Goodmorning and the White Girl," speaks of Teles Goodmorning, an American Indian who is nearing the end of his life and who is, like Anna, a spiritual guide for the poet. The last poem in this section, "Plain Song," is a death prayer that simultaneously returns the speaker to the earth ("Bring me to burn with a mesquite branch") and prepares the speaker to remain an immortal part of humanity ("and wear the bones that I leave/ around your necks").

In section 3, "The Place That Is Feared I Inhabit," the poet returns to the physical realm of the body; the title suggests that it is the woman's body that is feared. Several of the poems—"Taproot," "That Is Their Fault," "Year at Mudstraw," "Taking Off My Clothes," and "Kalaloch"—relate to the poet's perceptions of her sexuality. "Taproot" laments the loss of kinship between a young girl and a boy when the necessity to act according to tribally determined sexual roles interferes with childhood friendship. In "That Is Their Fault," the poet uses a metaphor of baking bread to narrate a multifaceted story of a neighboring family's poverty, violence, and squalor as a backdrop for childhood masturbation fantasies of degradation. "Year at Mudstraw" relates a new mother's powerful sexual needs, and "Taking Off My Clothes" details a woman's awareness that her sexual identity, as perceived by her male lover, is that of an object.

Hailed by Kunitz as possibly "the outstanding Sapphic poem of an era," "Kalaloch" is an erotic narrative of achieved mutuality between two women. Refusing to acknowledge the traditional taboo of lesbianism in Western culture, Forché's poem is a fitting culmination of the volume's primary themes, as the spiritual kinship of the poet and her grandmother identified at the volume's onset is reestablished in the physical union with the woman Jacynthe. It must be noted, however, that Forché is not advocating the rejection of men as a necessary condition for women's ability to connect; in the final poem, "White Wings They Never Grow Weary," and elsewhere, the poet intimates that men are important for companionship, intimacy, and the perpetuation of the tribes.

Analysis

Forché's poetic technique incorporates recurrent patterns of symbols throughout the volume, and she uses repetition to establish consistency in *Gathering the Tribes*. Perhaps the most persistent symbol in the book is whiteness: White is represented by snow, baking flour, the color of the poet's skin, and other images. Yet, whereas white has always been a symbol for women, particularly in regard to purity and virginity, Forché takes her symbolic use of white from other cultures. In countries such as Mexico, white traditionally symbolizes death. Therefore, in "Burning the Tomato Worms," the line that states "Cake flour clung to her face" in reference to Anna can be read as a foreshadowing of her death. The "muslin snow" in "What It Cost" symbolizes the death of the land for refugees who must leave it. In "Mountain Abbey, Surrounded by Elk Horns," white cattle slated for slaughter serve as symbols of faith for the abbey's bread-maker. "Your eyes are snowy," the poet writes in "Taproot," indicating that the boy she had once known is now dead to her. Yet death is never a finality in Forché's poetry; for example, even though Anna is dead, "Burning the Tomato Worms" indicates that she is "big under the ground," allowing for the possibility of Anna's rebirth.

Many of the symbolic purification and initiation rituals in *Gathering the Tribes* are spiritual ceremonies of connection and regeneration. Anna's religious rites in "Burning the Tomato Worms" serve to establish a "sacred and eternal" bond with her granddaughter; as Forché writes, "It was a timeless, timeless thing" that even death cannot destroy. Only the poet's furtive sexual initiation temporarily severs the kinship of grandmother and granddaughter. Following Anna's death, the poet seeks her presence in history, in the land, and in people she meets: Teles Goodmorning in "Goodmorning and the White Girl," Rosita in "Mientras Dure Vida, Sobra el Tiempo," and Jacynthe in "Kalaloch." In order to complete the cycle of the volume's poetry and restore her bond with Anna, the poet must purify herself from degradation and alienation.

In "Taproot," the boy's lust is awakened when he observes "a young monk" fondling the breasts of a statue, and the poet realizes that to satisfy him she must become the statue's physical manifestation. The woman in "Taking Off My Clothes" has desecrated her own body in order to please her sexual partner. In "That Is Their Fault," sexual release is only possible for the young girl masturbating herself to sleep by imagining acts of humiliation and violence. "Year at Mudstraw" describes the frustrating loneliness of a woman sexually rejected by her husband after she has given birth. The erotic poem "Kalaloch," conversely, is a sensuous celebration of women's bodies. Forché endows this poem with lush images of natural plenty that ironically contrast with the arid and violent imagery of her heterosexual poetry.

Read as a whole, *Gathering the Tribes* is a survival guide. The poetry urges the reader to recognize and embrace crucial common goals while it warns against self-destructive impulses to ignore history and the rhythms of nature. Mutuality is possible, Forché proclaims, once essential identifications are established among the tribes.

Context

Gathering the Tribes, Carolyn Forché's first volume of poetry, was published as part of the prestigious Yale Series of Younger Poets, an honor she shares with such distinguished poets as James Agee, Muriel Rukeyser, W. S. Merwin, and Adrienne Rich. *Gathering the Tribes* can be read in conjunction with other contemporary feminist poetry such as Rich's *The Dream of a Common Language* (1978) and *A Wild Patience Has Taken Me This Far* (1981) as similarly important poetic work actively seeking identity for women. While Forché does not consider herself to be the "feminist activist" that Rich is, her poetry reveals that she has been greatly influenced by women's concerns.

In *Gathering the Tribes*, Forché writes poetry that places a primary focus on women's heritages, experiences, and life rhythms. Rejecting conventional masculine poetic themes, in particular the Anglo-American heritage that centers on Western culture, Forché works with fragments of Slovak and Tewa (Pueblo Indian) language and myths, symbolically equating women's marginal status with other marginalized and oppressed peoples. She repudiates the traditional representations of women in male-authored poetry—stereotypes of the woman as lover, goddess, temptress, or deceiver. Instead, she develops full and complex portraits of women who fulfill a multitude of roles, and many of those roles serve independently of male expectations for women.

Forché's poetry focuses on spiritual and physical connections rather than on cerebral complexities; the poetry is both sensual and visual, and it derives from an inner comprehension. In other words, Forché expects her readers to see and feel her poetry instead of intellectually analyzing the poems for abstractions. Her frank exploration of women's sexuality, for example, and the myths and taboos that surround the subject, operates as a critique of women's traditional role as sexual object. Forché implies that women's spiritual kinship with their heritage, the earth, and their bodies engenders a sexuality which transcends mere physical union. *Gathering the Tribes* is ultimately an important part of the body of work produced by women authors challenging restrictive women's roles.

Sources for Further Study

Forché, Carolyn. "The Province of Radical Solitude." In *The Writer on Her Work: New Essays in New Territory*, edited by Janet Sternburg. New York: W. W. Norton, 1991. Forché writes an autobiographical account of her experiences with language, focusing in particular on her awakening political consciousness and her restless search for a poetic identity.

Gardner, Joann. "The Mirrored Self: Images of Kinship in Carolyn Forché's Poetry." *Women's Studies* 18, no. 4, (1991): 405-419. Gardner perceptively explores the themes of kinship and connection, mother figures, and sexuality in both *Gathering the Tribes* and Forché's second volume of poetry, *The Country Between Us* (1981).

Lerman, Eleanor. "Tribal World of Carolyn Forché." *Book Forum: An International Transdisciplinary Quarterly* 2 (Summer, 1976): 396-399. Lerman rejects the standard interpretation of *Gathering the Tribes* as poetry celebrating kinship and connection and offers an alternative reading; Lerman claims that Forché's poetry reveals a "deep sorrow at the ending of a way of life."

Ostriker, Alicia. "The Thieves of Language: Women Poets and Revisionist Mythmaking." In *The New Feminist Criticism: Essays on Women, Literature and Theory*, edited by Elaine Showalter. New York: Pantheon Books, 1985. A landmark feminist essay dealing with women's poetry, this article provides an excellent analysis of the feminist poets who aim to revise patriarchal language and traditional male-written myths.

Vertreace, Martha M. "Secrets Left to Tell: Creativity and Continuity in the Mother/Daughter Dyad." In *Mother Puzzles: Daughters and Mothers in Contemporary American Literature*, edited by Mickey Pearlman. New York: Greenwood Press, 1989. While the portion of this essay that specifically deals with Forché's poetry is not lengthy, Vertreace's discussion of the poems pertaining to Anna and her spiritual legacy provides useful insights.

Sarah Appleton Aguiar

GAUDY NIGHT

Author: Dorothy L. Sayers (1893-1957)
Type of work: Novel
Type of plot: Mystery
Time of plot: June, 1934, to June, 1935
Locale: Shrewsbury College at the University of Oxford, England
First published: 1935

> *Principal characters:*
>> HARRIET D. VANE, a highly successful author of mystery novels
>> and a graduate of Shrewsbury College
>> LORD PETER WIMSEY, a criminal investigator and the second son
>> of the duke of Denver, a wealthy scion of the British
>> aristocracy
>> MISS LYDGATE, an unworldly and gentle tutor of English
>> MISS DEVINE, a historian and a recognized expert on the subject
>> of Tudor finance
>> MISS HILLYARD, a historian
>> MISS MARTIN, the dean of Shrewsbury College

Form and Content

In *Gaudy Night*, Dorothy L. Sayers builds upon the basic structure of the mystery story to present a novel considering three separate but interwoven themes. At first glance, the mystery—ostensibly the reason for the novel's existence—seems comparatively tame: Shrewsbury College is plagued by a malevolent writer of "poison pen" messages. The plot involves the struggle to unmask the Poison Pen. As the story unfolds, it becomes clear that Sayers has employed this petty but malicious brand of crime to examine two far more critical issues; namely, the role of the intellectual woman in modern society and the proper relationship between a man and a woman bonded in marriage.

As the story opens, Harriet Vane nervously prepares to return to Shrewsbury College after an absence of several years. She attends the Gaudy, a reunion of old classmates, to discover that her rather public sins—she was wrongly accused of poisoning her lover and tried for murder—do not preclude her acceptance as an equal by students and faculty alike. Prospects of marriage and family may be closed off because of her past, but the world of the intellect lay open. The only event to mar her return is the discovery of two lewd and disgusting messages, crude notes which have no place at the University of Oxford. Some months later, Harriet is called back to consult with the Shrewsbury faculty. The college has been plagued by a series of vulgar sheets and malicious pranks; the Poison Pen has set to work to undermine the intellectual camaraderie of the college. When it becomes clear that the malefactor can only be one of the college servants (the "scouts") or a member of the Senior Common

Room (the dons and tutors of the faculty), Harriet reluctantly agrees to undertake the investigation.

In the ensuing weeks, the number and the gravity of the pranks escalate. Library books are damaged or destroyed, fuse boxes are ruined, and a student is nearly driven to suicide. Harriet struggles to establish alibis and thereby eliminate suspects, while at the same time keeping a careful record of all the activities of the Poison Pen. Yet she is unable to discern a pattern, not because of a lack of ability, but rather because of personal involvement and side distractions. The rigors of intellectual inquiry remain a powerfully attractive alternative to the unhappy emptiness of her past five years. Perhaps this is the life she should pursue, since the avenues to "normal" happiness seem closed off by the very public mistakes in her past. Yet, the thought that such an intellectual life might lead to the psychotic behaviors of the Poison Pen is horrifying.

The answers to Harriet's troubles seem to lie with Lord Peter Wimsey, who saved Harriet's life by uncovering the evidence that proved her innocence. As a criminal investigator, Peter is without equal. To ask for his help is dangerous, however, as he remains cheerfully determined to marry her. When the Poison Pen's activities assume dangerous proportions, Harriet finally requests Peter's assistance. Peter recognizes this as a crisis point, not only for the case at hand but also for their entire relationship. He treads lightly, gathering the threads of evidence and analyzing them for the patterns that will prove the malefactor's identity. Yet he is careful not to take over: This is Harriet's case; she must run the risks that she chooses. He will show her how to defend herself, but he will not defend her. Her life is her own.

The identity of the Poison Pen is successfully determined only after a last murderous attack on Harriet. Peter demonstrates that the individual's psychotic behavior grew out of an extreme and twisted ideal of domestic devotion. Shrewsbury's uncompromising devotion to women's education blunted and defeated the attack.

Analysis

Dorothy L. Sayers' career as a detective novelist flourished in the era immediately after the first great goal of the women's movement, the right to vote, was won. With such corollary rights as equal educational opportunity also in place, the essential feminist question for Sayers was to determine the proper role of women in society. Was it possible for women of talent and intellect to enter into marriage as equal partners with men? Did dedication to intellectual pursuit impede marriage, as it sacrificed domestic devotion to academic rigor? Were family and children the most important goals for a woman? Need she sacrifice her brain to achieve them? In *Gaudy Night*, Sayers set out to examine these important questions, structuring her story around the peculiar relationship between the aristocratic and sensitive Peter Wimsey and the intelligent but bitter Harriet Vane that had been developed in two previous novels. Unlike its predecessors, *Gaudy Night* concentrates almost exclusively on the thoughts and activities of Harriet. It is she who must wrestle with the question of head versus heart.

Sayers maintains that each woman must determine for herself what her proper "job" in life is to be. In a key conversation with Miss DeVine, Harriet Vane agrees that a proper job could be writing, research, or even traditional domesticity and devotion to a man. The important thing is to discover one's own proper job. Miss DeVine argues that when one does the correct job in the proper fashion, one does not make careless mistakes. Uncompromising determination makes such mistakes impossible. Harriet can ruefully confirm this; she made horrid mistakes in her personal life, but never in her writing. Harriet's job of writing precludes marriage unless she can find a partner willing to accept her as an equal and willing to accept her writing as a part of herself.

Over the course of ten novels, Sayers gradually shaped Peter Wimsey into her ideal of the proper man. Erudite and thoughtful, he is above all sensitive in his treatment of others. His misfortune has been to fall desperately in love with the one woman who seemingly can never be his equal, because he has saved her from the executioner. In the face of Harriet's at times savage resentment of the necessary gratitude, he must play act his passion as a kind of farce. By the time the events of *Gaudy Night* take place, five years of the farce have stripped him of all but his honesty. He not only accepts Harriet for what she is, both a woman and a writer, but also challenges her to become a better author, to write the book that she knows is inside of her. When he explains, almost offhandedly, that he loves Harriet for her own honesty, exhibited on the witness stand and ever after, she begins to examine the possibilities of marriage in a new light.

Still there are obstacles. Peter saved her life. They can only overcome that road-block if he can acknowledge that this life is indeed her own, to use and to risk as she sees fit. This he is finally able to do, being nowhere near when Harriet, understanding her danger, undertakes the activities that lead to the attack from the Poison Pen. Bloodied and very nearly murdered, Harriet is at last done with the necessity of gratitude.

The vicissitudes of Harriet and Peter's relationship are played out against the backdrop of scholarly achievement at Shrewsbury. The activities of the Poison Pen point up the strengths of the college. The women of the college, students and faculty, are exasperated and at times frightened by the Poison Pen, but they never waver from their task. Intellectual endeavor for women is not in any sense playacting or mere preparation for a "proper" life of domesticity. The harsh precision of Miss Devine and the gentle but firm analyses of Miss Lydgate exemplify scholarship at its most demanding, a higher calling to which both women and men of intellect must answer. The universal embrace of this calling creates a community of understanding which defeats the Poison Pen's efforts to discredit women's education.

Yet exercising the full abilities of the mind does not necessarily thwart the longings of the heart. As *Gaudy Night* concludes, Harriet Vane at last agrees, in Latin, on the grounds of the university, to marry Peter Wimsey. She will continue to write, and he will continue to investigate. They will support each other's endeavors and share in each other's honest love. For Sayers, it seemed ideally possible for a woman to possess both head and heart.

Context

Much to the surprise of Dorothy L. Sayers, *Gaudy Night* became a best-seller both in Great Britain and in the United States. Although she was unusually pleased with this particular work, she expected that the plot, turning on issues of women's roles in modern society, would not appeal to many readers. By weaving such issues into a superlative work in a popular genre, she successfully placed feminist questions before a widespread and atypical reading audience.

Sayers did not consider herself a feminist, arguing that she wanted to advance not merely the cause of women, but rather of the whole of humankind. To her mind, there was no particular woman's point of view to be promoted, but rather a need to free all people to exercise their abilities to the fullest in whatever occupation they choose. Her own field, detective fiction, was dominated by men, but this fact did not prevent her from exploring and extending her skills simply because she was a woman. To Sayers, the practice of writing understood no gender bias, nor did any other kind of occupation. To discriminate on the basis of gender was to inhibit the human race from getting on with its work.

In *Gaudy Night*, Sayers integrated these ideas into the character and experience of Harriet Vane. Because of her trial for murder, a significant segment of the public maintains that it is improper for Harriet to continue to write crime fiction. Yet that attitude denies Harriet her proper work merely on the basis of defined societal expectations, ideals bearing no relationship to her actual abilities. By continuing to write, Harriet upholds the duty of each human individual to undertake that which they do best, regardless of prescribed social norms.

Sources for Further Study

Brabazon, James. *Dorothy L. Sayers: A Biography*. New York: Charles Scribner's Sons, 1981. Generally accepted as the standard biography of Sayers, Brabazon's work is certainly the most thorough and includes a generous selection of primary quotations otherwise unavailable to researchers. Authorized by the Sayers estate to write the story of her life, Brabazon deals sympathetically with Sayers' passionate religious beliefs, but errs in casting her as desiring a too traditional female existence.

Dale, Alzina Stone, ed. *Dorothy L. Sayers: The Centenary Celebration*. New York: Walker, 1993. A collection of fourteen essays, including personal reminiscences of Sayers and analyses of her work, both the Wimsey novels and her later plays and translations. Especially pertinent are "*Gaudy Night*: Quintessential Sayers," by Carolyn G. Hart, and "The Marriage of True Minds," by B. J. Rahn, which details the entirety of the Wimsey-Vane romance.

Haycraft, Howard, ed. *The Art of the Mystery Story*. New York: Simon & Schuster, 1946. Still considered to be the best compilation of essays and commentary on crime fiction, this collection includes the observations of several noted detective authors regarding Sayers' work, generally acknowledging her as the "Queen of Crime." Most important, this book includes an essay by Sayers in which she details her long struggle to raise the detective story to the artistic level of the novel and to turn Peter Wimsey from a cardboard character into a human being.

Hone, Ralph. *Dorothy L. Sayers: A Literary Biography*. Kent, Ohio: Kent State University Press, 1979. Although necessarily less complete than James Brabazon's biography (above), Hone's book does include a number of sources neglected in the authorized work. Moreover, Hone, an American Baptist minister, is far more knowledgeable regarding Sayers' Christianity and more carefully attuned to her feminist ideas.

Reynolds, Barbara. *Dorothy L. Sayers: Her Life and Soul*. New York: St. Martin's Press, 1993. Reynolds worked closely with Sayers in the last years of her life and completed her translations of Dante's poetry. This biography provides perhaps the most intimate portrait of the artist at work. Includes an excellent selection of photographs.

Robert Kuhn McGregor

GEMINI
An Extended Autobiographical Statement on My First Twenty-five Years of Being a Black Poet

Author: Nikki Giovanni (1943-   )
Type of work: Autobiography
Time of work: 1950-1970
Locale: Knoxville, Tennessee, and Cincinnati, Ohio
First published: 1971

> *Principal personages:*
> NIKKI GIOVANNI, the poet herself
> LOUVENIA TERRELL WATSON, the poet's maternal grandmother,
>   an important influence on her life
> YOLANDE GIOVANNI, the poet's mother
> GUS GIOVANNI, the poet's father, a confident and fascinating man
> GARY, the poet's older sister and her friend
> TOMMY WATSON GIOVANNI, the poet's son

Form and Content

Composed of thirteen essays, most of them autobiographical and some previously published, *Gemini: An Extended Autobiographical Statement on My First Twenty-five Years of Being a Black Poet* records the coming-of-age of Nikki Giovanni as a black woman and her development and commitment as a black poet. Opinionated, honest, witty, and nostalgic, the collection offers the reader glimpses of selective moments in Giovanni's life. One follows the footsteps of the poet from her early girlhood and adolescence to her young motherhood and artistic success. Some essays in *Gemini* deal with Giovanni's relationship with her family while growing up, other essays focus on the relationship between black artists and the black community, the division of sexes between black men and black women, and the cultural differences between blacks and whites. Still others are devoted to why Giovanni becomes a writer and what her roles are as an African American female poet. The scope of her essays in *Gemini* is extensive.

To find out who she is in relation to her family, her community, and society at large was the focus of Giovanni's life in her first twenty-five years. As Giovanni makes it clear in one of her essays, this search for identity did not center on race. Rather, she still constantly defines and redefines herself in her own terms. From the essays in *Gemini*, one finds a most contradictory personality in Giovanni. As her best friend Barbara Crosby writes in the introduction to the book: "All I know is that she is the most cowardly, bravest, least understanding, most sensitive, slowest to anger, most quixotic, lyingest, most honest woman I know. To love her is to love contradictions and conflict. To know her is never to understand but to be sure that all is life."

Analysis

Nikki Giovanni firmly identifies herself as a black woman and black poet. She writes in one of the essays in *Gemini*, "On Being Asked What It's Like to Be Black," that any identity crisis she may have had never centered on race. The reader also gets the impression that she is not ambivalent toward her gender. Giovanni's strong belief in herself is attributable to the love and understanding that she has received from her family. Throughout her first twenty-five years, her family served as a buffer. In the essay "For a Four-Year-Old," Giovanni wittily accounts her idolizing relationship with her sister Gary, three years her senior. This is an important stage in Nikki Giovanni's life. In a four-year-old's eye, her all-knowing sister means everything to her. People would tease her "Can you do this?" or "Can you do that?" and she would always answer proudly, "No, but Gary can." She felt closely connected to Gary and was content to be simply "Gary's sister."

This interconnectedness is also seen with Giovanni and her grandmother, Louvenia Terrell Watson. The two developed a mutual understanding and respect. The house of her grandmother—400 Mulvaney Street, Knoxville, Tennessee—was always her spiritual home. *Gemini* begins with Giovanni arriving in Knoxville on a speaking tour and experiencing a sense of homecoming. Though both 400 Mulvaney Street and Louvenia exist no longer—the house has been destroyed by urban renewal and her grandmother is dead—Giovanni knows that this place is her source of strength and power. Although Giovanni did not know it at the time, she realizes later that Louvenia had been the force behind her to finish college. She was graduated from Fisk University on February 4, 1967, and Louvenia died on March 8 of that year.

Giovanni's parents, in their own way, were a steadying influence in her life. Her essay "A Revolutionary Tale" is about her involvement in the revolution for black power. Giovanni recounts how her mother made a firm decision that she either find a job or go to graduate school. Her father, all the time being sweet and understanding, quietly tells her that the revolutionary works in which she has engaged are ignorant of the realities of everyday black people. Giovanni's parents were trying to show her the importance of setting an example, of learning about a system in order to change it, and of understanding the people for whom and with whom you are working.

The discussion on the roles of black artists and their relationship with the African American community is an important theme in *Gemini*. Giovanni believes that musicians (as well as artists and writers) have always been in the forefront of the black experience and that music has been the voice of that experience, especially in the United States. In her essay "Black Poems, *Poseurs*, and Power," Giovanni expresses her concern about the danger of black artists slipping away from their roots. Black artists are the voice of their community, and they need to bring their art to the masses, not to make it elite. It seems that "the only thing that culturalists care about is assuring themselves and the various communities that they are the vanguard of the Black Revolution." They are competing for recognition and support from the whites, while poor people have always known that they are black. The black artists' task should be to find out where the community is going and to give voice to that dream.

Giovanni has a clear understanding of the cultural differences between blacks and whites. To her, these differences come from lived experience. As Giovanni claims in her essay "The Weather as a Cultural Determiner," "The culture of a people is an expression of its life style." She illustrates this point with the story of the ant and the grasshopper. Whites are ants, and blacks are grasshoppers. It is not that black people have no ability to delay gratification; it is simply the way in which they conduct their lives. Hence, Giovanni argues that African Americans must become the critics and protectors of their own, be it black music, art, literature, lifestyle, or culture. What is more, African American critics must view works from a black perspective.

Giovanni's understanding of the relationship between black men and women reflects, on the one hand, her profound love for black people and, on the other, her awareness of the sexist ideology in the black community. She is more concerned with the essence of this relationship rather than with its appearance. If a black man needs to know that he is leading by having his woman walking five paces behind him, then so be it. There is a historical truth embedded in black manhood: A black man's existence relies very little on his acts and more on his women—mother, sisters, and lovers. Commenting on the latent militarism of the black artistic community, Giovanni points out the sexist treatment of making African American women the "new Jews" in the Black Arts and Black Power movements. Recognizing the hidden hostility among black men and women, Giovanni advocates an honest communication between the two groups. At the same time, Giovanni ponders the possibility that "maybe men and women aren't meant to live with each other." Gender roles are already set up in the society to create conflicts in people's lives.

In her last essay, "Gemini—a Prolonged Autobiographical Statement on Why," Giovanni talks about how and why she became a writer and what she envisions for herself as a black female poet. She became a writer because she wanted to take a chance on feeling. She maintains that "love means nothing unless we are willing to be responsible for those who love us as well as those whom we love." She wants to show the world her love for her mother, her father, her grandmother, her sister, and her son. She remembers the people who have given her meaning in life. Her goal is to think a black, beautiful, and loving world.

Context

Gemini is an important book that marked a shift in Giovanni's life and writing. If her early writings are chiefly militant and revolutionary, her collections of poetry *Re: Creation* (1970) and *My House* (1972), written and published shortly before and after *Gemini*, are turned more to personal feelings and experience. Many of her poems written in the 1970's and 1980's focus on female identity, womanhood and motherhood, and the relationship between men and women. Giovanni has high praise for black women: "We Black women are the single group in the West intact. . . . It's clear that no one can outrun us." Her poetry has been read by young and old, black and white. She has achieved a popularity that is rarely experienced by living poets.

Nikki Giovanni has been a prolific writer. She has published several books of poetry, extended interviews with the older African American writers, such as *A Dialogue: James Baldwin and Nikki Giovanni* (1973) and *A Poetic Equation: Conversations Between Nikki Giovanni and Margaret Walker* (1974) that document the evolution of black artistic and aesthetic thinking; and poetry for children, including *Spin a Soft Black Song: Poems for Children* (1971), *Ego-Tripping and Other Poems for Young Readers* (1973), and *Vacation Time* (1980).

Sources for Further Study

Cook, Martha. "Nikki Giovanni: Place and Sense of Place." In *Southern Women Writers: The New Generation*, edited by Tonette Bond Inge. Tuscaloosa: University of Alabama Press, 1990. In this essay, Cook argues that the key to reading Giovanni is to place her in the rich tradition of Southern literature, in which the sense of place is a vital element. *Gemini* reveals Giovanni's strong link to the South, her spiritual home.

Fowler, Virginia C. *Nikki Giovanni*. New York: Twayne, 1992. Focusing on Giovanni's poetry, this book-length study not only offers a comprehensive analysis of Giovanni's poetry (with the exception of her children's poetry) but also provides the reader with some invaluable source materials on the poet's life and work, such as a chronology, a selected bibliography, an index, and an appendix. The appendix is a long, formal interview that Fowler conducted in Giovanni's study on October 12, 1991.

Giovanni, Nikki. "A *MELUS* Interview: Nikki Giovanni." Interview by Arlene Elder. *The Journal of the Society for the Study of the Multi-Ethnic Literature of the United States* 9, no. 3 (Winter, 1982): 61-75. In this first major interview with the mature Giovanni, the poet talks about the impact of a writer (do not think that writers have ever changed the mind of anyone or that a single poem can free all of humankind) and the relationship between the reader and the writer (the writer has the power over the reader but, at the same time, is vulnerable to the reader).

Harris, William J. "Sweet Soft Essence of Possibility: The Poetry of Nikki Giovanni." In *Black Women Writers (1950-1980): A Critical Evaluation*, edited by Mari Evans. Garden City, N.Y.: Anchor Press/Doubleday, 1984. Noting the contradictory fact that Giovanni has a large popular audience but has not gained the respect of critics, Harris claims that much of Giovanni's value as a poet derives from her insistence on being herself. She is a serious artist "because she tries to examine her life honestly."

Tate, Claudia, ed. *Black Women Writers at Work*. New York: Continuum, 1983. A collection of interviews Tate has conducted with fourteen important contemporary African American women writers, including Giovanni. Rather than writing from personal experience, Giovanni argues that writers write because they empathize with the general human condition. Her *Gemini* is not an autobiography, but an extended autobiographical statement, as the subtitle of the book indicates.

Weihua Zhang

GENERATIONS
A Memoir

Author: Lucille Clifton (1936-   )
Type of work: Memoir
Time of work: 1822-1969
Locale: Louisiana, Virginia, and New York
First published: 1976

> *Principal personages:*
> LUCILLE CLIFTON, an African American poet
> CAROLINE DONALD SALE, her great-great-grandmother
> SAM LOUIS SALE, her great-great-grandfather
> LUCILLE (LUCY) SAYLE, her great-grandmother
> HARVEY NICHOLS, her great-grandfather
> GENE SAYLE, her grandfather
> GEORGIA HATCHER SAYLE, her grandmother
> SAMUEL LOUIS SAYLES, her father
> THELMA MOORE, her mother

Form and Content

Dedicated to her father, Samuel Louis Sayles, *Generations: A Memoir* is African American poet Lucille Clifton's story of her family's genealogy. Written in prose, in five sections each named after a member of the family ("Caroline and son," "Lucy," "Gene," "Samuel," and "Thelma"), Clifton's memoir is a celebration of the strength of her family and of family ties, especially of her exemplary great-great-grandmother.

In her memoir, Clifton assumes the role of the griot, the African oral storyteller who passes on the record of the tribal history. She tells much of her family's story in the words of the original storytellers, her father and her great-great-grandmother. When she first began to think about the family stories, she worried about accuracy and demanded verification of the facts until her husband, Fred Clifton, told her "not to worry. . . . In history, even the lies are true." This observation is a significant one, for the family legends create their own truths by shaping the responses and beliefs of later generations of family members. Furthermore, history is always open to interpretation; its meanings depend upon the point of view of the historians. The stories of slavery, for example, will be different when told by descendants of slaves or by descendants of slave owners.

Generations starts with Clifton's conversation with a white collateral descendant of her family, a woman who has collected information about the family history. In this section, Clifton contrasts the position of the African American and white families. There is tension in the conversation: The white woman is puzzled and wary; Clifton is reassuring and conciliatory. The names of Clifton's branch of the family, the African American branch, are not listed in the white woman's records: Her slave ancestors are buried in unmarked graves. It reads like a short story which ends in triumphal affirmation: While the white woman is the last of her line, Clifton, on the other hand, is married and has six children. This section sets the pattern of the memoir, a pattern that reiterates the movement from slavery to freedom. In each section, Clifton combines tales of the past with present-tense narration. In all but two of the sections— "Caroline and son," section 6, ends with her brother whispering "We are orphans"; section 3 of "Samuel" ends with her father's burial—the movement is from difficulty to affirmation.

Next Clifton describes her journey from Baltimore to Buffalo for her father's funeral. Interspersed with memories of her father are his heroic stories of the family. The family matriarch, Caroline Donald (her names are slave names, because her real African name is not known) was brought as a slave to New Orleans and walked in a slave coffle from New Orleans to Virginia when she was eight years old. She married Sam Louis Sale, a slave from a nearby household who was forty-five years older than she was, and they had more than seven children. Caroline (known as Mammy Ca'line) became a midwife and was deeply respected by both whites and blacks. She took great pride in her African (Dahomey) heritage and repeated to her children "Get what you want, you from Dahomey women."

One of Caroline's children, Lucille (known as Lucy) had a child, Gene Sayle (the family added a *y* after emancipation), by Harvey Nichols, a white man who came from Connecticut after the Civil War. She shot him at a crossroads one night and waited there until she was found. Because of the whites' great respect for Caroline, Lucy was not lynched, but she was tried for the murder and became the first black woman legally hanged in the state of Virginia. After Lucy's death, Caroline took care of her child, Gene, and after Gene's death, she also took care of his son, Samuel Louis Sayle (Lucille Clifton's father).

Samuel Louis Sayle had little formal education, but he was an avid reader. After reading about plurals in a textbook, he thought "there will be more than one of me," and he changed his name to Sayles. He married Edna Bell, who bore a daughter, Josephine. After Edna died at the age of twenty-one, Sayles married Thelma Moore, who became the mother of Clifton and of Sammy Sayles. Thelma also died young, at the age of forty-four.

Samuel Louis Sayles was a proud man. He was born in Bedford, Virginia, and moved to Depew, New York, when a train came through the South offering jobs to black men. He had to have a leg amputated. Afterward, he "would smile and point to the empty place. Yeah, they got my leg, but they didn't get me, he would boast." He once walked twelve miles from his home in Depew to Buffalo to buy a dining room set, and he became the first African American man in Depew to have one. He surprised the family by buying a house. "Every man has to do three things in life," he said, "plant a tree, own a house and have a son." He had little education and could only write his name. When Lucille went to college, however, he spent all day writing a short letter to her. She writes, "I cried and cried because it was the greatest letter I ever read or read about in my whole life."

Thelma Moore was a plain woman. She spent most of her life caring for others: first her brothers and sisters, then her husband and her own children, and then her husband's daughter by a neighbor woman. She remained devoted to her husband, even though he openly carried on affairs with other women. Clifton describes her as "a magic woman." She did not go out much, but she used to sit in a rocking chair by the window. She suffered from epileptic seizures, and doctors were never able to determine the cause. The seizures were disturbing to her husband, and he worried that she was crazy. Lucille Clifton writes that facing this conflict in her family, "I wanted to make things right. I always thought I was supposed to. As if there was a right. As if I knew what right was."

In *Generations*, Clifton tells the family legends in simple and affirmative language. She regards each family member with a deep and quiet love and respect. She does refer briefly to problems in the family, but always in the context of love: Her father "did some things, he did some things, but he loved his family. . . . He hurt us all a lot and we hurt him a lot, the way people who love each other do, you know."

The memoir ends with an affirmation that "Things don't fall apart. Things hold." Clifton asserts that her six children continue the family tradition of "com[ing] out of it" better than their ancestors. "My Mama told me that slavery was a temporary thing, mostly we was free and she was right." Clifton imagines her great-great-grandmother Caroline nodding and smiling at her descendants. She then lists her generations, concluding with her own six children, and the promise that "the line goes on."

Analysis

Clifton's celebration of family is significant for women, whose central role (often in addition to paid employment outside of the home) is frequently that of mother and caretaker. In seeking to validate career opportunities for women and to encourage men to participate in family caretaking, some feminist writers of the 1970's and 1980's began to focus on the problems and limitations of maternal caregivers. This trend has been particularly prominent in the works of European American writers. African American women writers, on the other hand, have been more appreciative of women's nurturance. For example, Alice Walker, whose family history includes slavery (described in Walker's essay "In Search of Our Mothers' Gardens") stresses the importance of acknowledging her foremothers and paints a positive family portrait. Similarly, Paule Marshall, a black West Indian American novelist, has written in her essay "The Poets in the Kitchen" that listening to the stories her mother told her friends about her daily life taught her how to use language. The family memoirs of Walker, Marshall, and Clifton contrast with the work of European American women poets Anne Sexton and Sylvia Plath, who wrote of their families in negative or ambivalent terms, such as in Plath's poems "Daddy" and "The Colossus" or Sexton's poem "The Double Image."

Generations focuses primarily on matrilineage, in recognition of Clifton's powerful female ancestors. The family line in America begins with Caroline Donald Sale, who is described as "born free in Afrika in 1822, died free in America in 1910." This description of her great-great-grandmother sets the optimistic, positive tone of Clifton's memoir. She retells the story of her family by passing on the stories that her father told about her great-great-grandmother and her other ancestors. Although the lives set forth here were often difficult, Clifton's memoir is an affirmation of the strength of family ties and the value of the family.

Written in Clifton's characteristic simple, colloquial style, the memoir conveys strong emotions in plain, understated language. Clifton writes "I am interested in trying to render big ideas in a simple way. I am interested in being understood not admired. I wish to celebrate and not be celebrated." Yet although her language is simple, she brings a range of literary knowledge to her memoir. The quotations that introduce the work are drawn from the Book of Job and from her great-great-grandmother. Each chapter starts with a quotation from Walt Whitman's poem "Song of Myself," thus clearly placing Clifton's story in a tradition of American poetic autobiography.

Context

Lucille Clifton was named the Poet Laureate of Maryland in 1979, and in 1980 she was nominated for the Pulitzer Prize. She also received an honorary doctorate of humane letters from both Goucher College and the University of Maryland in 1980.

Clifton's memoir records her family's history in simple language, recognizing difficulties and problems, but affirming the strength of family love and connections in spite of hard times. Reflecting Clifton's affirmative vision, this book is important as a part of the ongoing reevaluation of the meaning of family and motherhood in women's lives that has been set in motion by the feminist movement.

Elsewhere, Clifton has written poems about her parents and her own children. She writes of her mother who "fell/ tripping over a wire at the forty-fourth lap." Clifton has also written children's books that describe the lives of young African Americans. Like her memoir, the children's books confront real problems with sympathy and love, as when Everett Anderson, who lives with his mother, says a prayer:

> Thank you for the things we have,
> thank you for Mama and turkey and fun,
> thank you for Daddy wherever he is,
> thank you for me, Everett Anderson.

In addition to the children's books *Some of the Days of Everett Anderson* (1970), *The Black BC's* (1970), and *Sonora Beautiful* (1981), Clifton has written several books of poetry, including *Good Times* (1969), *Good News About the Earth* (1972), *An Ordinary Woman* (1974), *Two-Headed Woman* (1980), and *Next: New Poems* (1987).

Sources for Further Study

Evans, Mari, ed. *Black Women Writers (1950-1980): A Critical Evaluation.* Garden City, N.Y.: Anchor Press/Doubleday, 1984. Essays in this book discuss the work of Clifton and other African American women writers, including Gwendolyn Brooks,

Paule Marshall, Toni Morrison, and Alice Walker. Each writer has written a short personal statement: Clifton's is "A Simple Language," which explains her intent in writing. The essays on Clifton are Audrey T. McCluskey's "Tell the Good News: A View of the Works of Lucille Clifton" and Haki Madhubuti's "Lucille Clifton: Warm Water, Greased Legs, and Dangerous Poetry." McCluskey's article includes references to *Generations*.

Lazer, Hank. "Blackness Blessed: The Writings of Lucille Clifton." *The Southern Review* 25, no. 3 (July, 1989): 760-770. Lazer examines how Clifton's use of language addresses political and aesthetic concerns, helping African Americans understand themselves.

Middlebrook, Diane Wood, and Marilyn Yalom, eds. *Coming to Light: American Women Poets in the Twentieth Century*. Ann Arbor: University of Michigan Press, 1985. This overview of the work of American women poets includes essays on Anne Sexton and Adrienne Rich. The essay on Clifton is Andrea Benton Rushing's "Lucille Clifton: A Changing Voice for Changing Times."

Karen F. Stein

GIFT FROM THE SEA

Author: Anne Morrow Lindbergh (1906-   )
Type of work: Essays
First published: 1955

Form and Content

While spending a week alone on the island of Captiva, Florida, Anne Morrow Lindbergh wrote *Gift from the Sea*, a collection of eight short essays inspired by the ebb and tide of the ocean. Each meditative piece focuses on a particular seashell, which Lindbergh uses to symbolize various perspectives on modern life. *Gift from the Sea* was on the best-seller list for more than six months, and it is still shared among women of all ages.

To become aware of inner rhythms, one must let today's tides erase yesterday's scribblings. With a mind free of responsibilities and time schedules, one is ready to receive the gift from the sea. Lindbergh uses these thoughts to introduce her collection of meditative essays. During her walks along the beach, she finds various shells; each unique design symbolizes different aspects of life, love, relationships, and identity.

The first shell is a channeled whelk, which is simple and bare. She realizes that her life is not simple since she has a husband, five children, and a home which require her attention. Her background, education, and conscience also contribute to the roles that she believes she must carry out in life. In satisfying external forces, she feels that she has lost a personal core, an individuality that lets her be herself. She wants to give to the world as a woman, an artist, and a citizen. Only when she has found her own means of giving will she feel an inward harmony that will be translated into an outward harmony. With a simple, unitary purpose that gives her direction, she will not feel fragmented by the multiplicity of life. She concentrates on removing the distractions that are inherent in her life and on replacing those tensions with a balanced core of inner peace.

The next shell is the moon shell whose spiral forms a solitary eye. To Lindbergh, this symbolizes that all people are alone. She claims, however, that people have forgotten how to be alone because they clutter their lives with constant music, chatter, and companionships. She encourages individuals to relearn how to be by themselves. When alone, people can get to know themselves, and in knowing themselves as individuals, they will be more willing to accept the individuality in others. Lindbergh goes on to explain that time alone is essential for women to replenish their wellspring of giving. She explains that women are forever nurturing children, men, and society. Time alone brings the quiet necessary to recharge resources. She addresses women who believe that their gifts are not needed by their families and society. To feel of value, women must turn inward. Time alone also brings out the creative life that resides within each individual and that may be expressed physically, intellectually, or artistically. She suggests that women do not need to compete with men in outside activities, that they need to develop their own inner springs.

Another shell is the delicate double-sunrise shell, which seems to wear a self-enclosed perfection. This beauty is used by Lindbergh to symbolize the early stages of relationships. She claims that the original pattern of ecstasy, that for which people hunger nostalgically, can never be held in an unchanging state. Life becomes too complicated and changes continuously, and so the love within that life must also change. She concludes that the ecstasy of early relationships is valid, but that validity is not dependent on continuity. Instead, it is one period in the ever-evolving spectrum of love.

Observing an oyster shell, Lindbergh sees a functional shell filled with many irregularities. She relates this to marriage after years have spread the relationship in many directions. Interdependencies and shared experiences are the bonds that keep the relationship together. She suggests that in middle age, people must begin shedding shells: "the shell of ambition, the shell of material accumulations and possessions, the shell of the ego." Then, they can become completely themselves by pursuing those intellectual, cultural, and spiritual activities that were set aside in their efforts to become worthy in society.

From the argonauta, Lindbergh meditates on the growth of relationships. Each partner must be given the space to grow in his or her respective direction. The distance that results must not frighten the partners because each is still strongly rooted in the marriage and in the family. The two separate worlds that result provide more to share with each other. She suggests that a couple should not look back to capture the ecstasy of the early relationship, nor should they look forward trying to define the future. Instead, they must be poised in the present, flowing with each day's tides. The couple must accept the ebb and flow of love, which is constantly in motion.

After greedily collecting shells, Lindbergh begins to realize that in the clutter of multiplicity, the beauty of individual shells is unappreciated. She realizes that in life people let too many activities, people, and possessions distract them from appreciating the significance of each. Only in simplicity can people retain a true awareness of life.

As Lindbergh departs from her week-long vacation, she reflects on what she has learned. She realizes that the "inter-relatedness of the world links us constantly with more people than our hearts can hold." She also reflects on America's appetite for the future, which results in rushing past the present. She concludes that people must make time for solitude, accept intermittency, and seek simplicity.

Analysis

During the 1950's, women's roles as housewives and mothers brought about some restless feelings. Women began to search for answers to ease their unhappiness. Lindbergh's book offered possible avenues for spiritual replenishment by suggesting that women simplify their lives. She wrote that technology, rapid changes, and the fast pace of modern life had cluttered women's lives. She suggested that women make time in their days to be alone, away from responsibilities, in order to nurture their spirituality.

In *Gift from the Sea*, Lindbergh discusses relationships between women and men. She encourages women to pursue personal growth and to accept growth in their mates. Although some distances may result from each spouse growing in different directions, Lindbergh concludes that the distances are not to be feared. The growth in relationships is like the growth of branches on a tree: each reaches in ever-broadening directions, but the trunk still remains stable in the ground.

Lindbergh also offers perspectives on love. She writes that love cannot be viewed as a permanent emotional condition that is without movement and change. Instead, love is constantly alive and altering in expression and feeling. By allowing for the fluidity of love brought about by growth, relationships are made stronger. Love must be given the freedom of ebb and flow.

As family members grow and begin to take independent paths, a mother's role is often left in limbo. Lindbergh addresses this issue and that of becoming middle-aged. Besides simplifying life in regard to time schedules, acquaintances, and space, women need to pursue activities that let them continue to give with purpose. For Lindbergh, this need is met by finding a solitary place where she can write, where she can forget herself, her companions, and the future. She suggests that women find their own creative activities to escape briefly the routines and responsibilities that surround them.

In solitude, women can nurture their inner lives, that aspect that is so often lost as one nourishes husband and family. In this way, women can find a sense of dignity as individuals, rather than letting themselves be standardized in thought and action. Lindbergh encourages women to nurture themselves as well as their families by finding a balance that allows for physical, intellectual, and spiritual development. Simplicity of time and space provides the environment in which such development can take place.

Context

Anne Morrow Lindbergh did not set out to write a book for women; she was writing meditations to resolve conflicts in her own life. Her friends persuaded her to put the essays into a book because all women could relate to her experiences. Lindbergh's *Gift from the Sea* was published eight years before *The Feminine Mystique* (1963), the groundbreaking feminist work by Betty Friedan.

Gift from the Sea is a unique piece of women's writing because Lindbergh does not ask women to abandon home life in order to pursue careers. As her several collections of diaries and letters reveal, especially the book *The Flower and the Nettle: Diaries and Letters of Anne Morrow Lindbergh, 1936-1939* (1976), Lindbergh devoted her life to her children and to her husband. Nevertheless, she also searched for time alone each day to write. Her lifelong practice of writing in every spare moment led her to Captiva and to write the meditations for *Gift from the Sea.*

Lindbergh did not encourage women to go out into the business world to seek meaning for their lives or to feel productive in society. Instead, Lindbergh encouraged them to find strength and meaning by turning inward, by nurturing their spirituality, and by expressing themselves creatively. Competing with men was not the answer that she offered; rather, simplifying life and nurturing the spirit would allow women to be the hub of a wheel around which the world turned. Without their inner strength, the wheel that represented all the lives that women touched would weaken. By finding and maintaining a balance of self—physically, intellectually, and artistically—women manage the distractions that occur in their everyday lives. They can utilize their inner strength to balance family life and social responsibilities.

Lindbergh acknowledged that life was stressful for women because of the constant demands to meet time schedules, to socialize with increasingly larger numbers of acquaintances brought about by mobility, and to maintain the numerous possessions resulting from industrialization. A woman's world was cluttered and could only be simplified by conscientious effort. Because it addresses the need for women to deal with the chaos of too many possessions, too many activities, and too many people, *Gift from the Sea* was popular when it was first released and remains so. Lindbergh's book offers encouragement to those women who want to be the hub of the wheel around which home life revolves. Lindbergh reveres the roles of mothers and wives without condemning those who choose professional roles. She presents a path by which those women choosing traditional roles can find self-worth and social meaning.

Sources for Further Study

Herrmann, Dorothy. *Anne Morrow Lindbergh: A Gift for Life*. New York: Ticknor & Fields, 1992. This candid biography focuses on Anne as an individual rather than as Charles Lindbergh's wife. Includes a bibliography of Anne's works, fine chapter notes, and an excellent bibliography for the study of Charles and Anne Morrow Lindbergh.

Lindbergh, Anne Morrow. *Dearly Beloved: A Theme and Variations*. New York: Harcourt, Brace & World, 1962. This book, like *Gift from the Sea*, was written during a dissatisfied period in Lindbergh's marriage. Using fiction rather then the nonfiction of *Gift from the Sea*, Lindbergh explores various conflicts in marriage, particularly the inadequacy of communication. Nevertheless, she firmly supports marriage for its sense of community.

——————. *The Flower and the Nettle: Diaries and Letters of Anne Morrow Lindbergh, 1936-1939*. New York: Harcourt Brace Jovanovich, 1976. A collection of diary entries and letters that are valuable in understanding Lindbergh's view of women's roles.

——————. *War Within and Without: Diaries and Letters of Anne Morrow Lindbergh, 1939-1944*. New York: Harcourt Brace Jovanovich, 1980. This final volume of Lindbergh's diary entries and letters covers the years of World War II. Anne discusses the Lindberghs' response to the accusations that Charles was a "traitor." She comments on the American attitude that raises individuals to hero status and then knocks them down by contempt and ostracism. She also reveals her personal struggles as she reconciles her devotion for her husband and their differing views about war.

Saint-Exupéry, Antoine de. *Wind, Sand and Stars*. Translated by Lewis Galantière. New York: Reynal and Hitchcock, 1939. This work was greatly admired by Lindbergh, who wrote a glowing review of it for the *Saturday Review of Literature*. Saint-Exupéry is often quoted in Lindbergh's writing because he was an aviator like herself and a writer who shared her perspective on the need for inner spirituality.

Linda J. Meyers

GIGI

Author: Colette (Sidonie-Gabrielle Colette, 1873-1954)
Type of work: Novella
Type of plot: Fairy tale
Time of plot: 1899
Locale: Paris, France
First published: 1944 (English translation, 1952)

> *Principal characters:*
> GIGI, a fifteen-year-old schoolgirl reared by a family of aging
>   courtesans to become a wealthy man's mistress
> GASTON ("TONTON") LACHAILLE, the heir to a sugar fortune and
>   a man of the world who falls in love with Gigi
> MADAME ALVAREZ, Gigi's grandmother, a former courtesan
> AUNT ALICIA, the matriarch of the family
> ANDRÉE ALVAREZ, Gigi's mother, a singer in the chorus of the
>   Paris Opera who never married Gigi's father

Form and Content

   Gigi is Colette's fairy tale of a young girl who grows up and marries her Prince Charming. Like the stereotypical fairy-tale princess, Gigi becomes the wife of a "prince" at the end of the story and will presumably live happily ever after; unlike the pristine storybook characters, Gigi is surrounded by sexual innuendo of which she is highly conscious. Indeed, she becomes the recipient of an indecent proposal herself before she takes control, shifting the balance of power away from others and into her own hands.

   It is no surprise that *Gigi* has translated so well to the stage and screen. The novella is composed largely of dialogue revealing the interaction between people rather than the private thoughts and interior journey that usually constitute the focus of the novel. Because of this, Colette's novella is sometimes called superficial; however, the conversations not only explore social customs and values but also reveal how off-center the customs and practices of this particular family of courtesans are. These women speak their minds to one another. They talk honestly and without euphemism so that the reader is able to become part of a web of relationships that centers on planning the future of Gigi.

   As a family friend, called Tonton ("uncle") by Gigi, Gaston Lachaille is charmed and amused by Gigi, who speaks without guile. It is through their repartee that he becomes enamored of her; it is what he does not say to Gigi that prompts her to refuse his offer to install her as his mistress in a fine home where he will take care of her. Finally, when she discloses to him that she would rather be miserable with him than without him—and he knows that she speaks from a pure heart—his own jaded persona melts away (his "silence seemed to embarrass her") and he asks for Gigi's hand in marriage. She accepts because he tells her that he loves her: "Oh!" she cried, "you never told me that."

The descriptive paragraphs do not attempt to penetrate the interior meanderings of the characters and, in fact, deal mostly with the outward appearances that reveal the personal quirks and tastes of these people who exist within a world of ritual, rigid rules, and planned reactions. Gigi's hair must be curled only at the ends, for ringlets all around would be too flashy. Madame Alvarez sleeps on a divan in the dining-sitting room waiting for her daughter to come home from the opera every night. Lachaille's preposterously lavish parties are dutifully given in order to satisfy what is expected of him, yet he is too often bored at his own soirées. Character transformations are clearly drawn using subtle changes of so-called outward demeanor that Colette reveals to the reader through her prose. At the beginning of the story, Gigi is a dishevelled and energetic schoolgirl dressed in childish clothing. Later, she is a well-dressed young woman asking for headache medicine. Gaston, who is the picture of perfection and pride in all his finery, must humble himself to Gigi in order to gain her hand in marriage. There are no superfluous moments in *Gigi*. Every detail serves to reinforce the notion of the fairy tale and to deflate it at the same time. Gigi begins as no beauty. She does not live in a castle, but she will. She begins the story an ordinary girl and by the end of the story becomes an extraordinary woman.

Analysis

When Colette wrote her captivating fairy tale *Gigi*, she was nearly seventy years old. It was 1944, and Europe had been conquered and destroyed by Hitler's Nazis. Colette's own husband, Maurice Goudeket, a Jew, had been arrested and sent to a prison camp in 1941. By the time that Colette published *Gigi*, both the author and the reader were in great need of a lovely story that took them to another place and time. The world of Gigi takes one back to the *belle époque* of Paris, when the world was optimistic and fun—a "once upon a time" for people surrounded by devastation.

Colette's attention to the small pleasures of daily French life—a warm cup of tea, a hearty plate of cassoulet—are intended to feed the reader's spirit at a time when food was hard to come by. Little candies and the gentle tug of a bead-embroidered bellpull are tiny memories that ring and echo in the memories of the Frenchmen during their most trying times. The fact that Colette chose sugar as the commodity controlled by the Lachaille family is indicative of her wish to spin her fairy tale with sweetness and light.

So many of the luxuries adored by the French are focused on in *Gigi* as symbols of the beauty and elegance that once surrounded them. Gaston brings Madame Alvarez bottles of champagne and *pâté de foie gras*. When Gigi is fitted for her feminine clothing, the seven and a half yards of rustling fabric, the wide flounced skirt of blue and white silk, recall the crisp, outdoor Impressionist paintings that captured only a moment before the subject moved on. Time moves on, warns Colette, and although the past seems even more desirable when the present cannot be endured, there must always be hope for a brighter future. Aunt Alicia, still living in the past, is described as having "fastidious taste." Elegance never goes out of style, good taste is timeless, and barbarians cannot remove beauty from the world. Aunt Alicia's apartment sparkles and shimmers: her tea set, the silver walls, her jewels, the knife blade one uses to cut lobster. It is a haven that is both luxurious and safe—the bed is covered in chinchilla, the rosary with seed pearls, the floor with Persian rugs.

Tantamount is the beauty of womanhood. Lest the gray world of 1944 plague men with grim, dull uniforms and plainly dressed women, Colette writes of a time when a woman was admired for "the turn of a wrist like a swan's neck, the tiny ear, the profile revealing a delicious kinship between the heart-shaped mouth and the wide-cut eyelids with their long lashes." Although the war that was being fought gave Colette and her countrymen some of their saddest moments, *Gigi* is, after all, a celebration of the triumph of woman. The fact that a young schoolgirl is about to begin a wonderful future is Colette's offering of hope to her reader. The future, for Gigi, will be a better one than anyone had dreamed for her.

Colette's novella, like the stories she had been writing for the French newspapers during the war, is about the world of women. Gigi is reared by women, is surrounded by female schoolmates, and has virtually no contact with men other than with "Tonton" Gaston. It is a feminine world that Colette has created choosing her symbols of nourishment and objets d'art about the home, portraying the inner sanctums where women have control. Once, when Gaston is visiting, Gigi's mother, Andrée, appears in dressing gown and curlers. Madame Alvarez comments: "It's plain that there's no man here for you to bother about, my child! A man in the house soon cures a woman of traipsing about in dressing-gown and slippers."

Man is a foreign intruder that one must work tirelessly to please and go to great extremes to suffer for. Aunt Alicia's discipline and beauty regimes are imparted to Gigi as essential to enhancing her face and figure. Although she is well past her prime, Aunt Alicia still retains these little tricks as if she were expecting a new lover at any moment. Liane d'Exelman, Gaston's girlfriend, attempts suicide when he discovers her with another lover. According to fashion, consuming an astonishingly painful overdose of laudanum is expected of the courtesan, and, in fact, she attempts suicide with predictability: "She has only one idea in her heart, that woman, but she sticks to it," remarks Andrée. Andrée is the only one of the four women who steps outside this female world to work at the opera. She has very little regard for men and, unlike her mother and aunt, does not view men as providers and rescuers. Her opinions, however, are not imparted to Gigi because, as a self-absorbed "artiste," she relinquishes her daughter's education to the older courtesans, whose lessons are decidedly of a sexual nature.

Context

Gigi is not a fairy tale for children. It is a book about the potency of women's sexuality and is replete with sexual metaphor. The matriarchal fortress serves to protect Gigi's virginity: "Don't get to know the families of your school friends, especially not the fathers who wait at the gates to fetch their daughters home from school." When Gaston innocently offers to take Gigi skating, Madame Alvarez forbids it, explaining that Gigi will be perceived by society to have been compromised. Gigi is told to "keep your knees close to each other, and lean both of them together," but she complains that it is too uncomfortable and that she would rather have her skirts lengthened because "with my skirts too short, I have to keep thinking of my you-know-what." Madame Alvarez explains that if Gigi's skirts were longer people would perceive her to be older and that would ruin her mother's career. In other words, her mother is still singing in the chorus not because of her great talent but because she is believed to be sexually vital. Although Gigi is still a virgin, she playfully asks Gaston to bring her "an eau-de-nil Persephone corset with rococo roses embroidered on the garters." Gigi, who was expected to be virginal nevertheless, was reared to be acutely aware of her sexuality. As Madame Alvarez instructed her, "You can, at a pinch, leave the face till the morning, when traveling or pressed for time. For a woman, attention to the lower parts is the first law of self-respect." A classmate of Gigi's is given a solitaire by a baron. Her grandmother immediately understands what this implies and forbids Gigi to remain her friend. Gigi has been made to know that the sexual power of women can be their most important asset. She considers falling into the trap set by the generations of women in her family but is saved from having to repeat history when Gaston asks her to marry him. At once, she has also saved her family and becomes their new matriarch, their heroine. Her potential for self-fulfillment becomes the happy ending.

Sources for Further Study

Cotrell, Robert D. *Colette*. New York: Frederick Ungar, 1974. Contrell provides a thorough biography of Colette and undertakes the task of applying her life to her various works. He also studies the symbols and tendencies prevalent in these works.

Lottman, Herbert. *Colette*. Boston: Little, Brown, 1991. Lottman's biography is an informative account of Colette's rise to fame and her life among the international set. Contains rare photographs of Colette's family.

Richardson, Joanna. *Colette*. New York: Franklin Watts, 1984. A comprehensive and well-researched book that studies the life and work of Colette in a most factual and methodical way.

Stewart, Joan Hinde. *Colette*. Boston: Twayne, 1983. Stewart sees Colette's theme as the shift of power away from men to women. *Gigi* is about a young woman who creates a new world where love is important, destroying an old order where sexuality was a commercial commodity.

Ward Jouve, Nicole. *Colette*. Bloomington: Indiana University Press, 1987. Ward Jouve discusses the theories of psychiatrist Sigmund Freud in relation to Colette's female characters and looks at the writer's singular contribution to the small list of women writers who, she claims, are neglected in school curricula.

Susan Nagel

THE GIRL

Author: Meridel Le Sueur (1900-   )
Type of work: Novel
Type of plot: Social realism
Time of plot: The 1930's
Locale: St. Paul, Minnesota
First published: 1978

Principal characters:
> THE GIRL, the unnamed narrator, the daughter of poor, rural
>   Minnesotans who finds work in a speakeasy
> CLARA, a frail and loving prostitute who befriends the Girl
> BUTCH, the Girl's love, who is shot while committing a bank
>   robbery
> GANZ, a gangster who rapes the Girl and shoots Hoinck and
>   Butch
> AMELIA, a woman who frequents the speakeasy distributing
>   leaflets for the Workers Alliance
> EMILY SCHAFFER, the Girl's mother
> HOINCK, a bootlegger who works in the speakeasy
> BELLE, the wife of Hoinck

Form and Content

The Girl is a novel built around the stories of women and men living under the shadow of the Great Depression of the 1930's in St. Paul, Minnesota. Meridel Le Sueur herself took down these stories from that time, when she was a member of the Workers Alliance and living in a warehouse with others. Although Le Sueur was unable to get her novel published in 1939—it was too radical, too pessimistic, too unconventional—by 1978 it was resurrected and acclaimed by feminist, literary, and historical scholars, as well as by the reading public.

In choosing an unnamed narrator, Le Sueur substantiates a basic tenet of her writing: to get rid of the "I," the egotistical, alienated, destructive hero-protagonist who must win or die at all costs. Instead, she seeks to verify the "communal I," the voices of the collective over the voice of the individual, the voices of cooperation over the voice of the competitor. In *The Girl*, a chorus of voices participate in the narrative. Gathering at the German Village, a bar and speakeasy, they tell their stories and write their lives. It is indicative of Le Sueur's emphasis on the collective voice that those who are outside the collective fail. For example, Butch, who insists that he wants to "beat out the other guy," that he always "must win," is killed.

The story begins with the arrival of the Girl from a village up the river in Minnesota. The daughter of a large, poor family, she is shy, sensitive, inexperienced, yet hard-working, and she soon wins a place among the others in the bar. The Girl is not only running away from being a burden on her family but also running toward a new life, new experiences, and new hopes. She finds work as a waitress at the bar and immediately falls in love with a young, lean man, Butch. Encouraged by Clara and Belle, women who suffer at the hands of men yet "can't live without them," the Girl and Butch take up with each other. The story takes place over four seasons, from fall through the next summer.

Poverty looms over the characters' lives, and they make desperate choices: Clara walks the streets; Butch's brother, Bill, is killed "scabbing" during a workers' strike; the Girl, lured by Ganz's offer of twenty-five dollars so that she can help Butch buy his gas station, is raped by Ganz and his lawyer, Hone; and Hoinck and Butch join Ganz in a plot to rob a bank and consequently are killed.

The women cooperate with one another in sustaining the men as well as themselves. Belle's rich stew, "booya," which she serves Saturday nights in the bar, symbolizes the unrequited nurturing and care that she and the other women disburse throughout the novel. It is they who clean wounds, prepare food, find money for warm rooms, and assist at death and at birth.

They also love men. Belle and Hoinck have been married more than thirty years, and they still quarrel and make love with passion. The Girl loves Butch, with his face as lean as a fox and his graceful body; he is the first man to make love with her. Even when he hits her, she is not deterred in loving him. His immaturity and bravado are endearing. Clara "loves" many men, for half an hour at a time, but religiously she holds onto the promise of the ideal man, whom she will one day marry and with whom she will live happily ever after.

The first half of the novel focuses on women and men, but after the bank robbery, which occurs midway through the novel, the men disappear for the most part. The women band together, first in a tenement and then in a warehouse, struggling to survive the loss of their men and to ward off the relief workers who advocate sterilization and electric shock treatments for the Girl and Clara. The novel ends with the death of Clara in the same hour as the birth of the Girl's baby, who is given the name Clara by the women attending her.

Analysis

Although on the surface the story of *The Girl* seems uncomplicated and straightforward, further consideration reveals mythic patterns and poetic rhythms that resonate beneath the story of a group of patrons of a speakeasy, a bank robbery, and a girl's pregnancy. Le Sueur envisions the narrative of *The Girl* as "cyclical," embodying the enfolding of the human spirit and destiny. She believes that a linear narrative denotes death (beginning, middle, and end), whereas a cyclical narrative embodies continuity. Thus at the end of *The Girl*, Clara's death juxtaposed with the birth of the Girl's baby represents the birth-life cycle. The stories of the women and men culminate in a circular movement toward this "end," out of which also comes a beginning.

The cyclical movement in the novel is twofold: interwoven from the course of the seasons, the gestation of the baby paralleling the Girl's maturation; and, from the men's and women's needs and desires, a dialectic circling through sex, love, death, and life. Other circular movements occur within the larger cycles. The Girl leaves the country for the city, leaving innocence and inexperience for growth and experience. Amelia lives in the word—she distributes leaflets for the Workers Alliance and is passionate about recording others' lives—but she also lives in action. Her acts, from the seemingly trivial to the significant, are made with a commitment to the community: She peels carrots for Belle's stew; helps the cat, Susybelly, which is having a difficult time giving birth to a first litter of kittens; organizes a milk drive for starving women such as Clara; and is midwife to the Girl's child. All is significant, and all is life; "glory," she says, is remembering it all.

The myth of Demeter and Persephone, an undercurrent in many of Le Sueur's writings, is present in *The Girl*. Through the seasons and through the search for the daughter (or the search for the mother), the women "write their stories." When the daughter, the Girl, leaves her mother after the father's funeral, she enters into the "underground" of criminality through her desire for sex and through her loyalty to the man who initiates her into both worlds. The bank robbery, planned by the gangster and rapist Ganz, takes place in the middle of winter. It is the time of Butch's death, but it is also the moment when the Girl announces that she has not had the abortion that Butch demanded: "I had to smile. I had already robbed the bank. I had stolen the seed. I had it on deposit. It was cached. It was safe." By the time that she makes her way back into the world of women and motherhood, it is summer. Thus the Girl, like Persephone, returns with seed from the underground for her time of fruition in the sun.

Not all the women in the novel follow this mythic pattern. Clara, the Girl's friend and guide in the city, ironically loses her way in its underground, as the Girl finds her way back. Through Clara, Le Sueur limns the antimyth, the Persephone whose mother fails to call her back. Clara's symbolic "mother" is a society that lives off the bodies of its young women and men. It is a society that promotes pandering for goods and dreams. Clara tells the Girl that she will meet "nice men, too, that'll give you lace tablecloths and peasant pottery." People such as Clara and Butch sell themselves for dreams of "two-bedroom homes in Florida" and lace tablecloths, or, in Butch's case, for a lease on a service station; in short, they sell themselves for the middle-class dream. In the stories of Clara and Butch, Le Sueur opens up another aspect of *The Girl*: the theme of class analysis, a political dialectic bridging gender and class.

Context

The Girl holds a unique place in women's literature for several reasons, one being because it is a text rich in the application of matters of literary theory, for those at home in the French school and for those at home in the British and American school. Whether one is interested in "writing the body," in the psychoanalytical approach to women's literature, in a historical class analysis, or in a revision of class and gender in women's revolutionary texts of the 1930's (as critic Paula Rabinowitz has written), *The Girl* is a gold mine.

In both form and content, the novel remains one of the most interesting works for feminist and historical scholars and for general readers, both women and men. Although the novel is set in the 1930's during the Great Depression, there is a community of women survivors who celebrate renewal and the human spirit. Among many contemporary women writers, except for some notable African American authors, one misses this perspective. In a time in which "the feminization of poverty" has become an issue, *The Girl* is contemporary in its perspective. Its view that women are exploited through economic systems is balanced by its view that they are, by the fact of being women, survivors. Le Sueur's language is a vital exploration of women's and men's sensibilities; she juxtaposes the elegiac and the profane, weaving both in prose closer to poetry than to exposition.

A revised edition by Le Sueur, edited by John F. Crawford, was published in 1990. This edition, with Le Sueur's afterword and afterwords by her daughter, Rachel, and friends Dr. Neala Schuleuning, a university professor, and Irene Paull, a Communist comrade from the 1930's, serves as a palimpsest of women's stories, issues, and lives.

Sources for Further Study

Barrett, Eileen, and Mary Cullinan, eds. *American Women Writers: Diverse Voices in Prose Since 1845.* New York: St. Martin's Press, 1992. The editors have included a concise biography of Le Sueur as a preface to her short story "Women Are Hungry."

Gelfant, Blanche H. *Women Writing in America: Voices in Collage.* Hanover, N.H.: University Press of New England, 1984. In a chapter entitled "Meridel Le Sueur's 'Indian' Poetry and the Quest/ion of Feminine Form," Gelfant explores the Hopi Indian influences on Le Sueur's language and structure. Although Gelfant is dealing primarily with poetry, her work also sheds light on Le Sueur's prose in general, emphasizing its cyclical, repetitive, rhythmic, and lyrical qualities, as well as its patterns of "continual return."

Le Sueur, Meridel. *The Girl.* Edited by John F Crawford. Albuquerque, N.M.: West End Press, 1990. Included in this edition is an essay by Crawford, "The Book's Progress: The Making of *The Girl*," in which he notes the changes made by Le Sueur since the novel was first published in 1978, with explanations as to why they were made.

_____. *Ripening: Selected Work, 1927-1980.* Edited by Elaine Hedges. Old Westbury, N.Y.: Feminist Press, 1982. In an extensive introduction, Hedges encapsulates Le Sueur's published writing, both descriptively and analytically. She traces the genesis of *The Girl*, noting previous publications of its segments or chapters.

Rabinowitz, Paula. *Labor and Desire: Women's Revolutionary Fiction in Depression America.* Chapel Hill: University of North Carolina Press, 1991. Rabinowitz places *The Girl* in a radical, historical, and feminist context. Le Sueur emphasizes feminine desire and maternity becoming historical narrative and identifies "the masses with the maternal."

Alice L. Swensen

GIRL, INTERRUPTED

Author: Susanna Kaysen (1948-   )
Type of work: Memoir
Time of work: 1967-1969
Locale: McLean Hospital, a psychiatric treatment center
First published: 1993

> *Principal personages:*
> SUSANNA KAYSEN, the author, who was committed to a mental
>   hospital as a teenager
> GEORGINA, her roommate
> DAISY, a teenager who commits suicide
> BRAD BARKER, a young patient who is judged "delusional" for
>   claiming that his father is a CIA operative

Form and Content

    Girl, Interrupted is Susanna Kaysen's idiosyncratic account of the nearly two years that she spent in a mental institution, after she was "interrupted in the music of being seventeen." In 1967, after having been interviewed briefly by a physician whom she had never seen before, Kaysen was put in a taxicab and sent to McLean Hospital, a private residential psychiatric treatment center.

    Initially, Kaysen's psychiatric treatment grew out of a failed—and fainthearted—suicide attempt involving fifty aspirin tablets, out of her failure to measure up to society's expectations:

> [M]y parents and teachers did not share my self-image. Their image of me was unstable, since it was out of kilter with reality and based on their needs and wishes. They did not put much value on my capacities, which were admittedly few, but genuine. I read everything, I wrote constantly, and I had boyfriends by the barrelful.

    This same diagnosis of social maladjustment, rendered with a particularly nasty misogynistic edge, is apparently what leads the psychiatrist to recommend Kaysen's commitment after concluding that she has been picking at a facial blemish because she has trouble with a boyfriend. Several chapters later, almost as an afterthought, Kaysen reveals that this same doctor was later accused of sexual harassment by a former patient. It is characteristic of her style that she makes little of this observation, but like her, the reader cannot help but wonder what sort of hidden agenda led to her incarceration, particularly when her release, occurring in the wake of a marriage proposal, seems equally arbitrary.

    Kaysen structures her memoir by interspersing brief chapters devoted to discrete incidents with pages taken directly from her medical records from McLean Hospital, which she secured with the aid of a lawyer twenty-five years after she was discharged. The effect of this juxtaposition is jarring. The official language of craziness, the dry, matter-of-fact way in which the details of her incarceration are recorded—for example, the episode in which she bites her hand until it bleeds in order to find the bones within is labeled one of "depersonalization"—is entirely at odds with the graceful simplicity that Kaysen employs in describing her state.

Kaysen notes that madness, the madness of those incarcerated at McLean in particular, has powerful artistic connotations, McLean having housed at various times poets Robert Lowell and Sylvia Plath and singers Ray Charles and James, Kate, and Livingston Taylor. She does not dwell overmuch on the nexus between her diagnosis and her own creative gifts, but she points out that in fact she did manage to make a life for herself out of boyfriends and literature. She has become a writer with published novels to her credit.

Analysis

Kaysen was not committed to McLean by her parents, but the depression that landed her there seems to have resulted from her inability to measure up to their image of what she should be. As Kaysen memorably puts it in *Girl, Interrupted*, "Lunatics are similar to designated hitters, Often an entire family is crazy, but since an entire family can't go into the hospital, one person is designated as crazy and goes inside."

Kaysen does not know if she was crazy in 1967, and she does not know if she is crazy still. As she said about that period of her life in an interview, "I was desperately unhappy, but I'm not sure it's the same thing." Indeed, Kaysen's diagnosis, something called "borderline personality disorder," partakes more of a sense of social maladjustment than of mental disorder. The symptoms of this malady seem to consist of "uncertainty about several life issues," such as self-image, sexual orientation, and long-term goals, which manifest themselves as promiscuity and excessive shopping. As one of her psychiatrists tells her, a "borderline personality" is "what they call people whose lifestyles bother them." Kaysen cannot help but note that the diagnostic manual says that this vaguely defined mental illness is "more commonly diagnosed in women," adding, "Note the construction of that sentence. They did not write, 'The disorder is more common in women.' It would still be suspect, but they didn't even bother trying to cover their tracks."

As Kaysen argues, most young people caught up in the turbulence of the late 1960's suffered from what the larger society perceived as personality disorders. She makes the case for the general craziness of the times most compellingly in a chapter called "Politics," which features a young inmate named Brad Barker. Brad has been committed because he has delusions that his father is an operative for the Central Intelligence Agency (CIA) who works with two individuals named Liddy and Hunt, "guys who will do anything." As Kaysen notes, what happens in the parallel world of the loony bin is a tryout for the real world: Years later, Bernard Barker, G. Gordon Liddy, and E. Howard Hunt would be connected with the break-in at Democratic Party headquarters at the Watergate Hotel in Washington, D.C.

Although she conveys her story of her tenure at McLean with considerable irony, Kaysen does not deride her experience there. She seems to have valued, above all things, the sense of protection that it afforded her at a time in her life when she was feeling extraordinarily vulnerable. While this protection did not come without a price—room checks every five, fifteen, and thirty minutes and barred windows that can only be opened by the staff—it provided a framework, a sense of stability around which to organize the chaos that raged within her. In a chapter entitled "Velocity vs. Viscosity," Kaysen describes with unforgettable acuity some of the thought patterns that constitute insanity:

> First, break down the sentence: *I'm tired*—well, are you really tired, exactly? Is that like sleepy? You have to check all your body parts for sleepiness, and while you're doing that, there's a bombardment of images of sleepiness, along these lines: head falling onto pillow, head hitting pillow, Wynken, Blynken, and Nod, Little Nemo rubbing sleep from his eyes, a sea monster. Uh-oh, a sea monster.

Her gifts as a writer show themselves in *Girl, Interrupted* not only in her philosophic explorations of the meaning of madness but also in her portraits of those who share her parallel world. Kaysen has admitted that she had to invent dialogue for her memoir, adding that, "My argument is that it's true even if it might not be the facts." Similarly, even though insanity might be said to have its own paradigms and patterns, Kaysen has surely added shape to the experiences of her fellow inmates. While her roommate Georgina may have "lacked affect" after Kaysen poured hot melted sugar over her hand, it is Kaysen the writer who makes the connection between Georgina's lack of reaction to being burned and G. Gordon Liddy's nightly ritual of holding his palm over a candle flame as a rehearsal for torture. While Daisy's father may have purchased an apartment for his daughter in a building surmounted with a sign reading, "If you lived here, you'd be home now," Kaysen's deft and subtle touch underscores the irony of Daisy's subsequent suicide in a space presided over by such an epigram, making symbolic use of an advertisement in much the same way as F. Scott Fitzgerald did with the eyes of Doctor T. J. Eckleburg in *The Great Gatsby* (1925).

As Kaysen makes clear, those who have crossed over into madness can never come back entirely. Getting there is easy—"most people pass over incrementally, making a series of perforations in the membrane between here and there until an opening exists"—but because of the fear that her stigma of craziness engenders in others (and in herself), Kaysen realizes she never will get entirely free of the alternative world that she inhabited in her youth.

In a memorable and moving coda to her memoir, Kaysen explains its title, taken from a Jan Vermeer portrait entitled *Girl Interrupted at Her Music*, which features a young girl with her music teacher. Kaysen contrasts this painting with two others by Vermeer housed with it in the Frick Collection in New York City. When she first saw Vermeer's girl, Kaysen was seventeen, and she did not notice the other two paintings, having been distracted by a warning that she believed the girl was trying to deliver. Sixteen years later, when she revisited the painting, it filled her with sadness, for she saw that, as had happened to her, one moment of the girl's life had been made to stand for all the others. Kaysen contrasts the girl at her music, who "sits in . . . the fitful, overcast light of life," with the subjects of the other Vermeers, both self-contained paintings illuminated by unreal light. Life is not, Kaysen implies, a sunny affair for anyone, sane or insane, and people cannot accurately judge others or even themselves. The division between the parallel worlds, both of which she has inhabited, is a matter of perception.

Context

Girl, Interrupted was published to nearly universal critical acclaim. Although it is a highly personal account of one person's journey through the world of modern psychiatric medicine, Kaysen manages to make her story emblematic of the dislocation experienced by young people—young women, in particular—beset at once by societal rigidity and social chaos. How, she seems to ask, can one grow into an individual when the slightest deviation from expected norms can result in a diagnosis of mental illness that will scar one for life? How, in the culture of the 1960's, could anyone tell what the norm was?

Kaysen's book is a poignant addition to the literature of women and mental illness, bringing to mind such classics of the genre as Charlotte Brontë's *Jane Eyre* (1847), in which the spurned first Mrs. Rochester is confined to the attic of her husband's mansion because she is deemed mad, and Jean Rhys's prequel, *Wide Sargasso Sea* (1966), which explains how youth and an alien culture served to "derange" Bertha Rochester. Kaysen's mastery of irony and understatement, and the grasp of metaphor that she demonstrates throughout her book (nowhere better than in her explanation of her distinctive title), all make a strong case for placing *Girl, Interrupted* in such exalted, and decidedly literary, company.

Sources for Further Study

Bell, Deborah, ed. *Lives in Stress: Women and Depression*. Beverly Hills, Calif.: Sage Publications, 1982. This series of essays by feminist therapists has special significance for Kaysen's story, asking why so many more women than men suffer from depression.

Bernay, Toni, and Dorothy W. Cantor, eds. *The Psychology of Today's Woman: New Psychoanalytic Visions*. Hillsdale, N.J.: Analytic Press, 1986. This series of essays by a variety of therapists offers a reassessment of feminine psychology in the light of new perceptions of femininity.

Chesler, Phyllis. *Women and Madness*. Rev. ed. San Diego: Harcourt Brace Javanovich, 1989. First published in 1972, this was one of the first books to popularize a feminist approach to psychotherapy. The 1989 edition updates advances in the field.

Gilbert, Sandra M., and Susan Gubar. *The Madwoman in the Attic: The Woman Writer and the Nineteenth-Century Literary Imagination*. New Haven, Conn.: Yale University Press, 1979. This groundbreaking work of literary criticism takes a fresh look at literary classics from a feminist point of view, pointing out how such works reflect their female authors' attempts to circumvent social constraints.

Penfold, P. Susan, and Gillian A. Walker. *Women and the Psychiatric Paradox.* Montreal: Eden Press, 1983. The research of two Canadian therapists explores the differential treatment accorded male and female psychiatric patients.

Lisa Paddock

GOBLIN MARKET AND OTHER POEMS

Author: Christina Rossetti (1830-1894)
Type of work: Poetry
First published: 1862

Form and Content

Goblin Market and Other Poems was the first book of poetry that Christina Rossetti published, although her grandfather had privately printed a collection of her juvenilia when she was seventeen. Despite its appearance at the beginning of her literary career, *Goblin Market and Other Poems* contains some of her finest and most enduring writing: the title poem, "Goblin Market," still her best-known work: "Up-Hill," "After Death," "Remember," "The Three Enemies," "A Better Resurrection," "An Apple Gathering," "Advent," "The Convent Threshold," "Dead Before Death," "A Triad," "Winter: My Secret," and "No, Thank You, John," among others. Though Rossetti would continue writing for another thirty years, no later poems surpassed these.

"Goblin Market," her most anthologized and discussed poem, is also, at 567 lines, one of her longest. A narrative poem (a rarity for Rossetti), it tells the story of two sisters, Laura and Lizzie, and their close brush with a sinister group of goblin merchants. The first of the twenty-nine irregular stanzas simply records the cries of the goblin men for someone to buy their magical fruits. In the following stanzas, Laura and Lizzie listen to the tantalizing cries; Lizzie warns Laura not to succumb to temptation, reminding her of the fate of their friend Jeanie who, after tasting the goblin fruit, wasted away with premature age and died. Laura ignores the warning, and, though she has no money, buys the enchanted fruit with a lock of her golden hair.

The fruit delights Laura, but leaves her wanting more, which she cannot have since she can no longer see or hear the goblins. Her addiction becomes her obsession, and she pines away for the fruit, not eating or sleeping and, like Jeanie, dwindling and turning gray. The only antidote is a second taste of the fruit, which the goblins withhold from their victims. When Lizzie realizes that her sister is dying, she goes to the goblins, whom she can still see and hear, and offers to buy their fruit. When they realize that her intention is not to partake of the fruit herself but to take it to the ailing Laura, the goblins try to force-feed her. Wearing down the goblin men with heroic resistance, Lizzie returns to Laura—not having tasted the fruit, but having its juice and pulp smeared all over her face by the struggle. When Laura kisses her sister, she tastes the juice, which removes the curse of the goblin fruit and restores Laura's youth and health. The final stanza is an epilogue in which the sisters, now married and with children of their own, use the story of the goblin market as an object lesson to their children of the salvific virtue of sisterhood.

Many of the shorter lyrics in *Goblin Market and Other Poems* demonstrate Christina Rossetti's characteristic and almost obsessive preoccupation with death as a release. Four Petrarchan sonnets in the collection treat the theme of love and death in four different ways. One, "After Death," surveys a deathbed scene from the point of view of a recently deceased maiden who triumphs in finally having captured the attention of a young man whom she had loved in vain. In another sonnet, "Remember," the young woman is alive but anticipates her death, urging her young man to remember her, but only if the memories will not make him sad. "Remember" utilizes the Petrarchan sonnet form to advantage, using the break between the octave (the first eight lines) and the sestet (the final six) to contrast the admonition to remember with the plea not to be sad.

A third sonnet, "Dead Before Death," laments the contrast between what one expects of life (and death) and what one gets. Unlike the other two sonnets, "Dead Before Death" makes no overt mention of romance, but the image of a fallen blossom which bears no fruit seems to refer to a love that could have been, the possibility of which is forestalled by death, who shuts the door. The octave begins the lament, while the sestet forms a kind of dirge in which the word "lost" is repeated six times. A fourth sonnet, "A Triad," looks at three women whose failed pursuits of love end in death: the first, a wanton whose indulgence in a sensual love brings her only shame; the second, a wife whose marriage is proper but "soulless"; the third, an unmarried woman who dies yearning for love. The octave describes the three women, while the sestet tells the results of their loves, all negative.

Analysis

The poetry of *Goblin Market and Other Poems* was immediately recognized as a significant contribution to English literature, and it set the tone for Christina Rossetti's later writing: Her metrical inventiveness, as well as her themes of death, ascetic renunciation, and thwarted love, were established here.

The theme of renunciation is central to the title poem "Goblin Market," and critics Sandra M. Gilbert and Susan Gubar have identified it as a key aspect of all Rossetti's writing. Though not overtly Christian or devotional as her later poetry, "Goblin Market" seems at first to express a traditional Christian attitude of renunciation of the sensual, of the flesh. Yet many critics have noted an ambiguity in the way in which sensuality, represented by the goblin fruit, is depicted in the poem. Laura's devouring of the fruit, paralleled later by her equally sensuous sucking of the juices off her sister's face, is described in a lushness of physical imagery unusual in Christina Rossetti's poetry (though typical of the verse of her brother, Dante Gabriel Rossetti).

The overt moral on the value of sisterhood, found in the final six lines of "Goblin Market," is often disparaged as an afterthought, unrelated to the rest of the poem, which is about renunciation. A close study of Lizzie's sacrifice for her sister, however, reveals that the themes of renunciation and sisterhood are related. Lizzie's resistance to the charms of the goblin fruit is merely temperance in the first scene, but when she seeks the goblin merchants after Laura's illness, her resistance takes on a heroic, sacrificial quality. Lizzie's Christlike self-giving defines sisterhood and makes her even more Christlike as Laura's savior, resurrecting her from the death-in-life caused by the evil fruit—an obvious parallel to the Eden story.

A few critics have been tempted to discover an autobiographical element in "Goblin

Market," which leads to a general question of how subjective a reader should consider Rossetti's poetry to be. Christina dedicated the poem to her sister Maria Rossetti, and her brother William speculated that Lizzie represented Maria and that the poem referred to some specific incident of "spiritual backsliding" on Christina's part, of which he was unaware. Violet Hunt picked up the hint in her study *The Wife of Rossetti: Her Life and Death* (1932) imagining that Maria had saved Christina from eloping with James Collinson, whose proposal Christina had refused nine years earlier and who had married another. Lona Mosk Packer's 1963 biography *Christina Rossetti* painted the same scenario, but with another married man, William Bell Scott. With nothing but circumstantial evidence for such speculation, most critics prefer to limit the interpretation of "Goblin Market" to its imagery and form, which are surely rich enough.

The meter of "Goblin Market" is much freer than that of most poetry of the mid-nineteenth century, which led to much criticism by her contemporaries. The first review of *Goblin Market and Other Poems*, in the April 26, 1862, issue of *The Athenaeum* (where much of Christina Rossetti's early verse had been published), praised the volume generally, yet lamented its "discords" and "harshness." The leading critic of the day, John Ruskin, made the same criticism in reading the work in manuscript, judging that no one would publish them because of their metrical irregularity. Yet Rossetti rightly trusted her ear rather than the metronome that her critics demanded, and by the twentieth century "Goblin Market" was recognized as a precursor of the metrically freer verse of modern poetry.

The theme of unsatisfied love in "The Triad" and the modulation of the fruit imagery from Genesis in "Goblin Market" are combined in one of Rossetti's finest lyrics, "An Apple Gathering." Actually a dramatic monologue, the poem is a young woman's lament for tasting love too early, and thereby losing her beau, "Willie." In the first stanza, she tells of plucking apple blossoms, so that when she returns to her tree at harvest time there is no fruit. In subsequent stanzas, she is teased by the sight of other young women who return with baskets full of apples. Here, as in "Goblin Market," Rossetti has altered slightly the traditional sexual connotation of the Edenic fruit image. The speaker's act of plucking the blossom before it could become fruit is an act of renunciation similar to Lizzie's in "Goblin Market." Instead of winning her Willie's love, however, it drives him to seek out "plump Gertrude" who passes the speaker arm in arm with Willie, her basket full of apples.

From the very first, critics have noticed, and sometimes lamented, the prevalence of the idea of death as a release from the oppressions of the world in Christina Rossetti's poetry. The reviewer for *The Athenaeum* mentioned above faulted her for overusing a melancholy tone. The frequency of the theme of death as release was ascribed simply to pious morbidity until 1980, when Jerome J. McGann noted its debt to an obscure Anabaptist doctrine of "Soul Sleep," the belief that the souls of the saved remained in a trance from the time of their deaths until Judgment Day. This explains the peculiarly static image of death as a bed in "Up-Hill" and of the newly dead speaker of "When I Am Dead" simply "dreaming through the twilight."

Context

Gilbert and Gubar have argued that the act of renunciation that forms the core of "Goblin Market" was emblematic not only for Christina Rossetti but for all women writers of the nineteenth century as well. To become a poet, Rossetti's life and poetry seem to imply, a woman must isolate herself. She must become that peculiarly nineteenth century phenomenon which the novelist George Gissing called the "Odd Woman," who refuses marriage in order to devote herself to her art, as if the two were at odds.

Whether Rossetti's refusal of three marriage proposals (two from one suitor, in 1848 and 1850, and one from another in 1866) was related to her writing, the picture of a young woman letting go of a young man who wants her is seen in many of the lyrics of *Goblin Market and Other Poems*—particularly "No, Thank You, John," which, as the title suggests, is the voice of a woman declining a marriage proposal. In "After Death," a dead woman smiles at the pity of the young man she is leaving behind, with perhaps an ironic double meaning in the closing line, "he still is warm tho' I am cold." While there are also painful images of unrequited love in this collection, there are just as many of love purposefully renounced.

Rossetti's tribute to sisterhood in the last six lines of "Goblin Market" can be seen in the context of this renunciation. Sisterhood is defined as a sort of self-giving in a fairy-tale world safe from the taint of men. As Gilbert and Gubar have pointed out, the only male figures in the poem are the hurtful and animal-like goblins. The counterpart to the divine "sister" is the diabolical "brother," as the goblins are twice described with negative adjectives: "brother with queer brother" and "brother with sly brother." The poem ends with marriages for Laura and Lizzie, but their husbands are not even mentioned; there are "children," but we are not told if any of them are sons.

Christina Rossetti was one of the first female poets about whom critics argued over the sexist term "poetess." In 1891, Richard Le Gallienne agreed that "Miss Rossetti is the greatest English poet among women," but that gender distinction "in questions of art" is a false one, "a distinction which has given us the foolish word 'poetess.'" In 1897, Arthur Symons, himself a leading poet who recognized Rossetti's superiority, used the offensive term, but only by way of saying that she rises above categories: "she takes rank among poets rather than among poetesses."

Sources for Further Study

Battiscombe, Georgina. *Christina Rossetti*. London: Longmans, Green, 1965. A handy starting point for studying Rossetti, this brief booklet offers a summary assessment of her literary accomplishment, as well as critical comments on a few selected poems. Battiscombe emphasizes the influence of pre-Raphaelitism and the Oxford Movement on Rossetti's poetry.

Bellas, Ralph A. *Christina Rossetti*. Boston: Twayne, 1977. Following the format of the Twayne English Authors series, this volume opens with a brief biography, then discusses critically Rossetti's works chronologically. The first part of chapter 3 is a pithy discussion of *Goblin Market and Other Poems*, including a summary of criticism to date.

Bowra, C. M. "Christina Rossetti." In *The Romantic Imagination*. New York: Oxford University Press, 1949. An illuminating study of Rossetti's poetry, but dominated and sometimes marred by Bowra's thesis that Rossetti was torn between being "the woman and the saint" and that her devotional verse is inconsistent with the rest of her writing.

McGann, Jerome J. "Christina Rossetti's Poetry." In *Cannons*, edited by Robert von Hallberg. Chicago: University of Chicago Press, 1984. After a thorough and valuable summary of Rossetti's poetic technique, McGann demonstrates that technique in Rossetti's most famous (and, he argues, most typical) poem, "Goblin Market."

Packer, Lona Mosk. *Christina Rossetti*. Berkeley: University of California Press, 1963. An exhaustive biography of Rossetti, this book also offers occasional literary comments where helpful. Its publication caused a little stir by Packer's assertion that Rossetti's love poetry was inspired, not by her two suitors, as previously assumed, but by William Bell Scott. Packer implies that Bell's love for another woman was an immediate influence on *Goblin Market and Other Poems*.

Woolf, Virginia. "I Am Christina Rossetti." In *Second Common Reader*. New York: Harcourt Brace, 1932. One of the earliest feminist studies of Rossetti by a leading twentieth century literary figure, this essay summarizes a 1930 biography, but warns the reader that biographies can distort. Tending toward the fanciful rather than the scholarly, Woolf's essay is a good antidote to the overanalysis of Rossetti's work found elsewhere.

John R. Holmes

THE GOLD CELL

Author: Sharon Olds (1942-   )
Type of work: Poetry
First published: 1987

Form and Content

Sharon Olds's third collection, *The Gold Cell*, is an extension and refinement of the strikingly singular woman's voice that she introduced in *Satan Says* (1980) and developed in *The Dead and the Living* (1983). Her first book of poems was not published until she was nearly forty, and the extended time that the poems remained in a formative process in her mind accounts for the candor and confidence that she projected in an unusually accomplished initial publication. Writing with energetic conviction in a mode she describes as "apparently personal poetry," Olds addressed subjects that had been previously approached tentatively or through indirection, covering areas of experience seemingly unavailable to men and often avoided by women. In poetry about her family, her body, and the hovering menace of the postmodern world—the essential subjects of her work—Olds dispensed with the conventional practice of shielding her thoughts behind elaborate conceits or cautious similes, and as critic Suzanne Matson puts it, "reclaims the power to speak for her own body."

The vivid, often uncommonly explicit language that Olds employed in descriptive passages about human sensory capacity in her first two books remains as an identifying characteristic of her style in *The Gold Cell*, while the impact of what Matson calls "the delightful voluptuous arrogance" of Olds's voice is deepened by a stronger linkage between physical sensation and the psychological consequences of closely examining the forces of sexual feeling and response. The immediacy achieved by poems that frequently begin with a directness of address, inviting and drawing the reader into the poet's realm, is maintained by such first lines as "When I saw my blood on your leg," "I lie on my back," or "As I stand with." The recollection or nearly literal re-creation of moments of intensely personal interaction with people identified as the poet's father, mother, children, and intimate male friends continues the "spectrum of loyalty and betrayal" across which Olds's work ranges.

The Gold Cell, like her earlier books, is divided into sections that concentrate the poet's attention in an area of particular importance. *The Dead and the Living* used specific headings such as "Public," "Private," "The Family," and "The Men," while *The Gold Cell*, following Olds's aim to stress the "partly metaphorical" rather than the "completely literal," is organized by parts that join poems with similar concentrations of interest. The first part includes poems that reflect Olds's troubled observations about the contemporary world, especially the "unreal city," as objectified by her well-known poem "On the Subway" that places the poet and a young black man in a matrix of influence and repulsion. In this section, Olds mixes commentary with an often acid wit, with "Outside the Operating Room of the Sex-Change Doctor" and

"The Solution" offering characteristically explicit description with sardonic sugges-tions about public and private versions of desire. The very serious and unsettling poem "The Girl" utilizes a propulsive, rhythmic structure to evoke the horror of assault and the impressive resilience of the human spirit.

The second part includes poems that continue Olds's careful, probing exploration of her relationship with her parents and focus on what may be the dominant concern of her work: her extremely complex, evolving understanding of the manner in which her father has figured in her life. Starting with the poem "Saturn"—which envisions a father as a ruler, controller (as a devourer akin to the Roman god of the title "eating his children"), and possessor of his children's life—Olds records her fear, fascination, and uncertain fondness for her father, examining need, necessity, and a growing knowledge about how she has been formed by their interaction. These poems antici-pate the even deeper discussions in her next book, *The Father* (1992), in which "scrupulously honest" poetry records her reactions to her father's death from cancer and her grief, gratitude, and perplexity about his life and hers.

Part 3 reaches back to Olds's youth and young womanhood and to the men who knew in a time of awakening to sexual possibility, a period of expanding horizons in which she discovered the power of revelation in mutual erotic exploration. Part 4 completes a cycle of growth and maturity as she focuses her attention on her own children, a moving away from a preoccupation with the self that paradoxically reveals the self through an illuminating alteration of position.

Analysis

Placed at a pivotal point in her work at the beginning of part 2 of *The Gold Cell*, the poem "I Go Back to May 1937" is a statement of Olds's intentions as an artist. She envisions her parents as "they are about to get married" and instinctively reacts to this decisive moment by feeling and then suppressing the urge to "say Stop,/ don't do it—she's the wrong woman/ he's the wrong man." Although Olds knows now that "you are going to do things/ you cannot imagine you would ever do," her knowledge of the pain and suffering for them and their children is overcome by her recognition that "I want to live" no matter the cost. Her declaration "Do what you are going to do, and I will tell about it" establishes her credo as a poet who will accept the burden of life and the obligations of art and indicates her awareness of the futility of much human action. What endures, she implies, is an effort to understand, and one of the keys to understanding for her is an attempt to be open and honest about her reactions and responses.

Since her poetry has dealt so intimately with the "apparently personal" and has covered instances of wrenching emotional disruption, she has often been compared to Sylvia Plath or Anne Sexton. While acknowledging the "gift" and "importance" of these writers, however, Olds cites Allen Ginsberg as a much more crucial influence. She recalls reading "Howl" at the age of sixteen and realizing that Ginsberg was looking at "a great force which dwelled in and through one." She initially identified this force as sex and says that Ginsberg "looking at his own sexuality with this great consciousness interested me," but as her own work developed, the importance of passion in the broadest sense emerged as a central theme.

Olds has spoken of "loosening some hinges in ourselves" as a means of seeing everything that shapes an individual's consciousness, which has meant not only an inclination toward complete candor but also an insistence on unveiling or exposing the basest urges and the most secret pleasures. The poems in part 2 that present passion-driven, self-absorbed incidents of parental indulgence (such as "What if God," "The Chute," and "San Francisco") are not designed as exposés. Instead, they function as a part of a strategy that promotes self-awareness as a method for escaping from the enclosure of the self—the "gold cell" of the title (words that recur separately throughout the book) that stands as a figure for both the inherent value and the limits placed on the core or original form of a person. It is almost as if Olds were writing these poems as retrospective instruction, the knowledge and insight available now at least for herself even as the subjects of the poems are beyond communication.

Similarly, the poems that chart the course of a woman's growth—from an adolescent realizing the excitement of sexual horizons widening ("First Sex") to the point that she learns that love must include loss ("First Love") to the ripening of full maturity when familiarity permits sensual abandon ("Greed and Aggression" and "It")—are not only expressions of extreme conditions of passion as a version of unleashed power but also investigations of primal, even archetypal human behavior. Olds recognizes the erotic realm as a crucial component of human consciousness, and her choice to conceal nothing about what she has thought or felt leads, almost paradoxically, to a tone that is vastly different from the self-consciousness and coyness of much traditional erotic poetry. As Olds observes, what she has done is to work in "an *unwritten* part of the tradition. But not unlived." Her ability to find a form for presenting a "return/ to the body/ where I was born" (as Ginsberg has it) is both a pioneering and an enduring aspect of her writing.

The emotional concentration evident in much of her work required a structure that would not permit energy to dissipate or attention to slacken. To answer this need, Olds almost exclusively works in a poetic arrangement that casts each poem as a single, long stanza, often twenty to forty lines advancing steadily—gaining momentum— with few breaks for capitalization and a sparse use of end-stops or periods. Even the relatively relaxed poems have a feeling of compression or urgency, rarely pausing or opening gaps for energy to leach out. After the establishment of a subject—usually in a direct, immediate declaration—the poems gather force through the accretion of detail and data, remaining tightly wound in an inner-focused accumulation of inventive consecutive or extended metaphors. As Olds observes, "There's just dancing and language, swimming underwater in language," placing her greatest emphasis on the relationships among words that reflect her attempts to understand and express the relationships between people whose common human qualities she is moved to portray.

Context

Donald Hall has said that "the poem exists to say the unsayable." His primary focus is on the poet's desire to confront and surpass the barriers inherent in language itself, but in a larger sense, he is addressing all the limits that conventional expectations place on artistic endeavor. For Olds, the "unsayable" has meant the entire cosmos of experience of a woman's life, including all the areas seemingly forbidden by the weight of centuries of customs designed by patriarchal social systems. Her work has been guided by the principle that there is nothing so sacred about a woman that it is beyond examination and nothing so supposedly obscene that it should be kept beneath a cover. Like Walt Whitman, whom she sees as spiritual kin in "Nurse Whitman," she "sings the body electric"—a subject that has been controlled through history by male prerogatives and choices. As Suzanne Matson points out, there is a "phallocentrically created special 'dirty' vocabulary for the private use of men," a select language to reinforce the "tradition of articulate male power over the mute female body." Olds does not diminish the power inherent in the physical self but attempts to give women equal access to its energy-delivering, generative forces through the instrument of a language.

Without disparaging the psychic struggles presented by the poetry of Sylvia Plath and Anne Sexton, Olds has repeatedly emphasized her admiration for Muriel Rukeyser (an in "Solitary," from *Satan Says*), whose lines "I'd rather be Muriel/ Than be dead and be Ariel" suggest the possibilities of resistive strength and individual pride as weapons against depression and discouragement. In her poetry, Olds assumes an equality or balancing of strengths and fears in her considerations of gender. She finds the greatest fulfillment in collaborative activity, as in "Greed and Aggression," in which she defines renewal as "I take you as if/ consuming you while you take me as if/ consuming me." She has staunchly resisted the term "confessional" for her poems, explaining that "confession is a telling, publicly or privately, of a wrong that one has done, which one regrets," and she believes that the concept of regret is an impediment to the kind of open inquiry that reveals aspects of human nature which might permit the formation of a humane morality for shaping behavior.

Similarly, her evolving sequence of poems about her father have not been written to judge or condemn, but to probe an extremely complex relationship, to work toward a more complete understanding of both parties, and in terms of feminine experience, to establish a dialogue with what Matson calls "a controlling male force" which must be addressed on the poet's (that is, woman's) terms rather than on his. The figure of "Our Father" as a cultural icon, an overwhelming presence combining theological, historical, and domestic patriarchal elements, is deconstructed in Olds's poetry. Two human beings are placed in a situation where individual need overcomes political privilege, where love and understanding lead to an individual's growth that respects but is not tied to gender.

Sources for Further Study

Franks, Elizabeth. "The Poet Stripped Bare." *Mirabella* 4 (December, 1992): 62-65.
A profile and appreciation combined with an interview. Emphasizes the sensual nature of Olds's poetry and her life as a mother, scholar, and artist.

Matson, Suzanne. "Talking to Our Father: The Political and Mythical Appropriations of Adrienne Rich and Sharon Olds." *American Poetry Review* 18, no. 6 (November/December, 1989): 35-41. Matson lucidly explicates Olds's poems about her father in *The Gold Cell* and places them in the context of feminist considerations of patriarchal power and its effects on women.

Olds, Sharon. Interview by Laurel Blossom. *Poets & Writers Magazine* 21, no. 5 (September/October, 1993): 30-37. A candid, revealing, and often pointed discussion of Olds's influences, attitudes, poetics, and ambitions.

Wright, Carol. Review of *The Dead and the Living*. *Iowa Review* 15, no. 1 (Winter, 1985): 151-161. A consideration of Olds's writing prior to the composition of *The Gold Cell*, showing how some of the poet's essential concerns were presented in her earlier books.

Leon Lewis

THE GOLDEN NOTEBOOK

Author: Doris Lessing (1919-   )
Type of work: Novel
Type of plot: Social criticism
Time of plot: The 1940's to the 1950's
Locale: London, England
First published: 1962

Principal characters:

ANNA WULF, a novelist experiencing writer's block who begins to write notebooks to figure out her life

MOLLY JACOBS, Anna's friend, a marginally successful actress rearing a teenage son alone

RICHARD PORTMAIN, Molly's former husband, an extremely successful businessman

TOMMY JACOBS, Molly and Richard's son

MARION JACOBS, Richard's present wife, an alcoholic who rebels against him

ELLA, a character in the Yellow Notebook who is a double for Anna, but without her political consciousness

SAUL GREEN, Anna's American lover

Form and Content

The Golden Notebook is divided into six sections that interlock and interact with one another to form a complex meaning. The first section, called "Free Women," is a conventional novel telling the story of Anna Wulf's and Molly Jacobs' lives in 1957 London. Anna and Molly are old friends who come together to talk about their experiences with men, politics, and life as "free women," women who are not living with a man. Anna is becoming bored with their talks and begins to suspect that their complaints about how they are treated by men contribute in some way to the continuation of these types of relationships. She wishes "to be done with it all, finished with the men vs. women business." Indeed, this is what she accomplishes by the end of the book.

In "Free Women," Molly's son, Tommy, goes through an identity crisis. His business tycoon father, Richard, offers him a job which he scorns as morally corrupt, but neither can he embrace his mother's socialism. He attempts suicide, is blinded, and then takes on Marion, Richard's alcoholic wife, as a protégé. Marion eventually leaves Richard and opens a dress shop. Molly marries a progressive businessman, Tommy follows in his father's footsteps, and Anna explores the meaning of life in her notebooks, then has a breakdown in her relationship with Saul Green. At the end of the novel, she goes to work as a marriage counselor with a man with whom she has worked at a magazine.

Every section of "Free Women" is followed by entries from each of Anna Wulf's notebooks. The Black Notebook deals with money, specifically with the royalties from her first novel, *Frontiers of War*; the notebook examines the part of her life about which the novel is written and later critical responses to the book. Anna and her group of communist intellectuals are in Rhodesia during World War II, and they spend their weekends at a resort hotel in the veld. One of Anna's friends becomes involved with an African woman who is the wife of the hotel cook, creating a scandal. The second focus of this section is how critics and producers try to manipulate her novel to serve their own political agendas.

The Red Notebook is an examination of Anna's relationship to the British Communist Party. In this section, she joins the Party, works for it for a while, and then eventually leaves. Anna's concern is with her relationship to political rhetoric, dogma, and slogans, how they function to control her thinking processes and sense of identity. The Yellow Notebook is a sort of novel, *The Shadow of the Third*, narrated by Ella, who is a shadow of Anna minus her political awareness. In this notebook, Ella explores her obsessive relationship with Paul, a married man with whom she has an affair. When Paul predictably leaves her, Ella tries to find out why she is so controlled by her need to be with a man, how the rhetoric of male-female relationships shapes her thinking and identity. In her attempt to escape this social conditioning, Ella begins to realize that a profound connection exists between reality and story. She writes a series of plot summaries of possible love relationships at the end of the Yellow Notebook that Anna reenacts with her lover, Saul, at the end of the novel. It is this reenactment which allows Anna to break free from her social conditioning as a woman.

The Blue Notebook is Anna's attempt to write a diary, a true account of her life with no political or sexual dogma, prearranged phrases, or plots intervening. Eventually in this notebook, words lose their meaning and Anna dissolves into a breakdown. The Golden Notebook is an account of how Anna comes through her breakdown into a new identity.

Analysis

The structure of *The Golden Notebook* is perhaps its most important feature and the most overlooked aspect of the novel when it was first released. Critics immediately pronounced the novel to be simply about the "sex war," a notion which provoked Lessing into adding a preface directing the reader's attention to the shape of the novel and the theme of "breakdown" which is reflected in the shape. Anna Wulf cannot write about her world as a whole, because it no longer fits together for her, so she breaks it down into parts in hopes that she can discover an underlying meaning which will bring a new order. Anna understands that she is herself internally divided when she examines the discrepancies in her belief system or sense of self and her actual behavior. By allowing herself to move into these contradictions and to live them rather than suppress them, Anna is eventually able to break through into a new paradigm.

A large part of this novel considers the function of language as ideology, and therefore a way to stop or to control the thinking process. Each section adds to this theme in its own way. The Black Notebook interrogates literature, the relationship between Anna's memories and the novel that she wrote out of them, and how literature is coopted by cultural ideology. The Red Notebook separates out and examines the ideology of political life. Anna discovers how she is manipulated, how her identity is shaped, by the surrounding cultural belief systems. She knows that the Communist Party has become corrupt, that members (including herself) will say one thing when alone or with one another and adopt or be taken over by another "viewpoint" while functioning in an official Party capacity. Yet this does not stop Anna from participating in all this activity even while she is ironically aware of its irrationality. The Red Notebook ends with clippings and a story about a man whose whole life was built on the delusion that the Russians would one day send for him to set the history of the Party straight.

The Yellow Notebook separates out sexual politics and examines the "woman in love" figure who emerges in the psyche of Ella. She is dismayed at her own conventional responses to her lover and realizes that she cannot stop herself from acting out cultural ideas and formulas. Paul, however, is as internally divided as Ella is, and he acts the parts of the irresponsible husband and the jealous lover seemingly against his will as well. Both genders are permeated by social ideology. Ella escapes these social formulas by writing out plot summaries in which she discovers pre-planned scenarios encapsulated in her head, thus purging herself of their influence.

In the Blue Notebook, Anna experiences "the thinning of language against the density of our experience." Language becomes inadequate to reflect reality. Try as she might, she cannot stop social ideology from contaminating her attempts to capture "pure reality" in her diary. Anna comes to understand slogans and ideology as substitutes for self-knowledge and independent action. The notebook ends with the purchase of the Golden Notebook, which contains the dreams that bring Anna out of the group of the cultural image of woman and the mind-containing slogans of politics and psychoanalysis.

Anna escapes the disintegration of her personality, which is intricately related to the social disintegration around her, by playing out all the possibilities of the male-female role with Saul Green, a man whose personality is as fractured as Paul's. By exploring each other's psychosis, by having both sides of the formula of gender available, Anna and Saul are able to break through their entrapment in the ideology of male-female relationships. Anna discovers in this process that individual con-sciousness is not isolated and discrete, as society would have her believe, but that consciousness is connected to culture and to other humans in a much more intimate way.

The "Free Women" section stands in ironic juxtaposition to the rich complexity of the journals. Lessing believed that the shape of the book would "make its own comment about the conventional novel," which would amount to "how little I have caught of all that complexity." The reader understands that this conventional novel fails because the surrounding source material of the notebooks is much richer, more complex, and interesting, but Anna Wulf has succeeded in creating a new definition of the nature of human consciousness and identity.

Context

The Golden Notebook was hailed as a feminist manifesto of sorts when it was first published, but Lessing was as dismayed by this simplistic reception of the novel as she was by the equally simplistic reaction against women speaking their minds that followed. Lessing makes it clear in her preface that, while she supports the aims of the women's movement, she is interested in a larger, although related, issue: the disintegration of Western society. She took the centrality of women's consciousness and problems for granted when she wrote the novel: "Some books are not read in the right way because they have skipped a stage of opinion, assume a crystallisation of information in society which has not yet taken place." Yet this novel is important to women's literature. In writing this book, Lessing was interested in capturing the cultural milieu of mid-twentieth century Great Britain and, in so doing, chooses a female narrator. Not only is Anna Wulf the narrator, but also her life and problems, the very structure of her psyche, serve as the vehicle for exploring Western culture at this point in time. For a woman's consciousness to serve as the center of a work of such scope was unusual even by the 1960's, although Lessing's Children of Violence series revolves around a similar female character.

The Golden Notebook expressed many women's experiences in print for the first time. The novel explores issues of intimate relationships, sexuality, and identity which had not previously been discussed in such detail or from a woman's perspective. Yet the novel does not stop there: It takes women's concerns and relates them to other issues. For example, Saul Green's continual barrage of "I, I, I, I" is likened to the rapid fire of a machine gun, and Anna and Saul's battle is considered part of "the logic of war." Lessing anticipates feminist writings of the 1970's and 1980's which explore the connections between the suppression of women and imperialism and the exploitation of the environment.

This novel also challenges Western culture's epistemology, the way in which it has defined human consciousness and the nature of reality. Anna Wulf breaks through into a new sanity by realizing that the divisions she tried to enforce in her notebooks are false—that she is not a discrete entity separate from all other people and events, but that her consciousness is part of everything and everyone around her. Western science established itself by suppressing the older European beliefs that humans were connected to nature, that knowledge came through bodily connection and intuitive insights, then spread the new worldview through several centuries of imperialism. Lessing challenges this worldview through a woman's insights about the nature of her own mind.

Sources for Further Study

Greene, Gayle. *Changing the Story: Feminist Fiction and the Tradition.* Bloomington: Indiana University Press, 1991. Feminist criticism of Lessing, among other writers. Examines how language plays an important role in *The Golden Notebook*.

Hite, Molly. *The Other Side of the Story: Structures and Strategies of Contemporary Feminist Narrative*. Ithaca, N.Y.: Cornell University Press, 1989. This work of feminist criticism offers a thorough discussion of Lessing's experiments with form.

Kaplan, Carey, and Ellen Cronan Rose, eds. *Approaches to Teaching Lessing's "The Golden Notebook."* New York: Modern Language Association, 1989. An excellent look at *The Golden Notebook*, with helpful applications of contemporary feminist theory.

Pickering, Jean. *Understanding Doris Lessing*. Columbia: University of South Carolina Press, 1990. Excellent summaries of the novels with helpful commentary.

Pratt, Annis, and L. S. Dembo, eds. *Doris Lessing: Critical Studies*. Madison: University of Wisconsin Press, 1974. A collection of essays on Lessing's work, containing an excellent interview with Lessing conducted by Florence Howe and some early feminist criticism.

Rubenstein, Roberta. *The Novelistic Vision of Doris Lessing: Breaking the Forms of Consciousness*. Urbana: University of Illinois Press, 1979. This book gives special attention to Lessing's focus on human consciousness, what the theme means in her work and how she challenges the limits of consciousness in her prose.

Sprague, Claire, and Virginia Tiger, eds. *Critical Essays on Doris Lessing*. Boston: G. K. Hall, 1986. A collection of insightful essays on Lessing's work.

Theresa L. Crater

GONE TO SOLDIERS

Author: Marge Piercy (1936-   )
Type of work: Novel
Type of plot: Psychological realism
Time of plot: World War II (1939-1945)
Locale: The United States, especially Detroit, and the battle zones of World War II
First published: 1987

> *Principal characters:*
> LOUISE KAHAN, a popular writer of women's fiction
> DANIEL BALABAN, the child of immigrant Jewish parents living
> in the Bronx
> JACQUELINE LÉVY-MONOT, a woman known by her Jewish name
> of Yakova, as Jacqueline Porell in order to disguise her
> heritage, and as Gingembre, her nom de guerre
> ABRA, a graduate student at Columbia University and the lover of
> Oscar Kahan, Louise's former husband
> NAOMI, a twelve-year-old at the beginning of the novel
> BERNICE, the unmarried daughter of Professor Coates, who joins
> the Army Air Corps as a pilot
> JEFF COATES, the artistic brother of Bernice, a member of the
> Jewish Resistance in France
> RUTHIE SIEGEL, a woman who works in a plant and attends
> school at night
> DUVEY SIEGEL, the brother of Ruthie
> MURRAY FELDSTEIN, a Marine who comes home to marry Ruthie

Form and Content

Gone to Soldiers offers an answer to the question that Albert Einstein asked in a July 30, 1932, letter to Sigmund Freud regarding the topic "Why War?" As the lives of ten major characters are played out against the backdrop of Word War II, "man's inhumanity to man" is revealed in the horrors of prejudice against Jews and women. War against an oppressive society and war within oneself is fought and won only against overwhelming odds.

Dedicated to Marge Piercy's grandmother, Hannah, *Gone to Soldiers* memorializes her as a storyteller who has a "gift for making the past walk through the present." The importance of memory in preserving the lessons of the past makes Jacqueline Lévy-Monot's mission a religious one as she affirms her identity as a women and as a Jew.

Jacqueline, whose stories are told in the form of a diary, is not the only character in the novel who is a teller of tales. Louise Kahan, the war correspondent, and Abra, in a series of interviews, mark their own quest for identity in the stories that they tell. Recounting the experience of her bleak childhood, Louise recalls being raped and having an abortion at the age of fifteen. Later, mired in dull wifehood, she finds it hard to juggle the demands of her daughter and philandering husband. When she divorces Oscar and strives to live as a single mother in a war-torn society, she learns that women have no military status, no privileges, no protection, and no insurance. It is only at the end of the novel that Louise learns that the lessons of the past enable her to reunite with Oscar and be healed. In one of the book's more important passages, Louise comes to several realizations.

> Miracles came seldom and rebirth more rarely yet and for countless and uncountable and never to be counted women like herself, her age, her body type, death had come from a machine gun, from blows of the butt end of a rifle, from poison gas, from poison injections, from starvation and typhus and neglect, from all the nasty ways to die warped minds in a violent and relentless system could devise. They had died of a lack of common respect and common love. They cried out to her, take him back and go live in peace as husband and wife and as Jews. Go make a home again and give thanks. Life is the first gift, love is the second, and understanding the third.

Abra, on the other hand, has to give up the role of mistress and separate from Oscar in order to find herself and to learn that a relationship of equals brings more fulfillment than subservient dependency. It is a hard lesson to learn—for men as well as for women. After the bombing of Hiroshima, Abra's beloved Daniel tells her: "I feel as if I looked out through a vast eye and saw the future of the world in a plain of ashes, of sand turned to glass, flesh vaporized, time itself burned up." When asked what can be done, Daniel replies, "First, put our opinions in the report if we can." *Gone to Soldiers* is the report and the answer to the question "Why war?" as each character reveals her or his own experiences of intolerance, misunderstanding, failures of communication, powerlessness, subjugation, and abuse.

Analysis

In an interview published in the anthology *Ways of Knowing* (1991), Marge Piercy says that *Gone to Soldiers* is the novel that caused her the most problems as she was writing it. Using ten viewpoints and moving regularly from one to another, she says that she thinks of the book as a cantata. Each character has her or his own social world, history, milieu, loved ones, and problems, and in wrenching herself from one world to another, Piercy does the same to the reader. The novel is not intended to invoke comfort or ease; it is designed to disrupt one's inner and outer worlds, as ideals and value systems are fought over and challenged.

Piercy is a major feminist writer espousing the causes of women; she is also perhaps the leading female Jewish novelist in the United States. The great-granddaughter of a rabbi, Piercy recounts in *Gone to Soldiers* the horrors of anti-Semitism, so that in Daniel's words: "No one will ever again call us dirty Jews. No one will make laws against us, ever again." The wars that take place in the novel extend beyond World

War II; they are fought on American as well as foreign soil and concern the misuse of women by society and by men. Like Piercy herself, Louise undergoes an abortion that almost kills her. Naomi is raped by Leib, her friend Trudi's husband who was shipped home because he lost a foot in the war, and finds herself pregnant. Bernice is told by her father that silly overgrown women do not run around in airports and that "real" women should not want to fly planes. "Real" women get married and exist to please a man; they do not pursue higher degrees. They want to bring babies into the world, yet Jacqueline comments that "a family is an accidental construct, a group of people brought together by chance and forced to cohabit in insufficient space." Even being Jewish is a matter of accident. "I was born Jewish," Jacqueline says, "but what does that mean?" She is unable to communicate with her Polish refugee aunt, uncle, and cousins—even about something as simple as tables and chairs, let alone her aspirations, feelings, and dreams.

That women should be victimized and used by men seems unconscionable in a prison camp, where they were forced to march and were clubbed to death if they stumbled from exhaustion, where they were fed soup every other day and took on the appearance of genderless, starved specters rather than human beings. Yet the subjugation of women is overlooked in a society that lacks tolerance of lesbians, blacks, and Jews and where women are deprived of equal jobs and equal pay. This insidious misuse of females results in women at war with themselves as they struggle to find their identity and sense of self-worth, not only in war-torn France or bombed London but also in Detroit and Alabama and throughout the United States, where prejudices make people victims and deny human rights.

In order to tell this story of war, Piercy chooses ten different voices, separating each story into segments as first one and then another character appears, disappears, and comes back again in various sections. The result, though it may seem disjointed, is part of Piercy's technique. She rejects the Aristotelian notion of plot as progressive movement from beginning to middle to end and selects instead a decentering format that weaves multiple threads of human existence into a unified whole. Men as well as women redefine their attitudes and adjust their ways of functioning in order to heal the abuses of the past.

Einstein's question of "Why war?" has a multitude of answers that are as complex as the lives of Louise, Daniel, Jacqueline, Abra, Naomi, Bernice, Jeff, Ruthie, Duvey, Murray, and the other characters in *Gone to Soldiers* whose lives, both separate and intertwined, encompass women's rights, the psychology of mother-daughter and father-daughter relationships, and the need to claim one's past on an individual, local, and global scale. Through an anatomy of war, Piercy shows that what Einstein called humanity's "lust for hatred and destruction" can only be overcome when men and women learn to heal, to have relationships of equals instead of those in which one nation, country, religion, class, or law victimizes another. Through storytelling, perhaps this lesson may be learned. As Naomi goes off to bear Leib's daughter, joy is brought back into the world, along with hope. Misfortune can be instructive, even though the end of one set of troubles is but the beginning of another.

Context

As one of the leading feminist writers in the United States, Piercy examines the situation of women in relation to marriage, education, work, and wealth, especially in terms of gender divisions of labor in employment, authority, leadership, and ethnic issues of race and religion. At the beginning of *Gone to Soldiers*, Louise begins the chronicle of issues that oppress women and Jacqueline laments the fact that people bring babies into the world so casually that often a birth is celebrated when it should be mourned.

Throughout her fiction, Piercy raises the question of what it is to be a "real" woman. In *Gone to Soldiers*, as in *Small Changes* (1973), men insist that a real woman directs her energy to, and derives her identity from, a relationship with a man. A real woman should not want to pursue a high educational degree; a real woman should not want to fly airplanes. Rather, a woman's duty is to stay at home, perhaps taking care of a lonely and aging father. The repression and abuse of women in *Gone to Soldiers* exists in other places at the concentration camp. It can be found within the family, in the workplace, and in interpersonal relationships. Women in the military can be dishonorably discharged for being lesbians, and Bernice finds herself forced to adopt a masculine identity in order to find a job in which she could support herself and live with her beloved, Flo.

Piercy shows that being "real" signifies a woman who can take control of her life and wrest it from any man who needs to subjugate her for his own selfish desires. Being real means being able to form a relationship with one's heart's desire without fear of losing a job and being court-martialed. It means that a woman can feel secure within herself and be assured of her own individual worth without having to do things she dislikes in order to keep a man. Being real means that women can earn higher degrees and equal pay, and it means that a woman can obtain positions of influence regardless of race and religion.

Piercy's feminist stance extends into a mission affirming her Jewish heritage. *Gone to Soldiers* engages the place of memory in keeping the past alive as a deterrent to future abuse. As Jacqueline promises, "I will live and tell the world about this. I will live and make them pay." Piercy's concerns enjoin social, ethical, and political wrongs in regard to the treatment of women and envision a society characterized by wholeness without barriers created by sex, race, religion, age, or class.

Sources for Further Study

Foster, David L. "Women on the Edge of Narrative: Language in Marge Piercy's Utopia." In *Patterns of the Fantastic II*, edited by Donald M. Hassler. San Bernardino, Calif.: Borgo Press, 1985. An interesting discussion of language as it reflects differences in status and power.

Jones, Libby Falk. "Gilman, Bradley, Piercy, and the Evolving Rhetoric of Feminist Utopias." In *Feminism, Utopia, and Narrative*, edited by Libby Falk Jones and Sarah Webster Goodwin. Knoxville: University of Tennessee Press, 1990. An important discussion on the differences in the ways that women and men communicate and how gender differences are revealed in language.

Piercy, Marge. *Parti-Colored Blocks for a Quilt*. Ann Arbor: University of Michigan Press, 1982. Presents insights into Piercy's attitudes on various feminist issues. Particularly interesting in view of its comments on education, body image, and issues of motherhood is the essay entitled "Through the Cracks: Growing Up in the Fifties."

Walker, Sue, and Eugenie Hamner, eds. *Ways of Knowing*. Mobile, Ala.: Negative Capability Press, 1991. A collection of critical essays, including ones on *Small Changes, Woman on the Edge of Time* (1976), *Stone, Paper, Knife* (1983), *Fly Away Home* (1984), and such topics as "The Renewal of the Self by Returning to the Elements," "Political Themes and Personal Preoccupations," and "A Sense of Place." Gives an overview of Piercy's work and includes an extensive bibliography.

Westerlund-Shands, Kerstin. *The Repair of the World: The Novels of Marge Piercy*. Westport, Conn.: Greenwood Press, 1994. A thorough critical assessment of Piercy's novels.

Sue Brannan Walker

GONE WITH THE WIND

Author: Margaret Mitchell (1900-1949)
Type of work: Novel
Type of plot: Romance
Time of plot: The Civil War and Reconstruction
Locale: Georgia
First published: 1936

Principal characters:
SCARLETT O'HARA, the spoiled, self-centered daughter of a
  wealthy Georgia plantation owner
RHETT BUTLER, a Southern aristocrat by birth and upbringing
  who scorns the idealism and hot-headedness that plunges the
  South into the Civil War
ASHLEY WILKES, Scarlett's great love, the representation of an
  aristocratic Southern idealism whose day is past
MELANIE WILKES, Ashley's cousin and his wife, the supreme
  representative of ideal Southern womanhood
FRANK KENNEDY, a fussy bachelor and the second husband to
  Scarlett

Form and Content

Gone with the Wind is a historical romance that uses Scarlett O'Hara as the symbol for Reconstruction in the South. Like Atlanta, which sheds its image of Southern gentility after the Civil War, Scarlett is allowed to break away from the conventionalities of proper Southern womanhood. The exigencies of war, its devastation and defeat, enable Scarlett to adopt behavior more suited to her energy and character as she struggles to support her family, to restore the plantation Tara to productivity, and later to become a commercially successful businesswoman in Atlanta, operating a general store, a lumberyard, and a mill.

Scarlett is motivated by her need to survive and to care for an extended family, which includes Ashley and Melanie Wilkes, their child, and the loyal family slaves. Only Scarlett has the determination, courage, and practicality—perhaps even the stubbornness—to accept the challenge of survival in the radically changed post-Civil War world. Her second and third marriages, to Frank Kennedy and Rhett Butler, are marriages of expedience, both for commercial gain.

Scarlett lacks both analytical and sensitivity skills, replacing them with her determined will to act. Thus, as she faces death, starvation, rape, exhaustion, loss of her beloved mother, and fear of losing Tara, as she acknowledges the commodification of sex and marriage disguised as romance by her culture and barters her body for tax money, she is forced to face the worst. Yet the novel is also about heroic growth to maturity for Scarlett. As she develops a sense of security about her survival, she begins to develop those qualities of sensitivity and concern for others that complete such maturity.

Intertwined with Scarlett's story of growth to heroic selfhood is a typical woman's romance tale. Rhett Butler, who moves in and out of Scarlett's life, plays the typical scoundrel hero so popular in this kind of fiction. He perceives Scarlett as a brave but naïve woman-child whom he can rescue and indulge after they are married. The romance formula is undermined, however, when Rhett neglects to come to Scarlett's rescue on several occasions, forcing her to develop the self-confidence and courage that he later rejects. Thus, Scarlett is empowered by the failure of both romantic heroes—Rhett and the ineffectual Ashley. Also at odds with the romance novel formula are Scarlett's three marriages, all occurring during the time that she is in love with a fourth man whom she no longer desires by the end of the novel. Also, when she finally "comes to realize" her love for Rhett, a central aspect of the formula, he no longer desires her. There is no happy ending or reconciliation of lovers; rather, Rhett walks out the door into a fog of confusion.

Gone with the Wind is also a story about land and agriculture. When she realizes that her mother has died, Scarlett's need to find comfort and security either on her mother's or Mammy's bosom is replaced by the stability and meaning that she finds in the red earth of Tara. It is farming about which Scarlett cares most, although her insistence on keeping Tara and restoring it to some degree of productivity requires her to leave it to marry Frank Kennedy. At the unhappy ending, Scarlett decides to return home to Tara and to its beloved earth in order to restore her sense of hope and of purpose.

Analysis

While it seems that Margaret Mitchell intended to create a formula-driven historical romance novel that celebrates the glory of war even in retreat, *Gone with the Wind* can also be understood as a kind of female *Bildungsroman*, a story of the growth to maturity that is traditional in Western literature that is generally reserved for male characters. Rhett Butler remains the stereotypical buccaneer throughout, but Scarlett begins as a spoiled adolescent flirt and becomes a sensitive, unselfish woman by the novel's end. Unfortunately, this process is slowed by Scarlett's very real fears of starvation and by her insecurity.

Mitchell portrays this process of development by sending Scarlett on a series of journeys which function as learning experiences for her, a typical part of the *Bildungsroman*. For example, returning home to Tara from a besieged Atlanta with Melanie, two children, and the maid Prissy, Scarlett realizes that she must be a survivor if her whole family is to survive. Her second journey is from Tara to a rebuilding Atlanta, wearing a dress made from green velvet drapes. In spite of the religious training that she received from her mother, Scarlett is willing to do anything to save Tara, including selling herself to Rhett as a mistress or, when that does not work, to Frank Kennedy, her sister's fiancé, in marriage. Scarlett's third journey is through human misery as she endures her father's death, the scandal over her most innocent hug from Ashley, her pregnancy and miscarriage, Rhett's rejection, her daughter Bonnie's death, and finally, Melanie's death. At this point, she realizes that financial security is not enough, but rather that compassion, community, and an understanding of reality are vital to her growth. Thus, her fourth journey is home to Rhett, as she is finally aware of how he also has been suffering. When Rhett rejects her, she prepares for a fifth journey—home to Tara to make a plan for her life.

In *Gone with the Wind*, Mitchell depicts several Southern female stereotypes—especially that of the helpless, passive, and sometimes silly woman, such as Scarlett's sisters and Ashley's sister, India Wilkes—and then undermines them by delimiting their roles. In Scarlett, she has created the stereotypical romance heroine who escapes the limits of her role and, in fact, is forced to expand her possibilities. Scarlett becomes the shrewdest businessperson among her old friends, and she has learned how to manipulate her feminine role to get what she needs for survival. Melanie Wilkes, who seems to typify the frail, passive, ideal woman, actually has a tough, pragmatic interior.

While Melanie lives within conventions, she sees beyond their limits. Thus she alone supports Scarlett through every contingency, however painful and difficult, including death, murder, and scandal. Against a background of conventional expectations for female behavior, Mitchell has set two women, seemingly complete opposites linked by courage, endurance, and pragmatism, into a bond of loyalty and support. The enduring and unexpected friendship between Scarlett and Mclanie subverts the patriarchal expectation that women will compete with other women for men, who are perceived as prizes. Scarlett resists Melanie's friendship at first because she was taught that women were weak and inadequate people with whom to make alliances. Soon, however, Scarlett perceives Melanie as armed with a sword so that she can act as Scarlett's loyal and passionate protector.

On the other hand, Mitchell critiques male romance roles and the sentimental longing for the old Southern plantation days by creating Ashley Wilkes, whose character, even in the beginning of the novel, seems limp and washed out. Ashley is brave enough as a soldier, but he has no real place either in the practical farm world to which he returns or in the world of commercialism that follows the war. Rhett's sense of dangerous mystery as a stock figure of melodrama is exposed by Scarlett's movement from being the central romantic heroine to being a person in a state of development. An understanding, compassionate adult cannot also be a childlike pet, to be protected and spoiled as Rhett has spoiled Bonnie. Rhett would prefer to spoil Scarlett rather than to accept her as an adult.

Mitchell warns that when independence is forced on women, they cannot readily be returned to a passive dependence, which she illustrates through both Scarlett and Melanie, as well as through Scarlett's mother, the figure of responsibility at Tara. The one-dimensional Rhett Butler ends his opportunistic adventurings by desiring a return to his genteel Charleston origins. In the end, Rhett gives up his role of romantic pirate to take on Ashley's role of perfect knight, while Ashley becomes only a burden inherited from Melanie by Scarlett.

Context

Margaret Mitchell worked steadily on *Gone with the Wind* for four years, from 1926 to 1929, but it was not published until 1936, receiving a Pulitzer Prize in 1937. It is an antiwar novel that depicts the devastation of war not only as it affects an entire region but also as it specifically affects the land and women's lives, forcing them into independence, poverty, and/or loneliness.

Like other Southern women writers, Mitchell identifies the Southern lady either with ideal passivity, selflessness, and exquisite moral virtue or with feminine beauty and flirtatiousness, at the same time that her main female character struggles against these limitations to become a person. Issues of women's work, independence, and need for wholeness, rather than role-playing, are typical issues faced by these writers, including Mitchell.

Mitchell raises two key feminist issues, but she leaves them for her readers to resolve. One occurs when the drunken Rhett carries Scarlett up the stairs to their bedroom. Many feminist critics condemn this as a rape scene which, therefore, may be used to romanticize rape, denying its pain and dehumanization in real life. The second issue revolves around the final scene in which Rhett rejects Scarlett's newly realized love for him and leaves her. Is Rhett Butler worthy of the person Scarlett is in the process of becoming? Can a strong male hero accept a strong female counterpart? These questions are made more problematic by the popular film version of *Gone with the Wind*, which came out in 1939. Although the film does a credible job of depicting Scarlett as a survivor in the period during and immediately after the Civil War, it does not allow her the growth that Mitchell has created for her in the novel.

Gone with the Wind also exists within a tradition of women's rural literature, which includes such novels as *So Big* (1924), by Edna Ferber; *Barren Ground* (1925), by Ellen Glasgow; and Willa Cather's *O Pioneers!* (1913) and *My Ántonia* (1918). These novels depict women as intelligent and capable farmers. In *Gone with the Wind*, Scarlett is primarily a farmer who must leave the farm in order to support it. Like Scarlett, these female farmers value the land that they successfully cultivate. It becomes more than a means to success, but a transcendent force that sustains them spiritually as well as economically.

A problem in *Gone with the Wind* that is unresolved by Mitchell is a racism inherent in her glorification of antebellum plantation life as an idyllic setting with happy slaves and bountiful land. Furthermore, her portrayals of Mammy, Prissy, and Big Sam all represent stereotypes developed to justify slavery and the plantation system as a benevolent institution. Unfortunately, Mitchell fails to provide any kind of serious critique of a plantation life that is based on slavery, although she readily undercuts many other aspects of Southern life, especially the limitations of women's lives.

Sources for Further Study

Edwards, Anne. *Road to Tara: The Life of Margaret Mitchell*. New Haven, Conn.: Ticknor & Fields, 1983. A biography of Mitchell which describes her as a mixture, like Scarlett, of Southern belle and emancipated woman, both conventional and rebellious.

Egenreither, Ann E. "Scarlett O'Hara: A Paradox in Pantalettes." In *Heroines of Popular Culture*, edited by Pat Browne. Bowling Green, Ohio: Bowling Green State University Popular Press, 1987. Places Scarlett O'Hara in the context of popular culture heroines while describing her resistance to such limits.

Harwell, Richard, ed. *"Gone with the Wind" as Book and Film*. Columbia: University of South Carolina Press, 1983. A series of essays from both scholars and the popular press that review the traditions of Southern and Civil War novels, Margaret Mitchell as person and writer, the novel and its characters, and *Gone with the Wind* as a film event.

Jones, Anne Goodwyn. *Tomorrow Is Another Day: The Woman Writer in the South*. Baton Rouge: Louisiana State University Press, 1981. Jones describes the influences from Mitchell's life that forged her sometimes contradictory positions regarding the roles of the traditional Southern man, the ideal Southern woman, the courageous woman, and the rebel.

Pyron, Darden Asbury, ed. *Recasting "Gone with the Wind" in American Culture*. Miami: University Presses of Florida, 1983. A collection of essays by various authors that explore *Gone with the Wind* from a critical perspective, as art, and in terms of its historical location.

Taylor, Helen. *Scarlett's Women: "Gone with the Wind" and its Female Fans*. New Brunswick, N.J.: Rutgers University Press, 1989. A collection of women readers' responses to survey questions about the novel and Scarlett, reflecting the basis for their constant popularity. Includes analyses of theme, character, biography, politics, and film and literary history.

Janet M. LaBrie

THE GOOD APPRENTICE

Author: Iris Murdoch (1919-   )
Tupe of work: Novel
Type of plot: Bildungsroman
Time of plot: The early 1980's
Locale: London, England, and Seegard, a country house
First published: 1985

Principal characters:

> EDWARD BALTRAM, a student at London University, the
> illegitimate son of painter Jesse Baltram and artist's model
> Chloe Warriston, who is driven to depression by the death of
> his best friend, Mark Wilsden
>
> JESSE BALTRAM, Edward's father, a famous painter who had
> affairs with both men and women
>
> HARRY CUNO, Edward's stepfather, a literary critic and novelist
>
> STUART CUNO, Edward's stepbrother, the novel's "good
> apprentice"
>
> MIDGE MCCASKERVILLE, Edward's aunt, a former fashion model
> who has an affair with Harry Cuno
>
> THOMAS MCCASKERVILLE, Midge's psychiatrist husband, who
> treats Edward's depression
>
> BROWNIE (BRENDA) WILSDEN, Mark Wilsden's sister

Form and Content

Set in England one summer during the early 1980's, *The Good Apprentice* focuses on Edward Baltram's search for redemption after accidentally killing Mark Wilsden, his best friend. Edward, who used LSD, invited Mark to his London apartment, slipped him the drug, and watched while he had a good trip. Just as Mark fell asleep, another student, Sarah Plowmain, asked Edward over to her nearby flat. Edward locked Mark in and spent the next half hour at Sarah's making love, forgetting his friend. When Edward returned, he found the window open and Mark dead on the sidewalk below. Edward's irresponsible acts destroy his own prospects. He lied at the inquest, claiming that Mark had asked for the drug and that he had left him alone only to take a ten-minute walk. He was ordered to receive psychiatric treatment from his uncle, Thomas McCaskerville.

Mark's mother, who does not believe Edward's story, sends him hate mail, and he is overwhelmed with guilt. Deeply depressed, he spends hours walking the streets. Neither the walks, nor the psychiatric sessions, nor the comfort of his family helps him. Then, one day he visits a séance on a whim. The medium brings a message for one who has two fathers. Edward thinks that this message is for him, for he has two fathers: his natural father, Jesse Baltram, and his stepfather, Harry Cuno. The message is to visit his father. Edward almost forgets about the message until May Baltram, Jesse's wife, invites him to Seegard, Jesse's country house. He accepts, hoping to find healing from his father, but Jesse Baltram is nowhere to be seen. (When Jesse finally appears, Edward learns that his father is insane and cannot offer him healing.) Instead, Edward meets May and his half sisters Bettina and Ilona, who live a cloistered, neurotic life. Edward is first attracted to Ilona, but then he meets Brownie Wilsden, Mark's sister, who is visiting a nearby cottage owned by Sarah Plowmain's mother. Brownie wants to understand Edward rather than to condemn him, and Edward falls in love with her.

Meanwhile, two parallel stories develop. In the first, Edward's stepbrother, Stuart Cuno, abandons his graduate studies at the University of Cambridge in order to live a life of goodness, much to his father's dismay. Stuart struggles with the interrelated problems of how to be good and how to do good, but initially only angers his friends. In the second, Harry Cuno and Midge McCaskerville, Edward's aunt, have an affair. Harry wants Midge to leave her husband for him, but she cannot quite bring herself to take that step. Although they keep their affair a secret from Thomas McCaskerville, Midge's son discovers it, plunging her into deeper turmoil.

Things come to a head when Stuart appears at Seegard, hoping to help Edward find forgiveness, followed by Harry and Midge, who blunder there after their car runs into a ditch. Stuart returns to London with Harry and Midge. His mere presence calls Midge back to her marital duties, and she breaks off the affair. Stuart visits Mark Wilsden's mother and persuades her to stop writing hate letters. Edward finds Jesse drowned in a river and returns to London freed from his debilitating guilt and able to bear the responsibility for his deeds.

Analysis

The central issue of *The Good Apprentice* is one that Iris Murdoch treats in many of her novels: the nature of good. Although Edward Baltram is the novel's focus of action, Stuart Cuno is the significant character, the one who gives the book its title. Edward is a young man growing into maturity and adulthood. Stuart is an apprentice, learning to be good and growing into goodness. Stuart's attempts at doing good fail, but he keeps trying to help Edward, Midge, and even Mark Wilsden's mother; eventually he succeeds, as an apprentice who perseveres will eventually succeed. Success comes when Edward takes Stuart's advice to talk to Midge. When Edward does help Midge clarify her own position, he heals himself. For Murdock, being good comes from doing good and helping others.

Murdoch paints Stuart as awkward, dull, and charmless, because for her the aesthetic is separate from, and sometimes opposed to, the ethical. (For example, Brownie Wilsden also is charmless and plain.) Murdoch implies that sometimes the false cloaks itself in beauty and sophistication, while simplicity and innocence usually accompany the good. When Stuart Cuno and Jesse Baltram confront each other at Seegard, Jesse stands for creativity, undisciplined passion, and ego, while Stuart stands for simplicity, disciplined moral spirit, and selflessness.

Underlying this issue is the harder one of how humans know what is good. God and revealed religion are not options for Murdoch. Harry Cuno, a thoroughgoing secularist, cannot understand why Stuart must learn about goodness on his own: "Don't you see you can't do all this alone? Human nature needs institutions. . . . Why not go to the church, to some church, ask for help, ask to be directed?" Stuart rejects this advice because he rejects traditional religious convictions: "That's just what I can't do. I can't go there. I don't hold their beliefs." Instead, Stuart believes that people are endowed with a moral intuition, a perception of good almost analogous to the perception of color. He also believes that morality is objective, not merely an expression of personal preference as Harry maintains. Stuart's views on ethics mirror Murdoch's own ideas. For many years a philosophy teacher at the University of Oxford, Murdoch focused her academic philosophical writings on ethics. After a lifetime of thought and experience, Murdoch says:

> I still cannot believe in a literal God, or a literal life after death, or the divinity of Christ, or any of the things which many people would regard as essential to Christianity. . . . I think somehow or other, what Christianity has been doing for us must now be done in a more general way by people, by thinking and by realizing that human life is fundamentally a matter of continuously making moral choices. We can live with Christ, but without all the other literalistic background.

Murdoch rejects the idea that moral choices are only the expression of personal preference, and she contends that the way to goodness is to imitate Christ.

Murdoch uses several techniques to express her views in *The Good Apprentice*. She juxtaposes pairs of characters to contrast her themes. Sarah Plowmain set against Brownie Wilsden contrasts beauty and simplicity, impetuosity and self-discipline, self-centeredness and concern for others. She uses mystical passages, such as Edward's dreamlike state at Seegard, the mysterious séance, or Stuart's experience of transfiguring joy while waiting for a train, to say that there is more to reality than what science and logic can reveal. She enters the heads of Edward, Harry, Midge, and Thomas to show what they are thinking. (Since she never enters Jesse's or Ilona's heads, and only rarely Stuart's, these characters are not as well developed.) She gives Harry, Midge, and Thomas a rapid-fire speaking style, as if to drown Stuart's call to goodness in a torrent of words. She creates interconnected strands to make things come out the way she wants. Sarah Plowmain and Edward Baltram make love as Mark dies. Sarah's mother knew both Edward's and Mark's mothers, and through that connection Edward meets Brownie Wilsden. The medium who called Edward to Seegard is a good friend of May and her daughters.

Finally, Murdoch resolves some of the conflicts with a device common among Victorian novelists, that of shipping characters off to the Colonies. Brownie rejects Edward's marriage proposal, instead marrying a student at an American university. She and her mother move to the United States, thereby resolving the question of their relationship with newly forgiven Edward.

Context

Murdoch's ambiguous views on women's issues leave their mark on *The Good Apprentice*.

> I am passionately concerned with the liberation of women. It's one of the most important things on the whole planet. But I am not of the mind that women are superior to men, that they are different, that they must have a world of their own. I think that is merely putting up another sort of cage—setting oneself off from the great stream of humanity. The point is to be *people*, ordinary people, and not to be persons living in a sort of ghetto.

Murdoch stresses the importance of equal relations between the sexes. In their relationship, Harry Cuno tries to manipulate Midge McCaskerville into leaving her husband, telling her that Thomas is a repressed homosexual who secretly wants to end their marriage. He dominates others even as he professes to detest dominating men. He makes Midge wait in her bedroom, "like a captive bride," and imagines her "as idle and artificial, an idle woman in a harem, a bored prostitute yawning as she waits for custom." Another example is Ilona Baltram. Edward secretly sees her dance at Seegard, entranced by her grace and beauty; but when she goes to London, becomes a stripper, and loses her virginity, she loses her grace. Edward watches her strip, thinking that her beauty would transform the seedy club but instead discovers that she cannot dance.

> . . . she was jumping about naked, smiling a strained stretched smile out into the dark. Her nakedness was pitiful, touching like that of a child, pallid, clammy, bare, the human form revealed in all its contingent absurdity. It was shameful and tragic. What in the other girls had seemed simply ugly and vulgar, here shone out as something sublimely obscene, like an exhibition of a deformity, which at the same time was little, pathetic, soiled and childish.

Here Murdoch combines her dislike of sexual exploitation with her belief that the beautiful and the good often are separate things. Because Ilona's dancing has ceased to be unspoiled, it also has ceased to be beautiful.

Murdoch deals tangentially with bisexuality when she relates Jesse Baltram's affair with a male painter who also had an affair with May Baltram. Murdoch does not explore this theme, using it merely as another example of Seegard's disorder. In another passage, Brownie asks whether Edward and Mark had been lovers; instantly, Edward realizes that an affair might have occurred had Mark lived. Murdoch does nothing with this idea. Instead, at the end of the book she relates how Brownie's husband, who had thought that he was homosexual, decided that he was heterosexual after all. It seems that the novel's process of redemption involves converting homosexuals to heterosexuals. Murdoch does not challenge conventional gender roles from that direction.

Moreover, the female characters, with the exception of Brownie Wilsden, are not especially admirable. Midge McCaskerville's redemption is to return to her husband and her wifely duties. May Baltram writes a sensationalistic account of her husband's life for money. Bettina and Ilona are inconsequential and talentless. Sarah Plowmain, although showing some change of character at the end of the novel, still seems insensitive and shallow. In *The Good Apprentice*, Murdoch focuses on the character development of two men and on the dangers of unrestrained sexuality.

Sources for Further Study

Bove, Cheryl Browning. *A Character Index and Guide to the Fiction of Iris Murdoch*. New York: Garland, 1986. Describes characters, places, and references from each of Murdoch's novels through *The Good Apprentice*.

_____ . *Understanding Iris Murdoch*. Columbia: University of South Carolina Press, 1993. Overviews of Murdoch's life and philosophical writings introduce discussions of her major works from *Under the Net* (1954) to *The Message to the Planet* (1989), her plays, and her minor novels. Includes an annotated bibliography.

Byatt, A. S. *Iris Murdoch*. Harlow, England: Longman, 1976. A brief pamphlet by one of the leading literary critics of the day. Full of insights, but written in an informal style.

Johnson, Deborah. *Iris Murdoch*. Bloomington: Indiana University Press, 1987. Analyzes Murdoch's novels from the dual perspective of feminist literary theory and psychoanalytical theory.

Ramanathan, Suguna. *Iris Murdoch: Figures of Good*. New York: St. Martin's Press, 1990. A well-written and clear explanation of Murdoch's ethical and religious ideas, focusing on figures of good in eight of her novels, including *The Good Apprentice*.

Tartt, Donna. "Iris Murdoch." *Interview* 22, no. 11 (November, 1992): 80. A brief but illuminating interview that explores Murdoch's philosophical and religious views.

Tucker, Lindsey, ed. *Critical Essays on Iris Murdoch*. New York: G. K. Hall, 1992. A collection of essays on several aspects of Murdoch's published work, including her religious views, philosophical perspectives, narrative style and structure, and character development. Includes a comprehensive primary bibliography.

Wolfe, Peter. *The Disciplined Heart: Iris Murdoch and Her Novels*. Columbia: University of Missouri Press, 1966. One of the first book-length studies of Murdoch, this work treats her novels from *Under the Net* to *The Italian Girl* (1964). Besides offering a still-useful account of the early works, Wolfe includes an extensive secondary bibliography that charts her early reception.

D. G. Paz

THE GOOD EARTH

Author: Pearl S. Buck (1892-1973)
Type of work: Novel
Type of plot: Naturalism
Time of plot: The late nineteenth century to the 1920's
Locale: Anwhei Province, East Central China
First published: 1931

Principal characters:

WANG LUNG, a Chinese peasant whose changing fortunes and those of his family are the novel's central concerns

O-LAN, Wang Lung's strong, raw-boned wife, a former slave of the wealthy Hwang family who is obedient, silent, and stoical

UNCLE, a brother of Wang Lung's father

LOTUS, a prostitute whom Wang Lung takes as a concubine when he becomes rich

CUCKOO, a former procurer who enters Wang Lung's house as Lotus' slave

PEAR BLOSSOM, a young slave girl in Wang Lung's house who is devoted to him

ELDEST SON, a scholar whose affections for his father are superficial

SECOND SON, a merchant who shows little affection for Wang Lung

YOUNGEST SON, a soldier who detests working the land

CHING, Wang Lung's faithful friend

Form and Content

Biblical in the simplicity of its language and cadence, *The Good Earth* traces the life of Chinese peasant Wang Lung from his youthful marriage to his death in his seventies. Living in Anwhei Province hundreds of kilometers west of Shanghai, Soochow, Nanking, and other cities of eastern China between the Hwang Ho (Yellow River) to the north and the Yangtze River to the south, Wang Lung must pin his survival upon the yields of his land. Above all else, the land preoccupies and absorbs him, as it did most of China's traditional, prerevolutionary peasantry.

Believing that the fate of his land compelled it, Wang Lung subordinated everything to the soil: family, friends, his beasts, and every ounce of his strength. To hold the land, he battled drought, devastating floods, plagues of locusts, bandits, the desires of his three sons, and jealous neighbors until midlife. Only on his deathbed was it clear that the land to which he had sacrificed so much—and which even as he was dying he sought to pass to his sons—would in fact be divided and sold by sons who had little affection for him.

Throughout the book's thirty-four chapters, Wang Lung is depicted as a changing, three-dimensional figure. Poor, unlettered, shy, traditionally dutiful, honest, thrifty, and indefatigable in his labors as a young man, his eventual attainment of riches provides ambit for his desires and moments of reflection. Self-absorbed and insensitive toward O-lan, his wife, and certain that his sons must unquestionably mold their lives to care for the land, he slowly perceives the depths of his wife's devotion and must grudgingly yield to his sons' contrary strengths while suffering their weaknesses.

Similarly, when wealth is gained Wang Lung becomes a caricature of his earlier self. Shyness gives way to airs and pomposity. Self-restraint is transmuted into desire and licentious folly. Once openly generous or at the least dutiful toward others, he hoards his wealth and appears shrewd, calculating, and greedy. He thinks of himself as powerful. Meanwhile, his vulnerabilities and weaknesses are transparent to everyone around him. His sons argue or whine their way out of serving the land as Wang Lung wished them to do. Eldest son takes schooling and becomes a fat, lazy, and duplicitous scholar. Second son becomes a merchant, eventually managing his father's money. Youngest son, fierce of temper, storms from the household to become a soldier.

After Wang Lung reaches midlife as a wealthy man, a landlord who lives off rents and interest, he purchases the house and lands of the decadent Hwang family and with his friend Ching as overseer hires labor to work his fields. Divorced from the soil, he indulges his follies, expanding his household to include his concubine (or second wife), Lotus, and her slave, Cuckoo, along with his uncle's family. None of these arrangements brings him the peace that he expected: Cuckoo mocks him; Lotus tires of him; O-lan dies; and the members of his uncle's family, on the strength of traditional duties, remain importunate. When the uncle reveals himself as the leader of local bandits, Wang Lung realizes that he has been immunized from their depredations.

His peace of mind has been destroyed by the demands of his household; by his sons' discontents, jealousies, and lack of affection; and by his own isolation—except for the love of his "fool" (a retarded daughter) and his last passion, the young slave Pear Blossom. Wang Lung grows more reflective about himself as he prepares for death. Old and alone, remorseful over the loss of his direct union with the soil, he seeks to ensure that his family retain his lands. Yet, even as his sons hoodwink him with promises of a grand funeral, they conspire to dispose of the earth that had been the focus of his life.

Analysis

Pearl S. Buck was the daughter of West Virginia Presbyterian missionaries who chose to serve in China. Her first husband, the distinguished agricultural expert Lossing Buck, was himself a China missionary. American China missions therefore accounted for Pearl Buck's language—as a child she learned Mandarin Chinese as she learned English—and the ambience, the substance, and the experiences upon which her most enduring novels were premised, none more so than *The Good Earth*.

As her second novel (*East Wind: West Wind*, published in 1930, was the first), *The*

Good Earth brilliantly reflects Buck's intimate comprehension of Chinese traditions and of Chinese life that she acquired during the first three decades of the twentieth century and renewed frequently thereafter. Combining the stark simplicity of Chinese peasant life as she knew it with the tones and rhythms of the King James version of the Bible (the basis of Protestant missionary teachings), she superbly adapted her prose to her subject. Accordingly, *The Good Earth* unfolds, much like Old Testament stories, as a chronological narrative. Its tenor suggests an objectivity expected in documentaries, recounting straightforwardly what happened during Wang Lung's life, how he perceived himself, and how others perceived him. As observer, the author maintains a certain distance from the characters that she has evoked and from the events that she has set in motion.

Yet, if Pearl Buck as narrator avoids didacticism and the passages dense with detail that frequently convey editorial comment on their subjects in lesser works (her own included), she is neither disengaged nor uncompassionate. Part of her genius in creating *The Good Earth* lies in the spare but therefore telling detail, as well as the symbolism associated with it, that teases out her own and her characters' humanity.

Much is implied about the early married relationship between Wang Lung and O-lan, such as when starving times force the decision to slaughter Wang Lung's cherished ox. Wang Lung cannot bring himself to wield the knife. Treated little better than a broodmare and beast of burden, it is O-lan who, drawing upon more profound reserves of practical character than her husband, drives home the knife herself. Even more is implied by the unforgettable fate of two pearls found by O-lan after others have looted a rich family's home. Possession of the jewels transforms Wang Lung from a starving, begging refugee into a landowner once again by furnishing the seed money from which springs his subsequent wealth. The source of her husband's good fortune, the self-effacing O-lan asks the now-rich Wang Lung only for two pearls, which she keeps close to her bosom. Poignantly, years later Wang Lung demands their return to ingratiate himself with Lotus, his newfound concubine.

Incidents such as these blatantly illuminate the Chinese peasant's perceptions of women: If worthy, they labor in the household, tending the needs of males and children and working alongside their men in the field; they produce sons; and they satisfy male sexual expectations. When cultural variations are stripped away, however, Buck asks by implication, if these were not general male expectations everywhere. The signature of Buck's genius, not only in these incidents but in many others in *The Good Earth* as well, was her unerring capacity to evoke the universal.

Context

Pearl Buck was a widely read and influential author. Previously unknown and lacking money or influential friends, she gained instant fame and international recognition because of *The Good Earth*. Published to rave reviews, *The Good Earth* became a Book-of-the-Month Club selection and in 1932 won the Pulitzer Prize. In 1935, it was awarded the William Dean Howells Medal for distinguished American fiction. The following year, Buck was also elected to the National Academy of Arts and Letters. These honors culminated in the Nobel Prize for Literature in 1938, for a corpus of work which also included two masterful biographies, *The Exile* (1936) and *The Fighting Angel: Portrait of a Soul* (1936), portraits of her parents, Caroline and Absalom Sydenstricker, respectively.

Before her death, Buck published forty novels, along with a score of nonfiction works, fourteen books for children, and several translations of Chinese works. Her novels in particular were themselves swiftly translated into more than fifty major languages and many others, testifying to the universal humanity of her works. This influence was of immense importance to the women of the world.

As a strong woman (although one often in conflict with herself), Buck created or portrayed memorable women throughout her life, starting with O-lan and Caroline. Such characters were embodiments of her own vocal rebellion against the situation that women, particularly creative ones, confronted in male-dominated cultures. She publicly exhorted women, in the tradition of Susan B. Anthony, Elizabeth Cady Stanton, and Lucretia Mott, to rail against the abuses, carelessness, and indifference with which they were so commonly treated by men in most societies. She was no less contemptuous of the "selfish, ignorant, self-indulgent American woman of wealth and privilege" and those who preferred life in "a mental vacuum." Rather than helping their sisters struggle against injustice, these women, Buck argued, pulled everyone down. Because of her sensitive strengths, Buck reached women as have few other authors. She understood their plights, but she also exhorted them to see themselves as the hope of civilization, as people capable of shaping the future of their countries and of the world.

Sources for Further Study

Buck, Pearl S. *House of Earth: "The Good Earth," "Sons," "A House Divided."* New York: Reynal & Hitchcock, 1935. A trilogy that begins with *The Good Earth* and thereafter unfolds the fate of Wang Lung's family after his death. Although critics thought less of the latter two novels, they nevertheless offer a wonderful portrait of the dissolution of traditional China. Contains a brief essay on the origins of *The Good Earth*.

——————— . *The Mother*. New York: John Day, 1934. A novel based on a woman named Mrs. Lu whom Buck had known in China. The central figure is a failed mother and unfulfilled peasant woman who Buck hoped would be seen as reflective of such women's lives everywhere. Biographers have perceived this character as a mirror of Buck's own emotions, many associated with the need for men and her lifelong care and love for a retarded daughter. Important for understanding Buck's appeal among a whole generation of women.

Doyle, Paul A. *Pearl S. Buck*. Boston: Twayne, 1980. Interesting for its excellent critical comments on the literary origins of Buck's novels and on the character and quality of her prose. A good survey of major points of Buck's life, but not intended as a profound assessment of a remarkable personage. Includes a chronology, notes, bibliography, and an index.

Harris, Theodore F. *Pearl S. Buck: A Biography*. New York: John Day, 1969. Written in consultation with Buck, this is tantamount to an official biography, by a man who was an intimate of hers for years. Not a rounded picture, but it contains many interviews with Buck that offer pertinent insights into several areas of her work. A bibliography of Buck's books and an extensive index are provided.

Stirling, Nora. *Pearl Buck: A Woman in Conflict*. Piscataway, N.J.: New Century, 1983. The ablest, most insightful, and most rounded biography of Buck. Reveals many details of her personal and emotional life. Deals with Buck's feminist convictions and the way in which they grew out of her own struggles and disappointments in a man's world. Contains a brief bibliography and a superb index.

Clifton K. Yearley

A GOOD MAN IS HARD TO FIND

Author: Flannery O'Connor (1925-1964)
Type of work: Short stories
First published: 1955

Form and Content

This collection of ten short stories demonstrates O'Connor's skill at using irony, violence, and the grotesque to create opportunities for redemption in the lives of characters who are often comical and always spiritually adrift in a realistic, yet highly symbolic world. At least one character in each story is somehow deluded and in need of an awakening by the Divine to reveal the true self and offer an opportunity for change.

Five of the stories include strong Southern women whose "sins" range from simple smugness to pride in one's physical and material attributes as virtues. In "A Good Man Is Hard to Find," a meddlesome but good-hearted grandmother inadvertently leads her entire family to their violent deaths at the hands of a criminal known as the Misfit. After the rest of the family has been killed, the grandmother experiences a profound spiritual change while talking to the Misfit as she accepts her connection to all living things. The Misfit acknowledges that she would have been a good woman if there had been "somebody there to shoot her every minute of her life." In "A Stroke of Good Fortune," Ruby Hill is a plump, judgmental woman returning from a visit to Madam Zoleeda, a fortune teller who informed Ruby that she is on the brink of a long illness followed by good fortune. The story ends with a stunned Ruby accepting the fact that she is pregnant, a condition she has carefully avoided and finds disgusting in others. In "A Circle in the Fire," Mrs. Cope is the proud owner of the best-kept farm in the county, but her worst fears come true when three boys, envious of her possessions, set fire to her farm. She watches, stunned, as a column of smoke rises over her woods, and she listens to their "shrieks of joy as if the prophets were dancing in the fiery furnace, in the circle the angel had cleared for them."

Mrs. Hopewell is a landowner in the story "Good Country People." She lives with her grown daughter, Joy, who has changed her name to Hulga because she believes it better suits her disposition, her physical ailments, and the fact that she has no illusions about life. Hulga finds out that she is not as smart as she thought when Bible salesman Manley Pointer tricks her into handing over her wooden leg as she tries to seduce him. The story ends with poor Hulga stranded in a hay loft while Pointer happily absconds with her leg. In "The Displaced Person," the parish priest, Father Flynn, persuades the wealthy Mrs. McIntyre to hire Mr. Guizac, a Polish war refugee or "displaced person," to assist the African American workers and Mr. Shortley, a hired white man, in running the farm. Mrs. Shortley, afraid that Guizac will take her husband's job, soon begins to undermine Mrs. McIntyre's impression of Guizac. Mrs. Shortley packs her family's belongings and, as they leave early the next morning, is overcome with a stroke and dies. Mrs. McIntyre decides that she must fire Mr. Guizac, but cannot seem to do it.

When a brake mysteriously slips on a tractor, Mrs. McIntyre, Mr. Shortley, and a young African American boy freeze, in a moment of collusion deciding not to help the displaced person as the tractor runs over him.

The other five stories in this collection seem to center around the theme of spiritual initiation. In "The River," Harry Ashfield is a young boy who changes his name to Bevel after his babysitter takes him to see a preacher by that name. Young Bevel's baptism in the river seems an appealing alternative to his neglected life with his parents. He returns to the river alone to baptize himself and to keep going until he finds the Kingdom of Christ. The story ends with the current pulling Bevel down and swiftly forward, "like a long gentle hand."

A precocious twelve-year-old girl receives her first intimations of sexuality in "A Temple of the Holy Ghost," as her two older cousins relay the story of a hermaphrodite they have seen in a freak show. After returning the cousins to their convent, the girl sees the sun as a blood-drenched Host. In "A Late Encounter with the Enemy," one-hundred-and-four-year-old General Sash (who was never really a general) attends his sixty-two-year-old granddaughter's graduation. Sally Poker Sash's grandfather is brought to the stage by wheelchair in a general's uniform with a sword across his lap, but the old man can recall nearly nothing of his own past. The final image of the story is of young John Wesley, a nephew in charge of pushing the general around for the day, lined up at the Coca-Cola machine outside with a wheelchair that now contains the corpse of General Sash.

"The Life You Save May Be Your Own" begins with Mr. Shiftlet, a drifter who wanders onto the farm of Lucynell Crater and her deaf and retarded daughter, who is also named Lucynell. Mrs. Crater slyly offers Shiftlet the late Mr. Crater's car, some money, and a home if he will marry Lucynell. After the ceremony, Shiftlet leaves Lucynell at a roadside eating place after she falls asleep waiting for her food. Shiftlet, ironically seeing himself as an honorable man, instructs the boy behind the counter to give her the food when she wakes up. Shiftlet picks up a young male hitchhiker so that he can carry on a dramatic monologue about mothers—especially his own, who was an "angel of Gawd." The young man suddenly tells Shiftlet to "go to the devil" and jumps out of the car.

Some of the most beautiful language in this collection is found in "The Artificial Nigger," the story that O'Connor said was her favorite. It is the story of a literal journey into the city of Atlanta, representing young Nelson's initiation into the real world, and a spiritual journey for the boy's grandfather, Mr. Head, who is forced to face the fact that he requires the mercy of God to be redeemed. Mr. Head is disdainful of Nelson's positive reaction to the city and to African Americans there. Determined to break the boy's independent spirit, Head sets up little tricks, culminating in his denial of his grandson at a moment when the boy needs him most. The day climaxes in a wealthy neighborhood with the sighting of "an artificial nigger," a chipped statue of a boy sitting on a wall, miserable, and nearly falling off. The two come to a mysterious understanding and head home together, the boy realizing that the grandfather is his mentor in the world and the grandfather recognizing his moral deficiency.

Analysis

It is sometimes difficult for readers to view O'Connor as a religious writer since none of her characters seem "good." Her tightly crafted narratives seem to bring readers to the moment where a "bad" character is ready to change, but one never sees the results. O'Connor considered herself a writer with "Christian concerns" and illustrated through her stories her vision of a world where what is normally thought of as progress is actually the opposite. She demonstrates humankind's need for the mysterious grace of God, a gift that is offered suddenly in ordinary settings. Violence is a means to wake up characters to their own moral deficiency, to burn away their virtues so that there is nothing left but a humbled self standing in perfect readiness to accept redemption.

O'Connor had a gift for being able to capture the natural speech patterns of the inhabitants of her South, and her ironic humor is unmatched. The stories in *A Good Man Is Hard to Find* also demonstrate her superior use of symbolism. The peacocks mentioned in "Good Country People," "The Life You Save May Be Your Own," and "The Displaced Person" are symbolic of God's presence; Father Flynn makes direct comparisons between the mysterious beauty of the peacock's tail and Christ's transfiguration. Descriptions of setting in O'Connor's stories are nearly always symbolic as well. The moon appears symbolically twice in "The Artificial Nigger," signifying the unknown aspects of himself that Mr. Head is about to discover and then the illuminating light of God's mercy.

The titles of the stories are nearly always ironic, as are the names of many characters. Mrs. Hopewell is annoyingly optimistic in "Good Country People," and her daughter is anything but filled with "joy." Bevel, the name that Harry Ashfield chooses for himself in "The River," can mean a device for adjusting slants, just as Harry is trying desperately to integrate the confusion and depression in his young life. Mr. Shiftlet certainly proves himself to be shiftless, or shifty.

For African American writer Alice Walker, O'Connor became "the first great modern writer from the South." Ironic humor, a rich use of symbolism and religious allegory, and characters that may falter but are always human are perhaps what continue to make O'Connor a favorite among readers and cause many to agree with A. L. Rowse's assessment that O'Connor was "probably the greatest short story writer of our time."

Context

While O'Connor died before the women's movement of the 1960's gained much momentum and never chose to identify herself openly with feminist concerns, her work itself is important to women's literature for several reasons. In her depiction of strong, independent female characters with as much of a chance at redemption as their male counterparts, O'Connor was responsible for presenting a new, more realistic picture of white Southern women. As Alice Walker has written, "when she set her pen to them not a whiff of magnolia hovered in the air." Walker was shocked and delighted at the humanity of O'Connor's characters, "who are miserable, ugly, narrow-minded, atheistic, and of intense racial smugness and arrogance."

Being a woman affected the way in which O'Connor was received during her time, particularly because the violence and general nastiness of her characters were often not admired coming from a "lady writer." Even those critics who praised her sometimes did so in carefully couched language. Evelyn Waugh once said of O'Connor's writing, "If this is the unaided work of a young lady it is a remarkable product." O'Connor was the first woman to be compared to the great male Southern writer William Faulkner. By taking her art seriously, and working hard during her tragically short life to achieve the status of a great American writer, O'Connor set a standard and paved the way for women writers to come.

Sources for Further Study

Cheatham, George. "Jesus, O'Connor's Artificial Nigger." *Studies in Short Fiction* 22, no. 4 (Fall, 1985): 475-479. Offers a brief discussion of the symbolism of the statue in "The Artificial Nigger."

Cheney, Brainard. "Flannery O'Connor's Campaign for Her Country." *Sewanee Review* 72 (Autumn, 1964): 555-558. Cheney's obituary for O'Connor describes her vocation as a Christian writer.

Getz, Lorine M. *Nature and Grace in Flannery O'Connor's Fiction.* New York: Edwin Mellen Press, 1982. Getz attempts to analyze the various actions of grace in O'Connor's work and the literary devices used to convey them.

Grimshaw, James A., Jr. *The Flannery O'Connor Companion.* Westport, Conn. Greenwood Press, 1981. An introduction to O'Connor's writings, both fiction and nonfiction. Features an introductory overview, a chronological survey of O'Connor's work, a catalog of her fictional characters, illustrations, and two appendices.

Zoller, Peter T. "The Irony of Preserving the Self: Flannery O'Connor's 'A Stroke of Good Fortune.'" *Kansas Quarterly* 9, no. 2 (Spring, 1977): 61-66. Zoller reads "A Stroke of Good Fortune" as a religious parable on the foibles of human pride. Calls the story "the *Divine Comedy* in modern dress."

Bonnie Flaig

THE GOOD MOTHER

Author: Sue Miller (1943-   )
Type of work: Novel
Type of plot: Psychological realism
Time of plot: The 1970's
Locale: Primarily Cambridge, Massachusetts, as well as rural New England and Chicago
First published: 1986

Principal characters:

> ANNA DUNLAP, a woman struggling to survive after she leaves a loveless marriage and takes her daughter with her
> BRIAN DUNLAP, Anna's former husband, a lawyer
> MOLLY DUNLAP, Anna and Brian's three-year-old daughter
> LEO, Anna's lover, an intense, gifted painter
> FRANK MCCORD, Anna's grandfather, who represents the repressive Calvinism that shaped her girlhood
> BUNNY, Anna's mother

Form and Content

  The Good Mother is told in the past tense, after Anna has survived her ordeal. Flashbacks to her childhood are interspersed with chapters narrating the recent past of her divorce, her affair with Leo, and the subsequent trial in which she loses custody of Molly. The scenes from Anna's childhood are important to the psychological realism of the novel, for it becomes clear that Anna, dominated by a mother who was in turn dominated by her father, has never had a strong sense of herself. Anna's marriage to Brian simply continues the pattern. Anna leaves Brian and attempts to build a more satisfactory life with Molly, and for a while she succeeds. Subsequently, she meets Leo, falls passionately in love, and creates a private Eden for the three of them. Yet Anna cannot close out the wider world completely. Her new lifestyle leads to indiscretions with Molly that cause disaster when they come to Brian's attention.

  The theme of a lost Eden is established in the first of the novel's fourteen chapters. While divorcing Brian, Anna rents a cottage in a New Hampshire village, a retreat for her and Molly. The warm, loving relationship between mother and daughter is evoked as they attend a film and stop for dinner at a small café. When they return to the cottage, Anna finds legal papers from Brian's attorney that she must have notarized and return the next day. Anna leaves Molly asleep in the car when she finally reaches the only available notary's home, and the chore takes longer than she expects. She returns to find Molly in a state of terror after she left the car to look for her mother and was attacked by a cat. For the first time, Anna questions whether she is strong enough, or good enough, to rear Anna alone. Their idyllic retreat has been violated by a world they have not managed to escape.

  Once resettled with Molly in an apartment in Cambridge, Anna finds a friend,

Ursula, among her piano students, and through her, a part-time job testing memory retention in rats at a Boston University laboratory. Molly adjusts well to her day-care center and provides all the companionship Anna needs. Anna, in fact, contentedly looks forward to their evenings together and to her private erotic explorations in the mornings. Then Anna meets Leo Cutter, a Cambridge artist whose life is as uncertain as hers, and she finds the sexual fulfillment she never knew with Brian. As their affair progresses, he spends more and more time at Anna's apartment. Molly grows to love Leo, and again Anna creates a private Eden outside the strictures of society.

The following summer, Molly goes to Washington, D.C., to stay with Brian and his new wife for a month. Anna enjoys her time alone with Leo until he goes to New York for his art show. After receiving a call from Brian informing her that he does not intend to return Molly and hinting that it is because of Leo, Anna falls into an agony of apprehension. Upon Leo's return from New York, Anna finds out what has upset Brian. Innocently responding to Molly's childish curiosity, Leo let her touch his penis when he was emerging from the shower.

Anna is soon surrounded by lawyers, family-service officers, and a psychiatrist as she struggles to retain custody of Molly. Another sexual indiscretion permitted by Molly comes to light. Anna ponders Brian's changed attitude toward her while the legal process grinds on, increasing the tension. On the witness stand, Leo lets himself be blamed for the sexual indiscretions, but he feels betrayed. Still, he is devoted to Anna and tries to salvage their love. When a conservative judge renders the decision to remove Molly from Anna's custody, Anna finds herself indifferent to Leo. Grief-stricken, she moves abruptly to Washington, D.C., to be near Molly, where she and the child struggle to come to terms with their losses.

At the end of *The Good Mother*, Molly has adjusted to her new family and moves back to Boston with her father and his newly pregnant wife. Anna returns to Cambridge to be near her and picks up the pieces of her life. Although Anna has consistently acted with good intentions, circumstances have conspired to separate her from what she loves most: her daughter and her lover.

Analysis

While Anna might be seen as a victim of circumstances, her own character is important in determining the course of her life. Her repeated attempts to create an idyllic haven outside society can be seen as vain efforts to re-create her childhood sojourns at her maternal grandparents' summer home in rural Maine. The "camp," as it was called, had no electricity or telephone, but Anna describes it early in the novel as "Edenic." When she moves into her Cambridge apartment, she paints Molly's room the same green and white as the buildings at her grandparents' camp, attempting to create something familiar and safe.

When Anna was fourteen, she moved with her family to Chicago, and her life changed. She spent her summers at a music camp, where her mother enrolled her in the belief she was musically gifted. After two years, however, Anna's teacher advised her not to return. Although the decision to be a pianist had not been Anna's, she believed that her life as a "serious person" was over. This lack of confidence led to the drifting quality of Anna's early life.

In addition to giving this careful depiction of Anna's inner life, *The Good Mother* takes on wider themes. While the primary conflict is apparently between Anna and Brian for custody of their child, another contest is between Anna's unconventional living arrangements and the traditional role that society demands of a mother. Anna dissolves a marriage that is outwardly successful, although she is unawakened sexually. Brian does not understand Anna's dissatisfaction, yet he is still generous in granting Anna custody of their child. Brian, traditional in his beliefs, is accommodating as long as Anna represents some subconscious ideal of a "virgin mother." As long as Anna centers her life exclusively on Molly, Brian is supportive.

When Anna steps beyond her chaste role as single mother and engages in a passionate love affair with Leo, she sets the machinery of retribution in motion. Her character changes as her sexuality develops: She becomes more sure of herself and has a firmer center. Brian's cooperative attitude changes: He realizes that Anna has become a woman he never knew. When Molly innocently reveals the sexual indiscretion she has experienced, Brian is ready to punish Anna in the harshest way he can—by legally taking the child from her.

Sue Miller has carefully constructed the novel so that the reader has no doubt that Molly's interests would be best served by her remaining with Anna. The psychiatrist who has studied the case also recommends that Anna retain custody. Yet when Anna enters the "real world" of the legal system to plead her case, she is helpless. Even Leo, powerful in his bohemian art world, appears foolish and inconsequential on the stand. Opposing them is Brian, a lawyer who believes in the system and knows how to use it. Once again, the private Eden that Anna lives in is destroyed. Although Brian had an affair with his present wife while he was still married to Anna, the law accepts this. A possible interpretation is that society tolerates a man's indiscretions more readily than a woman's, or perhaps Brian's later marriage provides him with an aura of respectability that Anna lacks. At any rate, Anna is punished for violating the rules of society. In living by her own rules, Anna has forfeited the protection and safeguards enjoyed by those who conform. She is twice punished: She loses custody of Molly and, through her own withdrawal, loses Leo.

In addition to teaching piano, Anna takes a part-time position training rats while she is in Cambridge. In a sense, the situation of the rats is a paradigm of her own condition. Each rat must run through a maze again and again until it learns in which direction a reward is waiting. When she tries to reach Molly in Washington, D.C., at the end of the novel, Anna becomes lost in a maze at the airport. This is one more failed attempt (piano, marriage, motherhood, love affair) in Anna's life, a series of events reflecting the lives of the animals that learn by trial and error, and then not very well.

Context

The Good Mother was Sue Miller's first novel. It sold well, earned good reviews, and was widely read and discussed. The themes of the novel are relevant to many of the social issues that dominated the public debates of the 1980's and the preceding decade. The breakup of the American family, opportunities for women, the changing roles of mothers, the sexual abuse of children, the personal in conflict with the public are all themes that are woven into the tight tapestry of *The Good Mother*. Notably, they are all items on the feminist agenda.

Far from suggesting answers to these questions, however, the novel simply follows them to their logical conclusions within the context of the plot. Anna loses everything she holds dear, and the only constant is her love for Molly. She never compromises that love or uses it for her own ends; in order to save Molly further turmoil, Anna decides not to appeal the decision of the judge. Some critics have suggested the popular appeal of *The Good Mother* is that it arouses women's deepest fear—the fear of being left alone. Yet that does not seem a satisfactory conclusion.

Among the many feminist themes in the novel, one of the most important is women's work. Anna is not talented enough to have a career as a pianist, but she is successful in her own small, private world. Yet that does not seem enough; Leo expresses some disdain for her attitude toward her work, which is not the consuming passion that his is. She defends herself by saying that her real commitment is to Molly and to performing her chosen tasks "carefully and well." By the end of the novel, it becomes clear that Anna's good qualities are not enough, for when she is forced to act on a larger stage she is unequal to the task. At a time when women are leaving their private worlds and entering the public sphere of work in great numbers, Anna's dilemma goes to the heart of the feminist debate.

Sources for Further Study

Drzal, Dawn Ann. "Casualties of the Feminine Mystique." *The Antioch Review* 46 (Fall, 1988): 450-461. A detailed feminist analysis that compares Anna with other fictional heroines who are in the same predicament: They are uncertain about their place in society because they are unable to find satisfying work. Drzal discusses what the role of motherhood means to these women.

Humphreys, Josephine. "The Good Mother." *The Nation* 242 (May 10, 1986): 648. Humphreys discusses the important contemporary issues that *The Good Mother* raises, and she finds that they overshadow the traditional character and plot underpinnings of the novel. She considers Sue Miller "brave" to raise such difficult questions in a first novel.

McManus, Barbara F. "Anna and Demeter: The Myth of *The Good Mother*." In *The Anna Book*, edited by Mickey Pearlman. Westport, Conn.: Greenwood Press, 1992. McManus gives the novel a mythical interpretation and concludes that Anna associates innocence and happiness with an asexual female world.

White, Roberta. "Anna's Quotidian Love: Sue Miller's *The Good Mother*." In *Mother Puzzles*, edited by Mickey Pearlman. New York: Greenwood Press, 1989. White interprets the novel as an affirmation of the greater value of the inner, private life, to the diminishment of the public life. Because Anna is driven to examine her life closely, *The Good Mother* raises important questions of responsibility and freedom.

Zinman, Toby Silverman. "The Good Old Days in *The Good Mother*." *Modern Fiction Studies* 34 (Autumn, 1988): 405-413. Zinman gives a quirky, original interpretation of the novel. She considers the longing for the innocent, happy days spent in childhood at her grandparents' summer home as the ruling motivation in Anna's life. Significantly, this was a women's world, for the men came up only on weekends, and they always seemed superfluous to Anna.

Sheila Golburgh Johnson

THE GOOD TERRORIST

Author: Doris Lessing (1919-   )
Type of work: Novel
Type of plot: Psychological realism
Time of plot: The 1980's
Locale: London
First published: 1985

Principal characters:
>ALICE MELLINGS, a member of a radical political group who restores their run-down house
>JASPER, Alice's partner of many years
>PHILIP, a working-class youth who looks to Alice and the house for opportunity
>JIM, the original inhabitant of the squat
>MONICA, a young and destitute mother who comes to the house for help
>FAYE, a lesbian, a victim of child abuse who is consumed by rage and pain
>DOROTHY MELLINGS, Alice's mother
>CEDRIC MELLINGS, Alice's beleaguered father
>MARY, REGGIE, BERT, PAT, ROBERTA, and JOCELIN, other members of the commune

Form and Content

The Good Terrorist depicts a group of disturbed middle-class young people who use radical politics as an outlet for their feelings of rage and deprivation. They are portrayed as politically irresponsible and personally reprehensible. The story is centered on Alice Mellings, the "good terrorist" of the title, an unsettling combination of maternal solicitude and destructive anger. She and her feckless companion Jasper move back to 43 Old Mill Road, one of the many abandoned houses in a poor section of London. Thirty-six-years old and still living the life of a political agitator, Alice occupies this "squat" with Jasper and other members of their group, the Communist Centre Union. For all of her radical politics, Alice takes on the caretaking and housekeeping responsibilities traditionally assigned to women. She almost single-handedly turns the filthy house into a livable home, tackling such thankless tasks as burying buckets of feces that the former tenants have left behind. She also nurtures the rest of the group, especially the only two genuinely working-class residents of the house, Jim and Philip.

Because the novel is told from Alice's point of view, and because she is shown energetically trying to improve a woefully neglected house, readers at first identify with Alice and her goals. Her skills as a homemaker and caretaker are offset, however, by her rage at everyone in the outside world, particularly her parents. Contemptuous of her mother and father, she depends on them to fund her radical activities. For all the group's political rhetoric, however, its efforts with the disadvantaged come to nothing and even do more harm than good. When a homeless young mother comes to the squat, Faye, a psychotic woman posing as a Cockney, flies into a rage and chases the frightened girl away. Alice herself alternates between solicitude and insensitivity toward this young woman and is similarly prone to bouts of irrational anger. After prevailing upon her father to employ the black, destitute Jim, Alice is responsible for his dismissal when he is blamed for stealing money that she has stolen herself. After she encourages the frail Philip to help her in restoring the house, he dies in a roofing accident.

While the group continues to make superficial political gestures, Alice locates her mother, who had moved and left no forwarding address in an attempt to rid herself of Alice's greedy demands. Sarcastic and bitter, Dorothy has no resources, either emotional or financial, left for Alice to plunder. Depleted by Alice, she no longer has the strength or love necessary to be able to be a good mother, and Alice, enraged, is no longer able to be a good daughter. Ironically, her parents are revealed as good liberals who espoused progressive causes. From Alice's perspective, however, they sacrificed their private life to these activities, leaving their daughter neglected and unloved. She has translated her sense of abandonment into a revolutionary identity that permits her to express all of her most negative feelings.

Her entire group is in fact drifting toward violence that is expressive more of psychological problems than of political principles. When Faye and Jasper drive a homemade car bomb to a large London hotel, the suicidal Faye refuses to leave the car. It explodes, killing her and five innocent bystanders and injuring others. This terrorist act leaves the group in disarray. At the end of the novel, a childish and confused Alice remains alone in the squat, about to be drawn into some unspecified action organized by professional terrorists.

Analysis

After a series of controversial science-fiction novels by Doris Lessing, *The Good Terrorist* was one of a series of novels that returned to the realism of *The Grass Is Singing* (1950) and the Children of Violence series (1952-1969). Inspired by the 1983 bombing of Harrod's department store and the assassination of Lord Mountbatten, which happened while Lessing was in Ireland, *The Good Terrorist* continues to reflect the disillusionment with communism found in earlier novels such as *The Golden Notebook* (1962). As in her analysis of the white colonial radicals in that novel, she sees contemporary British terrorism as a privilege assumed by a decadent leisure class. Her subject is the kind of self-styled revolutionary she believes can only be produced by affluent societies. Lessing's tone in this novel is as bitter and as sarcastic as that of Alice's mother, Dorothy Mellings, whose name is reminiscent of Lessing's own.

Alice's group, the Communist Centre Union, is only intermittently unified. In spite of its radical affectations, it replicates the social patterns of the wider society. The traditional divisions of labor between male and female are observed, as well as those between middle-class and working-class persons. While members of the group are theoretically in solidarity with the working class, they do not really further the interests of the disadvantaged or disfranchised. They are not a part of any true progressive party but instead use their political organization as a theater within which they can play out their psychological problems. Working-class members of the group, such as Jim and Philip, are seen as suffering from social, economic, and health problems that are not alleviated by the exhibitionistic political gestures of the middle-class radicals. Alice is singled out for using her politics to express an infantile rage at her sense of rejection by her successful, middle-class parents. The house she tends is almost a character in its own right, and it is the novel's central symbol. Its shabby, neglected character reflects Alice's own feelings of abandonment; it becomes a metaphorical substitute for herself, the unloved child.

Lessing very carefully refrains from introducing Alice's mother until the end of the novel, so that the narrative builds to a confrontation between mother and daughter. Although Alice has unconsciously modeled her own identity on that of her mother, taking her place in her own circle as homemaker, there is no empathic connection between them. Dorothy considers she has been drained of her good resources and left depleted. She has become an angry, remorseful alcoholic. Alice's father, who was once the head of a successful liberal printing press, is close to bankruptcy and on the verge of turning his daughter over to the police. Dorothy and Cedric Mellings represent a crisis in liberalism; their radical daughter has taken their progressive agenda and used it to justify nihilistic destruction.

The Mellings family also represents the fragmentation of the nuclear family. Cedric has left his wife for a younger woman; Dorothy has virtually disowned her daughter and her old identity as a wife and mother. Alice, though ideologically opposed to the bourgeois family, feels its loss intensely. Her nostalgia for family life contrasts so sharply with her identity as an angry activist that Lessing hints at a split personality. On the one hand, Alice is given to hysterical lapses of memory and uncontrollable fits of rage; on the other hand, she attempts to be the nurturing mother she herself longs to have. The splitting in Alice's psyche is reflected in the title's paradoxical description of her as a "good terrorist." Her conventional feminine self is in conflict with her alternate, angry self that finds expression in political agitation.

Alice's political activities meddle with innocent lives, demoralizing some and destroying others. Although Lessing's narrative method draws readers into identifying with Alice, they find that their sympathy for her has been undermined by the plot, which concentrates not on Alice's self-righteous attitudes but on the destructive consequences of her actions. Lessing's final picture of Alice is drawn with devastating irony. Like Alice in Wonderland, Alice Mellings is depicted as a child who has fallen into her own unconscious and is no longer in touch with the real world.

Context

Like Lessing's earlier novel *The Diary of Jane Somers* (1983), *The Good Terrorist* explores what is known as "women's work." Lessing suggests that the caretaking traditionally assigned to women is devalued and scorned in modern society. Alice, who gives her comrades a house, food, community, warmth, and order, is both exploited and unappreciated by her mates. Although Alice's domestic skills are wasted on her ungrateful comrades, her good offices transform her ragtag group into a terrorist gang. She keeps them together long enough for them to detonate a bomb.

The women in this radical group are depicted as both more competent and more enraged than the men. Jasper and Bert are weak and passive, babied by their respective companions, Alice and Pat. Only Pat and Alice are recruited by more powerful, international political organizations. Just as only Alice has the know-how to repair the house and deal with various government bureaucracies, Jocelin, another woman in the group, is the only member who has the expertise to make a bomb. Yet another woman, Faye, is both fearless enough and angry enough to execute the terrorist bombing. In *The Good Terrorist* it is women who are both the most efficient and the most violent political activists.

This is an important theme for Lessing, developed in earlier novels such as *The Golden Notebook*. Lessing believes that contemporary Western society fails to recognize the powerful capacity for aggression in women. For Lessing, female identity is socially constructed through a division between the conventionally socialized side of women, the good daughter or mother who "makes a house a home," and the repressed angry side, which seeks to destroy the powers that be. The political activity of the women in the novel becomes a way to express an identity that is split off from their expected nurturing selves. This construction of female identity divides a woman into two people—the mature, caring woman and the enraged and undeveloped self disallowed as unfeminine.

Ultimately, Alice's conventional feminine identity is subordinated to an intense rage that Lessing suggests is a product of her culture's failure to accept and socialize female aggression. Because aggression is seen as an inappropriate option for little girls, these qualities "go underground," where they eventually become unmanageable and irrational. It is the failure to integrate the disowned aggressive side that turns Alice into a "good terrorist."

Doris Lessing has always been known for her exploration of issues relevant to women. Her depiction of women is complex, incorporating questions of politics, religion, love, sex, children, and work. She is considered one of the most important writers of her generation.

Sources for Further Study

Bloom, Harold, ed. *Doris Lessing*. New York: Chelsea House, 1986. Includes an important review of *The Good Terrorist* by Alison Lurie, who praises it as one of the best novels she has read about the terrorist mentality since Joseph Conrad's *The Secret Agent* (1907). The book also contains some of the better-known articles, organized chronologically, indicating changing attitudes in Lessing criticism.

King, Jeannette. *Doris Lessing*. London: Edward Arnold, 1989. A reading along lines

developed by French psychologist Jacques Lacan, arguing that Lessing's work is implicitly feminist in its interrogation of a culture that ascribes value to what has been traditionally defined as male. Includes a brief chronology and an excellent analysis of *The Good Terrorist*.

Pickering, Jean. *Understanding Doris Lessing*. Columbia: University of South Carolina Press, 1990. A guide or companion for students. The analysis of *The Good Terrorist* emphasizes its depiction of radicals as an irresponsible leisure class supported by the lower orders.

Sprague, Claire. *Rereading Doris Lessing: Narrative Patterns of Doubling and Repetition*. Chapel Hill: University of North Carolina Press, 1987. Sprague considers *The Good Terrorist* in an examination of Lessing's characters and narrative patterns, especially the use of *A*, *M*, and *J* names and the numbers three, four, and five. She also discusses *The Good Terrorist* in the context of unresolved conflicts between mothers and daughters found in earlier novels.

Margaret Boe Birns

GORILLA, MY LOVE

Author: Toni Cade Bambara (1939-   )
Type of work: Short stories
First published: 1972

Form and Content

Gorilla, My Love is a collection of fifteen short stories told in the first person by female narrators who show the daily lives of ordinary people living in the black neighborhoods of Brooklyn, Harlem, and other sections of New York City, as well as parts of the rural South. As Toni Cade Bambara celebrates the life in these communities, she captures the culture, the traditions, and the unique speech patterns of the people who make up these neighborhoods.

The first story, "My Man Bovanne," deals with the generation gap that exists between Hazel, the older female narrator, and her children, who have become involved in the Black Power movement. In casting off their slave names for African names, the young people seem to be rejecting the values of the older people in their community. As Miss Hazel dances with Bovanne, the old blind man in the neighborhood, her children express their disapproval of their mother's actions and style of dress. For Miss Hazel, Bovanne, who used to fix skates for the children in the neighborhood, represents a familiar presence in a changing world.

Disillusionment as a part of growing up is the theme of three stories. In "Gorilla, My Love," Hazel, the young female narrator, must face the pain of realizing that her uncle—who jokingly promised to marry her when she grew up— is preparing to marry someone else. The story begins when Hazel and her friends are disgusted after they pay for tickets to see a film that the marquee advertised as *Gorilla, My Love*, only to be shown *King of Kings*, an old motion picture about Jesus. The story deals with the children's sense of betrayal when grown-ups do not keep their word. For Hazel, her uncle's betrayal is much more painful to accept than the false advertising of the film.

Another type of disillusionment takes place in the frequently anthologized story "The Lesson." The narrator is Sylvia, a tough, sassy, bright young girl whose class takes a field trip to F. A. O. Schwartz, an upscale toy store. Bambara is making a strong statement about American society as seen from the point of view of a group of poor children who cannot even imagine spending $1,195 for a toy sailboat. Miss Moore, the teacher, asks, "Imagine for a minute what kind of society it is in which some people can spend on a toy what it would cost to feed a family of six or seven. What do you think?"

One of the shortest stories in the book, "Sweet Town," deals with the disappointment and disillusionment of young love. Kit, the romantic young narrator, is softer than the tough-talking Hazel and Sylvia of the previous stories. Here is a woman narrator looking back at the sweet intensity of young love as she tells the story of her infatuation with the handsome B. J., who leaves her to travel west with a friend.

The theme of isolation dominates the story "Happy Birthday" as Ollie, a young black girl, must face the loneliness of spending her birthday with no one to notice or help her celebrate. This is one of two stories in the collection that features a third-person narrator.

Three of the stories focus on young narrators and their relationships with unconventional characters. In "Raymond's Run," Hazel Elizabeth Deborah Parker, known as "Squeaky," learns to care more for her retarded brother as she shifts her attention from her own abilities to see her brother in a new light. Even as she hears her own name announced as the winner of a race, Hazel makes plans to help her brother, Raymond, improve his skill as a runner. Hazel is a strong, honest, hardworking young girl who also comes to respect the abilities of Gretchen, a girl who has been her rival. The story ends with Hazel and Gretchen exchanging "this big smile of respect" that is "about as real a smile as girls can do for each other, considering we don't practice real smiling every day."

In "Maggie of the Green Bottles," Bambara shows the relationship between a young girl and Maggie, a strange older women who drinks too much and behaves in a bizarre manner. The young girl overlooks Maggie's eccentric behavior and sees her bottles as magic.

Manny, the male character in "The Hammer Man," disabled after a fall from a roof, is the crazy boy of the neighborhood. The unnamed protagonist, a young girl, watches Manny practicing basketball in the dark, trying to relive the last minutes of a game in his past in which he missed what could have been the final winning shot. When two police officers approach Manny to see what he is doing in the park after dark, he reacts in a confused manner and the policemen take him away in their patrol car. Although no act of violence takes place, Bambara shows that even a young child can show compassion and concern for others.

Analysis

Gorilla, My Love is a collection of stories about ordinary people who are part of the African American communities of large cities and small rural areas. The stories are told from the first-person female point of view and focus on the importance of family and the community. Bambara's characters speak in the black dialect of the street, with all its vitality and humor. It is this accurate portrayal of speech patterns that makes Bambara's characters come to life. Her characters are warm, lively, real-life people who show concern and love for their families and people in the neighborhood.

Bambara has written novels, such as *The Salt Eaters* (1980) and *If Blessing Comes* (1987), but she prefers the short story as an art form. In her essay "Salvation Is the Issue," Bambara expresses this preference: "Of all the writing forms, I've always been partial to the short story. It suits my temperament. It makes a modest appeal for attention, allowing me to slip up alongside the reader on her/his blind side and grab'm." In comparing short stories with novels, Bambara makes this observation: "Short stories are a piece of time. The novel is a way of life."

Bambara is interested in the cultural, social, and political activities of the African

American community. In her works, she seeks to portray the positive side of black family life and the strengths of the community. Her stories reveal the influence of black dialect, jazz, Negro spirituals, and the cultural traditions of her heritage. Her stories abound with warmth, humor, and pride.

Bambara writes about ordinary people living ordinary lives, showing their struggles and successes. In several of the stories, one sees the world through the eyes of a bright, sensitive, eight-year-old girl growing up in a world of economic and racial inequality. Other stories deal with the problems that women face in these communities. Bambara's stories take place in neighborhoods where characters of all ages interact. Although the emphasis is on the problems that young females face, older characters bring a sense of the past.

Bambara's stories are breezy, fast-paced, and full of vitality. Humorous exchanges and verbal banter characterize her work. As Bambara says in "Salvation Is the Issue,"

> What I enjoy most in my work is the laughter and the outrage and the attention to language. I come from a family of very gifted laughers. I was raised by family and community to be combatant. Forays to the Apollo with my daddy and hanging tough on Speakers Corner with my mama taught me the power of the word, the importance of the resistance tradition, and the high standards our community has regarding verbal performance.

Context

Toni Cade Bambara is a New Yorker who grew up in Harlem. She added "Bambara" to her name after she saw the word written on her grandmother's notebook in an old trunk. According to *Webster's Tenth New Collegiate Dictionary*, the word "Bambara" means "a member of an African people of the upper Niger" or "a Mande language of the Bambara people."

Bambara draws her material from the people living in black communities. In her commitment to portray strong female characters, she employs female narrators to tell stories that show women in a positive light. She says that she is "about the empowerment and development of our sisters and our community." Bambara's characters are young, hip, tough, humorous black women, much like the characters that Terry McMillan creates in her novel *Mama* (1987). When asked about the differences between African American male and female writers, Bambara says, "brothers generally set things out of doors, on open terrain, that is, male turf." Bambara's female characters, however, such as Hazel in "Raymond's Run," are out on the street. She creates strong female characters of different ages. The young girls are often spunky and outspoken, tough, sassy, and bright.

Bambara provides a realistic view of the world of African American communities in stories she calls "on-the-block, in-the-neighborhood, back-glance pieces." She is a novelist, short-story writer, editor, playwright, and lecturer. She won the American Book Award for her novel *The Salt Eaters* and the Best Documentary of 1986 Award from the Pennsylvania Association of Broadcasters for *The Bombing of Osage*.

Sources for Further Study

Bambara, Toni Cade. "Salvation Is the Issue." In *Black Women Writers (1950-1980): A Critical Evaluation*, edited by Mari Evans. Garden City, N.Y.: Anchor Press/Doubleday, 1984. In this essay, Bambara discusses her experiences as a writer and states her preference for the short story as a genre. The elements of her own work that she deems most important are laughter, the use of language, a sense of community, and celebration.

Burks, Ruth Elizabeth. "From Baptism to Resurrection: Toni Cade Bambara and the Incongruity of Language." In *Black Women Writers (1950-1980): A Critical Evaluation*, edited by Mari Evans. Garden City, N.Y.: Anchor Press/Doubleday, 1984. Burks provides brief summaries of the individual stories. Stresses the importance of language in Bambara's portrayal of black characters as she accurately records their experiences in their own voices. Burks notes that the rhythm and graphic descriptions of these narratives reflect the influence of Negro spirituals.

Hargrove, Nancy D. "Youth in Toni Cade Bambara's *Gorilla, My Love*." *Southern Quarterly* 22 (Fall, 1983): 81-99. Hargrove provides an in-depth analysis of individual stories, focusing on those that look at life from the point of view of a child. Notes that Bambara treats two sides of the African American experience, balancing the grim reality of violence and poverty with the positive portrayal of family ties and strong characters. Hargrove argues that Bambara deals with universal themes of isolation, disillusionment, and initiation, but that she also displays a warm sense of humor as she explores the pain, confusion, and joy of youth.

Tate, Claudia, ed. *Black Women Writers at Work*. New York: Continuum, 1983. In this collection of interviews with African American women writers, Claudia Tate explores their visions and styles. In her interview, Bambara reflects on the influence that being black and female has had on her work. She discusses the differences that she sees between male and female writers and talks about her own writing process.

Traylor, Eleanor W. "Music as Theme: The Jazz Mode in the Works of Toni Cade Bambara." In *Black Women Writers (1950-1980): A Critical Evaluation*, edited by Mari Evans. Garden City, N.Y.: Anchor Press/Doubleday, 1984. In discussing the importance of music in Bambara's works, Traylor emphasizes the way in which jazz encompasses the past and present. Shows that Bambara narrators reveal the importance of ancestry in the community. Traylor points to such older characters as Miss Hazel and Bovanne in "My Man Bovanne," Grandaddy Vale in "Gorilla, My Love," and the bluesman in "Mississippi Ham Rider," all of whom bring a sense of the past to the communities in which they live.

Judith Barton Williamson

GRACE NOTES

Author: Rita Dove (1952-   )
Type of work: Poetry
First published: 1989

Form and Content

Grace Notes, the fourth of Rita Dove's books of poetry and the first to appear after she was awarded the Pulitzer Prize for *Thomas and Beulah* (1986), is divided into five sections. A single poem, "Summit Beach, 1921," serves as an introduction to the whole work. At the center of this poem is a young woman who accepts the attentions of the young men at the beach, drinking the sassafras tea that they bring her, while at the same time holding her essential self in reserve. The poem is built on a balancing of attitudes: shyness combined with a sense of her own worth, desire in delicious tension with withdrawal, involvement in the moment played against the pull of memory. The whole adds up to a sense of heightened expectation, too luxurious to exchange for the banalities of fulfillment. The range of attitude and the quest for balance, linked to a black woman's perceptions, foreshadow some of the major strategies and themes of the book, as developed in the sections that follow.

The first section is made up of memory poems. "The Buckeye" establishes their setting as Ohio. One poem is specifically dated 1962, when Dove was ten, and the protagonist's tenth year is critical throughout the section. "Fifth Grade Autobiography" recalls a ten-year-old's examination of a family photograph taken when she was four. In "Flash Cards," a ten-year-old struggles to rise to her father's expectations. The child is not allowed over when her "Uncle Millet" comes to town, but she manages to memorize the stories that she has heard about her no-good relative. The pull and pain of memory are fully articulated in the last poem of the section, "Poem in Which I Refuse Contemplation." In a rambling letter, the mother of the protagonist, who is now an adult, informs her of the death by strangulation of her cousin Ronnie. Neither the protagonist's mother nor anyone else will know the intensity of the protagonist's memory of her cousin as he was, as they were together, when they were ten.

As memory poems, those in the first section of the book suggest the theme of time. The second section may be read as a series of variations on the protagonist's place in a natural and social environment. Specific locations are identified in titles: Mississippi; Roger Haggerty's house in Auburn, Alabama; Jerusalem. The poems "After Storm" and "Ozone" place their protagonist in the environment of the natural universe. Other people are also part of the environment, such as Roger Haggerty and students bicycling home. The first six poems of the section are uttered in the first person, the speaker either "I" or part of "we." In "Particulars," the seventh poem, a third-person protagonist, "she," finds that her best, though inadequate, strategy for engaging tears rests in agenda, in a structure of time and place, and in an involvement with objects provided by the immediate environment.

In these poems concerned with place, time still matters. In one poem, the speaker is turning thirty; many readers will regard this speaker as the ten-year-old of the first section grown up. The last two poems of the second section, "Your Death" and "The Wake," are addressed to "you" and acknowledge the power of time and of others as manifested in death: a day that was "ours," that belonged to the protagonist and her family, became and will always be "yours," since it was the day that "we" learned of "your" death.

The protagonist and her family are at the center of the book's third section. The delights of nursing her daughter and the afterglow of the experience are compared to the feeling of a young man whose partner's head rests on his chest after sex, inspiring a "Pastoral." In this "woman's poem," the comparison is bold, convincing, and generous: Men are admitted.

The book's fourth section turns toward a world of art, ideas, and intellect that Dove, an academic as well as a poet, knows intimately. One of the most powerful poems in the section, "Arrow," articulates a response to a white male lecturer whose bearing drips with a possibly unconscious and certainly unacknowledged contempt for African Americans and for women. There is anger in the poem, but even more strongly felt is the compassion of the speaker/protagonist of the poem toward the young women, at least some of them black, who have accompanied her to the lecture and whose techniques for coping may not be as sophisticated as her own.

On a casual first reading, the fifth section might seem a gathering of afterthoughts, of poems that do not quite fit anywhere else in the book. Yet the section has its own integrity. One notes a narrative impulse behind the lyrical voice in poems on the journeys of Catherine of Siena and on the conversion of Paul on the road to Damascus and, in general, in the strong emphasis on the third person in the section. The concerns that have informed much of the book extend now beyond the range of personal experience and contact to history and legend. Yet it is certainly as an African American woman that Dove writes of the great, and greatly troubled, black singer Billie Holiday. The unsentimental compassion that is a major strength of Dove's poetry generates the last line of the section. It is hard to resist reading it as a kind of summing up of the book: "Everyone waiting here was once in love."

Analysis

While *Grace Notes* is neither a poem nor a sequence, it is not merely a gathering of poems either; it is carefully and effectively shaped as a book. Not one of its five sections has the sort of unity that would lend itself to easy summation, yet each has its own thematic identity and makes a distinct contribution to the design of the whole.

The first section has the feel of autobiography. Without insisting upon it, the poems invite the reader to interpret them as moments in the life of a single protagonist, in some way descended from the girl encountered in "Summit Beach, 1921." The poems of the second section focus on their protagonist's awareness of the limits imposed on the self by what is outer and "other"—thus the emphasis on specific locations, on the natural environment, and on other people, as well as the "resolution" of the section in the acknowledgment of the death of another.

As in the first section, the emphasis in the third is on the personal and the familial, with the protagonist now assuming the role of mother rather than child. The mother is black, and the child's father is white. (Rita Dove married a German novelist.) Yet, as they discover when the child insists on comparing her vagina to her mother's, they are also pink, they are in the pink, the pink is in them. In this pivotal section of the book, and at one of its most intimate moments, Dove reminds the reader that diversity exists and is to be cherished, not only among groups but within the individual self as well.

The book's fourth section turns outward once again, gazing with reserves of irony, sometimes bordering on the satirical, on a milieu dominated by the intellectual and the academic. Moving beyond the personal and personally known in the last section of the book, Dove assimilates figures of the distant and recent past to her poetic vision. The poet thus remains true to the task of knowing herself by discovering and defining her place in the world.

Context

President Bill Clinton's appointment of Rita Dove to the position of Poet Laureate in 1993, making her the youngest person ever to hold that position, certainly constitutes a positive step for women's literature and, less dramatically, for the situation of women in general. Yet the career of Dove raises some provocative questions about the concept of women's literature itself. Her work may be seen as the enactment of one answer to the question of what, in the last quarter of the twentieth century, a women's literature might be.

This is a question raised by Judith Kitchen in "The Want Ad," an article that appeared in the *Georgia Review* in the spring of 1990. While responding most enthusiastically to *Grace Notes*, Kitchen uses the occasion to place a "want ad" for a poetry that explores a woman's way of knowing, rather than a poetry that seeks to forge a self. Perhaps, Kitchen suggests, a woman should turn to poetry after she has achieved a self.

For Kitchen, Dove's work is among the most compelling contemporary embodiments of the poetry that she seeks. For Dove, the self is where one starts, at least insofar as one is a poet. Dove is an African American and a woman: these are aspects of herself. In a period in which the value placed on cultural diversity leads some to define themselves in such categories, Dove has affirmed the diversity within the self. No one who reads *Grace Notes* with attention can fail to be aware that the book places the reader within the consciousness of a woman and an African American. Yet an adequate reading of the book must recognize the inadequacy of either category, or of both in combination, to a full understanding of the person who speaks in these poems.

Thus, Dove affirms a woman's identity but in a very special way. To adapt what Helen Vendler, an esteemed critic of modern poetry, says of Dove's affirmation of her racial identity, one may say that for Dove womanhood need not be her central subject, and certainly not her only one, even though it must be given an important place in her work. While some feminist critics may understandably find in Dove's stance an unacceptable compromise, many will believe that she provides a model for a mature women's poetry. Although Dove herself might feel more than a little uncomfortable at finding herself cast as a role model for other poets, one must be grateful for the poet that she is.

Sources for Further Study

Baker, Houston, Jr. Review of *Grace Notes*. *Black American Literature Forum* 24 (Fall, 1990): 574-577. A major African American critic and scholar addresses the question of Dove's relation to African American womanist traditions, finding the key in Dove's autobiographical lyricism and her astute precision in naming. She makes, says Baker, a cosmopolitan and common story out of everyday lives.

Costello, Bonnie. "Scars and Wings: Rita Dove's *Grace Notes*." *Callaloo* 14 (Spring, 1991): 434-438. In what must rank among the most perceptive articles on *Grace Notes*, Costello affirms the descriptive precision, tonal control, and metaphoric reach within uncompromising realism that are among its most impressive features. Many of the poems offer ways of coping with and transcending wounds, but Dove is also willing to remind readers that their vulnerabilities are real and often untranscendable.

Kitchen, Judith. "A Want Ad." *Georgia Review* 44 (Spring, 1990): 256-271. Admitting to feeling troubled by much of the women's poetry written by Dove's contemporaries, Kitchen praises Dove because, although she clearly cares about the issues that arise from being black and from being a woman, she does not assume that dealing with these issues makes her a poet. She resists ideology, preferring the inquisitive mind that discovers meaning. A provocative discussion of the book and of its cultural context.

McDowell, Robert. "The Assembling Vision of Rita Dove." In *Conversant Essays: Contemporary Poets on Poetry*, edited by James McCorkle. Detroit: Wayne State University Press, 1990. Although written before the publication of *Grace Notes*, this discussion illuminates that book as well as Dove's earlier work, as McDowell explores Dove's synthesis of striking imagery, myth, magic, fable, wit, humor, political comment, and knowledge of history. An eloquent tribute from one poet to another.

Vendler, Helen. "Blackness and Beyond Blackness: New Icons of the Beautiful in the Poetry of Rita Dove." *Times Literary Supplement*, February 18, 1994, 11-13. A critical survey of Dove's career by one of the most important critics of modern and contemporary American poetry. Vendler finds *Grace Notes* governed by Dove's discovery, as an African American poet, that blackness need not be her central subject but equally need not be omitted. The essay offers insights into a number of aspects of Dove's work.

W. P. Kenney

GRANDMOTHERS OF THE LIGHT
A Medicine Woman's Sourcebook

Author: Paula Gunn Allen (1939-   )
Type of work: Social criticism
First published: 1991

Form and Content

With its unique mixture of American Indian ethnography, history, philosophy, storytelling, revisionary myth, spirituality, and personal narrative, *Grandmothers of the Light: A Medicine Woman's Sourcebook* defies easy classification. Based on Allen's belief in thought's "magical" power and targeted at a wide, multicultural female audience, this text could almost be described as a mainstream self-help book. Allen implies that—read from the proper mythic perspective—the American Indian stories that she retells function as a guidebook for any woman interested in learning to develop her own shamanic powers and to "walk the medicine path, . . . to live and think in ways that are almost but not quite entirely unlike our usual ways of living and thinking." Drawing on her extensive knowledge of American Indian belief systems, Allen creates a holistic, woman-centered epistemology and a series of revisionary myths that emphasize native peoples' belief in a cosmic feminine creative intelligence. As she explains in the preface, the stories in *Grandmothers of the Light* provide women with guidelines enabling them to attain personal and collective agency. She implies that by fully participating in the "sacred myths" collected in her anthology, twentieth century English-speaking women of any ethnicity or cultural background can develop a spiritual mode of perception that empowers them to bring about psychic and material change. She combines theory, myth, and story to construct a twentieth century, feminist Pan-Indian worldview which she invites her readers to adopt.

Grandmothers of the Light can be divided into three parts: a preface and introductory chapter containing a brief discussion of Allen's holistic worldview as well as her interpretation of North American Indians' woman-centered metaphysical and social systems; a collection of mythic stories retold from Allen's distinctly twentieth century feminist, Pan-Indian perspective; and an informational "Postscript" and glossary of mythic figures. In her first chapter, "The Living Reality of the Medicine World," Allen provides readers with background information enabling them to comprehend the stories in the following section more fully. She discusses the similarities between native spirituality and other belief systems such as Taoism and Sufism, contrasts Eurocentric and American Indian conceptions of myth, and explores the transformational role that mythic narratives serve in oral cultures. Throughout this chapter, Allen underscores women's centrality in North American indigenous peoples' social and metaphysical systems. She outlines what she describes as the sevenfold path of medicine women—the way of the daughter, the householder, the mother, the gatherer, the ritualist, the teacher, and the wise woman—and explains that the stories in her collection teach readers how to follow this path.

The largest section of *Grandmothers of the Light* consists of Allen's versions of twenty-one myths drawn from a number of diverse North American traditions, including those of the Chippewa/Ojibwa, Aztec, Cherokee, Navajo, Flathead and Okanogan, Iroquois, Karok, Keres, Lakota, Lummi/Nootsac, and Mayan tribes. As Allen explains in the preface, she based her selection on two criteria: the stories' centrality to the construction of a woman-centered spiritual tradition and their importance in her own spiritual journey. As this emphasis on the personal indicates, Allen openly acknowledges the subjective nature of her revisionist myths. She does not attempt to present accurate ethnographic accounts, but instead reshapes traditional narratives in accordance with her own beliefs. Allen divides the stories into three chapters corresponding to the mythical eras that they reflect. "Cosmogyny: The Goddesses" contains her versions of creation accounts, including stories of the Keres Laguna Thinking Woman, the Iroquois Falling Woman, and the Navajo Changing Woman. While the tales in the first section focus exclusively on female creation figures, the stories in the second section, "Ritual, Magic, and Aspects of the Goddesses," examine the interaction between human and supernatural beings. According to Allen, the Keres Pueblo Yellow Woman and other mythic figures provide readers with empowering models of female identity. The stories in the final section, "Myth, Magic, and Medicine in the Modern World," serve a similar purpose. As Allen explains, they are designed to illustrate the continuing interaction between supernatural and human beings. Throughout these three chapters, Allen provides additional guidance for readers; she includes general overviews at the beginning of each section as well as supplementary background information concerning ethnographic sources and possible interpretations for each story.

Allen concludes *Grandmothers of the Light* with a brief discussion of the similarities and differences among the many peoples classified as American Indians as well as accounts of the ritual traditions and the precolonial and postcolonial histories of the peoples whose stories appear in her collection. It is significant that she does not present precolonial American Indians as powerless victims of European conquest; instead, she indicates that the shift to patriarchal structures had begun before European colonizers arrived.

Analysis

Throughout *Grandmothers of the Light*, Allen maintains a dual focus on education and transformation. As she informs her readers about American Indian peoples' woman-centered, holistic worldview, she attempts to alter their perceptions. She attributes the many problems facing Western culture to the spiritual imbalance that accompanied the shift to rational thought and patriarchal social structures and asserts that the worldview embodied in North American myths provides social actors with an alternative perspective. Moreover, Allen believes that native cosmology offers twentieth century women an important tool for achieving personal and social change, for it challenges the sexism and other forms of misogyny found in Western socioreligious belief systems. This desire to instruct and transform readers influences Allen's approach to her material. In order to reach a broad audience, she employs a conversational, nonacademic style and translates a highly sophisticated metaphysical system into accessible language and nontechnical terminology.

Myth plays a central role in the personal, social, and metaphysical changes that Allen advocates. She rejects Western ethnocentric conceptions of mythology as primitive belief systems, mystifying falsehoods, or nostalgic retreats into an irrecoverable past and maintains that mythic stories embody an alternate method of perceiving reality, as well as a highly complex metaphysics. In the introductory chapter, Allen equates myth with metamorphosis and transformation by defining it as a unique mode of communication, "a language contract that wields the power to transform something (or someone) from one state or condition to another." By associating myth's transformational power with the oral tradition, Allen constructs a unique theory of storytelling and a woman-centered, holistic epistemology that draw on language's performative effects to generate personal and collective change.

Allen's epistemology emphasizes women's agency. As she asserts, "Since all that exists is alive and must change as a basic law of existence, all existence can be manipulated under certain conditions and according to certain laws." By focusing their thought and channeling its energy in specific ways, she maintains, women can effect material change. Allen stipulates, however, that in order to utilize this transformative dimension of thought, people brought up under Western systems of knowledge must learn to perceive reality mythically. In other words, they must forgo their usual reliance on empirical knowledge and rational, linear thinking by entering into liminal space where alterations in consciousness can occur. Allen locates this liminal space, or what she calls "the universe of power," within mythic narratives, at the interface between the spiritual and mundane worlds invoked by the oral tradition. She explains that her stories guide readers through a series of myths designed to dislodge their conventional modes of perception. This challenge to Western thinking is especially evident in "A Fish of Another Hue" and "Someday Soon."

Allen's emphasis on nonrational thought forms is highly subversive, for it allows her simultaneously to critique the masculinist, Eurocentric bias in conventional forms of knowledge and to develop alternate ways of thinking. Her use of storytelling rather than logical proofs unsettles Western-educated readers' over-reliance on reason. As she uses paradox and ambiguity to expose the limitations of Western culture's confidence in the accuracy of logical rational thought, she provides an alternative to analytical forms of thinking. In "A New Wrinkle," for example, she describes the place of the Keres Laguna Grandmother Spider as both "far away" and "right among" human beings.

Context

Allen's revisionary myths have significance for twentieth century feminists in the United States of all cultural and ethnic backgrounds. By reinterpreting central female deities such as the Hopi Spider Woman, the Navajo Changing Woman, and the Keres Pueblo Thought Woman, Allen displaces the male Judeo-Christian God and challenges patriarchal beliefs concerning women's subordinate status. Yet unlike many twentieth century women revisionist mythmakers who rely exclusively on Greco-Roman mythic figures, and thus inadvertently reinforce conventional Western gender roles by associating female gods with biological reproduction, Allen redefines feminine creativity by associating her female creation figures with spiritual and intellectual power. The Keres Laguna Thinking Woman, for example, uses thought and song to create the entire cosmos—including nature, human beings, sociopolitical systems, literature, and the sciences. By thus positing a cosmic "feminine" intelligence, Allen simultaneously displaces Western cultures' traditional association of the body with the feminine and affirms women's intellectual and creative capacities. Furthermore, by emphasizing American Indian women's centrality in social, political, and religious structures, Allen exposes the ethnocentrism and racism behind stereotypes of native women as beasts of burden, dumb squaws, or traitors to their own people. Perhaps most important, by inviting readers of all ethnic backgrounds to walk the medicine path, Allen makes it possible to establish a transcultural community of self-empowered women.

In many ways, *Grandmothers of the Light* represents a remarkable departure from Allen's earlier, more conventional academic work as an American Indian scholar. Although she expands on the holistic, mythic worldview and the feminist themes found in *The Sacred Hoop* (1986), her collection of essays on native cultures and mythological traditions, in *Grandmothers of the Light* she adopts a distinctly personal approach and combines factual information with autobiographical commentary. By doing so, she challenges Western-educated readers' dualistic beliefs concerning the separation between objective and subjective forms of knowledge. Yet throughout her work, Allen is motivated by the desire to share her holistic, woman-centered American Indian worldview with people from all cultural backgrounds. Whether she intervenes in stereotypes of American Indians or invents alternate systems of meaning, her goal is transformation. By reclaiming and reinterpreting female North American creation figures such as the Keres Pueblo Thought Woman and the Mayan Xmucané (or Grandmother of the Light) and by retelling gynecentric tribal myths, she attempts to alter her readers' self and worldviews.

Sources for Further Study

Bataille, Gretchen M., and Kathleen Mullen Sands. *American Indian Women: Telling Their Lives*. Lincoln: University of Nebraska Press, 1984. In addition to discussing native women's autobiographical traditions, this study explores how the oral tradition and ethnographic accounts influence writings by Allen and other native women. Contains an extensive bibliography of primary and secondary materials.

Beck, Peggy V., Anna Lee Walters, and Nia Francisco. *The Sacred: Ways of Knowledge, Sources of Life*. Rev. ed. Tsaile, Ariz.: Navajo Community College Press, 1992. Compiled from interviews, conversations, speeches, songs, spiritual teachings, and prayers, this comprehensive account of North American indigenous peoples' "sacred ways"—their concepts, practices, belief systems, and worldviews

– enables readers to place Allen's work in a Pan-Indian context. Includes discussions of shamanism, storytelling and the oral tradition, peyote, and girls' puberty ceremonies, as well as a wide-ranging bibliography.

Hanson, Elizabeth I. *Paula Gunn Allen*. Boise, Idaho: Boise State University Press, 1990. Although published before *Grandmothers of the Light*, this brief study of Allen's work provides useful background information about her life, as well as summaries of creative and theoretical writings published before 1989.

Jones, David E., ed. *Sanapia, Comanche Medicine Woman*. New York: Holt, Rinehart & Winston, 1972. A personal narrative exploring a twentieth century Comanche woman's attempts to synthesize tribal and Christian belief systems.

Linderman, Frank Bird, ed. *Pretty-Shield: Medicine Woman of the Crows*. Reprint. Lincoln: University of Nebraska Press, 1972. This told-to narrative represents one of the few existing records of native life viewed from a woman's perspective. Pretty-Shield's discussion of her work as a medicine woman supports Allen's assertions concerning native women's social and spiritual power.

AnnLouise Keating

THE GRANITE PAIL
The Selected Poems of Lorine Niedecker

Author: Lorine Niedecker (1903-1970)
Type of work: Poetry
First published: 1985

Form and Content

The Granite Pail: The Selected Poems of Lorine Niedecker, edited by Cid Corman, presents an intriguing, if somewhat familiar, picture of Niedecker as a highly autobiographical poet whose primary concern is that which occurs in the domestic realm. Much of the work in this text focuses on the experiences of a female poet living on Blackhawk Island in rural Wisconsin; it tends to be devoid of the political concerns that critic Jenny Penberthy has argued are the source of many of Niedecker's lesser-known poems. The poet whom Corman reveals understands the complex way in which humans coexist with their environments, observing and rendering them in the language of experience and intellect. His Niedecker is thoughtful and fully engaged in the world around her, and though these "domestic," autobiographical poems are sometimes characterized as mere local color pieces, they tend to be highly learned. Several of the poems commonly considered Niedecker's best—poems that reveal the poet's strong interest and extensive reading in science, philosophy, Oriental poetry, and biography—are among those included in *The Granite Pail.*

Niedecker began her poetic career as a student of the Surrealists and ended it working toward an aesthetic theory she called "reflectivism," but the largest portion of her work shows great respect for the Objectivist ideals that Louis Zukofsky set forth in the February, 1931, issue of *Poetry* magazine. Zukofsky proclaimed that poets should think with "things as they exist" and write poems that exist as objects intrinsic to the environments from which they arise. To many, Zukofsky's mandate was difficult both to understand and to follow, but Niedecker was instantly drawn to it—and to Zukofsky; six months after reading that issue of *Poetry*, she initiated a correspondence with him which would continue for the next forty years of their lives. As a result, a number of Niedecker's earliest critics claimed Zukofsky as her mentor and argued that her best work was written under his tutelage. The poems that appear in *The Granite Pail* are highly influenced by Zukofsky's aesthetic, but they are also influenced by Niedecker's own reading and experimentation in such poetic movements as Surrealism and by her minimalist tendencies, her ability to capture in a word or two the complex realities of human existence.

The Granite Pail is arranged in three sections—"My Friend Tree," "North Central," and "Harpsichord & Salt Fish"—which Corman says represent the "earlier work," "central work," and "final work." While the chronology is accurate, this sectioning of Nicdecker's career can be a bit misleading, for the sections overlap considerably: The "earlier" work was written between 1935 and 1963, the "central" between 1958 and 1968, and the "final" between 1964 and 1970. Still, Corman's groupings are useful because they reveal the evolution of Niedecker's willingness to speak about and explore the unique experiences of the woman artist living and writing in the rural United States. Corman presents readers with a selection of Niedecker's poetry which highlights its allegiance to colloquial speech, the domestic realm, and personal growth, and the book's arrangement both within and throughout the sections illustrates the growth of Niedecker's aesthetic and intellectual awareness. Readers are likely to get from *The Granite Pail* some sense of the scope of Niedecker's art, as the poems in this book are simultaneously domestic and worldly, emotional and intellectual.

Analysis

In the editor's note, Corman says that the poems in the section "My Friend Tree" were written under Zukofsky's tutelage, and his reasons for making such an assertion are clear: These poems are marked by an adherence to the Objectivist mandate that poets think with "things as they exist." Readers should not make the assumption, however, that Niedecker was motivated only by the Objectivist aesthetic when she wrote these poems; they are influenced also by Niedecker's belief in the strength of minimalist expression, by her admiration of the lives and languages of those she called "common folk," and by her experimentation in what could be characterized as American haiku. Three poems in this section that clearly illustrate Niedecker's integration of Objectivist aesthetic principles with minimalist expression are "My Friend Tree," "Along the river," and the book's title poem, "Remember my little granite pail." The nine poems that close the "My Friend Tree" section of *The Granite Pail* are selected from a grouping Niedecker called "In Exchange for Haiku," written between 1956 and 1958. These elegant pieces arise from Niedecker's respect and admiration for the Oriental poetic tradition and foreshadow her movement toward a more considered integration of Objectivist and Surrealist elements.

Partly because of Corman's desire to present Niedecker's work chronologically, the poems in the "North Central" section of *The Granite Pail* are more mature and complex in content and in form than those in the previous section. Here, Niedecker moves toward an even fuller integration of Objectivist and Surrealist aesthetic principles as she comes to understand what Corman calls "her range and depth." These poems tend to find their sources in the intellectual realm rather than in the domestic, and many contemplate the implications of knowledge that Niedecker gleaned from her extensive reading in philosophy, science, and literature. For example, "Linnaeus in Lapland" is about an eighteenth century Swedish botanist, and "As praiseworthy" applies statements made by the first century Stoic philosopher Epictetus to life in twentieth century rural America. "North Central" is perhaps the most important section of *The Granite Pail* because it contains such poems as "Lake Superior," "Traces of Living Things," "My Life by Water," "Paen to Place," and "Wintergreen Ridge." Niedecker's longest poems, these five are considered by many critics the best in her canon. In each of these poems, she combines her astute poetic eye, her ability to say much in few words, and her learnedness. Niedecker also seems in these pieces to come to terms with the place of the poet's self in the poem, for while these pieces are finally no less autobiographical than those in the previous section, the autobiography is simultaneously more subtle and more direct.

The poems in "Harpsichord & Salt Fish," the final section of *The Granite Pail*, were written during the last decade of Niedecker's life, and they follow the precedent the poet set in the longer poems mentioned above. "Thomas Jefferson," "Three Americans," "Thomas Jefferson Inside," "His Carpets Flowered," and "Darwin" were inspired by Niedecker's readings of biographies and letters, and they reveal her intense interest in the way in which humans use language to create their lives. Interestingly, though, what unifies this portion of the text, what sets it apart from the rest of *The Granite Pail*, is that most of the poems in it are titled. Niedecker did not consistently title her poems; in fact, most of her poems were published either without titles or with first lines that double as titles. The consistent presence of titles in "Harpsichord & Salt Fish" indicates that, at the time of her death, Niedecker was still very much concerned with challenging her own aesthetic principles, with discovering and resisting the limitations of her work.

Context

Because Niedecker is most closely identified with Objectivism, a poetic movement whose other members are all male, and because her letters to Zukofsky and Corman never explicitly state an interest in feminist ideology, she is often seen as a "male-identified" poet. Further, even though such critics as Penberthy have shown that the relationship between Zukofsky and Niedecker was egalitarian, the critical tradition has been to view Niedecker as dependent upon Zukofsky both for recognition and for tutelage. This perception of her is not entirely unfounded: In her letters to Corman, Niedecker expresses very little interest in developing relationships with other female poets; her most pressing concerns seem to be her ongoing relationship with Zukofsky, domestic issues, and her art. It is necessary, though, to resist placing too much importance on the gender of the poets with whom Niedecker associated, for nothing mattered as much to this poet as did her art—not gender and not ideology. When read with this in mind, Niedecker's letters reveal a highly independent, motivated, and committed woman who devoted as much of her life as possible to her art.

While Niedecker did not consider herself a feminist, many of her poems actively reject the social ideologies that keep women from fully engaging in the world around them, and much of her work challenges those customs that value men's lives and art over those of women. Several of her poems deal with the implications of marriage in the lives of women, "I rose from marsh mud" and "I married" among them; others— "Who was Mary Shelley," for example—contemplate the manner in which women's identities are sometimes subsumed by those of their male counterparts. Further, Niedecker's autobiographical poems, especially those that appear in the "North Central" section of *The Granite Pail*, reveal that she shared with many feminists a belief in the validity and importance of personal knowledge and voice. Hence, Niedecker's work brings to American literature an organic feminism which arises from need and experience rather than from ideology.

Sources for Further Study

Heller, Michael. *Conviction's Net of Branches: Essays on the Objectivist Poets and Poetry*. Carbondale: Southern Illinois University Press, 1985. This book is the first to be entirely devoted to Objectivist poetics, to discuss in some depth the work of all the best-known poets in this movement. The chapter devoted to Zukofsky provides useful explanations of the Objectivist tenets that he set forth in the 1931 issue of *Poetry*. While it is perhaps true that Heller identifies Niedecker too singularly with the Objectivist movement, his readings of her work provide a number of useful insights into her poems.

Niedecker, Lorine. *"Between Your House and Mine": The Letters of Lorine Niedecker to Cid Corman, 1960 to 1970*. Edited by Lisa Pater Faranda. Durham, N.C.: Duke University Press, 1986. A complete collection of the letters that Niedecker wrote to Corman, this is as much a critical as it is an epistolary text because it contains lengthy, informative notes about Niedecker's intellectual, personal, and aesthetic life. Faranda also provides readings of several of Niedecker's poems and places her letters in a historical context.

_____ . *From This Condensery: The Complete Writing of Lorine Niedecker*. Edited by Robert Bertholf. Highlands, N.C.: Jargon Society, 1985. Unlike *The Granite Pail*, this book purports to be intended for Niedecker scholars and enthusiasts. While it has come under attack by Jenny Penberthy and others who lament its lack of scholarly apparatus and accuracy, it is the most complete collection available and is responsible for much of the recent scholarly interest in Niedecker.

Penberthy, Jenny. *Niedecker and the Correspondence with Zukofsky, 1931-1979*. New York: Cambridge University Press, 1993. This book not only makes available Niedecker's side of the correspondence with Zukofsky but also provides a discussion of the importance of the relationship to the personal and professional lives of both poets. Contains extensive readings of several of Niedecker's poems and discussions of the political dimensions of her canon.

Michelle Gibson

GRAVITY AND GRACE

Author: Simone Weil (1909-1943)
Type of work: Essays
First published: La Pesanteur et la grâce, 1947 (English translation, 1952)

Form and Content

Social philosopher Gustave Thibon compiled excerpts from Simone Weil's notebooks into a single volume for publication four years after her death. The finished product, *Gravity and Grace*, has drawn critical acclaim for Weil as a teacher, activist, philosopher, mystic, and writer; much serious study about her began after the appearance of this work in print. Emphasizing the principles of suffering and redemption, this collection delineates the scope of her human and mystical endeavors. Simone Weil did not merely advocate affliction; she deliberately sought it by pursuing the strenuous physical feats generally performed by men. Her passages give insight to the perils of mental stimulation, manual labor, and war—all of which she actually experienced. In her efforts to absorb all facets of oppression—she left her studies to work diligently on farmland, deserted her teaching post in favor of factory work, and actively participated in the Spanish Civil War—Weil demonstrated convictions relatively rare among women.

As its basis is personal belief and reflection, *Gravity and Grace* explores the mind of a woman who can only be categorized in terms of gender. Yet even in this aspect, she is exceptional. Weil's ideas are shaped by a plethora of sects and classes. Although she extracted her religious idealism from the Greek, Hindu, and Jewish traditions, her most prominent identification is with Christianity. This diversity of influences contributes to the abstruse inconsistencies that abound in the selections. While Thibon is responsible for the classification of the journal entries into chapters, the paradoxical tone and style are strictly Weil's; Thibon's only contribution to the text is his introduction, which unifies Weil's impact in the literary, social, and political realms. Weil mysteriously struggles to preserve the imperfections of humanity, which are in direct opposition to the doctrines of dogmatic faith. Despite vast influence, Weil's writing does not adhere to a specific religious or political agenda. Her chief aim is to reconcile gravity (which represents the baseness of the mortal condition) with grace (that divine power by which baseness can be lifted).

Beginning with a chapter on the parameters of gravity and grace, the collection explores myriad themes that derive from the title, including void and compensation, detachment, the self, love, evil, illusions, idolatry, and affliction. Each chapter consists of separate entries that relate to a central motif; these statements fuse the best features of Christianity with human limitations. Weil recognizes the ambivalence of the individual and of humanity, and she often refutes her own ideas antithetically as a means of illuminating the highest truth; she does this repeatedly in *Gravity and Grace*.

In her writing, she addresses a collective universe as "you" and "we" distinctly; never is mention given to "man," except when she makes a biblical reference (such as "man and wife"). She sees the inner soul as androgynous and does not dichotomize men and women. Weil, like Plato, incorporates her political views (as they pertain to human behavior) into her writing. Ideally, she would have an equal, harmonious society.

Analysis

Weil's tone appears to be highly philosophical upon an initial reading, but it does take cohesive form as her subject progresses. The central issue is the battle between good and evil. *Gravity and Grace* addresses the common teachings of Christianity, but it also condones the human tendency to sin. This seems contradictory, yet Weil argues that it is only through sin that one can acknowledge the existence of God. This duality is acceptable to her, because "Contradiction alone is proof that we are not everything. Contradiction is our wretchedness, and the sense of our own wretchedness is the sense of reality." Humanity is capable of performing ill, which is the required counterpart of righteousness, and this design presupposes conflict. For Weil, the two poles of spirituality are in some instances one and the same: An excess of goodness yields to the beginning of evil, so no crystal distinction can be made between them.

Gravity is the force that keeps the individual grounded; it is separate from grace (and therefore isolated from God). It is, as it were, the womb of sin. Grace is a celestial energy which prevails over void and gravity. Weil introduces the void as that area between human gravity and heavenly grace. The void is imperative for the animation of God—without a feeling of absence, there would be no longing. Humans are not capable of crossing this threshold that unites them with God; only the Supreme Being may cross over to meet them. Instead, they must only accept this void in the hope of future completion. Gravity holds people to themselves, and this attachment is a selfish desire for the present truth. God repudiates His essence to create humans; humans in return must become nothing to welcome God. This notion of "de-creation" pervades Weil's thought—the denial of one's own worth directly enables one to seek, and ultimately to reunite with, God. As an individual releases the self, so does gravity release that individual. Still Weil claims that without the concept of worth, there is no incentive to seek this union.

Affliction is the greatest means of denying one's own essence, and the ability to endure it is brought about only by grace. Yet an abundance of pain will debase the individual. Human existence tears at the spirit and beauty of the world; it brings all in the universe farther away from the divine. Suffering should not be regarded as something beneficial. If it is attributed to individuality, then it is without worth. Instead, the proper wish is to remain immune to its horrors, to endure it for its own sake without regard for the merit that it may bring. Given the mortal need for approval, it is impossible to achieve this state except through grace. Outside of its blessing, pain and enjoyment can never be separate emotional entities. Supernatural grace is second only to love, as it is love that allows one to receive grace. Weil adopts a Platonic vision of love as a spiritual relationship; all physical expressions of love are debased and removed from love itself. In Weil's mind-set, individuals must love themselves only because God loves them—and for no other personal intention.

If she was to be anything at all, Weil designed to remain a mediator between this world and the realm of God, to avoid intentional hubris and serve only when instructed to do so. Inspired by four mystical moments, she recorded her own understanding of these direct encounters with the divine. In addition, just as she describes the components of goodness, she also makes a point to define what it is not. Imagination is an illusion which fills the void, leading people to love their existing reality: themselves and their world, which are in fact illusory. It attempts to take the place of grace in filling the void. Time is another false measure of closing the chasm; it is a container which makes one feel comfortable with life. Properly, one may only be content to the extent that the void allows one to be. The ultimate striving is the inner desire for the infinite, that which cannot be realized, rationalized, observed, or seen.

Evil is a destruction of a degraded good, not a pure one. It is the origin of illusions and imagination. In its fullest definition, evil is an attempt to drive goodness down, and in this manner, it represents gravity. Weil holds that it is the way in which evil operates that deems it evil. Further, one should accept its presence and incorporate it into the process of suffering; by denying the liberty of performing evil, one in effect denies that it is a part of one's essential makeup. It is only by maintaining the greatest distance from God that humans can hope to come into His presence.

Context

As critics have noted, it is quite difficult to separate Simone Weil's life from her work. Her life itself was a cry for women to follow: She entered the École Normale only two years after the educational institution began to accept women. She thought nothing of her difficult duties on the land and in the Renault factory (where she spent one year of work) and would operate machinery with the same energy and determination as men—despite her frail stature. Without her posthumously published work, however, she might have been only faintly remembered, because what is known about her has been prompted by public interest in her literary work. Weil's writing as a reflection of her person has yielded an abundance of power for women.

Gravity and Grace was initially dismissed as the mystical creation of a mentally unstable, suicidal individual suffering from eating disorders. Yet Weil has come to be embraced as one of the most remarkable female intellectuals. Her spiritual idealism has been linked with Plato, and the Catholic church has praised her work; her political opinions have been compared to those of Karl Marx and George Orwell. She was not afraid to voice her opinion on any topic. Her gender was never a hindrance to her; in fact, it was not even a consideration—she was undaunted by society's expectations of the female role. This refusal to differentiate between the sexes is the core of the women's movement toward equality. Still, Weil did not know that she was lending herself to such a cause. Her involvement was in world issues—such as her refusal to eat when underprivileged persons were deprived of food, her determination to understand the social class structure, and her willingness to give her existence to the abolishment of oppression. Such acts have marked her as a woman to be imitated and remembered.

Sources for Further Study

Cabaud, Jacques. *Simone Weil: A Fellowship in Love.* New York: Channel Press, 1964. Cabaud examines the intellectual and political sides of Weil as secondary to her religious purpose. Includes an ample index and excellent primary and secondary bibliographies.

Dietz, Mary G. *Between the Human and the Divine: The Political Thought of Simone Weil.* Totowa, N.J.: Rowman & Littlefield, 1988. Structuring her work around Weil's writing, Dietz discusses Weil's clash of needs: the necessity for the soul to remain rooted in itself and the desire for it to join with God. This exploration attempts to rectify the public's view that Weil abandoned politics for religion, showing that Weil's task was in fact to link the two.

Hellman, John. *Simone Weil: An Introduction to Her Thought.* Waterloo, Ontario: Wilfrid Laurier University Press, 1982. Traces Weil's movement from politics toward religion, stressing her encounter with Marxism and her later disillusionment with it. Hellman mentions her writing in instances where it directly pertains to her thought.

Kovitz, Sonia. "Simone Weil's Dark Night of the Soul." *Midwest Quarterly* 33 (Spring, 1992): 261-276. Kovitz's article reviews the various phases of Weil's temperament: despair, bouts with thoughts of suicide, and the more enlightening desire for a knowledge of God.

McLellan, David. *Utopian Pessimist.* New York: Poseidon Press, 1990. This evaluation gives a condensed version of the main points in Weil's life. Attention is given to Weil's political participation and her seemingly contrary views on the essence of human behavior. Offers an appendix ("On Human Personality") and a chronology. The select bibliography includes original works in French and English translations, as well as secondary works.

Petrement, Simone. *Simone Weil: A Life.* Translated by Raymond Rosenthal. New York: Pantheon Books, 1976. Regarded as the premier source for an accurate, personal, and full background on Weil, this biography emphasizes the inseparability of Weil and the literary works that she produced. Petrement praises Weil's numerous accomplishments not usually attributed to women, and she presents Weil's political and religious excursions through memoirs of their shared academic setting and in accounts of Weil's trying work experiences.

Mary Dalton Jamieson

THE GROUP

Author: Mary McCarthy (1912-1989)
Type of work: Novel
Type of plot: Social criticism
Time of plot: 1933-1940
Locale: New York City
First published: 1963

Principal characters:

CATHERINE LEILAND STRONG PETERSEN (KAY), the leading
 figure in a group of young women who graduate from Vassar
 College in 1933
POLLY ANDREWS RIDGELEY, the only member of Kay's group
 who required scholarship money
ELIZABETH MACAUSLAND (LIBBY), a successful literary agent
HELENA DAVISON, a wealthy young woman
DOTTIE RENFREW LATHAM, a social worker in a Boston
 settlement house
ELINOR EASTLAKE (LAKEY), an art historian
MARY PROTHERO BEAUCHAMP (POKEY), the wealthiest member
 of the group, who had to be coached in order to pass her exams
PRISS HARTSHORN CROCKETT, an economics major who takes a
 job with the National Recovery Administration
NORINE SCHMITTLAPP BLAKE ROGERS, a classmate of the group
 who has an affair with Kay's husband
HARALD PETERSEN, a playwright and director who marries and is
 later divorced by Kay
GUS LEROY, an editor who has an affair with Polly
PUTNAM BLAKE, a politically active young man who is the first
 of Norine's two husbands
MRS. DAVISON, Helena's self-educated and widely read mother
MR. ANDREWS, Polly's eccentric father, who comes to live with
 her

Form and Content

The Group traces the lives of nine members of Vassar College's class of 1933 (eight of whom compose "the group"), from Kay's marriage shortly after their graduation until the day of her funeral. In a loosely woven narrative, Mary McCarthy documents the personal growth of each character and explores the ways in which their education had an effect upon their lives. Though McCarthy described *The Group* as illustrating the failure of America's "faith in progress," the novel should not be dismissed as mere satire. Far more than McCarthy's other works of fiction, *The Group* displays sympathy for its central characters at the same time that it dissects their values. It is thus as a chronicle of the beliefs shared by a class of educated and privileged young women that *The Group* makes its greatest contribution.

The novel is arranged chronologically in fifteen chapters, each of which is centered upon an incident in the life of one of the group's members. For this reason, the group itself rather than any individual serves as the novel's protagonist. Kay and Harald's wedding, for example, provides the author with an opportunity to demonstrate the personalities of all of her central characters. Kay herself appears adventurous and daring by inviting no parents to her wedding. Pokey displays her superficiality by speaking disdainfully of Harald's shoes. Lakey's angry reply to Pokey's remark reveals the contempt that she has even for other members of the group. Dottie, the most devout and traditional of the central characters, becomes uneasy at the unconventional nature of the ceremony.

Only in the first and last chapters of the novel do most members of the group appear together. In the intervening chapters, McCarthy shifts from character to character, focusing upon representative events in their lives. Two days after Kay's wedding, Dottie loses her virginity to Dick Brown, a young painter whom she had met at Kay's reception. Although she had been extremely conservative while in college, Dottie had been intrigued by the prospect of an illicit affair and agreed to Dick's suggestion that she be fitted for a diaphragm. One night, when Dick fails to meet her for a rendezvous, Dottie leaves the diaphragm under a park bench in Washington Square and returns to Boston.

The Group also explores the sexual awakening of its other major characters. Norine begins her affair with Harald when Putnam, her first husband, proves to be impotent. Libby fends off the advances of Nils Aslund, a Norwegian baron who manages a ski run. Polly has a lengthy affair with Gus LeRoy, Libby's former boss. Lakey returns from Europe with a lesbian lover. The explicit sexuality of *The Group* helped to make it the most widely read of all McCarthy's works, but it also suggests that *The Group* is largely a coming-of-age novel exploring the maturation of its group protagonist. The loss of virginity experienced by each of the book's central characters parallels the loss of innocence that the group itself faces after leaving Vassar and confronting the disappointments of the real world.

When the group reconvenes seven years later for Kay's funeral, each of them still possesses the traits delineated in the opening chapter. Yet each of them has also matured by having dealt in some way with a loss. Polly recovers from her affair with Gus and marries a young psychiatrist. Lakey has grown to accept her sexual identity. Norine emerges from an unsatisfying first marriage to a happy second relationship. Only Kay, the leader of the group and the first to marry, proves to be destroyed by the world that she encountered after college. McCarthy intentionally leaves unanswered the question of whether Kay's death was an accident or resulted from suicide.

Analysis

The Group documents, in a nearly journalistic fashion, the development of its nine central characters during their first years after college. The members of the group indulge in considerable experimentation, both political and sexual, throughout this entire period. Reacting against the conservative values of their parents, one character after another becomes attracted to left-wing causes. Several individuals are fascinated with Joseph Stalin's trials of other Bolshevik leaders from 1936 to 1938. Sympathies with trade unionists, socialists, Trotskyites, and Stalinists emerge, only to be set aside later for more conventional values. Characters in the novel thus appear to be trying on political causes like garments, attempting to find one that fits the person each has become.

Sexual experimentation is another means by which members of the group seek to find their identities. A number of the novel's major characters have affairs. Others go through successive marriages looking for the right partner. In the end, most of the characters' sexual roles are as ephemeral as their political affiliations. They experiment sexually because this gives them one more opportunity to rebel against the values of their parents and to discover something of their own identities.

The amount of detail that McCarthy has devoted to the group's political and sexual adventures serves two purposes. First, it reinforces the novel's role as a social commentary. Dottie's loss of viginity and her visit to an early birth control clinic are described in elaborate detail. In a similar way, the views of the Stalinists and the Trotskyites are explored at some length. This amount of detail helps the reader to enter into the minds of McCarthy's characters and to share the experiences of their social class. Second, the author's analytical style parallels the approach to life that her characters absorbed during their college education at Vassar. Members of the group have learned to distance their emotions from a situation, to gather relevant details, and to make judgments based upon the best information available. McCarthy's journalistic style thus applies this same approach to a study of her central characters.

Of special concern to the author are the ways in which this type of education either prepared or failed to prepare the group for the world awaiting it after graduation. Throughout the novel, there are repeated references to individual teachers and courses taken by the group at Vassar. Two of these instructors, "old Miss Washburn" and Hallie Flanagan, stand in opposition to each other. Miss Washburn, who taught a course in animal behavior, represents the rational side of the group's education. She is a teacher who had "left her brain to Science in her will," and she is frequently cited as a model of the modern analytical approach. Miss Flanagan, an influential instructor of dramatic production, represents the emotional aspect of the students' experience at Vassar. She fostered their ability to deal with their own emotions and cultivated their aesthetic sense. Appropriately, it is Kay, who has difficulty reconciling these two sides of her character, who was influenced most strongly by both of these teachers. Her fatal fall (or jump) occurs, appropriately, from the twentieth floor of the Vassar Club, suggesting the destructive role that her education has played in her life.

McCarthy was distressed to find her work greeted by acclaim from the public but condescension from the critics and anger from Vassar alumnae, who believed that both they and their school had been parodied in the novel. Largely because of this reaction, McCarthy regarded *The Group* as the least successful of her mature works.

Context

As a social commentary, *The Group* documents in elaborate detail the minutiae that filled most women's lives during the years between the two world wars. Enthusiastic plans for social work, agricultural school, and politics gradually give way to discussions of babies, toilet training, birth control, and dress patterns. To a certain extent, this is part of the characters' process of growing up. The group learns to reconcile its ambitions and cultural interests with the more mundane aspects of domestic life. Nevertheless, the novel also suggests that the restrictions of the traditional roles assigned to women prove to be more daunting than the characters initially believed. By the end of the novel, Kay is dead, Lakey has abandoned all pretense at conformity, and the other characters have settled for being far more similar to their parents than they once had wished.

McCarthy's depictions of male characters are generally unflattering. Harald is the one individual in the entire novel who shows no sign of maturity. Probably the most unappealing of all McCarthy's characters, his last appearance in the novel occurs as he tries to find a ride to New York City, away from the cemetery where Kay is about to be buried. Gus LeRoy, Libby's former boss and Polly's lover, "was ordinary. That was what was the matter with him." Mr. Andrews, one of the most engaging male characters in the work, is eccentric and probably insane. His continued spending after the family is impoverished by the stockmarket crash of 1929 nearly ruins Polly financially.

Therefore, members of the group face the double burden of limited opportunities and of men who make their lives all but unbearable. For this reason, nearly all the novel's central characters fail in some way. Kay has a nervous breakdown and may well have taken her own life. Dottie abandons her career as a social worker and her dreams of romance, settling for bourgeois respectability in Arizona. Priss becomes a reluctant subject in the behaviorist experiments adopted by her husband. Only Lakey, who turns her back on men entirely, fulfills her dream of European travel and study of art history. The portrait that McCarthy paints is thus a highly pessimistic one.

The Group has always enjoyed more success with the public than with its critics. Some readers have been attracted to the novel for its detailed descriptions of sexual seduction. Others have seen parallels between their own lives and the incidents described in the novel. The work's failure to characterize each of its nine central figures with equal clarity and its inability to suggest solutions to the problems that it addresses, however, have limited its impact upon women's literature.

Sources for Further Study

Auchincloss, Louis. "Mary McCarthy." In *Pioneers and Caretakers*. Minneapolis: University of Minnesota Press, 1965. Auchincloss criticizes *The Group* as an entertaining but disappointing book. He does not regard the central characters as sufficiently interesting or distinct from any other group of young adults.

Grumbach, Doris. *The Company She Kept*. New York: Coward-McCann, 1967. A biography of Mary McCarthy that contains some insightful literary analysis. Grumbach sees *The Group* as a "profoundly feminine" novel but argues that none of the characters matures through her experiences.

McKenzie, Barbara. *Mary McCarthy*. New York: Twayne, 1967. In this biographical and literary analysis, McKenzie interprets *The Group* as a social satire. Kay is presented as the one character who develops sufficiently to face her own failure.

Mailer, Norman. "The Case Against McCarthy." In *Cannibals and Christians*. New York: Dial Press, 1966. Mailer criticizes McCarthy for "not reaching far enough" in *The Group*. He sees the novel's main characters as largely identical and as anachronistic in their espousal of 1950's values during the 1930's.

Stock, Irvin. *Mary McCarthy*. Minneapolis: University of Minnesota Press, 1968. A concise and readable discussion of McCarthy's fiction. Stock considers *The Group* "not particularly successful" as a novel, but he refutes the view that its nine central characters are indistinguishable.

Jeffrey L. Buller

THE HABIT OF BEING
Letters

Author: Flannery O'Connor (1925-1964)
Type of work: Letters
Time of work: 1948-1964
Locale: Saratoga Springs and New York City, New York; Connecticut; and Milledgeville, Georgia
First published: 1979

Principal personages:

FLANNERY O'CONNOR, a writer of short stories, novels, and
  essays
REGINA CLINE O'CONNOR, her mother, with whom she lived in
  Milledgeville, Georgia
SALLY and ROBERT FITZGERALD, friends with whom she lived in
  Connecticut
ELIZABETH MCKEE, her literary agent
CAROLINE GORDON TATE, her mentor, the wife of critic Allen Tate
ROBERT GIROUX, her editor at Harcourt, Brace
"A," an anonymous woman in Atlanta
MARYAT LEE, a playwright from New York
KATHERINE ANNE PORTER, WALKER PERCY, J. F. POWERS, JOHN
  HAWKES, ELIZABETH LOWELL, ROBERT LOWELL, and
  ELIZABETH BISHOP, other writers with whom O'Connor
  corresponded

Form and Content

The title *The Habit of Being* alludes to "the habit of art," a concept that Flannery O'Connor admired in the writings of philosopher Jacques Maritain. Sally Fitzgerald, the editor of this collection of O'Connor's letters, explains in her introduction that "habit" refers not to mere mechanical routine, but to an attitude of mind; hence, the habit of art allows an artist to sharpen intellectual activity so that art becomes a virtue of the intellect. As O'Connor consciously worked to attain this quality in her writing, she acquired a secondary "habit of being": the essential quality of a mind perfectly alive to life. O'Connor's letters attest her achievement of this heightened consciousness.

Following Fitzgerald's introductions and editing notes is a brief biographical sketch. Born in Savannah, Georgia, in 1925, O'Connor moved to Milledgeville, Georgia, when she was twelve. After receiving her bachelor's degree from Georgia State College for Women and a master's degree from the State University of Iowa, she worked on her first novel, *Wise Blood* (1952), at Yaddo, a writers' retreat in Saratoga

Springs, New York. Here in 1948, O'Connor wrote Elizabeth McKee, asking her to be her literary agent; this letter appropriately begins the collection of selected correspondence.

The letters and editorial notes are organized chronologically into four parts. "Up North and Getting Home, 1948-1952" begins with O'Connor at twenty-three, writing *Wise Blood* and trying to publish it. She left Yaddo in the spring of 1949 and spent some time in New York City and Milledgeville. Then O'Connor lived with Fitzgerald and her husband from September, 1949, until December, 1950. On her trip home, she had an attack of lupus, a then-incurable disease of the blood vessels (her father died of lupus when she was fifteen). "Day In and Day Out, 1953-1958," along with the last two sections, details her daily activities at Andalusia, the O'Connor farm near Milledgeville, and her comments on her work and others' writing. "'The Violent Bear It Away,' 1959-1963" describes work on her second novel, *The Violent Bear It Away* (1960). The concluding (and shortest) section, "The Last Year, 1964," follows her rapid decline in health and her struggle to complete her last three stories: "Revelation," "Parker's Back," and "Judgment Day." Her last letter, a scrawled note written six days before her death at thirty-nine, is to her friend Maryat Lee. Fitzgerald illuminates these letters with explanations to clarify context, and an index allows quick access to specific letters.

O'Connor's letters provide wonderful insight into the mind of a major American short-story writer whose undeniable reputation has increased since her death. This book might owe its genesis to fellow author Katherine Anne Porter's comment that she would have liked some record of O'Connor that captured her finest qualities. *The Habit of Being* accomplishes exactly that: It is a picture reflecting O'Connor's true likeness, her inner self.

Analysis

O'Connor's letters paint a self-portrait in words. They offer an intimate glimpse of a woman perfecting her art and life despite a debilitating illness. She reveals her considerable intellect, modesty, self-confidence, honesty, and humor. Correspondence was very important to O'Connor. When she lived with the Fitzgeralds, she walked daily to the mailbox a mile away, always to find a letter from her mother, to whom O'Connor also wrote every single day. This writing habit became even more important once illness restricted her home. She writes a friend in October, 1951, that mail is very eventful for her. Occasionally she mentions the disagreeable effects of her cortisone treatments, but she remains cheerfully focused on her work and on her friends' lives. "Let me hear how you do" often occurs in her letters. They testify to her joy of life and her exploration of the full range of her talents. She enthusiastically and regularly wrote friends—(most often fellow writers), her agent and editor, clerics, academics, and even people whom she did not know well. Anyone could write her and get an answer, if not a correspondence.

Central issues in her letters include her and others' writing, philosophy, religion, contemporary politics, and day-to-day events. During the sixteen years covered,

O'Connor worked on two dozen short stories and two novels; thus, the letters often refer to the writing, publishing, and reviewing of her work. Half of writing, she confesses, is overcoming the revulsion felt when sitting down to it. She requests advice about her work from the Fitzgeralds, Elizabeth and Robert Lowell, Caroline Gordon Tate, Elizabeth McKee, Robert Giroux, and Maryat Lee. She also shared her writing with other writers who were establishing their own notable careers: Katherine Anne Porter, Cecil Dawkins, Elizabeth Bishop, Walker Percy, J. F. Powers, and John Hawkes, to name a few. This circle of writer friends supported her emotionally and professionally, allowing her to communicate freely with the outside world despite her restricted travel. She frequently discusses her extensive reading and expresses admiration for the work of Bernard Malamud, William Faulkner, and Thomas Merton, among others. Her most philosophical and theological letters are those to "A" (she prefers anonymity). In 1955, O'Connor tells "A" how pleased she is to find someone who recognizes her work for what she tries to make it, and how although the distance between them is eighty-seven miles, the spiritual distance is shorter. The correspondence with "A" leaves no doubt that O'Connor writes as she does because she is a Catholic and is very conscious of church doctrines of belief.

Besides discussing literature and religion, these letters also reflect O'Connor's observation of American society in the 1950's and early 1960's. Intrigued by rapidly changing events in the South, O'Connor comments on various social and political issues. She admires civil rights leader Martin Luther King, Jr., in his battle for racial equality and harmony, but she has serious reservations about militants who came South during this explosive time and about pious intellectuals who misread her stories as racist. Also, politicians bemuse her; her opinion of Vice President Richard Nixon as presidential candidate in 1960 is that King Kong would be preferable. Neither does she have a high regard for actors (who would later be politicians): Having sold the television rights to her story "The Life You Save May Be Your Own" to *General Electric Playhouse*, she imagines Ronald Reagan as Mr. Shiftlet, and she jokes that while they make hash out of her story, she and her mother will make ice in the new refrigerator that they bought with the money.

O'Connor's epistolary style reflects the same mastery of language and sureness of belief that mark her fiction; her letters are intelligent, interesting, amusing, serious, and precise. Her spelling could be as unique as her ideas. Fitzgerald suggests that O'Connor's ear was so fine that she got words down as they sounded to her. What emerges is a wide range of voices: intellectual and folksy, serious and playful, philosophical and mundane. For example, not wanting pity, she assumes a jocular tone about her crippling disease, writing that her crutches make her a structure with flying buttresses. She tells Maryat Lee in 1958 that she has a "DREAD DISEASE" that her father died of at forty-four but that scientists hope to keep her alive until she is ninety-six, thanks to pigs' pituitary glands. Writing more seriously about her illness to "A," she philosophically compares sickness to a place, more instructive than a trip to Europe—a place where there is no company. Thus, she sees sickness as one of God's mercies.

Context

O'Connor's most significant contribution to women's studies is that she succeeded as a writer at a time when men dominated the field. *The Habit of Being* clearly justifies her inclusion in the canon of modern American writers. Since writing is the dominant theme of *The Habit of Being*, readers come to understand the original literary genius and strong religious belief that infuse both her fiction and her nonfiction. Her body of work includes the short-story collections *A Good Man Is Hard to Find and Other Stories* (1955), *Everything That Rises Must Converge* (1965), and *The Complete Stories* (1971); the novels *Wise Blood* and *The Violent Bear It Away*; and essays, collected in *Mystery and Manners* (1969). Her book reviews have also been published. Attracting the most attention, however, are her stories, especially "A Good Man Is Hard to Find," "Good Country People," and "The Displaced Person," with their shocking violence and puzzling religious themes. Because of this fascination with O'Connor's works, her letters are all the more intriguing and insightful. Indeed, the large number of critical works on the writer is impressive, considering her relatively modest output

Reviewers have praised these letters for their wit, brilliance, intelligence, and precision of statement. Yet, because this volume does not reflect accurately the entire scope of O'Connor's massive correspondence, evaluating her views on women's issues proves difficult. Readers do not have here a sizable portion of O'Connor's letters (especially the daily letters to her mother), and they do not know the content of many passages deleted without ellipses to mark omissions. Fitzgerald's edition of *Flannery O'Connor: Collected Works* (1988), which devotes 340 pages to O'Connor's letters and includes twenty-two new letters, supplements *The Habit of Being*. Nevertheless, readers need a complete picture to assess O'Connor's views accurately. For example, Simone de Beauvoir, the author of the landmark feminist study *Le Deuxième Sexe* (1949; *The Second Sex*, 1953), is mentioned briefly in five letters in *The Habit of Being*. O'Connor writes that Beauvoir has probably led people to the Catholic church, yet readers do not know the full context of this comment. In another letter, O'Connor admits she has never read Beauvoir's works—and never intends to do so.

Judged on the content of her letters here, O'Connor remains peripheral to the feminist literary tradition. She is a woman writing about her day-to-day life without any particular focus on women's issues. Yet her true likeness is undeniably that of a remarkable writer and deeply spiritual person. The way she articulates her "habit of being" proves instructive to women and men alike.

Sources for Further Study

Asals, Frederick. *Flannery O'Connor: The Imagination of Extremity*. Athens: University of Georgia Press, 1982. This useful scholarly critique analyzes the texture and conflicts of O'Connor's fictional universe. A limited bibliography includes works from O'Connor's personal library.

Coles, Robert. *Flannery O'Connor's South*. Baton Rouge: Louisiana State University

Press, 1980. A psychiatrist offers a unique slant on O'Connor's depiction of characters' conflict and anxieties.

Feelcy, Kathleen. *Flannery O'Connor: Voice of the Peacock.* 2d ed. New York: Fordham University Press, 1982. Feeley, a Catholic nun, approaches O'Connor's work through the writer's nonliterary reading, drawing extensively on her essays.

Friedman, Melvin J., and Beverly Lyon Clark, eds. *Critical Essays on Flannery O'Connor.* Boston: G. K. Hall, 1985. Various critical approaches, an annotated bibliography of twenty-two books and articles, and "Reminiscences and Tributes" by Katherine Anne Porter, Allen Tate, Thomas Merton, and Alice Walker provide a broad view of O'Connor scholarship.

Montgomery, Marion. *Why Flannery O'Connor Stayed Home.* Vol. 1 in *The Prophetic Poet and the Spirit of the Age.* LaSalle, Ill.: Sherwood Sugden, 1981. Montgomery shows how Western culture's great philosophers shaped O'Connor's thought, making her a prophetic voice of the modern spiritual crisis. Rather than offering a detailed critical reading, this work synthesizes O'Connor's ideas.

O'Connor, Flannery. *The Complete Stories.* New York: Farrar, Straus & Giroux, 1971. Editor Robert Giroux provides a good overview of O'Connor's publishing career. The thirty-one stories range from those written for her thesis in 1947 to her last story, completed a month before she died.

_____ . *Mystery and Manners: Occasional Prose.* Edited by Sally Fitzgerald and Robert Fitzgerald. New York: Farrar, Straus & Giroux, 1969. O'Connor's essays provide an excellent companion to her letters, with topics ranging from religious belief to Southern writers.

Walters, Dorothy. *Flannery O'Connor.* New York: Twayne, 1973. One of the best critical overviews. Walters intelligently examines the theology and literary sources influencing O'Connor.

Laura M. Zaidman

THE HANDMAID'S TALE

Author: Margaret Atwood (1939-   )
Type of work: Novel
Type of plot: Fable
Time of plot: The future
Locale: Cambridge, Massachusetts
First published: 1985

> ### Principal characters:
> OFFRED, following the revolution that established the Republic of
> Gilead, a Handmaid, (surrogate mother) in the home of the
> Commander
> THE COMMANDER (FRED), a member of the administrative elite of
> Gilead and Offred's master
> MOIRA, a friend of Offred, who refuses to become a Handmaid
> but instead is forced to work in a brothel
> SERENA JOY, the Commander's wife, a former television
> evangelist
> NICK, the Commander's chauffeur and Offred's paid lover
> OFGLEN, a Handmaid who is a member of the underground

Form and Content

Margaret Atwood's *The Handmaid's Tale* takes place in the United States at the turn of the twenty-first century. A revolution sponsored by fundamentalist leaders has produced a monolithic theocracy called the Republic of Gilead. Although inspired by divine power, the administrators of Gilead rely on human control to implement their religion-based policies. Overt military control is conducted through a series of agents—such as Commanders, Eyes, and Guardians—who use electronic devices, blockades, and spies to maintain surveillance over the population. Those who are not members of the Gilead forces become servants, a role reserved almost exclusively for women.

Women, who the revolution was supposedly fought in part to protect, are relegated to serving in eight narrowly defined categories easily identified by the color of their prescribed wardrobe. The blue-clad wives of the Commanders are the most visible of all the women in Gilead. They are to preside over the Commanders' homes, create beautiful gardens, and attend social functions, which include public hangings and ritual beatings of men who break the Gilead rules. The green-clad Marthas are responsible for cooking and keeping the house clean. Econowives, women married to midlevel members of the Gilead administration, wear multicolored uniforms to designate their mixed functions as housewife, cook, maid, and mother. A small number of women wear black, widows whose life is ill-defined in Gilead; as a result, they are rarely seen. Two other groups of women are not seen in Gilead: the gray-clad Unwomen, those who refused to cooperate with the system and have been sent to work in the Colonies (where environmental pollution will soon kill them), and the women who work in the underground brothel, where the Commanders go for pleasures that are officially restricted by the republic. The remaining two categories of women rival the wives in importance. The Aunts, wearing Nazi-brown dresses, train the other group to become surrogate mothers. Because of the environmental pollution, the loss of life during the revolutionary fighting, and the age of some of the wives, sterility has become Gilead's most visible problem. The solution to this problem is the procurement of fertile women who will bear children for the Commanders, the red-clad Handmaids.

The Handmaid is limited to offering her body as a vessel for procreation during bizarre bedroom encounters with the Commander and his wife. Lying fully clothed in her red habit between the open thighs of the wife, the Handmaid receives the Commander, who is also clothed except for an open zipper. No communication between the Commander and the Handmaid is allowed. The sexual encounter becomes both asexual and pornographic at the same time.

The birth of a child consumes Serena Joy, the wife of one Commander, to such an extent that she accepts the private nighttime meetings of her husband and the Handmaid Offred in the hope that this might lead to a pregnancy. These private encounters allow both the Commander and Offred to assume more human qualities than either is allowed by the republic. Both at first relish the intellectual cat-and-mouse game that develops between them. Offred continues the game because the Commander provides items that she otherwise would never have, such as magazines, alcohol, and special soaps. The Commander pursues the game in the hope of creating a sexual intimacy that is not permitted during the procreation ritual. The game does not produce the desired result, however, for either the Commander or Serena Joy: Offred does not become pregnant. Desperate to produce a child for her house and bask in the rewards of Gilead's society, Serena Joy secretly employs the Commander's chauffeur, Nick, to have sex with Offred. At first hesitant, Nick and Offred discover a sexuality with each other that the republic forbids. Thus, even when the private meetings are ended by Serena Joy, Offred continues to sneak to Nick's room when possible. At about the same time, the Commander takes Offred for a nighttime excursion to an underground brothel. Once there, Offred is reunited with her college friend Moira, a rebel. Although glad to see her, Offred is dismayed that Moira is a prostitute. Moira explains that the decision was either to die in the poisonous Colonies or to remain alive and endure—to perhaps escape, as she has done twice before.

Moira's courage, Offred's revulsion to the brothel, and her exploitation by another woman, Serena Joy, lead to Offred's decision to attempt escape. Befriended by another Handmaid, Ofglen, who has contacts with the underground, and assisted by Nick, Offred escapes and attempts to reach Canada. During her trip north, she discovers a tape recorder and tells the Handmaid's tale.

Analysis

The Handmaid's Tale is a political fable whose purpose is to act as a cautionary tale for women. Dedicated to Perry Miller, the foremost authority on the Puritans and their influence in American history, and to Mary Webster, an ancestor of the Atwood family hanged as a witch in Connecticut, the catalyst for Atwood's concern was the self-proclaimed triumph of the religious Fundamentalists in elections held in the early 1980's. Like the Puritans of Colonial America, who hoped to create the model city upon the hill, the Religious Right hoped to create a moral, utopian society where their interpretation of the Bible prescribed the proper behavior and societal roles for men and women. Atwood uses science fiction to extend the logical outcome of such a society if the Fundamentalists held power; a woman must conform or be declared a threat, a witch.

The concept of the Handmaid is based upon the biblical story of Rachel and Jacob: "Behold my maid Bilhah, go into her; and she shall bear upon my knees, that I may also have children by her" (Genesis 30: 1-3). Thus the Handmaid's sole function in the Republic of Gilead is as a procreation device for the Commander and his sterile wife. The individual autonomy of the Handmaid is stripped away, beginning with her name. The Handmaids are provided new names that reflect their subservient status, patronymics: names composed of the possessive preposition and the Commander's first name, such as Ofglen, Ofwarren, or the central character in the novel, Offred.

Clothed in long red gowns, their faces hidden from view by veils and wimples, the Handmaids resemble a religious sect who have just emerged from a convent. Their daily rituals resemble the rules of a strict medieval order. Cloistered in a bedroom within the Commander's house, the Handmaid is not permitted any reading or writing materials, nor are objects that might assist suicide permitted. To suppress her identity further, not even a mirror is allowed in the room. Thus like a cloistered nun whose sole daily function is reflection and preparation for her relationship with God, the Handmaid is limited to one function, procreation, in order to ensure the future of the republic.

Despite the religious trappings of the Republic of Gilead, the purpose of the new order is not to protect women but to suppress them. Thus, Atwood's depiction of Serena Joy is a warning to the women supporters of the Religious Right that they must be careful what they wish for, for they might one day get it. Serena Joy, once a woman of some independence and social importance as a television evangelist, has been reduced to being an extension of someone else. She is the Commander's wife, and her world is his house and her roles as wife and mother. Unable to perform the latter role, Serena Joy must bear the presence of the Handmaid and the ugliness of procreation sex between her husband and this stranger who is a constant reminder that she is now wife in name only.

Atwood's tale also acts as a cautionary note for men who might support the phallocentric Republic of Gilead. Just as women are reduced to limited roles and role-playing, so too are the men. The full range of human sexuality becomes limited to the asexual procreation process—no joy, only duty. The pressure on men to be all things—father, husband, leader, and provider—creates an anxiety between Serena Joy and the Commander that makes their marriage a legal relationship but not a human one. The only interesting relationship that exists for the Commander is the one he establishes with Offred. The relationship is not equal, however, and thus not fulfilling for either participant. Each uses the other: The Commander hopes for an intimate sexual relationship, while Offred receives material items otherwise denied her. The unequal relationship is doomed when Offred, a slave, is reminded of her identity as the Commander's property when she is put on display at the underground brothel.

One woman in the novel remains admirable from the opening pages. Offred's old college friend, Moira, fights against the republic during the revolution, refuses to cooperate with the republic after its triumph, and even in captivity retains a personal identity by reversing the goal of her capturers and using her sex as a means to empower herself. Regardless of her situation, she maintains a level of integrity and becomes a catalyst for Offred's decision to chance escape.

The narrative force of the novel is the transformation of Offred from victim to hero, from passive to active. Throughout the novel, Offred reminds the reader that she is recording her Handmaid's tale in order to warn others that they must always be attentive and must realize that a time will come when they must act. As she declares in her tape recorder, "I intend to last."

Context

When it was first published, *The Handmaid's Tale* was immediately compared to the appearance almost forty years before of George Orwell's *Nineteen Eighty-Four* (1949). Both novels suggest that to create a world of perfect order and stability would require that the imperfections of human beings be brought under control. The future societies of both novels ban writing, the written word being a weapon feared by those in charge. Both worlds restrict relationships, reducing them to sterile, superficial role-playing. Violence as a method of control and citizen participation in that violence appear in both novels. Yet Winston Smith, the main character in *Nineteen Eighty-Four*, is a man and has at least a marginal sense of independence and identity. Offred in *The Handmaid's Tale* is a woman who has no independence and has been stripped of all identity.

Because of this difference, Atwood's novel is closer in relationship to the words spoken by the cofounder of the modern women's movement, Elizabeth Cady Stanton. At the end of the nineteenth century, Stanton was asked to speak on behalf of women's rights in the nation's capital. Her speech, quickly reprinted and published in newspapers throughout the United States, was about the "solitude of self." An appraisal of the forty years that had just passed and a speculation on the future, Stanton's address was a sober reminder that regardless of the success of the movement, women must realize that they are individuals first and that each must encounter the world alone. She implied that no utopia was imminent—nor should it be, because women are individuals and a collective success approved by all was neither possible nor, in the long run, desirable. The solitude of self was the acknowledgment of personal responsibility and the courage to endure—the qualities possessed by Moira and admired by Offred, and the reason that Atwood's character records *The Handmaid's Tale*.

Sources for Further Study

Grace, Sherrill E., and Lorraine Weir, eds. *Margaret Atwood: Language, Text, and System*. Vancouver: University of British Columbia Press, 1983. Includes nine essays examining Atwood's literary "system" and her development of style and subject matter up to the publication of *The Handmaid's Tale*.

Kostash, Myrna, et al. *Her Own Woman: Profiles of Ten Canadian Women*. Toronto: Macmillan of Canada, 1975. Contains a biographical essay by Valerie Miner, "Atwood in Metamorphosis: An Authentic Canadian Fairy Tale," that examines the evolution and maturation of Atwood's writing.

McCombs, Judith, ed. *Critical Essays on Margaret Atwood*. Boston: G. K. Hall, 1988. The best edition of criticism on Atwood. Contains thirty-two essays, arranged in the chronological order of her publications. The monograph contains an excellent analysis of *The Handmaid's Tale*.

Rigney, Barbara Hill. *Margaret Atwood*. Totowa, N.J.: Barnes & Noble Books, 1987. An analysis of Atwood as poet, novelist, and political commentator, all from a feminist perspective. Includes a useful bibliography.

Rosenberg, Jerome H. *Margaret Atwood*. Boston: Twayne, 1984. A concise literary biography of the Canadian novelist and poet that provides a useful introduction to her works.

David O'Donald Cullen

THE HARP-WEAVER AND OTHER POEMS

Author: Edna St. Vincent Millay (1892-1950)
Type of work: Poetry
First published: 1923

Form and Content

While other volumes of Edna St. Vincent Millay's poetry debated the struggle between life, love, and beauty versus loss, bitterness, and death, *The Harp-Weaver and Other Poems* was the first collection to focus on Millay's acceptance of death's inevitability. Love of life and adoration of beauty—two of Millay's prominent themes—are still present in this work, but they are relegated to a position of lesser significance as she concedes to perhaps the greater force. Her concession, however, is tinged with an ever-present defiance as she attempts to turn the ugliness of loss into another form of beauty.

Infamous for her many love affairs during her time spent in Greenwich Village, Millay finally settled down, marrying Eugen Boissevain, the widower of feminist Inez Milholland, in 1923. The poems of this collection reflect the maturation and commitment that Millay demonstrated in her marriage and subsequent lifestyle that same year. They also echo the strains of wistfulness that she may have felt as she entered her third decade and subdued her wilder ways. Many of these poems provide a voice for all women, restricted from individual expression or exploration of their identities by outdated patriarchal conventions.

The collection is divided into three parts—thirty lyrical and free-verse poems, twenty-two sonnets, and a seventeen-sonnet sequence—all of which comment on Millay's theories on beauty, love, or death. *The Harp-Weaver and Other Poems* suggests a more mature poet coming to terms with disillusionment and grief. "Call me in all things what I was before," she cautions in the sonnet "Say what you will," but in these poems she will "tell you I am what I was and more." The poems conclude with the image of the poet as a tree in autumn or a rose that "hugs the brown bough and sighs before it goes."

Analysis

"The Ballad of the Harp-Weaver," which lends its name to the collection, is its longest and most famous poem. Utilizing a deceptively simple ballad form, Millay spins the tale of an impoverished mother who dies, weaving garments for her little son on her magical harp. Millay's fantasy is rooted in the reality of her childhood, as her own divorced mother struggled to provide for her three daughters. She not only met their physical needs by working as a nurse but fed and clothed their minds and souls as well, sharing her talent for music and writing. The ballad is a tribute to Millay's own mother and to motherly love and its sacrifices everywhere; it is no surprise that the entire collection is dedicated to her.

The rest of the poems that make up the first third of the collection can be divided roughly into four categories in which Millay expresses her acknowledgment of beauty, grief, death, and acquiescence. Unlike many of her earlier poems on the adoration of the beautiful, these lyrics tend to demonstrate Millay's developing philosophy on the discovery of beauty in unexpected places. In "My Heart, Being Hungry," the poet claims to hunger for a "Beauty where beauty never stood"; in "The Wood Road," she defies even grief to deaden her appreciation of nature's dying loveliness. This love of nature is a theme introduced early in Millay's work and one that she never abandons, though her initial swift embracing of it may be less enthusiastic now. "The Goose Girl" is Millay's most outspoken comment on the theme when she states, "all the loveliest things there be/ Come simply, so it seems to me." "A Visit to the Asylum" illustrates Millay's respect for the unrespected in a tale of a little girl's visit to the local institution. Throughout the collection, Millay finds beauty where it may not typically be found and translates it into a language of appreciation.

Millay champions the expression of truth from the simplest, least expected natural sources, and she illustrates her philosophy with the deceptively simple method of lyricism that she employs in most of her poetry. A silk-spinning dragonfly becomes a metaphor for her own verse-making in "The Dragonfly"; however, the poet's identification with the unlovely takes on a threatening tone in "The Curse." Here, Millay describes her ashes, a metaphor for her poetry, as "a strange thing" that will continue to plague those who have not understood her, ever after her death.

The poet's acquaintance with grief seeps out in several other poems in this first third of the collection. "Scrub" identifies whatever deformities, literal or metaphorical, the poet may have acquired to her companionship with sorrow. The speaker in "Departure" cannot share her unidentified grief, covering her feelings with domestic busyness. This need to cloak one's sorrow with mundane industry is a repeated theme in Millay's work. "The Spring and the Fall" connects the change of the seasons with love's demise. While she can accept the inevitable death of things, in love as well as nature, she cannot help but grieve over the manner in which things die.

A member of the Provincetown Players, Millay wrote and acted with other famous writers, such as John Reed, Susan Glaspell, and Eugene O'Neill. "To One Who Might Have Borne a Message," written on the death of Reed, also recalls the death of a dear Vassar College friend, Dorothy Coleman. The simplicity of the final couplet belies the hidden and unexpressed sorrow that Millay restrains so well in her best poems.

In this more mature collection, Millay's early defiance of death is replaced by an acceptance, although a still-reluctant one at times. In "Autumn Chant," "the rose remembers/ The dust from which it came," and in the first of "Three Songs from 'The Lamp and the Bell,'" a play that Millay wrote for her Vassar classmates, the poet acknowledges that "Summer, for all your guile,/ Will brown in a week to Autumn."

In "Keen," Millay realizes that loving makes one vulnerable to death. "Never May the Fruit Be Plucked" carries this awareness further in its intimation that all love ends in death: "The winter of love is a cellar of empty bins." Death lurking beneath a mask of the ordinary is visualized in "The Pond," where a woman drowns herself in full view, covering her intentions with lily-plucking. Millay suggests that death waits in unexpected places, that it is inevitable however one attempts to elude it.

Finally, Millay demonstrates maturity in her ability to accept what she cannot change. Sometimes this acquiescence is a form of contentment, though often it is an exhausted last resort. "The Return from Town" suggests an appreciation for her new husband over many "a pretty lad." "The Betrothal" reveals the other side of perhaps the same situation when the narrator promises to "make a man a good wife," though she loves another. One of them might as well be happy, she muses, as "There's few enough as is." Millay's theme of acquiescence becomes concrete in "Spring Song," a fantasy in which spring no longer returns: "We shall hardly notice in a year or two./ You can get accustomed to anything."

The second third of the collection contains twenty-two sonnets, fifteen of which are written in the traditional Petrarchan form, already archaic in the early twentieth century. Many critics agree, however, that Millay restored the sonnet to respectability by perfecting its established form. These poems continue the themes established in the first third of the collection: "Love is not blind," "Still will I harvest beauty," and "Euclid alone has looked on beauty bare" particularly articulate Millay's own vision of the beautiful. "I know I am but summer," "Pity me not," and "Here is a wound" grieve over the demise of love; while "I see so clear," "Your face is like a chamber," and "Lord Archer, Death" (also written for John Reed) reflect Millay's acquiescence to death.

Context

Crowned "the greatest woman poet since Sappho" by critics of her day, Edna St. Vincent Millay personified the essence of her time. According to critic Anne Cheney, she became the "living symbol of women who would live, think, and love as freely as they chose." Her first published work, "Renascence," written at nineteen, won awards and secured her the opportunity for a Vassar degree. She followed its publication with three successive collections, introducing her smooth lyrical style and ensuring her place as the most popular poet of her day. Her next volume, *The Harp-Weaver and Other Poems*, however, was Millay's most mature work to that date and, many would argue, her greatest contribution to women's literature. It won the 1923 Pulitzer Prize for poetry.

Many of the sonnets in the volume add another dimension to Millay's established treatise on beauty, love, and death: an outspoken feminist perspective. "Oh, oh, you will be sorry" spews disdain on her "enemy," who thinks that women should be content as objects of physical love, rather than as free-thinkers. Though she plans to bide her time, playing the "sweet . . . soft" role for now, it will be a "sane day" when she leaves him to follow her own intellectual pursuits. She protests, too, the value that men place on physical love and the subordinate position to which they have subjected women in "I, being born a woman," finding "this frenzy insufficient reason" for her time or interest.

The sonnet sequence that concludes the collection, "Sonnets from an Ungrafted Tree," portrays a wife's care of a dying husband whom she no longer loves and may serve as a metaphorical narrative symbolizing Millay's probable resentment at being older and restricted, as well as a commentary on the plight of women of her generation. Though she burned her candle "at both ends" (as she describes in "First Fig") during her single days in Greenwich Village, acknowledged as "the It-girl of the Hour" according to critic Elizabeth Atkins, Millay recognizes her privilege of free expression as one not shared by many women of her day. She comes to identify with these less fortunate women when she joins the older, married ranks of her gender; the poems of this collection speak for all women who have known sorrow, constraint, and unfulfillment.

Anne Sexton, a 1950's poet, reportedly worried that she would be a "reincarnation" of Millay—maintaining poetic traditions, rather than creating new forms for her expression. She acknowledged Millay's significance as a writer, however, when she admitted that Millay was the only female poet she had ever read. Though Millay is not renowned for establishing new approaches to poetry, she sounded her feminist voice loudly and clearly to a receptive public. Though the critic Allen Tate remarked that she was "not an intellect but a sensibility," her personal approach to poetry spoke to and for a vast majority of women in her day and for later generations.

Sources for Further Study

Atkins, Elizabeth. *Edna St. Vincent Millay and Her Times.* Chicago: University of Chicago Press, 1936. Compiled during Millay's lifetime, this study addresses all the poet's work through 1934. A spokesperson of the times in which Millay lived and wrote, Atkins lacks the necessary perspective required for thoughtful scholarship, though her observations appear sound and insightful. Includes an index but no chronology or bibliography.

Brittin, Norman A. *Edna St. Vincent Millay.* Boston: Twayne, 1967. Brittin provides a detailed chronology, a bibliography, and an index, as well as thorough criticism of Millay's life and work. The chapter on *The Harp-Weaver and Other Poems* is succinct but adequate.

Cheney, Anne. *Millay in Greenwich Village.* Tuscaloosa: University of Alabama Press, 1975. Cheney examines Millay from a psychoanalytical approach, providing deep and detailed insight into Millay's personal life and promoting greater understanding about what she wrote and why. Includes a chronology, an index, and a bibliography.

Gilbert, Sandra M., and Susan Gubar. *The Norton Anthology of Literature by Women.* New York: W. W. Norton, 1985. Still the only adequate anthology of women's literature, this volume, which includes Millay and her more feminist contributions, is invaluable for women's studies. Regards Millay from a feminist perspective.

Gray, James. *Edna St. Vincent Millay.* Minneapolis: University of Minneapolis Press, 1967. This slim volume of criticism is intense, concise, and thorough. Gray provides an excellent introduction to Millay for the first-time student or a tightly constructed review for the returning scholar. A select bibliography is included.

Gurko, Miriam. *Restless Spirit: The Life of Edna St. Vincent Millay.* New York:

Thomas Y. Crowell, 1962. Gurko's well-written biography for the younger student includes a thorough bibliography.

Rebecca Luttrell Briley

THE HEART IS A LONELY HUNTER

Author: Carson McCullers (1917-1967)
Type of work: Novel
Type of plot: Psychological realism
Time of plot: The 1930's
Locale: A town in the western part of Georgia, bordering the Chattahoochee River
First published: 1940

Principal characters:
> JOHN SINGER, a deaf-mute who lives with his friend
> Antonapoulos
> MICK KELLY, an androgynous thirteen-year-old
> JAKE BLOUNT, a fanatic of social causes who believes that Singer
> can relieve his loneliness
> DR. BENEDICT MADY COPELAND, an African American doctor
> who believes himself a failure because no one will accept his
> ideas about social equality, birth control, and abortion
> BIFF BRANNON, the owner of the New York Café, who becomes
> obsessed with Mick

Form and Content

Carson McCullers' first novel, *The Heart Is a Lonely Hunter*, explores what Nathaniel Hawthorne called "the labyrinth of the human heart." Just as the spokes of a wheel revolve around a hub, the lives of Mick Kelly, Jake Blount, Dr. Benedict Mady Copeland, and Biff Brannon revolve around the deaf-mute John Singer.

The teenager, Mick, is the only character in the book who grows or changes; the sections that relate to her are a *Bildungsroman* that traces a young girl's movement from the instinctive emotionalism of childhood, through the advent of preadolescence and awakening sexuality, to the final thrust of maturity that brings disillusionment in love. Mick's first disappointing sexual experience with Harry West left her feeling very old, "a grown person now, whether she wanted to be or not." She gravitates toward Singer, who serves as her god until his suicide brings an end to her dreams. She knows that she will never become a famous musician and instead goes to work ten hours a day in a ten-cent store to contribute to the family income. Her childhood is over.

In her outline of *The Heart Is a Lonely Hunter*—published first in Oliver Evans' biography *The Ballad of Carson McCullers* (1965) and later in McCullers' *The Mortgaged Heart* (1971)—McCullers states that the theme of her novel is "man's revolt against his own inner isolation and his urge to express himself as fully as is possible." The escape from isolation is through the expression of love, but love is seldom reciprocal, and it is doomed to failure—for women as well as for men. As Biff Brannon points out, "By nature all people are of both sexes. So marriage and the bed is not all by any means."

The novel begins with a delineation of Singer's love for another deaf-mute, the grossly fat and retarded Spiros Antonapoulos, and the opening lines of the novel focus on their relationship: "In the town there were two mutes, and they were always together." Singer loves, indeed worships, Antonapoulos, and although he "never knew just how much his friend understood of all the things he told him, . . . it did not matter." What matters in Singer's life, and in that of the other major characters in the novel, is having a person to love, an all-too-human god to endow with qualities of compassion and understanding, though these traits exist only in the mind of the lover.

Singer finds himself isolated and alone when Antonapoulos is committed to the state institution. He visits Biff Brannon's New York Café and meets Mick Kelly, Jake Blount, and Dr. Copeland, who believe that he is able to assuage their loneliness. They tell him their hearts' desires, but when Antonapoulos dies, Singer has no reason to live and commits suicide. The other characters are likewise deprived of their beloved, and the altar of human "godliness" crumbles. The heart that is a lonely hunter is wrenched with pain.

Analysis

The loneliness of love and the oppressiveness of time are developed in *The Heart Is a Lonely Hunter* through the structure of a musical fugue. Singer's love for Antonapoulos, announced at the beginning of the novel, plays in counterpoint in the lives of Mick, Jake, Biff, and Dr. Copeland. McCullers explains that because of the fugal form, each character takes on a new richness when contrasted and woven in with the other characters; thus, according to her outline, Singer's love for Antonapoulos "threads through the whole book from the first page until the very end."

When Mick Kelly enters Brannon's cafe, Brannon finds that he can no longer keep his mind on reading the newspaper because a strange, new feeling of tenderness comes to him. Mick, however, does not share his interest; instead she turns to music, which becomes linked in her mind with Singer and with love. McCullers constructs a paradigm of Mick's character through references to music. At first the child's love is instinctive, and she responds to music with wonder and awe. "Nothing is as good as music," she says, and the songs of Wolfgang Amadeus Mozart are "the softest and saddest thing she had ever imagined about." As Mick develops, music becomes associated with sex and traces her evolution into adulthood. Innocence is symbolized by her misspelling the composer's name as MOTSART, and as Mick's growing sexuality is revealed, she scribbles "a very bad word—PUSSY" on the wall of an unfinished house. For McCullers, love should be essentially Platonic, and *agape*, or brotherly love, is the ideal. Sexual love leaves the lover feeling incomplete, and Mick thinks of it as bad and dirty.

The final fugal voices belong to Jake Blount and Dr. Copeland, who believe that Singer understands and shares their dreams. Blount thinks that Singer cares about social revolution. Copeland takes Singer on house calls because he will help make things better for the black race. Only Biff Brannon questions why everyone thinks "the mute was exactly as they wanted him to be—when most likely it was all a very queer mistake." This error is brought out in the irony of Singer's name, which links the themes of music and love. A deaf-mute cannot sing or hear, and his name is as false as are the impressions about him.

Part 2, the developmental section of McCullers' literary fugue, explores in counterpoint the one-sided relationship of lover and beloved established by Singer and Antonapoulos. The focus of the section is on Mick as Singer becomes increasingly the idol of her dreams. At first she seeks acceptance by her schoolmates and gives a grown-up dance in an attempt to belong to the group. The party, however, is a failure, and in her despair Mick turns to music to ease the emptiness that she feels inside. She sits outside a nearby house at night and listens to the music on the radio. Beethoven's Third Symphony, *The Eroica*, typifies Mick's spiritual condition, her passion and unfulfilled yearning to be in harmony with the grandeur and beauty of the song. The music is of strategic importance, as the symphony's initial whiplash of chords announces Mick's response: "The music came again, harder and loud," and it "left only this bad hurt in her." Mick's attempt to grasp the ecstasy of the music fails, as does her dream of living alone with Singer "in a little foreign house where in winter it would snow."

The music of *The Eroica* is a metaphorical rendition of Mick's situation, as well as that of the other characters in *The Heart Is a Lonely Hunter*. The fleeting feelings of radiance and peace when the lover shares the company of a beloved are part of each character's response to being in love. Yet McCullers' characters become disappointed by the heroes who are unable to respond to the needs and dreams locked in each lover's heart. Part 3 recapitulates the theme of love and shows each character's reaction to Singer's death. Blount leaves town, and Dr. Copeland goes back to his wife's farm and dies of tuberculosis. Mick works at Woolworth's, and the music within her heart is silent. The heart remains a lonely hunter in its unrequited quest for love.

Context

Carson McCullers' fictional concerns reflect her private confrontation with bisexuality, her feelings that she was "born a man." Virginia Spencer Carr reports in her biography, *The Lonely Hunter* (1975) that "Carson . . . spoke of herself as an invert and wondered if she would ever know the love of a woman who might answer her multileveled needs." McCullers said herself that she felt that her second novel, *Reflections in a Golden Eye* (1941) was the first open treatment of homosexuality in American literature.

Both Carson McCullers and the characters she created challenged the stereotypical notions of the Southern belle. Carr reports that Carson upset fellow writer Katherine Anne Porter by dressing in dungarees or men's pants, a man's white dress shirt buttoned at the top, and a boy's jacket. Additionally, her female characters such as Mick and Frankie, in *The Member of the Wedding* (1946), have short-cropped hair and bear names as genderless as her own. As Biff Brannon points out in *The Heart Is a*

Lonely Hunter, "Mick looked as much like an overgrown boy as a girl. And on that subject why was it that the smartest people mostly missed that point? By nature all people are of both sexes." McCullers denies the validity of erotic love between individuals, but she espouses *agape*, the humanitarian ideal that transcends love between the sexes and encompasses a love and feeling of responsibility for all humanity. Such love connects all people—those who work on a chain gang, such as the prisoners in *The Ballad of the Sad Café* (1951), and yet are able to sing, as well as those who believe they are freaks because they lack a strong identity as either male or female and are otherwise different.

McCullers confronted issues of sexuality in nontraditional ways and devised a "science of love" that would show the relationship between a man and a woman as a spiritual rather than a sexual communion. Her contribution to feminist literature is important in its representation and acceptance of relationships of difference rather than the typical heterosexual standards and values prevalent in the society of her time.

Sources for Further Study

Carr, Virginia Spencer. *The Lonely Hunter*. Garden City, N.Y.: Doubleday, 1975. This biography is a thorough and complete assessment of Carson McCullers' life and career. Shows how the people who influenced her life helped shape her fictional concerns.

Evans, Oliver. *The Ballad of Carson McCullers*. New York: Coward-McCann, 1965. Evans' intimate biography draws upon his long friendship with Carson McCullers. In addition to the facts of the author's life, the author presents a critical analysis of McCullers' novels. Contains the first published "Author's Outline" of *The Heart Is a Lonely Hunter*.

McCullers, Carson. *The Mortgaged Heart*. Edited by Margarita G. Smith. Boston: Houghton Mifflin, 1971. This book contains a selection of McCullers' short stories, essays, and poetry that were unpublished at the time of her death in 1967. Her essay "Loneliness . . . an American Malady" provides a comment that elucidates her vision of love and loneliness.

Walker, Sue. "Play Precious Play: Carson McCullers, Transition Music." *The New Laurel Review* 12 (1982): 31-36. This article shows how McCullers' early musical training became a part of her fiction as metaphor, symbol, structure, and form and as a psychological bridge that spanned the gap between self and other, between the need for love and the attempt to resolve its loneliness. Provides a reading of McCullers in the light of noted British psychoanalyst D. W. Winnicott's theory of the transitional phenomenon as the first attachment of the child.

Sue Brannan Walker

HEARTBURN

Author: Nora Ephron (1941-   )
Type of work: Novel
Type of plot: Satire
Time of plot: The 1970's
Locale: New York City and Washington, D.C.
First published: 1983

Principal characters:
RACHEL SAMSTAT, a cookbook writer and mother
MARK FELDMAN, Rachel's husband, a syndicated columnist who
   has had an ongoing affair with Thelma Rice since Rachel
   became pregnant with their second child
THELMA RICE, the "other woman" whose extramarital affairs are
   legendary in Washington, D.C.
ARTHUR and JULIE SIEGEL, Rachel and Mark's best friends
VERA MAXWELL, Rachel's therapist
THE SAMSTATS, Rachel's parents, an entertainer and an agent
RICHARD FINKEL, Rachel's former lover
BETTY SEARLE, Rachel's best friend

Form and Content

   The title *Heartburn* represents more than simply Rachel Samstat's constant diges-
tive distress during a pregnancy that seems unrelenting and endless. The word also
symbolizes the emotional pain that Rachel feels upon learning of her husband's
cold-blooded betrayal and his attitude of righteous indignation that she should have
the nerve to resent his love affair with Thelma Rice. Nora Ephron's novel is not simply
a comic story about pregnancy, nor is it merely a cookbook: It is a novel concerning
male-female relationships, truth, betrayal, guilt, self-pity, and one woman's romance
with food.
   The work is an ironic look at modern married life in the 1970's. Rachel Samstat and
Mark Feldman are typical of upper-middle-class professionals who have no more
control over their emotions than the average man or woman. Ephron is careful to
reveal Rachel's pain in tiny bits, like the pepper and spices added to a good sauce,
while simmering the whole question of love and betrayal, men and women, over a low
but steady flame of outrageous comedy.
   The narrator begins with a joke, her initial reaction to her husband's infidelity: that
"the most unfair thing" about it is that she "can't even date." She then discusses
Mark's character and her own, their relationship, and her cooking, trying to uncover
the key to his betrayal and the reason that she keeps falling for men who cheat on her
and lie about it, and badly. First she thinks that he is crazy, and then she blames his
mother, her mother, and the "other woman," Thelma. Finally Rachel leaves Washing-

ton, D.C., to go to New York City, staying in her father's apartment and rejoining her therapy group led by Vera Maxwell.

There are flashbacks revealing details of her romance and marriage to Mark, the significance of food in their lives, and her self-doubt, which reveals a pattern of choosing men who will betray her. Yet even in the depths of anger and pain, Rachel finds the humorous side to everything—she even suspects that Mark wants her to come back to him only so that he can find out the secret to her vinaigrette recipe. She is not far wrong, since Mark no longer loves her, treats her terribly, and only wants her to stay with him until the baby is born, for the sake of his own reputation.

Rachel's response to a crisis is either to laugh it off as one more humorous spectacle in a cruel world or to remember a particularly good recipe for sorrel soup or Key lime pie that allows her to forget the pain. Even when her therapy group is robbed at gunpoint and she must surrender the diamond ring that Mark gave her on the birth of their first child, Rachel wonders if the police officer who interviews her might be available for a date. Yet her attempts to understand men and her relationships with them are typical of the reactions of most women. People always wonder why she picked Mark, and Charlie before him, when in fact she (and other women) have made no conscious choice.

Throughout this episodic farce, the irony of Rachel's life reverberates in her self-mockery, her choice to be a "good girl" and return to Mark as expected, and even her willingness to give Mark the salad dressing recipe despite her gut instinct to keep it from him as punishment for his cruelty. Rachel survives and in that sense triumphs, with her good humor and sense of self intact.

Analysis

Nora Ephron is a journalist-writer-editor and commentator on popular culture. *Heartburn*, her first novel, received mixed reviews: Some admired her comic wit, while others denigrated her talent, plot, and characterization. Many questioned the appropriateness of writing a *roman à clef* (a story based on one's own life with characters who are versions of real people) in the wake of her own much-publicized divorce from Carl Bernstein, the celebrated journalist and Watergate investigator.

Ephron entertains her readers and sticks pins in the egos of her chief antagonists, her former husband and his paramour, hoping perhaps to reduce her own emotional anguish while increasing theirs. Although the plot twists in *Heartburn* seem awkward and coincidental, they nevertheless catapult the reader into the fray, held in Rachel's sly, ironic grip from her first discovery of the affair to the climactic childbirth scene. As a farce, *Heartburn* fulfills its expectations of both high and low comedy, and although its characters are not heroic, their reactions are believable.

Ephron's voice is occasionally strident, but she reveals her own faults with those of her former husband. It is this candor and appeal to the reader's humanity that is most effective in this suspiciously simplistic romp. One does not mind that Rachel's jealousy of Thelma reduces her to name-calling (she is "a clever giant" who "makes these gluey puddings"). As a cookbook author, Rachel is so focused on food that she really believes that Mark should not have had the gall to have an affair with a bad cook. It never occurs to her that there is more to marriage than sex and food.

Yet sex and food are the only things of importance in this book, even though fidelity is in no way a function of either. It is this same illogical view that enables Mark to have an affair with a woman who is in every way inferior to his wife and to feel no guilt for this betrayal. Mark's sense of loyalty is so warped that, after revealing his illicit affair, he angrily berates Rachel for a rumor that Mark's lover has a sexually transmitted disease. Thelma's minor embarrassment is a far cry from Rachel's sense of loss and humiliation, but Mark has other priorities. The supreme act of irony is Mark's insistence that Rachel remain with him until their second child is born, forcing her to submit to the ultimate betrayal: to give birth to her child while the baby's father cannot wait to leave her, to have the most intimate part of her life revealed to a man who despises her.

Rachel's ironic assessment of male-female relationships, love, sex, food, and fidelity enables her to swallow the bitter truth that, for all of their education, intelli gence, and common sense, men and women still act from the gut, not the brain. Rachel's trick of throwing in a recipe here and there is significant because food is a metaphor for love, fidelity, and trust. The kind of potatoes that she fixes for her lovers reveals the condition of their affair—meat and potatoes when falling in love, rotted potatoes in the cupboard midway, and mashed potatoes when the affair is over. The one true thing that Rachel knows is food. As long as one follows recipes, one always gets perfect potatoes. Yet life does not provide recipes for success. Instead, people are thrown into life to be reared by amateurs in a false and threatening world where even seemingly insignificant acts may be crucial to physical or emotional survival. For example, Rachel's not-so-subtle attempt to hide her diamond ring form a would-be mugger on the subway is directly responsible for the robbery of her therapy group.

To prevent *Heartburn* from being merely a diatribe against faithless men who debase the women (and children) who love them, Ephron includes the story of Rachel's former lover Richard losing his wife to another woman. Moreover, even at the lowest ebb of life's problems, everyone is polite and mannerly—even the man who robs Rachel's therapy group—as if to show that people may do bad things, but they are still "civilized." The humor is so tame that it reemphasizes the absurdity of the actions and choices of her characters. Rachel never answers her question of why Mark betrayed her or why she keeps choosing men who will betray her. In that sense, some argue, nothing much happens in this novel—no significant plot, no heroic or develop- ing characters, no resolution of problems—but it is a farce, after all, not a philosophi- cal treatise.

Context

Like Ephron's other books, which comment upon and poke parodic thrusts at the cogent issues and major figures of American popular culture of the 1970's, *Heartburn* allows the reader to share the writer's pungent wit directed at the battle of the sexes and love, sex, and food. Ephron ironically analyzes the contemporary scene from the perspective of a woman who is a feminist but who is also the first to admit her own weakness for emotionally abusive, faithless men. On the way, she examines psychotherapy, muggings, and modern technology.

Unlike some of the leading voices of women's liberation in the 1970's and 1980's, Ephron has a sense of humor and is willing to shoulder some of the blame for sexism in the United States. Rather than attempting to destroy the psyches and personas of her adversaries (Bernstein and his lover), Ephron is content to suggest that the unhappy ending of her marriage is more the fault of her obsession with food and with getting the last laugh than with any evil intent on their part. *Heartburn* is relatively free of malice, but it contains quite a bit of self-directed and self-imposed sarcasm and cynicism. The book has its temporary bouts with looniness, but at its core is a profound sadness about male-female relationships and their failures. This amusing, frisky, and rarely bitter farce may make Ephron's reputation as a comedic writer, but it has had little impact on serious women's issues.

In *Wallflower at the Orgy* (1970), a fun-filled but acerbic collection of interviews and analytical essays about major icons of popular culture, Ephron shows her wit, vitality, and penchant for pop-culture commentary and ego deflation. *Crazy Salad: Some Things About Women* (1975) explores the same biting but ironic truths about modern life and the polarity of the sexes, as Ephron attempts to deal with romance, the cultural fixation with large breasts, feminine hygiene, and sexism. Her book *Scribble, Scribble: Notes on the Media* (1978) is a collection of her critical commentaries and her parodies of the news media, her uncle the television carpet salesman, *Gourmet* magazine, and Palm Beach society.

Sources for Further Study
Bosworth, Patricia. "Dazzling Double Takes from a Marriage." *Working Woman* 8 (June, 1983): 124-126. A review of *Heartburn* which calls Ephron's work "witty and malicious." Speculates on the possibility that the story documents Ephron's own much-publicized marriage to and divorce from Carl Bernstein, famed Watergate investigative reporter who also publicly flaunted his affair with another woman while his wife was pregnant with their child. Bosworth also claims that the recipes in the novel are quite good.
Hoffman, Barbara. "Non-Fiction: *Crazy Salad.*" *Best Sellers* 35 (September, 1975): 171. Compares *Crazy Salad* to comic writer Jean Kerr's *Penny Candy* (1970), and gives Ephron credit for going beyond wit to find truth even behind the myth of feminism.
Jackson, Marni. "A Witty Woman's Revenge." *Maclean's* 96 (May 9, 1983): 62. This article calls Ephron's novel a *roman à clef* about her betrayal by Bernstein, yet asserts that Ephron refuses to show much malice, which is commendable under the circumstances.
Kent, Rosemary. "Nora Ephron's *Heartburn.*" *Harper's Bazaar* 116 (May, 1983): 30, 40. A very complimentary analysis of *Heartburn* that reveals the true identities of its leading characters while praising Ephron's use of "laughter as her best (antacid)

medicine" for marital heartburn. Carl Bernstein's real-life affair was with Margaret Jay, daughter of former Prime Minister James Callaghan and wife of former British Ambassador Peter Jay. Rachel's therapist is based on Dr. Mildred Newman, the coauthor of *How to Be Your Own Best Friend* (1971).

Koenig, Rhoda. "Yakety Yak (Don't Talk Back)." *New York* 16 (May 9, 1983): 78-81. Koenig dismisses the confessional strategy of *Heartburn* as lacking substantive content or graceful style, and she calls the novel flippant and hostile. Also argues that Ephron's plotting is unbelievable and that she dictates character traits rather than showing them in the actions of the characters.

Kriegel, Harriet. "Books: *Crazy Salud.*" *Commonweal* 103 (June 18, 1976): 412-413. Complains about Ephron's belief that beautiful or big-breasted women have no right to complain about America's sexist society. Kriegel is disturbed by what she calls Ephron's "feminine self-hatred."

Linda L. Labin

HEAT AND DUST

Author: Ruth Prawer Jhabvala (1927-   )
Type of work: Novel
Type of plot: Romance
Time of plot: The 1920's and the 1970's
Locale: Satipur, India
First published: 1975

Principal characters:

OLIVIA RIVERS, a beautiful, sensitive young English woman in
1920's India

DOUGLAS RIVERS, Olivia's husband, the Assistant Collector of
Satipur

THE NAWAB, the ruler of the princely state of Khatm, who has an
affair with Olivia

HARRY, the Nawab's English house-guest

THE NARRATOR, a young woman in the 1970's who is drawn to
India by her fascination with Olivia's letters

INDER LAL, the narrator's landlord, a simple Indian clerk who is
seduced by her

CHID, a confused English boy searching for salvation among the
Hindu swamis

Form and Content

Heat and Dust is the story of two English women who traveled to India, about fifty years apart in time, and recorded their experiences there in letters and journals. The stylistic arrangement of two parallel stories is creatively handled by means of excerpts from the narrator's journal interspersed with the details that she provides from the letters of the now-dead Olivia that she has in her possession. The reader needs to be alert to the constant shifts between the two tales as they trace fairly similar developments in the lives of the two women. The major historical difference that they encounter is that while Olivia came to India during a time when it was still a part of the British Empire, the narrator finds herself in a free country; the passage of time also means that there has been some progress in the way in which women are able to conduct their lives. The novel is focused on the lives of the two women and the decisions that they make fifty years apart: Though there are ironic similarities in the way in which their lives progress in India, their attitudes and actions are completely different in terms of personality. Through these differences, the author is able to convey the changes that have come about in women's lives through the years.

Olivia Rivers is bored and unhappy as the wife of a British colonial administrator in Satipur, India, and though she loves and adores her handsome husband, Douglas, she is moody and irritable until she meets the Nawab, a minor Indian prince of a neighboring state, and his English house-guest, Harry. The Nawab and Harry begin to provide the regular company and entertainment that Olivia craves, and though her husband and his friends disapprove of her friendship with a man of whom they are suspicious, she continues to see the Nawab, often without Douglas' knowledge. Aware that she is stepping in too deep, Olivia nevertheless seems powerless to stop her growing fascination with the handsome and unpredictable Nawab, until their closeness is sexually consummated. Meanwhile, Olivia and Douglas had been hoping to start a family, and when she finds herself pregnant, each man believes that he is the father (Douglas is unaware of her intimate relationship with the Nawab). Olivia, particularly upset when she learns from Harry that the Nawab is jubilant at the prospect of humiliating the British crowd when she gives birth to his child, arranges for an abortion; in the scandal that follows, she chooses to leave Douglas and go to the Nawab, who sets her up in her own house in the hills. She spends the rest of her days quietly, never leaving India, even after the death of the Nawab. Her only legacy is her letters, left with her sister Marcia.

These letters come into the hands of the narrator, who is Douglas' grandchild by his second marriage. She is inspired to trace Olivia's story in India more than half a century after it began in Satipur. The plain and unmarried narrator takes up residence in a house owned by Inder Lal, a simple Indian clerk with a life full of petty problems, and she keeps a journal of her life as she visits the buildings and places described in Olivia's letters and attempts to piece together the story of her life. Like Olivia, she ends up with two men in her life, the British boy Chid and her Indian landlord; unlike Olivia, however, she is married to neither and, in the progressive times in which she lives, is able to carry on her liaisons without scandal and without making any of them permanent. When she discovers herself to be pregnant, she decides to keep the child without informing the father, Inder Lal, and moves into the mountains where Olivia lived out her life. There she awaits the new phase in her own story.

Analysis

Ruth Prawer Jhabvala's central intention is to provide a voice for women, especially in the story of Olivia, which is chronologically earlier in time. A character such as Olivia is historically accurate, but very little is known about the thoughts of such people because they were never given a hearing. She is representative of the many English women who accompanied their husbands to India during the rule of the British Empire there and spent years in the country without ever recording or letting others know of their experiences or impressions; their lives were controlled by their husbands and the rest of the British community in India.

In fact, in *Heat and Dust*, Jhabvala is seen as rewriting the stories of such women in many colonial novels of the early twentieth century in which their opinions were not adequately voiced, the most well known of them being the English writer E. M. Forster's *A Passage to India* (1924). Even though Olivia's story, too, is regarded as a scandal by her own generation and is hushed up, the reappearance of her detailed letters to her sister makes it possible for the narrator to track down her life in India two generations later and to offer the reader her side of the tale. By cleverly juxtaposing her own experiences in India with those of Olivia, the narrator is also able to provide a sense of how women's lives changed all over the world in the course of the twentieth century.

Jhabvala, in both Olivia's and the narrator's stories, presents a range of strong women characters, against whom the men appear weak and ineffectual. Olivia must deal with the Begum, the Nawab's mother, who is a powerful matriarch in the palace. The narrator is befriended by Inder Lal's mother, who runs his household, as well as by Maji, an old woman of the town who is said to have supernatural powers. In contrast, all the men—Douglas, the Nawab, Harry, Inder Lal, and Chid—despite being the main political and social players, seem to lack strength, an indication perhaps that had women always been accorded the positions they deserved, all stories in history would have been different.

While the concept of a novel in the form of letters or journals is not original, Jhabvala's chosen form, excerpts from the narrator's journal interspersed with recollections from Olivia's letters, provides a new and interesting way of reading about two parallel lives lived many decades apart in the same Indian town.

Context

In the late twentieth century, the suppression of the woman's voice in history was given much attention. Jhabvala's *Heat and Dust* confronts the issue directly by telling the story of a woman who lived an unusually interesting existence in the early part of the century but was considered an embarrassment to her society because she did not live by the norms; by providing a voice for her through the interest of another woman, two generations later, Jhabvala seems to indicate not only that times have improved for women but also that only women can be relied upon to provide a fair hearing for other women; it is the duty of later generations of women to unearth the hidden lives of their forgotten female ancestors.

Besides providing a social commentary by two women living in times that are chronologically distant, *Heat and Dust*, one of Jhabvala's few historically based novels, offers a candid view of the life of a British colonial woman in India. It is a view that is rarely available in historical records or literary expositions of the time, despite the fact that there are hints in them of incidents and activities that make Olivia's fictional story believable.

Winner of the 1975 Booker Prize for fiction, *Heat and Dust* can be read in counterpoint to prior colonial novels based in India in which the woman is never given a strong voice. At the same time, it is a modern update on Olivia's story because the narrator's life and activities in India provide a glimpse of historical changes that have allowed women to make independent decisions about their own lives, without necessarily being criticized and ostracized by society.

Sources for Further Study
Crane, Ralph J., ed. *Passages to Ruth Prawer Jhabvala*. New Delhi: Sterling, 1991.

Contains ten previously unpublished essays that cover her novels and her short stories and delineate useful connections with other writers, such as E. M. Forster and Saul Bellow. Crane's essay "A Forsterian Connection: Ruth Prawer Jhabvala and *A Passage to India*" expounds on the important influence of the Forster novel on Jhabvala's work.

——————————. *Ruth Prawer Jhabvala*. New York: Twayne, 1992. One of the most comprehensive and useful critical appraisals of Jhabvala. Crane's analysis provides biographical details; readings of her work through the early, middle, and later Indian novels; analyses of the short stories and the American novels; and a commentary on the reception of her work by literary critics. Crane offers a time line of Jhabvala's life and work and a good bibliography for interested scholars.

Gooneratne, Yasmine. *Silence, Exile, and Cunning: The Fiction of Ruth Prawer Jhabvala*. New Delhi: Orient Longman, 1983. Building on work published in a number of earlier articles, Gooneratne has compiled an excellent, in-depth study of Jhabvala's fiction and her extensive work in writing for films.

Jha, Rekha. *The Novels of Kamala Markandaya and Ruth Jhabvala*. New Delhi: Prestige Books, 1990. Jha takes a thematic approach in considering the works of two major Indian women novelists in tandem; in her reading of Jhabvala's work, she concentrates on the novels to *Heat and Dust*, which is the writer's last fully Indian work of fiction, and provides a useful analysis of her major themes.

Jhabvala, Ruth Prawer. "The Artistry of Ruth Prawer Jhabvala." Interview by Bernard Weintraub. *The New York Times Magazine*, September 11, 1983, 64-65, 106, 110, 112, 114. Jhabvala speaks frankly about her early life and her career as a writer in this indispensable interview/profile.

Shahane, Vasant A. *Ruth Prawer Jhabvala*. New Delhi: Arnold-Heinemann, 1976. May be used as an introduction to Jhabvala's fiction up to *Heat and Dust*; a number of chapters have since been reprinted in journals and collections of essays.

Sucher Laurie. *The Fiction of Ruth Prawer Jhabvala: The Politics of Passion*. Basingstoke, England: Macmillan, 1989. Along with Ralph Crane's full-length study (above), an invaluable contribution to Jhabvala criticism that provides a feminist perspective to her work. Sucher discusses four of the novels (including *Heat and Dust*) and some related short stories in detail. She gives the reader a comprehensive overview of the passions of Jhabvala by tracing her quest for love and beauty in her fiction. Includes a selected bibliography.

Brinda Bose

THE HEAT OF THE DAY

Author: Elizabeth Bowen (1899-1973)
Type of work: Novel
Type of plot: Espionage
Time of plot: 1942-1944
Locale: London
First published: 1949

Principal characters:
>STELLA RODNEY, an attractive, upper-class, forty-year-old woman
>ROBERT KELWAY, Stella's lover, an army veteran who is attracted
>   to fascism
>ROBERT HARRISON, a counterspy who accuses Robert Kelway of
>   passing information to the Nazis
>RODERICK RODNEY, Stella's son, a soldier who is to inherit
>   Mount Morris, the family estate
>MRS. KELWAY, Robert's mother
>ERNESTINE, Robert's widowed sister
>COUSIN NETTIE, the widow of Cousin Francis
>LOUIE LEWIS, a lower-class working girl who picks up strange
>   men, usually soldiers
>CONNIE, an air-raid warden who befriends Louie

Form and Content

Set during the Blitz in the fall of 1942, *The Heat of the Day* is more than a spy thriller or a war novel. Although it has some elements of both, these genres rarely have a woman as the protagonist. Bowen makes the war a backdrop for Stella Rodney's ordeal and the issue of Robert Kelway's treason secondary to his betrayal of her. Stella faces the mutability and dislocation inherent in twentieth century life as she struggles to keep herself intact in a world that seems to be crumbling around her. Amid destruction and danger, class distinctions are broken down and emotions intensified. The people who have remained in London live without a past or a future. Caught in this external atmosphere of chaos, Stella's story is essentially the narrative of her expulsion from her self-defined Eden and her reconstruction of a new life.

As the story opens, Robert Harrison waits in Regent's Park for his meeting with Stella. Louie Lewis, a married working girl in the habit of picking up men in the park on Sundays, approaches Harrison. He rudely rebuffs her advances, but Louie's perception of Harrison as "funny" sets the stage for Harrison's obscene proposition to Stella. Stella has seen Harrison only once, at Cousin Francis' funeral, where he appeared looming over tombstones under a darkened sky. She imagines he is either a madman or a salesman. When he comes to her with his proposition that she become his mistress in order to stop or at least postpone her lover's exposure as a spy, Stella is overcome by uncertainty. She dismisses Harrison without an answer, but she cannot dismiss the seed of doubt that he has planted. The relationship that has sustained her and been the center of her life has been called into question. Stella is not horrified by Robert's treason so much as by what it reflects about the man she thought she knew perfectly. If Harrison's accusations are correct, Robert has betrayed more than his country.

The novel traces Stella's growing knowledge of the man she thought she knew. She prompts Robert to take her to meet his mother and sister at Holme Dene. There she realizes Robert has grown up amid lies and deceit, where language is meaningless and emotions are nonexistent. Visiting Robert's home forces Stella to give more credence to Harrison's accusations. Stella's son, Roderick, has inherited Cousin Francis' estate in Ireland, but because he is underage and in the army, he cannot attend to the affairs there. Stella must act on his behalf and visits Mount Morris, the scene of her honeymoon and where Roderick was conceived. Ireland remained neutral during the war, so Mount Morris provides a pastoral retreat from the devastation of London. Renewed by her visit, she confronts Robert with Harrison's story. He appears shocked at the suggestion but even more dismayed by Stella's keeping her suspicions to herself. The serpent has entered their garden and tainted their once-perfect understanding and trust. After the confrontation, Robert knows that he will be apprehended soon. Robert comes to Stella's apartment and confesses his guilt. He tries to escape his pursuers by climbing over Stella's roof but slips, or jumps, and is killed. Stella comes to realize the truth that Harrison and Robert are the destroyers of law, of morality, of identity.

Other truths come out as well. Roderick decides that he must visit Cousin Francis' wife, Nettie, at Wisteria Lodge, an institution for the mentally ill. Unlike the talk at Holme Dene, where nothing is said, the talk with Cousin Nettie brings to light the truth of Stella and Victor's divorce. Everyone assumed that Stella divorced Victor because of her involvement with another man, when in fact Victor fell in love with his nurse and left Stella to marry her. Stella allowed the fiction of her adultery because she would rather be an adulterer than a fool.

Amid these revelations, only Louie manages to create her own truth. Taken in hand by the competent Connie, Louie feels anchored and through the friendship gains some insight and knowledge. Her meeting with Stella overwhelms Louie and prompts her to reconsider her infidelities. Stella becomes for Louie an ideal of virtue until she reads about Robert's death. Without the ideal of Stella, Louie is forced to create an identity for herself. Inevitably, she becomes pregnant by one of her faceless lovers, but her husband is killed in action before she tells him of the child. When the boy is born, she names him Thomas Victor, even imagining a likeness between him and her dead husband. She returns to the South, presumably to devote herself to rearing her child. The novel ends with Louie holding up baby Tom so that he can see three swans flying west. Hence, the most positive solution to the issues of the novel is found by the most naïve and uncomplicated character.

Analysis

Although *The Heat of the Day* depends more on plot than Elizabeth Bowen's other novels, it is nevertheless thematic and, like her other novels, has at its center themes of dislocation and loss. In this novel, places serve as symbols of psychological and emotional loss. The two family homes, Holme Dene of the Kelways and Mount Morris of Cousins Francis and Nettie, are polar opposites. Stella's visit to Holme Dene is the beginning of her growth from ignorance to knowledge about Robert. The sign Caution: Concealed Drive greets anyone entering the place; the "drive" turns inward upon those unfortunates who live there. Holme Dene is a place where middle-class values of honesty and forthrightness are touted, while lies, deceit, and spying around corners are pervasive. It is, as Stella observes, a "man-eating" house, full of pretense and sterility—truly middle-class, but as Stella wonders, middle of what?

Mount Morris, on the other hand, is an illusion of pastoral innocence. To Roderick, it represents a future of possibilities that other characters in the novel lack and becomes the center of his imaginary life. Roderick understands the obligations of possession and heritage in a way that the inhabitants of Holme Dene do not. Holme Dene is perpetually for sale; Mount Morris cannot be sold. Yet it is the place where Cousin Nettie saw too much and was driven mad by it. As an Anglo-Irish aristocrat herself, Bowen is well aware of the colonial mentality, one shared by Cousin Francis. Stella is renewed by her visit to Mount Morris because it restores her vision of her heritage but, like Nettie, she realizes she could never live there. War-torn London is the ultimate symbol of emotional and psychological dislocation and loss. Because of the blackouts and bombings, all is reversed; day becomes night and night, day. People forget their past lives; Stella learns to ask no questions so that she will not have to answer any. Class differences are destroyed so much that Stella and Louie can becomes friends for a moment. The critical distinctions of past and present, truth and treason, exhilaration and despair have been shattered.

Bowen's finest achievement in the novel is her ability to create this psychological climate of war through language. The obscure and convoluted style of the novel, permeated by half-completed phrases, disrupted word order, and vague abstractions, reflects the state of mind of the characters. Stella's job at the War Office is to decode language. Louie is so unable to understand or express her experiences that she relies on Connie or the newspapers to do it for her. When there is no newspaper to describe her feelings, as when she meets Stella, she is inarticulate. Roderick understands the importance of language in the war, and Stella knows that those at the center of command use a language of calculated vagueness. Only Robert and Harrison refuse to believe in the power of language.

For Bowen, belief in easy language only leads to destruction and war. The war, then, is not a political issue but a psychological climate, a state of mind characterized by emotional disorder and expressed in language designed to avoid communication. In such a world, characters are not only lost and dislocated but have lost any hope of stability and purpose as well. At the end of the novel, Stella has moved to a much more dangerous apartment yet is engaged to marry a distant cousin: Love and death are the same. She has been able to keep herself intact but is unable to live meaningfully. Hers is the failure to connect the prose and passion of life. Throughout the novel, her private passion for Robert has been separated from the prose of public life, in this case the mutability and devastation of war. When the public war invades her private Eden, love is destroyed. The central thesis of Bowen's novel is that the only solution to the problem of deriving meaning in this world of endless change is through the individual, who must both be aware of and accept the essential dichotomy of life. In Bowen's terms, the connection must be made between the romantic passion and the necessary prose of life.

Context

Elizabeth Bowen was once heard to observe that when her friend Virginia Woolf discussed her feminist views, she was exceedingly tiresome. While Bowen may have been bored by Woolf's feminism, she certainly was not the upper-class conservative woman writer she was once thought. Her own life was filled with unconventional relationships, and she voiced repeatedly in her works a suspicion of "normal" conventional morality.

Her reputation as a writer of drawing room comedies of manners is inaccurate when one considers her longer fiction. In *The Heat of the Day*, Bowen questions traditional assumptions about the roles of women. She chooses the male-dominated genres of the war novel and spy thriller and makes her protagonist a woman. Further, the novel is not plot-centered, as are most novels of these genres. It is instead an examination of the emotional life of the female protagonist. Always wary of convention and normality, Bowen places Stella outside the role of moral anchor for her family. She dwells apart from any male idea of honor, either Harrison's or Robert's. Her homelessness is a willful choice, as is her perceived role as adulterer. Moreover, her relationship with Robert is not sanctioned by marriage. Louie, the other female character in the novel, is no more conventional in her behavior than Stella. Bowen may not have voiced active support for feminist issues, but in the case of this novel—as in her final work, *Eva Trout* (1968)—she shows her concern with women's issues and a deep understanding of the feminine psyche.

Sources for Further Study

Austin, A. E. *Elizabeth Bowen*. New York: Twayne, 1971. A study covering all Bowen's writings. An entire chapter is devoted to each novel, and her short stories are also discussed. Contains a good bibliography and concise critical comments.

Glendinning, Victoria. *Elizabeth Bowen: Portrait of a Writer*. London: Weidenfeld and Nicolson, 1977. Primarily a biography, with some literary criticism interspersed. Often referred to, it provides good background material.

Heath, William. *Elizabeth Bowen: An Introduction to Her Novels*. Madison: University of Wisconsin Press, 1961. Particularly concerned with placing her in the tradition of the English novel, but not necessarily as a woman writer. Contains an extensive bibliography of works about the theory of the novel and about Bowen.

Jordon, Heather Bryant. *How Will the Heart Endure: Elizabeth Bowen and the Landscape of War*. Ann Arbor: University of Michigan Press, 1992. An especially relevant topic when studying *The Heat of the Day*. Jordan discusses Bowen as an Anglo-Irish writer and the attitudes that she displays toward war as a result of her heritage. Not all the works are discussed, but the book contains a well-researched bibliography.

Lassner, Phyllis. *Elizabeth Bowen*. London: Macmillan, 1990. Analyzes Bowen's novels in somewhat technical prose with a feminist slant. Included is a brief summary of Bowen's life and a useful bibliography.

Rule, Jane. *Lesbian Images*. Garden City, N.Y.: Doubleday, 1975. Contains a chapter on Bowen but concentrates mostly on her final novel, *Eva Trout*. Focuses not so much on the literature as on how women writers fit into and influence the society of their times. Useful as background reading.

Jean McConnell

THE HEIDI CHRONICLES

Author: Wendy Wasserstein (1950-   )
Type of work: Drama
Type of plot: Feminist
Time of plot: 1965-1989
Locale: Largely New York City, with several scenes set in Chicago; Manchester, New Hampshire; and Ann Arbor, Michigan
First produced: 1988, at Playwrights Horizons, New York City, New York
*First published:*1989

Principal characters:
>HEIDI HOLLAND, a professor of art history at Columbia University
>SCOOP ROSENBAUM, Heidi's friend and sometime lover, who founds *Boomer* magazine
>SUSAN JOHNSTON, Heidi's high school friend, who becomes a legal clerk at the Supreme Court, a member of a women's health and legal collective, and an executive vice president for a television production company
>PETER PATRONE, a gay pediatrician who is one of Heidi's closest friends

Form and Content

The story of *The Heidi Chronicles* is told through a series of vignettes that extend from a high school dance in 1965 to Heidi's near future in 1989 (Wendy Wasserstein completed the play in 1988), when Heidi is a successful professor of art history at Columbia University. Throughout the play's thirteen scenes, the audience witnesses Heidi's development from an ordinary schoolgirl through her increasing dissatisfaction with her life before she finally develops greater acceptance of her career, her goals, and herself. The play also explores Heidi's evolving relationships with Susan, Peter, and Scoop, the three friends with whom she shares many of her most important moments.

While Scoop is always Heidi's friend, he is also occasionally her lover. She meets him in New Hampshire at an event supporting Eugene McCarthy's campaign for president. Heidi finds herself both attracted to and repulsed by Scoop's overwhelming confidence. His readiness to be judgmental exasperates Heidi, though she envies his self-assurance and the faith that he has in his own opinions. Unwilling to make a commitment to Heidi, Scoop ultimately marries Lisa, an illustrator of children's books who readily places Scoop's needs ahead of her own. By the end of the play, however, Scoop has grown as a human being. He sells his magazine, demonstrates concern for his children's future, and considers running for public office.

Peter functions in the play largely as an antithesis to Scoop. When he first meets Heidi in 1965, they form a close friendship through their youthful cynicism and the contempt that they display for conventions. Heidi comes to believe that, although she is strongly attracted to Scoop, Peter is the man with whom she has the most in common. On August 9, 1974, the date of Richard Nixon's resignation from the presidency, Peter reveals to Heidi that he is gay. From that time on, their friendship deepens as they share with each other the details of their romantic and personal relationships. On Christmas Eve of 1987, Heidi gives up her plans to accept a job at Carleton College, in Minnesota, so that she can remain near Peter, whom she has come to regard as a member of her own family.

Of all the characters in *The Heidi Chronicles*, Susan undergoes the most transformation. At the beginning of the play, she is a date-conscious teenager who cannot comprehend Heidi's indifference to the boys they meet at a dance. Throughout the 1970's and early 1980's, Susan experiments with several feminist causes. She is an active member of the Huron Street Ann Arbor Consciousness Raising Rap Group, considers founding a journal devoted to women's legal issues, and moves to Montana, where she joins a feminist health and legal collective. By the end of the play, however, Susan's shallowness has reemerged. She abandons her ideals and devotes her life to producing mindless situation comedies for television. With great insensitivity, Susan ignores Heidi's unhappiness and abruptly switches the topic to her plan for developing a comedy about women artists in Houston. One of the final references to Susan in the play occurs when Peter announces that she has contributed part of the profits from this television series to his hospital for children with AIDS: Susan's concern for others has degenerated to writing checks for popular causes.

Analysis

The Heidi Chronicles is Wendy Wasserstein's semiautobiographical play about life from the mid-1960's through the late 1980's. Although few of the incidents in the play have exact parallels in Wasserstein's life, Heidi serves as the author's witness to the confusion, frustration, and sense of disappointment that many young women felt during this period. It is not coincidence that the name "Heidi Holland" reflects the alliteration of Wasserstein's own name. Moreover, she also shares the name of the title character in the children's novel *Heidis Lehr und Wanderjahre* (1880; *Heidi*, 1884) by Johanna Spyri, about an energetic young girl who lives in the Swiss Alps. This character displays a mixture of youthful enthusiasm and maturity. While growing up, she helps the other characters deal with the problems that they encounter in their own lives. So, to a large extent, does the character of Heidi in Wasserstein's play.

This connection between Wasserstein's Heidi and the title character of Spyri's novel is reinforced during a climactic scene in the play when Peter wonders, "Did you know that the first section [of *Heidi*] is Heidi's year of travel and learning, and the second is where Heidi uses what she knows? How will you use what you know, Heidi?" Built upon this same structure, the first act of *The Heidi Chronicles* takes place in numerous locations as it follows Heidi's period of travel and learning. The second act, set solely in New York City, illustrates Heidi beginning to use what she knows and gradually coming to terms with herself and her own identity.

One of the most important lessons that Heidi must learn in *The Heidi Chronicles* is how to balance her career with her need to serve others and find meaning in her own life. This, in fact, is the goal that all the characters in the play are trying to attain. Peter becomes a successful pediatrician who develops a special ward for children with HIV infections. Scoop ultimately realizes the importance both of his children's future and of the political dreams he once had as a young man. Heidi finds a way of reconciling her need to love others with her desire to become a respected author and professor at Columbia University. In the final scene of the play, it is revealed that Peter has helped Heidi adopt a young daughter. Wasserstein indicates that this daughter, Judy, represents Heidi's hope for the future.

Other characters in the play fail to achieve Heidi's degree of balance. Susan, for example, tends to be motivated by whatever happens to be fashionable at the moment. During the mid-1960's, she is almost the stereotype of the teenaged baby-boomer. Her interests do not extend beyond dating, boys, and being popular. During the 1970's, Susan seems to have developed substantially and even appears to be more committed to feminist causes than Heidi herself, but this change of character is only a phase. During the economically aggressive 1980's, Susan forsakes both her feminist ideals and her friends, settling for financial success in the television industry. The picture of Susan that emerges is of a shallow individual who reflects the ideas of others rather than developing her own.

In a similar fashion, Jill, one of the members of the Huron Street Ann Arbor Consciousness Raising Rap Group, also fails to achieve the balance sought by the central characters. Though she speaks of her unhappiness in allowing everyone else to "lean on perfect Jill" while forgetting to take care of herself, Jill continues to demonstrate this fault. She nurtures the members of the discussion group as she had once nurtured her husband and children, always putting the needs of others ahead of her own. Lisa, too, prefers to serve Scoop and advance his career rather than satisfying her own needs. Her frustration with, and at times blindness to, Scoop's infidelity should prompt her either to leave home or to confront him with the situation. Lisa's habitual role of subservience to Scoop, however, prevents her from giving serious consideration to either of these options.

Of all the play's female characters, Heidi achieves the greatest balance between satisfying her own needs and meeting those of others. Nevertheless, Heidi still sees the final liberation of women as something that can be achieved only in the future. In 1986, she speaks to students of the girls' high school that she herself had attended and complains of feeling "stranded" as a woman. She had thought that "we were all in this together," and she is disappointed when other women fail to act this way. Even in the final scene of the play, she hopes that her daughter will "never think she's worthless unless [some man] lets her have it all. And maybe, just maybe, things will be a little better." For the moment, however, that hope has not yet been fulfilled.

Context

The Heidi Chronicles examines the frustration and disappointment that many women felt as they examined their opportunities and relationships throughout the 1970's and 1980's. The play explores these problems, however, without developing a tone of rancor toward men. Even Scoop, the one character whose cockiness and self-interest make him almost a villain for most of the play, is allowed to grow as a human being by the end of the drama. Fran, the character who is most bitter toward men and who blames them for most of the problems in the world, is a comic figure. Wasserstein's point is that women should regard men as sources of neither their self-worth nor their problems. If women hope to achieve balance in their lives, they must take charge of their own lives, realize that they are "all in this together," and create a future that will be more satisfying both for their daughters and themselves.

The importance of *The Heidi Chronicles* is that it expresses these ideas in a form that is palatable to a large popular audience. Rather than speaking of women's issues only to women, Wasserstein creates a work that entertains audiences of both genders. By including references to popular music, current events, and fashions that many viewers will remember from their own youth, Wasserstein presents characters with whom it is easy to identify. Because of its widespread appeal, *The Heidi Chronicles* won not only the 1989 Susan Smith Black Prize for the best play by a woman playwright but also the Pulitzer Prize for drama, the New York Drama Critics Award, and a Tony Award for the best play of 1989. Its success transcended boundaries of gender and allowed men and women alike to reflect upon the shared experiences of their young adulthood.

Perhaps for this reason, feminist reactions toward *The Heidi Chronicles* tended to be largely negative. Many critics did not regard Wasserstein as going far enough in explaining Heidi's unhappiness. A number of these authors also thought that the play dealt far too much with Heidi's romantic relationships and not enough with her work or her friendships with other women. The result, several critics have noted, is that Heidi gives lip service to feminist values but still appears to be dominated by the male characters in the play.

Sources for Further Study

Austin, Gayle. Review of *The Heidi Chronicles*. *Theatre Journal* 42 (1990): 107-108. Austin regards the play as simplistic and insufficiently feminist. She notes that Heidi is always depicted as deriving her happiness from the traditional roles of mother or lover and rarely from her work.

Hornsby, Richard. "Interracial Casting." *Hudson Review* 42 (1989): 464-465. In a scathing analysis of *The Heidi Chronicles*, Hornsby views the play's plot as aimless, its ideas as trite, and its characters as stereotypes. The critic attributes the play's popularity to "trendiness" and the fact that its author is a woman.

Keyssar, Helene. "Drama and the Dialogic Imagination." *Modern Drama* 34 (1991): 88-106. Keyssar regards *The Heidi Chronicles* as a failure since it depicts its title character only in reaction to an essentially male-dominated world, not in revolution against it. The author views few of the central characters as changing over the course of time.

Rose, Phyllis J. "Dear Heidi: An Open Letter to Dr. Holland." *American Theatre* 6, no. 7 (October, 1989): 26-29, 114-116. Rose argues that all art is political: It either supports or attacks the existing power structure. For this reason, she criticizes *The Heidi Chronicles* as focusing upon Heidi's relationship with men rather than the role that art or work plays in her life.

Weales, Gerald. "American Theater Watch, 1988-1989." *Georgia Review* 43 (1989): 573-575. The author questions why single parenthood seems to "fill the vacuum" in Heidi's life. Weales notes that Wasserstein lampoons most of the idealistic impulses of the 1960's and 1970's.

Jeffrey L. Buller

HERLAND

Author: Charlotte Perkins Gilman (1860-1935)
Type of work: Novel
Type of plot: Social criticism
Time of plot: 1914-1915
Locale: Herland, a remote and uncharted country populated entirely by women
First published: 1915 (serial), 1979 (book)

> *Principal characters:*
> VANDYKE (VAN) JENNINGS, a sociologist who is observant,
>   thoughtful, and introspective
> TERRY NICHOLSON, a wealthy explorer, pilot, and chauvinist
> JEFF MARGRAVE, a physician, botanist, and gentleman who
>   worships women sentimentally and uncritically
> ELLADOR, a young woman of Herland who marries Van and
>   prepares to accompany him on a reconnaissance of the outside
>   world
> ALIMA, a strong young woman who marries Terry but rejects him
>   when he tries to subdue her physically
> CELIS, an artistic young woman who falls in love with Jeff,
>   marries him, and becomes pregnant
> SOMEL, Van's tutor
> MOADINE, Terry's tutor
> ZAVA, Jeff's tutor

Form and Content

Herland is the first half of a witty, sociologically astute critique of life in the United States. This story concentrates ostensibly on three men—Van, Jeff, and Terry—who discover a small, uncharted country called Herland which, by force of an unusual accident of nature, has been governed and populated for two thousand years solely by women. Biological reproduction occurs miraculously by parthenogenesis (that is, without insemination). Charlotte Perkins Gilman exploits this contrived situation in order to contrast and compare the social features of a hypothetical woman-centered society to the harsh realities and crushing inequalities of everyday life found pervasively in male-dominated societies. The cohesive theme and primary purpose of *Herland* is the exposition of Gilman's interconnected ideas about economics, education, clothing, prisons, parenting, male-female relationships, human evolution, and social organization generally. In *With Her in Ourland*, the neglected sequel to *Herland* published in 1916, Gilman presents the second half of the Herland chronicle, dissects the patriarchal and technological madness of World War I, and points constructively to an alternative future based on the pragmatic application of feminist values. *Herland* is not fundamentally a utopian novel; rather, it is a lucid, persuasive analysis of modern life as Gilman saw it.

Gilman frames *Herland* as a series of narrative reminiscences told by Van, one of three male explorers who trek to Herland. Van recounts his easy capture, humane imprisonment, and gentle indoctrination to the language, culture, and history of Herland's all-female society. Van's detailed memoir includes recitations of the lessons taught to him and his male colleagues by three middle-aged female tutors, his firsthand observations and personal reflections, and the results of his supplemental readings form Herland's libraries. The effect is sometimes didactic. Readers learn many gazetteer-type facts: For example, Herland is ten to twelve thousand square miles in area, has a population of three million women, and supports a highly efficient, scientifically balanced agricultural economy based on tree culture. Van describes Herland as a pacific, highly evolved, and rationally ordered society molded by women who, beyond all else, value the happiness and welfare of their parthenogenically created children.

Gilman enlivens *Herland*'s didactic formula by having Van report verbatim several of his conversations (and those of his male companions) with Ellador and other Herland women. These frequently amusing and sometimes painfully ironic dialogues provide a point of direct contact where the men of Ourland and the women of Herland discover one another, argue, fall in love, and—in Terry's case—temporarily shatter the equality and powerful maternal calm of Herland. Unlike Terry, who never comprehends his chauvinism and its inherent destructiveness, Van finds his social consciousness raised through his discussions with Ellador. He is increasingly embarrassed by the massive shortcomings of the male-dominated culture that he represents.

The arrangement and style of *Herland* result in part from its publishing history. Gilman, unable to interest established publishing houses in her work, originally self-published the twelve brief chapters that comprise *Herland* as monthly installments in her feminist magazine, *The Forerunner*. The frequent restatement of central themes from chapter to chapter reflects Gilman's practical need to remind her readers of key elements in the story left unattended during the month-long intervals between issues of *The Forerunner*. *Herland* sparkles most brightly from within the pages of *The Forerunner* where, in many well-stocked libraries, *Herland* can still be read serially in context and in concert with Gilman's essays, poetry, and other major serialized fiction and nonfiction projects published during the brief but extraordinary life of *The Forerunner* from 1910 to 1916.

Analysis

By Gilman's own estimate, her novels failed as literary experiments. As a pedagogical device, however, *Herland* is an engaging, persuasive, and highly effective effort. The novel's light, patient, sympathetic voice is a worked example of the tolerant, noncoercive instructional mode employed by Herland's exemplary tutors: Somel, Moadine, and Zava. Sociological instruction through fiction is one of Gilman's literary strengths, and it is difficult to find a more straightforward instance of this genre than Gilman's own *First Class in Sociology* (1897-1898), a short novel of hypothetical classroom dialogue serialized in the *American Fabian*. Sociological instruction via fiction is a powerful educational tool utilized by several women sociologists: Examples include Harriet Martineau's *Illustrations of Political Economy* (1832-1834), Mari Sandoz's *Capital City* (1939), and Agnes Riedmann's *The Discovery of Adamsville* (1977). Judged pedagogically as a work that entertains and provokes while also teaching complex and sophisticated ideas, *Herland* is a superb sociological accomplishment.

The socially problematic issues that Gilman outlines in *Herland* echo the theoretical proposals of Lester F. Ward (1841-1913), a major American sociologist who admired Gilman and vice versa. Ward's concept of gynecocentric (that is woman-centered) social theory reinforces Gilman's strong belief in the fundamental rationality of women's values and social contributions. Gilman developed this perspective at length in her nonfiction works. *Herland* reflects, in greatly simplified form, sociological ideas comprehensively examined in Gilman's *Women and Economics* (1898), *Concerning Children* (1900), *The Home: Its Work and Influence* (1903), *Human Work* (1904), and the novel *The Man-Made World* (1911).

The overarching theme in *Herland* is that from women's roles and values as mothers springs a fundamentally important social current that society ignores at its collective peril. Mothering, in this view, is a social activity in which all members of society engage together. A social mother, Gilman maintained, is concerned with not only the welfare of her own children but also the support, happiness, and prosperity of all children. If the world were run from the point of view of social mothering, it would, presumably, evidence many of the positive social attributes of *Herland*: a healthy and well-educated populace, humane prisons, efficient use of resources, and so forth.

The premise that women's values provide an excellent basis for society was not unique to Gilman. Several prominent women sociologists, including American Nobel laureate Jane Addams (1860-1935), were feminist pragmatists who subscribed to a range of views similar to Gilman's. A brief and important precursor to *Herland* is Addams' witty and biting 1913 essay "If Men Were Seeking the Franchise," which was published in *Jane Addams: A Centennial Reader* (1960). Addams, who was a friend and colleague of Gilman, describes a hypothetical, bisexual society (otherwise similar in situation to *Herland*) in which women dominate the populace and have the political power to deny men the right to vote. Addams whimsically concludes that men, much like the men who venture to *Herland*, cannot safely be allowed to share in government until they abandon their selfish and destructive ideas.

Gilman's personal perspective as a mother is revealed in her autobiography, *The Living of Charlotte Perkins Gilman* (1935). Gilman's decision after a much-publicized divorce to give custody of her daughter, Katherine, to her former husband, Charles W. Stetson, is a consequential example of Gilman's idea that children should be reared by the one who is best at parenting—and that this individual is not necessarily the biological mother. The cooperative, mothering attributes of the society sketched in *Herland* no doubt comprise the kind of social situation that Gilman wished for her own daughter.

Context

The initial influence of *Herland* was restricted primarily to regular readers of *The Forerunner*, in which *Herland* was serialized in 1915. By extending reduced-price subscriptions of *The Forerunner* to participants, Gilman tried to encourage the formation of "Gilman Circles" in which the contents of her magazines, including *Herland*, were to be discussed by women in small, face-to-face groups. Poor sales, however, caused the demise of *The Forerunner* and the collapse of Gilman Circles. Overall, *The Forerunner* reached few readers, and thus *Herland* had minor social or literary force. From 1916 to 1979, the novel remained buried in the pages of Gilman's defunct magazine.

The impact of *Herland* increased dramatically when its chapters were collated and republished together in book form by Pantheon Books in 1979. *Herland*, forty-four years after Gilman's death and sixty-four years after the serialized first publication, reached a new feminist audience. The republication of *Herland* was promoted as the recovery of "a lost feminist utopian novel," and the work quickly attracted attention from feminists in the growing women's studies movement.

Yet, radically abstracted from the serial context of *The Forerunner* and divorced from *Herland*'s concluding sequel, the 1979 edition of *Herland* had a perplexing impact on the women's movement. Gilman was championed in some quarters as advocating the establishment and superiority of women-only communities of the type outlined in *Herland*, and the book version became a popular rallying point for radical separatists within the women's movement. That result, paradoxically, is opposite to Gilman's clearly expressed view that the future of the world depends crucially on the enlightened cooperation of men and women, mothers and fathers, laboring together side by side.

Other feminists, criticizing the 1979 book-length edition of *Herland*, find it sometimes naïve, ethnocentric, masculinist, and even racist. Superficial readings of Gilman's enthusiastic embrace of evolutionary principles and her complex ideas relating to race improvement brand Gilman in some quarters as politically incorrect. Such criticisms, however, often neglect the intellectual context in which *Herland* was originally published and ignore the precise ways in which Gilman defined her terms and offered cooperative solutions to many social problems. Gilman never intended the satirical, fictional romps that comprise *Herland* and *With Her in Ourland* to be definitive or comprehensive statements on the complicated moral and philosophical issues that she discussed at length in *The Forerunner* and elsewhere.

The potential impact of *Herland* on women's issues today remains largely unfulfilled. Whereas the work has become justifiably a recognized classic in women's literature, separatist politics and postmodern critiques deflect serious discussion of Gilman's insightful analyses of oppressive patriarchal social systems, as well as her dedication to constructive human advancement. When *Herland* is conjoined to *With Her in Ourland* and carefully studied in the context of *The Forerunner* and Gilman's nonfiction books, the progressive feminist ideas reflected in *Herland* may someday have the cooperative, forward-looking social impact that Gilman so ardently intended.

Sources for Further Study

Allen, Polly Wynn. *Building Domestic Liberty: Charlotte Perkins Gilman's Architectural Feminism.* Amherst: University of Massachusetts Press, 1988. An outstanding analysis of Gilman's interrelated ideas about homes, communities, and the social arrangement of the built environment.

Deegan, Mary Jo. *Jane Addams and the Men of the Chicago School, 1892-1918.* New Brunswick, N.J.: Transaction Books, 1988. This monograph is the major study of the Chicago women's sociological network, centered at Hull House, in which Gilman participated. Deegan's work is indispensable for untangling many of the relevant intellectual currents that defined Gilman's era, especially the concept of "cultural feminism."

Hill, Mary A. *Charlotte Perkins Gilman: The Making of a Radical Feminist, 1860-1896.* Philadelphia: Temple University Press, 1980. A major biography of Gilman and the one to which students should turn first. Hill presents an astute, well-documented, and trustworthy account of Gilman's early life and the origins of her ideas.

Karpinski, Joanne B., ed. *Critical Essays on Charlotte Perkins Gilman.* New York: G. K. Hall, 1992. An ambitious compendium of wide-ranging contemporary, reprinted, and original literary essays and critical assessments. Although somewhat technical, Lois Magner's study carefully explores Gilman's ideas on evolution and social Darwinism.

Keith, Bruce. "Charlotte Perkins Gilman (Stetson)." In *Women in Sociology*, edited by Mary Jo Deegan. New York: Greenwood Press, 1991. Presents a useful and straightforward overview of Gilman's work, writings, and stature as a sociologist. Keith includes a bibliography of Gilman's major works and a list of critical sources.

Lane, Ann J. *To Herland and Beyond: The Life and Work of Charlotte Perkins Gilman.* New York: Pantheon, 1990. This popular biography interprets Gilman primarily from a psychological perspective (an orientation that Gilman rejected) and stresses Gilman's family and interpersonal relationships. Unfortunately, Lane gives short shrift to major social issues and the intellectual milieu in which Gilman labored.

Meyering, Sheryl L., ed. *Charlotte Perkins Gilman: The Woman and Her Work.* Ann Arbor, Mich.: UMI Research Press, 1989. This compendium offers fourteen frequently referenced critical essays, three of which focus on *Herland*.

Scharnhorst, Gary. *Charlotte Perkins Gilman: A Bibliography.* Metuchen, N.J.: Scarecrow Press, 1985. This reference is indispensable for serious students. Scharnhorst lists 2,173 of Gilman's writings, including many found only in obscure magazines. This useful book also includes a compilation of published criticism, biographical materials, and relevant manuscript collections.

Michael R. Hill

HERSELF IN LOVE AND OTHER STORIES

Author: Marianne Wiggins (1947-   )
Type of work: Short stories
First published: 1987

Form and Content

Marianne Wiggins' volume *Herself in Love and Other Stories* includes thirteen stories ranging in length from a few pages to twenty-four. Each follows the general outline of the short story, focusing on one major character and one specific situation. Since the settings of the stories vary in time and place, Wiggins uses a style and language appropriate to the locale and type of character she has created. Likewise, the tone of each story varies from delightful humor to biting satire to lyrical pathos. Each story is almost a perfect miniature, making the volume a collection of thirteen perspectives on life. An examination of three stories can serve to illustrate the major aspects found in Wiggins' writings.

The story "Stonewall Jackson's Wife" is based on the life and death of the Confederate Civil War General Thomas Jonathan Jackson (1824-1863), known as "Stonewall" Jackson. It is evident that Wiggins has researched the history of the general's life at the time he was mortally wounded and the subsequent funeral for Jackson, who next to Robert E. Lee was the South's greatest and most loved general. Also evident is a fine portrayal of the facts surrounding his family life and home in the South; his deceased first wife, Eleanor; his second wife, Anna; and his daughter Julia.

The story is, however, not written in the traditional style of historical fiction. The narrator—a first person "I"—is the spirit of Stonewall Jackson's first wife, who comments, often disparagingly, on the events from the time that the news of the general's death first reaches the household in Richmond, Virginia, until the funeral train departs for Lexington, Kentucky. As narrator, Eleanor allows all the characters to speak in their own voices—ranging from the slaves who first report the death, to the dying words of the general, to the often unpleasant and unfeeling discourse of the genteel second wife.

It gradually becomes obvious that the personality of the general changed significantly during the time between his first and second marriages. The younger Jackson was a joyous and passionate man, while the older man seems concentrated on being a devout Calvinist engaged in long periods of prayer and a morose fighting man primarily intent on serving his country. The second wife is portrayed as a loveless woman whose only concern is to ensure that General Stonewall Jackson receives a burial befitting a great military hero. Anna feels slighted when the ongoing war makes it impossible for the military hierarchy to attend the funeral, she despises the masses of ordinary people and soldiers who come to mourn, and she cannot understand why those whom she ignores in turn reject her and pay homage to the general's daughter. There is a haunting similarity between the people's response to their young general—

who is called Jack by those who love him—and the funeral and cortege of another young Jack—President John F. Kennedy—who was also shot, dying exactly one hundred years after Stonewall Jackson.

"Gandy Dancing" is the story of a modern alienated man who, in a moment of recognition of his state of being, strikes out and does the unexpected. One day shortly before Christmas, a businessman arrives as usual by commuter train at New York's Grand Central Station. Rather than going to work that day, he decides to see the country by train. His itinerary has him fly to Atlanta, continue to New Orleans, board *The Sunset Crescent* to Los Angeles, and return immediately on the *Desert Wind* to Chicago, from where he will fly home. The entire trip should last eight days. Although the man's real name is not revealed until the last page of the story, during his journey he goes by the name of "Redcar," an epithet he acquired on the spur of the moment while still in college. It is obvious that this man can only enjoy life when fantasy allows him this special appellation; otherwise, he answers to a terribly common name.

On his journey through the United States, Redcar, like any other normal traveler, meets his equals: a zipper manufacturer from Wheeling who wears fancy lizard-leather shoes, a man and wife from Phoenix whose six-year-old son is probably a normal child (he claims to have forgotten his absent sister's name), or a group of inebriated gamblers en route from Los Angeles to Las Vegas. Yet Redcar does not recognize himself in these people while traveling in his dream world. His world is the world of trains: the long-distance trains with famous names, the architectural splendor of railroad stations, and most important, the train's operating personnel. He is especially drawn to the train's fireman, whose only duty these days is checking the condition of the tracks at redblocks (that is, when the signal lights adjacent to the tracks are red). The highlight of Redcar's journey comes when he is actually invited to join Thayer, the fireman, one night in Colorado as he examines the tracks. During this inspection period, Thayer tells Redcar in an almost mystical and highly lyrical language of the beauty of the world of empty tracks, suggesting that this experience was indeed "gandy dancing." Redcar had become one with the glorious world of the train's fireman and thereby fulfills his dream.

Although the theme of the alienated individual or life in a dream world has been used by other writers, Wiggins does not allow her protagonist to escape completely from the reality of his life. Redcar periodically realizes that he should have telephoned his wife, but he does not make the call until he arrives in Chicago. The climax of this story reveals that this vagabond dreamer has temporarily left a real family—a wife, two daughters, a suburban home, and a station wagon—who agonize over his disappearance. Despite the fact that the main character is an alienated man, the reader is reminded that there are also women and children in this alienated world.

The enigmatic tale entitled "Pleasure" offers the reader the story of two women and several children who watch a whale beach itself, return to the deep, and die by never surfacing again. Yet that is only the superficial plot of this story. Wiggins' primary purpose in this narrative is to consider the mystery surrounding the actions and demise of the largest and oldest known mammal and the corresponding mystery of the ultimate fate and destiny of the older of the two women. The reader who may ask about the cause of their deaths or the sins that they may have committed will receive no answers.

When the dying whale first comes ashore, these naïve but compassionate people are bewildered. They have never encountered such a creature in close proximity and react in a predictable but totally inappropriate manner. The children believe that by merely telling the whale to return to the sea, as they might address a pet, the whale will leave. They even attempt to push the huge creature with their tiny bodies. The younger woman is likewise unable to understand and is sent away with the children to fetch men and machines to right the problem of the dying whale.

Once alone with the whale, the older woman begins a discourse of passion and compassion; they become one in spirit. Just as this large sea creature is condemned to defeat and death for having lived a life of beauty and grace, so the older woman must suffer for her life of passion in a world that does not condone such human pleasure. They have met on the edge between land and sea, and they have learned of their fate. The whale returns to the deep, never to surface again, and the older woman returns to the land where, like Lot's wife, she is turned into a pillar of salt. "Pleasure" is perhaps the most complex story in this collection. Its symbolism and highly lyrical prose make for difficult but rewarding reading.

Analysis

Marianne Wiggins' short stories contain characters who represent a vision of human beings psychologically damaged in the course of attempting to live what could be perceived as normal lives. Her characters are real, sometimes even biographical, and yet they are always fictional. For example, in "Stonewall Jackson's Wife," Wiggins is ultimately not interested in describing the historical times of Stonewall Jackson's life and death, the behavior of his wife Anna, or what might have been if the first wife had not died. Instead, she offers a penetrating examination of the transformation that her characters have experienced. Wiggins also makes use of characters already established in literature or other art forms. In "Pleasure," she recalls the wife of the biblical figure Lot in order to exemplify the human agony experienced by the older woman. In this story, the reader observes how a story is used to create a new fictional reality capable of portraying great pathos.

The inclusion of considerable humor is a hallmark of virtually all Wiggins' writings. In "Gandy Dancing," this humor is evident not only in the caricature portraits of the secondary characters but also in the despair represented by the foolish actions of Redcar. It must always be remembered, however, that the use of humor is not Wiggins' goal but only a means of expressing the consequences of the main character's actions.

The main purpose of the short stories included in this volume is to offer a penetrating examination of the human world. Wiggins is—and yet is not—a moralist. She makes an unrecognizable reality understandable and a fiction real. Her characters continue to exist past the end of each story, forcing each reader to continue contemplating her portrait of an emotionally damaged human being.

Context

Almost all the characters in this collection of fiction are women, but Wiggins is by no means a writer who only writes and speaks about her own gender. She concentrates on that very fine point where her protagonists encounter an impossible world—indeed, where they attain the position of the classic heroine, but in modern dress.

One can only speculate and wonder what the outcome of the Civil War might have been if "Stonewall Jackson's Wife," Eleanor, had not died and could have continued to provide her husband with a life of reason, passion, and love, rather than the commitment to war he acquired after her death. Another unanswered question is raised in the story "Pleasure," answered even when it was first included in the book of Genesis. Neither story provides any evidence that the unnamed woman had committed a sin. She is turned into a pillar of salt, she falls accidentally from a state of innocence and grace into a sleep of woe for no apparent reason. Marianne Wiggins raises many such questions, but she does not supply answers. She believes that it is the task of the writer "to touch the nerve that otherwise, unwatched, falls or to certainly, only. I write about the things I fear." Her readers are taught to fear in that same way.

Sources for Further Study

D'Evelyn, Thomas. "Families, Satires, Kinship, Parody." *The Christian Science Monitor*, August 5, 1987, p. 17. A short, article which concentrates on "Quicksand" and "Candy Dancing."

Eder, Richard. Review of *Herself in Love and Other Stories*. *Los Angeles Times Book Review*, August 16, 1987, p. 3, 15. An article that examines Wiggins' writing, with special emphasis on "Herself in Love" and "Stonewall Jackson's Wife."

Kakutani, Michiko. "Books of the Times: *Herself in Love*." *The New York Times*, August 19, 1987, p. C20. A review article of this collection of stories, included discussion of "Candy Dancing."

Lattoon, Mark. "Adele Goes West." *London Review of Books*, September 19. A review of *Herself in Love and Other Stories* with a more extensive portion of "Stonewall Jackson's Wife."

Rich, Barbara. "Miniaturists at Work." *The Women's Review of Books*, 20. A review of the stories that examines Wiggins' language and particular.

Wiggins, Marianne. Interview by Michele Field. *Publishers Weekly*, July, 1989, 57-58. An interview with Wiggins that provides useful bibliographical information.

ultimate fate and destiny of the older of the two women. The reader who may ask about the cause of their deaths or the sins that they may have committed will receive no answers.

When the dying whale first comes ashore, these naïve but compassionate people are bewildered. They have never encountered such a creature in close proximity and react in a predictable but totally inappropriate manner. The children believe that by merely telling the whale to return to the sea, as they might address a pet, the whale will leave. They even attempt to push the huge creature with their tiny bodies. The younger woman is likewise unable to understand and is sent away with the children to fetch men and machines to right the problem of the dying whale.

Once alone with the whale, the older woman begins a discourse of passion and compassion; they become one in spirit. Just as this large sea creature is condemned to defeat and death for having lived a life of beauty and grace, so the older woman must suffer for her life of passion in a world that does not condone such human pleasure. They have met on the edge between land and sea, and they have learned of their fate. The whale returns to the deep, never to surface again, and the older woman returns to the land where, like Lot's wife, she is turned into a pillar of salt. "Pleasure" is perhaps the most complex story in this collection. Its symbolism and highly lyrical prose make for difficult but rewarding reading.

Analysis

Marianne Wiggins' short stories contain characters who represent a vision of human beings psychologically damaged in the course of attempting to live what could be perceived as normal lives. Her characters are real, sometimes even biographical, and yet they are always fictional. For example, in "Stonewall Jackson's Wife," Wiggins is ultimately not interested in describing the historical times of Stonewall Jackson's life and death, the behavior of his wife Anna, or what might have been if the first wife had not died. Instead, she offers a penetrating examination of the transformation that her characters have experienced. Wiggins also makes use of characters already established in literature or other art forms. In "Pleasure," she recalls the wife of the biblical figure Lot in order to exemplify the human agony experienced by the older woman. In this story, the reader observes how a story is used to create a new fictional reality capable of portraying great pathos.

The inclusion of considerable humor is a hallmark of virtually all Wiggins' writings. In "Gandy Dancing," this humor is evident not only in the caricature portraits of the secondary characters but also in the despair represented by the foolish actions of Redcar. It must always be remembered, however, that the use of humor is not Wiggins' goal but only a means of expressing the consequences of the main character's actions.

The main purpose of the short stories included in this volume is to offer a penetrating examination of the human world. Wiggins is—and yet is not—a moralist. She makes an unrecognizable reality understandable and a fiction real. Her characters continue to exist past the end of each story, forcing each reader to continue contemplating her portrait of an emotionally damaged human being.

Context

Almost all the characters in this collection of fiction are women, but Wiggins is by no means a writer who only writes and speaks about her own gender. She concentrates on that very fine point where her protagonists encounter an impossible world—indeed, where they attain the position of the classic heroine, but in modern dress.

One can only speculate and wonder what the outcome of the Civil War might have been if "Stonewall Jackson's Wife," Eleanor, had not died and could have continued to provide her husband with a life of reason, passion, and love, rather than the commitment to war he acquired after her death. Another unanswered question is raised in the story "Pleasure," unanswered even when it was first included in the book of Genesis. Neither story provides any evidence that the unnamed woman had committed a sin. She is turned into a pillar of salt; she falls accidentally from a state of innocence and grace into a state of woe for no apparent reason. Marianne Wiggins raises many such questions, but she does not supply answers. She believes that it is the task of the writer "to touch the nerve that otherwise, untouched, lulls us to complacency. I write about the things I fear." Her readers are taught to fear in the same way.

Sources for Further Study

D'Evelyn, Thomas. "Parable, Satire, Romantic Parody." *The Christian Science Monitor*, August 5, 1987, p. 17. A review article which concentrates on "Quicksand" and "Gandy Dancing."

Eder, Richard. Review of *Herself in Love and Other Stories*. *Los Angeles Times Book Review*, August 16, 1987, p. 3, 15. An article that examines Wiggins and her stories, with special emphasis on "Herself in Love" and "Stonewall Jackson's Wife."

Kakutani, Michiko. "Books of the Times: *Herself in Love*." *The New York Times*, August 19, 1987, p. C20. A review article of this collection of stories, with an extended discussion of "Gandy Dancing."

Lambert, Mark. "Adele Goes West." *London Review of Books*, September 17, 1987, 19. A review of *Herself in Love and Other Stories* with a more extensive examination of "Stonewall Jackson's Wife."

Rich, Barbara. "Miniaturists at Work." *The Women's Review of Books*, March, 1988, 20. A review of the stories that examines Wiggins' language and technique in particular.

Wiggins, Marianne. Interview by Michele Field. *Publishers Weekly*, February 17, 1989, 57-58. An interview with Wiggins that provides useful biographical and bibliographical information.

Thomas H. Falk

HIS OTHER HALF
Men Looking at Women Through Art

Author: Wendy Lesser (1952-   )
Type of work: Social criticism
First published: 1991

Form and Content

In this collection of thematically related essays in criticism, Wendy Lesser makes her subject the portrayal of women in works of art created by men. What she hopes will emerge is a deeper understanding of men's relationship to the feminine, as revealed through art. The context of *His Other Half: Men Looking at Women Through Art*, as Lesser sees it, is a climate of gender-theory obsession, a climate whose separatist pressures she resists. Specifically, she absolves the artists whom she discusses from the accusation of misogyny, although one of the criteria that had led her to choose these particular artists is their willingness to risk that charge—and, one might add, the willingness of some feminist critics to make it. While Lesser concedes that some male artists may justly be accused of misogyny, a mere exposé of misogyny is not her concern here.

Drawing on the psychoanalytic tradition inaugurated by Sigmund Freud, especially as developed in the work of the British psychoanalyst D. W. Winnicott, Lesser employs as an organizing device the Platonic myth of the divided self. According to this myth, found in Plato's *Symposium*, human beings were at an earlier time unified with—shared the body of—another being. The present gender isolation is not a natural condition, and people seek in their relationships with others to reestablish the primal unity that was lost. The myth may allude symbolically to the physical separation from the mother at birth and to the psychic separation that follows the physical. This separation, Lesser implies, is felt with special poignancy by the male child, since, for him, identification with the mother must be transcended as he grows to manhood. It is in severing himself from his mother that the male artist begins to become both man and artist. His achievement as artist will be more or less closely linked to the struggle between the desire to reunite with the maternal source of his being and the resistance to that desire that may seem vital to the artist's individual survival.

In the book's eleven essays, Lesser develops her thesis through the examination of the work of writers of fiction (among them Charles Dickens, D. H. Lawrence, George Gissing, and Henry James), one poet (Randall Jarrell), one painter (Edgar Degas), one photographer (Sir Cecil Beaton), and several film directors (including Alfred Hitchcock, Preston Sturges, King Vidor, and Billy Wilder). Two of the essays may at first seem out of place here, since their subjects—Marilyn Monroe and Barbara Stanwyck—are women. Lesser is interested in these women primarily as society knows them through their appearances in motion pictures directed by men. That is, although Monroe and Stanwyck were real women (known, however, by false names), Lesser examines them as, in a sense, creations of men.

Two principles of order determine the arrangement of the chapters. One is the progression from artist-as-child to artist-as-adult. The other is a progression in the view of women: Chapter 2 focuses on the woman as mother; the Degas and Gissing chapters on woman alone; the James and Hitchcock chapters on woman as opponent in the sexual battle; the Jarrell, Beaton, and Monroe chapters on woman as the artist's mirror; and the Stanwyck chapter on a recapitulation of all phases of the book. The last chapter closes the circle.

Chronological order is avoided. It is Lesser's position that works of art transcend their time, even though they are a part of their time. It is also her position that works of art transcend gender even as they partake of it.

Analysis

Woman-as-mother organizes chapter 2, in which Lesser discusses the work of Charles Dickens, D. H. Lawrence, and two of her contemporaries, Peter Handke and Harold Brodkey. For Lesser, it is through the exploration of autobiographical material, in which the death of the mother and the growth of the writer become intertwined, that these authors are able to free themselves as artists.

The painter Edgar Degas and the novelist George Gissing focus on woman alone. Degas' nudes, sometimes seen as evidence of misogyny, rather reflect his perception of woman as the hero of modern life. Not at all voyeuristic, these works articulate a definition of privacy. Their implications are finally utopian: They suggest an imaginary place in which a willingness to leave the other alone is somehow combined with an identification with the other's body to the point of feeling it as one's own.

George Gissing provides Lesser with her second example of an artist who focuses on woman alone. Lesser singles out for special attention *The Odd Women* (1893), a book so much in the spirit of feminism that, had it been written by a woman, it might be considered too polemical. Gissing transcends the familiar masculine-feminine opposition, urging both men and women to be womanly (by which he means "tender") not womanish (by which he means "weak"). In spite of his feminist values, however, Gissing implies that class is finally a more damning limitation than gender, an insight Lesser seems to endorse.

Woman as opponent in the sexual battle informs the next two chapters. Lesser's chapter on Henry James, while discussing several of his novels, emphasizes *The Bostonians* (1885-1886), a novel by which many feminists feel violated. In *The Bostonians*, the lesbian feminist Olive Chancellor loses the woman she loves to Basil Ransom, a man readers often perceive as an embodiment of sexism. The mistake that feminist critics too easily make, says Lesser, is to assume that James identifies with, or even much likes, his male character. Of all American novelists, Lesser notes, James is the master of multiple viewpoints. No one surpasses him in the exploration of the ways in which the right answer differs according to the position one assumes. This is the attitude in which he approaches the sexual battles of *The Bostonians*.

Lesser finds the films of Alfred Hitchcock supremely interesting for their examination of issues of strength, equality and inequality, and respect and trust in the relationship between men and women. Hitchcock's readiness to explore these issues has at times made him the target of accusations of misogyny. It is true, Lesser acknowledges, that women are often victims in Hitchcock's films, but at his best he probes the process of victimization, rather than merely inviting viewers to participate vicariously in that process.

Lesser's discussions of the poet Randall Jarrell, the photographer Cecil Beaton, and the film star Marilyn Monroe work variations on the theme of woman as the artist's mirror. Jarrell's divided sensibility and the importance in Beaton's work of mirrors, reflections, and siblings suggest the desire for reunion arising out of the division of self symbolized in Plato's myth. Marilyn Monroe, on the other hand, in part because of her unique combination of strengths and limitations, became a perfect mirror for all people. (When Lesser says "all," she means both men and women.) The male artist's realization of Monroe's possibilities, while undeniably involving exploitation and manipulation, contributes, at least to some degree, to a dissolution of the barriers of gender.

The chapter on Monroe brings the reader closer to the closing of the circle. Before that moment, however, Lesser recapitulates the phases of the book in the process of celebrating Barbara Stanwyck. A high point of this chapter is the discussion of *Stella Dallas* (1937), directed by King Vidor, a film that has for orthodox feminists often represented the unqualified triumph of patriarchal values. What Lesser sees in *Stella Dallas* is an unsurpassed exploration of the roles and relationships of women. In the character of Stella—played by a woman under the direction of a man—woman as mother, woman alone, woman as opponent in the sexual battle, woman as mirror, and woman as triumphantly and unapologetically herself are all embodied.

In her final chapter, Lesser states the criterion implicit in all of her judgments: Artists fail insofar as they make their creations the puppets of their ideologies; they succeed by setting their creations free. By this criterion, the subjects of Lesser's study must be respected as considerable artists, and their work recognized as evidence for Lesser's view that great art leaves behind both the "masculine" and the "feminine."

Context

Wendy Lesser's subject has significant implications for women, since women have a special interest in how their gender is depicted in art. That Lesser is primarily concerned with art produced by men acknowledges men's historical domination of the art world. Her subject, then, might have been chosen by any feminist critic in the last decades of the twentieth century.

Yet Lesser's relation to feminism is complex. Nowhere in her book does she describe herself as a feminist, and is frequently critical of what she calls "orthodox feminism." One of her tactics is to oppose her reading of a text to a feminist misreading. The climate of gender-theory obsession that she challenges has largely been the creation of feminist critics. Lesser's refusal to construct her argument on historicist lines would be viewed with suspicion by many feminists. Her claims that great art leaves behind the masculine and feminine; her suggestion that the circle can and should be closed; her reminder (borrowed from the novelist Dorothy L. Sayers) that, although women are different from men, they are more like men than like anything else in the world—all this might be seen by some feminists as a retreat to a supposedly discredited humanism.

Yet perhaps Lesser has opened up precisely the sort of questions that a vital feminism requires. Her fundamental assertion is that ideology offers at best a limited guide to reality. An ideology that rejects constant self-questioning is already far along the way to becoming an orthodoxy. If Wendy Lesser does not declare herself a feminist, she is no enemy of what is most creative in feminism. A feminism that did not have room for her critical spirit would be a poorer one.

Sources for Further Study

Hauser, Arnold. *The Social History of Art.* 2 vols. New York: Alfred A. Knopf, 1951. As the title suggests, a study of the arts in social context from prehistoric times to the film age. This sweeping study provides a useful context for Lesser's more narrowly focused investigation.

Hollander, Anne. *Moving Pictures.* New York: Alfred A. Knopf, 1989. A provocative exploration of the links between painting and cinema. The willingness to juxtapose supposedly high art and popular culture parallels Lesser's approach. Hollander was one of the original reviewers of *His Other Half.*

Hudson, Liam, and Bernadine Jacot. *The Way Men Think: Intellect, Intimacy, and the Erotic Imagination.* New Haven, Conn.: Yale University Press, 1991. A husband and wife who are also a scientist and a painter explore questions of creativity and gender that often echo Lesser's interests.

Paglia, Camille. *Sexual Personae: Art and Decadence from Nefertiti to Emily Dickinson.* New Haven, Conn.: Yale University Press, 1990. A provocative—some would say outrageous—journey across many cultures and most of the arts. Like Lesser, but more aggressively, Paglia distances herself from orthodox feminism, as well as from some other orthodoxies. Also like Lesser, she is concerned with questions of gender and artistic creativity. Paglia wrote an enthusiastic review of *His Other Half.*

Warner, Marina. *Alone of All Her Sex: The Myth and Cult of the Virgin Mary.* New York: Alfred A. Knopf, 1976. Examines the development in art and culture of one of the West's most powerful symbols of womanhood. The book, by one of the original reviewers of *His Other Half,* can usefully be compared to Lesser's work for subject, methods, and conclusions.

Winnicott, D. W. *Playing and Reality.* London: Tavistock, 1971. Winnicott is a major influence on Lesser, who includes five of his books, including this one, in her bibliography. By no means easy reading, but accessible to the general reader.

W. P. Kenney

HISTORY
A Novel

Author: Elsa Morante (c. 1912-1985)
Type of work: Novel
Type of plot: Historical realism
Time of plot: 1941-1947
Locale: Rome, Italy
First published: La Storia: Romanzo, 1974 (English translation, 1977)

> *Principal characters:*
> IDA MANCUSO, the protagonist, a simpleminded, timid young
> woman
> NINO MANCUSO, Ida's rebellious, streetwise teenage son
> GUNTHER, a nineteen-year-old German soldier who rapes Ida
> USEPPE, Ida's son by Gunther
> DAVIDE SERGE, a tormented, nonviolent, Jewish Marxist

Form and Content

History: A Novel is Elsa Morante's depiction of World War II from the point of view of ordinary Italians. Written in the sweeping tradition of nineteenth century realism, with aspects of Magical Realism, each of the nine chapters represents a year in the lives of one or more of the major characters. Each is preceded by a list of the principal events of world history, including battles, workers' strikes, and weapons development, lists created perhaps by the near-omniscient "I" who narrates the story. Throughout the novel, Morante shows the devastating effects of political events on the lives of common people, especially on Ida and her family.

The novel begins during Ida Ramundo's Sicilian childhood, during which she suffers from epileptic seizures accompanied by unconsciousness. In the 1930's after Italy's Fascist alliance with Adolf Hitler, Ida marries Alfio Mancuso, becomes a schoolteacher in Rome, and bears a son, Nino. When Ida's mother dies, Ida learns that her mother was Jewish. Terrified that someone will report her to the anti-Semitic fascist authorities, Ida keeps the secret, even as she begins to haunt Rome's Jewish ghetto. Her husband dies, and while Ida has tried to hold on to a middle-class lifestyle, his death marks the beginning of her slide into poverty and isolation.

One day, drunk and lonely, Gunther, a nineteen-year-old German soldier, rapes Ida, which triggers in her an epileptic seizure and unconsciousness. Gunther is killed three days later when his plane is shot down on its way to the North African front. Ida hides the pregnancy that results for fear of losing her job. After the birth, she tells Nino, who spends more time on the streets than at home, that she found the child abandoned. A deep affection develops between Nino and the baby Guiseppe, whom they call Useppe.

As the war in Europe rages, Rome's Jewish Ghetto becomes a ghost town, as trainloads of Jews are deported to "forced labor camps." Nino leaves to join the Italians fighting on the side of the Germans. When Allied bombs hit German-occupied Rome, Ida's apartment is destroyed, and she and Useppe move to a government shelter. There is little food, and Ida starves herself in order to feed Useppe. One of the inmates of the shelter is Marxist pacifist Davide Serge, a Jew. Detained by the Germans, he escaped and is hiding out at the shelter. A letter tells him that the members of his bourgeois family, whom he has rejected, have been killed in a concentration camp. When Nino shows up, having changed sides and formed a partisan band, Davide joins him. They carry out brutal attacks against Nazi soldiers.

After the war is over, Ida's school reopens, and she rents a room in a nearby slum. Nino visits the family occasionally, espousing the ideology of the revolution against the new Italian government. A black marketeer, he is smuggling guns to the revolutionaries. Not yet twenty-one, he is killed while fleeing the police with a cache of weapons. Ida keeps Nino's death a secret, but, uncannily, Useppe knows. The boy begins to have nightmares and epileptic "spells" similar to Ida's but much more violent.

Davide is also in Rome. Shattered by the brutalities of the war, he has become a drug addict, and just after a visit with Useppe, he dies of a heroin overdose. A few days later, Useppe dies from an epileptic seizure. On finding her six-year-old son's body, Ida's reason for life is gone and she goes mad. The story finishes with another list of world events, which include assassinations, nuclear testing, and bombing in North Vietnam, ending with the words, "and History continues."

Analysis

The saying goes that, "History is written by the victors." In this novel, however, Morante offers a history that focuses on the powerless, whose lives are tangled in the web of world events. The main characters have no hand in shaping the destructive political agendas of their country, but each deals with their terrifying consequences. Roman Jews whom Ida knows by name are killed because of the Fascists' alliance with Hitler. Once the Allies have won the war, Ida and Useppe no longer starve. Gunther's rape of Ida is also shown as another example of history's effect on the individual; it was only because of larger world events that the young German was in Italy at all.

Morante's use of historical circumstances and layers of documentary detail give this work a verisimilitude. By juxtaposing the words "A Novel" and "History," however, she calls into question any narrative, including hers, that stamps itself as truth. Moreover, she adds a nearly omniscient narrator and touches of Magical Realism to the narration of gritty everyday events.

The book is also Morante's platform from which to offer her mix of Christian and Marxist ideologies. Useppe's birth by a father of unknown origin, his supernatural powers, his blanket ability to love and generate happiness, and his several falls before his early death show him as a Christ figure. His otherworldly abilities—his ability to communicate with animals and understand the language of the trees, as well as his psychic connection to other people—also illustrate Morante's humanistic ideal: that all life is connected. Useppe's bright spirit offers the world a chance of redemption, but his frail power is not enough to change humanity. Traumatized by the catastrophes perpetuated by history, he dies after six years of life.

Useppe's mother is also a Madonna-like figure. Though a widow with a son, Ida's relatively scant sexual experience give her the qualities of a virgin. In addition, the rape, which produces the magical Useppe, takes on a supernatural air because of Ida's seizure. Ida's redemptive power is in her maternal devotion and self-sacrifice, the antithesis of the political forces around her. When her mothering role is destroyed by forces she cannot control—she blames history for her sons' deaths—she retreats into madness, silence, and eventually death.

The possibility of redemption is also the undercurrent in the ideology of Davide Serge. Through him, Morante airs her own Marxist analysis of world events. Davide sees the powerful economic forces shaping devastating political choices, and he articulates the idealistic vision of a humanistic workers' paradise. Davide's war experiences, however, leave him tormented, questioning his faith in humanity and his ideology. He turns to drugs in order to alleviate his psychic pain and dies another victim of the war and history. His redemptive potential, like Ida's and Useppe's, dies with him.

The story's ending is a pessimistic one, suggesting that the never-ending cycle of history, despite the tragic lessons of the past, will continue to crush goodness and humankind's attempts at personal happiness. Yet, Morante cannot finally sustain such hopelessness. On the last, otherwise blank, page, she offers these words of hope written by a political prisoner: "All the seeds failed, except one. I don't know what it is, but it is probably a flower and not a weed." It is Morante's hope that the book is a seed that does not fail to act on her readers as both warning and object lesson.

Context

The 1960's and 1970's were a time of great social protest in Italy, and Morante's Marxist polemics reflect a political position common at the time. As many feminists point out, however, Marxism finds the basis of women's oppression in economics rather than in sexual politics. With its strong Marxist focus, this work, while it follows the struggles of a female main character, is not representative of Italian feminist writing. Rather than protesting the limitations of orthodox female roles, Morante depicts traditional motherhood as a heroic, if ultimately powerless, force in a world gone mad with war. Played out against World War II, which was directed by men who sent the sons of their countries to kill and to die, Ida's self-sacrificing devotion to Useppe, her desperate focus on his survival, is a powerful force on the side of life. Despite near-starvation, air raids, deportations, and the deaths of countless others, Ida keeps her son alive, starving herself and even stealing in order to feed Useppe.

Unlike her mother, who had the outward appearance of womanly submission yet rebelled within the family, timid and simpleminded Ida grows up to accept her traditional role. During her short-lived marriage, Ida submits passively to her husband's authority, and while she does work as a schoolteacher, it is her own children that are her reasons for living.

Yet the all-consuming selflessness finally drives Ida into insanity and death. Having no other meaningful identity and unable to protect Nino and Useppe from death, Ida's mind snaps; the narrator notes that though she lives another nine years, she really died with Useppe. Ida's death is reminiscent of her namesake, the operatic character Aida, a slave who joins her entombed lover rather than live without him. Useppe's other protector, a female sheepdog, who is Ida's double, also dies, shot while fiercely trying to keep the child's body from being removed from the house.

Ida's madness, like her earlier "spells," does allow her to escape the patriarchal conditions, the dehumanizing effects of history, that have caused her so much hardship. Yet Morante's depiction of Ida's insanity does not seem a feminist protest against her character's limited life. Ida's madness seems more the natural consequence of both the emotional overload of her already simple mind and her selfless devotion, a devotion that Morante seems to applaud.

Sources for Further Study

Amoia, Alba della Fazia. *Women on the Italian Literary Scene: A Panorama*. Troy, N.Y.: Whitson, 1992. A survey of the works of nineteenth and twentieth century Italian women writers, including *History*, offering an overview of their place in that country's literary history. Includes a chronology marking the years between 1846 and 1991 when various women writers were born and dates of significant publications, a selected bibliography of primary and secondary sources, and a comprehensive index.

Aricó, Santo L., ed. *Contemporary Women Writers in Italy: A Modern Renaissance*. Amherst: University of Massachusetts Press, 1990. A collection of essays on twelve Italian women writers active since the 1940's. The chapter on Morante looks at autobiographical elements, as well as traumatic central motifs, in her body of work. There is a bibliography of works in Italian and in English on Italian literary history, general works about women authors, and literary theory, as well as comprehensive bibliographies for individual women writers.

Caesar, Michael, and Peter Hainsworth, eds. *Writers and Society in Contemporary Italy*. New York: St. Martin's Press, 1986. Prefaced by a description of post-World War II Italy's political and literary culture, this collection includes essays on ten influential Italian writers of the period. Each essay is followed by a bibliography of the author's work and suggestions for further reading. The chapter on Morante examines the use of imagination, Magical Realism, and the themes of childhood and history in her works.

Mandrell, James. "The Prophetic Voice in Garro, Morante, and Allende." *Comparative Literature* 42 (Summer, 1990): 227-245. A comparison of three female writers' historical novels, including *History*, suggesting that the narrative structures in women's historical novels differ from the male model.

Mora, Gabriela, and Karen S. Van Hooft, eds. *Theory and Practice of Feminist*

Literary Criticism. Ypsilanti, Mich.: Bilingual Press, 1982. This collection of essays first describes diverse feminist approaches to literary criticism, then offers analyses of the works of fiction using these frameworks. The short article on Morante focuses on her condemnation of the bourgeois Italian family structure and values in three novels, including *History*.

Kristen Montgomery

HISTORY OF WOMAN SUFFRAGE

Authors: Susan B. Anthony (1820-1906), Matilda Joslyn Gage (1826-1898), Ida
   Husted Harper (1851-1931), and Elizabeth Cady Stanton (1815-1902)
Type of work: History
Time of work: The late eighteenth century to 1920
Locale: The United States and Great Britain
First published: 1881-1922

> *Principal personages:*
> MARY WOLLSTONECRAFT, an eighteenth century British feminist
>   and author
> HARRIET MARTINEAU, a British novelist and economist
> LUCRETIA MOTT, an important American social reformer
> SARAH and ANGELINA GRIMKÉ, American sisters who worked for
>   the abolition movement
> MARGARET FULLER, an influential advocate for women's rights
>   in the United States
> CARRIE CHAPMAN CATT, one of the women responsible for the
>   passage of the Nineteenth Amendment granting women's
>   suffrage
> FRANCIS WRIGHT, an American women's rights activist
> LYDIA CHILD, an American women's rights activist

Form and Content

   History of Woman Suffrage, a chronological narrative with documents, comprises
six volumes averaging one thousand pages apiece. The broad purpose of this massive
work was to lend intellectual and moral support to feminists, and their male allies, in
their struggles between 1881 and 1920 to extend the franchise to women. Universal
white manhood suffrage had all but been accomplished by the mid-1840's, an area in
which Americans then led the world. In 1870, as a part of post-Civil War Reconstruction, ratification of the Fifteenth Amendment prohibited denial of the vote because of
race, color, or previous condition of servitude; thus the franchise was extended to
African American males, including those who had been freed from slavery by the
Thirteenth Amendment in 1865.

   The great discontinuity in such extensions of the franchise in the extension of
democracy was the general preclusion of voting by women. Despite the fact that in
some localities a few women had participated in voting during Colonial days and a
few subsequently enjoyed voting rights during the first half of the nineteenth century,
though still only locally, these were insignificant exceptions to the prevailing practices
of a male-dominated society. Whatever the opinions the majority of women may have
held regarding the value of the franchise to them during the eighteenth and nineteenth
centuries—and these are unknown—many thousands of educated and articulate

women certainly considered their denial of the vote a rank injustice. Abigail Adams had reminded her husband, John, of that fact during the drafting of the Constitution, and others like her had gained notoriety during each of the nation's nineteenth and early twentieth century cycles of reform. For example, the principal authors-editors of *History of Woman Suffrage*, Elizabeth Cady Stanton and Susan B. Anthony, had organized and led the famous gathering of feminists at Seneca Falls, New York, in 1848. Another author-editor, Matilda Joslyn Gage, had been an active participant in the agitations following it from the 1850's into the 1900's. Each advocated a wide range of women's rights, chief among them the right to the vote.

Not until 1879, late in their long careers as feminist reformers, did Stanton and Anthony decide to compile *History of Woman Suffrage*. Division between the American Woman Suffrage Association (AWSA), headed by Lucy Stone, and their own National Woman Suffrage Association (NWSA) lent impetus to the project. They sought primarily to establish the greater significance of their association, to emphasize the priority of suffrage reform over other feminist objectives, to provide subsequent generations of suffragist with documentation of their movement, and not least to make it more difficult for male historians (there were scarcely any other kind) to overlook their lifetime of struggle for all forms of feminine equality.

History of Woman Suffrage, was an intensely collaborative effort. To further their work, the principal authors-editors lived together for months at a time. Anthony, who for years had been collecting documents, continued to do so, while Stanton assumed general responsibility for writing most of the connective narrative passages. The somewhat younger Gage wrote three chapters of volume 1. Both Stanton and Anthony labored in unison over the tedious editing required for the three initial volumes, while Ida Husted Harper was browbeaten into superintendence over the latter three. Overall, the work includes references to and excerpts from newspapers, journals, and speeches and the writings of scores of outstanding feminists and female suffragists, as well as contributions by some of their male colleagues. There are reminiscences, notably by Stanton and Anthony; detailed reports of suffragists' efforts in many states, along with the legislative results thereof; records and proceedings of state and national woman suffrage conventions; documentation on the complex political and gender divisions over suffrage during Reconstruction; and accounts of the activities of woman suffrage organizations and the actions of state legislatures that led to the drafting and ratification of the Nineteenth Amendment in 1920, granting women the vote.

Analysis

With their suffrage proposals triumphant in only four western states when they died, Stanton, Anthony, and Gage nevertheless suffused the first three volumes of their history with their ebullience, with their unswerving belief in the justice of their cause, and with their informed high purpose, producing an élan that marked subsequent volumes as well. While they were confident of their own high principles, their advocacy of woman suffrage, as the work amply documents, was plagued nevertheless by the criticisms and indifference of society-at-large, crippled by personal animosities and organizational frictions among suffragists, and wracked by conflicts between suffragist priorities and those of other feminists and reformers. Yet despite the density and tedium of some of its inclusions, the tome of *History of Woman Suffrage* conveys frank good sense, as if with distant vision the suffragists had assumed the stance of future generations asking why, given the obvious justice of universalizing the vote for women, its attainment required so many years of struggle.

History of Woman Suffrage is more than a painstaking assemblage of speeches, journal excerpts, documents, legislative activities, and organizational vicissitudes. The first volumes, chiefly the handiwork of Stanton and Anthony, which they completed in 1886, are thus rich in historical context designed to deepen the suffragist movement's self-awareness. To this end, volume 1 traces the origins of suffrage reform within broader ranges of feminist reformism, discernible by the late eighteenth century and reaching an early pinnacle at the Women's Rights Convention assembled in Seneca Falls on July 19, 1848. During these years, as part of the expansive democratic sentiments that were affecting much of American society—most apparently during the presidency of Andrew Jackson—women's rights advocates promulgated a comprehensive challenge to traditional and predominantly male social values. In their thrust toward winning equality, they demanded legal reevaluations of marriage, divorce, and birth control, as well as reassessments of property rights for women. They were a principal force behind temperance movements and a vigorous adjunct to the increasingly vocal and influential antislavery movements of the 1850's. Within this wide spectrum, the demands for suffrage advanced by women such as Stanton, Anthony, Gage, and others became the key to achieving most other feminist objectives.

Because the authors-editors of *History of Woman Suffrage* recognized their own place within this environment of general reform, they were mindful of the importance of other feminist leaders whose principal goals did not center on the suffrage issue. For this reason, Stanton and Anthony respected, by inclusion, references to or the writings and speeches of the great British feminists Mary Wollstonecraft and Harriet Martineau, as well as foremost Americans such as Lucretia Mott, Sarah and Angelina Grimké, Margaret Fuller, Francis Wright, Lydia Child, and Carrie Chapman Catt. They also addressed the concerns of dozens of other figures less well known to later generations, such as Martha C. Wright, Eliza W. Farnham, Mariana W. Johnson, Harriot K. Hunt, Lydia Fowles, Pauline Wright-Davis, Ann Preston, and Mrs. Collins, who was also credited with being the founder of the first women's suffrage society. (The American Woman Suffrage Association is mentioned in the work, but Lucy Stone, the leader of these rival suffragists, refused to contribute).

The first volume is the record of a movement growing in confidence and influence, one supported on principle by a number of prominent male reformers, most of them leading abolitionists. This confident note continues into the early pages of the second volume, which cites women's contributions to the antislavery cause and their Civil War efforts; their subsequent support of the Thirteenth, Fourteenth, and Fifteenth Amendments to the Constitution; and the convening of the first postwar woman suffrage convention. Yet the suffrage movement, the history notes, fell upon hard times during Reconstruction (1867-1877). When erstwhile abolitionists and male legislators confronted what they perceived as a political choice between winning extensions of civil rights, including voting rights to African Americans (meaning at the time African American males) or universalizing the vote for women, they chose to back extensions of freedoms to black males and virtually abandoned the cause of woman suffrage.

Volumes 3 through 6, therefore, survey what were predominantly the campaigns of the National American Woman Suffrage Association (an organization created by the merger of the NWSA and the AWSA) in key states and localities, the strategies formulated in annual conventions, and legislative losses and gains year by year until the ratification of the Nineteenth Amendment in 1920.

Context

By the close of the twentieth century, *History of Woman Suffrage* was judged by male and feminist historians alike to be a major source for the study of nineteenth century women's rights movements, as well as an important source for the study of the lives and views of Stanton and Anthony. Accordingly, it was reprinted in 1970 by Source Book Press, while Mari Jo and Paul Buhle condensed and edited *The Concise History of Woman Suffrage: Selections from the Classic Work of Stanton, Anthony, Gage, and Harper*, published by the University of Illinois Press in 1978. Though the original work was never intended for general readers, later perceptions of its importance fully justified the efforts of Stanton and Anthony in launching this multivolume work and overseeing much of it to fruition. Judged within the context of its times—that is, the years from 1881 to 1922—*History of Woman Suffrage* may rank as the principal, if not the sole, scholarly contribution to literature concerning the struggle for women's rights in the United States.

History of Woman Suffrage is regarded as a monument in particular to the steadfastness and perseverance of Stanton and Anthony. In a social and political environment that was almost continuously hostile to their aspirations and objectives, they not only invested the six volumes with their emotional and intellectual substance but also drew heavily upon their own financial resources to bring them to publication. It was a feat accomplished amid extremely busy individual, familial, and public lives.

Sources for Further Study

Banner, Lois W. *Elizabeth Cady Stanton*. Boston: Little, Brown, 1980. A useful portrait of Stanton intended for nonspecialist readers. Banner focuses on Stanton's radicalism in the context of her times and the interplay of her conservative origins and radical bent upon her personality. Contains brief chapter essays on sources and an inadequate index.

Barry, Kathleen. *Susan B. Anthony: A Biography of a Singular Feminist*. New York: New York University Press, 1988. An excellent, enjoyable study which concentrates, as might be expected, on Anthony's character development, rather than on

History of Woman Suffrage. Offers many splendid photographs, chapter notes, and an extensive bibliography.

Dubois, Ellen Carol. *Feminism and Suffrage.* Ithaca, N.Y.: Cornell University Press, 1978. A clearly written, scholarly study of the independent women's movement in the United States from Seneca Falls (1848) through the early years of Reconstruction (1869). Excellent for its examination of the political complexities and divisions over suffrage and other women's rights. A bibliography and an index are included.

Griffith, Elisabeth. *In Her Own Right: The Life of Elizabeth Cady Stanton.* New York: Oxford University Press, 1984. A vigorous, scholarly study that treats the full range of Stanton's feminist activities and places her powerful advocacy of woman suffrage in an appropriate context. An important work since Stanton was widely recognized as the principal leader and chief advocate of women's rights during the nineteenth century. Excellent photographs, appendices, notes to pages, and a valuable index are provided.

Kraditor, Aileen. *The Ideas of the Woman Suffrage Movement, 1899-1920.* New York: Columbia University Press, 1965. An outstanding study which carefully traces its subject and important personalities through the ratification of the Nineteenth Amendment in 1920. When supplemented by Ellen Carol Dubois' study (above) and by perusal of *History of Woman Suffrage* itself, Kraditor's work completes a continuous history of woman suffrage. Contains a bibliography and an index.

Clifton K. Yearley

HOLY FEAST AND HOLY FAST
The Religious Significance of Food to Medieval Women

Author: Caroline Walker Bynum (1941-   )
Type of work: Social criticism
First published: 1987

Form and Content

Focusing on the lives of several hundred Christian women in Europe between 1200 and 1500 who were noted for their religious devotion, *Holy Feast and Holy Fast: The Religious Significance of Food to Medieval Women* is a groundbreaking exploration of their lives. These women's religious practices centered on the Eucharist: a rite of communion by which, in partaking of bread and wine, they received into their bodies the body and blood of Christ in all of its redemptive power. According to author Caroline Walker Bynum, in their elaboration of Eucharistic practices these women created distinct forms of spirituality with deep personal meaning and broad cultural influence.

Bynum's portrait of the lives of medieval holy women, marking a clear departure from previous studies of their lives, has inspired broad reassessments among historians about women of that era. Before Bynum, scholars who studied medieval women focused on their marginalization in society. While Bynum grants that women were subjugated, she argues forcefully that, generating their own distinct spirituality, numbers of women in the late Middle Ages exercised considerable power in relation to families, church authorities, and communities.

Bynum locates women's power in a piety centered on food: food from their tables that sustained the poor, food from their bodies (milk or other fluids) that healed others, and food of the Eucharist that united them with God. She establishes the variety of religious roles available to medieval women, outlines the significance of food practices to these roles, and demonstrates that, although food was featured in the religious life of all medieval Christians, it figured most prominently and distinctively in the lives of holy women. Refusing standard interpretations of medieval women's lives, Bynum summons a wealth of evidence to secure her larger claim: Medieval holy women employed resources available to them—especially food—to soar in triumph above the "tidy, moderate, decent, second-rate place" that society had intended for women.

Bynum's account is notable for its subject—the religious lives of medieval women—and also for its form: gender-sensitive historical analysis. Bynum's compelling study of medieval life establishes that the previously documented marginalization of women was produced, in part, by modes of inquiry hitherto favored by historians. Because scholars used tools of inquiry that did not permit a sophisticated grasp of gender in medieval society, they overlooked or misconstrued important facets of that society. The lives of holy women were misunderstood, as were the religious practices and social interactions of men and women in the larger society. By contrast, Bynum's tools of inquiry, fashioned expressly for the exploration of gender, not only bring women into focus but also illuminate a medieval world that is different from the one that scholars had observed previously. Thus, Bynum's work marks a turning point inn historical research for what she says about women's lives and for the means that she employs to build her case: a gender-sensitive mode of historical analysis that reshapes not only what is known about medieval women but also what is known in general about the Middle Ages.

Analysis

According to Bynum, food and food metaphors were featured prominently in thirteenth and fourteenth century Europe. Food divided rich from poor and informed a key cultural ethic: Overeating was a mark of privilege, and sharing food with the hungry was a primary symbol of benevolence. Food also had religious significance. Christians believed that those who luxuriated in food paid the penalty for the sin of gluttonly; those who renounced food through regular fasting obtained salvation. Moreover, in late medieval piety, Christians linked salvation with the individual reception of God in the Eucharist, which they described by appeal to graphic metaphors of nourishment. Tasting the broken body of Christ in the Eucharist, Christians became one with the suffering flesh crucified on the cross and obtained their salvation.

Notable among those for whom the Eucharist was central to faith were women who, in saintly asceticism, deliberately abstained from all food but God's food: the Eucharist. Hagiographic records which Bynum examines indicate that, although women were only 18 percent of those canonized as saints between 1000 and 1700, they comprised 23 percent of those who died from asceticism and 53 percent of those for whom illness was central to their sanctity. Moreover, the majority of Eucharistic visions and miracles were attributed to women: Of the twenty types identified by Bynum, only two were performed exclusively by men and those were linked to consecration of the Eucharist, which was a male prerogative in any case. Eight other types of miracles featured women primarily, and four were associated exclusively with women's spirituality.

Because hagiography is not entirely reliable in the reconstruction of history, Bynum supplements her argument with evidence drawn from the lives of religious men. Acknowledging that food asceticism and Eucharistic devotion can be located in the vitae of men, Bynum shows also that, in contrast to the holy women of the late medieval age, food in all of its miraculous and mystical powers was not at the center of men's religious lives.

Tracing further the special significance of food asceticism for holy women, Bynum observes its association with practical dualism: Some women, ascribing a negative value to their bodies and to nature, did cease to eat in order to discipline and defeat bodies that they perceived as sinful. Distancing herself, however, from historians who had claimed previously that dualism played a prominent role in medieval women's lives, authorizing and sustaining their subjugation, Bynum demonstrates that fasting by holy women was a "flight not so much from as into physicality." Believing that

God saves the world through the physical, human agony of the crucified Christ, these women viscerally embodied that theology: In their Eucharistic piety, these holy women incorporated as their own the suffering body of Christ and became the tormented flesh that saved. Subsequently, their bodies bore stigmata (bodily wounds like those of Christ) or produced fluids (like the blood of Christ) that healed others.

Moreover, citing the larger social significance of holy women's embrace of fasting, Bynum observes that, far from constraining women's lives, asceticism empowered women. Holy women could use their ascetic behaviors to manipulate parents into acceding to their wishes not to marry. Were they to vomit up the Host, testifying that it had not been consecrated and was yet human food, they could successfully challenge the authority and integrity of the priest who had offered it. More than one priest was run out of town, condemned in his sin by the testimony of holy women. Throughout Europe, many persons were drawn to the charismatic authority of women who saved others through the powerful example of their own suffering and their gift of healing. Escaping subjugation, these women were able to maneuver beyond societal limits in fulfillment of spiritual visions that also granted them significant social power.

Although Bynum's scholarly erudition is above reproach, some critics of her work have challenged her conclusions. That asceticism brought much physical pain to holy women, sometimes culminating in their deaths from self-starvation, has led some persons to qualify Bynum's assertion that holy women were personally and socially empowered by their religious practices. Nevertheless, few historians would subscribe today to a model of medieval religious life that would bypass Bynum's work, for the larger cultural context that she has so brilliantly illuminated is now viewed as a necessary point of departure for the study of asceticism and other aspects of medieval religious life.

Context

Bynum uses gender in *Holy Feast and Holy Fast* as a basic grid on which to lay out her research findings and deploys food, with all of its mystical and sacred potential, as a unifying theme on that grid. As a result, she brings the lives of late medieval women to visibility in ways that have required historians to recast their presentation of religious and cultural life in the late Middle Ages. Although the increased attention given by historians of the Middle Ages to issues of gender cannot be traced solely to Bynum's influence, she has played and continues to play a central role in these ongoing developments. That so many new assessments of medieval asceticism and/or the lives of medieval women bear the mark of her influence confirms that Bynum, more than other historians, is responsible for breaking the mold in which previous scholarship about women and the society of late medieval Christendom was produced.

Bynum's influence on the way in which gender is examined in the fields of history, literature, and the academic study of religion also has exceeded the boundaries of her own specialization in the late Middle Ages. That *Holy Feast and Holy Fast* has been received so positively in academic circles as a work of exceptional scholarship has energized an entire generation of women scholars who, conducting research on gender in a variety of fields in the wake of Bynum's intellectual achievements, have found that their efforts are taken more seriously by their colleagues. Because Bynum blazed such a broad trail with this work, the road traveled since by women scholars who study gender has been less rocky: They have consolidated earlier gains in scholarship on gender and have forged ahead in new directions, often using Bynum as a model for their own explorations of gender.

Sources for Further Study

Bell, Rudolph. *Holy Anorexia*. Chicago: University of Chicago Press, 1985. Using autobiographies, letters, confessors' testimonies, and canonization records, Bell examines the lives of more than 250 Italian holy women for signs of anorexia. He argues that these women, like some modern teenagers who engage in self-starvation, fasted as part of a larger struggle for liberation from a patriarchal family and society. Bell's quantitative data (enhanced by helpful charts) augments Bynum's research; however, Bynum's cultural analysis of the significance of food for medieval women is richer and more nuanced than Bell's, which focuses primarily on the psychology of women's fasting.

Bynum, Caroline Walker. *Fragmentation and Redemption: Essays on Gender and the Human Body in Medieval Religion*. New York: Zone Books, 1991. Written before and, in some cases, after *Holy Feast and Holy Fast*, these essays clarify the major themes of that larger work. Confirming Bynum's status as a preeminent historian of the late Middle Ages are her reflections on theological debates concerning the resurrection of the body.

_____ . *Jesus as Mother: Studies in the Spirituality of the High Middle Ages*. Berkeley: University of California Press, 1982. These early essays established Bynum's profile as an historian. Attentive to lay spirituality, Bynum explores religion in its social context without abandoning the ecclesiastical focus favored previously by historians. Already present are sustained reflections on gender that will distinguish Bynum's later work.

Catherine of Siena. *The Letters of St. Catherine of Siena*. Translated by Suzanne Noffke. Binghamton: Center for Medieval and Early Renaissance Studies, State University of New York at Binghamton, 1988. The first English translation of the entire corpus of Catherine's letters and a vital record of a woman whose role in medieval Catholicism was most significant. The centrality of fasting and Eucharistic piety in Catherine's life and her persistent appeal to metaphors of food and maternal nourishment in her letters establish Catherine as a key figure in Bynum's work.

Hadewijch. *The Complete Works*. Translated by Columba Hart. New York: Paulist Press, 1980. In poems, letters, and recorded visions written between 1220 and 1240, this Flemish poet and mystic employs images of hunger and food as principal metaphors in describing her relationship to God. Her prose illuminates and provides compelling support for pivotal claims made by Bynum in *Holy Feast and Holy Fast*.

Weinstein, Donald, and Rudolph M. Bell. *Saints and Society: The Two Worlds of Western Christendom, 1000-1700*. Chicago: University of Chicago Press, 1982. The major secondary source influencing Bynum's own book and a groundbreaking contribution to a social history of medieval Christendom. Demonstrates that explorations of the lives of saints illuminate the society in which they lived, even as an examination of that society enhances knowledge of holy men and women in that age.

Martha J. Reineke

HOME BEFORE DARK

Author: Susan Cheever (1943-　　)
Type of work: Memoir
Time of work: The 1920's to the 1980's
Locale: Massachusetts, New York, France, and Italy
First published: 1984

> *Principal personages:*
> JOHN WILLIAM CHEEVER, an author
> MARY WINTERNITZ CHEEVER, a poet and teacher, the wife of
>   John Cheever
> FREDERICK LINCOLN CHEEVER, Jr., the elder brother of John
>   Cheever
> SUSAN CHEEVER, a novelist, the eldest child of John and Mary
>   Cheever
> BENJAMIN HALE CHEEVER, the first son of John and Mary
>   Cheever
> FEDERICO CHEEVER, the youngest child of John and Mary
>   Cheever

Form and Content

In an attempt to cope with her feelings about her father's impending death, Susan Cheever began a journal in the autumn of 1981. Soon, she found that her writing triggered many memories of her family life, and she continued to write after her father died on June 18, 1982. Although she had never intended to become her father's biographer, Cheever found that her memories, her father's journals, and conversations with family members and friends led her to the discovery of the important story of an American writer's life and his impact on his daughter.

Cheever begins this biographical memoir with her father's childhood in Quincy, Massachusetts. Although Frederick Lincoln Cheever had been a successful business-man, by the mid-1920's John Cheever's father began a descent into financial ruin, forcing his wife to support the family. Both John Cheever, born on May 27, 1912, and Frederick, Jr., his elder brother by seven years, felt the disruption of their social standing and the ensuing marital problems of their parents. This feeling of displace-ment was compounded by John Cheever's sense that his branch of the Cheever family was poorer than the more aristocratic Cheevers.

John Cheever's feeling of being an exile from the more respectable members in his family was mixed with his pride in their independence and irreverence. Showing his own initiative and faith in his talent as a storyteller, he went to New York in 1930 looking for work and a market for his short stories. Although he struggled with poverty, soon he found friends who helped him be accepted into Yaddo, an elegant writers' colony in New York. While John Cheever did not achieve financial security until late in life, he always managed to live in elegant homes, such as the Vanderlip estate in which the Cheever family lived from 1951 to 1960. It was not until he was almost fifty that the Cheever family owned their own home in Ossining, New York.

Susan Cheever emphasizes the ambivalence that marked her father's life. For example, he despised vanity, but judged people on their appearance; he insisted that "literature is not a competitive sport," but enjoyed the fame that finally came late in life; and he maintained his marriage for forty years although it suffered from frequent strife and sexual infidelity. Susan Cheever, born in 1943, and her brothers, born in 1948 and 1957, often thought that their parents would divorce, especially during the 1960's and 1970's, but Mary and John Cheever defied predictions and stayed together until his death.

In her account, this author unflinchingly examines the triumphs and failures in her father's life. While noting his Pulitzer Prize, National Book Award, and election into the American Academy of Arts and Letters, Susan Cheever also chronicles his twenty-year struggle to write a novel and his difficulties with publishers. She details John Cheever's descent from heavy social drinking into a fifteen-year bout with serious alcoholism which finally ended in 1975 after his hospitalization for addiction. Furthermore, she reveals his many heterosexual affairs, his homosexual longings, and his relationship with his last lover, a man half his age. Although Cheever exposes the many contradictions of her father's life, her main objective is to show his struggle to transcend the ordinary in his art and in his life.

Analysis

In Cheever's attempt to open up her father's life and art to the reader, she also presents her family's history. The author divides John Cheever's life into roughly two parts. The first forty-five years or so were marked by his search for professional acceptance, financial security, a stable family life, and a home; the second half was dedicated to finding an escape from the upper-middle-class life that he had constructed and from the "pressure to continually surpass himself as a writer." During these two halves of his life, the Cheever children experienced their father's insecurity, depression, and inability to express his feelings.

The connection between John Cheever's life and his art are revealed in Cheever's evaluations of her father's stories. While he was trying to establish himself as a respectable gentleman, his short stories featured white, financially comfortable Protestants and contemporary suburban life. His first novel, *The Wapshot Chronicle* (1957), contained many autobiographical elements, including two brothers, an overbearing wife and mother, and a noble but humiliated father. A year after his hospitalization for alcoholism, John Cheever produced his most successful novel, *Falconer* (1977), which includes a homosexual love story and a protagonist who is an imprisoned heroin addict.

Cheever also reveals her father's many pretensions. The image that John Cheever presented to the world included genteel breeding, upper-class diction, a lovely home complete with hunting dogs, and a happy family. Cheever explains that her father was a high school dropout with an affected speech pattern, a stressful family life, and money worries.

Alternately generous and parsimonious, John Cheever treated his family to expensive travel yet refused small loans to his children. More injurious were his deeply sarcastic insults, which prompted his sons to call the dinner table "the bear garden" while his daughter likens it to a shark tank.

Cheever's relationship to her father is recounted. Explaining the choice of "Susan" as her daughter's name, Mary Cheever recalls her husband saying, "She'll have long blonde hair and drive a sports car and we'll call her Susie." Cheever states that she failed to live up to her father's fantasy of a beautiful adolescent, and her appearance became an area of conflict between father and daughter. When Susan Cheever was thirteen, her family lived in Rome for a year, and she and her father began "the intense, often uncomfortable intellectual discussions" that her interest in literature produced. Although John Cheever fascinated his daughter with his stories and ideas about books and language, she was bored with her teachers, and he was disappointed with her poor performance at an exclusive school after their return to the United States.

Despite her recognition of her conflicts with her father, Cheever acknowledges the great impact that he had on her development as a writer. Her many conversations with her father about literature and her exposure to his writing influenced her interest in fiction. Moreover, John Cheever encouraged his daughter to write about her feelings in order to understand them. When she decided to leave journalism and go to France to write her first novel, they wrote each other long letters two or three times a week. He never critiqued her stories, however, and she refrained from showing him her work until after it had been purchased by a publishing house. Even at this point, her father would only comment politely that her work was likable or "fine." By mutually agreeing to avoid detailed discussion of her output, Cheever avoided the influence that her father might have had on her stories, as well as decreasing family tension. She explains that they "never talked about the writing part of writing" and instead limited conversation to "agents and editors and subsidiary rights and publishing practices."

In the final pages of *Home Before Dark*, Cheever's generally elegiac tone is intensified as she describes her father's final battle with the invasive cancer that led to his death. She tells of his delight in her daughter, his first grandchild, and the importance of his family to him. She avoids sentimentality, however, by revealing John Cheever's ability to be sarcastic and cutting during his illness, despite his transformation into a kinder, gentler man after his recovery from alcoholism. Susan Cheever's memoir of her father's life is remarkable for its deeply affectionate but honest portrayal of his personality.

Context

Biography is generally regarded as a seventeenth century invention, and a number of women in that century used the writing of their husbands' biographies as a means of artistic self-expression. For example, Lucy Hutchinson, Lady Ann Fanshawe, and Margaret Cavendish fashioned their memoirs to describe their husbands' lives. Susan

Cheever, as a twentieth century woman writer, did not need the excuse of chronicling her father's life to write. In fact, she had published three novels before John Cheever's death. Cheever's biography is interesting, however, for its examination of the effect of a celebrated author upon his literary daughter. While artistic creativity has been described as a symbolic unleashing of Oedipal energy, this interpretation is not applicable to women writers. Contemporary women critics, such as those included in the collection of essays entitled *Daughters and Fathers* (1989) edited by Lynda E. Boose and Betty S. Flowers, investigate the role of the father in culture and literature by women.

Cheever outlines both her parents' genealogies in order to explain their interests and talents, presenting the reader with a detailed memoir of her father's difficulties with his family history. Moreover, she traces her mother's psychological development through her family's dynamics. Susan Cheever, while avoiding psychoanalytic jargon, reaches into the past to explain her parents' behavior. By describing their insecurities and pain, she presents the influence of their internal struggle on their art. Although her father was much more famous and prolific than her mother, Cheever reminds the reader that her mother was a poet and teacher. Through her poetry, Mary Cheever was able to express her anger about her marriage.

Home Before Dark provides a brief overview of Susan Cheever's own development as a novelist and shows the sacrifices that she made to afford the time to write. Unlike her father, Cheever did not find a mentor at an artists' colony, and she was afraid to ask her father for financial help. Instead, she saved, sold her car, and moved abroad to achieve her ambition. Yet her father was supportive when she received bad reviews and congratulatory when she was successful. Before John Cheever's death, his relationship with his daughter had improved, and she writes that, through the research for this biography, her knowledge of him was greatly increased. *Home Before Dark* is valuable for Cheever's disclosure of the special stresses that confront the daughter of a famous author, as well as for her insights into his life.

Sources for Further Study

Bosha, Francis J., comp. *John Cheever: A Reference Guide*. Boston: G. K. Hall, 1981. An invaluable reference for those in need of a relatively complete bibliography to Cheever's works.

Cheever, John. *Conversations with John Cheever*. Edited by Scott Donaldson. Jackson: University Press of Mississippi, 1987. A part of the Literary Conversations series, this work is useful for its insight into the conversation style of Cheever in a number of interviews.

—————— . *The Journals of John Cheever*. New York: Alfred A. Knopf, 1991. Taken from the twenty-nine notebooks left by John Cheever, this work represents approximately one twentieth of the estimated four million words in these journals. Although not intended for publication, these notebooks offer very personal reflections of Cheever. Permission was granted by the Cheever family for its publication.

—————— . *The Letters of John Cheever*. Edited by Benjamin Cheever. New

York: Simon & Schuster, 1988. Selected correspondence of John Cheever to friends, editors, and other authors. Edited by his son, with an interesting introduction entitled "The Man I Thought I Knew."

Coale, Samuel. *John Cheever*. New York: Frederick Ungar, 1977. A part of the Modern Literature Monographs series, this volume offers a brief criticism and interpretation of Cheever's work. Especially useful for beginning the study of Cheever.

Collins, R. G., comp. *Critical Essays on John Cheever*. Reprint. Boston: G. K. Hall, 1982. Respected criticism of Cheever by such noted authors as Cynthia Ozick, John Gardner, Granville Hicks, and Joan Didion. Organized into reviews, interviews, and criticism, this book includes a bibliography from 1978 to 1981 that includes primary and secondary work.

Donaldson, Scott. *John Cheever*. New York: Random House, 1988. A detailed biography of John Cheever based on 170 interviews with his family and friends, thousands of letters, and published writings.

Terri Hume Oliver

HOME TRUTHS

Author: Mavis Gallant (1922-   )
Type of work: Short stories
First published: 1981

Form and Content

Home Truths is a collection of short stories concerning the experiences of young people from Canada. Mavis Gallant, an expatriate who moved to Europe in the early 1950's, looks at the world through the eyes of a woman who has become completely independent in order to survive with her individuality intact. She assumes no fundamental change will ever occur in the state of inequality between the sexes and approaches the struggle not in a political arena, but in a very personal one. The stories in this collection loosely follow experiences from Gallant's early years. She grew up in Montreal and had the unusual distinction of becoming bilingual from a very early age. When her father died, she was still a young girl and was moved around two Canadian provinces and two states in the United States, attending a total of seventeen different schools. Her mother remarried soon after the death of her father and, eager to have a new life for herself, sent her daughter to boarding schools. The continual changing of school, language, religion, and culture left Gallant with a unique perspective which she has frequently used in her stories.

The sixteen stories that make up *Home Truths* were mostly written in the 1950's and make up her sixth collection of short stories. Divided into three sections, "At Home," "Canadians Abroad," and "Linnet Muir," the stories range in location from a small town in Quebec to Paris and in time from the Great Depression to the 1970's.

Eight-year-old Irmgard, in the first section's "Jorinda and Jorindel," learns that three is a crowd and picks one boy over another to share her summertime hours. She chooses while cycling down a steep hill out of control by squeezing shut her eyes and shouting out the chosen name. The act of choosing teaches her that she has taken a path with no return and that it is now impossible to return to her other friend.

"The Ice Wagon Going down the Street" is in the second section, entitled "Canadians Abroad." It concerns the selfish and heedless lifestyle of a formerly privileged young Canadian man who assumes that others will shortly come to their senses and offer him the easy life that he feels his name owes him. When he meets a plain, hardworking Canadian girl in Switzerland, he realizes they have more in common than simply their homeland; they also have the same drab destiny.

The third section of *Home Truths* contains the six Linnet Muir stories. Muir is Gallant's most important and well known character based very much on Gallant's own experiences. She is an eighteen-year-old who returns to Montreal from school in New York to establish her independence in her native city during World War II. In her new life, Linnet Muir is concerned with career rather than romance. She does marry, but any details about the marriage and its dissolution is missing from the stories, and that absence indicates her determination to be free; freedom is really what she cares about.

As soon as she finds work as the only woman in a governmental office, she comes face to face with the vast discrepancy in status between men and women, finding that her gender and not her abilities will direct her if she does not keep a sharp eye on her own interests.

Analysis

The major issues in the stories of *Home Truths*, and in all Gallant's fiction, are those of alienation, personal freedom, the low status of children, and the difficulties of being a woman in a man's world. Drawing from her observations of her father (who was an exile from England), of other refugees in Canada during World War II, and of her own experience of living in Europe as an expatriate from Canada, Gallant has created and explored characters who are alienated by choice or by fortune and who are trying, usually with little success, to find peace of mind in unfamiliar and indifferent places.

Having survived a childhood in which she was treated as an inconvenience, moving and changing schools at someone else's whim, Gallant frequently writes about issues of personal freedom. Linnet Muir placed a high degree of importance on attaining independence and vowed "that I would never be helpless again and that I would not let anyone make a decision on my behalf." Muir's fellow Canadians prefer the status quo and are uncomfortable with those who would veer from it. Gallant seems to take pleasure in having her heroine break from this rigidity. This need for freedom stems from a childhood with no freedoms, but when Muir succeeds in finding work as the first woman in a wartime government office, she finds there is never freedom, only different kinds of slavery. The men there are tied to unfulfilling jobs, and working with them does not make her a part of the group. She too has an unfulfilling job, but she is treated as a lesser person.

Gallant has made a deliberate effort to look carefully at her childhood and has concluded that children very often do not get the respect or rights that they deserve. In "Orphan's Progress," two young sisters are taken from their mother, who is deemed unfit. They are obliged to begin speaking French with their paternal relatives, only to be returned to English-speaking relatives when their grandmother dies. Finally, they are separated not only from their mother and their language but also from each other when only one is chosen for adoption.

In her short stories, Gallant describes the difficulties of being a woman, but she does not lay all the blame on men. Sometimes, it is women who participate in the practice of keeping women in their low status. Linnet's godmother insists that she has only godsons and leaves everything to them in her will. Unhappily married women only make Linnet more determined to attain financial independence. An older coworker, who is well educated and making inroads into the working world dominated by men, reveals that her husband beats and humiliates her.

More often that not, Gallant's voice is pessimistic and cynical. She does not use this approach without humor and interest, but unless her readers look carefully, they may think that she is too negative. Actually, writing with a cynical eye is Gallant's way of protesting the way things are; she zeroes in on the limitations rather than on the possibilities. Gallant prefers to write in English because she believes that it is more appealing than French. Her use of its sound and range and her playfulness with its ambiguities make the English language seem quick and easy to use. It may appear to the reader that she completes her stories in the first draft, but it is more usual for her to write a short story in two years than in six months. She is technically adept and thematically diverse; her narrative style is admirable for its realistic sense of place. Even so, the dreary Montreal streets, the petty habits of bored bureaucrats, and the commonplace experiences of ordinary people are not more believable than the psychological scars inflicted on a child who is ordered about in the same tone of voice used to discipline a pet. Gallant makes all of her descriptions lifelike. In *Home Truths*, the young orphans and unwanted children of the first section give way to the confused youths of the second section and become the strong-minded Linnet Muir of the third section.

Context

Mavis Gallant uses the quest for personal freedom and the plight of dependent children to make her case for the need for equality between the sexes. Her stories take an unsurprising and dreary look at the relationships between women and men, but they usually end with a solution that works for the heroine, if not for women in general. Gallant does not hope for any substantial change in the social or economic status of women. Instead, she looks for individual solutions for her female characters, exactly as she found an individual solution for herself. When she found her first job in journalism, Gallant was told that the reason for a male-journalists' club was not to exclude female journalists as much as it was to provide a haven for the men from their wives. Realizing that she would never be welcome in the newsroom, and not willing to settle for the dependence and nonexistence of housewifery, she began preparing to earn her living through her own writing. Such independence meant freedom from the inequalities of the pressroom and the working world in general, and it also meant personal freedom from economic dependence on a husband. Linnet Muir marries briefly, but only to prove to herself that marriage is only a dead end in the road to personal freedom.

Gallant's view of women is not clouded by a false belief in their moral superiority. If the men and women in her stories clash and conflict, so do the women among themselves. She not only writes about women wronged by men but also includes accounts of mothers hindering daughters and women betraying female friends. Those who are on lower social rungs scuffle for survival, leaving them no time or opportunity to work for economic or social change.

Mavis Gallant received Canada's respected Governor General's Award for *Home Truths* in 1982, a year after becoming an officer of the Order of Canada. In 1984, she received two honorary doctoral degrees, from the University of St. Anne in Nova Scotia and York University in Toronto, and served as writer in residence at the University of Toronto.

Sources for Further Study

Canadian Fiction Magazine: A Special Issue on Mavis Gallant, no. 28, 1978. Written by many Canadian essayists and critics such as Robertson Davies and George Woodcock, this special issue includes a collection of criticism, reviews of Gallant's work, and a listing of her publications to 1978.

Grant, Judith Skelton. "Mavis Gallant and Her Works." In *Canadian Writers and Their Works: Fiction Series*, edited by Robert Lecker, Jack David, and Ellen Quigley. Vol. 8. Toronto: ECW Press, 1989. An essay describing the evolution of Gallant's short fiction in terms of her successful narrative technique and themes.

Hancock, Geoff. "Mavis Tries Harder." *Books in Canada* 7, no. 6 (July, 1978): 4-8. this feature article praises Gallant for her contributions to Canadian literature and offers critical insight into her short stories and novels spanning decades and continents.

Hatch, Ronald B. "Mavis Gallant: Returning Home." *Atlantis: A Women's Studies Journal* 4, no. 1 (Fall, 1978): 95-102. A criticism claiming that Gallant's work has continued to change, from general observations about individuals and personal freedom to accounts of social upheaval and change stemming from her own experiences.

Keefer, Janice Kulyk. *Reading Mavis Gallant*. New York: Oxford University Press, 1989. A close look at Gallant's writing, covering criticism and the different periods of her work and her life. Childhood and women, two important areas of her work, are also examined, as is her nonfiction. Both sympathetic and analytical, Keefer provides a comprehensive interpretation of Gallant's writing.

——————— . "Strange Fashions of Forsaking: Criticism and the Fiction of Mavis Gallant." *Dalhousie Review* 64, no. 4 (Winter, 1984-1985): 721-735. A defense of Gallant's work, claiming that for the most part, she has received little recognition of the importance of her literary achievement. Keefer claims that Gallant's work not only has not been well received but also has been misinterpreted.

Ross, Robert. "Mavis Gallant and Thea Astley on Home Truths, Home Folk." *Ariel* 19, no. 1 (January, 1988): 83-89. A comparative study of the meaning and use of "home" in both Gallant's *Home Truths* and Astley's *A Boat Load of Home Folk*.

Marilyn Kongslie

THE HOME-MAKER

Author: Dorothy Canfield Fisher (1879-1958)
Type of work: Novel
Type of plot: Domestic realism
Time of plot: The 1920's
Locale: A town in the Midwestern United States
First published: 1924

> *Principal characters:*
> EVANGELINE (EVA) KNAPP, an organized and energetic woman frustrated with housekeeping
> LESTER KNAPP, her husband, a sensitive and poetic man unhappy with his job as an accountant
> HELEN KNAPP, the eldest of the Knapp children, who is like her father
> HENRY KNAPP, the middle child, who is small and sickly
> STEPHEN KNAPP, the Knapp's rebellious five-year-old, who is Eva's favorite
> JEROME WILLING, the owner of Willing's Emporium and the employer of first Lester and then Eva
> NELL WILLING, Jerome's wife and the advertising director for Willing's Emporium

Form and Content

The *Home-Maker*, by Dorothy Canfield Fisher (who published her fiction under her maiden name, Dorothy Canfield, and her nonfiction under her married name), explores the problems implicit in ascribing roles to individuals based on their gender, rather than on their specific talents, abilities, and desires. The turning point of the novel occurs when Lester Knapp loses his job in the accounting office at Willing's Emporium. Devastated by this development, Lester contemplates suicide, but he must make his death look like an accident if Eva and the children are to receive any insurance money. He sees his chance when his neighbor's roof catches fire. He slips and falls trying to put the fire out, but he does not die; instead, he is paralyzed and confined to a wheelchair.

The task of supporting the family now falls on Eva's shoulders, and she asks Jerome Willing to hire her. Although Eva keeps repeating to herself and members of her community the aphorism that a woman's first duty is to her home and her family, Eva loves her new job, which calls on her aesthetic abilities in working with fabric. Eva begins as a stock clerk in the ladies' cloak and suits department and quickly moves up to saleswoman. She takes great pleasure in knowing her stock and helping her customers find the clothes that will best suit them at a price they can afford.

Meanwhile, Lester runs the household, learning how to cook and devising creative ways to clean. Most of all, he devotes his time to getting to know his children. Because Lester has a greater imagination and a deeper perception than Eva, he is able to understand his children in a way that Eva never could. With her penchant for organization and love of detail, Eva is the perfect candidate for running a department, a fact that Jerome Willing soon realizes. Lester's imagination and his love for thought and storytelling suit him better for rearing children; he ignores the dusting and sweeping to talk to his children, to learn what kind of minds and hearts they have. They flourish under this kind of attention.

If socially prescribed gender roles are not flexible enough to allow house husbands and working women, individuals suffer. By the time that Lester unexpectedly regains the use of his legs, Eva is making more money than Lester ever did, and the children's physical ailments have disappeared; indeed, the children are much healthier physically, emotionally, and intellectually under Lester's patient care. It is clear, however, that if Lester is able to walk again, society deems that he must go back to work because he is a man; Eva must go back to what for her is the prison of home because she is a woman. The novel ends with Lester's decision that he will forgo the use of his legs so that the true homemaker can stay at home. His decision is a secret kept by Eva, Lester's doctor, and a relative, Aunt Mattie, who each agree, privately and without consulting one another, that it must be concealed from their community. Fisher makes it clear that maintaining this secret life is the only way that the Knapp family can be socially acceptable.

Analysis

After *The Home-Maker* was published, Fisher was disconcerted that many reviewers interpreted it as, in her words, a "whoop for women's rights"; her intention, she said, was to depict the rights of children. Fisher does spend much detail on the learning processes of the Knapp children, especially Stephen. For example, when Lester becomes concerned about Stephen's seemingly unmanageable temper, he devises a plan to harness the energy that Stephen expends in being angry. He gives him an eggbeater and challenges him to figure out how it works. Fisher devotes several pages to the description of Stephen's initial frustration with the tool and his eventual mastery of it. She demonstrates how the frustrations of a "problem child" can be alleviated by a creative, caring parent.

Yet, in devoting a fictional project to the subject of homemaking, traditionally women's work, Fisher is certainly writing about women's rights. When Aunt Mattie visits Lester at home and is dismayed to find him cooking and darning socks, he says to her, "Do you know what you are saying to me, Mattie Farnham? You are telling me that you really think that home-making is a poor, mean, cheap job beneath the dignity of anybody who can do anything else." He realizes that women's work in the home is never accorded the worth or respect that it deserves, largely because profit, at least in terms of monetary gain, is not involved. By making Lester her spokesperson, Fisher emphasizes the fact that homemaking should be everyone's job; she corrects the platitude "A woman's place is in the home" by showing that both men and women have places there.

Fisher also criticizes a burgeoning American consumerism through Lester, who finds Jerome Willing's tactics in drawing customers to his store morally reprehensible. This critique is countered, however, by the fact that both Willing and Eva find meaningful work in the department store. Thus, Fisher emphasizes the fact that all individuals should have the opportunity to find the work that sustains them.

The unsatisfactory resolution of the novel—Lester is metaphorically castrated, and there is no suggestion that he will be able to find satisfying work outside of the home to complement his work inside it—demonstrates that society should be more tolerant of individual needs and less rigid in inflicting work styles on people. In a perfect world, it would be acceptable for Lester to stay at home because he is the best caretaker for his children, not because he is crippled and unfit for anything else.

One can, in fact, interpret *The Home-Maker* as a novel about men's, women's, and children's rights. Fisher's shifting point of view is quite democratic, divided between all of her principal characters and a few minor ones. As a result, one can see the cost to each individual, and the community, when Lester and Eva Knapp are prevented from doing the work for which they are best suited. Fisher was a pioneer in using this method; Virginia Woolf, James Joyce, William Faulkner, and others were experimenting with it at this time as well.

Unlike Fisher's other novels, where the spirit of place is painstakingly described, the environment in *The Home-Maker* is fairly generic. There is no description of landscape at all; the town atmosphere is provided by the glimpses one gets into the minds of various townspeople. This is also a democratic move on Fisher's part because her implication is that Lester and Eva's situation can occur in any home, anywhere in the United States. Indeed, the novel is almost claustrophobic in its confinement to the minds of the characters and the inside of a limited number of buildings: the Knapp home; the Willing home; Willing's Emporium, which has as its motto the "home-like store"; the rectory of the church and the church itself as a spiritual home; and Aunt Mattie's home. This confinement reflects Fisher's belief that all the truly important developments in life—the building of self-esteem, the feeling of self-worth, the ability to love and be loved—happen at home and in its immediate environs.

In her fiction, Fisher is devoted to chronicling the aesthetic details of everyday life, such as the episode with the eggbeater. Art, according to Fisher, not only resides in art galleries and concert halls but also encompasses the creative solutions with which people correct problems of everyday living; Lester makes an art of being a father. This aesthetic determines Fisher's agenda in writing fiction. As she writes in her prologue to *A Harvest of Stories* (1956):

> no novel . . . is worth the reading unless it grapples with some problem of living. Beauty of description, a stirring plot, the right word in the right place . . . all these are excellent. But without that fundamental drive, they are only words—words—words.

Context

Fisher's themes remain constant in all of her work. First, she broadens the definition of the *Künstlerroman*, or the artist's coming-of-age plot, to include the domestic coming-of-age of her male and female characters. Second, she reimagines men's roles in the home, her male characters having, and needing, a significant place there. Third, she presents complex portraits of the minds and hearts of modern women who are struggling with the redefinition of self that resulted from the social evolution of the "new woman"—that is, women who, at the beginning of the twentieth century, pursued the same freedom and opportunity that was granted to men. Fisher's agenda is to show men who need home lives and women who need work lives in order to be fulfilled as human beings; she believed that neither men nor women could be totally satisfied with roles that were defined by gender.

The Home-Maker occupies a unique place in Fisher's canon; her sixth novel, it is the only one in which she imagines a total role reversal: a female provider and a male homemaker. It can be read as part of a continuing tradition of stories and novels by women that depict the limitations of gender roles and the psychological and emotional costs of such limits. Examples of this tradition include *The Story of Avis* (1877), by Elizabeth Stuart Phelps; *A Country Doctor* (1884), by Sarah Orne Jewett; *A New England Nun and Other Stories* (1891), by Mary E. Wilkins Freeman; *The Awakening* (1899), by Kate Chopin; *The House of Mirth* (1905), by Edith Wharton; *A Woman of Genius* (1912), by Mary Austin; and *The Song of the Lark* (1915), by Willa Cather.

Fisher's fiction differs from these other works because she takes into consideration the fact that men, too, are damaged by lives that have limits, lives that only include work outside the home. Her concern is always to present a balance for both men and women that includes fulfilling work in the public sphere and a supportive and satisfying home life in the private sphere. The fact that *The Home-Maker* was one of the ten best-selling novels of 1924 shows that achieving this balance was important in many American lives at the time; the reprinting of the novel in 1982, as well as the increasing attention to and reevaluation of Fisher's work, undoubtedly shows that it still is.

Sources for Further Study

Fisher, Dorothy Canfield. *Keeping Fires Night and Day: Selected Letters of Dorothy Canfield Fisher*. Edited by Mark Madigan. Columbia: University of Missouri Press, 1993. Fisher's lively personal voice is present in this excellent collection. In his introduction, Madigan provides a detailed chronology of Fisher's life and an examination of her friendship with Willa Cather. A thorough bibliography and an annotated list of Fisher's correspondents are included.

Madigan, Mark. "Profile: Dorothy Canfield Fisher." *Legacy: A Journal of American Women Writers* 9, no. 1 (1992): 49-58. A narrative chronology of Fisher's life and work. Madigan also discusses three of her novels as particularly worthy of critical attention: *The Brimming Cup* (1919), *The Home-Maker*, and *Her Son's Wife* (1926).

Rubin, Joan Shelley. *The Making of Middle Brow Culture*. Chapel Hill: University of

North Carolina Press, 1992. This well-researched study profiles the five people who made up the first Board of Selection for the Book-of-the-Month Club, a job that Fisher held for twenty-five years.

Washington, Ida. *Dorothy Canfield Fisher: A Biography*. Shelburne, Vt.: New England Press, 1982. The first critical biography to be published about Fisher, this book gives an overview of Fisher's prolific career. Also includes valuable information about Fisher's family and a good analysis of how Fisher drew on their varying influences in shaping her career. A good starting point for learning more about Fisher in general.

Yates, Elizabeth. *The Lady From Vermont*. Brattleboro, Vt.: Stephen Greene Press, 1971. First published in 1958 as *Pebble in a Pool*, Yates's book is a general biography of Fisher.

Anne M. Downey

HOPE AGAINST HOPE
and
HOPE ABANDONED

Author: Nadezhda Mandelstam (1899-1980)
Type of work: Memoirs
Time of work: 1919-1938
Locale: The Soviet Union
First published: Vospominaniya, 1970 (*Hope Against Hope,* 1970); *Vtoraya kniga,*
  1972 (*Hope Abandoned,* 1974)

> *Principal personages:*
> OSIP MANDELSTAM, a leading Russian poet of the twentieth
>   century
> NADEZHDA MANDELSTAM, Osip's wife, who stood by her
>   husband during their entire ordeal and preserved his poems
> ANNA AKHMATOVA, their faithful friend and another leading
>   Russian poet of the twentieth century

Form and Content

Nadezhda Mandelstam, the wife of one of the most accomplished Russian poets of
the twentieth century, Osip Mandelstam, spent most of her married life sharing the
good and the bad experiences of her husband's life. When he finally succumbed to the
reign of terror in Joseph Stalin's Soviet Union and perished in a concentration camp
on December 27, 1938, she took it upon herself to preserve for posterity her husband's
poetic works; without her gallant efforts, most of Osip Mandelstam's work would
have been lost forever, since he was prevented from publishing during the last decade
of his life. Her efforts are all the more remarkable since she herself was always in
mortal danger, in addition to having to struggle for basic life necessities in the years
after her husband's death.

The two volumes of her memoirs cover the nineteen years that the Mandelstams
spent together, from their first meeting on May Day, 1919, to their last moments
together on May Day, 1938; they also include the aftermath of Osip's death. The
eighty-three titled chapters of *Hope Against Hope* concentrate on Mandelstam's first
arrest in 1934, final incarceration in 1938, and eventual death later that year. *Hope
Abandoned,* almost twice as large but condensed in forty-two chapters, builds on that
foundation, complementing the earlier narratives but also providing lucid comments
on poetic, political, and religious subjects, as well as perceptive analyses of some of
Osip Mandelstam's poems and those of their closest friend, Anna Akhmatova. The
reader cannot avoid the conclusion that the author has used the second volume as her
final reckoning with her time, in order to say everything left unsaid in *Hope Against
Hope.* Both volumes contain appendices, with biographical notes on persons mentioned in the text and background information on the leading literary movements and
organizations of the period. The second volume includes a chronology of the Mandel-

stams' lives, paralleled by a time line of significant literary and political events.

The author follows, more or less chronologically, the genesis and development of the "case" against Osip Mandelstam that would eventually lead to his death. There are many digressions and flashbacks, and it is in these sections that Nadezhda's style reaches its most poignant level. She herself was a highly educated person, having prepared herself to teach literature, which she was prevented from doing not only because of her husband's precarious position but also because of her own liberal views. Her wide education enabled her to shed light in her memoirs on the true nature of the cultural life in one of the darkest periods, if not the darkest, in Russian history. The revelations of the personal side of their marriage and their struggle for survival against insurmountable odds are intertwined with her reminiscences about other important persons, in both literary and political life, and with comments about the system that brought suffering and death upon an untold number of innocent victims. Thus her books are not so much conventional memoirs as they are valuable documents of cultural history that are important in view of the extreme difficulties in ascertaining the truth in a totally lawless society.

For the most part, the memoirs deal with Osip Mandelstam and his travails, but there are other, highly interesting sidelights of the period, clearly showing that Mandelstam's tragedy was by no means an isolated case. One story tells of a man who deliberately ruined his health by refusing to leave his home for fear of being ordered to inform on his friends and neighbors ("Complete Retirement"). Another story is about a young woman who, like so many thousands, was sent to a prison camp; upon her release years later, she refused to dwell on her past and tried to make up for the lost time of her life instead ("Surviving with Honor"). Yet another concerns a good-hearted cobbler who helped the victims at the risk of being persecuted himself ("A Kind Person"). Through stories such as these, as well as those about her husband, Nadezhda Mandelstam tries to reach her main goal by saying, "We must go on talking of these things, over and over again, until every injustice and every tear is accounted for, until the reasons for what happened (and still happens) are made plain for all to see." The memoirs, therefore, read like a literary *j'accuse* of a lawless system of gigantic proportion.

Analysis

Nadezhda Mandelstam had firsthand experience with the Soviet system. As a result, her conclusions about that system are damning without reservation. She saw what happened in the Soviet Union not as an error of a few mistaken and misguided individuals, such as Stalin, but as the logical outcome of a system flawed from its most basic premises. Although she sees some of the Soviet leaders (Nikolai Bukharin, for example) in a less damning fashion, she believes that everyone in power is to blame. At the same time, she is reluctant to bring indictment against individuals "because everything was done not by human beings as such, but by a machine. People simply reacted to the instructions, signals and rhythms of an autonomous mechanism into which a monstrous program had been fed at some time out of mind." She regards with bitter irony all the "noble" goals set by leaders, to which an untold number of lives were sacrificed.

The role of the Russian people as a whole is a different matter. While Nadezhda Mandelstam is certain about the true nature of the communist system, she is less certain about the guilt of the Russians. In general, she has a very low opinion of her people's moral fiber. She paints an unflattering picture of those who "lost their soul" trying to save their lives and committed inhumane acts against their fellow humans and even against close relatives. She accuses these people of greed, envy, callousness, and gullibility, of being indifferent to the fate of others and collaborating with the authorities. To be sure, there were exceptions. She believes that the circumstances under which Russians were forced to live resulted in a state of collective mental sickness. She allows for extenuating circumstances, such as the instinct for self-preservation. Still, most people succumbed to the illness of the times ("a torpid state in which one could converse only with death"). Thus, the memoirs can be used for a psychological study of people living in a constant state of fear. Although far from being the best testimony to the terrors of the period, they have a convincing ring of truth because of their personal nature of the experience.

At the other end of the spectrum, the portrait of Osip Mandelstam that emerges from the books is highly inspirational. Nadezhda reveres her husband for both their relationship and love for each other and for his refusal to "respond to the demands of time." The granite character strength and rich inner resources enabled Osip to live a full life and approach the end whole and uncrushed. According to Nadezhda, he was devoid of affectation, displaying a naturalness about the things that were important to him. He had a rare ability to see the world at it was and, consumed by curiosity, absorbed every detail fully. He had faith in people's goodwill. He lived to work. His calm, seemingly haughty demeanor did not stem from his religious faith but from his humanism, acquired from his lifelong interaction with the high achievements of Western culture, which he held in the highest esteem. The picture of Osip Mandelstam in these memoirs is one of the best, and certainly the most genuine, of human beings and poets.

In that connection, Nadezhda Mandelstam corrected many falsehoods, perpetrated both in the Soviet Union and abroad, about her husband's character traits and idiosyncrasies. All these rumors the author rejects with indignation, in belief that they originated from Osip Mandelstam's outsider status and through the disinformation efforts on the part of the authorities. In the setting of records straight lies perhaps the greatest merit of the memoirs. The result is a portrait of a poet who literally gave up his life for "poetic rightness," which he believed to be the guiding light of his life.

Context

Nadezhda Mandelstam is a perfect example of an emancipated Russian woman. Though Jewish, both she and her husband were of the third-generation converts to Christianity, and they embraced this religion, not in the formal but in the spiritual and philosophical sense. Moreover, they were drawn more to the Western, Hellenic-

Mediterranean Christianity as embodied in the works of Dante, rather than to the Eastern Orthodox sect. Osip Mandelstam considered himself to be "the last Christian-Hellenic poet in Russia." Nadezhda, too, adhered to this position, as she often showed a remarkable compatibility with her husband's views. At the same time, she always displayed an independent mind and was not reluctant to offer her husband both advice and criticism. Thus, she is typical of a Russian woman—a strong individual, yet willing to synchronize her will with that of her husband and at times to submerge her will in his for the sake of harmony (as when she collaborated with her husband on some projects yet allowed them to be published under his name). Throughout her memoirs, however, her individuality breaks through, so that the two books can be read as a testimony to her own intellect and soul, even though she professed to have lived only to preserve her husband's name and poetry.

Nadezhda Mandelstam also made a lasting contribution to the genre of memoirs, in the long tradition of Russian writers. Her wide erudition—she was proficient in several languages, had translated widely, and had acquired a doctorate in English literature—enabled her to lace her reminiscences with lucid commentaries on times, mores, and cultures. Her most important contribution, however, can be seen in her enormous courage, not only while writing her memoirs but also throughout her married life. Without that courage she would not have been able to accomplish her main task of preserving Osip Mandelstam's poetry. In doing so, she proved to be an optimist, despite the cruel circumstances. It is interesting that the title in Russian in simply "memoirs"; "hope" in the English title is a play on the author's name. In fact, her full name is Vera Lyubov Nadezhda, which in Russian reads "Faith Love Hope." These three words summarize best her personality, as well as her achievements.

Sources for Further Study

Brodsky, Joseph. "Nadezhda Mandelstam (1899-1980)." *The New York Review of Books*, March 5, 1981, 3-4. An article by a Nobel Prize winner eulogizing Nadezhda Mandelstam and concentrating on her relationship with her husband and Anna Akhmatova.

Carlisle, Olga. Review of *Hope Against Hope*. *The New York Times Book Review*, October 18, 1970, 6. The reviewer touches upon the most salient points in the book, focusing on Osip Mandelstam as a poet but also on Nadezhda's courage in writing the book and on her optimism despite the unfavorable odds.

Ludwig, Jack. "Hope Without Hope." *Partisan Review* 41 (1974): 455-462. A review of *Hope Abandoned*, interspersed with an interview with Nadezhda Mandelstam and her remarks about various personalities affecting the life of her husband and her own.

Pevear, Richard. "On the Memoirs of Nadezhda Mandelstam." *The Hudson Review* 24 (1971): 427-440. A review article about both memoirs, evaluating them as literary pieces and seeing their value and explanation in Nadezhda's ability to harmonize her conscious will with an inner attentiveness. Also contains pertinent references to Osip Mandelstam's poetry.

Struve, Gleb. "Nadezhda Mandelstam's Remarkable Memoirs." *Books Abroad* 45 (1971): 18-25. A walk through *Hope Against Hope*, (actually an extended review) by a distinguished scholar of Russian literature. Offers pointed commentary highlighting the important passages and praising the literary value of the book.

Vasa D. Mihailovich

HOTEL DU LAC

Author: Anita Brookner (1928-   )
Type of work: Novel
Type of plot: Psychological realism
Time of plot: The 1980's
Locale: London and Switzerland
First published: 1984

Principal characters:
    EDITH HOPE, an intelligent, quietly forceful, and shy writer of
        romance novels
    GEOFFREY LONG, a personable but dominating and old-fashioned
        man whom Edith left at the altar
    PENELOPE MILNE, Edith's London neighbor
    DAVID SIMMONDS, Edith's married lover
    IRIS PUSEY, a rich, older hotel guest
    JENNIFER PUSEY, Iris' daughter
    MONICA, a hotel guest and the owner of the dog Kiki
    MADAME DE BONNEUIL, a comtesse and a lonely hotel guest
    PHILIP NEVILLE, a wealthy hotel guest with courtly manners

Form and Content

Hotel du Lac tells the story of Edith Hope, a writer in her late thirties who must face alternatives familiar to many women—and some not-so-familiar ones. She has left a tedious suitor at the altar; she has an attractive lover who will not leave his wife. She wonders if true love—marriage to a desirable and faithful man—can be found. Anita Brookner underlines Edith's problems by describing her occupation. Under the pseudonym of Vanessa Wilde, she is a writer of romance fiction in which happy endings are the rule.

Hotel du Lac is an elegant and expensive hotel on Lake Geneva in Switzerland. The chronology of the few autumnal weeks that Edith spends there is straightforward, but Edith's full story develops slowly. Although the novel opens as Edith arrives at the hotel, it is clear that something important has just occurred in London. Not until chapter 9, two-thirds of the way through the novel, does Brookner reveal that Edith has left her intended husband waiting at the church—literally. Brookner departs from ordinary chronology in other ways. Edith remembers scenes from her past. Hotel guests are not named immediately. Edith's letters tell much of what happens, and she often compares herself to the heroines of the romances that she writes.

The novel begins with Edith in her "veal-colored" room at Hotel du Lac, a quiet unspectacular setting appropriate to her mood. She prepares to work on her new novel *Beneath the Visiting Moon*. She yearns for David Simmonds, her lover, and begins a letter to him. She then descends to the salon for tea and to see the guests. During the next few days, Edith meets the hotel guests and slowly forms opinions about them. The countess, Madame de Bonneuil, does not speak English, but Edith cannot escape Iris and Jennifer Pusey, a wealthy mother and daughter. Later, she makes friends with Monica, the wife of a nobleman, and together they venture into the village. The central chapters of the novel show Edith trying to decipher these women and making up stories about them. By Mrs. Pusey's birthday party in chapter 8, Edith has discovered that her stories are very wrong.

What happens at the hotel is in the present; flashbacks and Edith's letters gradually reveal what has shaped her life. The reader hears about her childhood: Her screaming Viennese mother gave Edith a sample of life's terrors, and her wise father encouraged strength of character and advised her to avoid quick judgments. In London, she owns a pleasant house with a nice garden and has an interesting neighbor, Penelope Milne. At one of Penelope's parties, she meets David Simmonds and begins an affair. Because David will not leave his wife, Edith agrees to marry the dull, respectable, and possessive Geoffrey Long. Leaving him at the church brings such disgrace on her that she goes to Switzerland to do penance.

Into the hotel's female society, a man enters, bringing with him the complications that will push the novel to its conclusion. Philip Neville is tall, rich, and impeccably dressed. He somehow knows that Edith is Vanessa Wilde and regularly shows what seems almost an instinctive knowledge of her character. When they lunch at a restaurant, Neville chides her for being a romantic in love; he says pleasure should not depend on one person alone. Edith holds her ground, yet is both fascinated and repelled. Later they take a strange boat trip, and Neville proposes a marriage of convenience, a marriage which would give Edith prestige, money, and security—but not love.

Facing an uncertain future, Edith is tempted and writes David that she will marry Neville. Brookner has prepared readers for the novel's climax, taking them closer and closer to the Puseys' adjoining bedrooms, where Mrs. Pusey has accused a servant of assaulting Jennifer. Down the hall, Edith has heard strange noises in the night. So when early in the morning she goes to mail her letter, one is ready when she sees Neville emerge in his dressing gown from Jennifer's room. Marrying Neville, Edith now knows, would be spiritual death. She decides quickly that the uncertainty of the man she loves is preferable to the security of a man such as Neville. She will fly back to England immediately, and she sends a telegram to David: not the comfortable words "Coming Home," but only "Returning."

Analysis

Hotel du Lac is a character study of Edith Hope, a single woman facing her future on the brink of middle age. Brookner generally employs the point of view of limited omniscience; that is, she tells the story in the third person, but the reader is in Edith's mind most of the time. In spite of the impression that she makes, Edith Hope is a more accomplished and forceful woman than many other Brookner heroines. She is a success, owns her own home, and has a circle of friends. She is intelligent, well read, and witty. Although Edith divides people into hares and tortoises and identifies with the tortoises, she is not really so slow. She leads her life not safely but impulsively, so as to open possibilities of a fulfilling romance. She launches into an affair without a minute's hesitation and throws Geoffrey over in the most dramatic and public way possible. Nevertheless, she is prone to anxieties and feels the gnawing loneliness of most Brookner heroines. She is often so detached that she seems in a waking dream. Her character is so mixed that readers wonder what she will do with difficult choices.

Although *Hotel du Lac* is a superb character study, it also suggests much about fiction and writers of fiction. Edith's profession and her personal life are intertwined. She knows that a novelist must entertain and so must women in this less-than-romantic world; one suspects that her letters to David are edited to amuse. She also approaches the other women as a covert professional. She receives their confidences as a novelist who is storing up ideas. When she meets new people, she thinks that it is a novelist's duty to make up stories about them. One of the novel's most engaging ironies, however, is that her stories are never remotely true; Edith confesses that, though she can create characters in books, she cannot understand real life.

Edith is also conscious of the contrast between her romance novels and real life. (Edith learned about real life from the terrible complaints of her mother and aunt.) She knows that, in reality, the hares win and the tortoises lose. Her novels sell because her readers are tortoises, and she makes sure that tortoise characters win the desired males. This ploy costs her no sales because hares do not buy books: They are too busy having fun being hares. Once readers of *Hotel du Lac* are conscious of the contrast between fiction and reality, they may wonder about the stories that Edith has been told. They may wonder too about the difference between the wish fulfillment of escapist romances and the satisfactions of a novel such as *Hotel du Lac*.

These ideas are ones a reader expects of metafictional novels, but Brookner takes these ideas one or two steps further. In her final letter to David (perhaps to make him feel guilty), Edith tells him that both he and her publisher have assumed that she wrote romances "with that mixture of satire and trendy detachment that is thought to become the modern writer in this field. You were wrong. I believed every word I wrote. And I still do." Edith believes her unreal stories. So, it seems, does Brookner: In an interview, she acknowledged that she shares "practically all" Edith's characteristics. She noted that *Hotel du Lac* is a very personal story: "I meant it. Every word."

The story of this novel has some odd ingredients that the contrast outlined above will not explain. Readers get information from Edith's letters, which she must edit for David's amusement. The letters become more confusing when one begins to guess that they are never sent and when Edith refers to her husband before the reader is told that she was almost married. On the novel's opening pages, Brookner moves strangely in and out of indirect discourse and her omniscience is not always limited to Edith's mind. Sometimes it strays elsewhere, most notably and eerily when Philip Neville has a thought and immediately afterward Edith unaccountably says the same thing out loud. In fact, there is an eerie, dreamlike magic about much of the novel: the timeless hotel, the misty unstable weather, the odd and even monstrous guests, Edith and Neville's ghostlike boat ride.

It may occur to some readers that Brookner has a trick up her sleeve. Edith's romances are unreal; their plots move to happy endings, and their characters clearly embody good or evil. Yet in this novel, real life is not exactly the usual realistic world either. Some characters, the Puseys perhaps and most notably Neville, are not exclusively realistic. Every time that Neville comes on the scene, there is a whiff of sulphur in the air. Though he should not be identified with Satan, he has unnatural knowledge of Edith and her weaknesses. They spend the day on a chilling ship of fools. He tempts her with the world; she faces spiritual death. Even his affair with Jennifer, perhaps with Mrs. Pusey's connivance, suggests the horrible trio of Satan, Sin, and Death in book 2 of John Milton's *Paradise Lost* (1667). Brookner may imply that a person in real life can embody an abstract essence, like that of the devil.

Context

In 1984, *Hotel du Lac*, Brookner's fourth novel, won the Booker Prize, Great Britain's most prestigious award for fiction. From her debut as a novelist, Brookner has had a sizable general audience—not only a feminist one. Readers specifically interested in women's concerns will focus on Edith. Her loneliness and powerlessness seem particularly feminine, and so does her appreciation of nuances in clothes, decor, and social relations. Her goal in writing her novels is based on what women readers want; her goal in writing letters is to please her lover. Many women will see her as embodying traits that they try not to possess.

The critic John Skinner sees *Hotel du Lac* as a feminine novel at a deeper lever. Edith and the other women of the novel struggle against a male-centered bias in the very language that they use: The hotel has "patrons"; Neville "takes her" on a walk. Jennifer suggests the standard male separation of female intelligence from female sexuality; the status of each of the women is determined one way or the other by men.

Some say that women's novels are often more open-ended than those written by men. Though Brookner said in an interview that she began to write *Hotel du Lac* with the intention of writing a conventional ending in which love triumphs, she was not able to do so. Edith has escaped a closed ending, and there is no guarantee what will happen when she gets home.

That Brookner's works are read by many men as well as women may suggest that she is not a typical feminist novelist. In interviews, Brookner herself, though sympathetic with feminists, always distinguishes herself from them. Even though her heroines seldom find the ideal man, they usually look for a romantic ending with him. Brookner does not disapprove of those fictions and those dreams. In contrast, the heroine of Margaret Atwood's *Lady Oracle* (1976) is also a romance novelist, but Atwood is mainly interested in smashing the idols of romance. Despite her excellence as a novelist, Brookner is regarded by some feminists as a bit old-fashioned or not sufficiently radical.

Sources for Further Study

Hosmer, Robert E., Jr., ed. *Contemporary British Women Writers: Narrative Strategies*. New York: St. Martin's Press, 1993. In Hosmer's interesting essay, he analyzes Brookner's heroines in relation to biblical and other exiles. In *Hotel du Lac*, Edith is an archetypal exile: She walks aimlessly, searches her soul continually, experiences considerable guilt, and is literally exiled from England.

Kenyon, Olga. *Women Novelists Today: A Survey of English Writing in the Seventies and Eighties*. New York: St. Martin's Press, 1988. Kenyon treats *Hotel du Lac* briefly. Her chapter is most valuable when she discusses Brookner in relation to the traditional interests of women novelists and in particular to the plots of romance.

_____ . *Women Writers Talk: Interviews with Ten Women Writers*. New York: Carroll & Graf, 1990. Contains an interview in which Brookner describes how she began to write novels. There are interesting remarks on *Hotel du Lac*: Brookner started the novel wishing to write a story which contained a very surprising event and in which love was victorious. The novel's hotel resembles an actual hotel at which she has stayed.

Sadler, Lynn Veach. *Anita Brookner*. Boston: Twayne, 1990. Offers a valuable chapter on Brookner's life and works and one on *Hotel du Lac*. Emphasizes the book's humorous ironies and precise descriptions, and sets it in the context of Brookner's previous novels. Sadler likes Edith better than earlier Brookner heroines and finds the novel enjoyable to read.

Skinner, John. *The Fictions of Anita Brookner: Illusions of Romance*. New York: St. Martin's Press, 1992. The introduction describes critical opinions, Brookner's intellectual background, and the autobiographical nature of her works. In his section on *Hotel du Lac*, Skinner uses comparisons to other novelists and an array of contemporary theories to give the novel a feminist reading. Demanding but stimulating, especially on the novel's point of view, on Edith's anxiety, and on her fascination with Jennifer.

George Soule

HOUSE OF INCEST

Author: Anaïs Nin (1903-1977)
Type of work: Novella
Type of plot: Allegory
Time of plot: No particular time
Locale: No particular place
First published: 1936

> *Principal characters:*
> THE NARRATOR, a woman who introduces the reader to the other
>   characters and to the House of Incest
> SABINA, the narrator's lover and her complementary missing half
> JEANNE, a crippled figure tortured by her love for her brother
> THE PARALYTIC, a writer pained by the failure of language to
>   record the complexity of his inner life
> THE MODERN CHRIST, an empath so sensitive to other people that
>   he has essentially been flayed alive
> THE DANCER, a woman who lost her arms by clutching too firmly
>   everything she loved

Form and Content

House of Incest (first published as *The House of Incest* in 1936) is a difficult work to categorize or summarize. In reality, it is a prose poem with a breathtaking series of images and themes. Its characters and plot—if there really is one—remain deeply veiled. Overall, the atmosphere is distinctly dreamlike.

The book is prefaced by a brief statement and a somewhat longer fable, both of which indicate the work's deep psychological roots. The first section of the main text describes the narrator's previous idealized existence in a world of water—Atlantide. It ends with the narrator cast ashore like the skeleton of a wrecked ship. The second section opens with the narrator gazing at Sabina as she approaches in the haunting twilight. The narrator describes Sabina's appearance and personality, her compulsive lying and yet also her primitive vigor. "There is no mockery between women," the narrator states. It is clear that she is in love with Sabina. She also points out the fact that the women share an identity, that they are each other's missing halves: "YOU ARE THE WOMAN I AM," states the narrator. She closes with a passage about her own tormented inner fragmentation into many selves. Obstinate images and cracked mirrors surround her as she searches unsuccessfully for Sabina's face in a crowd. The brief third section presents more images, with the narrator "enmeshed" in her own lies.

The fourth section of the novella introduces the paradoxical Jeanne, who is oddly elegant yet also hampered by a withered leg. Jeanne is in love with her brother, married to a husband who does not understand her, and fixated on her own image in the mirror. In what appears to be a dialogue with the narrator, Jeanne describes her own fragmentation and concludes with the revelation that her love for her brother can never be realized.

In the fifth section, the narrator is finally led into the House of Incest by a mysterious "she." (Or is "she" the previous narrator and the new narrator a new character?) The house is described as having a room that could not be found. The narrator stumbles from room to room. In one, she sees the biblical figure Lot with his hand on his daughter's breast. From the city in flames behind them come the cries of incestuous lovers—fathers and daughters, brothers and sisters, mothers and sons. The narrator moves on to a forest of decapitated trees and then to a room of white plaster as the section comes to an end.

In the sixth section, Jeanne is looking through all the rooms for her brother. She begs for help. Coming to the conclusion that she loves nothing except the absence of pain, she stands for many years and dies. (Her crippled leg had previously kept her from escaping life.) Upon dying, she finds her brother asleep among some paintings. He says that he has been admiring her portrait, hoping that she would die so that she would never change. The two bow, but not to each other, according to the narrator. In truth, they bow only to their own likenesses in the other. They wish each other a good night.

In the seventh and last section, the narrator walks into her book to seek peace, is cut by sharp glass, and discovers that lies create solitude. She then returns from the book to the paralytic's room. The paralytic stares at blank sheets of paper. He writes nothing because to capture the truth he would have to write many different pages simultaneously; the whole truth defies self-awareness and defies language. The paralytic bows to the narrator, Sabina, and Jeanne, introducing them to the modern Christ. The modern Christ's painful sensitivity—"Do you know what it is like to be touched by a human being!"—is envied by the paralytic, whose nerves have been deadened. Together, the group long for escape from the House of Incest, where they can only love themselves in the other—that is, where they can engage only in narcissistic love. They are afraid, however, of the tunnel which leads away from the house to "daylight." They turn to see the dancer, whose arms had been forfeited because she clutched too firmly at the things she loved. Now her arms have been returned. Opening them in a Christlike invitation and embrace, she dances toward the daylight.

Analysis

Just as it is difficult to categorize and summarize, *House of Incest* is not easily interpreted. Indeed, it is not clear that Anaïs Nin wished to reveal her intentions clearly. She openly resisted fellow author Henry Miller's suggestion that she provide more clues for the reader. Perhaps she thought that analytic language could not capture poetic truths effectively, or that the absence of an authoritative interpretation would leave readers free to respond from the heart, just as her book was written from the heart. Perhaps Nin's high regard for surrealism led her to believe that reality is too multifaceted and perspectives too diverse for a work of complexity and depth to yield itself to a single interpretation.

Nevertheless, *House of Incest* has been subjected to intense interpretation from a number of perspectives. One likely approach, in the light of Nin's exhaustive diary, is to look at the work as autobiographical in nature. There is some basis for this approach. *House of Incest* was written at a time when Nin was engaged in a torrid and somewhat tortured love affair with both Henry Miller and his wife June, to whom Sabina bears a definite resemblance. *Henry and June* (1986), Nin's account of this relationship, repeatedly comes back to the theme of incest, with Nin's older lovers serving as father surrogates. More to the point, Nin had an incestuous relationship with her father just before *House of Incest* was published and is alleged to have been a childhood victim of incest at her father's hands. The House of Incest itself bears some resemblance to the home that Nin shared with her husband in Louveciennes—it, too, seemed to have a missing room. Finally, the dreamlike qualities of the book as well as its deep psychological probing of the subconscious bring to mind Nin's fascination with psychoanalysis at the time the book was written. Consistent with this approach is the prominence of lies and self-fragmentation (possibly the bitter fruits of incest in thought or deed) as themes in the work.

On the other hand, Nin denied any simple linear relationship between her life and fiction. Furthermore, there are many images in *House of Incest* that seem to defy biographical parallels. This is not to say that reading Nin's nonfiction of the period casts no light on the novella: The nonfiction does make the book's landscape more familiar. Yet it does not seem to explain all or even most of the book's many mysteries. A recommended strategy for unraveling *House of Incest* would be to read the book on its own terms if possible before putting it into a biographical context. Certainly, the book lends itself to being reread; indeed, Nin appears to have designed the work so that multiple readings are a requirement.

Despite Nin's persistent interest in the theme of incest, *House of Incest* is often interpreted as dealing primarily with narcissism, a vain self-love indicated by the conspicuous presence of mirrors throughout the text. According to this interpretation, incest in this case refers to the sterility of having a love affair with one's self as reflected in someone similar—another woman in the case of the narrator and Sabina, one's sibling in the case of Jeanne and her brother. The point is to escape this narcissism by truly loving another person, not one's self through another person. This is the "daylight" toward which the dancer is moving at the novella's conclusion. This theme hearkens back to the eighteenth century philosopher Jean-Jacques Rousseau's distinction between natural and vain self-love in his critique of modernity in the *Discours sur l'origine et les fondements de l'inégalité parmi les hommes* (1755; *A Discourse upon the Origin and Foundation of the Inequality Among Mankind*, 1761).

No matter what theme one ascribes to *House of Incest*, one thing that must be noted is the incredible richness of the book's language. Though stylistically unique among Nin's works, the novella resembles her other work—and Henry Miller's as well—in its seemingly limitless mastery over the English language. Each paragraph contains at least one pure reading delight, and there is an almost unending abundance of memorable images, described with exquisite precision and power. Even as one struggles, perhaps in futility, to find the meaning of *House of Incest*, the work's beauty remains transcendent and completely undeniable.

Context

The impact of *House of Incest* has been felt in two waves. It was her diary rather than any of her fiction that firmly established Nin's reputation as a writer, and only her volumes of erotica *Delta Venus* (1969) and *Little Birds* (1979) have achieved best-selling status. Yet *House of Incest*, which Nin essentially published herself in 1936, played a key role in her career by helping her to build a small but loyal following and laying the groundwork for her later fictional works and subsequent experiments by other authors, especially women writers. As such, the novella deserves credit for helping to inspire—along with works by authors such as Djuna Barnes—a proliferation of literature marked by striking candor, penetrating psychological realism experimental forms of narrative, and unorthodox styles. In short, even had Nin's diary never been published, *House of Incest* would have made its mark on literature despite what would have been a tiny readership.

With the publication of the diary beginning in 1966, Nin's readership and influence were greatly magnified. She became a major literary figure almost immediately. She also became a hot political property. Her liberated views toward female sexuality were seen as an effective antidote to the quickly unraveling double standard then current in society. Her work also fit in with the increasing desire to explore reverently the unique attributes of women, which for many promised liberation not only for women but for men as well. Finally, Nin's willingness to pursue her unorthodox writing career and lifestyle rather than conform to accepted norms brought a kind of personal admiration or aura. Nin presented an example of a woman triumphing on her own terms in a male-dominated world. Along the way, as Kate Millett pointed out in *Sexual Politics* (1970), Nin had even elicited words of praise and awe from the dreaded Henry Miller, disdained by feminists for his reputed ruthlessness toward women.

House of Incest also had political and social implications for feminists. The structure and behavior of family life was being examined in unprecedentedly critical ways during the late 1960's, with the incidence of incest being alleged to be far more common than anyone had been willing to admit previously. For this reason, the book has struck a particularly relevant chord, despite its resistance to any clear interpretation with regard to this issue.

Sources for Further Study

Evans, Oliver. *Anaïs Nin*. Carbondale: Southern Illinois University Press, 1968. One of the earliest critical studies of Nin's work. Evans, a Nin enthusiast since the mid-1940's who was personally acquainted with the author, provides detailed analysis of each of her fictional works, including *House of Incest*.

Fitch, Noel Riley. *Anaïs: The Erotic Life of Anaïs Nin*. Boston: Little, Brown, 1993. Fitch offers a thorough account of Nin's life and writing, showing the complex way in which the two were entwined. Special attention is paid to the relationship between Nin and her father, which Fitch believes to have been incestuous. Well referenced, with an excellent bibliography and index.

Franklin, Benjamin V., and Duane Schneider. *Anaïs Nin: An Introduction*. Athens: Ohio University Press, 1979. Provides a basic biography and assessment of Nin's work. Franklin and Schneider believe *House of Incest* to be Nin's finest work of fiction.

Harms, Valerie, ed. *Celebration! With Anaïs Nin*. Riverside, Conn.: Magic Circle Press, 1973. Proceedings from an informal weekend conference involving Nin, various acquaintances, and a variety of fans, all of whom discuss her life and work.

Knapp, Bettina. *Anaïs Nin*. New York: Frederick Ungar, 1978. Provides a sympathetic introduction to and chronology of Nin's life and work. Knapp devotes a chapter to *House of Incest*, linking it to Nin's experience with psychoanalysis.

Nin, Anaïs. *Henry and June: From the Unexpurgated Diary of Anaïs Nin*. San Diego: Harcourt Brace Jovanovich, 1986. Drawn form Nin's "unexpurgated" diary (earlier versions were edited severely for popular consumption out of consideration for Nin's husband, among others), this volume chronicles Nin's love affairs with Henry and June Miller and was written at about the same time as *House of Incest*. The prominent themes are those of incest, narcissism, psychoanalysis, and dreams.

——————— . *Incest—from a Journal of Love: The Unexpurgated Diary of Anaïs Nin, 1932-1934*. New York: Harcourt Brace Jovanovich, 1991. As with *Henry and June*, this volume was extracted from Nin's diary after having originally been heavily edited for publication. Details Nin's relationship with her father when they were reunited just after her thirtieth birthday.

Spencer, Sharon. *Collage of Dreams: The Writing of Anaïs Nin*. Chicago: Swallow Press, 1977. Spencer treats the full range of Nin's work available to her, likening it to the compositions of surrealistic art. Original and accessible.

Ira Smolensky
Marjorie Smolensky

THE HOUSE OF MIRTH

Author: Edith Wharton (1862-1937)
Type of work: Novel
Type of plot: Social realism
Time of plot: The late nineteenth century
Locale: New York City, upper Hudson estates, and Monte Carlo
First published: 1905

Principal characters:
> LILY BART, an unmarried New York socialite in need of a husband
> LAWRENCE SELDEN, a lawyer and a friend of Lily
> SIMON ROSEDALE, a wealthy Jewish capitalist and social climber
> MRS. PENISTON, Lily's wealthy but stuffy aunt
> GUS TRENOR, a wealthy capitalist married to Judy Trenor, who
> has adopted Lily socially
> MRS. HAFFEN, an impoverished charwoman
> GERTY FARISH, Selden's cousin, a poor but respectable
> philanthropist
> BERTHA DORSET, CARRY FISHER, MATTIE GORMER, and NORMA
> HATCH, four women of compromised reputations whose
> parties Lily attends

Form and Content

The House of Mirth is a work of social realism that criticizes a very specific world—that of wealthy, nineteenth century New York society—yet it is also much more than that. It is a moral fable with timeless insight into the problem of finding and keeping clarity of vision in a corrupt culture. The novel also reflects aspects of the feminine experience that are common, in one form or another, to modern Western culture. Lily Bart's moral failures are those of the world in which she lives. Edith Wharton leaves little doubt about her condemnation of that world. She does, however, leave some doubt about her protagonist.

From the very start, Lily both attracts and repels the reader. Her keen sense of independence, her astuteness about what motivates other people, her desire to rise above the petty concerns of those around her—all make her seem like a sound heroine. Yet repeatedly, Lily Bart disappoints the reader by making foolish choices that she seems not to have thought through. She cannot bear to plunge into the values of her social world, blinding herself to their stupidity, but she also fails to pull away from them altogether.

The reason for that failure is basic: money. Having grown up with luxury, with no real sense of how to manage money but a clear sense of how much power comes with having it, Lily wants badly to have a large fortune at her disposal. She has always been led to believe that her beauty alone will suffice to secure her the right marriage proposal, that she need only play the game right. Repeatedly, in the novel, one finds her on the brink of receiving a proposal; each time, she dodges it by committing some minor indiscretion that makes the match impossible. As the indiscretions add up, it becomes increasingly difficult for her to be marketed by her friends. They begin to seek some distance from their somewhat tainted acquaintance.

Lily's downward spiral is already hinted at in the novel's first scene, when she unwisely yields to the impulse to take tea in Lawrence Selden's flat. It is a typical move: Morally sound, like all of her indiscretions, it nevertheless breaks the rules of behavior for unmarried women in her set. It also gives two other characters some power over her reputation. A much more far-reaching indiscretion is the acceptance of a loan—disguised as a return on an investment—from Gus Trenor, her friend's husband. This move not only costs her the friendship of her primary protector on the marriage market but also results in the complete (and unjust) destruction of her reputation once it has become known.

Only after Trenor has tried to impose himself on her in the most alarming way does Lily turn to Simon Rosedale, the wealthy Jewish businessman who has long eyed her as a woman who might be the perfect wife to ensure his success in her social set. By this time, however, even Rosedale will not have her. Disinherited by her aunt, penniless, and denounced publicly by Bertha Dorset in most damaging (but again unjust) terms, she struggles to maintain herself as something of a social guide and parasite with a series of unappealing women. Eventually, she leaves that sorry business to try to support herself by working for a milliner.

Near the end of the novel, Lawrence Selden finds her in abject poverty and determines to try to help her. He comes too late: Before he returns to her rooms, she has taken an overdose of chloroform perhaps intentionally. Her death, readers realize, was already implicit in the novel's very first scene. At Selden's flat, Lily has both resisted playing by the rules and failed to find an effective substitute for them. There too, Selden appears to offer a tantalizing, real alternative to the vacuous bridge games of Bellomont, but he seems to fall just short. There, she is seen by the charwoman, who will be something of an emblem of her downfall: all the beautiful gowns and mansions of New York cannot protect her from the basic lowness, mean-spiritedness, and moral bankruptcy of most human beings around her.

Analysis

The House of Mirth is written in third-person narration, largely but not exclusively from Lily Bart's point of view. The narrator has a quick sense of irony, and irony pervades the work, both in its language and in the dramatic juxtapositions of its episodes. For example, the novel opens in New York's Grand Central Station, with Lawrence Selden catching a glimpse of Lily. The narrator notes, "It was characteristic of her that she always roused speculation." Wharton is playing ironically with all the meanings of the word "speculation." Selden, like the reader, is speculating about what Lily Bart's presence means at this moment. He is also, like the other men in the novel, speculating about her value and considering an investment. In a world in which money has such supreme importance, the concept of speculation introduces the range or ironies that the novel repeatedly brings into play.

The final irony may be that readers remain speculative about Lily Bart. The distant, sometimes witty narrator withholds clear judgment. Much of the critical response to the novel has focused on this question. How much is Lily to blame for her downfall? Is she a moral failure or a tragic heroine? Until her final weeks, she is consistently unable to choose between an immoral life of wealth and a rebellious life of morality and intellect, and the waffling costs her everything. Yet there is also some grandeur in her rise to moral superiority as she straightens out her affairs before her death, and critics have sometimes complained that the novel becomes positively sentimental in its closing pages.

One senses, however, that Lily is not fully to blame even for her worst lapses in vision: The choices available to her, as a woman, are few, and the chances to see beyond her world are nonexistent. As a woman in a rarified subculture, she has no opportunity to experience other ways of life and of thinking. Her failures, then, are also those of her culture.

It is a culture of speculation, in which money determines value and morality is confined to appearances. Wharton's scathing critique of this social world did not make her well-loved in it, and it should not be surprising that after this novel's immense success she chose to leave New York to live in Europe. Scarcely any character comes out looking good in the moneyed circles of the Trenors, the Dorsets, and the Gryces. Perhaps the one exception is Carry Fisher, a young mother twice divorced who supports herself by helping the nouveaux riches to master the nuances of the elite's social behavior. Some readers have wondered how she has been able to maintain some integrity, when every other character in the novel seems to have been warped by the culture's excessive emphasis on money and appearances. It is a culture in which nearly all live beyond their means and are badly behaved behind closed doors. Reputations rise and fall like (and with) fortunes. Speculation is the apt metaphor for this social world.

Even Lawrence Selden, whom many readers find to be a compelling figure, has major flaws. Recent critics have seen his flaws more clearly, in general, than earlier ones. Wharton's narrator describes him as a "reflective" man, and he seems generally more cultivated and less superficial than the other men in his world.

He has distinctly chosen to stay outside the money game (and the marriage game), preferring his independence on all counts. Yet he also allows his view of Lily to be colored in crucial ways by the questionable values of the culture that he pretends to disdain. At a crucial moment in the plot, he yields to the general suspicions about her reputation and avoids her in a cowardly way. At moments when he might intervene, he fails to, right up to the end. When he finally does arrive on the morning that she has died, the ironies do not end. Some readers have found that moment to be genuinely tragic, his sentiment for her sincere. Others have thought that on some level he prefers her dead, her beauty a kind of frozen icon, rather than have to engage in life with her and in all the challenges that such a life might represent. In either case, Selden does fail to provide a model for any proper response to the difficulties posed by Lily Bart. He remains a speculator, most aloof and disengaged.

It is precisely that stance of disengagement that the novel seems most incisively to criticize. The world of Lily Bart is a world in which all relationships appear to be transactions, in which as little emotional capital is spent as possible. Most recent critics note at least in passing that this novel's metaphorical language is the language of the marketplace. From the moment in which Selden notes that Lily Bart's beauty must be a real asset to the many relationships in which it becomes clear that running accounts are kept of every debt and gesture, the novel reveals a world in which value is almost never intrinsic. The characters show almost no moral sense; social position is purely a matter of effective manipulation of assets. Lily Bart seeks to rebel against that marketplace—ironically, by scrupulously paying back her debts. As one critic has claimed, that is the least effective form of rebellion, because it is swallowed up in the very marketplace that it seeks to replace. Lily Bart's life and death ultimately appear to have no meaning for her world. Their sense can only be measured in their larger impact on the world beyond the novel.

Context

The House of Mirth was an immediate success when it was published in 1905. It remained on the best-seller list for four months, and its sales became the basis for Edith Wharton's independent fortune. Readers immediately recognized the novel's attack on Old New York. Although some believed that the critique was unjust, more were concerned, ultimately, with its aptness as a subject for art. Despite its commercial triumph, the novel was not viewed as a real aesthetic success. Wharton was viewed as a poor imitation of Henry James, despite all the ways in which she deliberately distances herself from his art. She was also criticized for adopting too high a moral tone and for killing her heroine unnecessarily—two contradictory criticisms, it must be admitted.

Not until after her death in 1937 was Wharton's body of work, and especially *The House of Mirth*, taken seriously as the complex work of art and meditation on modern values most consider it today. It can be seen now as a kind of early feminist response to both James and Gustave Flaubert, whose *Madame Bovary* (1857) it resembles in certain ways. *The House of Mirth* represents most astutely and sympathetically the dilemmas of a woman living in a culture that does not permit her to work and that views her body and her sexuality as her most important capital.

Sources for Further Study

Goodman, Susan. *Edith Wharton's Women: Friends and Rivals*. Hanover, N.H.: University Press of New England, 1990. A study that moves back and forth between Wharton's relationships in life and her fictional characters.

Lauer, Kristin O., and Margaret P. Murray. *Edith Wharton: An Annotated Secondary Bibliography*. New York: Garland, 1990. A useful, extensive, and annotated bibliography of the criticism of Wharton's fiction.

Nevius, Blake. *Edith Wharton: A Study of Her Fiction.* Berkeley: University of California Press, 1953. A landmark study that is still highly regarded. The first book-length study to treat Wharton as a major author.

Wharton, Edith. *The House of Mirth.* Edited by Elizabeth Ammons. New York: W. W. Norton, 1990. This critical edition reprints some key essays about the novel and includes a full text.

—————————. *The House of Mirth.* Edited by Shari Benstock. Boston: St. Martin's Press, 1994. This edition offers five essays exemplifying different approaches to the novel, along with a complete edition of it, introductory essays by the editor, and a useful bibliography.

Sarah Webster Goodwin

THE HOUSE OF THE SPIRITS

Author: Isabel Allende (1942-   )
Type of work: Novel
Type of plot: Social realism
Time of plot: The early 1900's through the early 1970's
Locale: A South American country much like Chile
First published: La casa de los espíritus, 1982 (English translation, 1985)

> *Principal characters:*
> ESTEBAN TRUEBA, a landowner and conservative politician who
>   runs the plantation Tres Marias
> CLARA DEL VALLE TRUEBA, his wife, who can predict the future
>   and commune with spirits
> BLANCA TRUEBA DE SATIGNY, their daughter
> PEDRO TERCERO GARCÍA, one of the Tres Marías peasants, a
>   leftist leader, and Blanca's lover and the father of her child
> ALBA TRUEBA, the daughter of Blanca and Pedro and the adored
>   granddaughter of Esteban Trueba
> ESTEBAN GARCÍA, the evil son of Esteban Trueba's oldest
>   illegitimate child

Form and Content

The House of the Spirits is the story of a South American country much like the author's own Chile, shown by tracing a family through four generations and covering eight decades. Although in this society men control the church, the state, and the family, the major characters in Isabel Allende's work are the strong-willed women who refuse to be dominated or destroyed.

Appropriately, the story begins with a public confrontation between ten-year-old Clara del Valle and the fanatical priest Father Restrepo. After Clara makes a loud skeptical comment in church, the priest proclaims that she is possessed by the devil. Although Clara shows no signs of being evil, she does commune with spirits. Therefore, when after nine years of silence Clara announces that she is going to marry her dead sister's former fiancé, Esteban Trueba, it is understood that Clara is not merely mentioning a possibility, but foretelling the future.

Clara's spirits evidently have not told her how stormy the marriage will be. At first, everything goes well. Esteban stops appropriating peasant girls for his sexual needs and concentrates on pleasing his beautiful and willing bride, and before long, he is the father of a daughter and twin sons. Clara, however, not only is given to retreating in to the spirit world but also makes it evident that she cannot agree with her husband's political views. As a landowner, Esteban sees socialism and land reform as threats to his way of life. Clara, on the other hand, is an idealist who believes that Esteban's Conservative Party stands for oppression and injustice.

As his children become older, Esteban finds that he cannot govern them any more than he can his wife. In part because of her mother's liberalism and in part because of their childhood friendship, their daughter, Blanca, falls in love with and becomes pregnant by the fiery young leftist Pedro Tercero García. Infuriated, Esteban whips his daughter and forces her to marry a sinister count, and he tries to kill the young man. As a result, Clara stops speaking to her husband. Esteban also loses his twin sons, one to Eastern mysticism and the other, a doctor, to the needs of the poor and eventually to martyrdom for the cause of social justice.

Alba de Satigny, or Alba Trueba, as she chooses to call herself, dominates the final segment of Allende's novel. The daughter of Blanca and Pedro, Alba is born in her grandparents' home and soon becomes the center of her grandfather's world. Like her mother and her grandmother, however, Alba is idealistic. She is also strongly influenced by her father, whom she frequently sees in secret. At the university, Alba falls in love with Miguel, a revolutionary, and her involvement in the movement that he espouses results in her being imprisoned, raped, and tortured by the bitter and malevolent Colonel Esteban García, Esteban Trueba's illegitimate grandson. Perceiving the evil nature of the fascists he once supported, Esteban Trueba joins with Pedro to effect Alba's release and then arranges for Blanca and Pedro to leave the country together. In order to be near her own lover, Alba remains with her grandfather, and together they write *The House of the Spirits*, the story of their family and their country. At the end of the novel, Esteban Trueba dies, while Alba waits for the birth of her daughter, who may be the child of Miguel, but who is just as likely to be the child of her torturer.

The House of the Spirits is a complicated work, filled with dramatic incidents, crowded with characters, and characterized by dizzying leaps into the past and the future. The story is told in various voices. The first six words of the novel, for example, are quoted from one of Clara del Valle Trueba's notebooks, written fifty years before. Some segments of the work are written in the first person by Esteban, while the other first-person narrator is finally identified as Alba. Often, however, Allende adopts the voice of the omniscient author. It is a mark of her genius that this complexity of form and content in no way checks the progress of her novel or diminishes its powerful effect.

Analysis

At the beginning of *The House of the Spirits*, Alba Trueba says that she is writing "to reclaim the past and overcome terrors of my own." Like Alba, Isabel Allende began writing in order to make pain bearable. After her uncle, the Chilean president Salvador Allende, was murdered during a right-wing military coup, Isabel Allende, her husband, and her children were forced to go into exile. One of those she most regretted leaving was her autocratic but much-loved grandfather, upon whom she modeled the character of Esteban Trueba. Fearing that she would never see him again, Allende began to write a letter to her grandfather, in which she expressed her love for him and assured him that even after his death, he would live on in her memory. The letter was never sent; instead, it evolved into *The House of the Spirits*. Thus Allende's first novel was written to assuage her own pain and to call back into existence all that she had lost, her friends, her people, her country, her dream of social justice. While Allende insists that she is not Alba, she clearly shares with her narrator a faith in the power of the written word to defy repression and transcend time.

The House of the Spirits is built upon a number of contrasts and paradoxes. One of the latter can be seen in Allende's description of the world, which she shows as being at one and the same time ordinary and magical. Like other Magical Realists, Allende moves easily from one vision to the other, as when, having lined up the large Trueba family in a church pew, she mentions the fact that Rosa has green hair. Like their creator, Allende's characters have no problem with this dual view of reality. They incorporate Clara's habit of levitating salt cellars and her unfailing powers of prophecy into their everyday world.

The two dominant political views represented in the novel, however, are not so easily reconciled. Allende's own position is indicated by the fact that she chooses names associated with light, specifically "Clara," "Blanca," and "Alba," for her liberal heroines. In contrast, it has been noted that Esteban Trueba's Christian name means "crown," which is certainly consistent with his belief in a conservative, patriarchal system. Interestingly, all that Trueba bequeathed to the sadistic Colonel García was his first name and, seemingly, his belief that might makes right.

Yet, while Esteban García is so committed to revenge that he will not permit himself to feel pity, Esteban Trueba, though often blind to the needs of others, is capable of love. He tolerates Clara's peculiarities, even when she bars him from her bed; he welcomes the pregnant Blanca back into his home; and he feels such a strong attachment to Alba that he is determined to rescue her, no matter how radical the cause with which she is associated. One suspects that it is not only his disillusionment with the new regime but also the cumulative influence of these liberal women that causes Esteban Trueba to change his mind about politics. His literary collaboration with Alba, then, represents not only a personal and political reconciliation but also a fusion of age and youth, conservative ideas and liberal ones, and male and female viewpoints, which suggests that there is hope for the future.

Context

Isabele Allende dedicated *The House of the Spirits* "to my mother, my grandmother, and all the other extraordinary women of this story." As feminist critics have hastened to point out, her novel describes an inflexible patriarchal society which depends on traditional values and brute force to subjugate its poor, its powerless, and, therefore, its women. That so many women defy this society is evidence of their strength and their determination, and perhaps of the power of righteousness as well.

Clara, Blanca, and Alba, who Esteban Trueba says suffer from the inherited disease of idealism, are not the only "extraordinary women" who take part in the struggle against repression. There is Nivea del Valle, the mother of ten other living children besides Clara, who, though she has not yet discarded her corsets, is a "suffragette" in principle. There is Tránsito Soto, who by starting a cooperative of male and female prostitutes becomes, in effect, a union leader, but who is wily enough to maintain her power even under the Dictator. There is the once-beautiful Amanda, who, though debilitated by drugs, would rather die under torture than betray her brother Miguel. Then there are the heroic women in the prison camp, whose songs move even the men who guard them.

In her later novels, notably *De amor y de sombra* (1984; *Of Love and Shadows*, 1987) and *Eva Luna* (1987; English translation, 1988), Allende continues to show how the male establishment attempts in every way to destroy the identities, even the humanity, of women. In a patriarchal society, infused with the macho image, men expect to have full control over the sexuality of their women. They rape at will, force their wives into almost incessant childbearing, decide when and whom their daughters will marry, and, if any of the women under their control become recalcitrant, beat them into sense or insensibility.

While Allende's outrage about the wrongs done to women is always evident in her fiction, however, the sexual invasions that her heroines experience also symbolize a more general pattern of social injustice. When Pancha García is raped by Esteban, she represents all the peasants whom he considers little more than slaves; when Alba is raped by Colonel García, she symbolizes all the people, male and female, who lose their identities and their lives under a dictator's reign of terror. Thus the cause of women becomes only one part of a battle against oppression. Allende's fictional heroines stand for everyone, male or female, who has defied unjust authority for the greater good.

Sources for Further Study

Cunningham, Lucia Guerra, ed. Splintering Darkness: Latin American Women Writers in Search of Themselves. Pittsburgh: Latin American Literary Review Press, 1990. An essay on *The House of the Spirits* examines the effect of a male narrator's being controlled, or "framed," not only by a female writer but by a female narrator as well. In this way, it is suggested that, at least in fiction, women such as Alba can exert power over patriarchs such as Esteban Trueba.

Earle, Peter G. "Literature as Survival: Allende's *The House of the Spirits*." *Contemporary Literature* 28 (Winter, 1987): 543-554. Earle sees the basic conflict of the novel in Hegelian terms. Esteban Trueba, representing "the blind force of history," is opposed to Clara, Blanca, and Alba, who have "historical awareness and intuitive understanding."

Foreman, P. Gabrielle. "Past-On Stories: History and the Magically Real, Morrison and Allende on Call." *Feminist Studies* 18 (Summer, 1992): 369-388. A comparison of *The House of the Spirits* and Toni Morrison's *Song of Solomon* (1977). Notes that Allende attributes magic only to women characters, suggesting that as they transmit their magical powers, so women can preserve history for others through the magic of words.

Hart, Patricia. *Narrative Magic in the Fiction of Isabel Allende*. Rutherford, N.J.:

Fairleigh Dickinson University Press, 1989. The chapter on *The House of the Spirits* expands the definition of "spirits" to include such elements as vision, dreams, and ideals, as well as people, both living and dead. An interesting approach.

Jones, Suzanne W., ed. *Writing the Woman Artist: Essays on Poetics, Politics, and Portraiture*. Philadelphia: University of Pennsylvania Press, 1991. Critical essays from a feminist perspective. A discussion of *The House of the Spirits* considers the development of Alba Trueba as a writer.

Morgan, Janice, and Colette T. Hall, eds. *Redefining Autobiography in Twentieth-Century Women's Fiction: An Essay Collection*. New York: Garland, 1991. A perceptive essay compares Isabel Allende to Clarice Lispector. In *The House of the Spirits*, Clara's journal-keeping shows "a woman inserting herself into history" and asserting her right to self-expression.

Rojas, Sonia Riquelme, and Edna Aguirre Rehbein, eds. *Critical Approaches to Isabel Allende's Novels*. New York: Peter Land, 1991. A collection including three essays in English on *The House of the Spirits*. One concentrates on the importance of the prostitute Tránsito Soto, another on Allende's system of names, and a third on her theme of "Nation as Family."

Valis, Noël, and Carol Maier. *In the Feminine Mode: Essays on Hispanic Women Writers*. Lewisburg, Pa.: Bucknell University Press, 1990. Of particular interest is an essay on androgyny in *The House of the Spirits*. The author argues that merging of male characters with female may imply some hope for an end to gender conflicts.

Rosemary M. Canfield Reisman

THE HOUSE ON MANGO STREET

Author: Sandra Cisneros (1954-   )
Type of work: Novel
Type of plot: Bildungsroman
Time of plot: The mid-1960's
Locale: A Latino neighborhood in Chicago
First published: 1984

> *Principal characters:*
> ESPERANZA CORDERO, a preteenage girl and beginning writer
>   who narrates a chronicle of her Latino neighborhood in
>   Chicago
> SALLY, the beautiful older girl whom Esperanza tries to emulate
> ALICIA, a struggling university student whose mother has died
> ELENITA, the "witch woman" who reads Esperanza's tarot cards
> GUADALUPE, Esperanza's Aunt Lupe, who is terminally ill and
>   bedridden
> MINERVA, a girl slightly older than Esperanza who has two
>   children and an absent husband
> LUCY, Esperanza's new friend from Texas
> RACHEL, Lucy's little sister
> MAGDALENA (NENNY), Esperanza's little sister

Form and Content

Based on Sandra Cisneros' experiences growing up in a Latino neighborhood of Chicago, *The House on Mango Street* is the story of a girl's search for identity as she comes of age. The narrative covers one crucial year in her life. Esperanza Cordero, a young Chicana, draws her identity from her parents' Mexican heritage and from the culture of the Mexican American community in which she grows up. She narrates the stories, describing herself, her neighbors, their dreams, and the world of Mango Street. In the process, she gains an understanding of herself and her community.

Cisneros has described the forty-six vignettes that make up the novel as crosses between poems and short stories. The tiny chapters are written in intensely lyrical prose, highly charged with metaphor, like prose poetry. Esperanza's voice unifies the narrative. Her search for identity shapes the plot, which is otherwise loosely defined.

Esperanza's descriptions focus on the women whom she knows, their lives often made difficult by the men who dominate them. Her childish yet mature perspective illuminates the ways in which society-at-large oppresses Latin Americans. The Latina women whom Esperanza describes bear a double yoke. They live in a strongly patriarchal society, often in fear of violence. Their choices for survival and self-expression are limited. Meanwhile, many suffer along with their men from living in poverty. Their burden is the fate that the narrator wishes to escape. Esperanza describes her family's house on Mango Street as sad. She feels ashamed of it, as she did of the old apartment, and dreams of having her own house someday.

Keenly observant and intuitive, Esperanza describes her world with a child's innocence which is beginning to fade. She is approaching puberty, with its longings and confusion. Her older friend Alicia, a college student who wakes up with the "tortilla star" every morning to pack her younger siblings' lunchboxes, helps her and encourages her to write about herself. Esperanza's ruminations are emotional, troubled, and exuberant. In many vignettes, she tests her sexuality, marvels at her body's changes, and savors her adolescent emotions.

Sally, the beautiful girl in the neighborhood, influences Esperanza because she seems to know how to express her sexuality. Esperanza calls herself the ugly daughter, and Sally's self-assurance impresses her. One night, however, Esperanza is humiliated when she tries to rescue Sally from a group of boys only to find that Sally does not desire to be saved. Sally completes her betrayal by disappearing at the carnival. She leaves Esperanza, who is raped that night. Sally's marriage to a traveling salesman frees her from her abusive father but brings her to a new kind of prison.

As Esperanza matures, her interest in her identity grows. Latino society limits her to traditional roles. Esperanza calls marriage a ball and chain, and she recalls her grandmother pining for freedom at her windowsill. Esperanza is her grandmother's namesake, but she does not want to share her circumstances. Consequently, Esperanza rejects traditional roles and seeks those who can help her write. Her Aunt Guadalupe, who is terminally ill, encourages her. Minerva, a struggling mother her own age, exchanges sad poems with Esperanza. Elenita, the "witch woman," tells her that she will have "a home in the heart." Only later does Esperanza understand that this cryptic message means Mango Street will always be with her, even after she goes away, with her books and papers. The young writer will represent her community, becoming its voice and historian. She is devoted to the women of the community. She says in the end that she will have "gone away to come back. For the ones I left behind. For the ones who cannot get out."

Analysis

Cisneros' training as a poet is evident in her ability to capture voices in her fiction and to craft prose of great lyric intensity. She has suggested that although her book was written in English, the syntax, sensibility, and ways of seeing things are very culturally Mexican. To catch some of the subtleties and jokes, a reader might even need intimate knowledge of Chicana culture, although the author is very conscious of having an English-speaking or worldwide audience. Thus Cisneros attempts in the rhythms as well as in the content of her language to share her Mexicana culture, as she prefers to call it. For effect and mood, she sometimes uses Spanish phrases that an English-only speaker must comprehend from context.

The House on Mango Street is between genres, between poetry and fiction—an experiment. It could be described as prose poems, a chain of vignettes, or short stories unified by the narrator's voice and identity. The novel is not linear, but moves from one event to another, often revisiting settings and characters in much the same way that a young girl's conversation or inner thoughts might skip from story to story or person to person by association or some other trigger of memory.

Cisneros' primary concern is to chart a girl's struggle for selfhood, exploring how one accepts or chooses not to accept one's family, circumstances, and community. Throughout the novel, Esperanza insists, whimsically and desperately, that she must have a house of her own. She also intends to become a writer. The two needs are inseparable in the narrative. For Esperanza, the house symbolizes the act of writing, or a place in which to accomplish it. Her two wishes, to be a writer and to own her own house, are her prerequisites to freedom and self-identity. How artistic creation strengthens identity and provides dignity is an important theme. The house provides creative space.

Esperanza often thinks aloud about her identity, in subconscious or naïve ways. She is Chicana, or American by birth, and Mexican by parentage. This dual identity leads her to perceive two possibilities in everything that she encounters. One fundamental example is her name: In English it means "hope"; in Spanish it means "too many letters," sadness, and waiting. She says she would like a new name: Esperanza wants to re-create herself from scratch and build the house that will reflect and define her. The house symbolizes the book of stories that she wants to write and her freedom to express herself.

Alicia, Esperanza's mentor, is the woman who teaches her social responsibility. She shows her protégée that a woman can pursue her dreams despite male domination. Furthermore, Alicia tells Esperanza that she must come back to Mango Street. In the end, Esperanza acknowledges this tie, saying what she remembers most is the sad red house that "I belong but do not belong to." The stories that she tells release her from and also tie her to her past and her community, to the women to whom the book is dedicated. By handing down the stories of their lives to the girls of the next generation, she rescues them from anonymous oppression.

Esperanza often refers to racism and classism, although her child's voice suggests that her awareness of these social problems has only begun to deepen. Cathy, "Queen of Cats," and her family will move away from the neighborhood because "people like us move in," Esperanza notes. In the vignette "Those Who Don't," she talks about people from outside the neighborhood who come by mistake and are scared because "They think we're dangerous." Esperanza recognizes that racial solidarity creates both warmth ("All brown all around, we are safe") and isolation, which breeds further suspicion between the cultures.

Cisneros' careful treatment of Esperanza's narratives and her use of English phrasings that reflect Spanish idioms allow the author to share some nuances of the Mexican American culture that she cherishes. Thus Esperanza describes with pride and tenderness the strong ties that families and neighbors keep, especially the bonds between women. Yet she is also a strong critic of sexual and physical violence, an endemic problem in Esperanza's neighborhood and in Latino society in general.

Context

Sandra Cisneros dedicates *The House on Mango Street* "A Las Mujeres: To the Women." The feminism of these stories is not tied to the mainstream feminist movement in the United States, however, but to the struggle of poor, working-class, uneducated women of American Latino culture. Her fiction exposes male violence and deception from a girl's point of view, making the suffering of these women at the hands of the men in Chicano/Mexican culture seem even more devastating. Yet the female characters appear that much stronger in their opposition to these hindrances.

At the same time, Cisneros' novel exposes the myth of the traditional role of Mexican and Latina women. While her female characters may at first seem humble, tied to household duties, and self-effacing—exemplary of the so-called traditional Latina—they are actually tough fighters. Their fierceness and strength is evident in Guadalupe, Minerva, Alicia, and the narrator herself. They are underprivileged women; nevertheless, they fight patriarchy, fight for selfhood, and fight for education. Even Sally resists the role that her father—or society—plans for her, however unfulfilled she remains in her marriage bedroom (which the narrator describes in an ironic aside: "the ceiling smooth as a wedding cake").

The House on Mango Street, published in 1984, was Cisneros' first book of fiction. With its appearance, she becomes recognized as one of the most powerful of the young Chicana writers—writers such as Ana Castillo, Denise Chavez, and Gloria Anzaldua whose work first emerged in the 1980's. Cisneros has also published *Woman Hollering Creek* (1991), a collection of stories, and *My Wicked, Wicked Ways* (1987), a volume of poetry. These works also explore the themes of feminism, biculturalism, classism, family violence, artistic creativity, and personal identity. Cisneros' work offers insights into the lives of contemporary Latina women, and grapples with issues of power and selfhood that concern all women.

Sources for Further Study

Cisneros, Sandra. Interview by Reed Way Dasenbrock. In *Interviews with Writers of the Post-Colonial World*, edited by Feroza Jussawalla and Dasenbrock. Jackson: University Press of Mississippi, 1992. Cisneros discuses the genesis of her first novel, her use of voices, the effect that bilingualism has on her writing, her life in Texas, her parents' lives, feminism, her favorite writers, and her novel in progress.

De Valdés, Maria Elena. "In Search of Identity in Cisneros's *The House on Mango Street*." *Canadian Review of American Studies* 23, no. 1 (Fall, 1992): 55-72. The author systematically charts the stages of Esperanza's search for identity, complicated by her "double marginalization"—being both a Chicana and a woman. Reviews key chapters to suggest what ideas they contribute to major themes in the novel.

Kolmar, Wendy K. "Dialectics of Connectedness: Supernatural Elements in Novels by Bambara, Cisneros, Grahn, and Erdrich." In *Haunting the House of Fiction: Feminist Perspectives on Ghost Stories by American Women,* edited by Lynette Carpenter and Kolmar. Knoxville: University of Tennessee Press, 1991. Kolmar discusses the theme of the dual experience. Esperanza is both insider and outsider, Mexican and American. Her ability to live in two worlds lets her see the supernatural as natural, to recognize Mango Street as the fertile ground of her stories, and to see in the women "a vision of interconnectedness."

McCracken, Ellen. "Sandra Cisneros' *The House on Mango Street*: Community-Oriented Introspection and the Demystification of Patriarchal Violence." In *Breaking Boundaries: Latina Writing and Critical Readings*, edited by Asunción Horono-Delgado et al. Amherst: University of Massachusetts Press, 1989. Taking a feminist perspective, McCracken finds the novel criticizes capitalistic and patriarchal social structures which oppress Latin women. Esperanza desires her own house in order to reclaim her dignity. She writes in order to create this house.

Olivares, Julián. "Sandra Cisneros' *The House on Mango Street*, and the Poetics of Space." In *Chicana Creativity and Criticism: Charting New Frontiers in American Literature*, edited by Maria Hererra-Sobek and Helena Mari'a Viramontes. Houston: Arte Publico Press, 1988. Olivares argues that the house motif represents Cisneros' "house of story-telling"; the narrative charts a young artist coming into her own. Her real house represents confinement; her imagined house represents her ability to transcend her condition by writing about it.

JoAnn Balingit

HOUSEHOLD SAINTS

Author: Francine Prose (1947-   )
Type of work: Novel
Type of plot: Fable
Time of plot: 1949 to the late 1960's
Locale: New York City
First published: 1981

Principal characters:

> JOSEPH SANTANGELO, a butcher with a thriving business on
> Mulberry Street
> MRS. SANTANGELO, Joseph's mother, who makes the sausage
> from a secret recipe
> CATHERINE FALCONETTI, a woman who marries Joseph as a
> result of her father's losing a bet in a pinochle game
> THERESA SANTANGELO, the daughter of Catherine and Joseph,
> who is preoccupied with religion
> AUGIE SANTANGELO, Joseph's brother, who sold his share of the
> butcher shop
> LINO FALCONETTI, Catherine's father, the owner of a radio repair
> shop
> NICKY FALCONETTI, the son of Lino and the brother of Catherine

Form and Content

Combining ribald humor and extravagant mythos, Francine Prose tells a story about two Italian American families and makes them emblematic of the entire community of Little Italy. The novel is an attempt to reveal how religious beliefs and chance happenings determine a family's destiny.

Household Saints opens in the midst of a heat wave so severe as to cause the people in the neighborhood to eschew meat as part of their diet; thus for the period of the heat wave, Joseph Santangelo's business at the butcher shop is as bad as Lino Falconetti's radio repair shop is all the time. Not having much to do, the men while away time by playing pinochle. On one fateful evening, Joseph opens his refrigerator and a blast of cold air hits the men. When Joseph closes the door, Lino asks him to open it again, but Joseph refuses. The argument is settled by a bet—Lino's daughter against an open refrigerator door. Joseph wins and decides to claim Catherine for his wife. Catherine's acceptance of Joseph's proposal is a manifestation of her naïveté that has been nurtured by a steady diet of Hollywood films. For Catherine, Joseph is a kind of Humphrey Bogart, which must make her a kind of Lauren Bacall.

Mrs. Santangelo is not so accepting. She calls immediately upon Saint Gennaro, whom she believes to be her patron saint, to explain what Joseph could possibly see in Catherine. A statue of Gennaro occupies a prominent place on Mrs. Santangelo's altar, which takes up most of the family's mantelpiece. Next to Gennaro is a plaster Madonna and a photo of Mrs. Santangelo's late husband, Zio, who after his death is, Mrs. Santangelo believes, a frequent visitor.

At her marriage, Catherine, slightly tipsy from Champagne, thinks of her wedding overladen with food and drink as being similar to the marriage at Cana where Jesus is said to have changed water into wine. In *Household Saints*, miracles line up one after the other—some holy, some secular. Saint Gennaro holds back a volcano with his arms; Joseph opens Catherine with his thumb, which Catherine also thinks of as a miracle.

The power struggle that develops between Catherine and Mrs. Santangelo after the marriage becomes overt when Catherine brings African violets to Joseph's apartment and puts one next to Saint Gennaro. Though Mrs. Santangelo objects, Catherine wins the day; she wins the day again when, pregnant, she determines that she will help Joseph in the shop rather than take up housewifely duties. Mrs. Santangelo has other weapons, however, especially the power of prophecy, and when Catherine watches Joseph kill turkeys Mrs. Santangelo says that her baby will look like a chicken. Prophecy is strong, and Catherine's firstborn dies. Yet the young eventually win out over the old, and after a period of mourning the loss of her powers, Mrs. Santangelo dies.

Theresa's birth, the result of a second conception, takes place in almost exactly the midway point in the novel, and thereafter she becomes its focus, with Catherine and Joseph reacting to Theresa's turns and moves. Despite Catherine's best intentions to rear Theresa as a modern American child, somehow Mrs. Santangelo's influences seem dominant and Theresa turns out to be more religious even than Mrs. Santangelo. From the time that Theresa is old enough to go to school, she wants to go to parochial school, wants to be a nun, and desires to cultivate the saints. Despite her parents' efforts to turn her in different directions, Theresa pursues her calling much like a monomaniac.

Since her parents refuse to allow her to enter a convent and be a nun, Theresa latches on to the next best thing: She will be a saint like Saint Therese, the little flower, whose life was a testimony to modesty, humility, and service in the form of mundane and menial tasks. Theresa's sexual liaison with Leonard comforts her mother, who has been looking for some signs of normalcy in her daughter, and acts as the focal point for Theresa's breakdown. One day, Leonard returns to his apartment to find that Theresa has been ironing one red-and-white-checked shirt for eight hours. Theresa insists that there are many checked shirts and that Joseph has provided them as he has the loaves and fishes. Moreover, Jesus has been there with her and has thanked her for taking care of one of his flock.

Theresa does not recover, and soon after her death rumors start that all the patients at the hospital recovered immediately once she was dead, the patients and their relatives declaring that the hospital flowers had healing powers. The community also declares that since his daughter's death, Joseph never cheated customers again. This last statement, at least, is false, since Joseph begins to cheat more and more, and the women tolerate it as they have before. Soon people take sides about the consequences of Theresa's life. Only the elderly take the story as relevant to a saint's life. They shush one another and listen to the sound of the cards, for they believe that with that sound God is sending a saint.

Analysis

One of the important techniques that Prose uses in telling her story is the device of juxtaposition. Joseph's skill at cards, for example, is juxtaposed with Catherine's lack of cooking skills. At the wedding celebration, a female guest asks whether it is true that, one way or another, women win their husbands in card games. The question actually has been answered earlier when the dead Zio, manifesting himself to his wife, says that man deals but God stacks the deck.

This admixture identifies the holy and the secular as myths by means of whose strictures people order their lives. Sometimes the juxtapositioning points to the comic, and indeed the surreal, as when Catherine's dead baby looks to Joseph (who has been described as a bantam rooster) like a freshly slaughtered baby chicken; or when Catherine miraculously whips up a perfect batch of sausage at about the same time that she and Joseph whip up a new baby.

By the midway point in the novel, Prose has established a set of symbols and symbolic events that will guide the actions of the characters to complete the pattern, mainly through such juxtaposition. Joseph makes the point clearly at the end of the book. Theresa is, she tells her mother and father, playing pinochle with God, Jesus, and Saint Therese. God and Jesus are winning, however, and it looks to Theresa that Saint Therese is passing to God and Jesus every card she has. Moreover, God is cheating. After the game, God whispers to Theresa that of all the great miracles His favorites are tipping scales and cheating at pinochle. This has to be the way everything ends, Joseph insists; there must be a pattern by which he and Catherine, and now Theresa, are being governed. Indeed, it does seem so.

Catherine does everything that she can to direct Theresa toward a secular life. At Eastertime, Catherine dyes eggs and buys marshmallow bunnies. Theresa eschews these secular offerings and insists upon celebrating Easter as a time to reflect upon death and Resurrection.

Theresa's death is an occasion for another piece of the pattern to fall into place. When Joseph and Catherine enter the hospital after they have been informed of their daughter's death, they each perceive a strong scent of roses. Joseph finds on Theresa's wrists evidence of a stigmata; Sister Cupertino, the nurse, suggests that in another era people might have called Theresa a saint.

Yet there are other pieces of the pattern still to fall. At the funeral, every surface is covered with roses. Now even Catherine sees the pattern. First her own wedding "at Cana," then her daughter's shower of roses. Perceiving the pattern leads Joseph to bitterness, Catherine to anger. For Joseph, God was stacking the deck; for Catherine, her life was being planned without her being consulted.

Context

The women's issues that underlie *Household Saints* are related to a past time and place. The novel is set in New York City in September, 1949, four years after the end of World War II, a war that brought about a change in social mores lasting until the rise of the women's movement in the 1970's. The culture that arose after World War II called for single-family housing and a new kind of menu, typified in *Household Saints* by Augie and his wife's taste for white bread and bologna, which he offers as a substitute for Joseph's sausage. Augie sells his part of the butcher shop to Joseph, moves away from Little Italy, eschews Old World habits, and like most other Americans, buys into the new American culture.

Otherwise, life in the Italian community from the 1950's until 1966 is unchanged. The community lives untouched, it appears, by the outside world. No references are made to Martin Luther King, Jr., and the rise of the Black Power movement, much less to early attempts to define a new role for women. Children live in the same large apartments with their parents and then support their parents when the parents get older. Joseph cares for his mother in the way that she once cared for him. When he marries, Joseph brings Catherine into the house that is ruled by his mother, and Catherine adjusts to it, gradually making the changes that she believes are important. Power struggles develop, but they do not break up the families; divorces are forbidden in Catholicism. In the family, a man's role is that of breadwinner and arbitrator; a woman's role is that of wife and mother.

Left without a wife, Lino Falconetti expects his daughter to do the necessary cooking and cleaning; his son, Nicky, "works" with his father, though he is incompetent. In addition, Nicky accompanies his father to the men's pinochle games. The men understand that a newly married man will spend less time playing pinochle, but they also expect that in due time a wife will be pregnant and will turn the husband out of her bed for a given period. In addition, as women get older husbands spend less time at home, preferring the company of men. For the most part, women's social lives are limited to occasional outings with their husbands and daily trips to the market, where they meet other women like themselves. With few exceptions, a man and woman will marry at the appropriate time, have children, make do with each other, provide for older relatives, and die, mostly in their own beds. In *Household Saints*, there are few exceptions. One is Nicky, who kills himself in despair; others are priests or nuns, whose way of life is an acceptable alternative.

Sources for Further Study

Hogan, Randolph. "The Butcher Won a Wife." *The New York Times Book Review*, July 12, 1981, 12. Hogan's review is a critique of the novel. Lavish in his praise, he points out that in only a few pages, Prose is able to establish most of the elements that will form the pattern that dictates the direction of the lives of her characters, as well as the structure of the novel itself. Hogan makes more of the bad luck of the Falconettis than other reviewers do.

Kirkus Reviews. Review of *Household Saints*. 49 (April 15, 1981): 529. Calls the novel a folk-mystical/quasi-comedic tale, claiming that the characters in the novel are so well drawn that a reader accepts the miracles and the initial assumption—that even God tilts the scales and cheats at some gigantic pinochle game that affects the lives of people, in this case Joseph and his family and friends.

Nerboso, Donna L. Review of *Household Saints*. *Literary Journal*, June 1, 1981, 1244. Nerboso points to Prose's major achievement: the writing of a narrative rich in detail that meshes the ordinary and the extraordinary, the natural and the supernatural, and thus moves the characters from the commonplace to the mystic.

Strouse, Jean. "Sausages and Saints." *Newsweek* 98, no. 5 (August 3, 1981): 72. Strouse admires the novel's striking style, incisive characterization, texture in the details of setting and character, and impressive and illuminating meshing of madness and grace. Each of the characters is troubled with some aspect of the supernal, from Joseph's lucky thumb to Catherine's miraculous knowledge of Carmela's recipe for the sausage; from Nicky's obsession with Madame Butterfly to Carmela's sightings of her dead husband.

Mary Rohrberger

HOUSEKEEPING

Author: Marilynne Robinson (1944-   )
Type of work: Novel
Type of plot: Allegory
Time of plot: The late 1950's to the early 1960's
Locale: Fingerbone, Idaho
First published: 1980

Principal characters:

RUTH STONE, an awkward adolescent in search of her identity

LUCILLE STONE, Ruth's younger sister, who wants a
conventional lifestyle

SYLVIE FOSTER FISHER, Ruth and Lucille's mysterious aunt, who
comes to take care of them

SYLVIA FOSTER, the grandmother of Ruth and Lucille and the
mother of Sylvie and Helen

HELEN FOSTER STONE, the mother of Ruth and Lucille and
Sylvie's sister

LILY and NONA FOSTER, sisters-in-law to Sylvia Foster

MISS ROYCE, the home economics teacher who eventually takes
in Lucille

Form and Content

Narrated in the first person by Ruth Stone, *Housekeeping* examines a world of female relationships and experience. The sisters, mothers, aunts, and other relatives in the novel form a web of female kinship played out against the tensions of poetic vagrancy and stalwart rootedness. Set in the isolated town of Fingerbone, Idaho, *Housekeeping* reconsiders what it means to inhabit that traditional female space, the home. The book begins with Ruth's description of how her family ended up in the mountains of Idaho.

Edmund Foster, Ruth's maternal grandfather, arrived in Fingerbone, a frustrated artist who saw the world in his own way. Although he is never alive in the book, through the house he built, the objects and art that furnish it, even the decision to locate in Fingerbone, Edmund Foster and his choices conspire to define the physical and emotional space of the women in the novel. While working for the railroad, Edmund disappears with an entire train full of passengers in a spectacular derailment into the icy waters of the lake near Fingerbone. His widow, Sylvia, is left with her three daughters in the small town. For five years after Edmund's death, Sylvia and her daughters Molly, Helen, and Sylvie have lives of self-enclosed contentment. Masculine encroachment, however, claims the young women, one by one—Molly heeding a call from Jesus, Helen marrying Reginald Stone, and Sylvie leaving to visit her married sister and returning only once to her mother's home to marry Mr. Fisher in the garden. Left alone, Sylvia Foster realizes that she had not taught her daughters to be kind to her.

After her marriage fails, Helen returns with her daughters, Ruth and Lucille, to Sylvia's house in Fingerbone. Without explanation, Helen leaves the girls with Sylvia and drives the car that she borrowed from a friend in Seattle into the lake that claimed her father. Stunned by this event, Sylvia nevertheless manages to provide a good home for her granddaughters for the next five years. When Sylvia dies, her unmarried sisters-in-law, Lily and Nona Foster, come to care for the girls, but they are ill-prepared for parenting and constantly fearful of imagined disasters. By the end of the first two chapters, all biological mothers are dead and all fathers are absent. Sylvie, contacted by letter, arrives to care for Ruth and Lucille and free the unhappy Foster sisters. Sylvie, who has been living as a vagrant, is poised to take up both housekeeping and mothering.

Sylvie's notions about homemaking are unconventional, and after the girls discover that their aunt can add little to their store of information about their mother, Ruth and Lucille themselves begin a slow drift away from the society of Fingerbone. Frightened at the direction that their lives seem to be taking, Lucille attempts various schemes—such as dressmaking—to get back to a more mainstream lifestyle. Sylvie continues to inhabit her own world, occasionally including Ruth in some of her ventures, and the two grow closer. As Ruth and Sylvie become more alike, Lucille becomes determined to reenter what she considers the "real world." After several attempts to include Ruth in her plans, Lucille finally gives up and parts from her sister, though not without reluctance. Lucille cannot and will not live in Sylvie's dreams, and she moves in with her home economics teacher, Miss Royce.

After Lucille leaves, Sylvie takes Ruth on a journey onto the islands in the lake outside Fingerbone. Stealing a leaky rowboat, the two row over to a mysterious valley of abandoned and decaying houses, where Sylvie proposes they "watch for the children." Sylvie suddenly leaves Ruth in the cool, misty valley in a test or initiation into the world of transience to which Sylvie wishes to return. Left alone to muse over the unfamiliar landscape and her own losses, Ruth comes to terms somewhat with the loss of her mother, Helen. Cradled in the folds of the long coat that Sylvie wears, Ruth is reborn as a child of her mysteriously returned aunt.

The two return to Fingerbone by boat and freight train, where they are spotted by several townspeople. As a result, the sheriff comes to the house—the only living male to breach their space—to warn Sylvie that she cannot continue to care for Ruth in such a haphazard manner. Sylvie tries to conform to the notions of the town and its church women, but she is not able to persuade them of any change in her ability to "keep house." Thus, Ruth and Sylvie abandon housekeeping and any notion of permanence by setting fire to the house and fleeing Fingerbone by crossing the train trestle spanning the lake. The book ends with Ruth imaging Lucille in Boston waiting for them and the others who will not come and who are known only by their absence.

Analysis

Marilynne Robinson's lyrical first novel is concerned with mothering, female space, and cultural myths concerning mothering and family. The book suggests that in rejecting conventional norms of "housekeeping," women might gain autonomy, by embracing the transience of persons, events, and even memory rather than futile attempts at permanence. These themes are underscored by Robinson's major metaphor, water.

Water in its many forms flows throughout the work. The lake, for example, is the repository of the town's major event—the derailment of the Fireball—and of several Foster family members, including Edmund, Helen, and supposedly, Sylvie and Ruth. Like memory, the lake swallows up whole that which enters it, and surprising artifacts emerge—such as the suitcase, the seat cushion, and the cabbage—as the only tangible evidence of an event such as the derailment. Also, like memory, the boundaries of the lake are unreliable. Every spring, parts of the lake long forgotten rise up from the earth and flood Fingerbone, including the Fosters' orchard and house. Water inhabits the house and takes it over. Sylvie and Ruth row across the water to "watch for children" and, at the end of the novel, must cross the bridge over the lake to escape the confines of Fingerbone. Water appears in the forms of snow, ice, rain, mist, and frost throughout *Housekeeping.*

The Foster family home is another important element in the book. Its location on the edge of a town that itself is at the edge of a lake follows the Foster family tradition of being on the edge or fringe of things. Also, being close to the edge of town makes the house easier for Sylvie and Ruth to abandon. The presence of light and dark both within and without the house is noteworthy, as are the windows of the house. Ruth "spends too much time looking out of windows," which can be either mirrors or barriers to the world of possibilities. When Sylvie does attempt to "keep house," she does so by opening doors and windows to let the air in, and it does not occur to Sylvie to close either, so much of the outdoors comes indoors. When the house burns and Ruth and Sylvie escape across the bridge, the windows shatter with loud retorts. Lucille, who turns on the lights in the darkened house, also abandons "keeping house" in the sense that she leaves the Foster home. She moves in with her home economics teacher, however, and presumably will be adequately trained in the proper ways to keep house and shut windows at appropriate times.

The importance of names is constant throughout the novel. Ruth and Lucille are cared for by a series of "Foster" mothers until they are able to act on their own (Lucille to leave for a conventional life and Ruth to drift). Sylvie's married last name is Fisher, suggesting her connections to water, drifting, and perhaps Christ (in that she redeems Ruth). Helen, whose name suggests the mythical Helen of Troy, marries Reginald Stone, and like a stone, sinks to the bottom of the lake. Ruth's name—which she announces with a Melvillian directness ("My name is Ruth") in the first sentence of the book—has obvious biblical implications, while Lucille's name is never shortened. The name Sylvia brings to mind both a "sylph," a slender, graceful young woman, and "sylvan," one who frequents groves or woods. Even the name of the town, Fingerbone, has implications suggesting its insignificance and something perhaps not worth keeping.

Context

In *Housekeeping*, Robinson's protagonists Sylvie and Ruth abandon ownership of one of the objects most closely associated with defining women—the home. Instead of a traditional, functional nuclear family, Robinson presents readers with a family made only of women. Through death, fear, choice, or fate, these women are quite ready either to walk from or at least (even if only for a short while, as in the case of Lucille) to consider rethinking the whole project of "keeping" house. Transience, usually associated with male protagonists, is introduced as a possibility. Ideas about mothering and nurturing are also reexamined in *Housekeeping*.

For example, the woman who is a childless drifter—Sylvie—is the one most able to "mother" Ruth and Lucille while maintaining a somewhat autonomous existence herself. Judged by conventional middle-class American expectations, however, Sylvie is viewed as a failure at mothering. The women from the town and church visiting with casseroles and inquiries are appalled by what they find to be Sylvie's mode of acceptable housekeeping. The women call in the authorities in the form of the local sheriff who offers to take Ruth home with him. She refuses, and that night, with Sylvie, burns the house down, aunt and niece almost as one in their actions and intent.

It is when their Adamless Eden is invaded that the pretense of housekeeping, with all of its layers of meaning, totally falls apart. Robinson's point seems to be that women are certainly capable of making and inhabiting their own niches which do not have to be part of the patriarchal structure and that women are capable of walking away and abandoning that which has imprisoned them. Unlike previous female protagonists, Sylvie and Ruth do not suffer the traditional literary endings of marriage, madness, or death. Instead, like Mark Twain's Huck and Jim, they "light out for the territory." The choice is not without danger, but it is preferable to the slow suffocation offered by maintaining the fictions of housekeeping. As portrayed by Robinson, transience by choice is a poetic and viable alternative.

Winner of the Ernest Hemingway Foundation award for best first novel and the Richard and Hinda Rosenthal Award from the American Academy of Arts and Letters, *Housekeeping* also received nominations for the Pen/Faulkner fiction award and for a Pulitzer Prize. Robinson's evocative prose and persistent yet gentle characters combine to question the value of an enterprise supposedly entrenched within the cultural myths surrounding women.

Sources for Further Study

Aldrich, Marcia. "The Poetics of Transience: Marilynne Robinson's *Housekeeping*." *Essays in Literature* 5, no. 16 (Spring, 1989): 127-140. An in-depth discussion of the meaning of transience in relation to female choices and as a specifically female experience. This article also discusses mother-daughter relationships in *House-keeping*.

Booth, Allyson. "To Capture Absent Bodies: Marilynne Robinson's *Housekeeping*." *Essays in Literature* 5, no. 19 (Fall, 1992): 279-290. A provocative study of how metaphors of the body inform the novel. Includes a worthwhile discussion of some of the images and symbols in the book, such as the dresser painted by Edmund and other objects.

Champagne, Rosaria. "Women's History and *Housekeeping*: Memory, Representation, and Reinscription." *Women's Studies* 20, no. 3/4 (1992): 321-329. This essay considers how memory functions in the novel, as well as examining competing definitions as to what "good" housekeeping is within the parameters of the work.

Foster, Thomas. "History, Critical Theory, and Women's Social Practices: Women's Time and *Housekeeping*." *Signs* 14, no. 11 (1988): 73-99. Applies theories of deconstruction to *Housekeeping*. Also considers issues of how historical approaches to the public and private spheres of women and their roles are useful in thinking about the novel.

Meese, Elizabeth A. *Crossing the Double Cross: The Practice of Feminist Criticism*. Chapel Hill: University of North Carolina Press, 1986. An excellent study of feminist criticism, lucid and well written. Includes an informative chapter on *Housekeeping* that views the novel as "A World of Women."

Saltzman, Arthur M. *The Novel in the Balance*. Columbia: University of South Carolina Press, 1993. A useful and in-depth look at several modern novels, including *Housekeeping*. Offers the interesting juxtaposition of *Housekeeping* with John Hawkes's *Second Skin* (1964), Hawkes being one of Robinson's early mentors.

Virginia Dumont-Poston

HOW I GREW

Author: Mary McCarthy (1912-1989)
Type of work: Memoir
Time of work: 1925-1933
Locale: Minneapolis, Seattle, and Poughkeepsie, New York
First published: 1987

> *Principal personages:*
> MARY MCCARTHY, a writer remembering her life during her
> teenage years
> HAROLD COOPER JOHNSRUD, her first husband, an actor
> ETHEL (TED) ROSENBERG, her friend at a public high school
> MARK SULLIVAN, her uncle's friend, on whom she develops a
> crush
> FORREST CROSBY, her first lover
> MISS DOROTHY ATKINSON, her English teacher at Annie Wright
> Seminary

Form and Content

In *How I Grew*, Mary McCarthy constructs an intellectual autobiography of her adolescence, covering roughly the eight years between ages thirteen and twenty-one. In a sense a sequel to her earlier autobiographical work. *Memories of a Catholic Girlhood* (1957), it is the story of the orphaned McCarthy following the move from the Catholic, Minneapolis household of her McCarthy relatives to the Seattle household of her Protestant grandfather and Jewish grandmother, Harold Preston and Augusta Morgenstern Preston. McCarthy describes her intellectual awakening and development through recollections of influential family members, friends, and teachers. The book is also a literary exploration of the process of memory.

The book is a mostly chronological account of major and minor episodes in her life, largely centered on three sets of school experiences: her year at public school in Seattle; three years at the private girls' school, Annie Wright Seminary, in Tacoma, Washington; and her college years at Vassar College, Poughkeepsie, New York. Throughout, she manages a twofold focus: on her developing intellectual interests and influences (books, teachers, and friends) and on her adolescent social life (her forays into sexual and romantic adventure).

For example, she reveals the progress of her reading tastes, the books that she read and the people who influenced her, and her early writings and theatrical performances. Yet she also relates her first sexual experience (at age fourteen, in an automobile); her entry into Seattle bohemian society; her uneven relationship with her first husband, actor Harold Cooper Johnsrud; and her first, rather unflattering glimpse of her second husband, writer Edmund Wilson, when he speaks at Vassar. The narrative presents incisive portraits of a succession of persons whom McCarthy sees as having influenced her development into an intellectual.

Methodologically, the crux of the book is in the texture of overlapping and possibly contradictory memories, as McCarthy searches for as much truth as can be wrung from recollection, accompanied by an ever-alert awareness of memory's limitations. In addition, McCarthy's adult commentary is woven into the chronological narrative.

Analysis

McCarthy's introductory chapter is a whirlwind tour which ranges from her early childhood preciosity to the last of her disastrous attempts at acting while at Vassar. Throughout, the adult comments on the youth, often as the reader follows the author on her multipronged attempts to secure a memory. The texture of memory—of multiple, contradictory memories—is as much McCarthy's theme as her ostensible content, such as her final recognition that she was not destined to be an actress or her adult comment that this ambition probably reflected a desire to be considered beautiful. McCarthy carefully questions each reminiscence: An early recollection of a precocious questioning of language usage is swiftly followed by a recognition that this event was perhaps not as artless as remembered; she finally decides that she had been mimicking the artlessness of the child for effect.

This introductory chapter telescopes the movement from light to darkness brought about by becoming an orphan at age five (the subject of *Memories of a Catholic Girlhood*) into a few pages in a style characterized by a deadpan dryness. The anecdote about the precocious questions at prayers is quickly followed by the information that her prayers soon changed to include her parents in heaven. A brief reminiscence of the physical abuse that she received in Minneapolis provokes the adult comment that she has earned the right to satirize her abusers. Laughter, she admits, does dry out the feelings, allowing her to forgive, but removing the moisture needed not only for self-pity but for tragedy as well. Thus McCarthy provides a comment on her self-perceived limitations as a writer.

The move from Minneapolis to Seattle is a move again into light, from material and spiritual poverty into riches. McCarthy recounts how she devoured books (and bananas, another formerly forbidden pleasure) in the libraries that opened to her after the move. Some classic writers, she notes, such as Rudyard Kipling and Sir Walter Scott, are lost to her; she is now too old to embrace them. She recalls that her tastes ran to books written for young boys, as well as to adult escapist literature such as *True Confessions*.

McCarthy frames her account of her schooling and intellectual friendships with two ideas: that the choice of secondary school, though often haphazard, marks one's destiny and that friendships are necessary to the development of an intellectual. The heart of the text is the story of her years at Annie Wright Seminary. She notes that she alone was prepared to benefit from the elite education to be received there because she had already become an intellectual, ironically through a year at public high school in Seattle. In a chapter devoted to the year at Garfield, she examines her close friendship with Ethel (Ted) Rosenberg, with whom she shared books, but not tastes.

In a later chapter, Ted introduces McCarthy to bohemian life in Seattle.

The year at Garfield includes tales of theatricals and of an early crush on Larry Judson, with whom McCarthy acted. The account leads McCarthy to consider how it was that she eventually found out that he, like Ted Rosenberg, was Jewish. This series of recollections provides McCarthy with an opportunity to inventory her attitudes toward Jews and to uncover the memory of her own share of the prevailing anti-Semitism of the day, a theme which will preoccupy her later as she discusses her early writing at Annie Wright Seminary and attempts to trace the origins of its anti-Semitic stereotypes, as well as the subtle attitudes toward Jews and Catholics at that school.

McCarthy is also influenced intellectually by her uncle's friend Mark Sullivan, who provides her with reading suggestions and with whom she corresponds during her first year at Annie Wright Seminary. Ever writing the double narrative of the blossoming adolescent that coincides with the burgeoning intellectual, McCarthy also recounts how she pretends that Sullivan is her fiancé to boost her image with her new classmates and later, half-believing that she is in love with him, stages a dramatic suicide vigil outside his door.

As she opens the chapter that will begin the tale of her years at Annie Wright Seminary, she interrupts the narrative with the story of the loss of her virginity at the age of fourteen. She met her partner, Forrest Crosby, who was twenty-three, at Lake Crescent, where the family vacationed and where her grandfather provided a comical spectacle with his heavy-handed chaperonage of her. With mordant wit, McCarthy considers how she forced herself to overlook the inadequacy of Crosby's seduction, accomplished through letters, which she recognized as without style but on which she determined to forgo judgment. She describes her subsequent disappointment at the event as Crosby casually reveals his coarse indifference to her; she completes the act in resigned recognition of its meaninglessness, yet manages subsequently to persuade herself that she is in the midst of a love affair. McCarthy's accounts of these half-baked, souped-up emotions capture the texture of the adolescent's desire to be in love, as well as the adult McCarthy's vigilant pursuit of emotional honesty. It is echoed later in her account of her courtship with her first husband, to whom she determined to remain attached in spite of his indifference to her, succeeding in marrying him despite the disbelief of her Vassar classmates.

The years at Annie Wright Seminary are formative in a variety of ways. Set free for the first time in a library without supervision, McCarthy encounters literary periodicals and gains access for the first time to a collection of modern literature. Her English teacher, Miss Dorothy Atkinson, a Vassar graduate, inspires McCarthy with the desire to attend Vassar College. Atkinson advises McCarthy to send an early short story to essayist H. L. Mencken. Another story, about a prostitute, she sends to a young man at university, inspiring him to reply by writing her sexually explicit but not literary letters, disastrously intercepted by her overprotective grandparents.

McCarthy analyzes the social backgrounds of her classmates, linking background to character and finding them lacking distinction. On the other hand, she finds the teachers extraordinary, as well as the education. The emphasis is on English rather than American literature, which she reads on her own. She also studies French and takes accelerated courses in Latin to prepare for Vassar. At the same time, she is sneaking out to the woods after supper to smoke cigarettes with a local boy, as well as going out on illicit weekend excursions arranged through her young uncle, Harold Preston.

In the summer before junior year, McCarthy notices the actor Harold Johnsrud in a Magna Charta pageant in Seattle. Her Garfield friend, Ted Rosenberg, introduces them. Later, in New York, en route to Vassar, they meet and begin a courtship that is coterminous with her years at Vassar. During this period, her attention is split between the academic life and the New York theater world of Johnsrud, who exposes her to opera, the theologian Albert Parker Fitch, modern art, nightclubs, and speakeasies.

McCarthy describes her education at Vassar as largely a process of un-learning which she was presented under the tutelage of the Misses Kitchel, Sandison, and the hated Lockwood. Miss Anna Kitchel was McCarthy's influential faculty adviser. At Vassar, McCarthy also finds herself in New York society; ironically, it is Jewish high society that she experiences through a friendship with a classmate, Elinor Coleman. This memory prompts another examination of her anti-Semitism, her shame at having Jewish relatives, and her surprise at the anti-Irish sentiment that she encounters in Gentile country club society, to which she is introduced through another school connection.

The last quarter of the book describes the Vassar/Johnsrud years, including an amusing account of her first New York summer job, writing copy for a painter of dog portraits, as well as a portrait of her intellectual friendships at Vassar with classmates Frani Blough and the poet Elizabeth Bishop. With these two women, she joins in publishing an alternative to the Vassar literary magazine, which provokes outrage because it is unsigned. At the conclusion of the narrative, McCarthy graduates from Vassar and a week later marries Johnsrud. She ends the narrative with the image of herself in bed with her new husband, suffering remorse at her semiconscious recognition that she has married without love.

Context

How I Grew provides not only a background for understanding the fiction and nonfiction work by McCarthy, a prolific writer who made it into the mainstream of New York intellectual life, but also a picture of the social and intellectual culture of the period, especially as it pertains to elite women's education and sexual mores. McCarthy also provides an honest exploration of anti-Semitism. She does not examine the reasons for the ways in which her young self deviated from prevalent norms defining appropriate feminine sexuality.

On the other hand, the break with norms surrounding the educational goals and intellectual interests of young women of her class and upbringing is well analyzed. McCarthy portrays the impetus for her intellectuality as her early deprivation following orphanhood, which produced a craving and appreciation for the privilege of intellectual and aesthetic enjoyment. The loss of her parents, which made her some-

thing of an outsider, and the juxtaposition of her materially and spiritually impoverished childhood with her financially secure and elite adolescence also contribute to a
sociological outlook which permeates her descriptive interests and analysis, finding
expression in her close attention to the issue of social class and to social influence in
general.

McCarthy follows the development of her critical eye through a series of personal
influences, especially those of teachers. In this vein, she provides a depiction of a
continuity of female intellectual tradition carried on by graduates of elite women's
colleges who taught in a network of elite secondary schools during the period.

McCarthy received the National Medal for Literature, the Edward MacDowell
Medal, and two Guggenheim Fellowships. She was a member of the National Institute
of Arts and Letters and held the Stevenson Chair for Literature at Bard College. She
was the author of novels, such as *The Groves of Academe* (1952) and *The Group*
(1963); short stories; travel memoirs, such as *Venice Observed* (1956) and *The Stones
of Florence* (1959); essays, such as *On the Contrary: Articles of Belief* (1961) and
Ideas and the Novel (1980); and memoirs.

Sources for Further Study

Bennett, Joy, and Gabriella Hochmann. *Mary McCarthy: An Annotated Bibliography*.
New York: Garland, 1992. This bibliography contains summaries of critical responses to *How I Grew* at the time of its publication, as well as to McCarthy's work
as a whole.
Gelderman, Carol. *Mary McCarthy: A Life*. New York: St. Martin's Press, 1988. In a
well-researched biography that was written with McCarthy's cooperation, Gelderman attempts to show how McCarthy's public persona in her autobiographical
writing does not always correspond to her life.
Grumbach, Doris. *The Company She Kept*. New York: Coward-McCann, 1967. This
early biography analyzes McCarthy's novel *The Group*, relating it to her Vassar
years, and describes her studies at convent schools and at Annie Wright Seminary.
Includes examples of McCarthy's early essays written at Vassar.
McCarthy, Mary. *Memories of a Catholic Girlhood*. New York: Harcourt Brace
Jovanovich, 1957. This earlier autobiographical work by McCarthy covers some of
the same years and influences as *How I Grew*, with a different thematic emphasis
on how the narrator of memory constructs the narration in particular ways.
McKenzie, Barbara. *Mary McCarthy*. New York: Twayne, 1966. McKenzie relates
McCarthy's fiction and nonfiction to autobiographical materials—for example,
tying McCarthy's choice of satire as a literary mode to possible influences from her
Latin studies.

Allison Carter

HOW TO SUPPRESS WOMEN'S WRITING

Author: Joanna Russ (1937-   )
Type of work: Literary criticism
First published: 1983

Form and Content

In this witty analysis of the critical reception of women's literature, Nebula Award-winning science-fiction writer Joanna Russ explores the social connections of literature and art from a feminist perspective. Russ stresses that her discussion is not a history of oppression; rather, it is an investigation of the ways in which women's writing has been suppressed, discouraged, and marginalized.

How to Suppress Women's Writing traces patterns in the suppression of women's writing, mostly by male critics, drawing on examples from high culture of the eighteenth through twentieth centuries in Europe and the United States. Russ uses the examples of such diverse literary figures as the Countess of Winchelsea, Aphra Behn, Emily and Charlotte Brontë, George Sand, Emily Dickinson, and Anne Sexton to show how societal conditions and expectations are brought to bear on the creative efforts of women writers. Russ also provides illustrations of women artists and musicians to support her argument.

In her analysis of women's literary marginalization, Russ draws heavily on the work of other feminist critics, especially Ellen Moers, Elaine Showalter, and Virginia Woolf. The text begins with a prologue in which Russ uses her science-fiction background to create an alien society in order to draw a parallel with the earthly conditions about which she is concerned. Each succeeding chapter addresses one of the patterns of marginalization that Russ has identified, explaining how the pattern works to suppress women's creativity and giving many examples, both historical and contemporary, to support her argument. Chapters at the end of the text address literary women's response to their suppression (including Russ's own); a call for a redefinition of cultural aesthetics, which would move culture away from the center toward the margin; and the voices of women of color, who are often excluded from the literary canon.

Analysis

While admitting that women have not been subject to formal prohibitions against writing, as were black slaves in America, Russ nevertheless asserts that the informal prohibitions of poverty, lack of leisure, lack of education, and "climate of expecta-tion"—the belief in traditional gender roles, which placed women in the home—were instrumental in preventing women from writing. Many women, particularly in the nineteenth century, were financially dependent on their families or their husbands; their household duties as either daughters or wives left them little if any time to write; and if they still expressed a willingness to create literature, the pressure of gender roles was brought to bear upon them—artistic creativity was a masculine ability not to be attempted by women.

Most of the text, however, is devoted to an identification and analysis of the practice of what Russ calls "bad faith," a term borrowed from philosopher Jean-Paul Sartre. One displays bad faith by perpetuating the status quo in order to maintain discrimination. Women who insist on writing despite informal prohibitions are met with one or more of the following patterns of bad faith: denial of agency, pollution of agency, double standard of content, false categorizing, isolation, and anomalousness.

Denial of agency is used to refute a particular woman's claim of authorship by asserting that the work in question was written by a man, that the text wrote itself, that the "masculine" part of the woman did the writing, or that the woman writer is "more than a woman." Mary Shelley, for example, is denied authorship of *Frankenstein* (1818) by a male critic who asserts that she was simply a repository of ideas that were circulating "in the air around her." Similarly, critics generally agree that Emily Brontë lost control of *Wuthering Heights* (1847) and wrote an entirely different novel than she had intended (that is, a "good" one).

Pollution of agency calls into play traditional gender roles; a woman who writes is unfeminine, ridiculous, or immoral. *Jane Eyre* (1847), published pseudonymously by Charlotte Brontë, was judged by critics to be a masterpiece if written by a man, degrading if written by a woman. Russ contends that the designation of much twentieth century poetry by women as confessional, or highly personal and therefore shameful, is a contemporary version of the nineteenth century charge of impropriety against women writers.

The double standard of content privileges male experience over female experience and renders women's lives and experience invisible. Russ points out that critical assessment of *Wuthering Heights* changed from positive to negative after Emily Brontë's authorship (and gender) became known, and in *A Room of One's Own* (1929), Virginia Woolf notes that books which deal with war are judged to be more important than books about domestic life.

False categorizing occurs when women's artistic and literary contributions are subsumed under or eclipsed by men's. For example, the composer Gustav Mahler forbade his wife to write music even though she had been a composer before their marriage. Also included under the pattern of false categorizing is the renaming of women's literature so as to exclude it from serious critical consideration. Thus, Willa Cather and Kate Chopin are called "regionalists" in order to emphasize the limited scope of their works, or writing by women is rendered inferior because it does not occur in acceptable or "literary" genres, such as novels or poetry, but in "inferior" forms, such as letters or diaries. False categorization also includes the marginalization of women authors through biographical readings of their works in which traditional women's roles are assigned to them; these roles then become the lens through which their works are read. Elizabeth Barrett Browning, for example, becomes the Wife (therefore her political and feminist poems are ignored in favor of her love poetry) and Emily Dickinson is the madcap/sad spinster.

If a woman is admitted to the literary canon, Russ argues that she is subject to isolation, the pattern by which only one of her works is recognized and her others are ignored. The work that is chosen for inclusion is generally one which supports stereotypical notions of women's artistic abilities. Therefore, Browning's *Sonnets from the Portuguese* (1850) (her love poems) are frequently anthologized; *Aurora Leigh* (1856) (her feminist "epic novel") is not. Isolation also occurs when the work of a woman writer is "recategorized" and then marginalized. Woolf, for example, is frequently criticized for her elitist attitudes when, in fact, her essays were depoliticized by her husband after her death.

When a woman writer is admitted to the literary canon, she also suffers from what Russ calls anomalousness. The relatively low percentage of women writers included in literary anthologies (the average is 7 percent) obscures the notion of a tradition of women writers and strengthens the assumption that women do not belong in the male literary tradition. Anomalousness is also used to justify an individual woman's personal eccentricity. Dickinson, for example, is treated as an isolated spinster whose talent "came from nowhere and bore no relation to anything." Russ declares anomalousness to be the most powerful means of marginalizing women, for if the literary canon were opened to include a tradition of women writers, the possibility of other marginalized groups would also have to be entertained, and aesthetic standards would have to be revised.

The remaining chapters of *How to Suppress Women's Writing* discuss the effects of these patterns of bad faith on women writers and potential women writers. The resulting marginalization of women and their texts deprives women writers of a sense of a woman's tradition in literature; it deprives them of models, so that each new generation of women writers must invent its own tradition and find its own models.

Women respond to the challenges presented by these patterns of marginalization in several ways: They do not write; they agree that women writers are inferior to male writers; they deny that they are women; they assert that they are not "ordinary" women; they become angry; or they shift their focus to "woman centeredness," or a concern with other women. The work of feminist literary critics has led to the questioning of an absolute set of aesthetic values. Russ's solution to the problem is to propose aesthetic criteria that allow many centers of value, each based on historical fact. Therefore, in formulating a more inclusive set of aesthetic standards, one must move away from the center.

How to Suppress Women's Writing concludes with the author's confession of her own difficulties in visualizing the margin. She relates her reassessment of the work of Zora Neale Hurston and other black women writers, which she had always considered to be "different" and therefore not "literary," and concludes the text with excerpts from writing by women of color, including Audre Lorde, Rosario Morales, Maxine Hong Kingston, and June Jordan.

Context

The humor in *How to Suppress Women's Writing* makes the text amusing and easy to read (the title itself makes the text sound like a handbook for insecure male critics), but Russ's humorous tone throughout masks her serious intent. Like many feminists,

Russ uses humor to cushion the impact of her sharp social criticism. This is a scholarly text—each chapter contains a minimum of fifteen footnotes—but its contribution to the field of feminist criticism is not so much in the research, which is largely derivative, but in Russ's ability to relate the social and material conditions under which women live to the art that they create. Thus, *How to Suppress Women's Writing* represents an important movement in feminist literary criticism away from a preoccupation with images of women in literature toward a broader consideration of the impact of society on the production of art. The text tends to emphasize the victimization of women writers over their obvious successes in circumventing suppression, but the reader gains important insight into the ways in which the institutionalization of gender bias can influence what literature is read, how literature is read, and what constitutes the meaning of "literature" and "author."

How to Suppress Women's Writing is also important for its insistence on an alternative, more inclusive definition of culture which would include literature and art judged by standards other than the traditional Western, white, middle-class, and male orientation.

Sources for Further Study

Gilbert, Sandra M., and Susan Gubar. *The Madwoman in the Attic: The Woman Writer and the Nineteenth-Century Literary Imagination.* New Haven, Conn.: Yale University Press, 1979. This wide-ranging and groundbreaking work examines the responses of nineteenth century women writers to the male-dominated literary tradition in England. Psychologically rather than socially oriented, this text traces a female tradition in literature.

Poovey, Mary. *Uneven Developments: The Ideological Work of Gender in Mid-Victorian England.* Chicago: University of Chicago Press, 1988. Poovey's work is a sophisticated extension of the social perspective used by Russ. In it, she argues that nineteenth century representations of gender were sites of struggle for power and authority between the genders and reads such texts as Charles Dickens' *David Copperfield* (1849-1850) and *Jane Eyre* from this position.

Showalter, Elaine. *A Literature of Their Own: British Women Novelists from Brontë to Lessing.* Princeton, N.J.: Princeton University Press, 1977. A text from which Russ derives much of the support for her study, this book is one of the first analyses of a woman's tradition in literature. Like Russ, Showalter uses a social and literary approach as she compares women novelists to their female contemporaries in order to trace the complexity of women's literary relationships.

Spender, Dale, ed. *Living by the Pen: Early British Women Writers.* New York: Teachers College Press, 1992. This collection of essays traces the literary heritage of early British women writers in order to distinguish that tradition from the male tradition. Includes essays on the women themselves, the topics on which they wrote, and their achievements as artists.

Todd, Janet. *Feminist Literary History.* New York: Routledge, 1988. In this introduction to feminist literary theory, Todd seeks to defend the early sociohistoric enterprise of American feminist criticism, of which Russ's text is an example. She refutes the claim of French feminists that this criticism is historically naïve and, while admitting its limitations, attempts to place it within a larger context of feminist literary criticism.

Karen Volland Waters

THE HUNGRY SELF
Women, Eating, and Identity

Author: Kim Chernin (1940-   )
Type of work: Social criticism
First published: 1985

Form and Content

Emerging from the intersection of female identity and the prevalence of eating disorders among American women, *The Hungry Self: Women, Eating, and Identity* asks why so many women have a troubled relationship with food. In answering this question, Kim Chernin draws upon her work counseling women suffering from bulimia and anorexia. She argues that underlying women's obsession with food are the basic components of a rite of passage, the elements of a transition from one stage of life to the next. The problem of food thus becomes its failure as such a rite, its inability to enable women to move from one stage of life to another.

Throughout the book, Chernin recounts the stories that women have told her about the place of food in their lives. These are stories of obsession, descriptions of the compulsion to exercise, to ingest huge quantities of food and then vomit, and to allow calorie-counting to disrupt normal activities and behavior. Furthermore, as Chernin delves more deeply into women's stories, she explains how the problem of food cloaks a more fundamental problem of identity. Her thesis is that at a time when women are encouraged to forgo traditional feminine pursuits, eating disorders appear as sites for the struggle over the meaning and validity of female identity. In other words, an eating disorder signifies an identity crisis.

For example, some women develop eating disorders when turning to a new career after having spent a number of years mothering and caring for husbands and children. Others, generally younger and preprofessional, the first generation of women socialized to expect career and educational opportunities, take on the styles and manners of the group in power—men. These young women seek to rid themselves of the flesh that makes them feminine and often adopt the men's-wear look encouraged by the media. Both groups, the older as well as the younger women, are conflicted about their identities as women.

At the heart of this conflict, Chernin argues, is the relationship between mothers and daughters. Extending Betty Friedan's discussion in *The Feminine Mystique* (1963), she observes the change in the societal understanding of motherhood in America in the middle of the twentieth century. Whereas previous generations of women could find fulfillment in carrying out their natural duties to be good wives and mothers, once the "naturalness" of these roles came under scrutiny, a number of women could no longer see their self-sacrifice as serving a larger purpose or order. Once motherhood became a choice, the only reason to devote oneself to mothering was personal fulfillment.

Unfortunately, many women did not find the day-in, day-out work of housekeeping and child rearing especially fulfilling. Consequently, these women communicated this dissatisfaction to their daughters. As daughters have grown into adulthood, moreover, many of them have been reluctant to accept the opportunities and advantages denied to their mothers. Eating disorders emerge, in part, out of this sense of guilt. Feeling as if their mothers' lives were "shrunken," "impoverished," or "depleted," daughters act out these sufferings upon their own bodies, symbolically playing out the mother-daughter bond so as to save the mother.

This "playing out" tends to take on the character of a rite of passage. Analogizing the behavior of contemporary American girls with the tribal rituals described by Mircea Eliade in *Rites and Symbols of Initiation: The Mysteries of Birth and Rebirth* (1958), Chernin convincingly describes the retreat to infancy, separation, and dietary prohibitions common among female adolescents as aspects of a transition from one stage of life to another. She provides a stark and often shocking discussion of the social aspects of bingeing and purging on college campuses: Some girls, perhaps athletes or sorority members, engage in collective eating sprees; once they have eaten more than they can possibly hold, they may take turns vomiting or all purge themselves together. As they transform the traditional elements of ritual into an obsessive ritualization involving food and the body, eating disorders take on the functions of a rite of passage. Food becomes the vehicle for the daughter's separation from her mother: The daughter both takes control of what she eats and bonds with the girls around her through food rituals. Additionally, the preoccupation of food reconnects the daughter to her mother: Like her mother, the daughter, too, is engaging in food preparation.

Chernin concludes that women need to develop new rituals. As women take on different cultural roles, they have to find new, more authentic modes of transformation. She suggests that, in part, the new type of transition will require a revaluation of the work of mothers and a renewed investment of meaning in the rituals of food preparation that embody appreciation and forgiveness rather than obsession and guilt.

Analysis

In writing *The Hungry Self*, Chernin claims for eating the same sort of significance that Sigmund Freud and other psychoanalysts have found in sexuality. Like sexuality, eating is both a fundamental aspect of human existence and an activity with deeply symbolic meaning. Thus, just as Freud's work considers neurosis in the light of infantile memories and the cultural import of ancient and mythic rites and rituals, so does *The Hungry Self* analyze anorexia and bulimia with regard to early childhood experiences and tribal initiatory practices signifying the passage into adulthood. By linking the particular psychological experiences of individual women with larger societal issues involving the acceptance and inclusion of women as full participants in society, Chernin is able to provide a rich analysis of the epidemic of eating disorders disabling so many contemporary women.

Chernin describes the societal dimensions of eating disorders in stark terms. Using various studies from 1982, she estimates the number of girls and women suffering from anorexia and bulimia to range from one in a hundred between the ages of sixteen and eighteen and one in five college-age women. Given the vast number of women suffering from an obsession with food, weight, and body image, Chernin argues for the necessity of looking beyond each individual story to discover the larger social causes for this epidemic. Beginning in the 1970's and 1980's, women have been given more options, and pressures, than ever before: They are now able to move from the home into society at large. Yet many still find themselves feeling empty and confused, unsure of who they are and unable to turn to their mothers as role models in this new world. Thus, Chernin claims that women's eating disorders are not simply personal dilemmas, but a larger societal problem occasioned by women's ability to take on the rights and prerogatives of men.

Chernin neither belittles this advancement nor urges a return to traditional domesticity. Rather, she reads the messages of media and culture as signaling to women the need to be like men if they are to succeed in the workplace. Accordingly, the tight, muscular masculine body is more valued than the fleshy, maternal curves of feminine bodies. Not surprisingly, then, many young women attempt to rid themselves of the flesh that signifies their womanliness in an effort to measure up in this male-centered world. In yet another twist, however, the media also glorifies a particular image of femininity. In the bedroom, women are instructed to be sensual and seductive, garbing themselves in lingerie that reveals large breasts and lean, flat stomachs. The tension between the two messages traps women, giving them conflicting models of female identity.

Turning to the psychological level, a shift that some critics have found in need of further explication, Chernin locates even deeper sources for the epidemic of eating disorders in the relationship between mothers and daughters. Drawing from the work of the psychoanalyst Melanie Klein, Chernin explains the way in which infants experience both intense rage toward and a fierce attachment to their mothers. On the one hand, the mother is the source of food, whether from the breast or from the bottle. On the other hand, the child's sucking may take on a violent character, a way of expressing and acting out frustration and aggression. No matter how angry the infant becomes, the mother remains whole and comforting. As the child develops and begins to separate from the mother, however, her failings may seem to be the result of the infant's rage. For example, the child being weaned may come away with the impression of having sucked the mother dry, depleting her. The mother is no longer magically all-protective, but a human woman harassed by the inconveniences and inequities of daily life. The child thus finds that her own development required the diminishment of her mother.

Although boys also experience oral aggression toward their mothers, they do not develop the same debilitating sense of guilt that later plagues so many girls. Chernin explains this difference with reference to the gendered nature of child-rearing practices. From an early age, boys are taught that they are like their fathers and that, as men, they will have the same freedoms and opportunities. In contrast to the idea of autonomy imparted to boys, girls are offered an ideal of self-sacrifice. Reared to identify with their mothers, they are given to expect that they, too, will become mothers and hence must forfeit any plans of their own for the sake of marriage and family. Thus, when as adolescents girls are told that they need not make the same sacrifices as their mothers, they face a complex developmental problem. Should they choose an independent path of their own, they reenact the separation and depletion of the mother of infancy. Should they accept the maternal role, they make of themselves the food sacrifice their mothers were to them.

While the psychoanalytic dimensions of Chernin's discussion are not always convincing, her ability to link eating disorders with deeper societal and psychological issues provides an innovative way of considering anorexia and bulimia. Once these terrible disorders are exposed as aspects of an identity crisis experienced by many women, although in perhaps less damaging ways, it becomes possible to think more clearly about the way in which feminine identity develops now and the way it might emerge in the future.

Context

Kim Chernin's *The Hungry Self* is an important contribution to the understanding of the developmental issues particular to female identity. Perhaps more important, it is a shocking exposé of the horrors of eating disorders, both as aspects of a widespread phenomenon in American society and as deeply personal obsessions with food and weight. As one of the earliest nontechnical, book-length studies of anorexia and bulimia, it affected the way in which many women think about their own relationship to their bodies. Whereas previous feminist analyses of development had stressed sexuality, Chernin reminds her readers that while many contemporary women are comfortable expressing and acting upon their sexual desire, the vast majority of women experience deep guilt and ambivalence with regard to food. Eating is the new sin, the taboo to be secretly enjoyed and later absolved through penitential rituals. *The Hungry Self* further develops arguments and ideas Chernin raised in her book *The Obsession: Reflections on the Tyranny of Slenderness* (1981).

Sources for Further Study

Bordo, Susan. *Unbearable Weight: Feminism, Western Culture, and the Body.* Berkeley: University of California Press, 1993. A collection of critical essays exploring problems of the body for women. Includes discussions of anorexia, slenderness, and body image with reference to and elaboration on Chernin's work.

Brumberg, Joan Jacobs. *Fasting Girls: The Emergence of Anorexia Nervosa as a Modern Disease.* Cambridge, Mass.: Harvard University Press, 1988. An account of the scope and dimensions of anorexia, with attention to the historical context of the disease.

Bynum, Caroline Walker. *Holy Feast and Holy Fast: The Religious Significance of Food to Medieval Women.* Berkeley: University of California Press, 1987. An important discussion of fasting and other food rituals for medieval women. Contains an index and extensive notes.

Spitzack, Carole. *Confessing Excess: Women and the Politics of Body Reduction.* Albany: State University of New York Press, 1990. An analysis of contemporary dieting and weight loss literature which draws upon Chernin's work.

Wolf, Naomi. *The Beauty Myth.* London: Chatto & Windus, 1990. A general discussion of the media images of an ideal femininity. Draws upon Chernin's discussion of eating disorders and body image, providing later statistical data confirming the epidemic proportions of these problems. Includes a helpful bibliography.

Jodi Dean

I KNOW WHY THE CAGED BIRD SINGS

Author: Maya Angelou (Marguerite Johnson, 1928-   )
Type of work: Autobiography
Time of work: 1931-1945
Locale: Stamps, Arkansas; St. Louis, Missouri; and Los Angeles and San Francisco, California
First published: 1970

Principal personages:

MAYA ANGELOU, a poet and author who recounts her life from ages three to sixteen years

BAILEY JOHNSON, JR., Angelou's older brother and closest childhood friend

MRS. ANNIE HENDERSON, called Momma, their paternal grandmother

UNCLE WILLIE, their father's crippled brother

MRS. BERTHA FLOWERS, a teacher who inspires Angelou to read poetry

MRS. VIVIAN BAXTER, Maya and Bailey's mother

BAILEY JOHNSON, SR., Maya and Bailey's father

GRANDMOTHER BAXTER, Maya and Bailey's maternal grandmother

MR. FREEMAN, Vivian Baxter's boyfriend, who rapes Angelou

DADDY CLIDELL, Maya's stepfather

Form and Content

Maya Angelou's autobiography *I Know Why the Caged Bird Sings* tells her story: that of a Southern black girl moved from place to place, along with her brother Bailey, after their parents' divorce. The book is divided into thirty-six chapters and begins with a vignette, a sketch of the young Maya trying unsuccessfully to recite an Easter poem in church. She cannot remember the words. "Peeing and crying" in fear, she flees the church and concludes, "If growing up is painful for the Southern Black girl, being aware of her displacement is the rust on the razor that threatens the throat. It is an unnecessary insult." With this cultural setting, Angelou shifts to Long Beach, California, in 1931, where Maya and Bailey Johnson, Jr., ages three and four, are being sent by train to the home of their paternal grandmother, Mrs. Annie Henderson (called Momma), in Stamps, Arkansas. From there, the chapters are arranged chronologically and geographically, following Angelou's youth to the age of sixteen and the displacements of the children—to Stamps, to St. Louis, back to Stamps, to Los Angeles, and finally, to San Francisco. Along with the geographical displacements are familial displacements, as Angelou lives with her parents, with Momma and Uncle Willie, with her mother and Mr. Freeman, with Grandmother Baxter, with her father and his girlfriend, and with her mother and stepfather, Daddy Clidell.

Angelou wrote *I Know Why the Caged Bird Sings* after several requests from Random House publishers. Though it is an autobiography, it is also an exploration of survival. In a 1983 interview, Angelou says,

> When I wrote *I Know Why the Caged Bird Sings*, I wasn't thinking so much about my own life and identity. I was thinking about a particular time in which I lived and the influences of that time on a number of people. I kept thinking, what about that time? What were the people around young Maya doing? I used the central figure—myself—as a focus to show how one person can make it through those times.

Angelou talks about her survival as a black Southern girl in a society that devalues her beauty, talent, and ambition.

She contends that all of her work is "about survival." The sketches in *I Know Why the Caged Bird Sings* support her contention. Although parts of the book are humorous, such as the revival scene in chapter 6, when Sister Monroe knocks out Reverend Thomas' false teeth, many of the sketches deal with painful struggles for survival, such as the encounter between Momma and the racist white dentist who will not treat Angelou and the rape of the eight-year-old Maya.

In 1979, when Angelou was adapting *I Know Why the Caged Bird Sings* for film, she became keenly aware of the story line. She described it as "very delicate." It is the story of surviving both racism and childhood, and it culminates in a scene of the sixteen-year-old Angelou, having recently been graduated from high school, lying in bed and snuggling close to her three-week-old son, the result of a brief and loveless encounter with a teenage boy. Angelou's second autobiographical novel, *Gather Together in My Name* (1974), takes the story from there.

Analysis

I Know Why the Caged Bird Sings, its title taken from Paul Laurence Dunbar's poem "Sympathy," is an autobiographical story of survival. The vignettes, held together by time, place, and narrator, are joyous, angry, fearful, and desperate, but not bitter.

One of the most desperate and fearful events in the book is the account of Mr. Freeman raping the eight-year-old Maya. Angelou's candid narrative explores her childhood desire to be loved and her pain and horror at the psychological and physical violation of the rape. Mr. Freeman threatens to kill Bailey if Maya tells what she and Mr. Freeman did. By using the words "what we did," Mr. Freeman makes her feel responsible for his actions. When Bailey realizes that Mr. Freeman has somehow hurt his sister, he convinces her that Mr. Freeman, who has moved out of the house, can no longer hurt them. Trusting Bailey's judgment, she tells him about the rape. Angelou is hospitalized, Mr. Freeman is arrested, and the family comes to her aid. Bailey sits by her hospital bed and cries, her mother brings flowers and candy, Grandmother Baxter brings fruit, and her uncles clump around her bed and snort "like wild horses." After Mr. Freeman is sentenced to "one year and one day," his lawyer gets him released. Later he is "found dead on the lot behind the slaughterhouse," where his body has been dumped; he appears to have been kicked to death. Angelou, feeling responsible for Mr. Freeman's death, remains a mute until she is thirteen years old.

Angelou is often asked why she put the rape scene in *I Know Why the Caged Bird Sings*. In a 1983 interview, she said that she "wanted people to see that the man was not totally an ogre. The hard thing about writing or directing or producing is to make sure one doesn't make the negative person totally negative. I try to tell the truth and preserve it in all artistic forms." Angelou's profile of Mr. Freeman is, in fact, complex. Angelou also candidly explores, through this rape, the feelings of guilt in victims. In a 1987 interview, she said that guilt is still part of the victim's burden. Referring to child rape, she concluded that "the victim, especially if you are a member of a depressed class or gender or sex, is loaded with the guilt for that action against herself or himself." Nowhere else in *I Know Why the Caged Bird Sings* do the fear and desperation in survival surface more painfully. Nevertheless, Angelou consistently rejects bitterness as a response to pain, fear, and despair. She maintains that bitterness destroys the bitter person but has no effect on the object of the bitterness.

Connected to the theme of survival are flights from danger and searches for sanctuary. Ironically, the opening vignette shows Angelou fleeing the church, a traditional sanctuary, and seeking safety at home, where she knows that a beating awaits her. Again, when the teenage Maya flees her father's violent girlfriend, she seeks safety in the streets. An implied theme is that church and home, traditional sanctuaries, can fail and that survival depends on individual strength. In her journey to adulthood, Angelou comes to realize that her survival rests on believing in her own value, regardless of the low value that her culture places on her race and gender.

Context

In a 1973 interview, Maya Angelou was referred to as a Renaissance woman. The term is apt: She is an author of nonfiction, drama, and poetry; a stage and screen performer; a nightclub singer; a dancer; a producer; an editor; a television host of documentaries and educational films; a university teacher; and a social and political activist. Surviving her childhood rape, institutionalized racism, a teenage pregnancy, and, later, prostitution, Angelou emerged as a voice in American literature and politics.

In addition to her many honorary degrees, Angelou has received numerous other awards. In 1954 and 1955, Angelou, participating in *Porgy and Bess*, was sponsored by the United States Department of State to tour twenty-two countries. In 1959 and 1960, Angelou was appointed Northern Coordinator for the Southern Christian Leadership Conference. In 1970, *I Know Why the Caged Bird Sings* was nominated for a National Book Award. In 1972, Angelou became the first black woman to have an original script produced, and the same year, she received a Pulitzer Prize nomination for her poetry collection *Just Give Me a Cool Drink of Water 'fore I Diiie* (1971). She received a Tony nomination in 1973. In 1975, President Gerald R. Ford appointed her to the American Revolution Bicentennial Council. Angelou was named Woman of the

Year in 1976 by the *Ladies' Home Journal*. In 1977, she was named by President Jimmy Carter to the National Commission on the Observance of International Women's Year. Also in 1977, she received another Tony nomination, and she received the Golden Eagle award from the Public Broadcasting System for her documentary series *Afro-American in the Arts*. In 1982, she received a lifetime appointment as Reynold's Professor of American Studies at Wake Forest University in Winston-Salem, North Carolina. (This appointment, which lets her teach any subject in the humanities, is usually for two to five years. In an interview, Angelou remarked that her lifetime appointment "didn't sit well with some of the white male professors.") In 1984 and 1985, Angelou was appointed by Governor James B. Hunt to the Board of the North Carolina Arts Council. In 1992, Angelou accepted an invitation from President Bill Clinton to compose and read a poem at his inauguration.

Through these experiences, Angelou has continually reexamined her views, discarding those that she no longer accepts. For example, in her early years as a writer, Angelou called herself a "womanist" rather than a "feminist," because she believed that feminists lacked humor. In contrast, in 1986, when an interviewer asked Angelou if she were a feminist, Angelou responded, "I am a feminist. I've been a female for a long time now. I'd be stupid not to be on my own side." When the interviewer commented that she had not always held this opinion, Angelou admitted that her views had changed. Nevertheless, Angelou often contrasts black women's issues and white women's issues, believing that their positions in history and culture make their views different. In *I Know Why the Caged Bird Sings*, Angelou describes several black women: Momma, her mother, Grandmother Baxter, and Mrs. Bertha Flowers. It is not until her later books, such as *The Heart of a Woman* (1981), however, that Angelou begins to explore the significance of womanhood in general.

Sources for Further Study

Angelou, Maya. *Conversations with Maya Angelou*. Edited by Jeffrey M. Elliot. Jackson: University Press of Mississippi, 1989. An excellent collection of interviews with Angelou, arranged chronologically from 1971 to 1988. Contains a useful introduction, a chronology, and an index, as well as photographs of Angelou.

_____ . *Gather Together in My Name*. New York: Random House, 1974. This book, a combination of fiction and nonfiction, begins with a dedication both to Angelou's "blood brother" Bailey and to a group of "real brothers." A continuation of *I Know Why the Caged Bird Sings*, it explores Angelou's struggles as a single parent and provider.

_____ . *The Heart of a Woman*. New York: Random House, 1981. This autobiography, which begins with a dedication to a group of women that Angelou calls "Sister/friends," covers Angelou's early mature years as a writer. In it, she explores her creativity and her success.

_____ . *Singin' and Swingin' and Gettin' Merry Like Christmas*. New York: Random House, 1976. The autobiography covers the time of Angelou's stage debut through her international tour with *Porgy and Bess*.

Tate, Claudia, ed. *Black Women Writers at Work*. New York: Continuum, 1983. A collection of fourteen interviews with black women writers, this book focuses on creative processes. Though it lacks an index, the book offers a useful introduction, and each interview is preceded by a brief biographical sketch of the writer. The interview with Angelou includes some of her views on both women's and racial issues.

Carol Franks

I NEVER PROMISED YOU A ROSE GARDEN

Author: Hannah Green (Joanne Greenberg, 1932-   )
Type of work: Novel
Type of plot: Psychological realism
Time of plot: 1948-1951
Locale: Chicago and wards B and D of an unnamed mental hospital
First published: 1964

Principal characters:
DEBORAH BLAU, a sixteen-year-old undergoing treatment for
extreme schizophrenia
ESTHER BLAU, Deborah's mother, the one adult family member
who realizes the severity of Deborah's illness
JACOB BLAU, Deborah's father
DR. CLARA FRIED, Deborah's chief analyst at the hospital
SUZY, Deborah's younger sister
CARLA, a patient who becomes Deborah's friend when they are
confined to the various wards of the hospital
POP, Deborah's maternal grandfather

Form and Content

I Never Promised You a Rose Garden is a disturbing look at young Deborah Blau's descent into and eventual ascent from extreme schizophrenia. The severity of her illness is passed off by family members as being mere hysteria, an often-used explanation for women's emotional and psychological disorders.

The novel opens as sixteen-year-old Deborah, accompanied by her parents, is on her way to an unnamed mental health facility where she will be confined for three years to receive treatment for her mental illness. Deborah has suffered from schizophrenia since childhood, often tied to her fifth year, when she underwent two operations to remove tumors from her urethra and when her sister Suzy was born. Even though Deborah often demonstrates the severity of her illness through self-mutilation, her family denies that she is sick until she attempts suicide at the age of sixteen.

Many of Deborah's problems stem from her self-perceived need of punishment for her femininity, her Jewishness, and her earlier disdain for her sister. Throughout the novel, Deborah inflicts punishment upon herself by such masochistic acts as cutting and burning herself. Deborah also attempts to escape her mental torment by retreating into her imaginary world, the Kingdom of Yr. At the hospital, Deborah comes under the supervision of Dr. Clara Fried, who leads her toward mastering her problems rather than resorting to bodily harm or mental retreat. Dr. Fried bases much of Deborah's treatment upon techniques she learned dealing with Jewish patients in Germany during Adolf Hitler's rise to power.

Deborah moves between wards B and D as her mental health fluctuates. In ward D, she witnesses the most severe forms of mental illness that render patients either comatose or extremely violent. It is during this stay that Deborah's perception of her illness as a punishment is intensified when she meets Ellis, a conscientious objector who is spending his period of alternate service as a mental health worker. Unlike many other patients, Deborah is violent only to herself. She continues the acts of self-mutilation prevalent in her youth. Likewise, she continues escaping for varying periods of time to the Kingdom of Yr, where she comes under the influence of the voices of the Censor, Anterrabae, and the Collect.

While undergoing treatment, Deborah becomes acquainted with another patient, Carla, who is released and readmitted to the hospital on several occasions, a situation governed by her fluctuating psychological stability. Carla has a direct influence upon Deborah's acceptance of her situation as one of illness and not one of punishment.

The first significant indication of Deborah's coming to terms with her illness, and thus taking the first step toward recovery, is when she accepts her ethnicity, which is the source of both her self-punishment and the strength that she seeks. Toward the end of the novel, she admits that she has translated her strong-willed maternal grandfather into the persona of a dreaded Japanese soldier, which her subconscious had created to avenge the wrongs that had been thrust upon her.

The novel ends three years after the opening scene. Deborah, although not completely cured, has progressed sufficiently to win her release from the hospital. She resides in a halfway house and is continuing the education that had been interrupted by the onslaught of her illness.

Analysis

The complexity of *I Never Promised You a Rose Garden* arises from its power as both a work of fiction and an autobiographical psychological cleansing. This work stems from Joanne Greenberg's planned nonfictional account of her psychological collapse, treatment, and cure. Before the narrative could be written, however, Greenberg's analyst, Dr. Frieda Fromm-Reichman, died. Still intent on telling her story, Greenberg fictionalized the account and published it under the name of Hannah Green. When she learned that there was another writer using the name Hanna Green, Greenberg acknowledged authorship and admitted the autobiographical foundation of the novel.

However intriguing the autobiographical elements prove to be, *I Never Promised You a Rose Garden* is a novel and should be read as such. Green's central intention is to show the far-reaching effects that mental illness has upon patients, their families, and those entrusted with their care and treatment. Although there is melodramatic potential in the novel, Green does not allow herself to be trapped into taking the easy way out by depending upon atmosphere rather than content.

Green does not confine her readers within the walls of the mental hospital with the novel's protagonist, Deborah Blau; rather, she provides entry into the world that fostered Deborah's decline. Deborah's illness was both ignored and accelerated by the family and the society in which she found herself. The society that created Deborah also created the methods and attitudes dominating the treatment of mental illness during the novel's time frame.

Green does not approach male mental illness in detail, although there are male patients mentioned in passing. Instead, she focuses upon women who suffer psychological traumas and who confront them either through self-violence or through total introversion. By allowing Carla to earn release from the hospital only to be returned, Green demonstrates that quite often women patients were released when they were not yet ready and that many of the pressures that sent these women on their psychological rocky roads were on the outside waiting to confront them once again.

Green could easily have limited her narrative to the present-tense, psychologically confused world of the patients in wards B and D. To give her narrative substance and complexity, however, Green introduces the reader to the peripheral worlds of the patient's family and caregivers. In each instance, the patient's illness creates stress and confusion in those around her.

Green also complicates her narrative when she shows that the means of Deborah's salvation is, in fact, the cause of the conflict that eventually became insurmountable for her—her grandfather and the world that he represented. When she found herself in need of a psychological savior during those periods of adolescent torment, Deborah created from her grandfather the persona of a Japanese soldier who would, she believed, exact revenge upon her tormentors. Thus, the person who represented the Jewishness which creates Deborah's life of torment and self-punishment is the one who provides Deborah's subconscious with the will to combat the forces against her. When she becomes aware that she does want to fight back, Deborah realizes that she is able to defeat the demons within her.

Green does not rely heavily upon character development to carry the artistic merits of her novel. Instead, she develops her theme through the organic elements of the plot. One realization by Deborah leads to the next until the battle is won. No narrative contrivances facilitate the novel's denouement; the work's solution comes when the various events reach the point of resolution.

The tension and confusion governing Deborah Blau's world is re-created in the novel form. By switching from Deborah's confused present to her skewed memories of her past to her imaginary ventures into the Kingdom of Yr, Green presents a multilevel stream of consciousness that reflects the mental state of an extremely schizophrenic individual such as Deborah.

To maintain necessary realism, Green does not tie up all the loose ends. While Deborah has advanced to the point of being able to rejoin society, her psychological rebirth is far from complete. There is no indication that the forces which had sent Deborah into her psychological tailspin in the first place have been overcome or even diminished. Here lies the key to understanding the message of *I Never Promised You a Rose Garden*: One can overcome problems if they are identified, but they can easily return and throw the individual into the same turmoil from which one just escaped.

Context

I Never Promised You a Rose Garden is a frightening but accurate depiction of the onset and intensification of schizophrenia in a young woman. Like Charlotte Perkins Gilman's *The Yellow Wallpaper* (1892) and Sylvia Plath's *The Bell Jar* (1963), two classics of literature dealing with women's psychology, Hannah Green's novel is a fictionalization of the writer's own psychological decline, giving it a potency that would have been impossible if the writer had been a man or had only an intellectual familiarity with the subject matter.

Although the work has some weaknesses as a novel, *I Never Promised You a Rose Garden* offers a strong reaction to the ways in which women's emotional and psychological problems often have been pushed aside as being merely gender weaknesses and deserving nothing more than rest, as is suggested in Gilman's novella. Symptoms of acute schizophrenia are misinterpreted or not interpreted until Deborah comes under the watchful eye of a woman doctor. Only when Deborah is placed in the hands of Dr. Clara Fried is she set on the road to eventual recovery. Her problem is not a mere fit of hysteria or a case of the mystical "floating womb," two explanations once given for women's psychological problems. Rather, it is an emotional degeneration which can be altered when approached with a positive attitude rather than with gender-restrictive excuses.

I Never Promised You a Rose Garden will continue to prove significant because it tells of a woman's special psychological needs through the artistic endeavors of a woman who experienced similar needs. This work is a prime example of form following function; the story of a disjointed personality is told through a disjointed narrative, and breaks in the story indicate breaks in Deborah's emotional state. Green allows her audience to view the world of a young woman's mental collapse without any socially obscure rationalizations. This work has helped create more open discussions of mental and societal problems unique to women.

Sources for Further Study

Berman, Jeffrey. "*I Never Promised You a Rose Garden*: The Limits of the Fictional Psychiatric Case Study." In *The Talking Cure: Literary Representations of Psychoanalysis*. New York: New York University Press, 1985. Berman discusses how fictional works centering around psychological complications can be used as both teaching and diagnostic models. The chapter on *I Never Promised You a Rose Garden* discusses how this novel provides insight into the troubled world of the schizophrenic.

Greenberg, Joanne. "Go Where You're Sent: An Interview with Joanne Greenberg." Interview by Kenneth L. Gibble. *The Christian Century* 102 (November 20, 1985): 1063-1066. In this interview, Greenberg discusses how she enjoys not being pigeonholed as a certain type of writer. She writes about those topics that she considers important. Many of her works deal with the darker or more uncomfortable aspects of human existence.

_____ . "Interview: Joanne Greenberg." Interview by Susan Koppleman.

Belles Lettres: A Review of Books for Women 8 (Summer, 1993): 32-36. Greenberg discloses that much of her writing comes from unhappiness with her surroundings or social conditions. She tells how she joined the writing profession after becoming despondent while living in New York City.

_____ . "PW Interviews Joanne Greenberg." Interview by Sybil Steinberg. *Publishers Weekly* 234 (September 23, 1988): 50-51. This interview discloses Greenberg's interest in the lives of physically and emotionally challenged individuals and observes that she in no way condescends to her subjects. Much of Greenberg's works are based on the author's own experiences.

Wolfe, Kary K., and Gary K. Wolfe. "Metaphors of Madness: Popular Psychological Narratives." *Journal of Popular Culture* 9 (Spring, 1976): 895-907. Greenberg's novel is discussed in some depth as an illustration of works that have contributed to an increase in the popularity of fiction with a psychological foundation.

Thomas B. Frazier

THE ICE AGE

Author: Margaret Drabble (1939-   )
Type of work: Novel
Type of plot: Social criticism
Time of plot: November, 1975, to the spring of 1976
Locale: Yorkshire, England, and Wallacia, an imaginary Balkan country
First published: 1977

> *Principal characters:*
> ANTHONY KEATING, a partner in a property development firm
>   who has suffered a heart attack
> ALISON MURRAY, Keating's lover, an actress who gave up a
>   promising career to look after a younger daughter born with
>   cerebral palsy
> LEN WINCOBANK, a property developer serving time for fraud
> MAUREEN KIRBY, Len's girlfriend, executive secretary, and
>   partner
> JANE MURRAY, Alison's older daughter who is in prison in an
>   isolated Balkan country
> GILES PETERS, Keating's partner in property speculation

Form and Content

Margaret Drabble's *The Ice Age* uses property speculation to analyze English society during the 1970's. The novel begins on Wednesday, November 18, 1975, and concludes in the following spring. The Arab oil embargo and the October War of 1973 hurt Great Britain's economy, which is dependent on oil imports. The severe fuel shortage caused a three-day work week, labor unrest, a drastic drop in productivity, the collapse of the real estate market, and inflation that reached a rate of 26 percent in 1975.

Several intersecting stories make up the action of the novel. First comes that of Anthony Keating. Keating, from a stereotypical middle-class clergyman's family, studied literature at the University of Oxford and dabbled in light musicals with his wealthy friend Giles Peters. Married young, he could not afford professional training and took a job in television. As a producer, he was an intellectual with left-wing contempt for the philistine world of business. When he interviewed the property developer Len Wincobank in 1968, however, he decided that speculators took risks, had soaring ideas, and shaped the world. He quit his secure job to enter a partnership with Giles Peters and Rory Leggett. Their first development cost them £70,000, of which £65,000 was borrowed money, and they went on borrowing to develop properties in London. Their biggest scheme coincided with the oil crisis; Giles kept buying more property, but the crash came before they could unload. Suffering a heart attack on top of the economic collapse, Anthony left matters to his associates and moved to his country house, where he waits to learn if he is bankrupt.

Anthony's relationship with the former actress Alison Murray is the second story. The two hope to live together at the country house, but Alison's life present obstacles. Alison is in the communist country of Wallacia attempting to save her elder daughter, Jane, who faces prison for a fatal car accident. Her younger daughter, Molly, has cerebral palsy and needs constant care. Alison has left her husband, a successful actor though a terrible mate, but is not sure if she should make her life with Anthony.

The future of Len Wincobank and his girlfriend, Maureen Kirby, is the third story. Len is serving four years for fraud at Scratby Open Prison in Yorkshire, learning new ideas from his fellow white-collar criminals and monitoring outside developments such as the Community Land Act (real legislation preventing profit-taking in land development). Maureen wants to wait for his release, but she is attracted to her new employer. Len and Maureen, from working-class backgrounds, have no nostalgia for the past and revel in the affluence, the upward social mobility, and the sexual revolution that marked the 1960's.

Anthony seems saved when a buyer makes an offer on his London house and his partners sell their development under the Community Land Act; rescued from financial ruin, they may even make a profit. After a two-month drinking binge, he settles down with Alison. At this point, the foreign office official responsible for Jane Murray's case asks Anthony to visit Wallacia. The government is releasing Jane for humanitarian reasons, but a revolution is brewing, and he wants messages delivered to the Wallacian underground. Anthony agrees, delivers the messages, collects Jane, and is just about to return to London when the revolution comes. Jane boards the airplane, but Anthony misses it because his passport is being held. He is sentenced to a labor camp for spying. The book ends with Anthony meditating on the deeper meaning of life, Len preparing new ventures, Maureen sleeping with her boss, and Alison faced with Molly's care.

Analysis

Two themes underlie *The Ice Age*: the struggle between God and Mammon, and Great Britain's changing social and urban geography beginning in the 1950's. Anthony Keating is torn between religion and materialism. As an undergraduate and later in television, he rejects his family's religious views, but he retains their belief that education, arts, and politics are the most worthy spheres of activity. He becomes increasingly dissatisfied with his life, however, wondering if it is pointless and awakening in the night to ask, "What is it? What is what?" Alienated from work and society, Anthony was ready to embrace a new creed: "A political creed, but there wasn't one; a religious creed, but he had had God, along with his father and life in the cathedral close. So what would happen to the vacant space in Anthony Keating? What would occupy it?" The answer was Len Wincobank; the conversion happened in 1968. Anthony threw himself into property development heart and soul.

After the property market collapse, Anthony wonders whether his work is valuable. (In contrast, Len Wincobank and Maureen Kirby, remembering their childhood working-class privations, enjoy the prosperity before 1973 and find survival strategies afterward.) He returns to his home in the cathedral close when his father dies and reexamines the cathedral and the old values for which it stands, but is unable to accept them. Instead, he floats unmoored until he agrees to run errands for the foreign office. His name gets on a list of suspects, which causes Wallacian officials to hold his passport, which makes him miss his flight, which puts him in a labor camp. There Anthony regains health and faith. It is not faith in God, however, for he remains uncertain about God's existence. One of the few books in the camp is *De consolatione philosophiae* (*The Consolation of Philosophy*), one of the most popular examples of prison literature. Anicius Manlius Severinus Boethius (c. 480-524) wrote the work while awaiting execution for treason; it argues that the contemplation of God reconciles one to earthly misfortune. Anthony starts his own book justifying the ways of God to humankind, even though he himself does not believe in God. Drabble argues strongly that human choices are limited by fate, but that one has to behave as if one were a free agent.

The novel's second issue is Britain's changing society. Drabble argues that the trendy, middle-class Left values of the 1950's and 1960's are superficial, pseudo-socialist, and naïve.

> He and his clever friends . . . had dabbled and trifled and cracked irreverent jokes; they had thrown out the mahogany and bought cheap stripped pine, they had slept with one another's wives, and divorced their own, they had sent their children to state schools, they had acquired indeterminate accents, . . . they had worn themselves out and contorted themselves trying to understand a new system, a new egalitarian culture, the new illiterate visual television age.

Despite their efforts, however, nothing had changed: "Where was the new bright classless enterprising future of Great Britain? In jail with Len Wincobank, mortgaged to the hilt with North Sea Oil." Throughout, Drabble uses humor to illustrate British society's wrong turning. For example, she describes Chay Bank, Len Wincobank's favorite development, as "a noted success: remarkably few of its inhabitants had as yet gone mad, jumped out of high windows, murdered and mugged each other's grandmothers, or wantonly destroyed the children's adventure playground." In *The Ice Age*, Drabble effectively combines the domestic and the social, the tragic and the humorous, the personal and the political into a well-constructed piece of social criticism.

Context

Some critics called Drabble's first few novels—especially *A Summer Bird-Cage* (1963), *The Garrick Year* (1964), and *The Millstone* (1965)—lightweight "Tampax novels" or "soiled nappies novels" because her themes were how the coming of babies constricts choices and how women's physiology affects their lives. Those critics who so dismissed her reveal more about themselves and about their views of women than about Drabble's literary merits. As she wrote more explicit social criticism during the late 1960's and early 1970's, she continued to ground it in the domestic.

The Ice Age mixes domestic images with global concerns. On the novel's first page, Anthony buries a dead pheasant on his roomy estate; it reminds him that his London home had few spots suitable for burials, "and those that were suitable had been well stacked over the years with the small bones of mice and fish and gerbils." Critics with families know how important it is to find suitable spots to bury small animals. Again, she uses the image of Anthony's fried sausages—split open, burnt on the outside but raw on the inside—to reflect England's condition. Critics see this as an allusion to the philosopher Claude Lévi-Strauss' *Le Cru et le cuit* (1964; *The Raw and the Cooked*, 1969), which no doubt it is, but it also describes what happens when one cooks sausages. The most vivid example of Drabble's merging the domestic and the public, the humorous and the tragic, is a scene in which Alison sets out to buy tampons. Drabble's description of Alison, lugging her suitcase through pedestrian tunnels that open into traffic islands, looking across the oncoming flow of traffic at a drugstore as at a distant promised land, is darkly comic.

Drabble's very English, ironic, and low-key sense of humor has led astray some American critics, who find her insufficiently feminist. In several interviews she denied writing specifically for women, or writing feminist novels; she claimed that *The Ice Age*'s protagonist is a man because she was "fed up with women—slightly." Drabble is not impressed by the earnest and the self-important, and she certainly denies that ideology is the answer to human problems and that human needs should be sacrificed to ideology. Moreover, as a fatalist in human affairs she cannot write happy endings for her female characters. (That Anthony Keating's "happy ending" is to be incarcerated in a communist labor camp for six years qualifies as dark humor.) Nevertheless, she writes powerfully about the daily realities of women's lives and defends those daily realities against dismissal by showing that, far from being inconsequential, they offer a core of meaning that remains when all else fails.

Sources for Further Study

Hannay, John. *The Intertextuality of Fate: A Study of Margaret Drabble*. Columbia: University of Missouri Press, 1986. Studies four novels, including *The Ice Age*. The chapter on this novel argues that Drabble uses a providential model of fate, in which events occur as part of a larger plan, even though its existence cannot be discerned by the people involved.

Moran, Mary Hurley. *Margaret Drabble: Existing Within Structures*. Carbondale: Southern Illinois University Press, 1983. Analyzes Drabble's views of human freedom, choice, and constraints, using all the novels published up to 1983, including *The Ice Age*. Moran argues that Drabble sees human lives as determined by a variety of forces, including fate, nature, and the family. Hence, she rejects the existentialist idea that one is free to become what one wills.

Myer, Valerie Grosvenor. *Margaret Drabble: A Reader's Guide*. New York: St. Martin's Press, 1991. After a brief introduction, each novel from *A Summer Bird-Cage* to *A Natural Curiosity* (1989) is discussed. A useful introduction to Drabble's fiction.

Packer, Joan Garrett. *Margaret Drabble: An Annotated Bibliography*. New York: Garland, 1988. A comprehensive, annotated bibliography of Drabble's writings, both major and minor, and of English-language secondary works about Drabble published before May, 1986.

Rose, Ellen Cronan, ed. *Critical Essays on Margaret Drabble*. Boston: G. K. Hall, 1985. A collection of eleven essays tracing the evolution of Drabble's themes from the lack of choice for women to the question of the effect of equality on women. Five of the essays were written especially for this volume, and none of the six reprinted essays is older than 1977.

——————. *The Novels of Margaret Drabble: Equivocal Figures*. Totowa, N.J.: Barnes & Noble Books, 1980. Covering her works through *The Ice Age* from a feminist perspective, Rose complains that Drabble never releases her heroines from patriarchal trammels. Beneath the visionary message of strong women is the conservative message that women will never attain autonomy.

Sadler, Lynn Veach. *Margaret Drabble*. Boston: Twayne, 1986. Surveys how Drabble's vision is primarily autobiographical by focusing on the themes of young women, independent women, marriage, and coping with middle age. Includes the novels up to *The Middle Ground* (1980).

D. G. Paz

ILLNESS AS METAPHOR

Author: Susan Sontag (1933-   )
Type of work: Social criticism
First published: 1978

Form and Content

The first version of Susan Sontag's *Illness as Metaphor* appeared in *The New York Review of Books* in 1978, and the hardbound book appeared soon after. Not surprisingly, the public response to acquired immunodeficiency syndrome (AIDS) led Sontag to write another work, called *AIDS and Its Metaphors* (1989); the two long essays are available in one volume.

Illness as Metaphor is divided into nine sections. It is a polemic that approaches its arguments from first one angle and then another, quoting from doctors, scientists, poets, novelists, and anyone else who has described tuberculosis or cancer in metaphors. Sontag's splendid prose crackles with passion and indignation as she recounts the attitudes toward tuberculosis during the Romantic period and compares the myths surrounding that disease to later attitudes toward cancer. Sontag scorns author Norman Mailer as a "cancerphobe"—he had said that if he had not release some violent feelings by stabbing his wife he would have gotten cancer and died—and identifies psychologist Wilhelm Reich as mainly responsible for the identification of cancer with repression, which places the responsibility for cancer squarely on the patient.

To someone who has an illness, describing that illness in a metaphor is unhealthy. Illness is decidedly not a metaphor, and the best approach to it is to purge it of its metaphorical associations. To wrap up a disease in metaphor and mystery encourages thinking of it as morally contagious. Even the names of diseases such as tuberculosis and cancer can create a debilitating fear in many patients, a fact that has often led to concealment of their condition from many patients. Sontag points out that the 1966 Freedom of Information Act allowed withholding "treatment for cancer" from disclosure on the basis of its being "an unwarranted invasion of personal privacy." Cancer is the only disease thus privileged.

Cancer is viewed as obscene, Sontag says: "ill-omened, abominable, repugnant to the senses." There is no taboo or disgrace surrounding the collapse of the cardiac patient's heart, for the malfunction is purely mechanical. Tuberculosis and cancer, however, are "resonant" with the horror of "living processes" that feed on the body and dissolve it into something repulsive and alien.

Sontag spells out graphically the separate metaphors of the two diseases. The Latin word *cancer* means "crab," a metaphor that the ancient Greek physician Galen said derived from the swollen, extending (crablike) veins of an external tumor. The Latin word *tuber* for "bump" gives the diminutive form *tuberculum*, a little protuberance or growth. Thus until quite recently the two diseases overlapped in many ways typologically and were definitively separated only by studies in cellular pathology. Analysis with the microscope revealed that some cancers (for example, leukemia) do not always appear in the form of a tumor, and in 1882 tuberculosis was found to be a bacterial infection and therefore separate from cancer. In the 1920's, cancer began accumulating its own "modern fantasy" and taking on the vivid metaphorical heritage of tuberculosis, but with important differences in the popular conceptions of the two diseases.

Tuberculosis was frequently associated with poverty, whereas cancer is identified with rich diets and the toxic wastes of industrial affluence. Tuberculosis was thought to stimulate the appetite, but cancer therapy kills hunger and produces nausea. Tuberculosis was thought to be a painless disease that flourished in damp environs and was helped by travel; cancer resists alleviation by travel, has no favorite climates, and can be extremely painful. According to Sontag, "The dying tubercular is pictured as made more beautiful and more soulful; the person dying of cancer is portrayed as robbed of all capacities of self-transcendence, humiliated by fear and agony."

Analysis

Of the myths that surround cancer and tuberculosis, one of the most dramatic is the perception of them both as diseases of passion. The high fever of the tuberculosis patient was seen as a symptom of burning passion, and the disease itself becomes "a variant of the disease of love," a claim Sontag supports with quotations from John Keats and Thomas Mann. Tuberculosis has also been treated in literature as a consequence of sexual frustration, as in Henry James's *The Wings of the Dove* (1902) when Milly Theale's doctor suggests that a love affair will help her struggle with the disease. In one of Ivan Turgenev's novels, *Nakanune* (1860; *On the Eve*, 1871), the exiled hero, frustrated that he cannot return to Bulgaria, succumbs to his misery in a hotel room in Venice and dies after contracting tuberculosis.

Whereas James's and Turgenev's characters suffered from illness brought on by frustration, the hero of André Gide's novel *L'Immoraliste* (1902; *The Immoralist*, 1930) comes down with tuberculosis from repressing his homosexuality and then recovers upon accepting himself. Sontag says that today Gide's Michel would get cancer instead, following a common modern myth that the disease is rooted in sexual repression and an inability to vent one's emotions. The main source of this particularly pernicious myth—pernicious in that it puts the blame for the disease on the victim, who is perceived as failing to respond to life fully—is Reich, Sontag says. Reich was a disciple of Sigmund Freud who fell out of favor with the master and in his Maine laboratory invented the absurd orgone box, which he claimed trapped sexual energy that would cure many ailments brought on by repression.

Sontag adeptly finds many examples of her thesis in art and literature: Little Eva's peaceful death from tuberculosis in Harriet Beecher Stowe's *Uncle Tom's Cabin* (1852), the sudden wasting away of Michael Furey in James Joyce's story "The Dead," and the "emaciated" tubercular young women in the paintings of Edvard Munch. Sontag summarizes the complexity of this disease of sensitive, "interesting" people: "Above all, it was a way of affirming the value of being more conscious, more complex psychologically. Health becomes banal, even vulgar." In more recent years, Sontag says, mental illness has replaced tuberculosis as "the index of a superior sensibility."

Christianity encouraged a moral view of disease, Sontag says, and in the later book *AIDS and Its Metaphors* she cites the crude charges by Jerry Falwell and others that AIDS is God's punishment of homosexuals and drug users. She points out that in the seventeenth century, preacher Cotton Mather described syphilis as a curse "which the Just Judgment of God has reserved for our Late Ages."

Sontag's contempt for all these moral judgments is biting, but she is no less critical of the Reichian vision of disease as an inner failing than she is of the view that disease is "a punishment which fits the objective moral character." In fact, the Reichian view may be even more "moralistic and punitive." She acutely perceives that those who regard cancer as a "failure of expressiveness" lace their pity with contempt. As evidence, she quotes W. H. Auden's poem "Miss Gee," in which the young woman prays for deliverance from the sexuality that she sees all around her and then gets cancer. Miss Gee's helpless doctor ruminates: "Childless women get it,/ And men when they retire;/ It's as if there had to be some outlet/ For their foiled creative fire."

Sontag stiffens her polemic with a number of quotations that reveal the frequent use of illness as a metaphor in politics and ideology. Reich, for example, in 1933 claimed that fears of syphilis, among other factors, lay behind the politics and the anti-Semitism of National Socialism. In more recent times, support for "dangerous nostrums like Laetrile comes from far-right groups to whose politics of paranoia the fantasy of a miracle cure for cancer makes a serviceable addition, like a belief in UFOs." She also argues that the common perception of cancer as a disease of industrial civilization is without empirical support and derives from the mistaken notion that cancer is a "modern" affliction.

Context

By 1975, Susan Sontag had established herself as a significant force in American letters with two novels, *The Benefactor* (1963) and *Death Kit* (1967), and three much-discussed works of criticism and social commentary, *Against Interpretation and Other Essays* (1966), *Trip to Hanoi* (1969), and *Styles of Radical Will* (1969). She had also written and directed three films: *Duet for Cannibals* (1969), *Brother Carl* (1972), and a documentary on Israel, *Promised Lands* (1974).

Then in 1975, while finishing *On Photography* (1977), she learned during a routine physical exam that she had breast cancer. Her doctors estimated a 10 percent chance of her living for two more years. After a mastectomy, four other operations, and several years of chemotherapy, she was cured. Less than a year later, she was at work on *Illness as Metaphor*, completing it in a month and a half. She thought that other people would be encouraged by her book, and the many letters that she received proved her right. She has explained how much more important contact with people has become for her:

Now I debate with myself about the intensity of solitude that is required in order to write and the necessity for me to be with people. What saved my life, besides the extraordinary chemotherapy, was the effect of having received, not only from persons close to me, but also acquaintances and strangers who appeared suddenly, the sympathy they showed in such a marvelous way.

In *AIDS and Its Metaphors*, Sontag describes *Illness as Metaphor* as an "exhortation."

I was saying: Get the doctors to tell you the truth; be an informed, active patient; find yourself good treatment, because good treatment does exist (among the widespread ineptitude). Although *the* remedy does not exist, more than half of all cases can be cured by existing methods of treatment.

Sontag speaks to everyone, male and female, but for a highly visible woman to survive breast cancer and then write so profoundly about it must be of particular inspiration to women everywhere.

Sources for Further Study

Brooks, Peter. "Death of/as Metaphor." *Partisan Review* 46, no. 3 (1979): 438-444. Compares Sontag's views on metaphor to those of Alain Robbe-Grillet. Brooks doubts that people can truly free themselves from the need for metaphor and can only hope to expose metaphor for what it is. He hopes that Sontag will explore the subject further in the manner of Michel Foucault's "archeologies."

DeMott, Benjamin. "Susan Sontag: To Outrage and Back." *Atlantic Monthly* 242 (November, 1978): 98-99. DeMott reviews Sontag's career with open hostility to her modernism, but he finds *Illness as Metaphor* an encouraging turnabout in her thinking. In fact, he identifies the ideas behind illness metaphor as important to the whole body of thought named modernism. "Her happiest and least conventional book, it's also immeasurably her shrewdest," according to DeMott.

Jacobson, Dan. "Sickness and Psyche." *Commentary* 66 (October, 1978): 78-82. Argues that the representations of tuberculosis by nineteenth century poets and novelists cannot be compared with the remarks by more recent writers about cancer. Rejects Sontag's claim of a Romantic "cult" of illness. One of the sharper, more critical reviews.

Sayres, Sohnya. *Susan Sontag: The Elegaic Modernist*. New York: Routledge, 1990. Contains only occasional specific references to *Illness as Metaphor*, but the introduction and the biographical chapter are informative. The selected bibliography is indispensable.

Sontag, Susan. "Alone Against Illness: Interview." Interview by C. Kahn. *Family Health* 10 (November, 1978): 50-53. Sontag reviews the steps that she took before deciding on a radical mastectomy. She chose a Paris doctor who prescribed the largest number of drugs for the longest time, and she had thirty months of chemotherapy at the Sloan-Kettering Institute for Cancer Research in New York City. She also had immunotherapy, which was experimental in the United States at that time. She argues that cancer patients are undertreated.

_____ . "Susan Sontag: The Rolling Stone Interview." Interview by Jonathan Cott. *Rolling Stone*, October 4, 1979, 46-53. Another excellent interview that covers considerable ground. Sontag talks freely about her encounter with cancer, her resistance to it, and the book that she wrote about her experience. A wide-ranging interview filled with vivid comments.

Frank Day

IMMACULATE DECEPTION
A New Look at Women and Childbirth in America

Author: Suzanne Arms (1944-   )
Type of work: Social criticism
First published: 1975

Form and Content

Suzanne Arms, a photojournalist and mother, was motivated by her own sour experience with hospital obstetrics to research the American birth experience. She interviewed and photographed not only credentialed experts—midwives, nurses, and doctors—but also experiential experts—mothers. Based on these interviews and her research into the literature of giving birth, she wrote *Immaculate Deception: A New Look at Women and Childbirth in America.* She presents a well-constructed argument against routing all births through the hospital, an institution designed to intervene in pathological conditions. Arms's primary insight is that most births are normal births; that is, they are not pathological at all. The appropriate response to the healthy birth is watchful, unhurried support, not intervention. The appropriate source of this support is the patient and experienced midwife, not the highly paid medical doctor. In the hospital, with its predisposition to discern pathology, normal variations in labor are extremely likely to be labeled abnormal, which starts the laboring woman on a merry-go-round of intervention. Each obstetrical interference causes harm that requires another interference, until the woman loses all control of her own labor.

In *Immaculate Deception*, Arms interweaves several different types of presentation. Scores of photographs present the visual reality of the world that she describes in the text: harsh institutional labor and delivery rooms, masked doctors looming over trays of metal instruments or proudly presenting babies as if they had produced them themselves, the calm faces of midwives, the frightened eyes of young mothers, and one straining female hand, locked in a heavy leather handcuff. The photographs are generally small, literally "marginal" to the text, but they are nevertheless crucial to conveying on an emotional level the argument that Arms builds so solidly on an intellectual level.

Arms quotes many mothers, briefly or at length, on their experiences with hospital childbirth. With their birth stories, she also includes the words of American midwives, nurses, and doctors, as well as the bemused comments of foreign birth attendants, who often seem faintly puzzled as to why anyone would behave as Americans do toward birth. She not only presents the words of proponents of rehumanizing birth but also quotes from the doctors who frankly argue that modern women are unable to give birth safely without the assistance of their guardian angels, aggressive obstetricians. Arms supplies many facts and figures, with clear documentation of her sources. In tabular form, she presents statistical evidence, such as infant mortality rates that show the United States trailing behind many less wealthy nations. Arms's multifaceted presentation leaves her reader with a sense of the sturdiness of her position.

Analysis

Immaculate Deception situates contemporary childbirth in a broad historical context. In tribal agrarian cultures, Arms suggests, childbirth was not necessarily a fear-ful experience for women, because they lived face to face with all the processes of natural life. Birth, death, and reproduction had not yet become clandestine. Because childbirth was so mysterious to men, however, societies in which men were not allowed to witness the miracle often saw the development of peculiar male fantasies about its nature. Men's ambivalent fear and wonder thus led to attempts to gain control over the creative powers of women. Perhaps the most notorious of these is the curse in Genesis 3:16, where Eve is cursed to suffer in bringing forth children. This began the long trajectory of the Judeo-Christian self-fulfilling expectation of pain in childbirth.

With Christianity vanished any empiricism that the Greco-Roman tradition had brought to medicine. Pain became a matter of divine will or diabolic action, so that male religious authority moved in on childbirth. Midwives were identified with witches, with lethal results. Male barber-surgeons began to perform crude obstetrics. The Catholic church gathered sick and dying people, together with laboring women, into the early Christian hospitals, which became centers of massive dissemination of infectious diseases, especially childbed fever. The death rate in these "charity" hospitals was staggering; the possibility of labor and delivery in one of these virtual charnel houses greatly added to women's fear of childbirth. Into this atmosphere of helpless (and quite reasonable) terror came the invention of the forceps in 1588. This seemingly magical device, the nature of which was long kept a close secret by the men who invented and used it, finally seemed to consolidate the shift in the meaning of birth from "something a woman can give to a child" to "something a man can do for a woman." Then in the mid-1800's came obstetrical anesthesia which, by rendering them unconscious, completed women's surrender of the birth experience into the hands of male experts.

Arms's rich historical perspective contributes to another of the chief strengths of *Immaculate Deception*: its careful logical presentation of linked cause-and-effect sequences. For example, when male convenience dictated that a woman should labor flat on her back on a bed or a table, this diminished the effectiveness of her contractions (which are meant to work in the direction of the pull of gravity). Because of this, men devised metal implements for pulling the baby out of her, which made birth more painful and dangerous. Men then created anesthetic agents to relieve her pain and anxiety, but these further decreased the efficiency of labor and endangered her baby. This required further intervention, such as the medical stimulation of labor. Artificially stimulated labor is even more painful than natural labor, so even more pain-killing drugs are called for. Drugging the laboring woman, besides slowing labor and depressing the newborn, also takes away her ability to use conscious self-control and cooperate with the process. She ends up unconscious or strapped down to a table so that she will not hurt herself, which further retards labor. So it goes, with each medical interference taking the mother and child further away from the normal birth that would have been their due if patience and trust in nature's way reigned over childbirth.

Because she explicitly highlights such interlocking factors, Arms succeeds in showing birth not as an isolated event, but as a vortex of many of the streams that flow together in a woman's life: her taking or relinquishing responsibility, her connectedness or alienation from her body, her trust or fear of her own nature. The focus on chain reactions of intervention also tends to minimize blaming. Although Arms unapologetically opposes the practices of the obstetrical establishment, her understanding grasp of cause-and-effect relationships results in a text that is not adversarial, contentious, or aggressive. Instead, she simply shows how and why counterproductive obstetrical measures came to exist. She places responsibility on both the deceptive medical industry in control of birth and on the women who passively allow themselves to be so deceived and controlled.

Context

After many decades of scanty discussion of American birth customs, the mid-1970's saw an abrupt crescendo of public debate. Contributing to this sudden interest was the popular experiential psychology movement of the late 1960's and early 1970's. Many of the schools of thought within that movement (such as transactional analysis, Gestalt therapy, and primal therapy) placed considerable importance on the psychological aftermath of early childhood trauma. It was perhaps only natural that the earliest childhood trauma, birth itself, should finally receive some attention. In addition, the liberalization of sexual behavior of the same period led, as day follows night, to an interest in reclaiming that common accompaniment of sex, the birth of a child.

The year 1975 was a milestone in the reevaluation of technologized obstetrics. By a miracle of synchronicity, this year saw the publication of *Immaculate Deception*, Frederick Leboyer's *Birth Without Violence*, and Ina May Gaskin's *Spiritual Midwifery*. In addition to these soon-to-be classics, such lesser-known works as Doris Haire's *The Cultural Warping of Childbirth* (1972) and William Woolfolk and Joanna Woolfolk's *The Great American Birth Rite* (1975) also appeared. Even in the midst of this sudden abundance of material, *Immaculate Deception* stood out. Its fine balance of photojournalism, polished prose, sound research, careful logic, and emotional impact earned it generally good reviews. Poet Adrienne Rich compared it favorably to Leboyer's work.

Arms and her contemporaries left the American birth scene changed. By the very diversity of their approaches—the melodramatic prose of Leboyer, the hippie mysticism of Gaskin, and the good sense of Arms—they managed to establish beyond reasonable argument that American hospital obstetrical practices were damaging mothers and babies. Because of their attempts to demystify and reclaim birth, the intellectual landscape around reproduction shifted significantly. American women gained greater choice in how they can bring children into the world. Anesthetized, high-tech deliveries still occur, but the mother who wants a home birth, a birthing center, or rooming-in in a hospital can find these options if she takes the trouble to look. Breast-feeding is no longer considered odd and eccentric. Midwifery has gained public, if not legal, acceptance. Unfortunately, this progress in the United States has not halted the profit-oriented export of technologized birth fads to other countries. In the rush to Americanize, "progress" often comes to mean imitating the mistakes of the United States.

Sources for Further Study

Behuniak-Long, Susan. "Bibliographic Essay: Feminism and Reproduction." *Choice* 29 (October, 1991): 243-251. Lists and briefly describes scores of books that engage issues of reproductive technology from a feminist viewpoint.

Dwinell, Jane. *Birth Stories: Mystery, Power, and Creation*. Westport, Conn.: Bergin & Garvey, 1992. A midwife's casebook containing the stories of twenty-one specific births in American hospitals, homes, and birthing centers. Each is accompanied by discussion of the general issues of women's health care and spirituality that it exemplifies.

Ehrenreich, Barbara, and Deirdre English. *For Her Own Good: 150 Years of the Experts' Advice to Women*. New York: Anchor Books, 1989. Examines not only the victory of the obstetrical establishment but also the ascendancy of the other psychomedical experts who assumed power over women's lives: scientists, doctors, psychotherapists, home economists, and child-rearing specialists.

Gaskin, Ina May. *Spiritual Midwifery*. Rev. ed. Summertown, Tenn.: Book Publishing Company, 1978. This midwifery handbook and compilation of birth stories became one of the primers for the revolution against technologized hospital birth. It blends mysticism and practicality in a way that became typical of the resurgent midwifery movement.

Haire, Doris. *The Cultural Warping of Childbirth*. Hillside, N.J.: International Childbirth Education Association, 1972. This slender pamphlet is one of the sources to which Arms often refers in *Immaculate Deception*. Haire lists thirty hospital practices that tend to turn birth from a normal into a pathological process. Haire's well-documented appeals are based less on emotions and more on cognitive reasoning.

Leboyer, Frederick. *Birth Without Violence*. New York: Alfred A. Knopf, 1975. Uses highly emotional photography and rhapsodic prose to advocate gentle handling of the infant immediately after birth. Although this French obstetrician's method is decidedly doctor-centered, his focus on the experience of birth by the newborn was revolutionary in its time.

Mitford, Jessica. *The American Way of Birth*. New York: E. P. Dutton, 1992. Perhaps the most direct descendant of *Immaculate Deception*, this highly readable work surveys the history of power-hungry and profit-hungry male annexation of the traditional female territory of birth.

Rich, Adrienne. *Of Woman Born: Motherhood as Experience and Institution*. New York: W. W. Norton, 1976. Combining both historical-social and personal material, this in-depth analysis of the female nurturing role considers motherhood both as the self-defined potential relationship of each woman with children and her own powers of reproduction and as a socially defined institution directed toward keeping women under the control of men.

——————————— . "The Theft of Childbirth." *New York Review of Books* 22 (October 2, 1975): 25-30. A sensitive and sensible review which contrasts *Immaculate Deception* and *Birth Without Violence*. Also includes a concise review of the history of male intervention in normal childbirth, from the invention of the forceps and the first uses of obstetrical anesthesia, and gives a briefer treatment to some of the same concepts that are detailed in *Of Woman Born*.

Donna Glee Williams

IN SEARCH OF OUR MOTHERS' GARDENS
Womanist Prose

Author: Alice Walker (1944-   )
Type of work: Essays
First published: 1983

Form and Content

The essay collection *In Search of Our Mothers' Gardens: Womanist Prose* gathers nonfiction that Alice Walker, a novelist, short-story writer, and poet, wrote between 1966 and 1982. It includes book reviews published in scholarly journals and popular magazines, transcripts of addresses to groups and institutions, and articles for *Ms.* magazine. The earliest selection is the essay "The Civil Rights Movement: What Good Was It?" which won Walker a prize in the annual *American Scholar* contest when she was twenty-three. Among the latest is "Writing *The Color Purple*," which sketches how Walker wrote the novel that won her the Pulitzer Prize for fiction.

The title of the book is taken from the title of the major essay, a classic and groundbreaking discussion of the black woman writer's struggle for freedom of self-expression and her search for the roots of her creativity. The front matter includes a definition of "womanist" as a black feminist that distinguishes "womanist" from "feminist" as purple is distinguished from lavender. The publication acknowledgments at the back of the book provide detailed information on the original publication and presentation of the articles and speeches.

The thirty-six selections, ranging from three to twenty-nine pages, are arranged in four parts, each of which is loosely organized around several themes. A principal theme of part 1 is the artist's need for models, which Walker explores by discussing models important to her own development as a writer. Part 2 centers on the formative influence that Martin Luther King, Jr., and the Civil Rights movement of the 1960's had on Walker. These selections, such as a review of Langston Hughes's most radical verse, reveal Walker's recognition of the relationship between struggle and social change, her commitment to the struggle, and her recognition of the dignity of poor and oppressed persons. Part 3 begins with the title essay, "In Search of Our Mothers' Gardens." It also includes an interview in which Walker discusses a painful period while she was in college. Contemplating suicide, she wrote the collection of poems later published under the title *Once* (1968). The selections in part 4, the smallest section, address such issues as the danger of nuclear weapons and the Middle Eastern conflict. It concludes with a moving explanation of the dedication of the book to her daughter Rebecca and a joyous celebration of life. The publication acknowledgments at the back of the book provide detailed bibliographic data on the selections.

The style of the selections is personal and down-to-earth. A principal method is flowing from experience to insight, telling the story of an experience and reflecting on the meaning and value of that experience. The tone is honest, straightforward, and human, by turns serious and playful. The prevailing theme is a vision of what makes for the flourishing of human beings: the freedom of all persons to be themselves, to decide for themselves, to be respected, and to respect others. What emerges from the selections is a portrait of a woman who is aware, intelligent, searching, committed to seeing life as it is, and working to make it richer for the community of creatures who inhabit the planet.

Analysis

The book opens with the article "Saving the Life That Is Your Own: The Importance of Models in the Artist's Life." This text of a speech Walker gave to the Modern Language Association in San Francisco in 1975 sets the personal tone and direction for part 1. Walker asserts the importance of writers—especially those outside the mainstream of the literary tradition, writing not what others want but what they themselves want to read. In doing so, they not only set the direction of vision but also follow it. This integrity of purpose puts it in the power of the black woman artist to save lives and makes it her business to do so because she knows that the life she saves is her own.

Several of the other selections in part 1 explore the lives, work, and significance of several of Walker's literary models, especially Zora Neale Hurston, Flannery O'Connor, Virginia Woolf, Jean Toomer, and Rebecca Jackson. Wanting to write an authentic story drawing on black witchcraft, Walker undertook research into black folklore. She discovered that most research in this field had been published by white anthropologists, but in a footnote she discovered the work of Hurston. She found Hurston's *Mules and Men* (1935) the "perfect book," because of its "racial health," its depiction of black persons as "complete, complex, *undiminished* human beings." Recognizing Hurston as one of the "most significant unread authors in America," Walker visited Eatonville, Florida, Hurston's birthplace. Learning that Hurston had died in a home for the indigent and had been buried in an unmarked grave, Walker bought a tombstone to mark the gravesite. Walker recognizes the role this painful pilgrimage played in her own development as a black woman writer.

Walker, the daughter of Georgia sharecroppers, also made a pilgrimage to her own birthplace, Eatonton, Georgia, and to the home of another of her models, Flannery O'Connor. The daughter of Irish Catholic landowners, O'Connor lived in Milledgeville, Georgia, just down the road from Eatonton. Walker was drawn to compare herself with O'Connor, who is for her the first great writer of the South.

Part 2 opens with "The Civil Rights Movement: What Good Was It?," which Walker wrote at twenty-three. Her first published essay, it won the annual *American Scholar* essay contest. It sets the focus for the following selections: Dr. Martin Luther King, Jr., and the Civil Rights movement of the 1960's. King's heroism and the ideals of the movement stirred Walker to new life and to a commitment to work for social justice, for all oppressed peoples, especially African Americans.

As Walker began to realize the inadequacies in her education, she set about discovering and reading the black authors whose works had never been introduced to her. She began to see herself as a revolutionary artist. While her art might change nothing, she saw it as a way to preserve for the future the extraordinary lives of persons neglected by politics and economics.

In the extensive essay "My Father's Country Is the Poor," Walker reflects on her experiences in Cuba during a visit there during the Cuban Revolution. She was impressed by the compassion, intelligence, and work that the Cubans brought against all that oppressed them.

In part 3, Walker explores in depth the question of her roots as an artist in the lead essay, "In Search of Our Mothers' Gardens." Focusing on her feminine inheritance, she traces the images of black women in literature, such as the women in *Cane* (1923), the novel written by the Southern black male writer Jean Toomer, and the few women such as Phillis Wheatley, a slave in the 1700's, who were able to express themselves in poetry. The major contribution of this essay is its exploration of the legacy of creativity that slave women and black women after them passed on subtly and subversively to their daughters. Looked upon as mules of the world, denied the channels of creativity open to others, these black women expressed their creativity in gardens, cooking, and quilts. For Walker, the unique, imaginative, and spiritually powerful quilt made of rags and now preserved in the Smithsonian Institution in Washington, D.C., is a symbol of this legacy and a model for the exercise of her own craft as a writer.

Part 4, the smallest section of the book, includes reflections on having a child and writing the novel *The Color Purple* (1982). A principal theme of these selections is carried in the title of one selection, a speech Walker gave at an antinuclear rally: "Only Justice Can Stop a Curse."

Context

Alice Walker is one of the most prominent figures in the development of black women's literature in the United States. Winner of the Pulitzer Prize for fiction and the American Book Award in 1983 for her novel *The Color Purple*, Walker came to popular attention with the film version of the novel in 1985. Recognizing her own debt to the work of Zora Neale Hurston, folklorist and novelist of the early part of the twentieth century, she played a major role in rescuing Hurston's work from obscurity and expanding its audience. The essays, interviews, and book reviews in this collection reveal some of the persons, events, and experiences that Walker believes helped to create the person she is and the work she has done.

This collection demonstrates that Walker speaks out, often eloquently and passionately, against racism, classism, sexism, homophobia, and despoliation of the environment. Finding the term "civil rights" colorless and limited, she openly supports the movement toward human liberation: the right and need for all individuals to express themselves freely within the context of the earth community. Some critics find fault, however, with Walker's commitment to feminism and her portrayal of African American men.

This work is one of the first collections that emerged in the 1980's to express the struggle of African American women to define themselves in a society often indifferent and hostile to them and to see their experience recognized for its value in understanding the world. The collection reveals the process of self-discovery and self-development in which Walker has been engaged, some of the origins and changes in her thought, and the ideas that kindle her energy. Her search for understanding the significance of her mother's garden helps to unearth the tradition for contemporary black women writers that enables their efforts to claim their lives, assert their value, and articulate their meaning. It also contributes to an understanding of the nature of the artistry of black women writers. Among Walker's other works are the collection of poetry *Revolutionary Petunias and Other Poems* (1973), a collection of short stories about black women entitled *In Love and Trouble: Stories of Black Women* (1973), and the novels *The Third Life of Grange Copeland* (1970), *Meridian* (1976), and *The Temple of My Familiar* (1989).

Sources for Further Study

Blackburn, Regina. "In Search of the Black Female Self: African-American Women's Autobiographies and Ethnicity." In *Women's Autobiography: Essays in Criticism*, edited by Estelle C. Jelinek. Bloomington: Indiana University Press, 1980. Blackburn explores the themes occurring in the writings of black women: identity, pride, self-hatred and doubt, and the "double jeopardy" of being both black and female.

Christian, Barbara. *Black Feminist Criticism: Perspectives on Black Women Writers*. New York: Pergamon Press, 1985. A collection of a noted black feminist literary critic's previously published essays and lectures on contemporary black women writers and some of the issues and questions their work raises.

Evans, Mari, ed. *Black Women Writers (1950-1980): A Critical Evaluation*. Garden City, N.Y.: Anchor Press/Doubleday, 1984. This lengthy volume includes reflections of fifteen significant black women writing between 1950 and 1980 and critical essays examining their work, as well as brief biographies and selected bibliographies.

Gates, Henry Louis, Jr., ed. *Reading Black, Reading Feminist: A Critical Anthology*. New York: Meridian Books, 1990. Gates, a scholar in African American Studies, has collected a wide range of studies by and about some of the leading black feminist writers and critics whose shared structures and themes unify their works into a literary tradition.

McDowell, Deborah E. "New Directions for Black Feminist Criticism." In *The New Feminist Criticism: Essays on Women, Literature, and Theory*, edited by Elaine Showalter. New York: Pantheon, 1985. Recognizing the exclusion of black women writers by both white feminist and black male critics, McDowell points out some weaknesses of black feminist criticism.

Pryse, Marjorie, and Hortense J. Spillers, eds. *Conjuring: Black Women, Fiction, and Literary Tradition*. Bloomington: Indiana University Press, 1985. These articles raise questions about individual writers and their works, as well as their collective significance toward the goal of writing a literary history of black women novelists.

Smith, Barbara. "Toward a Black Feminist Criticism." In *The New Feminist Criti-*

cism: Essays on Women, Literature, and Theory, edited by Elaine Showalter. New York: Pantheon, 1985. In one of the first essays distinguishing the writing of black women from that of white women, Smith also protests the exclusion of black women writers, especially lesbian writers, from the literary tradition.

Walker, Melissa. *Down from the Mountaintop: Black Women's Novels in the Wake of the Civil Rights Movement, 1966-1989*. New Haven, Conn.: Yale University Press, 1991. Walker demonstrates how eighteen novels by black women relate both to the Civil Rights movement and to the historical conditions that brought about its rise and decline.

Christian Koontz

IN THE DITCH

Author: Buchi Emecheta (1944-   )
Type of work: Novel
Type of plot: Bildungsroman
Time of plot: The late 1960's
Locale: The slums of North London
First published: 1972

Principal characters:

ADAH, a young Nigerian sociology student rearing five small
children by herself

THE LANDLORD, a mean-spirited and hostile man

MRS. DEVLIN, a kindly Irish woman who lives above the
landlord's flat

WHOOPEY, a lonely, dependent, single mother of two children

MRS. COX, Whoopey's mother

MRS. COOK, a Jamaican mother of five children who chooses to
live without welfare assistance

THE SMALLS, a quarrelsome family consisting of Mr. Small, his
wife, and his mother, Granny

CAROL, a lonely, overweight, patronizing officer employed by the
Welfare Council

MR. PERSIAL, a patronizing, middle-class council clerk

Form and Content

Originally written as a collection of "observations" and published serially in *The New Statesman*, *In the Ditch*, Buchi Emecheta's first novel, is discussed almost always only in relation to *Second Class Citizen* (1974), its rightful chronological predecessor. Like its companion piece, *In the Ditch* is heavily autobiographical, following Emecheta's own descent into the "ditch" of welfare living and enforced dysfunctionality.

Adah, the protagonist of the novel, is an intelligent, hardworking woman who has to fight against considerable odds to keep from being driven insane by the degrading welfare system. The story chronicles her struggle to maintain her pride and dignity as a welfare recipient and her keen desire for independence for herself and her children. The novel begins at the point when Adah is newly separated from her husband. Alone and vulnerable, she battles the squalid conditions of the rat- and cockroach-infested room that she is forced to rent from an unethical landlord who uses his "juju" wiles to terrorize her and her children. Faced with a choice between one of two evils—enslavement and exploitation by the landlord on the one hand or a prisonlike existence of welfare living at the Pussy Cat Mansions—Adah opts for the latter, which she argues offers a qualified independence. The story concentrates on Adah's indoctrination to the slum life of the welfare system and chronicles her struggle to support and rear her children alone. Despite her desperation at the beginning of the novel, Adah is introduced as an ambitious evening-school student of sociology and a civil service librarian at the British Museum with middle-class and creative aspirations.

The burdens of an obviously stressful financial situation, parenting five small children between the ages of eight years and four months old, and the wiles of an unsympathetic and exploitative landlord set up a predictably negative framework for the novel. The novel's gloominess is evident in the constraining alternatives open to Adah and the desperate choices that she must make. Adah is inexorably pauperized as she must give up her job at the British Museum to qualify for the dole and membership in the ditch-dwellers' community. Consequently, the focus of Adah's story becomes the inevitable acceptance and rejection of the welfare system and its devastating psychological effect, which ironically is to dominate Adah's life and education literally and figuratively as a sociology student. The welfare system of council housing comes under scrutiny in a love-hate relationship. Adah's indoctrination into the slum life of the Pussy Cat Mansions estate chronicles the descent of bright, able-bodied, capable, and otherwise productive people such as Adah into the inevitable dependency inherent in the welfare system.

Officialdom defines the Mansions by dysfunctionality, by "problem families" who are characteristically large, possibly belonging to a minority group, and often headed by single parents, usually by "failed and rejected women" living on the dole and belonging to no particular class. It is to the oppressive hierarchy of this cult of ditch-dwellers that Adah must learn to yield and play dumb in spite of her pride. Survivor that she is, she learns to play the game just well and long enough to emerge from the experience more admirable, dignified, respectable, and wholesome than any of the other ditch-dwellers.

Analysis

Three central issues pervade Emecheta's writing: the oppression of women (especially African women), education as the means of their emancipation, and the effects of the conflict between tradition and Western influences on their development. Her central intention is to explore and protest the roots of women's oppression. This is a personal crusade. What she has uncovered and relentlessly critiqued in all of her novels is the enslavement of women by institutions in the private and public spheres: from welfare states that pauperize and deskill women to the insidious institution of slavery, the oppressive institution of marriage, and the martyrdom of motherhood. *In the Ditch* chronicles a series of journey-flights that the protagonist makes from one form of bondage to another, from a failed marriage to the den of an exploitative landlord to the demeaning snare of a welfare system.

In the Ditch illustrates the enslaving power of poverty, the symbolic embodiment of a caste system based on race, sex, class, and property. The society depicted is menacing to the poor, the economically deprived, and the uneducated, particularly women—the single, unsupported "mums." Emecheta's purpose is to present the hierarchy of the Pussy Cat Mansions as a microcosm of the oppressive hierarchies of society at large. The culture of poverty has its own hierarchy, its own protocol for socialization, and its own value system. If the blows of the treacherous Nigerian landlord's terrorism and exploitation have merely bruised Adah's self-esteem, then the verbal lashing with which the Mansions' white plumber, Mr. Small, indoctrinates Adah to Mansions living puts black, African, and female Adah in her place.

The hierarchy plays out entrenched attitudes and expectations. Adah quickly learns the characteristics of the culture of ditch-dwelling: forced unemployment, dependency, lack of initiative, dole lines, hopelessness, and overbreeding in an unhealthy community of unloved, neglected single mums. Although a camaraderie develops—a collective of sorts—among the women which allows them to cope with the bleakness of their situation and perhaps win some improvements here and there, the fragile basis of such group solidarity is ineffectual in the face of an indifferent, powerful welfare system. It is precisely for this reason that Adah feels compassion for the ditch-dweller mums but cannot bring herself to identify fully with them or their lot.

Steeling herself against the destructiveness of institutionalized dependency, with its inherent self-defeating inclinations of alcohol, overbreeding, and overeating, Adah reminds herself that her superior education, her goal to be a writer, her previous experience as a one-time wage earner, and her current status as a sociology student are her only guarantees to escaping the ditch—hence Emecheta's realism, her contention that the potential for choice rests ultimately with women. Where the ditch-dwellers such as Whoopey and Mrs. Cox continue to look to the system for their emancipation, Adah and perhaps the Jamaican Mrs. Cook entertain no delusions or faith in the welfare system to bring about equality or social change. Emecheta's vision of women's emancipation is fairly clear: Individual initiative, determination, and education are the liberating forces for transcending oppression and enslavement.

Adah's move to a new matchbox maisonette flat across from the famous Regent's Park, where "her own working-class council estate was cheek by jowl with expensive houses and flats belonging to successful writers and actors," symbolizes the triumph of the artistic and creative resourcefulness, empowering Adah to resist appropriating the ditch-dweller status of the welfare system. This final journey, though underscored by procrastination, chronicles Adah's emergence from the psychological ditch of dependence. Thus, despite the pervasive pessimism of Emecheta's prose, delineated by the ditch metaphor, the work offers crucial hope in its simple philosophy of indestructible strength of will. Although criticized for its thinness of style and simple language, and therefore rarely discussed, *In the Ditch* and its companion piece, *Second Class Citizen*, are important because they constitute the first *Bildungsroman* by a woman writer in African literature.

Context

Along with fellow second-generation African woman writer Mariam Ba, from Senegal, Buchi Emecheta has been described as a sustained and vigorous voice of feminist protest. Emecheta has dramatized in eight novels the entire realm of African women's experience: childhood, family, marriage and arranged marriages, perpetual pregnancy, childbirth, motherhood, widowhood, and polygamy. While she has pointedly disclaimed any feminist consciousness in her writing, many critics have avowed that her novels teem with a feminism more poignantly articulated than many avowed Western feminist novelists. Unlike first-generation writers of the 1960's—Flora Nwapa, Grace Ogot, and Rebeka Njau—Emecheta departed from the common themes of childlessness and marriage to the more complex issues of racism and sexism in a modern society in which tradition and modernization are at a crossroads. Her denial of conscious feminist writing not only has raised the issue of the genesis of African feminism but also has brought into focus the dire need for an African women's history, one which will historicize the important events in the lives of African women that colonialism has conveniently omitted.

Like her subsequent novels, *In the Ditch* provides a feminine perspective on the social issues of racism, injustice, the welfare state, and women and the culture of poverty. Compared to her predecessors' portrayal of African women, Emecheta's women characters are more profoundly sketched and better articulated. While her African women may still be marginalized by gender realities, they certainly are not depicted as the stock, stereotypic characters often found in portrayals by African male writers or the first-generation women writers. With Emecheta, characterization means not only recognizing the female stereotypes but also revealing sensitively and clear-sightedly how her female characters are both living out and transcending these stereotypes. Characteristic of her portraiture is a sense of identification with her characters—an identification nurtured by her personal experience of marginality—which enables her to articulate Nigerian women's reality both objectively and in the context of an ever-evolving culture.

In this regard, the immediacy of her women characters' existence and the articulation of their oppression challenge the masculinist practice of dismissing women in Nigerian and other African literatures as a monolithic unit. Also, all of her novels add a holistic and humanized (as opposed to a simply feminized) dimension to Nigerian and African literatures. While Emecheta demonstrates unequivocally women's ability to choose and to execute their choices, she is aware through her own marginalization of her strong, independent characters that social changes to a patriarchal mind-set provoke a backlash. *In the Ditch* began a tradition of the female *Bildungsroman* and unapologetic protest in African literature.

Sources for Further Study

Brown, Lloyd W. *Women Writers in Black Africa*. Westport, Conn.: Greenwood Press, 1981. A compilation of essays on the contribution of African women writers—the "other voices, the unheard voices"—to African literature. The introductory chapter gives a broad survey of African women writers and their articulation of the female experience. Chapter 2 offers an excellent introduction to the curious indifference to female voices of protest. Chapter 3 provides criticism of Emecheta's first five novels.

Frank, Katherine. "The Death of the Slave Girl: African Womanhood in the Novels of Buchi Emecheta." *World Literature Written in English* 21 (Fall, 1982): 476-497. An extensive critical examination of the protest tradition of Emecheta's novels, with particular attention to her fourth novel, *The Slave Girl* (1977). Frank tends to argue for a strictly feminist reading of Emecheta's account of African womanhood.

Katrak, Ketu H. "Womanhood/Motherhood: Variations on a Theme in Selected Novels of Buchi Emecheta." *The Journal of Commonwealth Literature* 22, no. 1 (1987): 159-170. Discusses the major theme of Emecheta's concern in her major novels, especially *The Joys of Motherhood*.

Porter, Abioseh M. "*Second Class Citizen*: The Point of Departure for Understanding Buchi Emecheta's Major Fiction." *The International Fiction Review* 15, no. 2 (Summer, 1988): 123-129. Argues against the persistent attempt by some Western scholars to read many of Emecheta's novels only within the feminist tradition. Demonstrates the danger of focusing almost exclusively on her feminist themes at the expense of the universality of her novels. Discusses *Second Class Citizen*, the companion piece to *In the Ditch*, as a powerful example of the *Bildungsroman* in Africa.

Pamela J. Olubunmi Smith

IN THE SHADOW OF THE WIND

Author: Anne Hébert (1916-   )
Type of work: Novel
Type of plot: Tragedy
Time of plot: The summer and autumn of 1936 and the autumn of 1982
Locale: Griffin Creek, a fictional place between the city of Québec and the Atlantic
   Ocean
First published: Les Fous de Bassan, 1982 (English translation, 1983)

> *Principal characters:*
> NICHOLAS JONES, a clergyman
> IRENE JONES, Nicholas' wife, who hangs herself in 1936
> OLIVIA ATKINS, a seventeen-year-old in 1936 who is murdered
>   and returns as "Olivia of the High Seas"
> NORA ATKINS, a fifteen-year-old in 1936 who is murdered with
>   her cousin Olivia
> STEVENS BROWN, the first cousin of the Atkins girls
> FELICITY JONES, the mother and grandmother of the central
>   characters
> PERCIVAL BROWN, Stevens' younger brother who can only
>   communicate by shrieks and cries
> PAM and PAT BROWN, the twin sisters of Stevens and Percival
>   and the servants of their Uncle Nicholas
> JOHN ERWIN MCKENNA, a detective sent to investigate the
>   disappearance of the Atkins girls

Form and Content

   In an atmosphere marked by the mysterious influence of the sea, Anne Hébert uses multiple narrators to reveal different facets of the central events and characters of *In the Shadow of the Wind.* The plot revolves around the sexual maturation of two young girls and three violent deaths precipitated by the erotic tension that they innocently produce. As the novel opens in 1982, Nicholas Jones laments the dwindling of Griffin Creek in a broken echo of his former voice. As pastor of an Anglican congregation in French Catholic Québec, he speaks for God to an isolated community. Closely related to his flock, he is invested with patriarchal power, which he abuses. In 1936, he lusted after his nieces Nora and Olivia, driving his wife to suicide. In 1982, he tyrannizes his aging twin nieces, Pam and Pat Brown. The only surviving women of the old community, they nurture each other and somehow contrive to resist his domination. Nicholas attempts to re-create the old Griffin Creek by painting his male ancestors, begetting fathers in his own image. The twins counter with vivid paintings of female ancestors, especially Irene Jones and the cousins Nora and Olivia Atkins. Nicholas Jones's rambling reminiscence of 1936 sets the stage for a tragedy presented in fragments by succeeding narrators.

Stevens Brown is next, with a series of letters from the summer of 1936. He explains his motives and past to a friend in Florida, "Old Mick," giving a clear sense of his home and family and of the "buried child," prey to terrible memories of abuse, hidden in his man's body. He inspects the landscape of his childhood and identifies with its harsh northern beauty. This is a landscape that he intends to reclaim only during summer, an intense season corresponding to the brief bloom of Nora and Olivia, whom he describes in their delectable beauty. Stevens closes his last letter on the night of August 31, planning to start on a return to Florida the next day.

Nora follows with an inner monologue which covers many of the same events as Stevens, vividly rejoicing in life and the strength of her erotic potential. Every male is a potential "first," and her reaction to an attempt at seduction by her Uncle Nicholas is to wish for someone her own age and unmarried. Her narration stops in the same moonlit evening as Stevens', declaring, as he does, that summer is over.

Percival, Stevens' brother, opens the next section, gazing out at the moonlit scene from his window. A double murder has just occurred; he sees a small boat heading out to sea, but only later knowledge indicates that it contains the bodies of the Atkins girls. As an "idiot," he is naïve in tone, but acute in his perceptions. Percival's vision is both poetic and earthy. He understands the relationship between his grandmother Felicity and the sea, guesses at the transmutation of his cousin Olivia to a pure spirit of sea. He also knows people by their smell—Nora and Olivia by a scent of green ferns and blood, the detective McKenna by a fecal, greasy odor. He ignores proprieties; his concern is for the people he loves. The reader is privileged in sharing Percival's vision, since his communication with his family is essentially nonverbal. He and his father discover Nora's remains on the beach after a storm.

Percival alternates with the distinctive voices of the collective community and an unidentified "objective" voice. The people of Griffin Creek worry about presenting a united front. They preserve appearances, stress sightings of strangers. The neutral voice presents the actions and words of Griffin Creek as it discovers its loss and continues with the investigation of the crime. Several plausible suspects with possible moments and motives are presented, including unknown men in big American cars or boats offshore. All three narrative voices talk about John Erwin McKenna, the Anglophone detective sent from Montréal, and his investigation. Eavesdropping with Percival, the reader hears McKenna interrogate Stevens, hears the clack of the typewriter which swallows his living words. This segment ends with Percival lamenting the loss of his brother and cousins as he stares out to sea.

Olivia of the High Seas follows, speaking in a present independent of time, joined to a larger consciousness which continues after Olivia Atkins' death. She has become a disembodied spirit of the waters and communes with the dead women of Griffin Creek. While Nora's voice is warm sunlight, Olivia's is cool water. Born by tides of water and memory, she moves effortlessly through time, echoing events recounted in earlier narration, reliving a memory of sunlit communion with Stevens and the violence of his father's reaction. Consciousness of her murder waits on the shores of

Griffin Creek, but fear of a second death drives her far out to sea, before she can recount her story.

It is Stevens' last letter, dated 1982, that reveals the final horrors to "Old Mick." Stevens has escaped from a government hospital, where he has been confined, surrounded by men shattered in mind and body by World War II. The deaths of the Atkins girls are almost incidental in this context, but seabirds, his personal furies, prey upon his mind and fill his ears with their cries. He plans suicide after writing one last time. Thus, in a Montréal apartment, he evokes the stormy sea and winds that echoed his fury as he "punished" and killed Nora, raped and killed Olivia. The "mystery" of their deaths is solved, even though Stevens has long ago been acquitted of the murders.

Analysis

The text of *In the Shadow of the Wind* is a complex one. It quotes the Bible and Hébert's own poetry. It presents itself at times as letters, at times as inner thoughts, and even as the choral voice of a whole community. Dominated by marine images—the sea wind, the voices of seabirds—the novel is continually swept by the tides of different voices, reflections on the same events, each tied to the others in mounting sexual and social tension. The central themes of the novel are similarly complex. Certainly the text supports a reading as a mystery, yet, as successive narrators draw the reader into deeper complicity with the characters, there is less and less doubt as to the identity of the killer. Yet determining guilt for the deaths of Irene, Nora, and Olivia is more difficult.

One facet of the text is Nicholas Jones's description of his portrait gallery. A failed patriarch, he has no issue. Instead he paints his male ancestors, stiff figures dressed in black and white, all with his face. In turn, Pam and Pat Brown paint the women of Griffin Creek, vibrant with colors, flowers, and lace. In the borders, the twins intertwine, endlessly repeated, the word "summer" and the number "1936." The forbidden faces and names of Irene, Nora, and Olivia appear, surrounded by symbols of the sea. All three women are victims of men (although one was a suicide), and they are placed in the sisterhood of women, in opposition to their male ancestors. A feminist rejection of patriarchy and the victimization of women, further developed in the violent deaths of the three women, is obvious.

It is also important, however, to remember that the women of Griffin Creek live in complicity with their men. Stevens' mother approves of his father's attempts to kill him. In spite of her seemingly supernatural motherly powers, Felicity rejects the love of her sons and grandsons and chooses to perpetuate the system of life of Griffin Creek, a closed community settled by Loyalist refugees after the American Revolution. Its geographical isolation is doubled by its linguistic and religious isolation. It is in miniature what Québec is within Canada, an isolated patriarchy which maintains an identity alien to the larger nation. Identified with the northern shore of Québec, Griffin Creek is a model of traditional Québecois society, offering another possible reading of the novel.

Nevertheless, the specific setting of Griffin Creek's tragedy in 1936 also renders it a microcosm of the world then germinating World War II, in which Stevens serves after his acquittal. Stevens is already a victim of his parents' abuse. His combat psychosis, his years of suffering in a military hospital, and his planned suicide make him a victim of society's war, even as his cousins were victims of his rage. Hébert does not intend to exempt present society from guilt. The first settlers reached Griffin Creek in 1782; thus 1982, the date of the framing texts of Nicholas Jones and Stevens Brown, is both a bicentennial and the year of the novel's publication. All society is implicated in the horrors of Griffin Creek.

Context

Anne Hébert won early fame as a poet, one of the first of the women of Québec to reach an international audience. Her bestseller *Kamouraska* (1970; English translation, 1973) became a widely distributed film, and in 1982, she won the prestigious French literary prize, the Prix Femina, for *In the Shadow of the Wind*. Her works are intense, intricately crafted in language, and emotionally dark and violent. Thematically consistent, they deal with the destruction of innocent victims: by vampires in *Héloïse* (1980), by Satan worshippers and cloistered nuns in *Les Enfants du sabbat* (1975; *Children of the Black Sabbath*, 1977), and by the inbred violence of the isolated patriarchy of *In the Shadow of the Wind*. The oppression of the individual by patriarchal cultural patterns is consistently a pretext for tragedy.

Paradoxically, it is also in meticulous patterns that some hope can be found. Although Nicholas and Stevens use biblical language for their destructive ends, the beauty of the language and images in the Bible can have positive uses. The Song of Solomon sets Olivia dreaming of love and Nora speaks of her parents' happy home as an ark. Hébert even ties this novel to her own poetry, by having Olivia of the High Seas quote the poem "There is certainly someone . . ." from *Le Tombeau des rois* (1953; *The Tomb of the Kings*, 1967). The patterning of privileged words, scripture, and poetry is a source of positive pleasure, as is the cultural and spacial pattern that governs the Griffin Creek community in the central barn dance scene. The balanced interplay of men and women in the dance is erotic, but not violent. Stevens is able to swing through the line of women, touching them all, and does no damage. Dance, fully cooperative and pleasurable, is a model for the male-female community. When Irene Jones sits aside from the dance, she prefigures her suicide. When Nicholas Jones exceeds the pattern and frightens Percival by his predatory kissing of his nieces, he prefigures the violence that Stevens will carry into action.

Female desire, in Nora and Olivia, is a positive, constructive force, while Hébert's predatory males are destructive. Still, her women are not all passive victims. They have also cooperated in the victimization of other women and their own children. Like Felicity, they have chosen resentment and have refused to use their full creative power, both erotic and maternal. Hébert identifies women, through Felicity and Olivia, with the vast, untapped fertility of the sea. *In the Shadow of the Wind* is a text saturated with marine images, charged with the violence of sea and wind and the predatory birds and fish that flash between them. The novel may seem despairing in the destruction that it chronicles, but in its poetic beauty it offers the hope of creation.

Sources for Further Study

Gould, Karen. "Absence and Meaning in Anne Hébert's *Les Fous de Bassan.*" *French Review* 59, no. 6 (May, 1986): 921-930. This study considers the poetic language and formal construction of the novel and shows them to be subversive and feminist. Citations are in French.

Green, Mary Jean. "The Novel in Québec: The Family Plot and the Personal Voice." In *Studies on Canadian Literature: Introductory and Critical Essays*, edited by Arnold E. Davidson. New York: Modern Language Association of America, 1990. This essay provides a historical context for Hébert's novel within the rubric of novels dealing with Québecois culture, although it analyzes only Hébert's early novella *Le Torrent* (1950, 1963, 1965; *The Torrent*, 1973). Contains a useful bibliography of Québecois family novels and criticism devoted to them.

Rea, Annabelle M. "The Climate of Viol/Violence and Madness in Anne Hébert's *Les Fous de Bassan.*" In *Québec Studies*. Vol. 4. Hanover, N.H.: Northeast Council for Québec Studies, 1986. Analyzes the violent physical and psychological climate of *In the Shadow of the Wind* and the images used to present it, in particular the use of seabirds. Quotations are in French. Includes extensive notes.

Slott, Kathryn. "Submergence and Resurgence of the Female Other in Anne Hébert's *Les Fous de Bassan.*" In *Québec Studies*. Vol. 4. Hanover, N.H.: Northeast Council for Québec Studies, 1986. Examines the passive role of women in Hébert's novel, referring to categories developed by Simone de Beauvoir in *Le Deuxième Sexe* (1949; *The Second Sex*, 1953). Quotations are in French.

Smart, Patricia. *Writing in the Father's House: The Emergence of the Feminine in the Québec Literary Tradition*. Toronto: University of Toronto Press, 1991. This study of French-Canadian literature from a feminist perspective attempts to analyze and generalize "within national and gender contexts." Chapter 4 studies Hébert's poetry. Smart argues that traditional novels are based on the "founding murder" of a woman, and her brief analysis of *In the Shadow of the Wind* in chapter 6 asserts that Hébert's novel demands cultural transformation by exposing this murder. Offers a bibliography and an index.

Smith, Donald. "Anne Hébert and the Roots of Imagination." In *Voices of Deliverance: Interviews with Québec and Acadian Writers*. Translated by Larry Shouldice. Toronto: Anansi Press, 1986. This interview with Hébert focuses on her verse and earlier prose. Particularly interesting as a personal context to Hébert's work.

Anne W. Sienkewicz

INDIANA

Author: George Sand (Amandine-Aurore-Lucile Dupin, Baronne Dudevant, 1804-
1876)
Type of work: Novel
Type of plot: Psychological realism
Time of plot: The early eighteenth century
Locale: France
First published: 1832 (English translation, 1833)

> *Principal characters:*
> INDIANA, a beautiful, melancholy young woman
> NOUN, Indiana's maid
> COLONEL DELMARE, Indiana's husband, an elderly retired soldier
> SIR RALPH BROWN, Indiana's cousin
> RAYMON DE RAMIÈRE, the lover of first Noun and later Indiana

Form and Content

Indiana is devoted to exploring women's position in society, the marital relationship, and the family and to condemning the laws that govern women's existence. The
book begins on a rainy autumn evening in Brie, when Colonel Delmare, hunting
charcoal poachers, shoots Raymon de Ramière. Raymon, brought into the house and
revived, claims that he slipped over the wall to examine the machinery in Delmare's
factory, but he has actually come to meet Noun, Delmare's maid.

When Raymon wearies of Noun, he re-encounters Indiana, the colonel's young
wife, at a party in Paris and is struck by her beauty and delicacy. He woos her ardently,
and Indiana begins to reciprocate his passion. A letter from Noun announcing her
pregnancy forces Raymon to meet her at the Delmare estate. Sensing that her lover's
interest has waned, Noun prepares a seductive nest in Indiana's own boudoir. Her tears
and pleas persuade Raymon to make love to her—although, drunk, he imagines that
she is Indiana.

Raymon tells Noun that he will not marry her, although he offers her a substantial
settlement. Indiana returns unexpectedly, and Noun, panic-stricken, hides Raymon
behind a curtain. Indiana discovers Raymon, who covers himself by claiming that his
love for her has brought him there. Indignant, Indiana orders him away and reproaches
Noun for aiding him. Although she says nothing, Noun realizes that Raymon loves
Indiana. The equally unexpected return of Sir Ralph Brown, Indiana's devoted cousin,
forces Raymon to flee. The following day, Indiana discovers the body of Noun, whose
despair has led her to drown herself.

Two months later, Colonel Delmare invites Raymon to inspect his factory. Indiana
avoids Raymon, but eventually they are thrown together and her love for him revives.
Ralph tries to separate them but is unable, resigning himself to keeping the affair from
Delmare. When Delmare breaks his leg, Raymon visits him daily in order to see

Indiana, and he and Ralph, although forced to appear friends, develop a strong antipathy for each other. Delmare leaves on a business trip, and Ralph sets up a vigilant watch over Indiana and tries to warn her by revealing the cause of Noun's suicide. When Raymon comes to her that night, she questions him. As he is admitting his culpability in Noun's death, Ralph slips a note under the door alerting them to Delmare's return.

When Delmare plans to retire to Île Bourbon, Indiana declares her willingness to abandon him, and Raymon's ardor cools. Indiana runs away from Delmare and comes to Raymon, who reproaches her and tries to send her away, saying that it would be dishonorable to accept her sacrifice. She replies that since she has not spent the night beneath her husband's roof, she is already disgraced in the eyes of society. Raymon forces Indiana from the house. Leaving, the distraught Indiana throws herself in the river, seeking to follow Noun's example. Ralph rescues her and brings her home. Her husband demands to know where she spent the night, but she refuses to tell him. Delmare and Indiana leave for Bourbon, accompanied by Ralph.

Raymon falls ill and begins to regret Indiana's loss, imagining her nursing him. On a whim, he writes her a letter urging her to leave her husband and come to him, but he then forgets about the letter. Meanwhile, Delmare reads Indiana's journal and discovers her affair. He attacks her and subsequently suffers a stroke. When Raymon's letter arrives, Indiana finds a ship going to France and bribes the captain in order to arrange passage. Meanwhile, Raymon courts and wins Laure de Nangy, a wealthy heiress. Upon Indiana's arrival, she is met by the sardonic Laure, who sees in the confrontation a chance to forever gain the upper hand over her new husband. Raymon puts Indiana in a carriage for Paris, where she finds Ralph, who brings news of her husband's death. Ralph reveals his love for Indiana, and the two resolve to commit suicide. They do so, but in the contradictory final chapter, the reader discovers the two living in solitude on Bourbon.

Analysis

Indiana deals with the freedom of the individual; in it, George Sand tries to do away with romantic notions of choice and to present humans made thoroughly miserable by the structures and imposed silences of society. She observed in the preface to the 1832 edition that "the being who tries to free himself from his lawful curb is represented as very wretched indeed, and the heart that rebels against the decrees of its destiny in sore distress." Throughout the novel, an atmosphere of gloom and melancholy prevail, while physical love is presented as a hallucinatory delusion. Indiana and Ralph, the most sympathetic characters, are shown as passive beings driven almost mad by the pressures of society, while the guileless Noun is impelled to kill herself from similar pressures.

Speech is the way in which these characters attempt to declare their autonomy; throughout the work, characters engage in lengthy monologues or equally lengthy letters, which Sand reproduces in full. Ralph, inarticulate at the beginning of *Indiana*, is by the end able to utter the prolonged statement which preludes his and Indiana's suicide attempt; Indiana, silent and dreamy, pens lengthy missives to Raymon and finally silences him with her eloquence. It is their final breaking through to articulation which allows them to remain unsilenced by the attempted suicide and to emerge in the final chapter as beings who speak directly with the narrator for the first time. Those movements toward eloquence reflect a similar movement in the author; Sand repeatedly emphasized that *Indiana*'s writing was a process of inspired rush, of finding and claiming her authorial voice. Certainly, the publication of *Indiana* moved Sand from anonymity to literary celebrity.

It is not only the characters of Ralph and Indiana who speak. Delmare employs the diction of a soldier from the onset, but he accompanies it with actions designed to silence those around him, such as shooting Raymon or killing Indiana's dog. Raymon himself is a creature, it seems, purely of words. His words allow him to win Indiana, while his letters rekindle their love every time that she tries to repudiate him; in fact, his letter leads Indiana to the final desperate act of fleeing Bourbon and coming to him. Both these characters employ a speech recognized and validated by society—the language of warfare, politics, or seduction by men. Sand stresses that both characters, whom the reader comes to see as despicable, are working within society's rules and are defined by society as good and valued individuals, despite any feelings that the reader might possess to the contrary.

The ending is ambiguous. Although Indiana and Ralph have survived, they live in a state of exile, which seems to indicate that an ideal relationship between a woman and a man can exist only outside society, and their relationship can also be read as an incestuous one. This ambiguity is troublesome when one reads the work as the story of the individual's development. Indiana does learn to look beyond the narratives presented to her by society, such as the idea that she, like Sleeping Beauty, will be awakened and brought to psychological fruition by a Prince Charming such as Raymon. Yet the story that becomes her life is one of isolation and a hermit's existence, which admittedly seems preferable to the claustrophobic scene that opens the novel.

At the same time, the ending returns the reader to the beginning of the story when the narrator's relationship to the story is explained: He is simply retelling the story told to him by Ralph at the end of the book, which implies that the individual's struggle for autonomy will never achieve resolution.

Context

Indiana, one of Sand's earliest novels, is a strongly feminist work which analyses the restrictions that a patriarchal society places on women, and it explores the individual's options in trying either to obey or to circumvent those restrictions. The device of using a narrator marked as male who is strongly sympathetic to a female character demonstrates the move toward androgyny that permeates Sand's work. *Indiana* was originally assumed by critics to have been written by a man with the assistance or input of a woman; when it became known that the author was female, she was hailed as an extraordinary being. The book was affirmed one of the most important works of the year; Honoré de Balzac called it "delightfully conceived" and asserted that its success was inevitable.

The book is, to some extent, autobiographical, but the reader who focuses only on this aspect will lose much in doing so. The text represents an attempt to reclaim the novel—a form becoming at that time increasingly respectable and hence increasingly masculine—for women. The protagonist is presented as a being as sensitive and introspective as any male character of the time. Indiana's impassioned speeches condemning the system of power that has brought her to an oppressive marriage were cited as examples of Sand's interest in women's rights, and certainly an assertion of those rights was a major theme throughout her writings. Sand points out repeatedly that Delmare, who abuses his wife and condemns her to stultification and isolation, is considered by society a "good" man and that, in fact, he is only obeying society's rules. Simultaneously, the characters of Noun and Indiana allow Sand to show that the two roles traditionally assigned women, either the chaste upper-class angel or the sexually active lower-class servant, are equally fraught with difficulty and frustration.

Women's studies scholars have revived interest in George Sand: Her work was largely ignored at the beginning of the twentieth century, and it was not until feminist scholars began to explore women's writing that interest in her substantial body of work revived. Scholars finally began to move away from the distorted caricature of Sand as a cross-dressing libertine with literary ambitions.

Sources for Further Study

Cate, Curtis. *George Sand: A Biography*. Boston: Houghton Mifflin, 1975. This biography of Sand may help readers understand parallels between the subject matter of *Indiana* and her own life. Also provides an account of how *Indiana* was received.

Crecelius, Kathryn J. *Family Romances: George Sand's Early Novels*. Bloomington: Indiana University Press, 1987. An interesting and invaluable work, this text limits itself to Sand's works published between 1827 and 1837. Looks at the ways in which her early novels employ and alter conventional forms, and spends considerable attention examining how Sand describes women's psychological development in terms of a female Oedipal structure.

Datlof, Natalie, Jeanne Fuchs, and David A. Powell, eds. *The World of George Sand*. New York: Greenwood Press, 1991. Contains papers presented at the Seventh International George Sand Conference at Hofstra University in 1986. The topics range widely; a number of articles will prove useful to *Indiana* scholars, such as Marilyn Yalom's "George Sand's Poetics of Autobiography" and Margaret E. Ward and Karen Storz's "Fanny Lewald and George Sand: *Eine Lebensfrage* and *Indiana*."

Moers, Ellen. *Literary Women*. London: Women's Press, 1978. This overview of women's literature devotes considerable space to George Sand, exploring motivations for and themes in her works.

Naginski, Isabelle Hoog. *George Sand: Writing for Her Life*. New Brunswick, N.J.:

Rutgers University Press, 1991. This book avoids the biographical approach common to Sand criticism. Identifies four specific periods of Sand's writing and examines each, focusing on common themes rather than on a detailed analysis of each work.

Powell, David A., ed. *George Sand Today: Proceedings of the Eighth International George Sand Conference—Tours 1989.* Lanham, Md.: University Press of America, 1992. Contains essays in French and English. Of particular interest are Tamara Alvarez-Detrell's "A Room of Her Own: The Role of the *lieux* from Aurore to *Indiana*" and "The Politics of George Sand's Pastoral Novels," by Marylou Gramm.

Thomson, Patricia. *George Sand and the Victorians: Her Influence and Reputation in Nineteenth-Century England.* New York: Columbia University Press, 1977. While not focusing on *Indiana*, this work provides an excellent overview of the reception given Sand's work in England and underscores many of the gender-related issues raised by reviewers and critics.

Catherine Francis

INTERCOURSE

Author: Andrea Dworkin (1946-   )
Type of work: Social criticism
First published: 1987

Form and Content

In *Intercourse*, Andrea Dworkin attributes women's societal subordination to their becoming a colonized people through the act which intimately connects them to their oppressor—sexual intercourse. She asks if since women have no physical privacy—that is, they must be entered for intercourse—can they truly be free? Her answer is no.

In the first section, "Intercourse in a Man-made World," Dworkin discusses the portrayal of intercourse and sexuality in works of five male authors: Leo Tolstoy, explaining how his writings reflect repulsion at being sexual; Kōbō Abe, whose images of intercourse invoke the sense of going beneath the skin, sometimes through its removal; Tennessee Williams, who connects sexual expression in females with a negative stigma; James Baldwin, who illustrates the pain which must be experienced for two people to commune with each other sexually; and Isaac Bashevis Singer, who provides an example which Dworkin uses to suggest that, for women, intercourse is destructive and requires being possessed. Attitudes and behaviors depicted in the fiction are treated as reflecting real-world attitudes toward the sexuality of women.

In part 2 of the text, Dworkin examines "The Female Condition" first through changing views of virginity, as evidenced in the lives of Joan of Arc and the fictional characters of Madame Bovary and Dracula's female victims, and then through woman's agreement or collaboration in being "occupied" by man.

In part 3, "Power, Status, and Hate," Dworkin examines religious and secular laws that limit men's behavior in intercourse and encourage men to experience erotic feeling through violating laws. Here she looks at images which connect woman with filth and death (using comments by psychoanalyst Sigmund Freud), as well as at sexual violence perpetuated against women in Nazi concentration camps and other settings.

Dworkin carefully scrutinizes what men say, think, and do regarding female sexuality and speaks the truth as she sees it; namely, that the social subordination of women is perpetuated through the sexual domination of women, and that the difference between men's behavior toward women in the matrimonial bed from that evidenced in sadistic torture is one of degree, not of kind.

Prior to the publication of *Intercourse*, Dworkin had written extensively on the topic of woman-hating and violence against women. Her book *Pornography: Men Possessing Women* (1981) is a starting point for most feminist discussions of the subject, whether individuals agree with her conclusions. With Catherine MacKinnon, Dworkin authored a description of pornography as violating the civil rights of women in 1983, later published as *Pornography and Civil Rights: A New Day for Women's Equality* (1988). *Intercourse* represents an attempt by Dworkin to broaden the discussion, which has focused on violent pornography, to include popular works deemed acceptable and even celebrated literature. It is interesting that *Intercourse* was published the same year as Dworkin's first novel, *Ice and Fire* (1987), a work in which sex within marriage is the most violent form that the female protagonist experiences. Her novel, like *Intercourse*, was greeted by a few supportive and many strongly negative reviews.

Dworkin's tone has been referred to as elegant, passionate, profound, shocking, and even comic at times; others describe it as crass, self-absorbed haranguing and as rhetoric stuck in the 1960's. *Intercourse*, which includes a thirty-five-page bibliography, twelve pages of notes, and a ten-page index, draws the reader into exploring the real-life sex lives and attitudes of men and their portrayal and treatment of women and women's sexual behavior.

Analysis

Dworkin opens the discussion with "Intercourse in a Man-made World," examining men's repulsion at sex with women. Using Leo Tolstoy's short novel *Kreutserova sonata* (1890; *The Kreutzer Sonata*, 1891), she contrasts the male protagonist's killing of his wife with Tolstoy's behavior. The man in the novel kills his wife not only by stabbing her but also by having intercourse with her, resulting in many pregnancies which drain her youth and energy. Tolstoy uses his wife for sexual release for which he in turn "blames and hates" her; she gives birth to thirteen children. Dworkin uses Tolstoy to argue that celibacy would help establish equality between the sexes.

In "Skinless," Dworkin examines novels by Kōbō Abe, including *Suna no onne* (1962; *The Woman in the Dunes*, 1964) and *Tanin no kao* (1964; *The Face of Another*, 1966). The metaphor for sexual intercourse that Dworkin draws from these works is the need for people to touch, not merely skin to skin but with that below the skin as well. She describes the difficulties that Abe's male characters have in achieving this touch without violence.

In Tennessee Williams' plays, Dworkin explores the stigma for women attached to intercourse and sexual desire. In *The Rose Tattoo* (1951), a wife is mystically marked by her husband's tattoo when she becomes pregnant. Stanley Kowalski's animalistic rape of Blanche in *A Streetcar Named Desire* (1947) drives her insane and destroys her relationship with her sister Stella, Stanley's wife. In *Summer and Smoke* (1947), Alma loses her aspirations for the ethereal communion of souls and ends her life addicted to pills and meaningless sex with strangers.

In "Communion," Dworkin uses James Baldwin to support the need to examine whether sex is good. Baldwin's male characters in *Giovanni's Room* (1956) and other works want to experience "not doing it, but being the beloved." In attempting to attain this state, they cause their sexual partners and themselves great pain; by the time that they are ready, they have destroyed those whom they desire.

Through *Sotan in Goray* (1935; *Satan in Goray*, 1955), by Isaac Bashevis Singer, Dworkin illustrates that sex to a woman means being taken over (possessed), and to a man means conquering (possessing). The female protagonist is possessed: by her father; by an uncle who wants to marry her; by a husband who possesses many wives, shaming each because of his impotency; by a lover who forces her husband to divorce her and then marries her himself; and lastly by the devil. As a result of the last possession, she dies. All these possessions are sanctioned by rules of the community that protect male power.

Throughout part 1, Dworkin draws primarily from fictional representations of sexuality. Some object that while writers of fiction mine the societal psyche for material, it is fiction, not reality. Others support Dworkin's mixing of the real and unreal, citing a tradition from Plato to Jean-Jacques Rousseau "that condemns representation as dangerous and corruptive."

In part 2, "The Female Condition," Dworkin explores virginity, with Joan of Arc exemplifying the power that a woman can obtain if she is celibate and if she rejects female trappings. Flouting tradition, however, causes Joan's downfall; she burns because she defies the male power. Returning to fiction, Madame Bovary, the title character in Gustave Flaubert's 1857 novel, is a woman who has an extramarital affair in which she begins to enjoy sex. The affair and her enjoyment violate social restrictions on women's sexuality, and Madame Bovary is ruined. In Bram Stoker's *Dracula* (1897), virgins Lucy and Mina, unlike heaven-protected Joan of Arc, draw evil to them. They couple passionately with Dracula with the "place of sex moved to the throat." To regain purity, Lucy is mutilated by men who wanted to marry her, and Mina's demon lover is killed. Dworkin sees in *Dracula* inspiration for pornographic "snuff" films in which women are taped being tortured and murdered.

"Occupation/Collaboration" has been cited to suggest Dworkin believes that women's subordination is "natural." Man must enter woman if the human race is to continue; hence, woman, according to Dworkin, is doomed to "have a lesser privacy, a lesser integrity of the body." Furthermore, a woman initiates her own degradation by allowing her own colonization and experiencing pleasure in her own inferiority. Dworkin argues that individual men and women cannot escape negative societal expectations of women's subordination and men's domination and that intercourse can never be an equal, loving event. Some cite Dworkin's experiences with men, some extremely abusive, as reason for her analysis. Others attribute it to her being a radical feminist lesbian. Still others claim that Dworkin receives negative reviews because she dares to ask forbidden questions about the nature of intercourse.

In part 3, "Power, Status, and Hate," Dworkin explores how law, both religious and secular, has defined acceptable sexuality. Here it becomes clear that Dworkin believes women's inferiority is a social construct, as she says that "Laws create and maintain male dominance." These same laws also create excitement for men in violating women sexually.

In "Dirt/Death," Dworkin ventures into attitudes toward and treatment of women by professors of gynecology, in concentration camps and prisons, and in comments by philosopher Friedrich Nietzsche and Freud. Sex is dirty because it is with women whose bodies produce slime and filth; female circumcision cleans women who "carry death between (their) legs."

Context

In *Intercourse*, Andrea Dworkin has added a new dimension to the pornography debate, showing how much mainstream literature (in addition to so-called actual pornographic literature) includes themes expressing men's perception that women's sexuality exists to be controlled and punished, often violently.

Dworkin believes as Baldwin does that, "It is really quite impossible to be affirmative about anything which one refuses to question." Hence, addressing sex-role conditioning, Dworkin has posed a previously unasked question; namely, whether sex is an inherently intrusive act perpetuated on women by men and whether as such it stands in the way of truly equal and loving relationships between women and men.

Some reviewers have referred to Dworkin's language as filthy, not reprintable, and mimicking the very pornographic speech that she would see eliminated. Others have reacted to it as powerful and lyrical. Response to *Intercourse* has been overwhelmingly negative, in part because of Dworkin's language usage and tone and in part because of her ideas, which have not been popular among women and which have made some men too angry to consider the work rationally. After such a negative reception, it is interesting to note that references to *Intercourse* are almost nonexistent in many late 1980's and early 1990's publications that cite other works by Dworkin, such as *Pornography: Men Possessing Women*, *Right-Wing Women* (1983), and *Letters from a War Zone* (1988). References to *Intercourse* do appear in discussions on changing views of masculinity, much of it written by men. While references to *Intercourse* may not occur directly in feminist conversations on female subordination, male domination, popular literature, sex-role conditioning, and pornography, the questions that Dworkin has asked will remain an undercurrent in these discussions.

Sources for Further Study

Assiter, Alison. *Pornography, Feminism, and the Individual*. London: Pluto Press, 1989. Assiter dedicates two chapters to examining works by Dworkin, *Pornography: Men Possessing Women* and *Intercourse*. She argues that Dworkin's rhetoric is impressive but that her theories are flawed, mainly because they rely on individual action for change and deny the need for collective responsibility.

Booker, M. Keith. *Literature and Domination: Sex, Knowledge, and Power in Modern Fiction*. Gainesville: University Press of Florida, 1993. This text is for those well versed in literary criticism. Issues of domination are examined in works including Vladimir Nabokov's *Lolita* (1955). Types of domination range from female-male relations to class relations.

Brittan, Arthur. *Masculinity and Power*. New York: Basil Blackwell, 1989. Although making no reference to *Intercourse*, Brittan does mention two of Dworkin's earlier works. This feminist author explores connections between masculinity and social and political power, what men could do about imbalances, and why they do so little.

Ferguson, Ann. *Blood at the Root: Motherhood, Sexuality, and Male Dominance*. London: Pandora, 1989. In this text, the author's theory "weaves together . . . key insights of radical feminism, Marxism and Freudianism while avoiding some . . .

problems." Ferguson devotes six pages to an analysis of the Dworkin/MacKinnon antipornography ordinance, passed in Minneapolis and later ruled unconstitutional by the U.S. Supreme Court.

Rosen, David. *The Changing Fictions of Masculinity.* Urbana: University of Illinois Press, 1993. Like Dworkin, Rosen examines literature for what it can "tell about men." Using an "Anglo-American feminist perspective," he explores works from English literature, including *Beowulf,* William Shakespeare's *Hamlet, Prince of Denmark* (1600-1601), John Milton's *Paradise Lost* (1667, 1674), and Charles Dickens' *Hard Times* (1854), garnering stereotypes about masculinity in general rather than in female-male relationships.

Russell, Diana E. H., ed. *Making Violence Sexy: Feminist Views on Pornography.* New York: Teachers College Press, 1993. In this collection, many articles refer to Dworkin's work on pornography. Some reactions are negative; most, however, are extremely positive. Although *Intercourse* is never referred to, here is a mostly appreciative audience for Dworkin's ideas about pornography. Contains an extensive bibliography of feminist works.

Segal, Lynne. *Slow Motion: Changing Masculinities, Changing Men.* New Brunswick, N.J.: Rutgers University Press, 1990. The author explores "masculinities" in the hope that understanding differences between men will assist in the "struggle for change" in male behavior toward women and one another with reference to women's liberation and gay liberation. Segal refers to Dworkin and other radical feminists and finds their work lacking because of its emphasis on sexual power and the penis as the basis of male dominance.

Su A. Cutler

INTERVIEW WITH HISTORY

Author: Oriana Fallaci (1930-   )
Type of work: Current affairs
First published: Intervista con la storia, 1974 (English translation, 1976)

Form and Content

A regular contributor to the Italian news magazine *L'Europeo* and a successful free-lance journalist, novelist, and essayist, Oriana Fallaci became famous primarily as one of the most original and controversial interviewers of her time. The essence of her style is captured in *Interview with History* (translated into English by John Shepley and published in the United States in 1976), her best-known work of journalism. It might be more accurate, however, to call the genre in which she works "contemporary history," a term she herself uses in her introduction.

The fourteen interviews in this anthology first appeared in *L'Europeo* between 1969 and 1974, although most are concentrated around 1972-1973. The dominant news stories from that era are reflected in the interviews themselves: the Vietnam War, the Middle East crisis, the war between India and Pakistan, the military takeover in Greece. The first three interviews rise out of the Vietnam War: Henry Kissinger, shortly before Richard M. Nixon named him secretary of state and put him in charge of peace negotiations, South Vietnamese president Nguyen Van Thieu, and North Vietnamese general Vo Nguyen Giap. These interviews set the pattern that Fallaci followed, with some variation, in each of the others: The subject is often a man or woman who is involved in a violent political conflict and works for or against the forces of oppression. Frequently, the interviewee is a public figure from whom it is extremely difficult to obtain an interview, as with each of the first three subjects, and who subsequently tries to disavow his or her careless declarations. Fallaci recounts the story of each interview and its aftermath in brief introductory essays.

The protagonists of the Vietnam War fare badly under Fallaci's questioning—as is often, but not always, the case. Kissinger's comparison of himself to a "cowboy who rides alone into the town, the village, with his horse and nothing else" became one of his most famous quotes, a point of ridicule, and almost caused irreparable damage to his relationship with Nixon. Thieu comes across as a puppet dictator, too weak to design a policy that does not come straight from Washington, D.C. Giap is a Napoleonic figure, a brilliant, ruthless military strategist whose ego is in direct inverse proportion to his tiny stature. The interviews with Palestine Liberation Organization (PLO) leader Yasir Arafat, President Ali Bhutto of Pakistan, and Mohammad Reza Pahlavi, Shah of Iran, clearly show the hostility, at times bordering on revulsion, that Fallaci often has for her subjects.

In the light of Fallaci's often confrontational attitude, she herself expresses surprise that so many major figures agree to grant her an interview. Also surprising was the effect some of the interviews had upon publication. The temporary falling out between Kissinger and Nixon is one example. A second example is the near-derailment of peace negotiations between India and Pakistan because of the unflattering things that Indira Gandhi said about Ali Bhutto and the even more insulting things he said about her. Similar immediate effects of the unexpected candor of Fallaci's subjects have occurred throughout her career as an interviewer. The unguarded honesty of her subjects, who are usually seasoned politicians, has often been held up as evidence of the validity of her controversial methods. Such incidents reverse the traditional role of the journalist, who instead of being a witness to history in the making, actually influences history.

Fallaci's unusual ability to relate to her subjects as human beings rather than merely as players on the geopolitical scene reaches its apogee in the final interview, of the Greek revolutionary Alexandros Panagoulis. He had just been released from prison, where he was held for his role in a failed assassination attempt against the dictator George Papadopoulos in 1967. Panagoulis was clearly the incarnation of Fallaci's ideal of the revolutionary poet, but their relationship rested on much more than his ability to conform to an idealized image. The entire interview expresses Fallaci's profound empathy, admiration, and finally love for her subject. They left Greece together after the interview and lived a passionate and turbulent life until Panagoulis was killed three years later. Fallaci chronicles this period in *Un Uomo* (1979; *A Man*, 1980), another of her most famous works, which functions as a kind of sequel to *Interview with History*.

Analysis

Fallaci makes her interviewing approach clear from the outset: She is not in the least interested in conventional journalistic principles of objectivity or detachment. In order to get at the truth, she considers it essential to challenge people on the intellectual and emotional levels and to exhibit, rather than hide, her own feelings, opinions, and emotions. Her ability to break down barriers between interviewer and subject makes her entire enterprise more closely related to psychoanalysis than to traditional journalism or historiography.

Several overriding concerns unite all the interviews in the collection. First of all, Fallaci exhibits, and proudly claims, a violent hostility toward power. She is both fascinated and repelled by the process that turns ordinary human beings, with their share of qualities and faults, into politicians, tyrants, and victims. Because she sees power as "an inhuman and hateful phenomenon," her sympathies lie primarily with revolutionaries and outcasts. Heads of state, even if they are wise and well intentioned (as is the case with Israeli prime minister Golda Meir in her interview, for example) cannot escape the corrupting influence of their position. Among Fallaci's other concerns are whether "great" men and women, as opposed to the masses, are the real architects of history and her claim that journalism is a potentially more direct means of arriving at the truth than history.

These interviews and their accompanying essays can convey tremendous warmth and admiration as easily as they do hostility. At first glance, it would seem that the people whose political viewpoint Fallaci opposes the least are those who come off the best, such as Pietro Nenni, the aging patriarch of the Italian Socialist Party, or Archbishop Makarios III, the president of Cyprus who was exiled after a coup d'état orchestrated by the Greek military regime in 1974. Yet Fallaci's affection for these individuals is not simply a matter of ideological compatibility. She responds viscerally, almost instinctively, to the human individual behind the public persona. While it is only natural that, as an avowed and even militant socialist, she should find authoritarian dictators more or less contemptible, her approach also leads her to criticize those with whom she clearly feels a deep personal and political bond; such is the case in her ambivalent interview with Indian prime minister Indira Gandhi. Fallaci mentions in the introduction to this piece how she publicly condemned Gandhi and renounced her personal affection for her when she suspended the Indian Constitution in 1975 rather than resign in the face of political opposition. Yet in the interview, which goes on at length about the war against Pakistan that India had just won, Fallaci had already managed to portray Gandhi as a pragmatic leader driven by a thirst for power, and not a genuine socialist, in spite of the intimate rapport that the two women were able to construct.

Context

Fallaci has always proudly worn the mantle of militant feminism. In *Interview with History*, this is shown in a number of ways. She presses her female subjects (Meir and Gandhi) to speak as women, as wives and mothers, in order to break through the façade of the head of state. By making Meir talk about how being a woman has made her try harder for what she achieved or about the condescending remarks made to her by political mentors such as David Ben-Gurion, Fallaci brings feminist issues to the forefront. In a similar fashion, she suggests that Gandhi's admiration for Joan of Arc is a sign of her determination to succeed in a male-dominated world in spite of being a woman.

In both interviews, Fallaci clearly attempts to bring to light an issue that has dominated much twentieth century feminism: whether the goal of feminism is simply to put women on an equal social and political footing with men so that they can compete effectively, though in a world whose rules were written by and for men, or whether there is a specifically female alternative to the male worldview. Both Meir and Gandhi seem to come across as holding very conservative viewpoints on this issue. They both emphasize that there is no fundamental difference between men and women and that their effectiveness as heads of state is neither diminished nor enhanced by their gender. Gandhi states most emphatically at one point that she is not a feminist. Although Fallaci never explicitly states her own opinion on that particular topic in her questions or introductions, she implicitly suggests that the two women are prisoners of their decision to fulfill political responsibilities in a male-dominated world. Simply by identifying themselves with power, the two women have bought into the system in which male tyranny is the ruling principle.

Again, it must be emphasized that Fallaci does not present such a feminist perspective outright. At no point does she say, for example, that conventional political power and its inevitable corollary, political oppression, are specifically male phenomena. She clearly suggests that resistance to oppression, however, is an activity with which women, as a group, are very familiar. The male subjects of her interviews who are on the side of the oppressed, such as Makarios and Panagoulis, are credited with being more feminine than the more authoritarian leaders whom she interviews, or at least not as completely under the sway of masculine clichés.

The achievement for which Fallaci has received the greatest amount of recognition is having revolutionized the style and function of the interviewer within the journalistic profession. She often uses gender as a means of escaping from what she might term the pseudo-objectivity of traditional interviewing style. For example, she establishes a complicity with her female subjects based on their common experience as women. With male subjects, she will force them to respond to her as a woman, not only as a journalist. Such prominence given to gender in a sphere in which it had never played such an overt role has earned Fallaci the distinction of being perhaps the first feminist interviewer in the history of the genre.

There is much more to Fallaci's influence on feminism than her journalistic work on "contemporary history." Among her published books, perhaps the two most relevant to the topic are *Il Sesso inutile* (1961; *The Useless Sex*, 1964), a survey of women's conditions in different parts of the world, and her novel *Lettera a un bambino mai nato* (1975; *Letter to a Child Never Born*, 1976), in which she argues in favor of a woman's right to have an abortion. Many readers have discovered that throughout her entire work, however, Fallaci presents women as having a privileged understanding of the dynamics of oppression and also as having the means to devise effective ways of resisting them.

Sources for Further Study

Arico, Santo L. "Breaking the Ice: An In-depth Look at Oriana Fallaci's Interview Techniques." *Journalism Quarterly* 63 (August, 1986): 587-593. Most of the response, favorable or unfavorable, of the journalistic profession to Fallaci's techniques has appeared in the popular press. Arico's article is one of the few to present a more studied and careful critique of Fallaci from the perspective of a professional colleague.

Burke, Jeffrey. "Fallaci Records." *Harper's* 261 (November, 1980): 98-99. Primarily a review of the novel *A Man*, this article contains many references to *Interview with History* and provides some useful insights into Fallaci's career up to that point.

Cott, Jonathan. *Forever Young*. New York: Random House, 1978. Among Cott's interviews compiled in this anthology is one with Fallaci which first appeared in the June, 1976, issue of *Rolling Stone* magazine. Of all the interviews given by Fallaci, this is perhaps the most famous. In addition to turning the tables on Fallaci by having her answer questions instead of asking them, this interview is important in that it provided her with a forum to explain and justify some of the techniques for which she became famous.

Griffith, Thomas. "Interviews, Soft or Savage." *Time* 117 (March 30, 1981): 47.

——————— . "Trial by Interview." *Time* 115 (January 21, 1980): 71. In these two very brief articles, Griffith comments on Fallaci's celebrity as an interviewer and the controversy that surrounds her. He gives a balanced account of the ethical and professional issues involved and expresses a degree of respect and admiration for Fallaci's success, both in obtaining interviews from inaccessible people and in expressing her personal style. In "Trial by Interview" he also mentions several other journalists who have contributed to revolutionizing the genre of the interview.

M. Martin Guiney

THE ITALIAN
Or, The Confessional of the Black Penitents

Author: Mrs. Ann Radcliffe (1764-1823)
Type of work: Novel
Type of plot: Romance
Time of plot: 1758
Locale: Italy
First published: 1797

Principal characters:
>ELLENA DI ROSALBA, a seamstress orphaned very young and
>   reared by her aunt
>SIGNORA BIANCHI, Ellena's aunt and guardian
>VINCENTIO DI VIVALDI, the eldest son of aristocratic parents, who
>   is in love with Ellena
>MARCHESA DI VIVALDI, Vincentio's mother, who conspires with
>   Father Schedoni to separate the young couple
>MARCHESE DI VIVALDI, Vincentio's father, a Neapolitan nobleman
>SCHEDONI, the Marchesa's confessor, who intends to kill Ellena
>   in order to receive the high church office promised by the
>   Marchesa
>SPALATRO, Schedoni's hired assassin

Form and Content

The Italian: Or, The Confessional of the Black Penitents places the story of two young lovers, Vincentio di Vivaldi and Ellena di Rosalba, in a gothic setting. Ellena is a seamstress, and Vivaldi is the eldest son of an old and noble family. The Marchese and Marchesa di Vivaldi oppose the union so vehemently that Ellena's life is endangered and Vivaldi is held captive and subjected to torture by the Inquisition. Vivaldi is warned early on by the mysterious archway monk to stay away from the Villa Altieri where Ellena lives. Most likely Schedoni's agent, the mysterious, cowled figure reappears to repeat his warnings.

Vivaldi asks Signora Bianchi for Ellena's hand, and the signora accepts with the reservations that their different class positions will cause problems. Soon after, she dies mysteriously. The Vivaldis soon begin trying to persuade their son to abandon Ellena. When he refuses, the Marchesa enlists the aid of her confessor, Father Schedoni, a mysterious monk of whom little is known except that he is of the brotherhood at Santo Spirito.

Vivaldi assumes that Schedoni has caused the death of Ellena's aunt. When he confronts him about it, he enrages Schedoni and incurs his vengeance. Schedoni is instrumental in causing the many problems for the young couple. Abductions abound in *The Italian*, the first of which occurs when Ellena is getting ready to go into temporary seclusion with the nuns at Santa Maria della Pieta. She is driven instead to a horrid convent presided over by a wicked abbess who is obviously in the Marchesa's employ. The abbess confronts Ellena with a choice: either take vows and become a nun or marry whomever the Marchesa chooses for her. She refuses both choices. As a result, she is kept in close confinement in a threatening atmosphere and shown tenderness only by Sister Olivia.

As the narrative pans back and forth between Ellena and Vivaldi, Vivaldi and his servant Paolo also become imprisoned when Paolo shoots at the archway monk. They then follow the blood-dripping form and find themselves locked in a room with a pile of bloody clothes and the recurrent sound of moaning. It is here that Paolo tells Vivaldi the story of a particular confession heard by a penitentiary (an officer of the Catholic church appointed to act in behalf of a bishop) named Ansaldo di Rovalli. When Ansaldo heard the confession, it caused him to go into convulsions.

Sister Olivia plays an inexplicably important part in Ellena's life, advising her to follow the directions of the abbess to take the veil and promising to risk her own safety by helping Ellena escape when she hears that the abbess intends to confine Ellena in a room which certainly would mean her death. Sister Olivia's kindness, her resemblance to Ellena, and her willingness to exceed the expectations of a nun in her position indicate a blood tie.

Finally about to be married in a chapel at Celano, Ellena and Vivaldi are abducted, this time by representatives of the Inquisition. They are separated again, and Ellena is taken to the house of Spalatro by the Adriatic shore, where Schedoni's hired assassin keeps close watch over her. By this time, the Marchesa and Schedoni have concurred that Ellena must be killed.

The turning point of the story occurs when Spalatro refuses to kill Ellena, his remorse getting the better of him. Schedoni vows to do it himself, but just as he has his dagger raised, he shudders at his own horrific nature and sees on Ellena a miniature portrait of himself as a young man. He undergoes a character change, thinking Ellena to be his daughter. He tries to get Vivaldi released from the Inquisition, but to no avail, for Schedoni has plotted himself into his own disgrace and disclosure: A mysterious adviser visits the imprisoned Vivaldi, telling him to disclose Schedoni as a fraud. He is not a monk at all, but rather Count Fernando di Bruno. Vivaldi is told to ask Ansaldo di Rovalli about the confession that he heard in 1752.

Vivaldi follows these instructions, which reveal that Schedoni was a count, the younger son of a noble family, and that he had his brother killed in order to obtain his position, property, and wife. He abducted the woman and raped her, and she married him out of propriety. When, though, he found her speaking with a visitor in their home, he (apparently) killed her in a jealous rage. The visitor turns out to have been the grand penitentiary himself, Ansaldo di Rovalli, and the woman was Sister Olivia, the former Countess di Bruni, and Ellena's mother. Olivia, who survived the attack on her, affirms Ellena to be Schedoni's niece, and not his daughter. In order to escape the indignities that will clearly be his fate at the hands of the Inquisition, Schedoni poisons himself.

Analysis

Acclaimed as the best-crafted novel by the most highly acclaimed romance novelist of her day, *The Italian* is a tale of revenge, remorse, and reversals in addition to being a gothicized sentimental story of true love. Schedoni, the villainous monk, is the most imposing character in all Ann Radcliffe's work and the only one continuously praised as a masterwork in the art of characterization in the gothic genre. It has been said that he is the prototype of the Byronic hero. In a sense, *The Italian* is Schedoni's story because he is the character drawn with the greatest psychological complexity: He is the one who moves the action of the story and who undergoes significant change. In fact, he experiences a kind of illumination—or at least thinks he does when he sees the picture of himself in Ellena's necklace and knows it to be himself in his former days, before he was guilty of rape and fratricide. Radcliffe's development of the character of Schedoni makes *The Italian* unique among her works as well as among other horror gothics; here, the characterization creates the gothicism to a greater extent than does even the stock gothic paraphernalia.

Nothing supernatural happens in *The Italian*, so nothing needs to be explained away. Gothic effects derive from the specter of murder looming over the narrative and the instruments of murder, such as the gleaming dagger of Schedoni and the rack of the Inquisition, and from the motif of mysterious Catholicism, specifically, the Inquisition as a force as unreasonable to deal with as the supernatural. The Inquisition, in essence, becomes Schedoni's antagonist, a force against which he cannot fight. Because he has contrived to have Vivaldi arrested by the Inquisition, he has woven a web for himself which even he cannot undo. It is ironic that he has earlier had Ellena arrested for pretending to be a nun, because he will have to face the Inquisition on charges of what amounts to impersonating a monk.

Radcliffe's moral and aesthetic goal in writing *The Italian* was most likely to write a corrective to the base vulgarity of Matthew Gregory Lewis' *The Monk* (1796), a novel which represents the pinnacle of depraved eighteenth century horror fiction, containing debased and debauched sexuality, matricide, and Satanism. Although it may seem that Ellena's constant flight from the threat of murder constitutes a criminal, twisted, gothic situation, it seems normal when compared to the world of Lewis' monk Ambrosio, who rapes his sister on a pile of rotting corpses.

The romance of the lovers was pleasantly familiar to the eighteenth century audience. Vivaldi is the hero of significant sensibilities who adores and weeps, although he is capable of outbursts of aggressive emotion. Ellena, like Emily in Radcliffe's *The Mysteries of Udolpho* (1794), is significantly affected by the sublime forms of nature, which lead her to a contemplation of the goodness of the Deity. She weeps and faints, but she always recovers and rises to the task before her, which is usually that of escaping from the imminent threat of death.

Scenery plays its part in showing the relative moral worth of the characters: Ellena can almost always be inspired, or at least be affected by, images in nature—Schedoni, never. Also, the whole of the novel is covered over with half-light, daylight serving only as its contrast. As in all Radcliffe's work, the picturesque plays a significant role, with the poetry of Thomas Gray and James Thomson and the paintings of Salvator Rosa, Claude Lorrain, and Nicolas Poussin providing the inspiration for the imagery that becomes the backdrop against which the story unfolds.

The world of *The Italian* is one in which the innocent young lovers are confined, controlled, and threatened with murder by parental and religious forces, which are actually forces of evil motivated by avarice and pride. The goal of this sentimental heroine and hero is to escape the subterranean gothic world, which is as loaded with terrifying surprises as an abandoned mine field, and to emerge into the light of day with its promise for the future. Schedoni poisons himself, the Marchese condones the marriage, and at the wedding celebration, Vivaldi's faithful servant Paolo exclaims, "*O! giorno felíce!*" (Oh, happy day!).

Context

Like Emily St. Aubert in Radcliffe's *The Mysteries of Udolpho*, Ellena di Rosalba is a self-conscious heroine who has the capacity to imagine herself among the ruins of a tower. She is similar to Emily in other ways as well. Of highly refined sensibilities, she can feel empathy for even Spalatro, having, she says, suffered so much herself. Like Emily, she is a victim who fights against her oppression, and even within the constraints of the gothic world of evil, she manages to win. Insofar as Radcliffe's heroines gain some power of action, Radcliffe has considerably ameliorated the image of the heroine in the novel.

The character of Schedoni, though, is commonly seen as the great contribution to literature of Radcliffe in *The Italian*. The prototype for the romantic hero-villains to follow, Schedoni, it has been said, is the character upon whom George Gordon, Lord Byron, modeled himself, and upon whom he modeled the heroes in *The Giaour* (1813) and *Lara* (1814). In the wide spectrum of his feelings, Schedoni broadens the range of the gothic villain.

Most of the major romantics admired Radcliffe's works, and some wrote about them, including Sir Walter Scott and Samuel Taylor Coleridge. She was an acknowledged innovator in several respects, among which are her use of atmosphere and imagery as elements that give information about the moral, mental, and emotional states of the characters; her combining of the heroine and hero of the novel of sensibility with those of the horror novel; and her resulting creation of the "respectable" gothic romance. *The Italian* extends the possibilities of the gothic to include credible situations and developed characters, thus paving the way for the coalescence of the gothic and the realistic found later in the nineteenth century. Radcliffe's precursors are Tobias Smollett's *The Adventures of Ferdinand, Count Fathom* (1753), Horace Walpole's *The Castle of Otranto* (1764), Clara Reeve's *The Old English Baron: A Gothic Story* (1777), and Sophia Lee's *The Recess: Or, A Tale of Other Times* (1783-1785).

The Radcliffean gothic romance continued through the nineteenth and twentieth centuries in a variety of manifestations. Radcliffe's influence may be seen in the works of Mary Shelley and Edgar Allan Poe. The influence of her work continues to be seen in the "formula gothic," best-selling mass-market paperbacks which are currently being analyzed by feminist critics for their social implications regarding women's issues. The horror novel, which evolved out of the same period, became a separate type and survives also in paperback books and films.

Sources for Further Study

Ellis, Kate Ferguson. " 'Kidnapped Romance' in Ann Radcliffe." In *The Contested Castle: Gothic Novels and the Subversion of Domestic Ideology.* Urbana: University of Illinois Press, 1989. Discusses the gothic in terms of domestic relations. Ellis sees Schedoni as fulfilling his own wishes to be first in a family circle by insinuating himself into the Marchesa's confidence. See also herein Ellis' chapter "Otranto Feminized: Horace Walpole, Clara Reeve, and Sophia Lee."

Flaxman, Rhoda. "Radcliffe's Dual Modes of Vision." In *Fetter'd or Free?: British Women Novelists, 1670-1815*, edited by Mary Anne Schofield and Cecilia Macheski. Athens: Ohio University Press, 1986. Recognizes Radcliffe as developing a "new descriptive mode and technique," that mode and technique including something akin to cinematography.

Murray, E. B. *Ann Radcliffe.* New York: Twayne, 1972. An excellent overview of all Radcliffe's novels; contains long passages from obscure eighteenth century novels. Provides psychological and ethical perspectives on *The Italian.*

Ronald, Ann. "Terror-Gothic: Nightmare and Dream in Ann Radcliffe and Charlotte Brontë." In *The Female Gothic*, edited by Juliann E. Fleenor. Montreal: Eden Press, 1983. Discusses and compares these authors' works in terms such as the journey and the images in fairy tales.

Ruff, William. "Ann Radcliffe: Or, The Hand of Taste." In *The Age of Johnson: Essays Presented to Chauncey Brewster Tinker*, edited by F. W. Hilles. New Haven, Conn.: Yale University Press, 1949. Ruff discusses Radcliffe's real contribution to literature as "the novel of taste" in which everything becomes "ladylike."

Varma, Devendra P. *The Gothic Flame, Being a History of the Gothic Novel in England: Its Origins, Efflorescence, Disintegration, and Residuary Influences.* London: Arthur Barker, 1957. A standard work which examines the development of Radcliffe's techniques of terror and suspense, the explainable supernatural, and atmosphere. Also discusses her influences, specifically those from the Renaissance.

Donna G. Berliner

I'VE BEEN A WOMAN
New and Selected Poems

Author: Sonia Sanchez (1934-   )
Type of work: Poetry
First published: 1978

Form and Content

For Sonia Sanchez, politics and poetry have always been inextricably linked. She wrote one of her first poems about an aunt who spat in a bus driver's face when he ordered her to leave a bus that was filling up with white people and published her first book of poetry, *Homecoming*, in 1969 after becoming involved with the organization of a black studies curriculum at San Francisco State College in the mid-1960's. "One of the things which has propelled me all my life is when a principle is violated. America has violated many principles as far as black people are concerned," Sanchez states, and the selections from her earlier volumes that are gathered in *I've Been a Woman: New and Selected Poems* are a record of her attempts to "eradicate" these violations of human rights, civil liberties, and social justice.

In discussing the origins of her work, Sanchez recalls both the racial slights ("There were simple things, like going to a house where my grandmother worked, and we were in the kitchen and heard the way she was talked to") and the sexual contempt ("I watched white men pinch black women on their behinds") that she recognized as a child. When the surge of inspirational energy released by the doctrines of Black Pride and Black Power swept out of the 1960's, Sanchez found a direction, a style, and a voice for the feelings that she had been harboring since her youth. Because the dominant mode of expression for writers involved in the Black Arts movement was one of defiance mingled with rage, and because there was a sense of exhilaration and liberation produced by speaking without restraint, Sanchez's poetry in the selections from *Homecoming* are informed by the confidence engendered by a new realization of the self's possibilities. "Homecoming" asserts that the poet has "returned/ leaving behind me/ all those hide and/ seek faces," while "Poem at Thirty" is critical of the boundaries imposed by her father (and other men). There is a strong strain of criticism directed toward American society but a balancing, positive element in a recognition of individual strengths ("but i am what i/ am. woman. alone/ amid all this noise") and in the encouraging example of people such as Malcolm X, who Sanchez celebrates ("he was the sun that tagged/ the western sky") and mourns.

We a BaddDDD People (1970) moves directly into the heart of the political process. "Blk/Rhetoric" is written in the characteristic rhythms and with the pungent vernacular of street talk, with inventive spelling and punctuation designed to convey the new spirit of a community enjoying its own styles and forms of discourse. Yet Sanchez knows the cost of following any trend blindly, and poems such as "Summer Words of a Sistuh Addict" and "Indianapolis/Summer/1969/Poem" indicate her awareness of the sometimes destructive aspect of people swinging wildly between poles of excitement and despair. The selections from this volume are somewhat limited, and some of Sanchez's wit—as in "221/1424 (San/francisco/suicide/number)"—is not represented.

Perhaps to widen her perspective, the next selections are from *Love Poems* (1973), in which the focus is primarily on an individual consciousness exploring various aspects of love, from a love for family ("Father and Daughter"), for a mate ("Magic" and "Prelude to Nothing"), for oneself ("Why"), and for words (in several shorter lyrics and haikus) to a consideration of the mysteries and power of love itself. The section concludes with "Poem No. 8" which provides the title for the volume, its first line "i've been a woman" leading to an assertion of feminine desire and circumstance.

The poems chosen from *A Blues Book for Blue Black Magical Women* (1974) concentrate on the themes suggested in "Poem No. 8" from a personal perspective— " . . . this is how I got here." Sanchez observed that the book examines the experience of being female in a society that "does not prepare young black women, or women period, to be women." The book is divided into sections: "The Past," "The Present," "The Future," and "Rebirth." The collection concludes with a group of "Haikus/ Tankas & Other Love Syllables" which demonstrate Sanchez's control and discipline in working with specific, traditional forms and tight, compressed images. They are followed by several longer poems, including a sonnet of reconciliation, "Father and Daughter"; two tributes to Sterling Brown, the "griot of fire" who represents "part of a tradition of black writers"; and "Kwa mama zetu waliotuzaa," a eulogy for the widow of W. E. B. Du Bois and Sanchez's stepmother, the title meaning "for our mothers who gave us birth."

Analysis

Sonia Sanchez has always been direct and specific about her aims as a writer. Responding to both the immediate demands of her social and historic situation and the timeless requirements of her craft, her focus has been to combine the lyric power of an accomplished writer with the impassioned political consciousness of a self-aware African American woman. One of her most effective methods has been to transform traditional poetic devices into the language patterns of the black community. The poet and publisher Haki Madhubuti has observed that Sanchez "more than any other poet has been responsible for legitimizing the use of urban Black English in written form." To do this, Sanchez has restructured conventional English grammar, integrated "rapping with reading" by creating rhythmic structures from folk styles such as "the dozens," worked at reproducing some of the sonic qualities of jazz and some of its improvisational aspects in terms of a theme-and-variations mode akin to the call and response of the classical African American sermon, utilized the moods of the blues, and rejected the restrictions of narrow academic definitions of poetry.

Her success in establishing a singular voice that has its roots in the culture of the black community and its foundations in the world of multicultural classical literature depends on her familiarity with and mastery of form, so there is always a reason for a particular choice. Free verse "also has discipline," Sanchez notes, echoing T. S.

Eliot: "There's a reason for having one word on one line." Therefore, her inventive spelling, including the addition and subtraction of letters, places emphasis on a word by interrupting the reader's or listener's familiar manner of comprehension. The use of standard punctuation—especially the dash, the solidus, and the ampersand—between syllables and in other unexpected locations alters the flow of the line so that unique and often striking rhythmic arrangements influence the psychological mood of a poem.

The range of Sanchez's technical proficiency is evident in the selection from *A Blues Book for Blue Black Magical Women*. Sanchez wrote this poem during her brief membership in the Nation of Islam, spending more than a year on its composition. She wanted to produce "a spiritual autobiography" (as the critic George Kent notes) in which both visionary illumination and pointed social commentary operate within the scope of the history of African American women. The first part (not included in this anthology) is subtitled "Queens of the Universe" and was written for a women's group in Pittsburgh "to keep them holding together." This is basically an entrance to the wider field. The section "Past" is written in four stanzas, each one set as a block of type, positioned in an angular configuration, and containing either one or two long, segmented lines. The placement on the page concentrates the psychological condition of the woman/artist as a figure for the mind and soul of a people. The next division consists of a separation of "Woman" into different realms: mythic Earth Mother becoming individual black woman growing through adolescence toward maturity. The invocation to the Earth Mother to give the poet strength is built upon a series of romantic images:

> rise up earth mother
> out of rope-strung-trees
> dancing a windless dance
> come phantom mother
> dance me a breakfast of births
> let your mouth spill me forth
> so i creak with your mornings.
> come old mother, light up my mind
> with a story bright as the sun.

The section "Earth Mother" is orchestrated like a musical score with directions ("*old/woman's/voice*") and rhythmic repetitions leading toward the rapid, scattered explosion of energy of a young girl depicted in the darting motion of a child's game. She is thrust into an awareness of the adult world with the arrival of another in a succession of stepmothers in the section "young/black/girl." This part of the poem extends, with additional stage direction, into the pressures of sexuality, which Sanchez conveys through the hard language of angry slang. The final parts of the poem, "Present" and "Rebirth," move back in cyclical fashion toward the eternal, first showing a woman moving toward adulthood and the complexity of choice with the employment of compound adjectives and linked words ("soft/black/woman," "long/legged/daughter," and "blue/black/magical/woman"), then carrying the woman/ poet beyond life in the United States to other continents inhabited primarily by people of color, where human life and the natural world fuse into a cosmic conception transcending a racist society. The versatility that Sanchez displays in this longer poem is characteristic of her capability to shape her work in accordance with its purpose.

Context

In order to help her students understand the conditions of her life and art, Sanchez has asked classes in black autobiography, in a consideration of Zora Neale Hurston, "What was it like to have been a Black woman artist in your grandmother's time?" Noting the prevalence of "the chauvinism that exists today," she is attempting to give her classes a picture of what has been called a revolution within the revolution, wherein black women have had to confront, in the critic Stephen E. Henderson's words, their position as "victims not only of racial injustice but of a sexual arrogance tantamount to a dual colonialism." Within this context, Sanchez has dedicated her second book *We a BaddDDD People* to "blk/wooomen: the only queens of this universe" and has specifically mentioned that her enduring contribution to the Nation of Islam was her fight against the inferior status that it assigned to women. Yet she has also made a particular point of not permitting women to see themselves only as victims, because she believes that people should not be "programmed for defeat and victimization."

Instead, her work has been designed to demonstrate the persistence and determination of women across time, frequently using the specific facts of her own life and experience as an anchor in an unsteady flux of communal and national assaults. She chose to publish her first book with Dudley Randall's Broadside Press, a publishing house supporting black writers, rather than seeking a more prominent established publisher, and she was willing to face the criticism of a generally supportive fellow artist such as Madhubuti, who "did not understand" her experiments in language in *We a BaddDDD People*, because she thought that she could not give in to fear in her own life when she was exhorting her readers about the "values of change." Without suggesting that women are superior to men, Sanchez does believe that "Women are quite different from men in what they feel and think and how they view the world. I use feminine imagery that is drawn from ancient cultures." An indication of the success and impact of her work are comments from Madhubuti that "Sanchez has been an inspiration to a generation of young poets" and that "in a real fight, this is the type of black woman you would want at your side."

Sources for Further Study

Evans, Mari, ed. *Black Women Writers (1950-1980): A Critical Evaluation*. Garden City, N.Y.: Anchor Press/Doubleday, 1984. One of the essential critical texts for a study of African American poets. Includes an interview with Sanchez and several incisive critical essays.

Gibson, Donald, ed. *Modern Black Poets: A Collection of Critical Essays*. Englewood

Cliffs, N.J.: Prentice Hall, 1973. Includes an essay by R. Roderick Palmer, "The Poetry of Three Revolutionists," that covers Sanchez.

Melhem, D. H. *Heroism in the New Black Poetry*. Lexington: University Press of Kentucky, 1990. A compilation of critical essays and interviews with Sanchez and some of her peers, such as Jayne Cortez, Gwendolyn Brooks, Haki Madhubuti, Amiri Baraka, and Dudley Randall. Includes a useful bibliography.

Sanchez, Sonia. "Exploding Myths: An Interview with Sonia Sanchez." Interview by Herbert Liebowitz. *Parnassus: Poetry in Review* 12-13, nos. 2-1 (Spring-Winter, 1985): 357-368. A pointed, probing discussion with Sanchez conducted by the publisher of *Parnassus*.

Tate, Claudia, ed. *Black Women Writers at Work*. New York: Continuum, 1983. Contains an interview with Sanchez in which the poet expresses her opinions and ideas about politics, black studies programs, poetics, and her early life. Provocative, candid, and appealing.

Leon Lewis

IVY DAYS
Making My Way Out East

Author: Susan Allen Toth (1940-   )
Type of work: Memoir
Time of work: 1957-1963
Locale: Ames, Iowa; Northampton and Boston, Massachusetts; England; and
  Berkeley, California
First published: 1984

> *Principal personages:*
> SUSAN ALLEN TOTH, a student at Smith College
> CHRIS MORGAN, her friend and a rival student at the woman's
>   college
> MRS. KURTZ, Toth's art professor, whom she admired
> MR. ABERNATHY, Toth's English professor, with whom she was
>   infatuated
> MRS. STEVENS, the housemother of Toth's dormitory
> MR. SHEIK, a professor whose criticism discouraged Toth from
>   writing

Form and Content

Ivy Days: Making My Way Out East is a wry first-person narrative that examines the impact on an innocent Iowan of attending Smith College, an elite woman's college in Northampton, Massachusetts. Toth scrutinizes the difficulties and doubts, largely unexamined at the time, that she faced as a scholarship student in highly competitive Lawrence House, where she lived while attending Smith from 1957 to 1961. An unsophisticated young woman from Ames, Iowa, a small town in a rural setting not far from Des Moines, she longed to see and experience the East that she had read about in American literature. Instead, the awe that she felt at the wealth and confidence of the Easterners she met was tempered by her own isolation and claustrophobia.

The introductory section of the book, "Ivy Days," is written from Toth's viewpoint twenty-five years later as a divorced single parent and a college professor herself. This strategy, also used in Toth's earlier memoir *Blooming: A Small-Town Girlhood* (1981), sets the pattern for the chapters that follow: Each is preceded by a brief italicized vignette featuring Toth's experiences and opinions long after college.

"Out East," the first chapter, depicts the process of cracking the unfamiliar codes of clothing styles and the Honor System, speculating about the wild students who attended parties in New York, and enduring nude pictures to determine posture flaws. Her homesickness for her mother, widowed when Toth was seven, nearly overwhelmed her. In fact, her first semester was so difficult that she describes returning to Smith after Christmas vacation as one of the most difficult things she ever did. Gradually, however, she began to feel at home. Chapter 2, "Learning to Live with

Women," examines the pressures of living in small, enclosed spaces; describes beginning to care passionately about food; and laments the way in which the residents of Lawrence House hid their thoughts and feelings from one another. In "Intellectual Butterfly," the third chapter, her flirtation with various majors and eventual switch from a history to an English major branded her an intellectual butterfly, a designation she eventually accepted with some pride because of the exhilaration that she continues to feel when using the habits of mind that were the lasting gifts of an education at Smith. "In the Swim" describes the blind dates, mixers, and college weekends that Toth blundered through at Smith. She depicts herself as lonely and longing for warmth, but frightened and confused by sex. "Summa" deals with the agonizing academic pressure that Toth felt in her last two years at Smith, especially from her friend and classmate Chris Morgan but also from other students and even from her professors. Her senior year was dominated by her rivalry with Chris and by the expectation that she would be one of a handful of young women to graduate summa cum laude. Failing to do so was a crushing blow.

"Up, Up, and Away," the final chapter, describes Toth's forays beyond Smith, including a summer working in Boston that fell far short of her expectations and a return to Boston five years later during which she lost and miraculously found her thousand-dollar engagement ring in a bin of bargain purses, evading the chance to confront the facts of her failing marriage. While still at Smith she spent a wonderful summer in England, which began a romance she describes at length in *My Love Affair with England* (1992). *Ivy Days* ends by portraying Toth's experiences in graduate school at the University of California, Berkeley, where she came to terms with how driven she was and decided to marry and begin what she thought of as real life.

Analysis

Toth recaptures a past in which men were absent from women's colleges and academic achievement was a priority, at least among the students she knew. Critics have praised Toth for her balance: She neither yearns nostalgically for her college days nor implies that everything is far better today than it was in the 1950's and early 1960's.

She writes perceptively about relationships, affectionately recalling the love and support that she received from her mother, whom she wanted to please all of her life. Toth recognized only belatedly that her burden of perfectionism was self-imposed. The most telling example of this misperception is her anguish over not being able to present her mother with the achievement of a summa cum laude degree when her mother was entirely satisfied with the magna cum laude degree that Toth received.

Toth celebrates friendships among women and expresses her regret over the lack of trust and honesty that was typical of the late 1950's and early 1960's. She warmly recalls her friendships with her beautiful roommate Sophie and her campus big sister, Dulie, who advised her about what courses to take and coached her on drinking and smoking. Most of the young women with whom she lived and worked, however, kept their hidden selves secret from one another. Toth puzzled over the wild students, fantasizing that she knew which of them were among the third of her senior class who admitted in a poll to being nonvirgins, but she was never able to talk frankly about sex herself.

Toth ruefully acknowledges that the isolation she felt at Smith was worsened by her confusion over sex and her fallible taste in boyfriends. She details awkward entanglements with nice young men and painful attractions to aloof and angry ones, bemoaning the passivity and game-playing that the times imposed on social life, yet offering forgiveness to the timid person she once was. Most regrettable, she implies, were the lasting consequences of the wrong choices she and her contemporaries made because of what they did not know about sex and about themselves.

The expectations for women's careers that Toth found at Smith in the 1950's were high, and they conflicted with other aims that were in the air at the time—marriage and children seemed at odds with the life of the mind as it was represented by her female professors, most unmarried and apparently asexual. The male professors, on the other hand, were perceived as having fascinating sexual lives and fulfilling careers. Toth idolized some of her professors, such as Mrs. Kurtz, who taught Art II, an intensely demanding course that fascinated and terrified Toth. For women, however, the price of academic achievement appeared to be high—too high, Toth implies, though the ideals and achievements of intellectual life exerted a powerful appeal for her.

Toth's writing has been criticized as banal, as not angry enough. Despite her quiet approach, however, she exposes weaknesses in others and in herself. Mona, a housemate, took a nasty pleasure in repeatedly scheduling late-night fire drills. Mr. Sheik, a creative writing professor, wrote "Oh, God!" on a story of which Toth was proud, discouraging her from writing another story for eighteen years. Toth herself failed to understand and sympathize with Mrs. Stevens, the determinedly cheerful housemother of Lawrence House who eked out a dreary existence in a tiny, noisy suite of rooms. Only much later did Toth acknowledge the connections that she might have made with other students and with professors. Some regret for what might have been filters through this otherwise cheerful book. Had her mentors and models and the constraints that she felt been different, her life could have been happier and more fulfilling.

In her acknowledgements, Toth reveals that the incidents described in the book took place but that she changed the names of many people. These name changes freed her to provide witty, truthful accounts of such incidents as fending off a drunken date in the backseat of a hearse, enduring an excruciatingly boring weekend at Yale University, and arranging for a sex education lecture by a doctor who compared having sexual intercourse with helping a boyfriend change a tire. Most humiliating to Toth was her attempt to impress Mr. Abernathy, the English professor with whom she was hopelessly in love, and getting her foot entangled in his typewriter instead.

Context

    Ivy Days continued the account of Susan Allen Toth's life begun in *Blooming* and resumed in a collection of essays on middle age, *How to Prepare for Your High-School Reunion* (1988). It solidified Toth's reputation as an amusing, insightful essayist. *Ivy Days* has influenced women's studies by helping to extend the range of subject matters, tones, genres, and degrees of accessibility considered appropriate to women's writing. By demonstrating that one rather unremarkable woman's experience and character have compelling interest, *Ivy Days* has encouraged other women to value their own everyday experiences and to write more personally themselves.

Toth's honest, personal tone has fostered a powerful sense of connection between herself and her readers, many of whom think of her as a close friend, just as Toth herself once thought of Clarissa and Lovelace in Samuel Richardson's novel *Clarissa* (1747-1748) as her friends. Some readers believe that Toth tells their own stories as no one else could (though others question whether anyone could have been quite as innocent as she claims to have been). Interest in *Ivy Days* is not limited to people who moved from the Midwest to the East or who attended Ivy League colleges in the 1950's. Toth's description of the stresses of forging a social life and grappling with questions about career choices and marriage have a much wider appeal. Toth's book encourages a reassessment of the costs of intense academic competition, but it also invites generous forgiveness of women's own past selves.

Although the genre of memoir has often been considered minor, even inconsequential, the achievement of *Ivy Days* has helped to legitimize memoir and to validate a woman's life as deserving scrutiny. It helps to fill a gap in literature much devoted to men coming of age but not providing enough honest accounts of women doing so. The accessibility of Toth's straightforward prose style is a welcome antidote to the prolixity, jargon, and doctrinaire quality of some personal narratives. Toth is genuine and candid, giving the impression that she has little need to fictionalize her past experiences or lie to protect herself. Her warmth, wit, quiet tone, and clarity make *Ivy Days* a useful model for other women writers.

Sources for Further Study

Benstock, Shari, ed. *The Private Self: Theory and Practice of Women's Autobiographical Writings*. Chapel Hill: University of North Carolina Press, 1988. This collection of essays provides theoretical frameworks for interpreting *Ivy Days*. Its first section presents six essays on theories of autobiography, and the final six essays examine various forms of women's autobiographical writings across three centuries.

Culley, Margo, ed. *American Women's Autobiography: Fea(s)ts of Memory*. Madison: University of Wisconsin Press, 1992. This collection provides historical context for understanding the tradition out of which *Ivy Days* comes. The essays, which are arranged chronologically by subject, reflect trends in the theory and criticism of autobiography from the late 1980's and early 1990's. They trace the roots of American women's autobiography, analyzing the stories of slaves, suffragists, and homesteaders, as well as narratives by Gertrude Stein, Mary McCarthy, and Dorothy Day.

Heilbrun, Carolyn G. *Writing a Woman's Life*. New York: W. W. Norton, 1988. This short book argues for new ways to interpret women's lives. Heilbrun urges women to reject the limitations imposed by patriarchal society not only on what can be discussed in biographies and autobiographies but also on what women can do. Like *Ivy Days*, this book addresses the issues of identifying the buried self, admitting and achieving ambitions, and sustaining friendships among women.

Personal Narratives Group, Joy Webster Barbre, et al., eds. *Interpreting Women's Lives: Feminist Theory and Personal Narratives*. Bloomington: Indiana University Press, 1989. International in scope, this collection surveys the contexts and forms of the life stories of women, ranging from a Victorian maidservant and a Prussian aristocrat to abortion activists in Fargo, North Dakota, in the 1980's. It also investigates the relationship between narrators, who tell their own stories, and the people who interpret the narratives. Its authors include anthropologists, historians, and specialists in women's studies.

Sarton, May. *Journal of a Solitude*. New York: W. W. Norton, 1973. One of the precursors of *Ivy Days*, this memoir is cited by Carolyn Heilbrun as a turning point in women's autobiography because of its honest anger. Like Toth, Sarton chronicles the events of a woman's everyday life and does not shy away from describing her own pain.

Barbara J. Daniels

THE JAILING OF CECELIA CAPTURE

Author: Janet Campbell Hale (1947-   )
Type of work: Novel
Type of plot: Bildungsroman
Time of plot: The latter half of the twentieth century
Locale: The American northwest and an Indian reservation in Idaho
First published: 1985

> *Principal characters:*
> CECELIA CAPTURE, the protagonist
> NATHAN WELLES, Cecelia's husband
> WILL CAPTURE, Cecclia's father
> MARY THERESA CAPTURE, Cecelia's mother
> BUD DONAHUE, a young soldier who dies in Vietnam and the
> father of Cecelia's son
> JIM, one of Cecelia's lovers
> THOMAS RUNNING HORSE, a Sioux man whom Cecelia meets at a
> bar in Oregon
> MISS WADE, a welfare caseworker

Form and Content

Although *The Jailing of Cecelia Capture* begins with Cecelia's incarceration and ends three days later with her release, Janet Campbell Hale also uses the jailing as a metaphor for the "prison" in which Cecelia has lived throughout her life. Most of the chapters begin in the present in the jail, but Hale soon has her protagonist remembering events from her past. These flashbacks, which occur in associational rather than in chronological order, fill in the details of Cecelia's life, her case history. That history is one of entrapment and confused identity—the novel depicts the protagonist's journey toward freedom and selfhood. Cecelia Capture Welles becomes Cecelia Capture, which involves the shedding of her "white" past and acquired "white" identity and the embracing of her American Indian heritage.

Cecelia spends her first twelve years on an Indian reservation in Idaho, where her father's past shapes her life. Because of his failed "white" academic and athletic career at Notre Dame, he desperately wants a son to become the lawyer and athlete he tried to be. Cecelia senses his disappointment and attempts to become a worthy substitute for the missing son. Will Capture insists that she speak English and enrolls her in public school, where the white students make her miserable. Knowing that she must be better than they, she overachieves academically and athletically; but when she loses at a track meet, she understands that her lack of self-confidence has cost her the race. Shortly after the race, the family moves to Tacoma, Washington, where her isolation from her family is represented by her escape to the library, which becomes a retreat and refuge for her. To assert her independence, she refuses to do housework, alienating herself from her mother, Mary Theresa, and her three older sisters. When Mary Theresa leaves Will and takes her daughters to the Yakima Valley Reservation, Cecelia effectively opts out of academic life and seeks to "belong," which is more important to her.

After Will buys a house in Wapato, Mary Theresa and her daughters rejoin him, but sixteen-year-old Cecelia soon drops out of school and moves to San Francisco. There she meets Bud Donahue, a young soldier who, during an intense three-day relationship, impregnates her before leaving for Vietnam, where he dies. After Corey is born, Cecelia goes on welfare, decides to return to school, and resolves to become a "criminal" by getting a job which she does not report to her caseworker, Miss Wade, who discovers her secret and threatens her with criminal charges. During this period, Cecelia rejects a marriage proposal from Jim, who offers her security, and meets Nathan Welles, a doctoral student in English at the University of California, Berkeley. She completes her undergraduate degree, marries Nathan, and moves to Spokane, where he takes a position as an English professor at a community college.

Although they have a daughter, Nicole, and things go well for a while, eventually Nathan's behavior alienates Cecelia. He disparages her abilities, treats her condescendingly, and finally makes a revealing joke about Wounded Knee; Cecelia, who interprets the joke as bigotry, decides to go to law school and leaves her family behind. At the prestigious law school, she lives frugally, indulges herself in a few affairs, and then, on her birthday, gets arrested for driving under the influence of alcohol. The welfare charge resurfaces, and she spends the weekend in jail. When she is finally released on bail, she buys a gun, apparently to commit suicide after the trial; but when she is released, she says goodbye to Nathan and then to Bud at this grave. After shedding her wedding ring and discarding the gun, she is free to start a new life.

Analysis

Hale's somewhat autobiographical novel ostensibly concerns the memories of an American Indian woman who is incarcerated for drunken driving and for an old welfare fraud charge. Her jailing, however, is metaphorical as well as literal. As a child, Cecelia conforms to her father's expectations for a boy, and her chosen sport appropriately is running. Her childhood dreams of flying and of angels with wings reflect her desire to escape: "She thought that her favorite song ['Oh, if I had the wings of an angel, over these prison walls I would fly'] must have been made up by a little girl like herself, another secret angel, who had been imprisoned." Cecelia's story is, in fact, a series of flights, of attempted escapes, that ironically result in her "capture" before she finally escapes over the walls of exploitation and oppression. Late in the novel, she recognizes that she feels much as her mother had, the prisoner of "circumstances and an inability to imagine anything beyond the prison," both in loveless marriages, traps of their own making.

Circumstances such as racism have led not only to her exploitation and oppression but also to that of all American Indians unable to see beyond the walls. Using Cecelia as a spokesperson, Hale points out that American Indians did not receive citizenship until 1924, that separate-but-equal schools are not equal, and that whites introduced disease through blankets given as "gifts" to American Indians. It is, however, the insidious, less obvious racism that produces the "sidewalk Indians," those marginalized individuals without futures. The lack of self-confidence that cost Cecelia her race is fostered by bureaucrats such as Miss Wade, who suggests vocational courses for Cecelia, and by whites such as Nathan, who advocates a "more realistic career goal" such as "social worker or a teacher of young children"—both choices, unlike law, have less status than college professor. Even her mother, Mary Theresa, attacks Cecelia's (and her own) American Indian heritage and asserts the superiority of their Irish American ancestors, the Harrigans, whose white skin Mary Theresa has inherited. Since both American Indians and Irish Americans endured abuse and became "displaced persons," Mary Theresa's racial prejudice seems ironic and tragic.

Like her parents, Cecelia has contradictory feelings about her identity. Will attempted to lead a "white" life and failed, but he seems determined that Cecelia achieve his goals, which include becoming a lawyer. While she speaks English, attends white schools, and adopts stereotypical white academic behavior, Cecelia believes that she belongs on the reservation, where she gives up academic pursuits. While she identifies with the "sidewalk Indians," she also has little in common with them. As Thomas Running Horse points out, she is an "educated squaw." Both fathers of her children are white, and she takes Nathan Welles's name. Hale depicts Nathan as the quintessential white Anglo-Saxon Protestant, the son of a concert pianist and the descendant of a *Mayflower* family. When she marries him, she moves into a white world where she cannot survive. She is, in Nathan's eyes, another Lupe, a Mexican prostitute to whom he once proposed marriage. Both women appeal to him because they represent the "other" and because his supposed love for them reinforces his self-image as a liberal. When Cecelia sees herself as Nathan sees her, the member of an inferior race with lowered expectations, she leaves him to return to law school, but she is not free until she sees herself as Cecelia Capture, not Mrs. Welles.

Cecelia's ambivalence about her identity leads her to adopt another persona, Carmen, which becomes her "drinking name" because she says it derives from Carmen Miranda, a star but also "foreign," and because Carmen is the femme fatale and title character of a famous opera. Cecelia also does not want to use her real name in bars. Later in the novel, she reveals her childhood fantasy about escaping from "these Captures" and being reunited with Carmen Miranda, her "real" mother. Before she acquires her own identity, she has to stop frequenting bars as Carmen, shed the clothes of a white law student, discard Nathan's ring and name, and bid farewell to Bud, whose memory ties her to the past. Ironically, she gains her freedom and a new life at the cemetery where Bud is buried. There she rejects suicide, resolves to live, makes plans for her future, and passes through the iron gates of the cemetery.

Context

In *The Jailing of Cecelia Capture*, Hale examines an American Indian woman's struggle to achieve her identity and freedom. Since the novel is narrated primarily from her protagonist's point of view, Hale offers a feminist critique of many social ills, among them punitive welfare agencies, dysfunctional families, male chauvinism, mother-daughter conflict, and inadequate health care for the poor (suggested by Corey's unnecessarily painful birth). Although Nathan, Cecelia's most oppressive male character, is white, men of color are also criticized. Thomas Running Horse, for example, disparages "educated squaws," and Raoul, her lover in law school, treats her as a gynecologist would—clinically. In fact, male characters in the novel typically fail their women or abuse them.

Since the novel spans the thirty years of Cecelia's life—she is jailed on her birthday—it is essentially a *Bildungsroman*, a belated coming-of-age story about a character's quest for identity and adulthood. Yet this novel is about a woman of color, not a white male. Sex, education, career—Hale treats all these traditional subjects, but from a woman's perspective. For example, a young man's sexual experience often liberates him, impels him toward maturity; Cecelia's first sexual experience results in pregnancy, welfare motherhood, and dependency on men and institutions—in effect, her "jailing."

While she occasionally evokes the past (Cecelia imagines herself and Thomas Running Horse on the early plains), Hale focuses on the present and uses a fairly conventional narrative to tell Cecelia's story, which seems to have much in common with Alice Walker's *The Color Purple* (1982). Hale's autobiography, *Bloodlines: Odyssey of a Native Daughter* (1993), and her first novel, *Owl's Song* (1974), written for "young adults," concern the same themes as *The Jailing of Cecelia Capture*: reservation life, emotional imprisonment, the effect of the past, the struggle to establish identity, and the problem of coping with urban environments. As some critics have noted, she is one of the few American Indian writers dealing with urban problems. While her work concerns the past, it does not stress many of the themes found in other American Indian novels, such as myth, folklore, the oral tradition, the mixture of poetry and prose, and writing about narrative itself.

Sources for Further Study

Cole, Diane. "The Pick of the Crop: Five First Novels." *Ms.* 13 (April, 1985): 14. A generally sympathetic review of the novel, although Cole believes that the cards are stacked against Nathan, the small-minded husband who is almost a caricature. Cole also examines the theme of physical and emotional imprisonment in the novel.

Hale, Janet Campbell. *Bloodlines: Odyssey of a Native Daughter*. New York: Random House, 1993. An autobiography that reveals ties between the lives of Hale and her protagonist in *The Jailing of Cecelia Capture*. Like Cecelia, Hale was reared on a reservation, had white ancestors (Hale's was Dr. John McLoughlin, the "Father of Oregon"), had a verbally abusive mother and an alcoholic father, lived in San Francisco, married a white man, had a son and a daughter, and had to come to terms with her past in order to establish her identity.

Library Journal. Review of *The Jailing of Cecelia Capture*. 110 (March 15, 1985): 72. A short review which stresses the themes of alienation and imprisonment. Finds the protagonist's emotional entrapment more severe than actually serving time in jail.

Ruoff, A. LaVonne Brown. *American Indian Literatures: An Introduction, Bibliographic Review, and Selected Bibliography*. New York: Modern Language Association of America, 1990. Offers a brief overview of Hale's life and discussions of *The Jailing of Cecelia Capture* and *Owl's Song*, both of which deal with reservation alcoholism, suicide, and other problems in the urban landscape.

Wolitzer, Meg. "In Short: *The Jailing of Cecelia Capture*." *The New York Times Book Review* 90 (April 7, 1985): 14-15. Wolitzer considers the flashback structure a bit awkward and finds the prose "flat" in the second half of the novel, but she also believes that the details of Cecelia's life are moving and that the sense of alienation is effectively portrayed.

Thomas L. Erskine

JANE EYRE

Author: Charlotte Brontë (1816-1855)
Type of work: Novel
Type of plot: Bildungsroman
Time of plot: The nineteenth century
Locale: England
First published: 1847

Principal characters:
 JANE EYRE, an independent, spirited woman
 EDWARD FAIRFAX ROCHESTER, the master of Thornfield Hall and
  Jane's primary love interest
 ST. JOHN RIVERS, Jane's cousin, a minister
 BERTHA MASON ROCHESTER, Edward's wife, who has become
  insane
 SARAH REED, Jane's cruel aunt, who reared her until she was ten
 HELEN BURNS, Jane's friend at Lowood, a school for poor
  orphaned girls

Form and Content

Charlotte Brontë's *Jane Eyre* traces the personal development of a young woman who must struggle to maintain a separate identity and independence in the suffocating pressures of her culture. She grapples with the societal expectations of her gender, which frequently conflict with her intuitive sense of self. Each setting and situation that Jane encounters denotes a phase in her personal progress, teaching her and preparing her for the next experience.

The linear organization of Jane's maturation process is attributable to the viewpoint of the narrator. The narrator is not the child, teenager, or young woman that Jane is during the course of the narrative, but the adult wife and mother who is recounting her story. With hindsight and from a mature perspective, Jane can recognize the pivotal, shaping events of her life. She takes account of her life, selecting events so that a pattern of personal development becomes apparent, what all people do in making sense of their past. The reader also senses Brontë's voice. Although the novel is not an autobiography, it contains autobiographical elements—Brontë's experience at the Clergy Daughter's School is similar to Jane's years at Lowood, for example. Certainly Brontë draws from her own experience as a maturing young woman in describing the life of Jane Eyre.

Each setting indicates a stage of growth for Jane. Under the cruel treatment of her aunt, Sarah Reed, at Gateshead Hall, Jane learns as a child to rely on her own inner strength. The strong self-reliance that she develops as a protective mechanism in this brutal environment sustains her throughout her life. At Lowood, Jane finds sincere friendship in Helen Burns and a compassionate mother-figure in Maria Temple. Jane learns from Helen's religious stoicism, but realizes that she is too much in need of human companionship to accept such a solitary existence completely. When Miss Temple leaves to get married, Jane believes that she also must leave, having matured enough to break free from this surrogate mother.

As governess in Thornfield Hall, Jane finds in Edward Fairfax Rochester a kindred spirit equal to her in passion and strong individualism, but also suffering from a faltering sense of identity in regard to what he is and what is expected of him. Bertha, Rochester's insane wife, who lives in the attic, haunts them both as a symbol of their still-unresolved identities. They cannot truly be united until each has worked out these inner problems.

Jane finally finds real family support with her three cousins at Moor House. She attains self-confidence from her success with the school and financial independence from her uncle's inheritance. From her unemotional relationship with her cousin St. John Rivers, a zealous minister, she realizes that she needs a passionate love, and her inner standard of religious morals are further solidified in contrast to his frigid piety.

Jane Eyre contains gothic, Romantic, and Victorian elements. Elements of these styles do not simply exist for their own sake, but underscore the major theme of Jane's personal progress. The gothic and Romantic elements—Bertha's ghostlike haunting, Thornfield's dark and castlelike image, the spiritual connection between Rochester and Jane, nature's sympathetic response to Jane's emotions with storms and sunshine—are symbolic of Jane's dark struggles with her identity and her romantic tendency to follow her intuition. The Victorian emphasis on realism, on domestic concerns of marriage and family, and the reconciliation of feeling with reason also pervade the novel.

Analysis

Belonging to a family is a major theme in *Jane Eyre*. Family was extremely important to a woman in the Victorian period. It provided emotional and financial support to her as a child and an unmarried woman. Later, it defined her as a wife and mother. As an orphan, however, Jane is cast into a Victorian domestic wilderness, without a mother to prepare her for her proper place in society and without a father to care for her until her husband can replace him.

The absence of family creates a mixed effect in Jane. Her painful solitude spurs her to spend much of her young life in search of a family. Many of the characters serve as symbolic mothers for Jane. The harsh mothering of her aunt Mrs. Reed causes Jane to suffer, forcing her to withdraw into a lonely shell for protection. Miss Temple at Lowood is Jane's first positive mother figure, showing compassion and caring and leading her on the path to self-fulfillment by encouraging her studies in French and literature.

The novel's structure buttresses the theme of Jane's search for a family. Beginning with the false, hurtful family of Mrs. Reed and her spoiled children, Jane encounters

increasingly more rewarding versions of family coinciding with her personal maturation. At Lowood, Helen Burns and Miss Temple are a caring sister and mother. At
Thornfield, Jane becomes a pseudo-mother to the sweet Adele and Mrs. Fairfax is a
comforting mother-figure, but Jane is not yet able to be Rochester's wife.

At Moor House, she encounters an even stronger sense of familial belonging with
Diana, Mary, and St. John Rivers, her cousins. She lovingly prepares the house for
their Christmas reunion and shares her inheritance with them. Therefore, the strange
coincidence of Jane ending up on the doorstep of Moor House should not be seen as
a rupture in realism, but a thematic device. She rejects St. John's proposal of an
authoritative, loveless marriage as a warped confusion of brother, husband, and father
roles. Finally, Jane returns to a more enlightened Rochester to start a true family.

Jane's lack of family also has instilled in her a strong sense of self-reliance and
independence. Even as a child in Sarah Reed's house, Jane recognizes the essential
injustice of her predicament. She rejects the qualitative judgments that society makes
on the basis of class and recognizes her cousins for the shallow, self-indulgent children
that they are. Her personal standard of ethics tells her that Reed's children are not her
superiors. She also balks at Mr. Brocklehurst's estimation of her as dishonest, recognizing his hypocrisy in demanding that his pupils live humbly and poorly, while his
wife and daughters are bedecked in plumes and furs. Jane seems most humiliated and
angered when her integrity is in question.

Jane's self-reliance and personal ethics allow her to recognize the unfairness of
many societal conventions. She is belittled and ignored as a "mere governess" by
Rochester's upper-class guests, but she recognizes them as arrogant and self-centered.
Although she ranks far below Rochester in social rank and wealth, a profound
impediment to a marriage in the Victorian era, she feels equal to him in soul,
understanding his true nature. Jane finds his courting of the frivolous Blanche Ingram
for her political and social connections disturbing because she knows that she herself
is more his intellectual and spiritual equal.

Rochester's courtship of Blanche is particularly ironic in the light of his marriage
to the insane Bertha, who he was tricked into marrying for the sake of monetary and
political gain. It is significant that the primary symbol of hypocritical societal propriety, Thornfield Hall, in which Rochester lives a sham life of decorum, must be
destroyed by fire before he and Jane can live together happily and truthfully.

The most convincing evidence of Jane's strength and independence, however, is her
narrative voice. From the very beginning of the novel, the reader is struck by the sense
of confidence and control in the narrative voice. Brontë cleverly manipulates reader
response through the compelling voice of Jane. At times, one is brought close to the
narrator in an intimate relationship in which Jane makes the reader a confidant,
revealing inner feelings and weaknesses. Yet she never allows herself complete
vulnerability as a narrator. Often Jane addresses readers directly, never letting them
forget that she is aware of their presence. Readers are not eavesdroppers as in a
third-person narrative, but invited guests of Jane, who is in complete control of the
narrative. She creates suspense by withholding information from readers, such as the

identity of Rochester when he is disguised as an old gypsy, playing with them to heighten their interest. Jane's voice is so commanding that her reliability and sincerity do not come into doubt.

Context

Published in 1847, *Jane Eyre* was a popular success. Although many women writers were read by the Victorian public, true literary respectability required a masculine name; hence Brontë used the pseudonym "Currer Bell." The popularity of this intelligent novel should force one to reconsider the often belittled and maligned tastes of the largely female reading public of the period. One can imagine that the novel appealed to women then, and today, because it reflects the frustratingly limiting condition of women in the nineteenth century. Although the novel's end suggests a happy, typically Victorian domestic solution to Jane's problems—the reconciliation of Jane and Rochester—this conclusion does not assuage the more pervasive difficulties that Jane encounters in defining her identity as a woman within nineteenth century constraints. Modern readers appreciate Jane's strength and independence and her admirable struggle to live with integrity within a culture stifling for women.

For example, Jane's job as a governess exemplifies only one confusing female role in the 1800's. Women had very few alternatives for survival. If not supported by a father or a husband, an educated, middle-class woman likely was forced to become a governess, a position of lifelong servitude and repression of personal desires. As a woman who possesses the education, tastes, and behaviors of upper-class decorum so that she can teach them to her charges, the governess was frustrated to be treated as simply another household servant. Much of Jane's confusion about her identity at Thornfield stems from her contradictory role as governess.

Marriage, however, was no saving grace. Jane expresses the very modern fear, practically unheard of in the nineteenth century, of losing her identity in marriage. She resists compromising her identity and denigrating herself in conforming to Rochester's idea of a wife. In her wedding dress, she does not recognize herself before the mirror, nor can she write "Mrs. Rochester" on her luggage. As St. John's wife, she fears she would be "always restrained, and always checked—forced to keep the fire of my nature continually low." When Rochester is maimed and socially ruined, essentially bringing his physical strength and social position equal to that of Jane, the threat of domination no longer exists. Jane announces her decision in the powerful, self-asserting words of the final chapter: "Reader, I married him."

Sources for Further Study

Blom, Margaret Howard. *Charlotte Brontë*. Boston: Twayne, 1977. This introductory work asserts that *Jane Eyre* reflects Brontë's own contradictory struggle to be both independent and controlled by a man. Using biographical information as a springboard for analysis, the work examines Brontë's novels in separate chapters, including notes, an index, and a bibliography.

Gilbert, Sandra M., and Susan Gubar. *The Madwoman in the Attic: The Woman Writer and the Nineteenth-Century Literary Imagination*. New Haven, Conn.: Yale University Press, 1979. This feminist work examines recurrent themes in the works of major nineteenth century female writers. Interprets *Jane Eyre* as a progress novel tracing Jane's maturation, emphasizing the complex meaning of Bertha. Although 700 pages long, the book's extensive index and chapters divided by writer and work make it convenient for research.

King, Jeannette. *"Jane Eyre."* Philadelphia: Open University Press, 1986. An effective introduction to *Jane Eyre*, the book is arranged by literary elements with chapter headings such as "Characterization," "Language," and "Structure and Theme." Based on a tutorial approach in which readers are asked to reread certain chapters before reading discussion portions carefully examining the passages.

Macpherson, Pat. *Reflecting on "Jane Eyre."* London: Routledge, 1989. The author's conversational style and humor make this an entertaining work of criticism. Offers extensive character examinations of Jane, Bertha, and St. John and suggests that Brontë is practicing biting social criticism behind the disarming disguise of feminine confession.

Nestor, Pauline. *Charlotte Brontë's "Jane Eyre."* New York: St. Martin's Press, 1992. Arguing that Jane does not control her own actions, this work of new feminist criticism rejects previous estimations of Jane as a feminist hero. Offers interesting analyses of the themes of motherhood, sexuality, and identity and surveys the work's historical background and criticism. Includes an index, notes, and a bibliography.

Pinion, F. B. *A Brontë Companion*. New York: Barnes & Noble Books, 1975. A good reference work on all the Brontës, including biographical material, chapter-length analyses of their novels, a section on characters and places, an index, an annotated bibliography, and illustrations.

Heidi Kelchner

JOURNAL OF A SOLITUDE

Author: May Sarton (1912-   )
Type of work: Diary
Time of work: September 15, 1970, through September 30, 1971
Locale: Nelson, New Hampshire
First published: 1973

> *Principal personages:*
> MAY SARTON, a poet, novelist, and memoirist
> PERLEY COLE, Sarton's friend, neighbor, and hired hand
> X, Sarton's lover
> JUDY, a friend of Sarton for nearly thirty years
> ANNE THORPE, Sarton's seventh grade teacher in Shady Hill
>   School and a lifetime friend
> THE WARNER FAMILY, Sarton's neighbors
> CAROLYN HEILBRUN, a literary critic
> MILDRED, Sarton's housekeeper
> ANNE WOODSON, a painter
> ELEANOR BLAIR, another "old true friend" of Sarton

Form and Content

Journal of a Solitude, an illustrated account of May Sarton's life at Nelson in New Hampshire between 1970 and 1971, is Sarton's debunking of what she calls "a myth of a false Paradise" that she inadvertently created in her memoir *Plant Dreaming Deep* (1968). Sarton hoped, through *Journal of a Solitude*, to correct a false view of the ease of her life and to "come to terms with a depression."

Though a number of people appear fairly often in the journal, Sarton successfully shows readers that her life is "often frightfully lonely" and that she corresponds and works with many people she does not "know and will never know." Countless letters from readers show Sarton that the myth in *Plant Dreaming Deep* needs to be destroyed. She concludes, "If I should wear the mask of that mythical person *Plant Dreaming Deep* has created in readers' minds, I would be perpetuating a myth, not growing . . ."

The journal begins with the words "BEGIN HERE. It is raining." According to critic Carolyn Heilbrun, Sarton lets readers into "the rages, the assaults from critics, the despairs." Intertwined with these emotions are some of the flaws in Sarton's mythical paradise. Early in the journal, for example, she describes the death of Perley Cole, her "dear old friend," who is dying a lonely death in a nursing home. Later, Sarton offers a poignant sketch of the captured, half-wild cat that she sends to be euthanized. She speaks of her despair in breaking its trust, of the cat's final snarl, of the pain and practicality of her decision to prevent the overpopulation of cats on her property. Finally, Sarton relates the fading of her love relationship with the unidentified X. The journal concludes with Sarton's half-lament, half-resignation: "Once more the house and I are alone."

Analysis

According to Sarton, *Journal of a Solitude* was written with publication in mind. The journal focuses on specific themes, and Sarton herself says that she consciously leaves much unsaid in the journal. For example, in a 1983 interview, Sarton says of X: "X is my lover, is neither male nor female, has no name, no profession, no place of habitation, on purpose, because . . . I had to protect this person." Nevertheless, X is a critical part of the journal because of Sarton's themes, among them the value of solitude, the difficulty of being a creative woman, passion that goes beyond youth, and the value of maturity.

Sarton introduces the first of these themes, solitude, in the title. At the time she begins the journal, her parents are dead. She lives alone. What Sarton has—and values—is space and time, essential luxuries for creativity. She says of solitude that one of its chief values is that "there is nothing to *cushion* against attacks from within," and throughout the journal, she explores the meaning of her situation: "The fact that a middle-aged, single woman, without any vestige of family left, lives in this house in a silent village and is responsible only to her own soul means something." She learns through her introspection that creativity requires both time and space, luxuries not available to most women, particularly to those who are married and, even more so, to those who have children.

In exploring the theme of creativity in women, Sarton repeatedly questions how and if women can take on marriage and children and still be creative. She speaks of two young women students, at Wellesley College, who both married and quit writing poetry. Sarton contends that, for women, marriage is an "earthquake" but, for men, marriage changes their goals much less. She sees a traditional marriage relationship as an obstruction to creativity for women and concludes, "No partner in a love relationship (whether homo- or heterosexual) should feel that he has to give up an essential part of himself to make it viable." Though Sarton notes some improvement in twentieth century marriages, she still sees marriage as a greater obstacle to creative women than to creative men. In a 1977 interview, Sarton laments the difficulties that married women (particularly mothers) face, yet realizes that "the women who have had children and been married can say certain things which I, unmarried and without children, cannot say."

Sarton, a person of passion herself, also explores that quality, contending that, in the United States, people are terrified or offended by the idea of passion beyond youth. Her candid exploration of passion—both among the young and old, both homosexual and heterosexual—has made her an inspiration to her readers. Early in *Journal of a Solitude*, she writes of coming into one of the most passionate relationships of her life in her fifties. Sarton, who identifies herself as bisexual, lets her passion for X remain universal. While readers do not know X's gender, they know that both Sarton and X are almost sixty years old and that they are lovers.

Both in *Journal of a Solitude* and in later journals, Sarton explores the themes of aging and maturity. She avoids sentimentalizing aging, but she balances the losses of aging with the gains of maturity. Among Sarton's bleaker sketches on aging is the death of Perley Cole. Sarton visits Perley in a nursing home, where he is dying a lonely death. Ultimately, he dies while being transferred by ambulance to a hospital. Perley's death is unmarked by a memorial service, and his body is shipped unattended from Nelson to Cambridge, Massachusetts, to be cremated. Sarton calls Perley's death "the loneliest dying and the loneliest death I ever heard of." She asks how one can accept such a death, with people "discarded at the end like an old beer can." Later, during a depression, Sarton battles her own view of herself as an aging American. In one journal entry, she writes, "I feel old, dull, and useless."

While Sarton cannot always buffer herself from cultural attitudes on aging, she recognizes the value of maturity, one of the foremost concerns in her journals. She explores ways of sustaining creativity, with mature passion, throughout a long life. She berates American culture for making maturity so undervalued that people in their thirties mourn "their lost youth because we have given them no ethos that makes maturity appear an asset."

Through Sarton's voice, readers begin to sense the meaning of her life as a woman "responsible only to her own soul." Her explorations of solitude, womanhood, passion, and maturity speak to the human need to seek solitude, to become responsible for the soul. Sarton ends her journal by ending her relationship with X. In doing so, she faces aloneness, but with a sense that this aloneness will return to solitude.

Context

Sarton, a novelist, poet, memoirist, and journalist, has used her writing to explore issues central to women. For example, in her novel *The Bridge of Years* (1946) Sarton depicts a marriage in which the wife earns the income from a business that she inherited from her mother. Sarton explores another controversial relationship with *Mrs. Stevens Hears the Mermaids Singing* (1965), a novel that Sarton calls a gentle introduction to the theme of homosexuality.

In *Journal of a Solitude*, Sarton explores women's lives and issues through nonfiction. She says in the journal that, during the time of writing the journal, she thought "a lot about the lives of women, their problems and conflicts." She voices her awareness that "now we are increasingly aware that women must fight a difficult and painful war for their autonomy and wholeness." Sarton's work, including more than seventy books, has become an integral part of women's and gender studies, and her books are read internationally by a diverse audience. As Elizabeth Evans says in her critical analysis *May Sarton, Revisited* (1989), Sarton's journals have "spoken the unspoken for women who could not express anger, deal with regret, welcome the love of women, risk passion in middle or in old age." Sarton has become a role model for women of all ages.

Sarton, who has received many awards and honors, maintained, in a 1988 interview, that she has never won "the great prizes" for her work. She believes that her literary statement, rather than being embodied in a specific work, is a cumulative vision of life. Among Sarton's work, however, *Journal of a Solitude* has had particular success. Sarton has said that it has sold two thousand copies a year for twenty years. In speaking of the many letters from readers who say her books have changed their lives, Sarton concludes, "I feel loved by so many people. Let's face it, that's better than money."

Sources for Further Study

Evans, Elizabeth. *May Sarton, Revisited*. Boston: Twayne, 1989. Sketches Sarton's early years and focuses on the development of themes in her writing. Contains a chronology, notes, an index, and a series of letters to Sarton from her editor, Eric Swenson, to whom Sarton dedicated *Journal of a Solitude*.

Kallet, Marilyn, ed. *A House of Gathering: Poets on May Sarton's Poetry*. Knoxville: University of Tennessee Press, 1993. Gives close attention to Sarton's work in the 1980's and 1990's. Contains not only poets' reviews of Sarton's poetry but also Sarton's comments on her work. An introduction, a bibliography, a list of Sarton's works, a chronology, and an index are also provided.

Sarton, May. *At Seventy: A Journal*. New York: W. W. Norton, 1984. Beginning on May 3, 1982, and ending on May 2, 1983, this journal focuses on Sarton's views on solitude and aging, reflecting upon her seventy years of life.

_____ . *Conversations with May Sarton*. Edited by Earl G. Ingersoll. Jackson: University Press of Mississippi, 1991. This series of interviews is organized chronologically from 1972 to 1990. Contains an introduction, a chronology, and an index.

_____ . *The House by the Sea: A Journal*. New York: W. W. Norton, 1977. This illustrated journal is set in Sarton's house on the seacoast of Maine and covers the time from November 13, 1974, until August 17, 1976.

_____ . *I Knew a Phoenix: Sketches for an Autobiography*. New York: Rinehart, 1959. A series of Sarton's memoirs, arranged chronologically, from childhood in Massachusetts to her early twenties, when Sarton left the theater for poetry.

Sibley, Agnes. *May Sarton*. New York: Twayne, 1972. The first chapter is a biographical sketch of Sarton, and the remaining four chapters explore her poetry and novels. Contains notes, an index, and a chronology.

Carol Franks

THE JOY LUCK CLUB

Author: Amy Tan (1952-   )
Type of work: Novel
Type of plot: Psychological realism
Time of plot: The 1910's, the 1940's, the 1960's, and the 1980's
Locale: San Francisco and China
First published: 1989

> *Principal characters:*
>
> SUYUAN WOO, the founder of the Joy Luck Club, who dies two
> months before the book opens
>
> JING-MEI (JUNE) WOO, Suyuan's daughter, who learns that she
> has two half sisters in China
>
> LINDO JONG, Suyuan's competitive and critical best friend
>
> WAVERLY JONG, Lindo's daughter, a divorced woman with a
> five-year-old daughter
>
> AN-MEI HSU, a member of the club whose mother brought
> disgrace on herself in China and poisoned herself
>
> ROSE HSU JORDAN, the third of An-mei's seven children, whose
> husband, Ted Jordan, wants a divorce
>
> YING-YING ST. CLAIR, the wife of an American man who calls
> her "Betty"
>
> LENA ST. CLAIR, Ying-ying's daughter, who is unhappy in her
> marriage to the self-centered and success-oriented Harold
> Livotny

Form and Content

Amy Tan's *The Joy Luck Club* is a narrative mosaic made up of the lives of four Chinese women and their Chinese American daughters. Because of its structure, the book can only loosely be called a novel. It is composed of sixteen stories and four vignettes, but like many novels, it has central characters who develop through the course of the plot. The daughters struggle with the complexities of modern life, including identity crises and troubled relationships, while the mothers reflect on past actions that were dictated by culture and circumstance. The lives of the older women are bound together through their similar situations as immigrants and their monthly mah-jongg games at Joy Luck Club meetings.

Each of the stories is a first-person narration by one of the Joy Luck Club's three mothers or four daughters. Each narrator tells two stories about her own life, except for Jing-mei (June) Woo, who stands in for her deceased mother, telling a total of four stories. The tales are arranged in four groups, with a vignette preceding each group. The first group is told by mothers (plus June), the second and third groups by daughters, and the fourth by mothers. Jing-mei's final story, in which she learns her mother's history, concludes the book.

Since *The Joy Luck Club* is concerned with the relation of the present to the past, many stories take place in more than one time period. For example, in the last group of stories, the mothers begin their narration in the present time of the 1980's but then recall incidents that occurred when they were girls or young women: An-mei's mother's death, Ying-ying's first marriage, and Lindo's immigration to the United States. The narratives of the daughters are set in the 1960's, the time of their youth, or in the 1980's, with flashbacks to various earlier times. The first group of daughters' stories focuses on significant childhood experiences, while their second stories explore issues that they are experiencing as adults.

The daughters' tales are all set in the San Francisco Bay area, whereas the mothers' stories span two countries, China and the United States. Both rural and urban scenes in prewar China are depicted, and details related to festivals, customs, dress, housing, and food provide a rich backdrop to the central events in the narratives. June's final story, "A Pair of Tickets," takes her to a more modern China, where she finds Western capitalistic influences making inroads after nearly forty years of Communist Party rule.

The book examines a number of sociological issues from a woman's perspective: the death of parents, husbands, and children; marriage, adultery, and divorce; childbirth and abortion; and aging. The exploration, however, is often indirect. Situations are presented and later their consequences are shown. For example, Ying-ying's guilt over aborting her first child haunts a later pregnancy, and her daughter Lena's bulimic episode as an adolescent affects her eating habits as an adult. Exotic touches are added to the book's realistic rendering of emotions and incidents by means of references to Chinese folklore and superstition. Tan balances Eastern and Western points of view in her portrayal of the significant events of life.

Analysis

At first glance, *The Joy Luck Club* may seem randomly structured, but in actuality the book's organization is complex. Tan's use of multiple narrators and connecting vignettes shows the influence of writers such as William Faulkner and Louise Erdrich, but the narrative scheme is also patterned after the game of mah-jongg. Each family is represented once in every group of stories, just as each family is represented at the mah-jongg table at the Joy Luck Club. In mah-jongg, after each of the four players has started a round, a series is complete and the players change positions round the table. Likewise, the order of narrators changes after each group of stories. The first storyteller in the book is June. This corresponds to the position that she assumes at the mah-jongg table, the East wind, which always starts the game.

The stories in *The Joy Luck Club* are structurally self-contained. Built around a central incident or conflict, each one can be read without reference to the other stories. Yet there are numerous links among the stories that give unity to the book as a whole. Characters appear in one another's narratives, as when the Jongs eat Chinese New Year's dinner with the Woos in June's story "Best Quality." A recurring motif throughout the work is misunderstanding caused by cultural differences. All the mothers are perplexed by their American-born daughters, as are the daughters by their Chinese-born mothers. A more subtle device occurs in the third and fourth sections of the book. Each of the daughters' stories in the third group mentions the narrator's mother in the first sentence. Likewise, each of the mothers' stories in the fourth group begins with a reference to the narrator's daughter. The effect is not only to create unity within each group but also to suggest a close tie between the pairs of mothers and daughters. What one thinks, says, and does is important to the other, even in relationships where conflict is pronounced, as with Lindo and Waverly.

The short vignettes between groups of stories are an important structural feature as well. They are narrated by an omniscient voice, and their fablelike quality derives from their depiction of universal situations, such as a child challenging her mother's warnings against danger and a grandmother musing aloud to her infant granddaughter. The vignettes introduce important thematic concerns, such as preserving hope in the face of loss and passing on one's cultural legacy.

The quest for personal identity is the central theme in *The Joy Luck Club*. The death of Suyuan Woo causes Jing-mei to realize that she knew very little about her mother's life, and in her stories she ponders the meaning of her own life. Her discovery that she has two half sisters in China prompts her to take her cultural heritage seriously for the first time in her life. Rose, Lena, and Waverly are also engaged in various stages of the quest for selfhood. Rose and Lena are both learning to think and act independently of their husbands, and Waverly is discovering that her mother is not an adversary that she must outsmart. The author depicts the mothers as having resources that the daughters lack. Suyuan, An-mei, and Lindo were all severely tested by circumstances when they were young and found the strength to survive cruelty and hardship. Although Ying-ying lost her inner drive for many years, her daughter's unhappy marriage inspires her to try to regain her true nature in order to show Lena how to survive.

Context

The Joy Luck Club highlights the influence of culture on gender roles. The Chinese mothers in the book, all born in the 1910's, grew up in a hierarchical society in which a woman's worth was measured by her husband's status and his family's wealth. When they were young, the women were taught to repress their own desires so that they would learn to preserve the family honor and obey their husbands. The difficulties in marriage encountered by Lindo and Ying-ying as well as by An-mei's mother emphasize how few options were open to women in a tightly structured society in which their economic security and social standing were completely dependent on men.

Consequently, when the mothers immigrate to the United States, they want their daughters to retain their Chinese character but take advantage of the more flexible roles offered to women by American culture. The postwar baby-boomer daughters, however, are overwhelmed by having too many choices available. They struggle to balance multiple roles as career women, wives or girlfriends, and daughters. The

materialistic focus of American culture makes it difficult for the daughters to internal-
ize their mothers' values, particularly the self-sacrifice, determination, and family
integrity that traditional Chinese culture stresses.

In addition to gender roles, mother-daughter relationships are an important focus
of the book. Mothers are shown to have profound influence over their daughters'
development, yet their influence is constrained by the surrounding culture. As girls,
the Chinese women wanted to be like their mothers, whereas the American-born
daughters are estranged from their mothers. This contrast is consistent with a difference between cultures: Americans expect their children to rebel against parental
authority, while the Chinese promote obedience and conformity. The daughters in *The
Joy Luck Club* think that their mothers are odd because they speak broken English and
miss the subtleties of American culture pertaining to dress and social behavior. They
also tend to see their mothers as pushy. Waverly and June rebel against their mothers'
expectations without understanding that Lindo and Suyuan are trying to give their
daughters the opportunities that they never had themselves. As adults, Waverly and
June struggle with the conflicting desires of pleasing their mothers and developing
their own individuality. Because they perceive their mothers' guidance as criticism,
they are slow to understand the depth of their mothers' love and sacrifice for them.

Despite such generational and cultural gaps, the author suggests that daughters
resemble their mothers in character as well as in appearance. Waverly possesses
Lindo's shrewdness, and Rose shares An-mei's passivity in the face of suffering. By
developing four central mother-daughter relationships rather than only one, Tan
reveals that the factors which shape family resemblance, both negative and positive,
are varied and complex.

Sources for Further Study

Chan, Jeffery Paul, Frank Chin, Lawson Fusao Inada, and Shawn H. Wong. "An
    Introduction to Chinese-American and Japanese-American Literatures." In *Three
    American Literatures*, edited by Houston A. Baker, Jr. New York: Modern Lan-
    guage Association of America, 1982. Arguing from the viewpoint that white
    supremacist thinking controls American culture, the authors detail the origins of a
    distinctly Asian American literature, a category not readily recognized by critics.
    The stereotype of the Asian American "dual personality" is rejected.
Fong, S. L. M. "Assimilation and Changing Social Roles of Chinese Americans."
    Journal of Social Issues 29, no. 2 (1973): 115-127. Examines the influence of
    acculturation and assimilation on traditional Chinese family structure and Chinese
    social hierarchy. Conflicts over parental authority and changes in sex roles and
    attitudes toward dating are discussed.
Kim, Elaine H. "Asian American Writers: A Bibliographical Review." *American
    Studies International* 22, no. 2 (1984): 41-78. Provides a useful overview of various
    types of Asian American writing and its special concerns, such as the Vietnam War
    and gender issues, and discusses problems in the criticism of Asian American
    literature. A bibliography of primary works is included.

——————. " 'Such Opposite Creatures': Men and Women in Asian-American Literature." *Michigan Quarterly Review* 29, no. 1 (Winter, 1990): 68-93. The author briefly discusses mother-daughter relations in *The Joy Luck Club* in her examination of the different ways in which Asian American men and women portray gender and ethnicity in their writing.

——————. *With Silk Wings*. San Francisco: Asian Women United of California, 1983. Following twelve profiles and forty short autobiographical sketches of Asian American women, this well-illustrated book provides the social and historical background of various groups of Asian women immigrants to the United States.

Tan, Amy. Interview by Barbara Somogyi and David Stanton. *Poets & Writers* 19, no. 5 (September 1, 1991): 24-32. In an informative interview, Tan talks about the origins of *The Joy Luck Club*, its autobiographical elements, and its portrayal of mother-daughter issues.

Patricia L. Watson

JUBILEE

Author: Margaret Walker (1915-   )
Type of work: Novel
Type of plot: Historical realism
Time of plot: 1839-1870
Locale: Georgia and Alabama
First published: 1966

Principal characters:
VYRY, the daughter of the slave Sis Hetta and John Dutton, the master of the plantation
RANDALL WARE, a free black man who earns his living as a blacksmith and marries Vyry in a slave ceremony
INNIS BROWN, a former slave who acts as Vyry's protector
JOHN MORRIS DUTTON, the master of the plantation and Vyry's father
SALINA DUTTON (BIG MISSY), John Dutton's wife, who hates Vyry
LILLIAN DUTTON, the daughter of John and Salina Dutton
AUNT SALLY, the Dutton's cook
ED GRIMES, the overseer of slave labor on John Dutton's plantation

Form and Content

Jubilee is a fictionalized account of the life of Margaret Walker's maternal great-grandmother, Margaret Duggans Ware Brown, the character of Vyry in the novel. She lived through slavery, the Civil War, and the Reconstruction and died a month before Margaret Walker was born. Walker's grandmother passed on the history of her mother's life in the form of bedtime stories that she told her granddaughter. From this oral history, Walker reconstructed the events of that period of American history from antebellum days through Reconstruction. In doing so, she shows the everyday life from the point of view of a slave woman. Walker began the novel when she was nineteen and finished it thirty years later.

Jubilee resembles a true slave narrative based on Vyry's experiences as a slave and her search for freedom. The novel begins and ends with childbirth. As the book opens in 1839, Sis Hetta is giving birth to her last child. The novel ends in 1870 with Vyry looking forward to the birth of her fourth child. *Jubilee* is divided into three sections following the structure of the slave narrative: bondage, escape, and freedom.

The first section, "Sis Hetta's Child—the Ante-Bellum Years," begins when Vyry is two years old. After Sis Hetta, Vyry's mother, dies giving birth to her fifteenth child, Mammy Sukey takes over as Vyry's surrogate mother. When Mammy Sukey dies of the plague, Aunt Sally, the Duttons' cook, takes Vyry into her cabin. Aunt Sally teaches

Vyry how to cook and how to use herbs and roots for medicinal purposes. As a young child, Vyry plays with Lillian, the Duttons' daughter and Vyry's half sister by the plantation's owner, John Dutton. Later, Vyry works in the "Big House," where she is badly mistreated by Salina Dutton, John's wife.

Vyry falls in love with and marries Randall Ware, a freeman who tries unsuccessfully to secure Vyry's freedom. When Randall Ware is forced to leave the state of Georgia, he urges Vyry to leave with him. Unwilling to desert her two children, Minna and Jim, Vyry attempts to flee, taking her children with her. She is captured and returned to the plantation, where Salina orders her flogged.

The second section, "Mine Eyes Have Seen the Glory—the Civil War Years," deals with the changes that occur as a result of the war. After the war, Vyry stays on the plantation waiting for Randall Ware. When she hears that Ware is dead, she marries Innis Brown, a former slave who has acted as Vyry's protector. A series of tragedies befalls the Duttons. Johnny Dutton and Lillian's husband both die as a result of wounds that they received in the war. Lillian suffers from severe depression and is unable to care for herself or her children. John Dutton dies of complications from the injuries that he sustained when he fell from his horse. After Salina dies of a stroke, Vyry takes over the care of Lillian and her children until a family member comes to take them home with her. Knowing that Lillian will be cared for frees Vyry to leave the plantation and begin a new life with Innis Brown.

In the third section, "Forty Years in the Wilderness—Reconstruction and Reaction," Vyry and Innis move from place to place trying to make a living by farming. Ku Klux Klan members drive them off of their land, but they are finally accepted in a community in Greenville, Alabama, where they have a home of their own. At the end of the novel, Randall Ware returns to claim Vyry and his children. Although Vyry chooses to stay with Innis Brown, Jim goes with his father to get an education. The book ends with Vyry secure in her own home knowing that her children will succeed in the world.

Analysis

In the essay "How I Wrote *Jubilee*," Walker explains that she "always intended *Jubilee* to be a folk novel based on folk material: folk sayings, folk belief, folkways." She also "wanted the book to be realistic and humanistic." Walker succeeded in creating a novel whose main character, brought up in a culture rich in folklore, exemplified a humanistic approach to life. Vyry is a product of the African American community and continues this close connection throughout her life. She is nurtured by black women, and she speaks in black dialect. Walker shows the strengths and skills of the black women who lived during this time. Older women instruct younger ones on food preparation, needle crafts, and the medicinal value of herbs and roots. Walker's detailed descriptions of the hard work involved in food preparation provide a realistic look at the everyday lives of the women who spend their lives cooking and caring for others. In addition to cooking for the family in the "big house," these women must also cook for their own families. For example, Vyry cooks ham for the owners in the "big house," but fixes possum and collard greens for her own family's Christmas.

Walker portrays the everyday realities of plantation life from the point of view of the slaves. In contrast to Margaret Mitchell's romanticized view in *Gone with the Wind* (1936), Walker deals with the speech, behavior, hardships, fears, and hopes of the slaves. She treats the horrors of slavery, the realities of the Civil War, the rise of the Ku Klux Klan, and the problems that former slaves faced in the aftermath of the war. Walker draws on her investigation of African American oral tradition, historical accounts of slavery, and newspapers to support the oral history as told to her by her grandmother.

Walker also succeeds in her attempt to create a folk novel based on folk music and folk material. Chapter headings include excerpts from spirituals, folk songs, or folk sayings that correspond to the plot. The title of the book comes from a traditional Negro spiritual, "Jubilee," the last line of which is "Do you think I'll make a soldier in the year of Jubilee?" Jubilee refers to the rejoicing at the time of freedom. Throughout the novel, Walker includes verses from such spirituals as "Steal Away," "I Got Shoes," and "I Am a Poor Way-faring Stranger." The novel also contains descriptions of folk medicine as women pass their knowledge of herbal medicine from one generation to the next. Vyry makes a salve of barefoot root to treat rheumatism and a mullein bath for swollen feet.

The novel is sprinkled with folk sayings that Walker learned from her grandmother and put into the mouths of her characters. When Randall Ware asks Vyry to marry him, she replies, "When you buy my freedom, then I marriage with you, and not before! And I'll tell you like the monkey say to the parrot when they was fighting over the brush-broom, them's my final words of dust you eating, Mr. Coon." Later, when Ware tries to explain to Vyry that white people up north are talking about slavery being wrong, Vyry says, "Talk don't get you nowhere. Don't pay no attention to what the guinea hen say, cause the guinea hen cackle before she lay."

Context

In 1965, Walker received a Ph.D. at the University of Iowa, using *Jubilee* as her dissertation. In 1966, she received a Houghton Mifflin Literary Fellowship for the novel. *Jubilee* has been translated into several languages. Walker's chief contribution to the world of women's literature is her portrayal of the daily lives of black women during the time of the Civil War. Walker shows the strengths of these women who survived the hardships of slavery. Unlike other writers who use such stereotyped characters as mammies and pickaninnies, Walker portrays realistic female characters with individual personalities and strengths. She points out the important contributions these women made in the arts of healing, food preparation, and needlework. She shows the hard work and skill that went into the preparation of food for so many people. She describes the nursing skills of women such as Vyry who act as midwives for other women. Throughout the novel, Walker portrays a community of women who worked together to care for one another and for their children. Older women taught the younger ones the skills necessary for survival. Through the oral tradition the women handed down the history necessary to preserve a sense of family. In presenting history from a black woman's point of view, Walker shows the strengths of these women.

She treats the problems that existed in the relationships between black and white women during this period of history. On the one hand, the women formed close bonds, but white women were often jealous and threatened because their husbands were having sexual relations with the black women. Ambivalent relationships resulted. Thus, Salina Dutton treats Vyry with extreme cruelty, but Vyry continues to serve Salina and is even able to forgive her. Lillian and Vyry have a close relationship; it is Vyry who feels responsible for her care after Lillian's husband dies.

Vyry rejects racial bitterness as she forgives Salina in spite of the terrible cruelties that she endured at the hands of her master's wife. Racial reconciliation is seen in Vyry's charitable feelings toward other white women. Vyry is a nurturing woman who cares for all women. She shares her food with the families of her white neighbors and acts as a midwife for the white women in her area. Walker's treatment of interracial relationships between Southern women in the nineteenth century is optimistic; her work is based on humanism instead of racism.

Sources for Further Study

Goodman, Charlotte. "From Uncle Tom's Cabin to Vyry's Kitchen: The Black Female Folk Tradition in Margaret Walker's *Jubilee*." In *Tradition and the Talents of Women*, edited by Florence Howe. Chicago: University of Illinois Press, 1991. Goodman argues that *Jubilee* deserves a place in the literary canon because of Walker's detailed account of the lives of black women during the Civil War period. Shows how Walker grounds her novel in the folklore, music, and folk beliefs of the black folk tradition.

Gwin, Minrose. "*Jubilee*: The Black Woman's Celebration of Human Community." In *Conjuring: Black Women, Fiction, and Literary Tradition*, edited by Marjorie Pryse and Hortense J. Spillers. Bloomington: Indiana University Press, 1985. Gwin regards Walker's novel as a celebration of humanist values, as portrayed by the black characters who endured slavery, the Civil War, and Reconstruction to emerge victorious in their struggle for freedom. Calls *Jubilee* a "synthesis of folk tradition, imagination, and moral vision."

Klotman, Phyllis Rauch. "Oh Freedom: Women and History in Margaret Walker's *Jubilee*." *Black American Literature Forum* 11 (Winter, 1977): 139-145. Klotman shows that *Jubilee* is an important work because Walker's account of her great-grandmother's struggles and triumphs reveals the hardships that slave women endured. Argues that *Jubilee* comes out of the tradition of the slave narrative and praises Walker's research into this tradition to support the oral history that came from her grandmother.

Walker, Margaret. *How I Wrote "Jubilee": And Other Essays on Life and Literature*. New York: Feminist Press, 1990. Walker traces the thirty-year project of research and writing that went into the making of the novel. She shows how she visited places where her grandparents had lived and talked to people who knew her grandmother. She checked congressional records, newspapers, diaries, letters, court records, books, and slave narratives to provide accurate information for the novel

Judith Barton Williamson

THE KEEPERS OF THE HOUSE

Author: Shirley Ann Grau (1929-   )
Type of work: Novel
Type of plot: Social realism
Time of plot: The late 1950's and the early 1960's
Locale: A small town in The Delta of the United States
First published: 1964

Principal characters:
> ABIGAIL TOLLIVER, the granddaughter of William Howland,
>   whose life is tied to his life and to that of three generations of
>   Howlands
> WILLIAM HOWLAND, a kind, good-hearted man who, after his
>   wife dies and his daughter leaves the house, marries a mulatto
>   woman whom he meets in a magical setting
> MARGARET HOWLAND, William's second wife, whose ancestry is
>   one-half white, part black, and part American Indian
> JOHN TOLLIVER, Abigail's husband, a budding politician
> ROBERT, NINA, and CRISSY, William Howland's children by
>   Margaret
> OLIVER, William's black servant

Form and Content

The Keepers of the House is divided into four sections and an epilogue. Abigail's point of view dominates three of the sections: the first, the fourth, and the epilogue. The inner chapters, told by Abigail through the consciousness of William and Margaret, provide the poetic base for the novel, for the force that leads William to Margaret and Margaret to William, shaping their destinies and those of their children and the children of their children, is strong enough to transform a chance meeting into a necessity and every coincidence into part of a pattern of ultimate destruction.

As Abigail tells the reader, her memory goes back well beyond her birth. The house in which she lives was built by generations of her family. The stories that are a part of her heritage become stories that surround her, figures of people who parade in front of her. Abigail is able to speak through the minds of William and Mary because these stories form a ring around her and become so much a part of her that they constitute a portion of her own consciousness.

The Howland story starts in 1800, when the first William Howland finds a place to settle. Succeeding generations, each with a William Howland, add to the house and acquire more land and more wealth. The first William is killed in an Indian raid, and his sons avenge his death with even greater violence. One Howland is married and dies in the Civil War. Abigail's grandfather, however, is not a violent man. He slaughters animals for food but never kills wild things, although hunting is part of the way of life of the area. William knows the kind of woman he should marry to bear his children, and when he finds an appropriate girl, he courts and marries her within two weeks. She dies in childbirth. A daughter, Abigail, lives and grows and marries and gives birth to the Abigail who is the protagonist of the novel.

Seventeen years later, William meets Margaret. He has spent two days in the swamp on a bet, and when he emerges, he is not certain where he is. A sense of mystery prevails. Soon he realizes that he is at New Church, the home of a group of black settlers who have intermarried with Indians. Margaret is invisible to him until the third time his eyes circle a creek where she is washing clothes. Everything is silent, and William thinks she might be a part of the morning fog. In his imagination, she becomes Alberta, a legendary black woman who marries a demon figure, Stanley Albert Thompson, and whose presence is still recounted in stories. The morning sounds of birds and rustling leaves and moving water add to the magic of the scene.

The identification of Margaret with a mystical figure foreshadows her account of her first recollections—nothing but cold and noise and her mother as a shadow figure with no face. Margaret, the daughter of a black American Indian woman and a white man, is able to see ghosts—especially that of her dead great-grandmother, who has a jagged cut, a mark of ceremonial magic, on the back of one hand. Margaret is able to talk with her dead grandmother and to experience herself growing bigger than houses until she can hear the sound of the stars. When Margaret first sees William, she thinks he is a spirit like others she has seen, and then she recognizes him as someone for whom she has been waiting.

With this story as a component of her own being, Abigail accepts Margaret's and her grandfather's liaison in the same way that she accepts her stepbrother and his younger sisters, with whom she plays until each in turn is sent off to school, never to return. Abigail also accepts the role her husband conceives for her.

Here, more than halfway through the novel, is where the narrative returns more or less to present action, which it had left at the end of Abigail's first section of narration. Events move more rapidly in the present than in memory; moreover, all of history's pieces have been offered. It remains only to watch them fall into place.

Analysis

Although most critics, reviewers, and scholars who have offered comments on *The Keepers of the House* speak of the many excellent qualities of the novel, some accuse Shirley Ann Grau of being so far outside her work that it has no moral center; others accuse her of adhering too strictly to Southern literary idioms, so that the novel emerges as a grand cliché. Both negative observations seem more self-serving than true. The first observation suggests that author and character are one and the same and that Abigail's condition is to be equated with the author's psyche. Only the critically naïve would suggest such an identification. At the end of the novel, Abigail is in a state of almost total collapse. She has acted in a way that she believes her grandfather would act; she has used her wit and intelligence; she has risked bodily harm to protect her house because she now is its only keeper. When he died, Howland owned the major part of the town, and now Abigail does. She determines that she will destroy the house—the city—she will deprive the townspeople of work, and she will exert a kind of godlike power to bring punishment to the people of the earth. As Ecclesiastes states (12:3-5), "the keepers of the house shall tremble and the strong men shall bow themselves and the grinders cease. . . ."

This novel is no Southern "romance," more sentimental than ironic. No author faces a void more severe than the stark vision that Grau imparts in this novel, in which necessity drives humans to the inevitable ends that their beliefs and actions demand. Abigail is as steady in her condemnation of Margaret's children as she is in that of her husband, and she is as ruthless toward Robert as she is toward the townspeople. She will tear down all of their houses, although she knows there will be nothing left for her to salvage, but she no longer cares. She has, she says, "her own sob-racked echoing world," and she is locked into it.

It no longer seems to matter where the fault lies. What is left is to reject the mentality that invented and sustains master/slave relationships, as Abigail rightly does.

Context

Shirley Ann Grau rejects the idea that she is a feminist and likewise abhors the appellations of "Southern" and "female"—the former term carrying with it a set of assumptions she does not totally accept and the latter term being, she believes, disparaging and limiting. She is a writer, she maintains, who is not limited by subject matter or by the assumptions of other people. Some of the strongest characters she has created are women, but some of the more fascinating characters she has created are men.

Probably, the novel of Grau's that is most concerned with women's role in society is her second, *The House on Coliseum Street*, which was published in 1961. The protagonist of the novel, Joan Mitchell, involves herself with a professor at the university she attends. When she becomes pregnant, her mother acts with dispatch to arrange an abortion and thus put everything back together, but events act on Joan in a different way. She responds not only to the abortion but also the sterility and lack of commitment in the world around her, and she enters into a kind of psychotic disassociation that leads her to lie about her consensual relationship with the professor, thus causing his dismissal.

In *The Keepers of the House*, Grau measures the history of the Howland family in terms of fathers and sons, a patriarchal lineage that shows no evidence of breaking down until a decade after this novel was written. The taking of the father's name is important thematically in the novel, since the "black" children of William and Margaret use their mother's name while in their father's house. Away from the South, these now "white" children are free to use the name that the marriage license legally obtained for them—their father's. The attitudes of the 1960's are also reflected in Abigail's ready acceptance of the role of wife and mother until circumstances force her to engage in aggressive behavior.

Another of Grau's strong women is Lucy Henley in *Evidence of Love* (1977). Lucy is married to Stephen Henley, a Unitarian minister and a classical scholar, but the closeness of her relationship with him is based not on sexual love but rather on a kind of identification and trust. Stephen's father, Edward Milton Henley, is a self-indulgent sensualist who is incapable of love. Edward's carefully planned sensual experiences are matched by his son's carefully planned intellectual experiences, and Lucy, finally, is content to be freed from both men.

The volume of Grau's that is most closely concerned with women's issues as they come to be defined in the 1970's is the story collection *Nine Women*, which was published in 1985.

Sources for Further Study

Gossett, Louise Y. *Violence in Recent Southern Fiction*. Durham, N.C.: Duke University Press, 1965. Gossett traces the motif of violence (which can be found in Caldwell, Faulkner, and Wolfe) in several later Southern writers, including Robert Penn Warren, Flannery O'Connor, Truman Capote, and Shirley Ann Grau, among others. Among such writers, themes of loneliness, exploitation, and the inability to escape the past have accompanied new literary approaches. Gossett sees the violence in Grau's work (including the violence of natural setting and human isolation) as a denial of the romantic notion that "the elemental man is a free agent protected by his environment."

Pearson, Ann. "Shirley Ann Grau: Nature Is the Vision." *Critique* 8, no. 2 (1975): 47-58. Pearson sets out to discover a relationship between Grau's use of natural setting and her use of theme, but she ultimately concludes that Grau consistently "shortchang[es] herself" by failing to integrate the two fully. Stating that Grau is otherwise a "virtuoso," the author finds this same flaw in *The Black Prince*, *The Hard Blue Sky*, *The House on Coliseum Street*, *The Keepers of the House*, *The Condor Passes*, and *The Wind Shifting West*.

Rohrberger, Mary. "Shirley Ann Grau and the Short Story." In *Women Writers of the Contemporary South*, edited by Peggy Whitman Prenshaw. Jackson: University Press of Mississippi, 1984. Attributes the critical failure to recognize the complexity of Grau's work to the misapprehensions of early critics and reviewers who tended to categorize Grau as a regionalist. Mistaking the smooth surfaces of Grau's fiction for evidence of a detailed but facile narrative style, critics have ignored the underlying patterns of image and symbol which carry the richest meaning. Argues that, from the beginning, Grau's stories show both traditional and epiphanic modes of construction and an intuitive mastery of image and structure.

Ross, Jean W. "Shirley Ann Grau." In *The Dictionary of Literary Biography*, edited by Jeffrey Helterman and Richard Layman. Vol. 2. Detroit: Gale Research, 1978. Ross supplements biographical information with discussions of Grau's major works—particularly the novels. Ross traces Grau from an emerging Southern writer compared favorably to Eudora Welty and Ernest Hemingway because of her "precise, impersonal descriptions of nature" and "meticulous craftsmanship" through her development in terms of style, theme, and narrative stance toward multiple points of view.

Schlueter, Paul. *Shirley Ann Grau*. Boston: Twayne, 1981. This indexed, book-length (but somewhat short) study provides a fairly thorough introductory account of Grau's career and work up to 1980. Contending that it is appropriate to call Grau a "Southern writer" only because she demonstrates such a strong sense of place, Schlueter does not believe that Grau's work should be deemed regionalist in any narrower sense. Schlueter concludes that Grau is an important short story writer and that her strength as a novelist rests in style rather than construction; she is a "fine example of a regional novelist whose best work surpasses mere regionalism."

Mary Rohrberger

KINDRED

Author: Octavia E. Butler (1947-   )
Type of work: Novel
Type of plot: Science fiction
Time of plot: The early nineteenth century and 1976
Locale: The eastern shore of Maryland and Los Angeles, California
First published: 1979

Principal characters:

EDANA (DANA) FRANKLIN, a twenty-six-year-old black woman and a newly published author who is suddenly transported to the antebellum South

KEVIN FRANKLIN, Dana's husband, a white man who must pose as her master when he is transported to the past with Dana

RUFUS WEYLIN, Dana's great-great-great-grandfather, a white plantation owner in antebellum Maryland who summons Dana to the past when his life is endangered

TOM WEYLIN, Rufus' father, a stereotypical white slave owner

MARGARET WEYLIN, Rufus' mother

ALICE GREENWOOD, Dana's great-great-grandmother, a freed-woman whom Rufus passionately loves

SARAH, the plantation cook

CARRIE, Sarah's daughter

NIGEL, Carrie's husband and father of her children

Form and Content

In *Kindred*, a young black woman is mysteriously transported to the antebellum American South, where she must adapt to a society in which the vast majority of black people are slaves and where she too confronts enslavement. In order to survive, she must acquire basic skills that, as a modern woman, she has never learned, including cooking on an open hearth, sewing, and doctoring without the benefit of modern medicines or antisepsis. She must also determine whether she has the strength of character required for survival in a world that is rough and crude, in which black people are believed to be subhuman and are kept as chattel, and where physical and psychological punishments are daily tribulations.

On an elemental level, *Kindred* questions whether a modern person is equal to the challenge of living in a preindustrial world and whether modernization has resulted in fundamental losses of resiliency and strength. Because Dana is a black woman, there are racial dimensions to her struggle. Through Dana, Butler explores the nature of slavery and slave-master relations, the special strengths or weaknesses of character that allow slaves to survive as chattel, and the relationships between white men and black women both in the present (1976) and in the past.

The reader is first introduced to Dana in her hospital room after she has returned, injured and mutilated both psychologically and physically, from her final voyage to the past. In a series of flashbacks, Dana describes the six different trips in which she was called, against her will, to an antebellum Maryland plantation. After her first two excursions, Dana understands the purpose, if not the method, by which she returns to the past. In order to ensure her own birth, she must protect the life of her accident-prone great-great-great-grandfather Rufus, whom she first meets as she rescues him from drowning when he is a young boy. She quickly discovers that she can return to her present only when her life appears to be threatened. With each trip to the past, several years have passed for Rufus, while only a few hours or, occasionally, days have passed in Dana's time. Because Dana cannot safely return home at will, she must endure lengthy intervals, often months, with Rufus.

As they realize that she is about to be transported on her third trip, Kevin embraces Dana, thereby traveling with her to the past. His presence enables her to feign the role of his slave and grants her time to learn the techniques necessary for her own survival. She must prepare a place for herself against the expectation of later trips to Rufus' future. Although it eases her way in the past, Kevin's presence worries Dana. She fears the effects that the antebellum South will have on her tolerant and compassionate husband. In order to survive, he will have to tolerate, if not condone, life in the nineteenth century. Her fears seemingly realized, Dana's life is again threatened, and she returns home without Kevin. He remains for five years until she is newly summoned to Rufus' aid.

Analysis

Initially, because she underestimates her own courage, which has never been properly tested, Dana doubts that she has sufficient fortitude to survive in the nineteenth century. As *Kindred* unfolds, it becomes clear that she does, indeed, have abundant courage and stamina. Butler effectively utilizes a common technique in fiction whereby an individual becomes heroic by transcending his or her base humanity by drawing on hidden inner resources. Dana is tested in her second trip to the past when she is nearly raped by a white man who is part of a patrol—the forerunner to the Ku Klux Klan. Never before having experienced physical abuse, initially Dana is reluctant to act. She fails to disable him by gouging his eyes, thereby losing her only chance for escape. She learns from the experience, however, knowing that in the future she will be ready and willing to harm or kill if necessary. Ultimately, she frees herself from the past by killing Rufus with a concealed knife as he attempts to rape her.

While Dana is discovering her own strength of character, she learns of the various forms that courage assumes among the plantation slaves. Sarah, whose own children—with the exception of the mute Carrie—have all been sold, nevertheless protects and loves other children of the plantation. She refrains from attempting escape for the sake of Carrie, but she does so with dignity and with anger. Although marriages between slaves are not legally sanctioned, slaves have developed their own rituals of union. Nigel, a carpenter, uses his craft and his slightly privileged position with Rufus to work for hire in his spare time. Rufus receives a percentage of Nigel's wages, but Nigel, with his share, builds a relatively substantial house for his wife and three children. Dana learns that, despite the omnipresent fear of separation, slaves establish and maintain families.

Dana also discerns the manifestations of slave resistance. She overhears, for example, Luke telling his son Nigel how to behave. Nigel is to refrain from arguing or admitting anger; instead, he must visibly acquiesce to his master's order and then do as he pleases when no one is watching. Eventually, Luke is sold when his master tires of his attitude, but Dana successfully acts on his advice. In a similar vein, she learns from a field hand to work slowly so that the overseer believes she is working to capacity. Once he sees her working quickly, he will always expect a high output from her.

From the other slaves, Dana learns endurance. In order to protect themselves, their families, and their communities from retaliation, few attempt escape. The punishment—attack by dog pack, sometimes mutilation, beating, and often sale to the deadly sugar, rice, or cotton plantations of the deep South—is perceived as too great a risk for most. Instead, they learn to live and to adapt as slaves and in so doing evolve and maintain unique cultural traditions.

In *Kindred*, Butler explores the nature of power in the form of interracial relationships, particularly those between black women and white men, and in the broader relationships of males and females. Dana and Kevin's marriage is clearly a marriage of equals. As orphans, they shared a similar upbringing, and as young adults, both worked menial and often demeaning jobs before becoming moderately successful authors. Jointly, they weather racial prejudice when their relatives are angered by their proposed interracial marriage. They know that their relationship would not have been tolerated in the previous century, and they discover that their marriage still elicits notice even in late twentieth century Maryland, where they travel when their ordeal is completed. Yet Dana worries about the changes that might occur in Kevin if he is forced to remain for long in the antebellum South. Even after a separation of five years, however, longer even than the couple had been married in the present, their relationship is intact. Kevin does not succumb to racist or sexist influences, and in his absence from Dana he symbolically moves farther and farther north until Dana hears upon her return that he was last living in Maine. Kevin's tolerance is deeply ingrained, and Butler's message is optimistic. Although race relations continue to be strained, the improvement from the early nineteenth to the late twentieth century is obvious.

Context

As is the case in many of Butler's novels, *Kindred*'s protagonist is an able black woman. Yet Dana, like others among Butler's characters, is not designed exclusively to carry a feminist or antiracist message. Instead, *Kindred* is a story of the universal striving of human beings to transcend their base humanity in the face of adversity. Using a familiar science fiction technique in which a character develops strategies for survival in an alien environment—in this case, the slave-holding South—Butler chronicles Dana's developing inner strengths. In the process, she examines the nature of power and the dynamics of racial and sexual relations. Butler's characters are multidimensional, and no group, either racial or sexual, has a monopoly on strength, courage, or goodness. Her worlds are multiracial, sometimes multispecies, and, at least among some human individuals and in her alien worlds, tolerant of gender differences.

Through her several successful novels, including those of the "Patternist" series— *Patternmaster* (1978), *Mind of My Mind* (1977), *Survivor* (1978), *Wild Seed* (1980)— and others, such as her trilogy *Xenogenesis* (1987, 1988, 1989) and *Kindred*, her only book to be published in the general market, Butler has developed an extensive readership as well as a cult following among black women. In a genre that traditionally has been nearly exclusively populated by white male authors and white male characters, Butler is a pioneer black woman writer. Her work has received acclaim from a broad readership as well as from critics and other writers. She has won science fiction's highest awards: the Nebula, voted by other science fiction writers, in 1984 and 1985; the Hugo, voted by readers, in 1985; and the *Locus* award from *Locus* magazine.

In many ways, Butler's life parallels that of Dana. Her father died when she was a baby, and Butler was reared by her mother, who had worked as a maid from age ten, and her Louisiana-born grandmother, who had endured a life of hardship on sugarcane plantations. At age twelve, Butler began writing science fiction as a means of shielding herself from the meanness of her family's existence by creating her own stimulating intellectual world. At Pasadena City College and at the University of California at Los Angeles during 1968 and 1969, Butler studied anthropology, an interest that enriches her writing. After spending several early years working in menial jobs, chronicled in *Kindred*, Butler succeeded as an author. As a pioneer woman writer who has broadened the scope of a predominantly male genre and as a black woman among predominantly white writers, Butler is clearly a role model for women, both black and white.

Sources for Further Study

Beal, Frances M. "Black Women and the Science Fiction Genre: Interview with Octavia Butler." *The Black Scholar: Journal of Black Studies and Research* 17 (March-April, 1986): 14-18. In this interview, Butler discusses *Kindred* and the difficulty she had in publishing it. It was not considered science fiction, yet it did not fit readily into any other category. Butler discusses her intentions in writing *Kindred* and talks about her childhood experiences.

Crossley, Robert. Introduction to *Kindred*. Boston: Beacon Press, 1988. Crossley describes *Kindred* as a modern slave narrative. He provides context for *Kindred* in his history of the science fiction genre, in which very few writers are blacks or women.

Foster, Frances Smith. "Octavia Butler's Black Female Future Fiction." *Extrapola-*

tion 23 (Spring, 1982): 37-49. Although her article is not specifically about *Kindred*, Smith analyzes the strong female characters portrayed in Butler's fiction. Foster also presents her case that Butler is a major science fiction writer who has made significant contributions to the genre.

Friend, Beverley. "Time Travel as a Feminist Didactic in Works by Phyllis Eisenstein, Marlys Millhiser, and Octavia Butler." *Extrapolation* 23 (Spring, 1982): 50-55. Friend describes the use of time travel as a means by which "current freedom" and "past oppression" can be contrasted. Her analysis of Eisenstein, Millhiser, and Butler is didactic, for she uses her article to proclaim that modern women are educated to be helpless and probably could not survive without men.

Govan, Sandra Y. "Connections, Links, and Extended Networks: Patterns in Octavia Butler's Science Fiction." *Black American Literature Forum* 18 (Summer, 1984): 82-87. Although Butler denies that *Kindred* is related to her Patternist books, Govan finds in all of them a similar theme of "caring for family" and psychic bonds between individuals—in *Kindred*, Rufus and Dana.

Salvaggio, Ruth. "Octavia Butler and the Black Science-Fiction Heroine." *Black American Literature Forum* 18 (Summer, 1984): 78-81. Salvaggio discusses Butler's strong female heroes in her first four Patternist novels, illustrating the types of heroism found in four different women, each surviving in a male, racist world.

Mary E. Virginia

THE KING MUST DIE

Author: Mary Renault (Mary Challans, 1905-1983)
Type of work: Novel
Type of plot: Historical realism
Time of plot: Pre-classical Greece
Locale: Greece and Crete
First published: 1958

Principal characters:
> THESEUS, the son of Aegeus, the king of Athens
> PITTHEUS, the king of Troizen and the grandfather of Theseus
> AITHRA, the princess of Troizen and the priestess of Mother Dia (Demeter)
> PERSEPHONE, the queen of Eleusis, who takes a husband yearly who is killed in a wrestling match at the end of his year
> AEGEUS, the king of Athens and the father of Theseus
> ARIADNE, the princess of Crete and the daughter of King Minos, who falls in love with Theseus
> ASTERION THE MINOTAUROS, the prince of Crete and the half brother of Ariadne
> MINOS, the king of Crete, who is fearful of Asterion's lust for power
> POSEIDON, the god of bulls, horses, earthquakes, and the sea and Theseus' patron god

Form and Content

The King Must Die is the story of the early years of Theseus, the legendary king of Athens. Set in pre-classical Greece and told by Theseus himself, the novel chronicles Theseus' childhood, adolescence, and early manhood as the fatherless grandchild of King Pittheus of Troizen. As a young man, Theseus leaves Troizen in search of his father, King Aegeus of Athens, and in the process becomes involved in a lifelong struggle against the worship of Mother Dia, or Demeter, the goddess of fertility. The novel also describes in vivid detail Theseus' adventures as a bull-dancer in Crete and his triumphant return to Athens.

Setting is of great importance in The King Must Die, and Renault organizes her novel in sections named for the places where events transpire. Book 1, "Troizen," introduces Theseus as child in the court of King Pittheus, focusing on his difficulties with not knowing who his father is and his hope that he may be the son of the god Poseidon. He reveals to the reader his bravery, his sensitivity about his small stature, his highly sexed nature, and his desire to excel. The section culminates in his mother's revelation that Theseus is the son of the king of Athens. As a result, he decides to journey to Athens to reveal himself to Aegeus.

In Book 2, "Eleusis," Theseus accomplishes the dangerous crossing of the Isthmus, which joins the Peloponnesian Peninsula with Greece. When he arrives at Eleusis, a town outside Athens, he is forced to kill Kerkyon, the young husband of the queen of Eleusis, and to marry the queen. This marriage will ostensibly only last one year, when Theseus will be killed by the new king. Predictably, Theseus immediately begins to overturn the matriarchal rule of Eleusis and eventually succeeds in vanquishing the queen, establishing in her place a patriarchal form of government.

In Book 3, "Athens," Theseus finally arrives at his father's palace, but initially he does not tell Aegeus who he is, with the result that he is almost poisoned by his father's mistress Medea, the famous Asian sorceress who has taken up residence in Athens. When Theseus does reveal his identity, Medea flees, but not before cursing Theseus, a curse that will eventually come to pass. Theseus has little time to establish a relationship with his father, for he volunteers to go to Crete as part of the tribute that the Cretan King Minos exacts from less-powerful kings. Before Theseus leaves for Crete, Theseus and Aegeus agree that if he lives to return, an unlikely possibility, he will put a white sail on his ship to signal that he lives.

The fourth and longest book of the novel, "Crete," details Theseus' experience in Crete as a bull-dancer, where he organizes his group of Athenian young men and women into the famous bull-team The Cranes. He immediately becomes the enemy of Asterion, who is supposedly the son of King Minos and his former wife Pasiphae but was actually fathered by a bull-dancer. When Theseus becomes the star of the bull-ring, Ariadne, the daughter of Pasiphae and Minos, falls in love with Theseus and the two become lovers. She, her father King Minos, and Theseus plot against Asterion, who is attempting to take over Crete. When an earthquake partially destroys the House of the Ax, or the "labyrinth," Minos asks to be killed by Theseus. After Theseus organizes a battle and emerges as the leader of Crete, he and Ariadne quickly arrange to travel to Athens.

In the final book, "Naxos," they stop off at the island of Naxos, where they encounter another mother-worshipping culture in the process of sacrificing its year-king as part of a celebration in honor of the wine-god Dionysos. Horrified because Ariadne participates in the dismemberment of the young king, Theseus abandons her on Naxos and proceeds to Athens. After asking for a sign from Poseidon, he fails to paint his sail white, and Aegeus, thinking that his son is dead, commits suicide. The novel concludes as Theseus prepares to take up his rule as king of Athens.

Analysis

Mary Renault is famous for the uncompromising historical accuracy of her novels that are set in the ancient world. Although she is not academically trained in classical culture, her extensive reading and research enable her to construct novels that give the reader a real sense of the culture and everyday lives of the Greeks. In *The King Must Die*, she combines history, myth, legend, and archaeological evidence to provide a fascinating and believable background for the adventures of young Theseus.

Having Theseus tell his own story in first-person narration lends an immediacy and liveliness to the novel that are matched by the fast-paced chronological development of the plot. Theseus' personality pervades the novel and keeps the reader intimately involved in his plight. He is intelligent but not intellectual, sensitive, highly sexed, and sometimes misogynistic, and he unfailingly provides precise details about the people, places, and cultures he encounters. Although unabashedly proud of his Hellenic heritage, he is curious about Eleusis and Crete, which enables Renault to provide readers with the fruits of her research into these cultures. For example, the emotional center of the novel is located in the "Crete" section. Theseus' descriptions of the sophisticated, pampered lifestyle of the Cretans, their artwork, and the lives of the bull-dancers have an almost documentary-like realism.

Mary Renault's enormous knowledge of Greek mythology is also an important component of the *The King Must Die*, in which she uses several of the most important Greek myths to illuminate Theseus' exploits. Myths, for Renault, are modern misreadings of what were originally true events. Mythic characters such as Medea, Ariadne, King Minos, and Theseus himself are repeatedly revealed as all-too-human individuals whose histories have been exaggerated and distorted by later accounts. Medea, for example, is treated as an intelligent, powerful woman who effectively manipulates the fears of those around her to gain her ends. The legendary King Minos is characterized as an ill, aging, fearful ruler who wants to ensure his daughter's safety so that he can die in peace. Renault's rewriting of the mythic Minotaur as the depraved, power-hungry Asterion humanizes the myth and sets up a plausible conflict between him and Theseus.

Even more creative is Renault's refashioning of several of the most important myths that surround the character of Theseus. Always searching for rational explanations of the more fantastical elements of mythology, Renault has Theseus acknowledge that his legendary journey across the Isthmus, when he supposedly accomplished larger-than-life feats, was wildly exaggerated even during his own lifetime. His successful battles with human monsters such as Sinis Pinebender are explained as political moves in his attempt to unify Athens, and his failure to change the color of his sail to signal his return to his father is depicted as the result of his special relationship with Poseidon. Perhaps most interesting is Renault's explanation of why Theseus abandoned Ariadne. This action is justified by Ariadne's behavior during a Dionysian festival rather than being a consequence of Theseus' brutality or indifference. In fact, it is another example of Theseus' canny political agenda, for the reader realizes that his plans for a strong, invulnerable Athens cannot include a woman from a female-centered, decadent culture such as that of Crete.

Renault's knowledge of Greek culture and ideas is central to the historical integrity of her novels. *The King Must Die* serves as an excellent introduction to the various dimensions of Hellenic life. A conversation between King Pittheus and a very young Theseus contains an excellent description of the concept of *moira*, or fate, in Greek culture, just as Renault's depictions of the deaths of the young Eleusinian king and the young king of Naxos provide insight into the *pharmakos*, or scapegoat, ritual of killing certain individuals to ensure the health and safety of the group. The profoundly religious nature of Greek thinking and the relationships between gods and humans are explored in depth, particularly the notion that human beings cannot ever hope to rival the gods in any area of life. Mary Renault's love and respect for the Greeks make this novel a testimonial to Greek culture.

Context

Mary Renault did not consider herself a feminist and did not wish to be discussed as a "woman writer." Her novels, including *The King Must Die*, almost always focus on male protagonists and, as Carolyn Heilbrun has observed, fail to present powerful, independent women; instead, they depict female characters as vulnerable and weak. Gender issues do, however, appear in her fiction, and the tension between male and female power is an essential structuring principle of both *The King Must Die* and its sequel, *The Bull from the Sea*.

In *The King Must Die*, the powerful female principle represented by Mother Dia is resisted by Theseus, who wishes to transform earlier, earth-centered matriarchal structures into the male-dominated, sky-father worshipping culture of the Greeks. Theseus is frightened by the tremendous power of Mother Dia, a power that is based on her fecundity and regenerative potency, but he is always confident that masculine thinking, particularly in its political aspects, can overthrow the female principle. The depiction of women and female power in this novel is almost always unreservedly negative. Persephone, the queen of Eleusis, and Medea are presented as vicious, power-hungry women, and Ariadne is finally revealed to be capable of bloodthirsty, despicable action. Masculinity is equated with the Apollonian virtues of reason, light, order, and creativity, and it is no accident that Theseus flees to Apollo's birthplace, the island of Delos, after abandoning Ariadne. The female principle is the enemy of true culture and civilization in this novel.

It is obvious that Mary Renault identified and concurred with Theseus' belief in the superiority of masculine consciousness. An avid admirer of Apollo who named her own home "Delos," she is quoted in David Sweetman's biography of her as stating that Theseus' fight against the female principle is "primitive man struggling to defend his new-found ego against the surrounding jungle of the unconscious . . ." In spite of Renault's approval of Theseus' behavior and orientation, however, *The King Must Die* inevitably forces the reader to speculate on the nature of female power.

Sources for Further Study

Burns, Landon D., Jr. "Men Are Only Men: The Novels of Mary Renault." *Critique* 6, no. 3 (Winter, 1963): 102-121. Burns analyzes *The King Must Die* and *The Bull from the Sea* as "legendary romance" rather than historical fiction and believes that the most important aspect of both novels is Theseus' progression toward his "tragic maturity."

Dick, Bernard F. *The Hellenism of Mary Renault*. Carbondale: Southern Illinois University Press, 1972. Although Renault's earlier novels set in contemporary England are discussed briefly, this book focuses on the fiction that takes place in the ancient world. Chapter 3, "To Be a King: The Theseus Novels," looks at the sources of *The King Must Die* and *The Bull from the Sea* and analyzes both novels.

Heilbrun, Carolyn. "Women Writers and Female Characters: The Failure of Imagination." In *Reinventing Womanhood*. New York: W. W. Norton, 1979. Heilbrun believes Renault to be representative of women writers who are unable to create characters that reflect their own autonomy and freedom and instead affirm patriarchal structures. Renault is discussed within the context of other women writers, including Willa Cather, Iris Murdoch, and Penelope Mortimer.

Sweetman, David. *Mary Renault: A Biography*. New York: Harcourt Brace, 1993. Sweetman looks at every aspect of Renault's life and integrates discussions of her novels with the personal events of her life. This work, the only biography of Renault available, does an excellent job of introducing her to the reader.

Wolfe, Peter. *Mary Renault*. New York: Twayne, 1969. This is the only full-length critical book on Renault that analyzes all of her work. Chapter 5, "The Mainland Savage," contains an extended analysis of *The King Must Die* and *The Bull from the Sea*. This study includes a chronology and bibliography, including secondary sources.

Angela Hague

THE KINGFISHER

Author: Amy Clampitt (1920-1994)
Type of work: Poetry
First published: 1983

Form and Content

The first nine poems of *The Kingfisher* present the coastal panorama of Maine. In these short poems, Clampitt established four contexts: first, the circular flow from private to public life, in which privileged moments give way to confusion; second, the topographical movement from waterfront toward the heartland, representing anguish and guilt, with a return to birth and creativity, symbolizing patterns in a woman's life; third, the geographical displacement westward from European civilization (primarily Italy and Greece), through New York City (the media capital) and the Potomac/Pentagon (military headquarters), toward California (Hollywood and the Asian influx)—a journey that notes that midwestern values, like the poet's mother, are "curtained in Intensive Care" ("A Procession at Candlemas"); fourth, the vertical flow up and down language through fog over rocks toward "a texture . . . along the horizon" ("Gradual Clearing").

In this spiritual odyssey from composure to Armageddon, Clampitt presents numerous opportunities for divergence or an attempt at new directions; hence, part 5 of *The Kingfisher* is entitled "Watersheds." Part 4, with three short poems ("Triptych"), represents a religious interlude. The poet ponders human fate and concludes that violence, apathy, and injustice are the offspring of evolution. Enlightenment is confirmed, but only through loss of innocence. Despite the elegiac mood of this section, the poet is able to transcend human limitation in order to return to God, the "already half-imaginary with distance/ toward the improbable" ("The Reservoirs of Mount Helicon").

The Kingfisher takes its title and epigraph from a poem by Gerard Manley Hopkins in which the tiny bird, associated through its blazing color with the Pentecostal Dove, announces the themes of redemption and the gift of tongues. Clampitt places the title poem (twenty-third out of fifty) in part 2, "Airborne, Earthbound," at a pivotal moment when idealism is challenged by the disarray of life, as if the fiery plumage of the kingfisher represents the odd, brief moment associated with the calm of halcyon days. As memory, sorrow, grief, and remorse are interrogated, Clampitt makes felicitous use of the literary allusions established by T. S. Eliot, in whose "Burnt Norton," part 4, "the kingfisher's wing/ Has answered light to light," and by Hopkins, in whom she recognized the power and fertility in order and light. Indeed, many of the poems are imbued with the four natural elements of earth, air, fire, and water, but light alone is endowed with sacramental grace, the by-product of fire and water—"the absolving smile of rainbows" ("Or Consider Prometheus").

Clampitt's organization follows a pattern through which the fleeting habitats of a vagabond existence produce a kaleidoscope of sounds and images. Three long poems draw the reader toward the cyclical nature of reality; death is followed by redemption, and withdrawal edges toward commitment. The shorter poems, clustered around people and events situated in public and private domains, are rich in anecdote and local color; they shine with an effervescence distilled through precise observation. "Beach Glass" epitomizes these traits. The ocean is compared to the human mind that produces human artifacts, what Clampitt refers to in "A Cadenza" as "an apotheosis of merchandise." The last poem of *The Kingfisher*, "The Burning Child," is consistent with Clampitt's purpose because it offers a choice between disaster and "the nurture whose embrace is drowning." This total immersion, the return to the womb of ocean, brings the reader back into the poet's abode in such a way that the concrete poetry of the Great Plains is linked with the abstract configurations of Clampitt's sensitive mind, producing an expressionist fantasy of aesthetic illusion.

Analysis

The most striking characteristic of these poems is the vigorous use of extension, by means of which metaphors and concepts are given full carrying power and amplitude. For example, the sound of buoys and bells appears as a leitmotif representing frozen moments in time. Ubiquitous plants and birds symbolize raw elements of human emotion. Women's work is cataloged, and diligence and labor are given epic stature. Insects and flowers are magnified. Landscapes are projected into memory. The poet's personal shatterings and dilemmas are universalized into archetypes of bewilderment. The poetry is loaded with associations and suggestions, as in "Antiquity unshrouds on wimpling canvas,/ adjunct of schoolhouse make-believe" ("Imago"). "Wimpling canvas" is typical of Clampitt's inventiveness, since the playful, clever "wimpling" conjures an image of heavily draped art that allows ancient ("dead") history to unfold in the mind of an elementary school student taught by nuns wearing "wimpled" habits.

Other extrapolations include westward trekking—associated with the forced migrations of American Indians. Water is identified with music, as in "tambourines of rain" ("The Edge of the Hurricane"). In part 2, there are numerous ghostly presences. Memory is connected to physical movement—"the ancestral flyway" ("A Procession at Candlemas"). Destruction is related to "the unseen filament . . . that runs/ through all our chronicles" ("The Dahlia Gardens"). Such density implies not only linguistic control but also fairly rigid structures. As a result, the longest poems are formally proportioned: "A Procession at Candlemas" is written in triplets; "Rain at Bellagio" is composed of twelve stanzas neatly permeated with reciprocal sounds. "The Dahlia Gardens" is arranged in a similar fashion, with alliteration acting as a controlling device. In lines 13 to 22, fourteen words beginning with the letter *c* establish an eerie sequence of associations: "clash," "counterpart," "concrete," "cushioned," "chariots," "calculus," "carrying," "clocks," "chronicles," "calibrations," "clerks," "chain," "concentric," and "corridors." This poem is replete with an equal number of alliterative *f*'s, *d*'s, and *w*'s. In addition, Clampitt's use of enjambments, at least by conventional standards, provocative.

About one-third of the poems in *The Kingfisher* are geometrically organized with clearly established forms. For example, "Or Consider Prometheus" is written in ten quatrains; iambic pentameter, often extended into alexandrines, is the dominant feature. Poems with stanzas of equal measure appear often, with the number of lines varying from three ("Berceuse") to twelve ("Times Square Water Music"). "The Cormorant in Its Element" is a variation on a sonnet.

The Kingfisher pulls into focus Clampitt's attempt to identify contrasts and contradictions: everyday life and intellectual finesse, home life and travel, commitment and rejection, past and present, myth and history. The narrative voice reflects these tensions as the poetry swings from personal appeal to ironic self-detachment. In the same way, the tone shifts from the elegiac and defiant to the capricious and wistful; the poet rarely instructs, yet confidence gained from experience produces an edifying effect. Clampitt offers subtle clues to underscore her intentions: Males have for too long possessed an unfair social advantage, and consequently they have disrupted the female conscience by attempting to define women's destiny. Clampitt's signature poem, "Rain at Bellagio," identified the process by which continuous observation fuses "the fragments of experience into . . . a single scheme." By this method, cadences rise and fall in an unpredictable arch of conjurations.

Context

The Kingfisher, like Clampitt's other books of poetry, is laced with interpolated voices of poets who have influenced her: Stéphane Mallarmé, W. H. Auden, William Butler Yeats, Wallace Stevens, Hart Crane, Walt Whitman, and A. A. Milne. Her poems refer indirectly to the struggle to achieve recognition. This somewhat reluctant self-exposure brings her close to Emily Dickinson and to John Keats, about whom she wrote an endearing sequence of poems, *A Homage to John Keats* (1984). Additional publications since the appearance of *The Kingfisher*—*What the Light Was Like* (1985), *Archaic Figure* (1987), and *Westward* (1990)—have advanced the ideas crystallized in this collection. Clampitt reinforces her belief in the manifold capacities of women, who, like Medusa figures, can appear erratic, threatening, beautiful, and mournful. In her poetry, she strives for a conclusive, deep act that asserts a woman's dream of being.

This intense focus has brought Clampitt into the forefront of American poetry. She is often associated, stylistically, with poets of a younger generation, such as Gjertrud Schnackenberg and Louise Erdrich, rather than with the women writers who contributed to her formation: Marianne Moore, Louise Bogan, Elizabeth Bowen, Elizabeth Bishop, May Sarton, and Denise Levertov. The numerous awards that she has received (Guggenheim Fellowship, 1982; Academy of American Poets, 1984; American Academy and Institute of Arts and Letters, 1984; honorary doctorate, Grinnell College, 1984; writer-in-residence, College of William and Mary, 1984-1985; visiting professor, Amherst College, 1986-1987; Hurst Professor, Washington University, 1987-1988; Phi Beta Kappa Poet of the Year, 1987) bear witness to the insistent, unsentimental, plucky intelligence that affirms the exalted state of female consciousness.

Clampitt's poetry sketches the contours of a modernist perspective in which the sources of "a deaf anxiety" ("Tepoztlán"), though partially revealed, generate a response to bondage; the protest against "a terrain as barren/ as the dust of bones" ("The Quarry") is identified with "tantrums of spring and summer" ("The Woodlot"). Such autonomy in submission lends an energizing force to Clampitt's vision. Certain poems illustrate the intricacy of women's work ("Marine Surface, Low Overcast"), while others examine the legacy of the past. "Imago," in particular, traces the sexual evolution of the female who, liberated from the abyss of history, reaches a state of fulfillment akin to Margaret Fuller's ideal of being simultaneously all intellect and all feeling. To express this duality, Clampitt chooses the image of a mermaid who is born out of antiquity and who partakes of a double life—a sea creature thriving on land, diving spontaneously into the picturesque.

Sources for Further Study

Clampitt, Amy. "An Interview with Amy Clampitt." Interview by Jan Huesgen and Robert W. Lewis. *North Dakota Quarterly* 58, no. 1 (1990): 119-128. A valuable addition to scholarship on Clampitt, this interview summarizes her life-long attachments: regional traditions, ancient Greece, ocean vistas, Italian Renaissance paintings, and travel.

Howard, Richard. "The Hazardous Definition of Structures." *Parnassus: Poetry in Review* 11, no. 1 (Spring/Summer, 1983): 271-275. This study connects Clampitt to *The New Yorker* poetry establishment and illuminates the craft that transforms "grammar into glamour." The title of Howard's essay refers to Clampitt's description of the poetic process in "Beach Glass."

McClatchy, J. D. Review of *The Kingfisher*. *Poetry* 143 (December, 1983): 165-167. An insightful analysis of Clampitt's verbal invention, moods, and preoccupations by a critic who has assiduously followed her career and enthusiastically praised her poetry.

Olson, Paul A. "The Marryings of All Likeness." *Prairie Schooner* 57 (Spring, 1983): 99-102. The title of this essay refers to Clampitt's description of the search for meaning and coherence in patterns of disorder. Olson views Clampitt's work as a fusion of medieval religion and Great Plains poetry, a passage from guilt to purification.

Vendler, Helen. "On the Thread of Language." *The New York Review of Books* 30 (March 3, 1983): 19-22. In this deeply reflective essay, Vendler examines Clampitt's meditative scope. Working from the idea of a "thread" of language implanted in "The Reservoirs of Mount Helicon," Vendler underlines the aesthetic quest in which Clampitt spans "the gulfs of the mind and world."

Robert J. Frail

THE KITCHEN GOD'S WIFE

Author: Amy Tan (1952-   )
Type of work: Novel
Type of plot: Social realism
Time of plot: 1921-1990
Locale: China and San Francisco, California
First published: 1991

Principal characters:
    WEILI "WINNIE" JIANG, the protagonist and chief narrator
    JIMMY LOUIE, Winnie's second husband, an American-born
        Chinese minister
    WEN FU, Winnie's first husband, a Chinese air force pilot who is
        a cruel husband and father, a womanizer, and a gambler
    PEARL, Winnie's American daughter, who has been diagnosed
        with multiple sclerosis
    HELEN (HULAN), Winnie's partner in a florist shop in San
        Francisco
    GRAND AUNTIE DU, Helen's aunt
    PEANUT, Winnie's cousin

Form and Content

The Kitchen God's Wife focuses on Weili "Winnie" Jiang's attempt to narrate her life in China in a culture that denigrates females to her forty-year-old American-born daughter Pearl so that her daughter will understand and appreciate how her mother's experiences have forged her identity. For example, the Chinese culture taught Winnie that a married woman is expected to defer to her husband's opinions and preferences even to the point of submitting to depraved sexual abuse. Chinese law even supported her husband's unilateral right to control his wife's actions and to retain custody of his son, to the point of imprisoning Winnie because she ran away from her brutal husband and sent her son north, where he died in an epidemic. It is in the context of her life as a woman without rights that Winnie is trying to defend her decisions to a daughter born in a home that fostered her self-confidence and in a country that guarantees her civil rights.

The book opens and concludes in contemporary San Francisco. Winnie's supposed sister-in-law, Auntie Helen, insisting she is dying of a brain tumor, informs the mother and the daughter that she will reveal the secrets of each one to the other if they do not disclose them before the Chinese New Year. Within the exigencies of this framework, Winnie Louie proceeds to narrate her life story in China, beginning when she is a six-year-old child abandoned by her mother and culminating in her escape in 1947 when she is thirty. On the eve of her departure to the United States, Winnie is raped by her husband, Wen Fu, after she tricks him into signing divorce papers. Nine months later her daughter Pearl is born. Winnie's secret seems to be that Pearl is the child of this sadistic man, although she disclaims this paternity, telling her shocked daughter that she would not let that bad man be her daughter's father. Pearl is the daughter of the kind, spiritual Jimmy Louie, who had loved her mother during a seven-year absence and helped her to escape.

The shift of voice from that of a strong, seventy-five-year-old immigrant woman holding on to her superstitions depicted in the opening chapters to that of the sensitive, bewildered, naïve voice of the young wife and mother of the central narrative impresses the reader as well as the daughter. Pregnant Winnie's ride in the back of a truck over fog-filled highways up a mountain, her wrenching search for a son missing during a Japanese air raid, her powerless witnessing of her small daughter's physical abuse and death at the hands of her brutal father—all these experiences make her "the weak but strong" woman whom Jimmy Louie and the reader learn to love.

Hearing her mother's painful story enables Pearl to reveal her secret—she has been diagnosed with multiple sclerosis. Her mother's outpouring of love breaks down the "protective shell" that Pearl had built around her fears, a shell that kept her not only from confiding in her mother but also from discussing her feelings with her husband. By the conclusion of the novel, Pearl recognizes that the "lies" that she believed pervaded her relationship with her mother could also be interpreted as a form of loyalty of an extraordinary caliber, like that of the Kitchen God's wife for her unfaithful husband.

Analysis

Like Pearl in *The Kitchen God's Wife*, author Amy Tan spent years in cultural conflict with her mother. She decided to learn more about China by visiting there with her mother Daisy in 1987, and she met the two half sisters whom her mother was forced to leave behind when she chose to divorce her husband and leave China. Inspired by the insights she experienced listening to her mother's history, Tan expressed some of them in the vignettes that constitute *The Joy Luck Club* and then decided to write one unified story, *The Kitchen God's Wife*.

In *The Kitchen God's Wife*, there is a striking contrast between the educated, sophisticated but harassed voice of daughter Pearl in the opening and concluding chapters of the novel and the strident voice of her mother. Pearl's annoyed, long-suffering tone dominates from the opening sentence, where she says, "Whenever my mother talks to me, she begins the conversation as if we were already in the middle of an argument." The stress of being split between loyalty to her Chinese mother and loyalty to her American husband is evident in her efforts to find compromises. What is amazing is that the reader who is initially sympathetic to Pearl's forebearing, educated tone succumbs so quickly to the appeal of Winnie's linguistically halting narrative.

When the mother's voice begins her narrative, her domineering tone shifts to that of a wounded, lonely, naïve person. It contains a sense of wonder as Winnie recalls her ongoing efforts to please her self-centered husband and later becomes poignant when Winnie realizes that one of the soldiers, Gan, actually believes that she is worth his attention and admiration. Frequently, Winnie returns to the fatalistic tone and view of life that she identifies with females—specifically, her mother and herself—and with Chinese culture. Most pervasive in the novel, however, is the apologetic tone: Winnie finds it difficult to explain what she identifies as her failures within the context of her culture as she speaks to a daughter who has no experience of humiliation as a "sex machine." In the conclusion, Pearl terminates her tight control over her voice by collapsing in tears in her mother's arms.

In *The Kitchen God's Wife*, the barrier between the American-born daughter Pearl and her mother Winnie's Chinese culture is symbolized by the altar to the Kitchen God, which Pearl inherits from her recently deceased Grand Auntie Du. Although she can barely restrain her impatience with this gift, Pearl admits that she feels guilt when she tries to ignore the gods of her Chinese culture. This guilt seems to connect what she rationally identifies as superstition with her denial of her Chinese ancestry.

As is implied by the title of the novel, Winnie believes that her life embodies the legend of the Kitchen God's wife, which she narrates to her daughter. This "valiant woman" whose hard work provided her husband's prosperity is thrown out of her home so that her husband can put a younger woman in her place. After the husband loses all of his possessions, he receives charity at the hands of his former wife. Ironically, the Jade Emperor not only forgives the husband's selfishness but also makes him the Kitchen God, the arbiter of each year's good and bad luck. The legend of the Kitchen God's wife provides a connection with China's cultural past and a context for understanding Winnie Louie's abused, unappreciated life. Eventually, it affords a bridge for change, for Winnie goes to the Shop of the Gods to find a more appropriate model for her daughter than the Kitchen God or his wife.

This new version of the Kitchen God's wife is a goddess—"Lady Sorrowfree"— who will offer Pearl the support that she believes she has been missing. Winnie says to her daughter, "See how nicely she sits in her chair, so comfortable-looking in her manner [unlike the excitable, aggressive Winnie]. . . . I heard she [like Winnie] once had many hardships in her life. . . . You should tell her everything."

Tan's use of mythology expresses both the cultural differences between mother and daughter and the final accommodation between them. Instead of trying, like her mother, to placate a capricious male god who does not deserve his position of respect, Pearl is given a female goddess who offers a refuge of compassion and understanding. The use of mythology closes the gap in communications between the mother and daughter; it also expresses the survival of Winnie's human spirit in spite of adverse cultural conditioning.

Context

Like Tan's previous novel, *The Joy Luck Club*, *The Kitchen God's Wife* presents the life of a woman in China as one without legal rights or human dignity. Whether poor, like Winnie's mother, or the daughter of a rich man, like Winnie, women are treated as little more than possessions. Without legal protection and opportunities for financial independence, a life of starvation and destitution was the fate of a woman in China prior to the communist takeover.

In *The Kitchen God's Wife*, the narratives of several characters depict harrowing choices. Winnie's mother, a "replacement" of a second wife, a doubly ignominious situation in the polygamous household of a rich merchant, preferred to abandon her child and join a revolutionary group. Similarly, Winnie's cousin Peanut, married by her parents to a hermaphrodite, prefers to jeopardize her life by joining the communist underground. The most tragic story is that of Little Yu, who preferred suicide to being the wife of a wealthy, mentally deficient man. Finally, Winnie Louie, the protagonist, announces at her trial for being a disobedient wife that she prefers sleeping on a concrete floor in a prison cell to returning to a husband who enjoyed humiliating her. Throughout these narratives, Tan is dramatizing the need to change religious, social, political, and economic structures that strip women of the right to participate in the decisions that govern their lives.

One of the main concerns of the women's movement has been to discover whether women can communicate their needs in male-dominated literary forms or whether they need alternate ones. Out of such studies as *Women's Ways of Knowing* (1986), by Mary Field Belenky et al., and *Revising the Word and the World* (1993), edited by Vèvè A. Clark et al., psychologists and feminist literary critics have identified the narrative as the form females prefer for learning and expression because it presents the voice and the issues important to women. The effective use of narrative in *The Kitchen God's Wife* to express the voice and the feelings of Winnie Louie and her daughter Pearl and to present issues significant to women attests the validity of the research done in this field.

Sources for Further Study

Burkhardt, V. R. *Chinese Creeds and Customs*. 3 vols. Hong Kong: South China Morning Post, 1953-1958. Illustration of the Kitchen God and description of the male ritual connected with him (no females may participate) are included in "The Twelfth Month." The account describes both the celebration of the Chinese New Year and the gifts given to gain the good will of this capricious but powerful god.

Dew, Robb Forman. Review of *The Kitchen God's Wife*. *New York Times Book Review* 96 (June 16, 1991): 9. This review commends the epic proportions and domestic detail of this compelling but bitterly humorous story.

Iyer, Pico. Review of *The Kitchen God's Wife*. *Time* 137 (June 3, 1991): 57. Iyer sees the book's main theme as forgiveness: To understand the miseries of Winnie Louie makes it difficult to judge her.

Shapiro, Laura. "From China, with Love." *Newsweek* 117 (June 24, 1991): 63-64. This review of *The Kitchen God's Wife* applauds Tan as a storyteller who touches the heart of the reader but criticizes her characterization and thematic development as superficial.

Tan, Amy. "Lost Lives of Women." *Life* 14 (April, 1991): 90-91. Using a group photograph, which she calls "a picture of secrets and tragedies," Tan narrates a microscopic version of the genesis of her novels.

Yglesias, Helen. "The Second Time Around." *Women's Review of Books* 8 (September, 1991): 1, 3. The universal appeal of *The Kitchen God's Wife* lies in the immigrant's experience: the contrast between the rigid class structures and male domination experienced by the female in China and the culture shock of the nonspeaking Chinese wife and mother in America.

Agnes A. Shields

KRISTIN LAVRANSDATTER

Author: Sigrid Undset (1882-1949)
Type of work: Novels
Type of plot: Romance
Time of plot: 1306-1349
Locale: Jörundgaard and Husaby, Norway
First published: 1920-1922 (English translation, 1923-1927); *Kransen* (1920; *The Bridal Wreath*, 1923), *Husfrue* (1921; *The Mistress of Husaby*, 1925), *Korset* (1922; *The Cross*, 1927)

Principal characters:

KRISTIN LAVRANSDATTER, the daughter of landowner Lavrans Björgulfson and Ragnfrid, the wife of Erlend Nikulaussön, and the mistress of Husaby

LAVRANS BJÖRGULFSON, Kristin's father and an important influence on her

BROTHER EDVIN, a Franciscan monk who is Kristin's spiritual guide

ERLEND NIKULAUSSÖN, Kristin's husband, a knight

SIMON ANDRESSÖN, Kristin's first fiancé, with whom she breaks her engagement

LADY AASHILD, Erlend's kinswoman, who is reputed to be a witch

ULF HALDORSSÖN, Erlend's henchman at Husaby, who is accused of adultery with Kristin

NAAKKVE and BJÖRGULF ERLENDSSÖN, Kristin and Erlend's sons, who leave the homestead to become monks

GAUTE ERLENDSSÖN, Kristin and Erlend's third son, the heir to Jörundgaard

Form and Content

In the trilogy *Kristin Lavransdatter*, which is set in fourteenth century Norway, Sigrid Undset tells the story of Kristin Lavransdatter, from her childhood to her death by plague in 1349, while reproducing the historical atmosphere of that period. One of the novel's main events, the conspiracy to usurp King Magnus VII (King of Norway, 1319-1343) by a group of his courtiers, is historically authentic. Although it operates within a specific historical-cultural framework, *Kristin Lavransdatter* at no time demands the reader to be a historian. Undset's medieval characters are clearly defined personalities, and her aim is to explore certain permanent conditions of the human heart, such as love, loyalty, and grief, in relation to the social, political, and religious circumstances in which they occur. Kristin Lavransdatter is a product of her culture and her particular moment in history, but she is also a strong-willed woman who rises above these conditions to create her own destiny. Her character embodies the anxieties of any woman who dares to reject the familiar, comfortable norms of her society for the sake of the unknown.

Kristin's first act of self-assertion is to defer her marriage to Simon Andressön, the man her father had picked for her, and eventually to break that betrothal to marry Erlend Nikulaussön. In her youth, Kristin submits to the passions of her heart. Kristin's split loyalties are represented in the figure of the elf-maiden, a wild pagan spirit whose apparition beckons her in the woods while she is still a child, and in the figure of the crucified Christ, whose face seems to her not "mild and sorrowful" but "upturned and harsh." Kristin's boldness is evident in the manner in which she allows herself to be courted by Erlend. While staying in a nunnery in Oslo, she steals away to meet him in the woods and houses of infamy. She conceives Erlend's child in secret and forces Simon to break off their engagement.

Undset does not exaggerate Kristin's courage. Kristin's courtship with Erlend breaks her spirit: She is fearful of her actions, she is guilty of having tainted her own and her father's reputation, and she fears for her unborn child because it was conceived in secret. Part 2, *The Mistress of Husaby*, is almost entirely concerned with Kristin's attempts to restore her own good name as the lawful wife of Erlend Nikulaussön and as the mistress of his manor, Husaby. An efficient housewife, devoted mother, affectionate daughter, and kindly neighbor, Kristin rebuilds her own sense of self-worth. Her relationship with Erlend is a tempestuous one. Kristin is angered by Erlend's inattention to husbandry, and Erlend is angered by her complaining, proud nature: Both are tormented by the shady history of their courtship.

Ramborg, Kristin's sister and a conventional bride and wife, is a marked contrast to her sister. *The Cross*, part 3, aims at psychological realism in exploring the internal and external meanings and values of kinship. In the confrontations between Simon and Erlend in which Simon reveals his love for Kristin, in the meeting between Simon and Kristin in which Simon refrains from telling her that he loves her, and in the confrontation between Ramborg and Kristin after Simon's death, when Ramborg reveals Simon's love for Kristin, the characters simultaneously express their innermost feelings and reinforce the necessary kinship roles, dues, and sacrifices.

Kristin Lavransdatter ends with the onset of the Black Death in Norway in 1349. Kristin passes from the domestic stage of her life to the monastic one in the section called *The Cross*; she joins the Rein Cloister at Trondheim, and her crowning act of self-assertion is to help the victims of the plague. Her husband and four of her children are dead; Kristin no longer prays to God for gifts for herself. *Kristin Lavransdatter* ends with Kristin's submission of her will to Christ and her painful yet peaceful death as a thin layer of new snow covers the pestilence-stricken land.

Analysis

In *Kristin Lavransdatter*, the life of a woman is divided into the stages of childhood, marriage, motherhood, and religion. In each stage, the corresponding identity of a woman is primarily defined in terms of her relationship with others: daughter to parents, wife to husband, mother to children, and votary to God. Although such a schematization of life-stages might sound rigid, in practice, it seems to contain a logic of its own; Undset seems to be aware of the biological, social, and religious impulses that constitute human life. In the first book, *The Bridal Wreath*, young Kristin, burdened with guilt over her younger sister's crippled existence, barters to God her youth for a life in the cloister, in exchange for her sister's well-being. It is instructive that Undset moves Kristin from that path and places her into a passionate romance that is at once sweet and bitter. Kristin goes through a stormy marriage with a vain, fickle, irresponsible man who turns out to be a good lover and an acclaimed knight but a negligent husband and father. It is precisely that experience, however, that molds the strong and mature personality of the adult Kristin; Undset seems to say that it is only through suffering that one can know one's true limits, one's special strengths and resources.

Undset ranks the occupation of motherhood very highly in this scheme of a woman's life. Kristin bears eight children to Erlend, and the births and the mothering process are described in considerable detail. Kristin's tenderest introspections favor her children; she is at once elated, fearful, proud, and possessive about her sons. The experiences of pregnancy and motherhood are described in a language that swells with images of fertility and sweet happiness; Kristin feels shriveled and barren when she is not carrying Erlend's child. Yet this glow is balanced with harsh outbursts about the burdens of fertility to women—the realities that sensual love involves the risk of conception and that women are the primary care-givers for their children.

Suffering is a key emotion in Undset's characters' coming to grips with their true natures, and in this respect *Kristin Lavransdatter* may be termed a Christian romance. The suspense-filled, love-hate relationship between Erlend and Kristin is filled with suffering, as are the unexpressed emotions between Lavrans and his wife Ragnfrid, and so it is with Simon, who cannot speak of his love for Kristin anymore, because of their kinship bond. This affliction originates with each character's personal relationship with and interpretation of God's nature and power; at a crucial moment when Brother Edvin advises Kristin to stay away from Erlend and from ways of sensual temptations, she tells him, "When I was a girl at home 'twas past my understanding how aught could win such power over the souls of men that they could forget the fear of sin; but so much have I learned now: if the wrongs men do through lust and anger cannot be atoned for, then must heaven be an empty place."

Such reassuring thoughts notwithstanding, Kristin and the other characters live in perpetual fear of being "discovered" by God; the psychological introspection of most characters is transformed into self-critiques of real, imagined, and potential transgressions that cannot be hidden from the eyes of God. One exception is the character of Erlend Nikulaussön. Erlend becomes aware of his transgressions against fellow human beings and God only when Kristin reminds him of them; he is portrayed as the pagan with the heart of gold, ineffectual in practical life but enchanting to the opposite sex. He dies with a smile on his lips because he has been able to forgive Kristin for her share in their troubled life, while Kristin feels ashamed to stand before God, because she has been self-righteous and proud.

Erlend and Kristin's marriage, marital disharmony, and eventual separation offer a unique perspective on the dynamics of medieval Norwegian society. The husband and wife seem to inhabit two different elements: Kristin of Jörundgaard inhabits the earth and fields, while Erlend, the knight and courtier, is most comfortable with the sea or in remote mountains. They could very well belong to two different cultures. The lush descriptions of geography and landscape in this extraordinarily lengthy novel highlight the conflicting models of life that Kristin and Erlend harbor in their minds.

Kristin is a unique female hero in her sense of her difference from others and her boldness in speaking and acting her mind, but in fourteenth century Norway her spheres of action are limited to the home and the church. What makes her character compelling and three dimensional is the manner in which Undset binds Kristin's personality intensely with both the pagan and Christian landscapes: From wandering to the woods to see the elf-maid, to watching their church burn to the ground, to gathering flowers with her sons, Kristin projects herself into nature so wholeheartedly that she seems to develop a complex grandeur.

Context

Sigrid Undset's *Kristin Lavransdatter* is a medieval Christian romance with a moralistic residue to it; life is conditioned by the strife between the flesh and the spirit, and the necessary values associated with these two apparently conflicting paths. Although she followed the school of realism practiced by Henrik Ibsen (1828-1906) and August Strindberg (1849-1912), Sigrid Undset achieved fame for her realistic treatment of medieval Norwegian themes. It was primarily for her novels about life in medieval Norway that she was awarded the Nobel Prize in Literature in 1928.

Undset was well read in medieval archaeology and history, but her medieval novels are not period pieces disconnected from the rest of history. She is acutely aware of the continuity of history, and her artistic vision seems to focus on what is common to humanity across centuries. Her medieval novels, moreover, are testaments to her passionate faith in the Catholic church as the only true church of Christ. The Middle Ages, in which Christianity and non-Christian practices existed together, provided her with the perfect religious, philosophical, and social frameworks for novels that dealt with the split desires of the human mind: desire for sensual union versus desire for union with God.

Almost all Undset's works challenge the stereotype of woman as the passive erotic object; her women are passionate and eager to experience erotic love and are "erotic-subjects" themselves. Although her final thoughts on the subject seem to emphasize the frailty of fleshly love, her novels serve as interesting commentaries on the topic of the sexuality of women.

Undset also introduced the modern professional woman into Norwegian literature. In her contemporary novel *Jenny* (1911), a young, liberated woman painter with high moral standards falls in love with an older man who does not love her as purely and freely as she loves him. After a series of disastrous turns of events, Jenny takes her own life. This novel was much discussed in the feminist circles in Norway in 1911 because of its frank treatment of Jenny's erotic life and because Jenny seems to devalue her life as an artist in her pursuit of men and romantic love.

Sigrid Undset was neither a militant feminist nor an antifeminist. She believed that women should be allowed to practice any art or profession or occupy themselves in any manner of work without losing the right to love and have a family. Undset's novels are significant because they explore in great imaginative detail the dynamics of the man-woman relationship in all its permutations and combinations. In particular, the role of the woman as a wife and a mother and the importance of family are key themes in *Kristin Lavransdatter* and in many of Undset's later works.

Sources for Further Study

Allen, Walter Gore. *Renaissance in the North*. London: Sheed & Ward, 1946. This study contains an informative essay by the author on Sigrid Undset's conversion to Catholicism at the age of forty-two, discussing its influence on both her contemporary-based and medieval-based works.

Bayerschmidt, Carl F. *Sigrid Undset*. New York: Twayne, 1970. This book-length study of Undset argues that it was the empirical side of Christianity that Undset emphasized rather than the dogmatic. A comprehensive biography.

Gustafson, Alrik. "Christian Ethics in a Pagan World: Sigrid Undset." In *Six Scandinavian Novelists*. Minneapolis: University of Minnesota Press, 1966. An interesting and useful reading of Undset's medieval novels as documents of her own spiritual growth. Includes a very interesting discussion of the "sombre" mood of *Kristin Lavransdatter* as characteristic of an acute religious sensibility.

Winsnes, A. H. *Sigrid Undset: A Study in Christian Realism*. Translated by P. G. Foote. New York: Sheed & Ward, 1953. This book-length study of Undset as a writer in the realist tradition interprets, among other things, Undset's tendency to indulge in lengthy descriptions and analyses of mental states.

Gayatri Devi

LAGUNA WOMAN

Author: Leslie Marmon Silko (1948-   )
Type of work: Poetry
First published: 1974

Form and Content

Leslie Marmon Silko is of mixed ancestry—American Indian, Mexican, and white—but she grew up in Laguna Pueblo in New Mexico, and the title of *Laguna Woman*, her first book, announces not only her sense of her American Indian identity but also the persona and the cultural perspective of the voice that is heard throughout this collection of eighteen short poems. The poems can be appreciated for their unpretentious use of ordinary language to achieve striking and memorable scenic effects; for the conciseness of their form, which is firmly anchored in the free-verse and imagistic tradition of modernist verse; and for the precision of their images.

Because of Silko's frequent mention of specific places and dependence on allusions to cultural assumptions and oral traditions of storytelling with which many readers may be unfamiliar, appreciation of the content of the poems is considerably less direct and immediate than appreciation of their form. Knowledge of the geography of the American Southwest and of its indigenous cultures, however, especially the Laguna and Navajo cultures from which the poems spring and to which they constantly refer, reveals layers and complexities of meaning that are belied by the simplicity of the poems' form.

Among those features of Laguna culture that are most relevant to an understanding of *Laguna Woman* are its strong sense of continually being in the presence of spirits, its belief in the primacy of tribal rather than individual welfare and survival, its belief in the interrelatedness and mutual dependency of all forms of life, and especially the matriarchal nature of Laguna society. Laguna culture puts women at the center of its theology and its social and economic well-being, and it makes clan membership, which defines the individual's place within the universe, dependent on matrilineal descent. Thus, *Laguna Woman* is related to women's issues and concerns not only in the general sense that it was written by a woman and that its subject matter is focused on female experience but also in the more specific sense that it reflects a woman-centered theology and a matriarchal, matrilineal social structure.

Although none of the poems is specifically about a particular place, all are closely related in one way or another to the landscape of the relatively small reservations of the Laguna Pueblo and of its close geographical and cultural neighbor, the Acoma Pueblo, in west-central New Mexico, as well as the much larger Navajo reservation to the northwest. With the obvious exception of a poem dealing with a trip to the Pacific Ocean, the poems are set within the confines of these three reservations.

Although *Laguna Woman* is firmly anchored in a specific locale and time, it is an important part of Silko's perspective that the present is always connected to the past, not only through the constant of place but also through traditional stories and songs.

The organizing principle is not chronological but thematic, based on the intertwined cycles of human life and death and of nature and the seasons. The volume begins with paradoxical images of conception and abortion and ends with paradoxical images of the life-sustaining nature of death.

Among the influences of Laguna culture that are apparent in the poems are such elements as the trickster theme ("Toe'osh: A Laguna Coyote Story"); sexual encounters ("When Sun Came to Riverwoman," "Love Poem," "Si'ahh Aash'," and "Mesita Men"); the interconnections of nature, animals, and human beings ("Sun Children," "Indian Song: Survival," and "Hawk and Snake"); love and respect for animals ("In Cold Storm Light," "The Time We Climbed Snake Mountain," and "Horses at Valley Store"); the cyclical nature of time ("Where Mountain Lion Laid Down with Deer" and "Slim Man Canyon"); the spirit world ("Four Mountain Wolves"); and the "truth" of myth ("Prayer to the Pacific").

Analysis

The thematic organization of the collection is announced in the first poem, which provides an example of the way the poems center on female experience and concerns and which also serves as a thematic map illustrating mixed cultural influences and the conjunction of story, place, and time—both present and past. It is titled "Poem for Myself and Mei: Concerning Abortion" and is headed by a note that reads "Chinle to Fort Defiance April, 1973." Although Silko does not say so, Mei refers to her friend Mei-mei Berssenbrugge, who is also a poet and who is treated here as an alter ego in the phrase "Myself and Mei." Chinle and Fort Defiance are towns on the Navajo Reservation in northeastern Arizona. The poem grows out of an automobile journey that the two women took, and like several other poems in the collection, it is divided into four sections: Four is the sacred number in Laguna culture and in most American Indian cultures. The first two sections present images of conception (the sun comes "unstuffed with the yellow light of butterflies" [butterflies are commonly associated with children in pueblo culture]) and images of gestation (the winter "snowed mustard grass/ and the springtime rained it").

The third section presents a seemingly irrelevant image of horses seen from the highway, and the reader is told that the white horse was "scratching his ass on a tree." The allusion here is to the poem "Musée des Beaux Arts" (1939) by the English poet W. H. Auden, in which Auden in turn alludes to two paintings, *Icarus* and *The Massacre of the Innocents*, by the sixteenth century Flemish painter Pieter Bruegel the Elder, both of which deal with the deaths of children. Auden observes that old masters such as Bruegel understood the nature of suffering, understood that tragedies of even mythic proportions work themselves out while "the torturer's horse/ Scratches its innocent behind on a tree." Silko's allusion to Auden connects her with the mainstream European American literary tradition for the moment, signifying that the "myself" of the poem's title (who is also the Laguna Woman of the book's title) is a person of mixed cultural heritage who of necessity must operate in both American Indian and European American cultural spheres, although the center of her being is firmly rooted in the former.

The fourth section of the poem presents an image of tragedy comparable to that of the death of Icarus; the butterflies "die softly/ against the windshield" of the car, where their "iridescent wings/ flutter and cling/ all the way home." When one remembers that Icarus died when he ventured too close to the sun, melting the wings of wax his father Daedalus had made for him, the wings of the butterflies become especially significant, connecting Icarus' abortive and fatal flight with the abortive and fatal flights of the butterfly children. Furthermore, the biblical slaughter of the innocents has its modern counterpart in the practice of abortion. Thus, Silko opens vistas of suggestivity and complexity through the effective use of allusions, and at the same time she emphasizes the continuing relevance of the stories of the past to the circumstances of the present and the interrelatedness of the natural world and man and animals.

Among the poems that depend most clearly on American Indian motifs is the second in the collection, "Toe'osh: A Laguna Coyote Story," which is dedicated to the Acoma poet Simon Ortiz and is dated July, 1973. "Toe'osh" is the Laguna name for coyote, the preeminent trickster figure in American Indian traditional literature. Coyote not only tricks others but also is the victim of tricks to which others subject him. Coyote stories are favorites among the Indians, and Silko begins by remembering how on winter nights her family would sit by the stove drinking Spañada, a cheap wine, and tell traditional stories about how coyote lost his original fine coat in a poker game and got his "ratty old fur coat/ bits of fur/ the sparrows stuck on him/ with dabs of pitch." Navajo coyote stories are also mentioned, and then the myths of the ancient past are applied to the present when coyote is identified with the white men who came to Laguna and Acoma more than a hundred years ago to exploit the native peoples, fighting over their land and their women. Next, the mythical range of reference is brought up to the present when the reader is told that the descendants of those white men can now be heard "howling in/ the hills southeast of Laguna."

Contemporary politicians are also equated with coyote, whose stories often emphasize his insatiable sexual appetite, when Silko mentions Charlie Coyote, who wanted to be elected governor of the pueblo so that he could "run the other men off/ the reservation/ and keep all the women for himself."

In the final section of the poem, coyote is identified with Simon Ortiz himself in a manner typical of the way in which Silko identifies her own persona with characters from Laguna mythology. Toe'osh is said to have howled and roared and "scattered white people/ out of bars all over Wisconsin" by bumping into them "at the door/ until they said/ 'Excuse me'/ And the way Simon meant it/ was for 300 or maybe 400 years."

This poem thus connects the coyote trickster myths of the Laguna and Navajo oral traditions with the author's own childhood, when storytelling was a means of passing on the culture and sense of identity that enable Silko to see herself as "Laguna Woman," and it also shows how storytelling is a means of binding a family together and of connecting with friends such as Simon Ortiz. Furthermore, the poem is an excellent example of the fluidity of coyote as trickster figure—sometimes animal, sometimes human, sometimes perpetrator and exploiter, sometimes victim and dupe, and sometimes even rising to the level of culture hero, as when Simon bumps into white people to extract revenge for centuries of exploitation or when the Laguna people accept the hams and turkeys politicians give them to get their votes and then stay home on election day, eating the turkeys and laughing at the politicians.

Trickster is not the only figure in *Laguna Woman* who shifts back and forth from animal to human form. Such transformations, which are sometimes confusing to non-Indian readers, are related to the Laguna belief in the interrelatedness of nature and the animal and the human worlds, and they are quite common in traditional Laguna stories. Several poems in *Laguna Woman* deal with such transformations. For example, "Indian Song: Survival" ends with lines in which the speaker identifies her being with that of nature and those of the animals: "taste me,/ I am the wind/ touch me,/ I am the lean grey deer/ running on the edge of the rainbow." In "Sun Children," the wild ducks that migrate with the sun and are his children at the beginning of the poem have, by its conclusion, merged with human life, spring grass, and deer until all forms of life are seen to be "sun children."

Context

Laguna Woman went virtually unnoticed when it was first published, although Silko was gaining a measure of national recognition because of her short stories published at almost the same time. After the publication of her first novel, *Ceremony*, in 1977, Silko was recognized as the leading American Indian woman writer, and she began receiving considerable critical attention, but her reputation as a writer of fiction has continued to eclipse her reputation as a poet. Indeed, since *Ceremony*, she has largely devoted herself to fiction, her next work being the very long and complex novel *Almanac of the Dead* (1991).

Laguna Woman, although it is written from an explicitly female point of view, presents the female experience, perspective, and range of interests as being not very different from the male. Silko has commented that Laguna culture is very different from mainstream white, middle-class culture, which typically segregates the sexes. In Laguna culture, boys and girls range freely and are not exposed to the division of labor that prevails in white culture. Consequently, Silko grew up participating in activities shared by both sexes and is able to portray male experience as convincingly as female experience. Her close observation of the natural world and her interest in wild animals, which presuppose considerable time spent outdoors, are not as exclusively identified with male experience as they are in middle-class white culture, and the persona in *Laguna Woman* is able to climb mountains, go horseback riding, and hunt deer without losing her femininity. She is able to look directly at ugliness and cruelty—the dead sheep beside the road with its belly bursting open and its guts oozing out or the "green eyes wolf/ as she reaches the swollen belly elk"—which are as much a part of nature as its beauty, just as she is able to speak directly of the coyotes in the trickster tale who hung "down over the cliff/ holding each other's tail in their mouth making a coyote chain/ until someone in the middle farted/ . . . and they/ all went tumbling down."

Sources for Further Study

Allen, Paula Gunn. *The Sacred Hoop: Recovering the Feminine in American Indian Traditions*. Boston: Beacon Press, 1992. A good explanation of American Indian gynocracy is contained in the introduction and the first two essays, "Grandmother of the Sun: Ritual Gynocracy in Native America" and "When Women Throw Down Bundles: Strong Women Make Strong Nations."

Seyersted, Per. *Leslie Marmon Silko*. Boise, Idaho: Boise State University, 1980. A good introduction to Laguna culture and to Silko's early work.

Silko, Leslie Marmon. *Yellow Woman*. Edited by Melody Graulich. New Brunswick, N.J.: Rutgers University Press, 1993. Contains an excellent biographical introduction by Graulich and an important interview with Silko by Kim Barnes.

Silko, Leslie Marmon, and James Wright. *The Delicacy and Strength of Lace: Letters Between Leslie Marmon Silko and James Wright*. Edited by Anne Wright. St. Paul, Minn.: Graywolf Press, 1986. Contains considerable autobiographical information and important comments by Silko about her poetry.

Wiget, Andrew. *Native American Literature*. Boston: Twayne, 1985. This is the longest discussion (but only one page) of Silko's poetry to date, with comments on "Toe'osh: A Laguna Coyote Story" and "Where Mountain Lion Laid Down with Deer."

Dennis Hoilman

THE LAIS OF MARIE DE FRANCE

Author: Marie de France (c. 1150-c. 1215)
Type of work: Poetry
First published: Lais, c. 1167 (English translation, 1911)

Form and Content

Marie de France is the earliest French woman poet whose name is known today. Her major work, *The Lais of Marie de France,* consists of twelve poems that range in length from 118 to 1,184 lines. Although these poems were composed over a number of years, Marie decided at some point to collect the *lais* into a single book. She added a fifty-six-line prologue dedicating the volume to a "noble king" whom she never names. For more than a century, scholars have attempted to determine this king's identity—and even the land that he ruled—but the matter remains a mystery. One leading possibility is that Marie's "noble king" was Henry II, the English ruler who came to the throne in 1154. Like Marie, Henry was of French descent but lived in England, where a large number of the *Lais* were set.

The word *lai* (plural *lais*) that Marie adopts for her poems is a French borrowing of the Provençal term for "ballad." Originally, *lais* were short, lyric poems sung to the accompaniment of a stringed instrument. By Marie's time, however, the term *lais* had expanded to include nonmusical poems intended to be read, either privately or as part of a court entertainment. In Marie's *Lais,* references to such figures as the Roman poet Ovid, the medieval grammarian Priscian, and the legendary Babylonian queen Semiramis make it clear that these works were intended for a highly educated audience. Marie herself appears to have been quite learned. She knew both Latin and English and attained a wide reputation for her poetry during her own lifetime.

The Lais of Marie de France were written in Old French with rhyming couplets of eight-syllable lines. Each of the poems presents a romantic crisis that leads the central characters to an adventure. Some stories, such as "Equitan," attempt to teach a moral lesson; most are pure entertainment. A few of the *lais,* including "Chaitivel" and "The Two Lovers," end tragically. The majority of the poems, however, represent love as ultimately triumphant over obstacles arising during the course of the story.

Analysis

The Lais of Marie de France are important both as folklore and as literature. As Marie herself says at several points, most of her stories originated in the oral legends of the Bretons. As a result, poems such as "Lanval" contain many plot elements found in oral traditions all over the world. Like Elsa in the Germanic legend of Lohengrin or Psyche in the Greco-Roman legend of Cupid and Psyche, the hero Lanval temporarily loses his beloved by breaking his promise. Like Potifar's wife in the Old Testament or Anubis' wife in the Egyptian tale of Anubis and Bata, Guinevere falsely claims that a man molested her when he had actually refused her advances. In "Eliduc," the king of England's daughter is restored to life in a manner almost identical to that by which both the healer Asclepius and the seer Polyeidus were said to have revived Minos' son Glaucus in Greek mythology.

By recording the legends of the Bretons, Marie preserved these tales at a time when oral traditions throughout Europe were being obliterated by a rapidly expanding literary culture. Even as Marie was preserving these stories, however, she was also reshaping them, giving them a distinctly literary form. She added geographical names and a touch of the archaism that she found in such chronicles as Geoffrey of Monmouth's *Historia Regum Britanniae* (c. 1135; *History of the Kings of Britain*) and Geoffrey's Gaimar's *Estoire des Engleis* (c. 1150; *History of the English*). In "Chevre-foil," she adapted the familiar legend of Tristan, the same story that would later be treated by such authors as Béroul (c. 1200) and Gottfried von Strassburg (c. 1210).

Like Chrétien de Troyes in the late twelfth century and the other writers of medieval romance, Marie combined supernatural elements with heroic exploits. Her character Guigemar, like Galahad and Parzifal before him, boards an enchanted ship that carries him to a distant land. Bisclavret is transformed into a werewolf, and Yonec's father becomes a hawk. The hero of "The Two Lovers" uses a magic potion that greatly increases his strength. In addition to these supernatural details, Marie also borrowed a number of unrealistic situations from the romantic tradition. In many of her stories, her hero and heroine fall in love without ever having met: The mere report that a woman is beautiful or that a man is noble is enough to stimulate the deepest affections. Spouses, parents, and other impediments to the marriage of the central characters conveniently die or vanish from the story at the appropriate moment so that the lovers may be united.

Beneath this layer of fantasy and wish fulfillment, however, Marie's poems reflect many values that would have been familiar to her aristocratic audience. Nearly all Marie's heroes are either kings or noblemen. Nearly all of her heroines are kings' daughters or ladies of the court. In every case, the characters adhere to the complex set of social conventions that came to be known as *courtoisie* (courtesy). Medieval authors represented courtesy through such traits as generosity, fidelity, valor, and romantic love. Discourtesy is usually introduced by Marie only to be punished quickly and severely. Equitan, for example, is killed by the same plan that he had intended for his steward. Bisclavret's wife and her lover are banished because they have plotted against the hero. Guigemar kills Meriaduc for the discourtesy that he displayed to the hero's beloved. Situations such as these helped to reinforce the values of Marie's aristocratic audience and encouraged readers to identify with the noble figures de-picted in her poems.

While the central characters of Marie's *Lais* thus generally follow the code of behavior known as courtly love, this does not mean that they are constrained by every precept of that code. For example, lovers are occasionally unfaithful or even treach-erous. Eliduc, although married, takes a lover when he is sent into exile. The heroine of "Chaitivel" has four lovers, all of whom she loves equally. Moreover, the knights in Marie's poems rarely suffer the prolonged period of "languishing" that was common in courtly romances. The female figures in *Lais* are neither as disdainful as the heroines of many romances nor pure, unattainable women such as Beatrice in the *La divina commedia* (c. 1320; *The Divine Comedy*) of Dante Alighieri (1265-1321). To the contrary, Marie's heroines are usually amorous women who succumb to their lovers shortly after their first meeting. In part, this departure from the romantic tradition is attributable to the short length of the *lai*, which did not permit Marie to describe long periods of unfulfilled passion. In part, too, it was attributable to the age in which Marie was writing, a time when all the conventions of courtly love had not yet been firmly established.

One of the most important values shared by Marie's original audience was the view expressed in "Equitan" that honorable love can exist only between social equals. While it is true that Marie continues this discussion by saying that a man who is poor and honorable is of far greater worth than a king who is discourteous, strict social boundaries still separated the two classes. Humble individuals, Marie notes, will come to disaster if they search for love above their station. In fact, all the central characters in Marie's poems are aristocrats. Unlike such literary forms as the *fabliau*, the *lai* was a type of poem written *about* the nobility *for* the nobility. It dealt with characters who had sufficient wealth and leisure to devote to such activities as falconry, tournaments, courtship, and listening to ballads.

The values of Marie's social class also help to explain her emphasis upon male characters, often at the expense of women. Since Marie herself was a woman author, the reader might expect the heroines of her stories to be prominent. In fact, this rarely occurs. While most of Marie's heroes have names, most of her female characters are referred to only by their titles. In "Guigemar," the hero concludes (incorrectly) that a woman whom he sees cannot really be his beloved since "all women look rather the same." In "Eliduc," the hero's wife humbly retires to a convent so that her husband will be able to marry his lover. These situations reflect the conventions of the literary genre that Marie had adopted and the aristocratic values of the late twelfth century. There is no way of knowing whether they also reflect the feelings of the author herself. Nevertheless, it should be noted that Marie gives roughly the same attention to the romantic plights of her male and female characters. She portrays women as highly creative, even as the guiding forces in several stories. In "The Two Lovers," for example, it is the female character who suggests that the hero travel to Salerno to acquire the magic potion. In "Milun," a noblewoman rather than the hero develops the plan by which her pregnancy is kept a secret.

Context

Marie de France was a pioneer in women's literature not because she limited herself to issues of concern to women but because she achieved prominence in a genre that would long remain dominated by men. Throughout the entire Middle Ages, Marie was the only woman author of romantic tales to achieve a status equal to that of Chrétien de Troyes, Guillaume de Lorris, Jean (Clopinel) de Meung, Gottfried von Strassburg, and Wolfram von Eschenbach.

As a result of both the conventions of medieval romance and the culture of her time,

Marie often gave more attention to the male characters in her poems than to the female characters. With the exception of Le Fresne ("Ash Tree") and La Codre ("Hazel Tree"), whose names are central to the plot of the story, few women in Marie's *Lais* are even named. Most women simply have titles, such as "Meriaduc's sister" and "Eliduc's wife," that define their position in terms of their male relatives. Even Guinevere, who appears as a minor character in "Lanval," is called simply "the queen." Nevertheless, Marie's success in her genre prepared the way for such later women authors as Marguerite de Navarre (1492-1549), whose *Heptaméron* was based upon the structure of the *Decameron* (1348-1353; English translation, 1702), by Giovanni Boccaccio (1313-1375). Moreover, Marie's aristocratic and intellectual poetry anticipated the later works of such authors as Anna, Comtesse de Noailles (1876-1933) and Catherine Pozzi (1882-1934).

Sources for Further Study

Burgess, Glyn Sheridan. "Chivalry and Prowess in the *Lais* of Marie de France." *French Studies* 37 (April, 1983): 129-142. Burgess argues that the *Lais* are primarily an upper-class phenomenon presenting twelfth century knights in the context of their social superiors. This article also studies the vocabulary that Marie adopts for various courtly virtues.

_____ . *"The Lais of Marie de France": Text and Context.* Athens: University of Georgia Press, 1987. The best general analysis of the *Lais*, this work deals with such matters as chronology, chivalry, character analysis, vocabulary, and the status of women in the poems. Includes an extensive bibliography.

Damon, S. Foster. "Marie de France: Psychologist of Courtly Love." *Publications of the Modern Language Association* 44 (1929): 968-996. This article argues that, since Marie was writing before the "laws" of courtly love were established, she was freer than later authors to develop the actions of her characters. Also includes a useful chart analyzing the hero, heroine, and villain of each *lai*, as well as the solutions to the romantic crises of the poems.

Jackson, W. T. H. "The Arthuricity of Marie de France." *Romanic Review* 70 (1979): 1-18. Jackson suggests that Marie's purpose was to question the assumptions of the courtly romance. As a result, she created almost a parody of that genre.

Mickel, Emanuel J. *Marie de France*. New York: Twayne, 1974. Intended for the general reader, this is a good introduction to many aspects of the *Lais*. Contains a discussion of Marie's possible identity, the sources of her works, a historical background, and a concise discussion of each poem.

Jeffrey L. Buller

LATER THE SAME DAY

Author: Grace Paley (1922-　　)
Type of work: Short stories
First published: 1985

Form and Content

Later the Same Day is Grace Paley's third collection of short stories. As in her first two anthologies, *The Little Disturbances of Man* (1959) and *Enormous Changes at the Last Minute* (1974), many of the stories in *Later the Same Day* are so short (two to four pages) that some reviewers doubted they were stories at all, calling them nervous, haphazard sketches or too underdeveloped to allow Paley's artistry to shine through. For example, "Love" seems to be an inconclusive episode in which a man tells his wife about his past loves, one of whom is a fictional character in her own book. "Lavinia: An Old Story" is a brief monologue in which a black woman tries to talk her daughter's suitor out of marrying her. "At That Time: Or, The History of a Joke" is itself little more than a joke in which the virgin birth becomes the source of several satiric jabs at the Christian religion.

The stories "Anxiety," "In This Country, but in Another Language, My Aunt Refuses to Marry the Men Everyone Wants Her To," and "Mother" seem sketchy, cryptic, and irresolute. "Anxiety" consists primarily of a woman's warnings to a young father who is taking his daughter home from school, "In This Country" is a two-page prose poem in which a female child tries to determine whether her maiden aunt has a life of her own, and "Mother" is a two-page memoir brought on by a woman's hearing the song, "Oh, I Long to See My Mother in the Doorway." The two short pieces "A Man Told Me the Story of His Life" and "This Is a Story About My Friend George, the Toy Inventor" are more like brief parables than fully developed narratives. In one, a man who is unable to fulfill his dream of being a doctor saves his wife's life because of his diagnostic ability; in the other, a man invents a pinball machine that is a poem of the machine, its essence made concrete.

It is not these brief pieces that have attracted readers to Paley's stories, however, but rather the more developed stories, especially those that focus on the friendships of women, such as "Friends," "Ruthy and Edie," and "The Expensive Moment." In "Friends," a story that Paley has said is about grief for the children, Paley's character Faith, who has appeared in a number of Paley's stories, goes with her friends Ann and Susan to visit another friend, Selena, who is dying. The story is a Paley experiment in creating a collective narrator; she has said in an interview that it is based on her own female friends, with whom she had a kind of collective existence.

"Ruthy and Edie" begins with the relationship between two young girls who talk about the "real world of boys" and fight their fear of a strange neighborhood dog; then the story shifts to Ruthy's fiftieth birthday, when she invites three friends, including Faith and Edie, to her apartment for a celebration. The story ends with Ruthy's anxiety about her success as a mother as she struggles with the hopelessness of protecting her granddaughter from the hard world of "man-made time." Faith appears again in "The Expensive Moment," in which the network of women, a frequent theme in Paley's stories, broadens to include a Chinese woman whom Faith and Ruthy have met at a meeting of a women's governmental organization sponsored by the United Nations. Over tea in Faith's kitchen, the three women wonder about their children and whether they were right to rear them as they did.

Faith also appears in several other stories in the collection, as either a character or a narrator. In "Zagrowsky Tells," the reader gets an unsympathetic perspective of her from the point of view of a pharmacist whom Faith and her friends had once picketed for racism. In "The Story Hearer," Faith compiles a list of incidents in response to her husband Jack's standard question "What did you do today?" but makes it clear that she purposely does not mention her meeting with Zagrowsky or her encounter with what she calls "new young fathers"—probably the same fathers she warns from her window in the story "Anxiety."

Analysis

The key words in the titles of several of the stories in *Later the Same Day* are "telling," "listening," "hearing," and "story," for the nature of narrative talk is central to all of them. Paley's central concern is the basic characteristics of story; specifically, the characteristics of oral narrative specifically associated with women. In "Listening," at breakfast, Faith tells her husband Jack the two stories "Anxiety" and "Zagrowsky Tells," stories that she neglected to tell him in the story "The Story Hearer." Jack complains that these are stories about men and urges her to tell him the stories told by women about women. Although Faith says they are too private, many of Paley's stories are indeed about the very private talk between women.

Paley's concern with the nature of story moves many of her narratives into the realm of self-reflexive fiction or metafiction, for they are about reality as a language construct. Although her stories lack the kind of tight intentional patterning of the well-made short story since Poe, they are not "realistic" in the usual "slice-of-life" sense. Paley is too self-conscious a writer to be content with straightforward mimetic treatments of real people in the real world. As a result of Paley's refusal to build her stories around a clear conflict and thus move them toward an emphatic sense of resolution and closure, a number of critics have often been puzzled about how to discuss her stories about women.

Paley's very brief stories have also been the source of critical reservations, for they are so short and seemingly inconsequential that they challenge the lower limits of storyness. Paley has sometimes been classified among those contemporary short-story writers known as minimalists, although her minimalism has been more accepted than that of Ann Beattie, Mona Simpson, Amy Hempel, and Mary Robison because of her use as subject matter of the urban Jewish community and the community of women. In spite of the politically correct nature of her characters, she has been criticized for self-indulgently engaging in meaningless memoirs and desultory dialogues that, although they contain socially significant ideas, are not really stories at all.

This is the same kind of criticism that once was lodged against Anton Chekhov, the originator of the tradition of short-story "realism" to which Paley belongs. Although Paley's stories seem like mere slices of life without intentional pattern, they are actually quite carefully crafted narratives in which simple objective description takes on symbolic meaning through a careful structure of repetition and interconnection of motifs. She believes that stories should be "like life," or at least like the way life should be—that is, open-ended, full of hope, promise, and possibility. Stories should not be governed by the inevitability of plot, particularly plot determined by the goal-directed nature of male culture. If life is like a story, then Paley insists that all individuals should be storytellers, each writing his or her own stories and forming communities of stories with others.

Writing for Grace Paley is a collaborative, social act, not merely in the obvious sense of centering stories on social issues but also in the more complex and profound sense of writing as the creation of a community of speakers and listeners sharing the same values. Not content to remain the prisoner of a language system based on the dominant male culture, Grace Paley has devoted her art to the creation of a language-based community made up of talk by women to women.

Context

Grace Paley's concern with "women's stories" has made her the center of current discussion among feminist critics about whether women's mode of storytelling is truly different from that of men. The basic issue seems to focus on the goal- or end-directed nature of male stories as opposed to the less linear and more open-ended stories of women. Moreover, Paley's stories raise the issue of whether male stories are more egoistic and self-centered than the communal and collaborative stories written by women. If such distinctions do exist, they not only raise significant issues about the nature of story in its most basic sense but also suggest some of the reasons that the stories of women have often been undervalued in a culture that is basically goal oriented and egoistic. Whether such distinctions can be supported or not, Paley herself has said that as more and more women talk to one another, such issues will have to be faced. Moreover, she is well aware that there are significant social implications of women banding together and talking to one another more.

Later the Same Day is perhaps Paley's most emphatic treatment of the importance of language communities and the collaborative nature of story, for the stories here are more interrelated than they were in her earlier two collections, and her concern with the basic characteristics of "telling" and "listening" is more direct and insistent here. Because Paley's stories not only are "about" women but also raise the more crucial issues of a distinctive woman's "voice," Paley will no doubt continue to be at the very center of subsequent discussion and debate about the unique nature of women's literature.

Sources for Further Study

Aarons, Victoria. "Talking Lives: Storytelling and Renewal in Grace Paley's Short

Fiction." *Studies in American Jewish Literature* 9 (Spring, 1990): 20-35. Argues that although Paley's characters try to reinvent themselves by telling stories, she ironically undermines their attempts to do so. Through storytelling, her characters build communities of women; the telling of stories becomes the saving of identity.

Baba, Minako. "Faith Darwin as Writer-Heroine: A Study of Grace Paley's Short Stories." *Studies in American Jewish Literature* 7 (Spring, 1988): 40-54. Focuses on Faith as a middle-aged woman in the 1970's and 1980's in such stories as "Friends," in which she visits a dying friend, and "Listening," in which she shares stories with her new husband Jack. Argues that Faith's career shifts from domesticity to social awareness to the knowledge that storytelling is the means of preserving humanity.

Criswell, Jeanne Salladé. "Cynthia Ozick and Grace Paley: Diverse Visions in Jewish and Women's Literature." In *Since Flannery O'Connor: Essays on the Contemporary American Short Story*, edited by Loren Logsdon and Charles W. Mayer. Macomb: Western Illinois University Press, 1987. Compares and contrasts the thought and art of Paley with Ozick; argues that whereas Ozick writes from a classical feminist perspective, Paley manifests a feminine consciousness of empathy with her characters.

Lyons, Bonnie. "Grace Paley's Jewish Miniatures." *Studies in American Jewish Literature* 8 (Spring, 1989): 26-33. Discusses how Paley's stories are grounded in Jewish experience. They embody an oral framework of belief practiced by the Jewish culture and constitute a coherent Jewish vision. Argues that her stories convey the sense that in a patriarchy, the little person—one of Paley's most frequent concerns—is usually a woman.

Schleifer, Ronald. "Grace Paley: Chaste Compactness." In *Contemporary American Women Writers: Narrative Strategies*, edited by Catherine Rainwater and William J. Scheick. Lexington: University Press of Kentucky, 1985. Discusses the purposeful lack of closure in Paley's stories, which creates a sense of "open" lives rather than contrived climaxes. Focuses on several of Paley's "minimalist" stories and stories that seem irresolute and open ended and thus challenge "storyness."

Taylor, Jacqueline. *Grace Paley: Illuminating the Dark Lives*. Austin: University of Texas Press, 1990. This is the most detailed discussion of Paley's "woman-centered" point of view. Taylor analyzes Paley's recognition of the problems women face when trying to use a language based on male categories. Separate chapters deal with Paley's humor, her narrative structure, her link with the oral tradition, and her experimentation with undermining the authority of the narrator.

Charles E. May

THE LEFT HAND OF DARKNESS

Author: Ursula K. Le Guin (1929-   )
Type of work: Novel
Type of plot: Science fiction
Time of plot: The future
Locale: The imaginary planet of Gethen, also called "Winter"
First published: 1969

> *Principal characters:*
> GENLY AI, a young man from Earth who has come to Gethen as
>   the envoy of a benign interplanetary league, the Ekumen
> THEREM HARTH REM IR ESTRAVEN, the Lord of Estre in Kerm
>   and Ai's ally
> ARGAVEN XV, the mad king of Karhide
> TIBE, Argaven's cousin, who gains power in the court and causes
>   Estraven's exile from Karhide
> FAXE THE WEAVER, an Indweller at Otherhord Fastness and a
>   member of the Handdarata
> FORETH REM IR OSBOTH, Estraven's former lover, or
>   "kemmering"
> OBSLE and YEGEY, two of the thirty-three Commensals who rule
>   the nation of Orgoreyn
> COMMISSIONER SHUSGIS, a politician in Mishnory, the capital of
>   Orgoreyn
> ESVANS HARTH REM IR ESTRAVEN, the Lord of Estre, Estraven's
>   father
> AREK HARTH REM IR ESTRAVEN, Estraven's brother, who vowed
>   kemmering with Therem
> SORVE HARTH REM IR ESTRAVEN, the heir of Estre and the son of
>   Arek and Therem

Form and Content

The Left Hand of Darkness is one of several novels describing the results of experiments carried out on other planets by beings from the planet Hain. On Gethen, the Hainish established a race of ambisexual humans. Gethenians are usually androgynous and asexual; once a month, however, they enter a state called "kemmer." During this period sexuality predominates over everything else. In kemmer, Gethenians develop male or female characteristics, but their specific gender is completely arbitrary and may vary from one cycle to another.

The novel takes place thousands of years later, when Genly Ai comes to this ambisexual world as an envoy from the Ekumen. Gethen has evolved into a complex society, shaped not by gender differences but by the alternation of frigidity and sexual activity; it has also developed two national superpowers (Karhide, a monarchy, and

Orgoreyn, a communist state) and two principal religions (the Handdara and the Yomesh). *The Left Hand of Darkness* traces Ai's adventures on this planet in the course of fulfilling his mission. He gradually convinces the Gethenians—in particular, Estraven—that his stories of other worlds are true. Equally important, he himself comes to understand Gethen.

The novel begins in Ehrenrang, Karhide's capital, where Estraven has arranged Ai's audience with the king. Ai does not trust Estraven, however, and he is scarcely surprised when Estraven tells him that he can no longer represent Ai's interests to the king. The following morning, however, Estraven is gone, banished from Karhide on pain of death; the king condemns him as a traitor and shows no interest in the Ekumen. Despondent, Ai decides to leave Ehrenrang.

He goes to eastern Karhide to learn more of the country and to learn the answer to a question. In eastern Karhide are the Fastnesses, retreats for practitioners of the Handdara. Like Taoism, this religion advocates living in the moment as a meaningful response to the one certain fact known by every person: He or she will die. In order to demonstrate the uselessness of all other knowledge, the Handdarata perform a ritual in which a "weaver" foretells the answer to a stranger's question. Handdarata legends confirm both the answers' accuracy and the questions' essential irrelevance. Nevertheless, Ai asks this question: Will Gethen join the Ekumen within five years? Hours later, he receives his answer: yes.

When Ai arrives in Orgoreyn, he finds Estraven already there, garnering support for Ai's cause among the ruling Commensals. Yet Ai still does not trust him, even though Estraven's kemmering, Foreth, begged him to assist Estraven in his exile. To Ai, Estraven's presence in Orgoreyn merely confirms his treachery and his political expediency. Ai therefore ignores Estraven's warning that his life is in danger. The next morning, he is arrested and sent to a work farm—where he almost dies, but for Estraven's brilliant rescue.

By crossing the dangerous Gobrin Ice, Estraven and Ai hope to return to Karhide, where Ai's mission may fare better now. On this journey, they risk starvation, injury, and death—and become true friends. Ai teaches Estraven a form of telepathy that precludes misunderstanding; they call each other by their first names; and, when they reach Karhide, Estraven skis directly toward the border guards' guns—a sacrifice that facilitates the political success of Ai's mission in Karhide.

Karhide does join the Ekumen, confirming the Foretellers' answer to Ai's question. Yet as Ai journeys to Estre to tell Estraven's father of his son's death, he realizes that question's irrelevance to what he has learned on Gethen. At Estre he meets Estraven's son Sorve, who asks a better question in the book's final sentence. Rather than assuming a yes or no answer, Sorve begins a dialogue: "Will you tell us about the other worlds out among the stars—the other kinds of men, the other lives?"

Analysis

In form as well as content, Ursula K. Le Guin's novel emphasizes that the whole is greater than the sum of its parts. Ai's mission asks the Gethenians to look beyond their personal interests, to join in solidarity with other lives and other worlds. Estraven is the only Gethenian capable of such large-mindedness, and even so, Ai initially thinks him disloyal or unpatriotic, because he does not care whether Karhide or Orgoreyn is the first to join the Ekumen. By the end of the novel, however, Ai understands the selflessness of Estraven's motives. He tells Argaven XV that Estraven had served neither Karhide nor its king, but the same master that he himself served. When the king asks suspiciously whether that master is the Ekumen, Ai answers that it is humankind. Similarly, *The Left Hand of Darkness* asks readers to look beyond gender roles and sexual identities, and to focus instead on the common humanity that all people share.

The novel's title emphasizes this theme. "Light is the left hand of darkness/ and darkness the right hand of light," according to a poem of the Handdarata that Estraven recites to Ai as they cross the Gobrin Ice. The novel consistently acknowledges dualities such as light and dark, left and right, but emphasizes that they are complementary rather than opposed. Together, they make up something greater than either alone, as the poem's ending suggests:

> Two are one, life and death, lying
> together like lovers in kemmer,
> like hands joined together,
> like the end and the way.

It is fitting that a sacred poem from an imaginary religion, which one character recites to another, should gloss the title of *The Left Hand of Darkness*. The novel is filled with embedded texts that add depth and verisimilitude to the story. Chapters that develop the plot alternate with others that feature Karhide folk tales, Handdarata or Yomeshta writings, Orgota creation myths, or the field notes of the first Ekumenical investigator on Gethen. Each interlude provides a mythic, religious, or anthropological context for an episode in the novel's plot; it also generates suspense, since the reader is anxious to return to the main story line. Most important, these fragments of other writings serve as complements to the story of Ai and Estraven.

In chapter 6, Le Guin's narrative strategy becomes more complicated. Up to this point, the chapters developing the main story line are narrated in the first person by Ai. Now they are narrated alternately by Ai and Estraven, as each describes his own adventures in Orgoreyn; later, the two take turns describing their shared adventures on the Gobrin Ice. The reader gradually understands that Ai, the novel's frame narrator, believed that he could most accurately describe his experiences by including other voices and other texts in his report to the Ekumen. As he explains on the novel's first page, "I'll make my report as if I told a story. . . . The story is not all mine, nor told by me alone." The novel's narration thus reiterates the theme that the whole is greater than the sum of its parts.

Context

The Left Hand of Darkness can be compared to other works of fantasy or science fiction that concentrate on gender. Charlotte Perkins Gilman's separatist feminist novel *Herland* (1915; 1979) imagines an entire society of women. Herland—whose architecture, economy, industry, and religion is described in considerable detail—is a land of peace, harmony, and creativity. So, at first, is the society of hermaphrodites that Theodore Sturgeon describes in his classic science-fiction novel *Venus Plus X* (1965); Sturgeon's novel darkly suggests, however, that such utopias can only be attained by means of genetic engineering. Doris Lessing's science-fiction novel *The Marriages Between Zones Three, Four, and Five* (1980) suggests the difficulty and necessity of leaving behind separatist models of men's and women's "zones."

Because science fiction facilitates imagining alternatives to contemporary society, many feminists choose this genre to express their ideas. Yet *The Left Hand of Darkness*—which won both Hugo and Nebula Awards for best science-fiction novel of 1969—stands out among other works, for both the originality of its conception and the care with which it is worked out. The novel was a "thought-experiment," as Le Guin explains in her introduction, in which she tried to imagine a world without gender. Le Guin's solution to this problem—making the Gethenians utterly androgynous and asexual, except in kemmer—also enabled her to imagine a world in which sexuality is separate from daily life. On Gethen, no one is limited by predetermined gender roles; which partner bears children, for example, is a matter of chance. On Gethen, war and rape do not exist. Yet cruelty, violence, and injustice still flourish there—along with kindness, compassion, and pursuit of truth. Significantly, this planet of androgynes is neither a utopia nor a dystopia. Indeed, *The Left Hand of Darkness* resists such dualistic thinking. Le Guin's novel forgoes separatist feminism in order to establish common humanity beyond assigned gender roles.

The Left Hand of Darkness is not without flaws. Early critics claimed that the Gethenians' ambisexuality was a gimmick and was unimportant to the plot; however, careful reading shows that this is not the case. Other critics have claimed, more convincingly, that the novel is not truly feminist, because it emphasizes a masculine perspective rather than a feminine or androgynous one. It is true that *The Left Hand of Darkness* tends to express its humanist vision in terms of men and masters. In her essay "Is Gender Necessary?" Le Guin admits that her consistent use of male pronouns fails to convey the Gethenians' androgyny.

Le Guin's essay also makes clear, however, that she considers *The Left Hand of Darkness* an ongoing experiment to be completed in the minds of individual readers. In this sense, the novel is certainly successful: Critics continue to debate its merits in the contexts of feminist theory, male feminism, and gay and lesbian studies. Ultimately, however, *The Left Hand of Darkness* is a feminist novel because it challenges readers to transcend gender and discover a common humanity shared by both men and women.

Sources for Further Study
Barrow, Craig, and Diana Barrow. "*The Left Hand of Darkness*: Feminism for Men." *Mosaic* 20, no. 1 (Winter, 1987): 83-96. This insightful essay suggests that Le

Guin's feminist novel was specifically intended for male readers.

Bloom, Harold, ed. *Ursula K. Le Guin*. New York: Chelsea House, 1986. A collection of chronologically ordered and previously published essays tracing the general critical reception of Le Guin's work.

_____ . *Ursula K. Le Guin's "The Left Hand of Darkness."* New York: Chelsea House, 1987. This useful collection contains nine previously published essays, arranged in chronological order, which examine the novel in various contexts: archetypal narrative patterns, social criticism, feminism, and speech-act theory. Martin Bickman's essay on the novel's unity persuasively counters earlier charges that the Gethenians' ambisexuality is irrelevant to the plot.

Cummins, Elizabeth. *Understanding Ursula K. Le Guin*. Columbia: University of South Carolina Press, 1990. The third chapter of this book compares *The Left Hand of Darkness* to Le Guin's other novels about the results of Hainish experiments. Good annotated bibliography.

Frazer, Patricia. "Again, *The Left Hand of Darkness*: Androgyny or Homophobia?" In *The Erotic Universe: Sexuality and Fantastic Literature*, edited by Donald Palumbo. New York: Greenwood Press, 1986. Frazer's essay discusses issues of sexuality—rather than gender—in the novel. The collection features an excellent annotated bibliography on sexuality in science fiction.

Le Guin, Ursula K. "Is Gender Necessary?" In *The Language of the Night: Essays on Fantasy and Science Fiction*, edited by Susan Wood. New York: G. P. Putnam's Sons, 1979. In this important essay, Le Guin critiques her own novel as a feminist experiment—not wholly successful—in which she tried to discover the essence of humanity by eliminating gender.

Rhodes, Jewell Parker. "Ursula Le Guin's *The Left Hand of Darkness*: Androgyny and the Feminist Utopia." In *Women and Utopia: Critical Interpretations*, edited by Marleen Barr and Nicholas D. Smith. Lanham, Md.: University Press of America, 1983. This essay cogently argues that the novel's exploration of androgyny is undermined by Le Guin's own patriarchal bias.

Spivack, Charlotte. *Ursula K. Le Guin*. Boston: Twayne, 1984. A good overall introduction to Le Guin's work in fiction and other genres.

Susan Elizabeth Sweeney

LESS THAN ANGELS

Author: Barbara Pym (1913-1980)
Type of work: Novel
Type of plot: Domestic realism
Time of plot: The 1950's
Locale: London
First published: 1955

Principal characters:

> CATHERINE OLIPHANT, a writer of romantic fiction and articles
> for women's magazines who lives with Tom Mallow
> TOM MALLOW, a rising young anthropologist working on his
> Ph.D. thesis and shortly to return to Africa for more fieldwork
> DEIDRE SWAN, a first-year student of anthropology who becomes
> romantically involved with Tom
> MABEL SWAN, Deidre's mother
> RHODA WELLCOME, Mabel's sister
> ALARIC LYDGATE, a recently retired colonial administrator who
> lives next door to the Swans and writes scathing reviews of
> anthropology texts in scholarly journals
> DIGBY FOX, a promising, impoverished, and hardworking young
> anthropology student
> MARK PENFOLD, Digby's friend, who is also a hardworking
> anthropology student
> FELIX MAINWARING, a retired professor of anthropology
> ESTHER CLOVIS, a secretary at Mainwaring's new research center
> GERTRUDE LYDGATE, an expert in African languages who shares
> a flat with Esther Clovis

Form and Content

Less than Angels moves between three different worlds: that of London anthropologists competing over research grants, the suburban world with its secure and tidy routines, and a briefly sketched upper-class world in the English countryside. These worlds intersect through shifting romantic alliances, which are seen largely from the women's point of view, and often point to the unequal relations between the sexes.

The novel begins with a party at a new anthropological research center, which gives Pym an opportunity to poke fun at the jargon of anthropologists and introduce Mark and Digby as wry observers of some of the absurdities of the academic world.

The main plot line concerns the love of three different women for Tom. Tom returns from two years of fieldwork in Africa and, although he still lives with Catherine, strikes up a friendship with Deidre. She falls in love with him, although Tom regards her as no more than a good listener for his talk about his work.

Later, Catherine spots Tom and Deidre talking intimately in a restaurant. Catherine reacts mildly, but as they discuss the matter later, Tom says he will move out of her flat. He moves into a room in the flat occupied by Digby and Mark. Tom has no intention of starting a serious romantic relationship with Deidre, and he sees her only as often as is needed for his sense of well-being, which is less than Deidre had hoped for.

Interspersed with the romance, Pym creates some fine comic scenes, particularly the one in which Digby and Mark take Miss Lydgate and Miss Clovis out to lunch. The students have only a small amount of money in their pockets and suddenly develop a great liking for all the most inexpensive dishes, only to find at the end that the women insist on paying. Also providing comic material are the scenes involving Mabel and Rhoda, as they go through the routines of suburban life, organizing tea parties and the like (through which they become acquainted with Catherine and the anthropologists) and observing their neighbors. It is during one of these episodes that Catherine meets Alaric and finds him, in a careful foreshadowing, quite attractive.

Tom visits his family at their country home in Shropshire but no longer fits into that environment. He meets his first love, Elaine, who still loves him. Tom is uncomfortably reminded of his lost youthful self, and he wonders whether the change has been for the better, one of several occasions when he questions the value of anthropology. Nevertheless, having completed his thesis, Tom departs for more fieldwork in Africa.

Four candidates for the two research grants, Digby, Mark, and two young women, spend the weekend at Felix Mainwaring's country home for informal interviews. Just before they leave, they learn to their dismay that there will be no grants after all, because Father Gemini, another anthropologist, has persuaded the rich American widow who was donating the money to award it all to him.

Just before Christmas comes the news that Tom has been killed in Africa, shot in a political riot to which he was a spectator. Several weeks later, Catherine, Elaine, Deidre, and Tom's sister meet for lunch to discuss their memories of Tom and decide what to do with his papers. Each is well able to go on with her life. Deidre becomes engaged to Digby, who is to receive the unexpired portion of Tom's grant. Catherine sees more of Alaric, whom she has persuaded to burn his anthropological notes. The novel ends optimistically, with a hint of a future marriage between them.

Analysis

Barbara Pym often commented on the similarity between the work of the anthropologist (which she knew about through her work as assistant editor of the journal *Africa*) and the novelist. Each is concerned with the detached, objective observation of human behavior. Part of the humor of *Less than Angels* lies in the fact that the tables are turned: The observers become the observed, and the anthropological profession does not come out of it well. Its rituals, consisting of jargon-ridden seminar papers, scholarly articles, the sending of offprints to all the right people, and periodic spells of fieldwork, are subjected to Pym's gentle but pointed satire. Even the anthropologists find their own profession unfulfilling. Tom questions the value of it, Mainwaring is no longer much interested in it, Mark leaves it, Alaric finds liberation through rejecting it, and Catherine mocks its "cowardly" caution, in contrast to the aplomb of poets and novelists, who do not fear to rush in with their analyses of the human mind, heart, and soul.

Pym saw the literary uses of anthropology, realizing that it was not confined to the study of "primitive" African tribes. One minor character in the novel, a French anthropologist, observes English culture as if he is doing fieldwork, and Pym's narrator frequently looks with a detached eye at English social customs and rituals, such as a debutante ball and a flower-and-vegetable show in Shropshire, and suggests that the customs of faraway tribes in Africa may not be any more strange than English ones.

Mabel and Rhoda are also anthropologists of a kind, since they spend a large amount of time at their upper windows, observing the eccentric (at least to them) activities of Alaric. Yet they never approach the objectivity of the anthropologist, judging what they see only by the narrow standards of suburbia—it is not proper, for example, to beat the carpets in the evening (if everyone were to do it, "just think of the noise!")—and their attitude contradicts one of the first tenets of anthropological research, that the observer must never exhibit disapproval or disgust, however unusual the activity being observed (this according to Miss Clovis, who quotes from an anthropological manual that she once read).

One main theme of the novel that Pym's literary anthropology unveils is relationships between men and women. Pym suggests that men arrange these relationships to their own advantage. Digby's facetious remark to Deidre about the probable relationship between Tom and Catherine, "the woman giving the food and the shelter and doing some typing for him and the man giving the priceless gift of himself," has some general application. Another telling moment comes when Rhoda agrees to wash Father Tulliver's clerical clothes, because his wife is sick and he has no intention of learning how to wash them himself. Rhoda does wonder why he cannot send the clothes to the laundry, but the thought seems disloyal, and she suppresses it. Deidre protests, conveniently forgetting that she has been doing typing for Tom. Even Catherine, who is usually an independent spirit and has a moderately successful career of her own, experiences the unequal relationship between the sexes, commenting on "the general uselessness of women if they cannot understand or reverence a man's work, or even if they can." Yet the dominant note is not one of anger but one of a woman's acceptance of her subordinate and limited role. "I don't think we can ever hope to know all that goes on in a man's life or even to follow him with our loving thoughts," Catherine says.

Yet there is a paradox, brought out by Catherine's observation that men need women stronger than themselves. Tom, the principal male character, is shown to be weak. Even as he moves out of Catherine's flat, he looks to her for comfort (Catherine has to look to herself for comfort), and he ends up exiled from those who love him. His death is not heroic.

Catherine sees that behind the forbidding exterior of another important male character, Alaric, lies the insecure little boy. Alaric feels the burden of his life lessen only when he burns his anthropological notes in a celebratory bonfire, and there is a hint that he is now able to adopt Catherine's values. Asked what he is going to do now, he replies that he is free to do whatever he wants: "I could even write a novel." One is reminded that anthropology, with its emphasis on understanding human life through rational, orderly analysis and classification, is presented as a predominantly male world, and it must be supplemented by a female sensibility if it is to be of any value.

Context

Less than Angels was Pym's fourth novel, and the first to be published in the United States (1956). In England, the novel did not receive as much attention from reviewers as Pym's earlier novels had, and its sales were lower. In the United States, the book had almost no impact, and it was not until after her death in 1980 that Pym began to acquire a reputation across the Atlantic.

Like Pym's other novels of the 1950's, *Less than Angels* (the title is derived from a poem by Alexander Pope) provides a snapshot of middle-class social relations in England before the revolutionary changes of the 1960's. Although the unequal relations between the sexes are made abundantly clear, there are also some hints that times are changing and that the men are unsettled by shifting social mores. Returning home from a party, for example, Digby suggests to Mark that one of them should have seen Deidre home. Mark says he must cure himself of such an old-fashioned idea, and Digby replies, "Yes, of course, one's apt to forget that women consider themselves our equals now. But just occasionally one remembers that men were once the stronger sex." There are also some backward glances at the conventions of an earlier era that suggest how times have changed. Deidre sees a daring play with her boyfriend, and Mabel remarks that when she was young, in the 1920's, she would have been embarrassed to have seen such a play with a man. She does not think, however, that relations between men and women, although they have changed, are any more satisfactory.

One relationship in the novel, that between Tom and Catherine, seems to look forward beyond the 1950's. The casual way in which they share a flat without being married shocks no one in their bohemian circle, but the fact that Tom's aunt pays Catherine a visit and is ready to censure her for her conduct reminds the reader that she is indeed still in the 1950's, before the sexual liberation of the 1960's and 1970's made such arrangements more common.

Sources for Further Study

Burkhart, Charles. *The Pleasure of Miss Pym*. Austin: University of Texas Press, 1987. Starting from the premise that Pym wrote for pleasure and to please, Burkhart analyzes what that pleasure consisted of, for Pym and her reader. Topics include the importance of anthropologists and Africa, relationships between men and women, and the Anglican church. *Less than Angels* receives its share of comment.
Cotsell, Michael. *Barbara Pym*. New York: St. Martin's Press, 1989. Includes a

concise reading of *Less than Angels*, which Long sees as depicting a crueler, harder world than that displayed in Pym's earlier novels (contrast Nardin's view that *Less than Angels* is the most serene of Pym's early novels). Pym sets professional anthropology against "literary" anthropology, to the advantage of the latter.

Long, Robert Emmet. *Barbara Pym*. New York: Frederick Ungar, 1986. Includes detailed analysis of *Less than Angels*, which Long sees as having the form of a maze in which characters try to understand and form relationships with one another. It is concerned also with the isolation of women. Includes a useful bibliography that lists reviews of *Less than Angels*.

Nardin, Jane. *Barbara Pym*. Boston: Twayne, 1985. This book-length study of Pym's work surveys her major novels. Includes a brief but interesting reading of *Less than Angels*. Pym plays with ideas prompted by the realization that the novelist can effectively use methods of observation—detached, tolerant—that are essentially anthropological.

Wyatt-Brown, Anne M. *Barbara Pym: A Critical Biography*. Columbia: University of Missouri Press, 1992. Describes Pym's life and work in much more detail than does Hazel Holt's biography *A Lot to Ask* (1990). Argues that Pym's art allowed her to triumph over dejection and social constraints; her creativity was spurred by her personal dissatisfactions. *Less than Angels* represents a temporary triumph over despair; its subtext is Pym's survival as a writer.

Bryan Aubrey

LETTERS FROM THE FIELD, 1925-1975

Author: Margaret Mead (1901-1978)
Type of work: Letters
Time of work: 1925-1975
Locale: Samoa, New Guinea, Bali, the West Indies, and Nebraska
First published: 1977

Principal personages:
> MARGARET MEAD, one of the leading figures in anthropology in
> the twentieth century
> REO F. FORTUNE, a New Zealand-born anthropologist whom
> Mead married as her second husband in 1928 and who
> accompanied her on field trips to the Admiralty Islands and
> New Guinea
> GREGORY BATESON, British anthropologist whom Mead wed as
> her third husband in 1936 and who collaborated with her in
> fieldwork on the island of Bali

Form and Content

Margaret Mead's *Letters from the Field, 1925-1975* is a selection of letters written by Mead while on anthropological field trips to provide "one record, a very personal record, of what it has meant to be a practicing anthropologist over the last fifty years." She recognizes that fieldwork is only one aspect of the anthropologist's work. She even admits the inevitable subjectivity to be found in any individual observer's account. Yet she emphasizes that fieldwork—"immersing oneself in the ongoing life of another people, suspending for the time both one's beliefs and disbeliefs, and of simultaneously attempting to understand mentally and physically this other version of reality"—has supplied the data on which anthropology rests.

Modern fieldwork was just starting when Mead entered anthropology in the mid-1920's—invented by British anthropologist Bronislaw Malinowski and Columbia University's Franz Boas. The methods of fieldwork were, and remain, grounded "in certain fundamental theoretical assumptions about the psychic unity of mankind and the scientists' responsibility to respect all cultures, no matter how simple or exotic." Letters written to associates, friends, and family from the field have a special role in the fieldwork experience. "One must somehow maintain," Mead explains, "the delicate balance between empathic participation and self-awareness. . . . Letters can be a way of occasionally righting the balance as, for an hour or two, one relates oneself to people in one's other world."

Most of the recipients of the letters are, unfortunately, not named, but they appear to fall into two groups. Some letters are written to such respected mentors as Boas and Ruth Benedict of the Columbia Anthropology Department, sociologist William Fielding Ogburn, and Clark Wissler, the chair of the ethnography department of the American Museum of Natural History. Most of those written during the early years of

Mead's career, however, were intended to keep informed persons with whom she had a close personal relationship—such as members of her family and intimate friends. As time passed, however, the letters become more formal accounts, almost on the "record," intended for a broader audience. Their chronological arrangement follows the trajectory of Mead's professional life.

Analysis

Margaret Mead was born on December 16, 1901, in Philadelphia, Pennsylvania, one of five children of Edward Sherwood Mead, a University of Pennsylvania economist, and Emily Fogg Mead. After attending DePauw University for one year, Mead switched to Barnard College, Columbia University. Taking a course with Boas during her senior year led her to make anthropology her life work. After receiving her B.A. from Barnard in 1923, she did graduate work at Columbia under Boas and Benedict. She wrote in 1925 for her Ph.D. a library-based dissertation titled "An Inquiry into the Question of Cultural Stability in Polynesia." Her first field trip was to the Samoan Islands in 1925 and 1926, where she studied female adolescence in Samoan society.

The resulting book, *Coming of Age in Samoa: A Psychological Study of Primitive Youth for Western Civilization* (1928), made Mead's reputation in anthropology and was a popular success. The book pictured adolescence in Samoa as a happy, carefree time without the stress and turmoil associated with adolescence in the United States. Mead's findings were widely read as an indictment of the sexual repressiveness of American society. Even more significant were the work's implications for the ongoing nature-versus-nurture controversy. Mead underlined that her findings indicated the decisive importance of culture—rather then biology—in determining human behavior. That conclusion became the center of renewed controversy when Derek Freeman's *Margaret Mead and Samoa: The Making and Unmaking of an Anthropological Myth* (1983) accused Mead of misunderstanding not only Samoan adolescence but also the larger Samoan culture. Although he exonerated Mead from deliberate falsification of data, Freeman charged that her ideological commitment to cultural determinism had distorted her interpretation.

The letters from the Samoan trip in *Letters from the Field* reveal Mead's excitement, even awe, at "being in a strange land." They also show a literary artist's talent for describing vividly the physical landscape, the dress of the people, and ceremonies and customs. The materials shed no direct light on the Freeman-Mead controversy, but there is evidence confirming the superficiality of Mead's immersion in Samoan culture. At the primary site of her investigation, for example, she lived at the house of the local representative of the United States naval administration rather than in a Samoan household, to avoid "the loss of efficiency due to the food and the nerve-wracking conditions of living with half a dozen people in the same room, in a house without walls, always sitting on the floor and sleeping in constant expectation of having a pig or a chicken thrust itself upon one's notice."

After her return to the United States in 1926, Mead was appointed assistant curator of ethnology at the American Museum of Natural History. She would remain associated with the museum for the rest of her career. A Social Science Research Council fellowship in 1928-1929 allowed her to make her second field trip—this time to Manus Island, one of the Admiralty Islands off the coast of New Guinea and part of the Melanesian cultural area—with her second husband, Reo F. Fortune, to study the thought patterns of primitive children. The outcome was her *Growing Up in New Guinea: A Comparative Study of Primitive Education* (1930).

In the summer of 1930, Mead made a third field trip—to study an American Indian tribe, focusing upon the changing life of American Indian women. In her *The Changing Culture of an Indian Tribe* (1932), she used the tribal alias of "Antler" to protect the tribe studied, but her introduction to the letters from this expedition identifies the tribe as the Omaha Indians of Nebraska.

Between 1931 and 1933, she and Fortune were in New Guinea investigating the formation of the social personalities of the two sexes by studying three sharply differing tribes—the Arapesh, the Mundugumor, and the Tchambuli—each with its own stylized set of sex roles. Her book *Sex and Temperament in Three Primitive Societies* (1935) portrayed how "different societies emphasize the same or contrasting temperaments as the basis of the expected personalities of men and women."

The "longest and in many ways the most complexly organized" of Mead's field trips was her stay during 1936 and 1939 on the island of Bali, then part of the Dutch East Indies, now part of Indonesia. Her collaborator was her third husband, Cambridge University anthropologist Gregory Bateson. The large collection of stills and films they collected was the basis for their jointly authored *Balinese Character: A Photographic Analysis* (1962).

World War II made field trips impossible abroad. In 1953, however, Mead returned to Manus to report on the changes that had taken place since her previous stay. That trip—resulting in *New Lives for Old: Cultural Transformation—Manus 1928-1953* (1960)—was the last in which she did the major part of the fieldwork herself.

The last segment of *Letters from the Field* is made up of letters written during brief visits between 1964 and 1975 to research projects by younger associates and friends in the Admiralty Islands, New Guinea, and Montserrat, West Indies. Mead died on November 15, 1978, in New York City from pancreatic cancer.

Context

In the post-World War II years, Margaret Mead was popularly regarded as America's—indeed, the world's—foremost anthropologist. When the women's movement revived in the late 1960's, she was accordingly regarded by many younger feminists as a role model for their own aspirations for personal autonomy and professional achievement, Her argument—most fully articulated in *Sex and Temperament*—that gender-role behavior was culturally rather than biologically determined became a cardinal article of the feminist creed.

In *The Feminine Mystique* (1963), however, Betty Friedan complained that Mead, despite her "revolutionary vision" of what women might achieve, had increasingly become guilty of glorifying women's childbearing role, and Mead had ambivalent feelings about the new women's movement. Her biographer Jane Howard relates that Mead thought word formation such as "chairperson" silly, was scornful of middle-aged women who complained about discrimination when they had never even tried anything except marriage and children, and was offended by the "which side are you on?" mentality of many feminists.

Sources for Further Study

Foerstel, Lenora, and Angela Gilliam, eds. *Confronting the Margaret Mead Legacy: Scholarship, Empire, and the South Pacific*. Philadelphia: Temple University Press, 1992. This collection of papers reassessing from a left-wing perspective the treatment of South Pacific peoples by Western anthropologists faults Mead and her followers for promoting a sensationalized image of the Pacific peoples as oversexed primitives.

Freeman, Derek. *Margaret Mead and Samoa: The Making and Unmaking of an Anthropological Myth*. Cambridge, Mass.: Harvard University Press, 1983. An Australian anthropologist with extensive fieldwork experience in Samoa, Freeman provoked a major controversy when he accused *Coming of Age* of misinterpreting not only adolescence in Samoa but also the larger Samoan culture. Although exonerating Mead of deliberately falsifying data, Freeman charges that her ideological commitment to cultural determinism led her to distort what she saw and heard.

Friedan, Betty. *The Feminine Mystique*. New York: W. W. Norton, 1963. The chapter "The Functional Freeze, the Feminine Protest, and Margaret Mead" complains that Mead's increasing "glorification of women in the female role—as defined by their sexual biological function" (most strikingly in her 1970 book *Male and Female: A Study of the Sexes in a Changing World)*—had become "a cornerstone of the feminine mystique" that keeps women subordinate.

Grosskurth, Phyllis. *Margaret Mead*. London: Penguin Books, 1988. A brief interpretative synthesis that takes a debunking view of Mead, emphasizing her egotism, her pretentiousness and self-certitude (her "being sure she was right about everything"), and her publicity-seeking and hunger for adulation.

Howard, Jane. *Margaret Mead: A Life*. New York: Simon & Schuster, 1984. The fullest and most thorough biography available. Howard interviewed a host of Mead's associates, friends, and family relations and did extensive research in manuscript collections, including Mead's papers in the Library of Congress. Although she is not uncritical, Howard is sympathetically admiring.

Rosenberg, Rosalind. *Beyond Separate Spheres: Intellectual Roots of Modern Feminism*. New Haven, Conn.: Yale University Press, 1982. Includes a perceptive analysis of Mead's contribution in promoting a cultural deterministic approach to male-female differences that emphasized the crucial importance of social conditioning in shaping sex roles and downgraded the significance of biological differences.

John Braeman

THE LETTERS OF EDITH WHARTON

Author: Edith Wharton (1862-1937)
Type of work: Letters
Time of work: 1874-1937
Locale: The United States, Italy, France, England, and Africa
First published: 1988

Principal personages:
EDITH WHARTON, an American novelist
BERNARD BERENSON, an Italian Renaissance art historian
MARY BERENSON, his wife
WALTER BERRY, an American lawyer and Wharton's adviser and
  companion
EDWARD L. BURLINGAME, the editor of *Scribner's Magazine*
WILLIAM CRARY BROWNELL, a literary consultant for Charles
  Scribner's Sons
CHARLES SCRIBNER, Wharton's publisher
WILLIAM MORTON FULLERTON, an American journalist and one
  of Wharton's lovers
HENRY JAMES, a writer and Wharton's mentor
GAILLARD LAPSLEY, the don of medieval history at the
  University of Cambridge and Wharton's literary executor
SARA (SALLY) NORTON, a well-read and knowledgeable woman
  who wrote an admiring letter to Wharton, beginning their long
  friendship
EDWARD ROBBINS WHARTON (TEDDY), Edith Wharton's husband
  from April 29, 1885, until their divorce in April, 1893

Form and Content

As a healthy adult, Edith Wharton mailed approximately six letters per day. Still in existence are an estimated four thousand letters of a personal nature and approximately four thousand business letters. In *The Letters of Edith Wharton*, editors R. W. B. Lewis and Nancy Lewis include not quite four hundred. These were chosen as characteristic examples of the author's letters, exemplifying her different styles, her personality, and her differing emotional states, and reflecting the stages of her important relationships.

The well-edited book includes a comprehensive introduction as well as introductions to each section, detailed footnotes (although foreign-language passages are rarely translated into English), photographs, chronologies of Wharton's life and her writings, and a thorough index. A biographical framework is used, and the letters are organized into seven periods of Wharton's life.

The vital, emotional character who emerges through the letters contradicts Wharton's public image as a reserved, austere woman. The letters reveal a woman who was spontaneous and adventurous, who lived in the moment, and who could be relied on to celebrate with or to give support to others in good and bad times.

The oldest known letter and the first in the collection, dated September 23, 1874, is addressed to Pauline Foster Du Pont. Written when Wharton (then Edith Newbold Jones) was only twelve years old, the letter reveals an extremely bright and confident girl, whose interest in and aptitude for satirical commentary on social events is already developing.

The next letter, dated almost twenty years later, on November 25, 1893, is written to Edward L. Burlingame, who that month had suggested the publication of a volume of Wharton's stories. In 1894, Wharton plunged into an identity crisis, which manifested physically in exhaustion, nausea, and depression. She stopped writing for sixteen months. This period resulted from the combination of a disappointing and unfulfilling marriage (both emotionally and sexually) and professional discouragement (her response of March 26, 1894, to Burlingame's criticism of one of her stories shows her disappointment and self-doubt). In 1896, she began the collaboration for *The Decoration of Houses*, which was published in December of 1897.

In 1898, she wrote a series of short stories and began to get treatment in a "rest-cure" program. A volume of her stories was published in 1899. In her response to praise for this work from Barrett Wendell of May 15, 1899, she refers to her illness. At this time, she also begins the criticism of the handling of her work by her publishers.

Sara Norton is introduced in Wharton's letter of February 28, 1901, at the point in their relationship Wharton first began addressing her in a colloquial manner, signing the letter, "Edith or Pussy as you please." In their letters, peppering this collection from 1901 through June 14, 1916, the two women avidly discuss literature and the events of their lives.

With the publication of *The Valley of Decision*, Wharton became acknowledged as a successful American author. One result was the commission to write articles on Italian villas for *Century* magazine. Wharton and her husband, Teddy, left for Italy in 1903. In the second section of letters, Wharton discusses her feelings about moving from one continent to another and about the inhabitants of both areas. She expresses awe on arriving in Europe, and disappointment on the return to America, exclaiming: "the tastes I am cursed with are all of a kind that cannot be gratified here."

Henry James encouraged her to write again about America, and she published *The House of Mirth* in October of 1905. The novel was an enormous and immediate success. In 1906, Wharton worked with American playwright Clyde Fitch to adapt the novel to the stage. Unfortunately, the production was a failure and closed shortly after its appearance in New York City.

During her 1906 stay in France and England, Wharton was introduced to the Parisian literary world. When the Whartons returned to Paris in 1907, they rented the residence at 58 Rue de Varenne, beginning the establishment of Wharton's European home.

The first letter of this section is written to Sara Norton, acknowledging birthday greetings. Wharton has just turned forty years old. Immediately, the reader is drawn into the living quality of the work, feeling the sense of a real person living and changing year after year. The letters also reveal that much of the fullness of Wharton's life occurred late in her life.

This section begins to cement an understanding of Wharton as a wonderful, loving friend. Besides telling the "news," she jokes, sends comfort and affection, and pleads with her friends to visit. Her epistolary relationships with Sara Norton and Scribner's continue, and new ones are established. At the end of the section, W. Morton Fullerton is introduced. The third chapter focuses primarily on Wharton's affair with Fullerton. During this time, she was also working and socializing widely. She traveled to England and entered society there. In addition, she spent time caring for her mentor and friend Henry James, who was severely depressed.

Teddy Wharton, who also was depressed, began to require much of Edith Wharton's attention. Wharton reveals in her letters the energy she spent arranging his activities, attempting to care for his health, and trying to bolster their marriage. The Fullerton letters are Wharton's most free and open letters, vacillating between confident and insecure, exuberant and desperate, contented and longing. She repeats a cycle of being jubilant, becoming terribly insecure as a result of his silence, and indignantly wanting her letters back. The editors examine her masterly June 8-11 letter in detail. By 1910, she begins to suggest sincerely that the intimacy stop, but she continues to waver. The depth of her feeling is absorbing—she has come to passion late in life and loves fully. Although her letters in chapter 4 detail her attempts to establish an amicable relationship, the difficulties between Wharton and Teddy were not resolvable. After a period of conflict with an unpredictable Teddy, during a social stay at the home Wharton built in Massachusetts, called The Mount, Wharton returned to Europe. While abroad, she learned that Teddy had sold The Mount, ending her attachment to the United States.

Once in Europe, Wharton traveled extensively with Walter Berry. She firmly established her friendship with the Berensons and produced an enormous amount of work, including *The Reef* and *Ethan Frome*. In 1913, she suffered from problems with her brother Harry, a misunderstanding with Henry James regarding a birthday present (an event she believed she would "never get over!"), and her divorce.

As indicated by the letters continued in the fifth chapter, when World War I broke out, Wharton immediately established a workroom for unemployed seamstresses in Paris. Elisina Tyler, whose important relationship with Wharton began in 1912, worked closely with Wharton on the war efforts. Tyler oversaw the programs in Wharton's absence. Confident that the projects were stable, Wharton drove to the front lines in 1915—she was the first woman to witness the war at the front. She wrote letters to Henry James describing her experience, accounts that he treasured.

For her relief efforts, Wharton received prestigious awards. She poured all of her efforts into that work for the first two years of the war. "The Refugees" was the only piece of fiction she wrote during that time. She did publish journalistic pieces, however, as well as a compilation of stories written earlier. *Summer* was published in *McClure's* magazine in 1917. *The Marne* came out in 1918.

Egerton Winthrop, a friend and mentor of Wharton's, died during the war, as did

Henry James, after a stroke. Wharton's letters are filled with mourning and with strong comfort for others. When the United States declared war, the tone of her letters became more hopeful. She began traveling again and in 1918 decided to buy a villa outside of Paris.

In the period represented in chapter 6, Wharton primarily focused on refurbishing her two homes, welcoming visitors, and writing. In fact, she wrote so prolifically that it was difficult to keep track of her projects. For her work, she was paid extremely well. *The Age of Innocence* won for Wharton the Pulitzer Prize for fiction, although the jury originally selected Sinclair Lewis' *Main Street*. Wharton wrote Lewis a kind, sincere letter expressing her admiration for his work and her pleasure in learning that he read hers. Wharton continued to travel. On her last trip to America, she became the first woman to receive an honorary degree from Yale University. In 1926, Wharton rented a yacht and with some friends took a ten-week cruise through the Aegean. In 1927, Walter Berry died. Wharton writes of sitting with him for his last three days in a letter to John Hugh Smith which, like her other grieving letters, is heartfelt, touching, honest, and filled with love. September of 1928 and the release of *The Children* marked Wharton's peak in her fiction career in terms of popularity and financial compensation. She was disappointed by the reviews, however, which she called "drivel." Soon afterward, the harsh winter destroyed her gardens, and Wharton contracted a severe case of pneumonia.

Although it affected her later than others, Wharton felt the effects of the Depression—primarily in terms of rejection of her writing as a result of subject matter or resistance to paying her high prices. Because she always stayed in touch with her publishers, many letters to Rutger B. Jewett (the editor of D. Appleton) are included in this section. Wharton was very troubled by the political occurrences of the time (such as the rise of communism and fascism and the riots in Paris), and she became more conservative. Her interest in the church increased as well. In this period, Wharton continued to acknowledge her suffering in her letters—particularly that caused by the deaths of her personal maid, Elise, and her friend and housekeeper, Catharine Gross. Nevertheless, her production in the 1930's was remarkable, and her financial standing was entirely reestablished with some of her work running successfully on Broadway. She was making great progress in the promising novel *The Buccaneers*.

Wharton's last letter before her death on August 11, 1937, was written after she had a stroke. A replication of the letter is included in the photo plates. The letter to Matilda Gay is full of the life and character that are found in her other letters, although the handwriting is shaky.

Analysis

Like her fiction, Wharton's letters combine elements traditionally considered "female," such as the detailing of daily activities, with elements traditionally considered "male," such as consciously literary prose. Both she and her correspondents were conscious of her ability to work outside traditional gender limitations. When Fullerton addresses Wharton as "Cher Ami" (French for "Dear Friend"), he purposely uses the masculine form of each word. Wharton herself commented on a distinction between writing by men and by women in a response to criticism of her novel *The Fruit of the Tree*.

> I conceive my subjects like a man—that is, rather more architectonically & dramati-cally than most women—& then execute them like a woman; or rather, I sacrifice, to my desire for construction & breadth, the small incidental effects that women have always excelled in, the episodical characterization, I mean.

In her June 8-11 letter to Fullerton, she says that they share the combination of these traits, the ability to feel the "dream-side of things" as well as clearness of thought. Then she aligns herself with the goddess of reason—a phrase that (if she is associating "reason" with maleness) combines the "female" and "male" worlds.

Wharton not only goes back and forth between the two styles but also combines them, a characteristic most clearly evident in the Fullerton letters. This intermingling of highly intellectual discussion and extremely charged emotional feeling with do-mestic, human, or mundane events and concerns is what makes her letters particularly interesting and gives the reader insight into her life and mind.

Wharton's remarkable intellect and knowledge of texts is evident in her letters. She quotes and discusses a wide variety of books from different time periods, cultures, and languages, ranging from literary to scientific to artistic to philosophical to religious. Many of the references in the letters are obscure, and it is clear that reading and learning were essential to her being and development.

Wharton's style of letter writing reflected her taste in literature. Wharton originally liked the Jamesian novel, but after 1920, she started to prefer the Victorian novel. Her letters reflect this shift as they become more free and casual, filled with anecdotes, random thoughts, and gossipy questions and stories.

Wharton was conscious that the style of her letters varied depending on her correspondent, noting in a letter to Berenson, "Goethe always Schillered when he wrote to Schiller, didn't he?" Her letters to her editors and publishers are generally consistent. They are formal business letters. Although Henry James burned all but a few of her letters, those Wharton wrote to him about the war reflect his style. Nevertheless, although her voice alters slightly depending on the recipient, it is always her distinctive voice.

Context

History is an imperfect science, often changing and being reinterpreted depending on the sources from which it is gathered. Much of female history has been neglected, since it has not been recorded in history books. Wharton's contribution to literature is extensive. Her work is important not only for literature but also for women, because she wrote about society—which included the position of women in the cultures she knew. Her letters also give insight into the changing times through which she lived and give the reader the personal view of an aware woman of the day.

Wharton lived during a time when letters were written, and she continued to write them after their heyday had passed. In addition to being prolific, she is among those epistolary writers who are admired for the elegance of their letters. She distinguishes herself from this group by the intense personal content and high literary quality of the letters.

Until recently, Wharton was not considered a feminist by many, since she did not fight politically for social advances for women and avoided well-known feminists of the time. To characterize her as a misogynist, however, is far from the truth. Wharton's writing clearly shows her strong feelings about the predicament of women in society. Furthermore, her writing reflects social history and therefore the social entrapment of women during her lifetime. For example, her letters show her sympathy for women stuck in unhappy marriages because of social mores—a situation that she knew personally.

Wharton was a role model and a trailblazer. Often, she was the first woman in an arena in terms of both activity and recognition by award. In addition to being a fine writer, she was a savvy businesswoman. Throughout her life, she expressed her feelings about how her publishers were handling her affairs. She headed committees. Her letters describe her self-reliance in both professional and domestic situations.

The Letters of Edith Wharton is both a chronicle of the great author's life and a literary test. These letters not only reveal historical events from a highly intelligent and thoughtful personal perspective but also draw the reader into a community of artists, a world of literature, and a creative mind.

Sources for Further Study

Auchincloss, Louis. *Edith Wharton*. Minneapolis: University of Minnesota Press, 1961. An integrated review of Wharton's life and work.

Coolidge, Olivia. *Edith Wharton: 1862-1937*. New York: Charles Scribner's Sons, 1964. In this straightforward biography, Coolidge divides Wharton's life into various periods of time, from "The World of Little Miss Jones" to "Fight with a New World."

Joslin, Katherine. *Edith Wharton*. New York: St. Martin's Press, 1991. Joslin discusses Wharton's life and work from a feminist perspective in a series of essays.

Lewis, R. W. B. *Edith Wharton: A Biography*. New York: Harper & Row, 1975. A remarkably thorough and well-written biography revealing the complexity of Wharton's character.

Lindberg, Gary H. *Edith Wharton and the Novel of Manners*. Charlottesville: University Press of Virginia, 1975. Wharton is often called a "novelist of manners." Lindberg analyzes her work in terms of this view, dividing his book into categories of social manners.

McDowell, Margaret B. *Edith Wharton*. Boston: Twayne, 1976. McDowell takes a new look at Wharton's work, emphasizing Wharton's important position in American literature.

Ursula Burton

THE LETTERS OF MARGARET FULLER

Author: Margaret Fuller (1810-1850)
Type of work: Letters
Time of work: 1817-1849
Locale: The United States, England, Italy, and France
First published: 1983

Principal personages:
> MARGARET FULLER, an intellectual and feminist
> JAMES FREEMAN CLARKE, a Unitarian clergyman
> WILLIAM HENRY CHANNING, a radical theologian and
> socialist
> RALPH WALDO EMERSON, a leading Transcendentalist and
> Fuller's early mentor
> MARGARETT CRANE FULLER, Fuller's mother
> TIMOTHY FULLER, Fuller's father, a congressman and lawyer
> FREDERICK HENRY HEDGE, a leading Transcendentalist
> JAMES NATHAN, a German businessman who rejected Fuller's
> love for him
> GIOVANNI ANGELO OSSOLI, Fuller's lover, the father of her child,
> and probably her husband
> SUSAN PRESCOTT, Fuller's teacher at Groton
> CAROLINE STURGIS, a lifelong close friend of Fuller

Form and Content

The Letters of Margaret Fuller, comprising five volumes and almost nine hundred letters, provides a rich and complex record of the life and ideas of this prominent nineteenth century American intellectual and feminist. The letters cover virtually her entire life, beginning with one she wrote at age seven and concluding with those of 1849, less than one year before her death. They are organized chronologically by year; each volume has a separate preface that summarizes the major events, both personal and historical, of the years of that volume. Additionally, volume 1 contains an introduction that discusses Fuller's life, her work, and textual issues concerning the publication of the letters. Robert N. Hudspeth, editor for all five volumes, has taken great care to present all the surviving letters that Fuller wrote, providing a less biased view of Fuller than that of the often unreliable *Memoirs of Margaret Fuller Ossoli*, written and edited after her death by her close friends Ralph Waldo Emerson, William Henry Channing, and James Freeman Clarke.

The letters provide insight into Fuller's many moods, the range of her intellectual and social interests, and her highly diverse professional career. Moreover, because Fuller knew many of the major thinkers, writers, reformers, and artists of her day, her letters provide a fascinating social history of the early to mid-nineteenth century, in Europe as well as in her native United States.

Volume 1 begins with Fuller's childhood letters, mostly to her father (who was often away in Washington, D.C., serving in the House of Representatives), and detail her early education. Her early intellectual achievement is marked by impressive precocity; she became a teacher, first in Boston and later in Providence, Rhode Island. After returning to Boston, she began her "Conversations," designed to enable women to discuss leading issues and writings of the time. In 1840, she became editor of *The Dial*, a literary magazine and the leading publication for Transcendentalist thought. She wrote of her travels out West in her letters and published an account of this trip in *Summer on the Lakes, in 1843*, which reflected her growing attention to cultural analysis rather than literary criticism. She published her most memorable work, *Woman in the Nineteenth Century*, in 1845. This landmark piece of American feminist thought seriously investigated the condition of American women, an issue whose development can be traced in the letters.

In 1844, Horace Greeley, editor of the *New York Daily Tribune*, hired her as his book reviewer. As the newspaper's first female reporter, she covered the burgeoning New York literary scene and later furnished Greeley with travel letters, detailing her observations during her first trip to politically charged Europe. This trip proved to be one of the most important events in her life, for in Europe she met with leading writers, reformers, and politicians: in England, with the Romantic poet William Wordsworth, writer-reformer Harriet Martineau, and critic-novelist Thomas Carlyle. Her introduction to the Italian revolutionary Giuseppe Mazzini in London led to her involvement with the Italian revolution the following year. In Paris, she met with the French novelist George Sand (whose novels she had earlier defended to a scandalized American audience) and the Polish poet and politician Adam Mickiewicz.

Volume 5 of the letters ends in December, 1849, when Fuller was making plans to leave Italy. There she met and fell in love with Giovanni Angelo Ossoli; she gave birth to their son, Angelo, in 1848. The final letters signal her disappointment and weariness with the turn of events in the Italians' struggle for political unification, yet they also indicate her contentment with her new family life.

Analysis

As a record of the private and public life of one of the nineteenth century United States' leading literary figures, *The Letters of Margaret Fuller* conveys a wide range of moods and ideas. The tone of the letters can be lofty or playful, highly intellectual and serious, bright and witty, consoling, passionate, and reflective. The style of her prose can likewise be complex and even convoluted; at other times, her directness and simplicity prove to be suitable for expressing her lucid, even brilliant, insights. The addressees of Fuller's letters are as various as their content and styles. She wrote newsy, often hurried, letters to her parents and siblings, informing them of her activities while she was away or summarizing news at home in her parents' absence. Letters to close women friends often show aspects of Margaret Fuller's personality that seem at odds with her very confident, assertive public persona: She sometimes expresses doubts about her abilities or admits to disappointments (in love or in her professional life). Given the span of years covered by the five volumes of *The Letters of Margaret Fuller*, they also trace her development from a precocious child who avidly sought her father's approval to an accomplished and famous woman who had become a citizen of the world.

The more famous addressees of Fuller's letters indicate the breadth of her association with public figures, both in the United States and in Europe. An early letter to Ralph Waldo Emerson thanks him for giving her a copy of his book *Nature* (1836); their friendship had an important impact on Fuller's ideas, even though in later years—especially after her travels in Europe—she was less close to him, both intellectually and personally. An 1841 letter to Henry David Thoreau, written while she was editor of *The Dial*, thanks him for a poem he submitted and gives both praise and criticism for it. Volumes 1 through 3 contain letters whose addressees are predominantly family, friends, and public figures in New England.

One of the more striking features of volume 4 is the many love letters Fuller wrote to James Nathan, a German businessman from Hamburg whom she met in New York. Fuller's letters to Nathan are often deeply passionate; her other letters—even other love letters—rarely attain the same level of emotional intensity. The letters to Nathan show Margaret Fuller as a lover, one of the many roles presented to the reader throughout *The Letters of Margaret Fuller*. As an informal, unstructured form of autobiography, the letters show Fuller as a dutiful daughter, caring and advice-giving sister, and respectful granddaughter and niece. They also show her as a concerned friend, thoughtful student, astute editor, and insightful cultural and literary critic. As Fuller matured and her horizons broadened to include life in other countries, her roles as political commentator and political activist, social reformer and social critic, expand the portrait of her as an impressively accomplished, dedicated, and intelligent woman.

The letters provide so much diversity of material that summarizing them into one or two central issues is nearly impossible, yet an important overarching theme does emerge from the five volumes taken as a whole: the tension between the private and the public personas of Margaret Fuller. She was deeply devoted to her family and friends, and she sought romantic love even after several serious rejections. She was also extremely committed to ideas and ideals, to an intellectual and later an activist existence, which often took her away from her more personal involvements and occasionally even seemed at odds with those relationships. Yet the letters, which are at once personal and interpersonal, fill an important gap between these two disparate facets of Fuller's rich and complex life. Letters that she wrote to close friends and relatives allow a glimpse into the private Fuller's thoughts and activities, and provide Fuller's more personal commentary on her professional involvements. In a similar fashion, the letters she wrote as editor of *The Dial*, as reporter for the *Tribune*, and while in Europe show that this intensely brilliant and intellectually demanding woman was not without humor, wit, and charm.

Context

Fuller is perhaps best known for *Woman in the Nineteenth Century*, an early and highly influential work of feminist thought first published in 1845. It was one of the first works to deal seriously with the social conditions of American women. Fuller was an avid reformer, both in the United States and abroad, and she was concerned with issues such as poverty, prison reform (in particular for women prisoners), and the conditions of prostitutes. She was also an important literary critic, editor of *The Dial*, translator of several important works in German, essayist, and—as a columnist for *The New York Daily Tribune*—the newspaper's first woman reporter.

Fuller set an example of woman's independence throughout her life, marrying only later (and that after she had borne a child), and she was censured by her more conservative contemporaries for this and other radical acts. She received an education that was unusual for a woman at the time; she read widely throughout her life, and the range of her knowledge is prodigious.

Fuller's "Conversations" in Boston are often identified as forerunners to the modern consciousness-raising groups, for they provided women with a forum for discussing intellectual issues that were pertinent at a time when women's roles were in transition.

Fuller is truly a "woman of letters," not only because of the copious and highly varied correspondence that is gathered in these five volumes. She was one of the nineteenth century's most prolific and diverse writers, and her work is characterized by keen insights and probing analyses of culture, people, trends, and ideas.

Unlike other important women intellectuals of her time, Margaret Fuller never limited herself to any one particular movement, cause, or genre of writing. Even during her lifetime, Fuller was considered an anomaly: Her work was considered more "masculine" than "feminine." She gave no sustained attention to issues that involved other important women reformers, such as the abolition of slavery, the temperance movement, and women's suffrage. Rather, her wide-ranging contributions were predominantly intellectual.

Margaret Fuller provided the inspiration for two of American literature's most memorable characters: Zenobia in Nathaniel Hawthorne's *Blithedale Romance* (1852) and Olive Chancellor in Henry James's *The Bostonians* (1885). Although neither of these portraits is completely flattering (nor based on Fuller alone), they do indicate the powerful effect that Fuller had on those she met, and ultimately on her culture in general.

Sources for Further Study

Allen, Margaret Vanderhaar. *The Achievement of Margaret Fuller*. University Park: Pennsylvania State University Press, 1979. Vanderhaar explores the range of Fuller's intellectual and professional accomplishments. Also shows the importance of two major influences, in chapters on Goethe and Emerson.

Blanchard, Paula. *Margaret Fuller: From Transcendentalism to Revolution*. New York: Delacorte Press/S. Lawrence, 1978. This extensive biography aims to correct the misconceptions about the Margaret Fuller of the "myth" by providing a fairer, more realistic, and more historically factual view of her than previous critics have done. Blanchard covers both Fuller's involvement with Transcendentalism and her later social activism.

Brown, Arthur W. *Margaret Fuller*. New York: Twayne, 1964. A useful, concise survey of Fuller's life and work. Contains a selected annotated bibliography of secondary sources.

Capper, Charles. *Margaret Fuller: An American Romantic Life*. New York: Oxford University Press, 1992. The subtitles of these two volumes, *The Private Years* and *The Public Years*, indicate Capper's concern with the tensions between the private (family-oriented) and the public (intellectual) Fuller. Both volumes are remarkably detailed regarding Fuller, her family, and her contemporaries.

Chevigny, Belle Gale, comp. *The Woman and the Myth: Margaret Fuller's Life and Writings*. Old Westbury, N.Y.: Feminist Press, 1976. Chevigny's anthology includes excerpts from Fuller's writings, illuminating commentary about her by contemporaries, and useful section introductions that summarize various aspects of Fuller's life and career.

Fuller, Margaret. *Margaret Fuller: American Romantic*. Edited by Perry Miller. Gloucester, Mass.: Peter Smith, 1969. Miller's anthology provides selections from Fuller's writings and correspondence, and contains an insightful foreword.

Slater, Abby. *In Search of Margaret Fuller*. New York: Delacorte Press, 1978. Slater's biography gives a very readable and accessible account of Margaret Fuller's complicated life, including her family background, romantic interests (and disappointments), and friends—both the famous and the lesser-known.

Ann A. Merrill

THE LETTERS OF VIRGINIA WOOLF

Author: Virginia Woolf (1882-1941)
Type of work: Letters
Time of work: 1888-1941
Locale: England
First published: 1975-1980

> *Principal personages:*
>   VIRGINIA WOOLF, a prominent British novelist and essayist
>   VANESSA BELL, Virginia's sister and close companion, an artist
>   who married Clive Bell
>   VIOLET DICKINSON, Virginia's childhood friend and adult
>   romantic interest
>   ROGER FRY, a painter and critic and the originator of
>   Bloomsbury's Omega Art Workshops
>   JOHN MAYNARD KEYNES, an influential economist and a member
>   of the Bloomsbury group and the Charleston artist colony
>   VITA SACKVILLE-WEST, an aristocratic writer, Harold Nicolson's
>   wife and Virginia Woolf's lover
>   THOBY STEPHEN, Virginia's brother, who died in 1906 of typhoid
>   contracted in Greece
>   LYTTON STRACHEY, a historian and a member of the Bloomsbury
>   group
>   LEONARD WOOLF, Virginia's husband, a politician, historian,
>   author, and social and political activist

Form and Content

Edited by Vita Sackville-West's son Nigel Nicolson and Joanne Trautmann, some 3,800 letters by Virginia Woolf appear in these six volumes. The letters begin with a note written by Virginia Stephen at the age of six; they end with her suicide letters to Vanessa Bell, her sister, and Leonard Woolf, her husband, in 1941 at the age of fifty-nine. In between these dates, Woolf's letters provide a personal chronicle of her life, her writing, her friends, and her feelings. They also provide insight into the core of the Bloomsbury group, a loosely-knit group of writers, artists, and intellectuals who form a bridge between the aesthetics and philosophies of Victorian England and the aesthetics and philosophies of modernism in British and American art and literature.

Among Woolf's early correspondents in the Bloomsbury circle are her brother Thoby Stephen, her sister Vanessa, Vanessa's husband Clive Bell, Lytton Strachey, Roger Fry, John Maynard Keynes, Violet Dickinson, her half brother George Duckworth, and her husband Leonard Woolf. Later volumes also include letters to contemporary writers such as T. S. Eliot, George Bernard Shaw, Rebecca West, H. G. Wells, and James Joyce. Throughout the volumes are letters to Vita Sackville-West and her husband Harold Nicolson; Sackville-West was to become Virginia's lover and the model for the title character of her novel *Orlando* (1928), described by the editor of the letters, Nigel Nicolson, Sackville-West's son and Woolf's nephew, as the longest and most charming love letter in literature.

Despite her last request to Leonard that he destroy all her papers, these documents still exist, a record of the social intercourse of one highly accomplished writer with other brilliant minds. They reveal much about the personality of a woman who at times fought mental instability, if not insanity. They also reveal the genius of a woman who devoted her life to writing, to articulating the world around her. Though sometimes hastily composed, the letters reflect a life lived at a time when carefully written words were the predominant method of social interaction.

The volumes cover the time periods as follows: volume 1, 1888-1912; volume 2, 1912-1922; volume 3, 1923-1928; volume 4, 1929-1931; volume 5, 1932-1935; volume 6, 1936-1941. Each volume is extremely well-indexed; some photographs are included. Volume 6 contains letters left out of previous volumes, as well as a speculative dating of Woolf's final letters explaining her intention to kill herself.

Analysis

The scope of such a collection of letters makes possible many different avenues of study. Their importance too derives from differing sources. In their most literal sense, they record the personal correspondence of a talented and influential writer. They also document the social interactions of the Bloomsbury group of artists, writers, and intellectuals, both within the group and with various social, political, and business contacts. They describe a time and a place, London and the English countryside in the early part of the twentieth century, a time and place of two world wars.

These letters also document a life. They provide a comprehensive record of the life of a writer considered by many to be a genius, who was plagued by periods of depression, even insanity. The letters demonstrate her personal and social life from her childhood to her death. In so doing, they offer insight into her personality, self-image, and attitudes toward people, places, and other contemporary writers. The editor of the letters, Nigel Nicolson, suggests that, while important and enlightening diaries may continue to be written, this collection of letters may never be surpassed, either in artistic merit or sheer number.

Especially in the earlier volumes, Woolf is an expressive and self-aware writer. Her tone is often playful, mocking, or sarcastic in correspondence to her childhood friends, even as they enter adulthood. The tone matures in later volumes, however, retaining the self-deprecating and reflective quality of earlier letters when Woolf's audience is a personal friend, and leaning further toward formalized gentility when she is addressing a social or business acquaintance. Thus, the earlier volumes reveal much more about her developing personality and aesthetic preferences, while the later volumes record the mature life of a Bloomsbury writer and intellectual.

By the second volume, Woolf has married and has begun to work on her earliest novels, *The Voyage Out* (1915), *Night and Day* (1919), and *Jacob's Room* (1922).

These letters record the evolution of the manuscripts, offering some insight into how the composing process is progressing, but more often addressing the issues of a novel's publication and its subsequent critical reception. Although her *Diaries* (1977-1985) reveal more about the writing process than do the letters, the latter address such items as press runs, income from writing, and the problems of printing. The Woolfs, Leonard and Virginia, began the Hogarth Press during this time, publishing for the first time the works of many writers who would become well known, such as T. S. Eliot and Katherine Mansfield.

Woolf expressed the thought that nothing in fact existed until it had been put into writing. Accordingly, her letters strongly suggest that Woolf is interpreting, if not creating, the world and the people she describes. The letters are often full of metaphor and analogy, their poetic qualities on a par with those of her novels. Whereas some sentences and entire letters appear to be well-formed thoughts, others indicate the writer's thought process behind the composition, the initial vision and subsequent revisions of an idea.

The third volume allows the reader to follow Woolf's evolving feelings for Violet Dickinson and for Vita Sackville-West especially. In letters to Vita, the salutations change from a formal, social tone to an intimate, endearing one. The contents trace the relationship of Woolf and Sackville-West, ranging from objective analysis of their passions and their social positions to discussions of the real or imagined reactions of others. Woolf writes her most enduring novels during this period: *Mrs. Dalloway* (1925), *The Common Reader* (1925), *To the Lighthouse* (1927), and her genre-breaking and gender-bending "autobiography" of Orlando. During this time, Woolf's correspondents also include Gerald Brenan, Lady Ottoline Morrell, Jacques Raverat, David Garnett, and Dora Carrington, as well as Keynes, Strachey, and Fry.

The fourth and fifth volumes follow the most productive period of Woolf's career. Her career as a writer is well established, and her correspondence reveals that her earlier self-doubt and self-deprecation has grown into a reflective analysis of her strengths and weaknesses, her passions and her humanity. During this time, she has published *Orlando* and the nonfiction work *A Room of One's Own* (1929). She is working on her most complex, possibly most innovative, novel, *The Waves* (1931).

Woolf's social life and career dominate these letters, including her close relationships with Vanessa Bell, Vita Sackville-West, and her newly acquainted admirer, the egotistical and cantankerous Ethel Smyth. She corresponds with her eventual biographer Quentin Bell, complains to Logan Pearsall Smith, and relishes the social activities of the Bloomsbury circle. During this time she writes *The Second Common Reader* (1932), publishes her mock biography of the dog *Flush* (1933), and works on the manuscript of *The Years* (1937). The Woolfs travel abroad, and Virginia writes numerous letters during their travels; Leonard's Jewishness causes Virginia some concern in prewar Germany in 1935. Her correspondence also addresses the death of two of the Bloomsbury originals, Lytton Strachey and Roger Fry.

The final volume records the letters sent as many of the Bloomsbury circle were either growing distant or dying. The coming world war becomes a frequent topic of discussion. Her letters reveal ambivalence about the quality of her final manuscript of *Between the Acts* (1941), which her husband Leonard published after her death, against her wishes. Her final thoughts are captured by the letters, some hopeful and some in despair, sent to friends and acquaintances in her last days.

Context

The collected letters provide insight into a woman's struggles in her personal and professional life. Though she elsewhere recounts the discrimination she witnesses against women throughout history, her letters reveal little of the economic deprivation of women in general. Her tone, attitude, and comments, however, indicate the subtle discriminatory attitude she faced as a woman writer, a professional career woman, soon after the Victorian era of English history had ended. The letters describe the social roles and formalities expected of a woman; occasionally, they demonstrate the conflicts created when a woman of that time filled what were considered to be men's roles. Ultimately, the letters record the social interaction of an articulate person, providing a study of life, literature, gender, and society in the person of Virginia Woolf and in the context of the Bloomsbury group, both highly representative of the evolving status of all these areas in the transitional period between the Victorian era of the nineteenth century and the modernist era of the twentieth century.

Sources for Further Study

Bell, Quentin. *Virginia Woolf: A Biography*. London: Hogarth Press, 1972. Written by Virginia Woolf's nephew, the first complete biography of Woolf was first published in two volumes (now combined). It includes numerous photographs, a chronology, references, and a short bibliography. Bell, as a family member, drew on Virginia's letters and diaries, but his work was completed before all of Woolf's letters and diaries had been compiled.

DeSalvo, Louise A. *Virginia Woolf: The Impact of Childhood Sexual Abuse on Her Life and Work*. Boston: Beacon Press, 1989. A detailed study of Woolf's life and personality based on her diaries, letters, and biographical sources. Although the abuse is predicated on vague diary entries about her half brother George Duckworth, this work provides a feminist analysis of Woolf's lesbianism.

Edel, Leon. *Bloomsbury: A House of Lions*. London: Hogarth Press, 1979. Ignoring their collective reputation as elitists, Edel sympathetically chronicles nine "Bloomsberries" (including Woolf) as they live, love, and marry, and as they debate and experiment with new forms for their lives and their arts.

Raitt, Suzanne. *Vita and Virginia: The Work and Friendship of V. Sackville-West and Virginia Woolf*. Oxford, England: Clarendon Press, 1993. An analysis of the relationship, both personal and professional, of two women, one an aristocrat and the other an artist, based on sources such as the *Diaries*.

Sackville-West, Vita. *The Letters of Vita Sackville-West to Virginia Woolf*. Edited by Louise DeSalvo and Mitchell A. Leaska. New York: William Morrow, 1985. Providing only letters, this work highlights the sometimes intimate correspondence between two fascinating women whose romance is recounted in the thinly veiled autobiography *Orlando*.

Woolf, Virginia. *The Diary of Virginia Woolf*. 5 vols. Edited by Anne Olivier Bell. New York: Harcourt Brace Jovanovich, 1977-1984. Though vast, these volumes are well indexed and provide the most authoritative source for any study of Woolf or her politics and philosophy. Contains an introduction by Quentin Bell.

Bradley R. Bowers

LEVITATION
Five Fictions

Author: Cynthia Ozick (1928-   )
Type of work: Novella and short stories
First published: 1982

Form and Content

In *Levitation: Five Fictions*, Cynthia Ozick presents the reader with four short stories and a novella, all of which focus on the problematic relationship between the Jewish artist and history. This book, Ozick's third collection of short fiction, features women protagonists whose lives are disrupted by their own creations.

"Levitation," the work that opens and names this collection, begins as a couple named Feingold try to rise above their secondary status as authors by giving a party for famous writers. Although no stars attend, the Feingolds' apartment fills with minor writers. In the dining room, the guests are either gentiles or very secular Jews. In contrast, the living room is dominated by a Holocaust survivor surrounded by Mr. Feingold and the more intense, serious Jewish guests. Standing in the hall between the two groups, Lucy Feingold, a convert to Judaism, realizes that she rejects the Jews and their fascination with history and anti-Semitism. A dual vision ensues, allowing her to see the living room, with its human links to the past, rise upward toward the ceiling; meanwhile, she imagines herself joining a pagan festival in a park, emphasizing her choice of Hellenism over Hebraism.

"Shots" also focuses on the difficulties posed by an artist's struggle to understand her relationship to the past; the unnamed, first-person, female narrator has become a photographer in order to freeze people into a moment of time. After capturing a murder on film, the narrator becomes aware of the power of "shooting" someone with a camera. Appropriately for someone fascinated with preserving the past, the narrator develops an infatuation with an unhappily married historian. The story ends as the narrator remains entrapped in this asexual, nonproductive relationship, referring to her camera as "my chaste aperture, my dead infant, husband of my bosom."

The short pieces entitled "From a Refugee's Notebook" are introduced with a short passage that explains that two "fragments were found in the vacated New York apartment of an unidentified refugee from an unspecified land." The first relic is a meditation on a picture of Sigmund Freud's study in Vienna in which the narrator notes the presence of hundreds of small, carved, ancient stone gods. Speculating that Freud has attempted to become a god by "standing apart from nature" through the invention of the id, ego, and superego, the essay contrasts Freud's paganism with Moses' monotheism. The second fragment, "The Sewing Harems," continues the exploration of the dangers of disrupting nature's rhythms. Making the locale for this story the planet Acirema, a word meant to be read backward, Ozick satirically comments on America's fascination with issues of reproduction. In Acirema, women decorate themselves by sewing their skin with thread, and some of these artists of the body band together, sewing up their vaginas to reduce the world's population. Their plan backfires when these "sewing harems" actually increase the population after societal reaction produces a cult celebrating fertility and motherhood.

The problems of social change are more gracefully explored in the Puttermesser stories; the first of these stories has the long, three-part title "Puttermesser: Her Work History, Her Ancestry, Her Afterlife." Although she is a New York lawyer and an independent, unmarried woman, Ruth Puttermesser longs for her lost Jewish tradition and imaginatively constructs conversations in which a long-dead uncle teaches her Hebrew. This story ends with a challenge to Puttermesser's biographer, Ozick herself, to imagine where to go with Ruth's story.

Ozick picks up Puttermesser's life history twelve years later in the novella *Puttermesser and Xanthippe*. Now forty-six, Puttermesser loses her married lover when she prefers reading Plato to having sex; further, her life is complicated by periodontal disease and her demotion at City Hall. In response, Puttermesser, in a sort of fugue state, draws on her knowledge of Jewish folklore and forms a golem, an artificially formed being reputed to aid Jewish communities in times of trouble. Although the golem, Xanthippe, initially helps Puttermesser become mayor, institutes a plan for an urban utopia, and restores order to the city, it ultimately grows out of control. Puttermesser finally unmakes her creation, and the city reverts to its previous, ungovernable state.

Analysis

In her fiction, Ozick's central concerns are the conflict between Hebraism and Hellenism and the fear that the production of art is a breach of the Second Commandment's prohibition against creating idols. Ozick is particularly harsh with those characters who abandon their Jewish identity in favor of pagan imagination, but she is also sensitive to the dangers of a personality that focuses on history and forgets to produce the future. With the exception of the essay "Freud's Room," *Levitation: Five Fictions* focuses particularly on women artists and the difficulties surrounding their efforts to create both identity and art.

In "Levitation," the title story, the reader first believes that the author-couple are solidly united by their literary ambitions. Their main connection, however, is a rejection of their respective traditions. Feingold has chosen a non-Jewish wife, and Lucy abandons Christianity to convert to Judaism. Although this alliance seems superficially happy, both are dissatisfied by their secondary status as writers. Their minimal production, one book each, is reflected in the absence of their actual children, who are mentioned but never appear. During a party that the Feingolds give, Lucy's visions make her realize that she is stifled by Jewish monotheism, and she chooses instead the goddesses of fertility, the Madonna and Astarte. Meanwhile, Feingold has joined the group of Jews who are repeating the stories of their shared history. Although the story ends without a resolution, it is Lucy's failed conversion to Judaism that is most problematic: How will she proceed with her marriage and her art? How can Jewish history be reconciled with creativity? Ozick leaves these questions unanswered as she leaves the room of Jews suspended in the air.

In "Shots," the dominant imagery emphasizes the sterility and stagnation of this female photographer's life. Although she becomes infatuated with a historian named Sam, he loses his umbrella with a horse-head handle at their first meeting. Horses generally indicate virility, but Sam has lost his sexuality, at least in relation to the protagonist, and refuses to betray his wife sexually. The narrator's artistry, motivated by her desire to capture time, is unable to create life. Instead, one of her photographic shots coincides with the subject's death by gunfire. While the photographer visits Sam, his wife, named Verity, truthfully predicts the photographer's future when she drapes her in a nun's habit, thus consigning the narrator to an antique infertility.

The weakest stories in this collection are the pair referred to by Ozick as "From a Refugee's Notebook." Their juxtaposition, however, is interesting because of the inclusion of the stone idols that fascinate the narrator of "Freud's Room." The idolatry of stones is repeated in the companion piece "The Sewing Harems," in which the children of the harem members erect stone vulvas everywhere in their deification of motherhood. Because the children are themselves failures of their mother's intention to artistically render themselves sterile, the new idolatry is an ironic reversal of the old idolatry: Both are obsessed with the reproductive choices of women.

In contrast, Ruth Puttermesser is one of Ozick's most interesting creations; she represents a woman clearly defined by her name, which means "butter knife." Puttermesser has no edge, no effectiveness. Giving up on private law practice because of barriers erected by sexism and anti-Semitism, Puttermesser leads a quietly nonproductive life in New York's bureaucratic maze. Instead of producing or reproducing, Puttermesser consumes, thinking of heaven as a place where one could read all day without distractions and consume candy without contracting gum disease. Unfortunately, time will not leave Ruth alone; she is forced from her comfortable nest in her parents' apartment, and her job is taken over by a political appointee. Although she wishes to avoid change, she is unable to stop history.

In the Puttermesser stories, Ozick presents a character who learns about her religious tradition but does not participate in it, thus opening a door for disaster. When she is enraged by her treatment at City Hall, she unthinkingly forms a golem/daughter to help her achieve power and change New York for the better. This act of creativity, however, while proceeding from Puttermesser's knowledge of folklore, lacks both religious faith and the necessary participation of other Jews. In folk tales, golems grow too large and become destructive; Puttermesser, by acting alone and transgressing her tradition, has amplified the danger involved. When Puttermesser is finally forced to destroy her creation, she experiences the pain of destroying her only child and her hope of participating in the future.

Context

Levitation: Five Fictions reflects Cynthia Ozick's fascination with the problems of creativity for a Jewish artist. For Ozick, the artistic act always carries within it the danger of creating false idols, thereby betraying monotheism. In this collection of stories, the central characters are female, and the challenges inherent in Ozick's view of creativity are seemingly complicated by the protagonists' gender. Ozick's previously published fiction, however, which includes male protagonists, illustrates that the temptations that she presents to her protagonists apply equally to males and females. Although all of her characters in this collection are women who fail to achieve satisfaction personally and artistically, Ozick clearly indicates that their sterility emanates from their inability to uphold tradition without fossilizing it.

Ozick states in her introduction to *Bloodshed: Three Novellas* that her function as a writer is "to judge and interpret the world." Ozick's harsh judgment of her characters and the twentieth century that they inhabit is reminiscent of Flannery O'Connor or Muriel Spark. This author demands that her protagonists struggle with a world in which the wrong moral choice inevitably leads to violence, death, or slow decay. Through her device of emotionally distancing characters from the reader, Ozick allows their actions to be seen clearly, almost as case studies.

Ozick often inserts magical elements into otherwise ordinary stories to alert the reader to the metaphysical struggles that are present. Through her use of the fantastic, she underscores the displacement of her characters in the world and their resultant inability to produce, physically or creatively. The failed woman artist is the representative artist; by "judging" and "interpreting" such failures, Ozick provides cautionary tales for those women who desire to create.

Sources for Further Study

Bloom, Harold, ed. *Cynthia Ozick*. New York: Chelsea House, 1986. This collection covers Ozick's works up to 1983. Although many of the pieces are merely brief book reviews, Victor Strasberg's contribution includes a brief but illuminating discussion of Ozick's novellas. Bloom's introduction is interesting for its treatment of Ozick's essays.

Currier, Susan, and Daniel J. Cahill. "A Bibliography of Writings by Cynthia Ozick." *Texas Studies in Literature and Language* 25, no. 2 (Summer, 1983): 313-321. This complete listing of Ozick's works up to 1983 is dated, but it is helpful in that it cites works that are not usually cited in other listings.

Friedman, Lawrence S. *Understanding Cynthia Ozick*. Columbia: University of South Carolina Press, 1991. An entry in the *Understanding Contemporary Literature* series, this book is designed for those who are unfamiliar with works that use nontraditional literary forms and techniques. Particularly helpful introduction for first-time readers of Ozick's fiction.

Kauvar, Elaine M. *Cynthia Ozick's Fiction: Tradition and Invention*. Bloomington: Indiana University Press, 1993. A close reading of Ozick's fiction that avoids theoretical approaches. In the chapter that deals with the stories in *Levitation*, Kauvar emphasizes the links between the stories and their symbolism. Ozick's sources and references are exhaustively explored.

Lowin, Joseph. *Cynthia Ozick*. Boston: Twayne, 1988. A very readable interpretation of Ozick's fiction, this book is also useful for its chronology, selected bibliography, and first chapter, which provides a brief biography of Ozick.

Pinsker, Sanford. *The Uncompromising Fictions of Cynthia Ozick*. Columbia: University of Missouri Press, 1987. A brief analysis that includes a short chapter on *Levitation* entitled "Dreams of Jewish Magic/The Magic of Jewish Dreams."

Zatlin, Linda. "Cynthia Ozick's *Levitations: Five Fictions*." *Studies in American Jewish Literature* 4 (1985): 121-123. An investigation of the tensions between creativity and Judaism in *Levitation*.

Terri Hume Oliver

LIFE BEFORE MAN

Author: Margaret Atwood (1939-   )
Type of work: Novel
Type of plot: Domestic realism
Time of plot: October 29, 1976, to August 18, 1978
Locale: Toronto, Canada
First published: 1979

Principal characters:
>ELIZABETH, a woman who has had a string of affairs, most
>   recently with a temperamental artist at the museum who
>   committed suicide
>NATE, Elizabeth's estranged husband, who has also had a series
>   of extramarital affairs
>LESJE, Elizabeth's coworker and Nate's new love interest
>WILLIAM, Lesje's roommate
>MARTHA, Nate's most recent lover
>CHRIS, Elizabeth's most recent lover, a talented artist
>MURIEL, the sister of Elizabeth's alcoholic mother
>MRS. SCHOENHOF, Nate's mother

Form and Content

Life Before Man has fifty-eight short sections, each dated and identified with one of the characters in a romantic triangle. Eighteen sections are narrated from Nate's point of view, eighteen from Lesje's, and twenty-two from Elizabeth's. The narrative covers twenty-two months in their lives, from Nate's first gesture in Lesje's direction to a tentative hope that they have a future together. There are longer breaks in time as the story unfolds. Part 1 follows the three main characters through a single weekend; part 5, the last, covers almost a year. There are flashbacks throughout, as the three come to terms with their own pasts; two sustained flashbacks are dated to the fateful moments when Nate learns of Elizabeth's affair with Chris and when he last sees Chris.

Ever since childhood, when she was dominated by her aunt, Elizabeth has seized control of every relationship. She breaks off the affair because she is terrified by Chris's possessiveness, then she is angered and depressed by his suicide. The depression throws her marriage off balance, nudging Nate away from a tepid affair with Martha and toward Lesje. The triangle becomes a foursome when Elizabeth seduces William for pure revenge, but the real foursome involves Chris, whose memory lingers in everyone's mind. At first, Lesje cannot imagine what made him commit suicide, but her affair brings out new passions. Although she is tempted to take an overdose of pills and kill herself, she decides to get rid of her birth control pills. She destroys her museum career, at most, when she becomes pregnant with Nate's child.

Even before Lesje and Nate begin their sexual relationship, Elizabeth senses something between them. She invites Lesje and William to a dinner party at which the guests play "lifeboat" and explain why they should be allowed to stay on board when supplies dwindle. Elizabeth says she has a strong "survival instinct" and will take at least one person with her if they throw her overboard. Nate says he will sacrifice himself for the common good. Lesje says lamely that she can identify bones, then panics and runs away. The game brings out their differences. Elizabeth is a fighter and trusts no one. Nate cannot assert himself because, Elizabeth realizes, he has been reared as a pacifist and uses pacifism as a cover for indifference. Lesje is also unassertive, afraid of her emotions. Before their stories can be resolved, they must face the gaps opening up in their lives.

Elizabeth realizes that she has lived a double life. She is sophisticated but scrappy, a street kid who will stop at nothing to get her way. She realizes she is shockingly like her aunt in that she rebuffed her mother and so, perhaps, pushed her loyal sister into insanity and death. At her aunt's funeral, Elizabeth faints and returns to her senses, more herself than before. Nate, meanwhile, discovers that he has been reared to respect the rules. He imagines Lesje to be unruled and unruling. At his mother's house one evening, he imagines (in an interesting anticipation of Robert Bly's wild man) that he growls and breaks through a glass door, chasing the desirable Lesje. When he tries to lead a "divided life," however, living in two houses, he falls apart. Meanwhile, Lesje discovers that she wants more than she had thought from the relationship. When William is alerted by Elizabeth and tries to rape Lesje in a last-ditch effort to keep her, she moves out and rents a house that Nate promises to share. She wants him to spend more time there; later, she realizes that she wants to have his child.

Analysis

The novel's title has different meanings for the main characters. For Elizabeth, "life before man" means that she must place her own life before any man; she must never allow a man to manipulate her, as Chris has done, or become addicted to a man's image of her, as she has done with Nate. For Nate, it means that life as people know it now is not fully human, is not "the ethical life" to which he is committed. For Lesje, it means paleontology first of all, the study of life forms predating *homo sapiens*. It may also refer to her life before she knew what a man-woman relationship could involve and to her decision to become pregnant and thereby affirm that life itself is more important than the problems of men and women. In the long-range perspective of geological time, she realizes that life may well outlast the human race; however, she does not share William's indifference about the future of humankind.

Atwood's working title for the novel was "Notes on the Mesozoic." As Lesje reflects in a moment of musing, "Mesozoic" means "mid-life" and is used for the broad geological time span when the dinosaurs lived. It comes between the Paleozoic and Neozoic—that is, the old life and the new life. Elizabeth and Nate are going through mid-life crises in the novel, and Lesje, who is undergoing more of a youthful identity crisis, plays a central role in Nate's mid-life change. Atwood's working title helps to explain the two epigraphs that she chose for the novel. The first quotation, from a book on dinosaurs, makes the reader think that the characters are symbolically fossils, frozen forever at the moment of their deaths—that is, at the moment when life becomes art. The second is from a work of fiction and suggests that the story is like an icicle in the hands of a reader—outside the reader but also inside, dead but also alive. The characters are predatory in an eat-or-be-eaten world, and their stories are no more than a scientist's field notes until they strike a response in the reader.

The novel is set in Toronto, Canada, and abounds with names and places—bars and restaurants, streets and parks—that evoke much for readers who have been there. Atwood makes Toronto her city and sends a message to Canadians who grew up reading British and American novels: Our places are important too. Elizabeth grieves for Chris on Remembrance Day (Veterans Day in the United States). Nate watches the news at a bar on the day after the separatist Parti Québecois came to power, already thinking about separation from Elizabeth. This is a Canadian novel as well as a women's novel, a domestic novel about life in changing times.

Life Before Man represents a turning point in Atwood's career. *The Edible Woman* (1969), *Surfacing* (1972), and *Lady Oracle* (1976) all concern a young woman struggling to survive in a male-dominated world and arriving at a distinctly female solution. She feasts or fasts, gets herself pregnant or cuts off her hair. She is apolitical, whereas the politically involved characters, usually male, are mere caricatures. *Life Before Man* has more politically conscious characters, and the next two novels are increasingly political—*Bodily Harm* (1982) is set in a small Caribbean country during a revolution, and *The Handmaid's Tale* (1985) is set in a futuristic theocracy where patriarchy runs wild. Atwood's seventh novel, *Cat's Eye* (1989), is a retrospective work with elements of the earlier ones. Like the first three, it concerns a woman's personal quest; like the next three, it shows a growing political consciousness as she becomes involved in consciousness-raising groups. Atwood's eighth novel, *The Robber Bride* (1993), resembles *Life Before Man* in that it is written from three points of view.

Context

From the beginning, readers have responded favorably to the realism of *Life Before Man*, which was named notable book of 1980 by the American Library Association. Readers have complained mostly only that they need a sequel to know what really happened. For, as with many of Atwood's novels, the ending seems ambiguous, the plot unresolved. The most controversial aspect of the ending is Lesje's pregnancy. Some readers see it as a selfish, manipulative decision on her part. Others see it as a life-affirming act. There may be truth in both views, but insofar as there is hope for Nate and Lesje, the act is necessary. Atwood told critic Alan Twigg that Lesje is "tired of being put down for not being the mother," tired of hearing the parents demand all the consideration.

Elizabeth is a survivor, like all Atwood's heroines. She is among Atwood's most fully realized characters because she is shown as Nate and Lesje see her, not only as she sees herself. She is a sympathetic character, but not always a pleasant one; she can be a nurturer and a bitch. Nate, meanwhile, is Atwood's best answer to critics who say that she cannot create a plausible male character. Some complain that he is very much a woman's man, dominated by his mother and wife, even by his daughters and lovers, and unable to stand up for himself against the more aggressive Chris. In that sense, however, Nate is typical of his generation; he is a sensitive man, trying to do his share in the marriage, uncertain about his role at home or at work. Atwood has resisted the view that only women should write about women, only blacks about blacks, and so forth. In her introduction to *The Best American Short Stories, 1989* (1990), she says she could not bear the logical result: a world in which one could only write, or read, about oneself.

Atwood's early novels are at once witty and poetic, with the poetry making the heroine's plight more intense and the wit adding a wry perspective on the world in which she struggles to survive. In *Life Before Man*, the poetry and wit are more subtly blended in the characters' self-understanding. A few readers have found the setting, plot, and characters as drab as tourists once found Toronto, but many more have seen the novel as a statement of literary high fashion, completely in the know about mid-life crises in the upper-middle classes during the decade after the women's movement resurfaced. Atwood has been compared to Doris Lessing and Muriel Spark, novelists whose clever descriptions and dialogues bring ideas, as well as people, to life.

Sources for Further Study

Davidson, Arnold, ed. *Studies on Canadian Literature: Introductory and Critical Essays*. New York: Modern Language Association of America, 1990. Includes the essay "Margaret Atwood and the Politics of Narrative" by the feminist critic Annette Kolodny, which is helpful for its comments on *Life Before Man*.

Grace, Sherrill. *Violent Duality: A Study of Margaret Atwood*. Edited by Ken Norris. Montreal, Quebec: Véhicule Press, 1980. An introduction to Atwood's early poetry and prose. The postscript has special interest as an early and intelligent response to *Life Before Man*.

Grace, Sherrill, and Lorraine Weir, eds. *Margaret Atwood: Language, Text, and System*. Vancouver: University of British Columbia Press, 1983. A collection of nine essays on Atwood's texts and contexts. Linda Hutcheon's essay discusses the narrative technique and character development in *Life Before Man*.

Ingersoll, Earl G., ed. *Margaret Atwood: Conversations*. Princeton, N.J.: Ontario Review Press, 1990. A collection of interviews with Atwood, including one with Alan Twigg, conducted shortly after the publication of *Life Before Man*. There is an index of names and titles mentioned in the interviews.

McCombs, Judith, ed. *Critical Essays on Margaret Atwood*. Boston: G. K. Hall, 1988. A collection of early reviews and criticism of Atwood's work. Contains a bibliography of Atwood's publications through 1986.

Moss, John George. *A Reader's Guide to the Canadian Novel*. Toronto, Ontario:

McClelland & Stewart, 1981. A standard introduction to the Canadian novel. The entry on Atwood discusses her first four novels, finding fault with *Life Before Man*.

Rosenberg, Jerome H. *Margaret Atwood*. Boston: Twayne, 1984. An overview of Atwood's creative output through the 1970's, written with Atwood's cooperation.

VanSpanckeren, Kathryn, and Jan Garden Castro, eds. *Margaret Atwood: Vision and Forms*. Carbondale: Southern Illinois University Press, 1988. A collection of original essays on Atwood's work, all written from a feminist perspective.

Thomas Willard